Sales and Sales Management

Ralph W. Jackson
University of Tulsa

Robert D. Hisrich
Case Western Reserve University

PRENTICE HALL, Upper Saddle River, New Jersey 07458

Library of Congress Cataloging-in-Publication Data

Jackson, Ralph W.
    Sales and sales management / Ralph W. Jackson, Robert D. Hisrich.
        p.   cm.
    Includes bibliographical references and index.
    ISBN 0-13-606161-3
    1. Sales management.   2. Selling.   I. Hisrich, Robert D.
    II. Title.
    HF5438.4.J33   1996
    658.8'1—dc20
                                                                95-36814
                                                                CIP

Sr. acquisitions editor: Donald Hull
Editorial assistant: John Larkin
Assistant editor: Melissa Steffens
Editorial/production supervision
    and interior design: Linda B. Pawelchak
Copy editor: Mary Louise Byrd
Cover design: Wendy Alling Judy
Manufacturing buyer: Vincent Scelta
Cover photo: Leo De Wys, Inc.

 © 1996 by Prentice-Hall, Inc.
Simon & Schuster/A Viacom Company
Upper Saddle River, New Jersey 07458

Printed in the United States of America

10   9   8   7   6   5   4   3   2   1

0 - 13 - 606161 - 3

Prentice-Hall International (UK) Limited, *London*
Prentice-Hall of Australia Pty. Limited, *Sydney*
Prentice-Hall Canada Inc., *Toronto*
Prentice-Hall Hispanoamericana, S.A., *Mexico*
Prentice-Hall of India Private Limited, *New Delhi*
Prentice-Hall of Japan, Inc., *Tokyo*
Simon & Schuster Asia Pte. Ltd., *Singapore*
Editora Prentice-Hall do Brasil, Ltda., *Rio de Janeiro*

Contents

PART II   THE PERSONAL SELLING PROCESS

Chapter 6
The Selling Process—Preparation   121

Chapter 7
The Selling Process—The Sales Presentation   148

Chapter 8
The Selling Process—Closing the Sale   171

Chapter 9
The Selling Process—Handling Objections   189

Chapter 10
The Selling Process—The Follow-Up After the Sale   203

PART III   MANAGING THE SALES FORCE

Chapter 14
Training the Sales Force   315

Chapter 15
Forecasting Sales and Establishing Goals and Budgets   345

Preface

As the twenty-first century approaches, the sales profession is going through unprecedented changes. The globalization of business has opened up new markets and has altered the nature of competition. The speed of communication, along with the amount of accessible information, has irrevocably changed the nature of the selling job. Salespeople must be able to respond immediately to customer problems through the tools and know-how provided by their sales managers. This requires that sales professionals be knowledgeable about and skilled in using the latest computer technology. However, at the same time, sales professionals must be skilled in developing customer relationships. Successful sales professionals in the twenty-first century will be the ones who understand customers and are able to propose and develop effective solutions to customer problems.

In writing this book, we tried to approach the sales profession from an international human relations perspective. Increasingly, the terms "relationship marketing" and "partnering" are being used to describe the dynamics of the buyer-seller interaction. Trying to bring about one sale and then moving on to the next one without adequately ensuring that customer needs are being met is a vestige of an earlier time. We take the view that sales professionals are chiefly in the "people business," in that their major objective involves developing effective, long-term relationships. Both salespeople and sales managers are in the business of helping others solve problems. Doing so requires that they possess a great deal of knowledge not only about the products they sell but also about the people with whom they interact, the industry in which they operate, and the companies with which they compete.

THE AIM AND ORGANIZATION OF THIS BOOK

In writing this book, we wanted to address both personal selling and sales management because we believe that these are inextricably related to each other. It is difficult to grasp the complexities of managing salespeople without an adequate understanding of personal selling. We also believe that sales management is more or less an extension of personal selling, and, therefore, these two areas, though distinct, have some common themes. We address the topics from an international perspective because, increasingly, the terms "marketing" and "international marketing" are synonymous. There are few instances today in which marketing decisions do not have cultural and international overtones.

This book is intended for use with undergraduate students in colleges and universities that have a comprehensive course in the sales area. Additionally, it can be used in schools that have both a course in personal selling and one in sales management and yet want to have greater linkage between the two. Although the book is aimed primarily for undergraduates, it is written with sufficient rigor that it can be used in a graduate-level course as well.

The book has four major parts. In Part I, Chapter 1, we provide a background for the study of both personal selling and sales management. Chapter 2 discusses organizational buying, presenting both its human and the organizational side. A sales professional must understand and empathize with customers and appreciate the process that buyers go through in making a purchase. The topic of communication is covered in Chapter 3. Both selling and sales management depend on an individual being able to understand what another person really means. We take the view that "words don't mean—people do." Chapter 4 addresses the topic of motivation. Both salespeople and sales managers work to motivate people. Salespeople attempt to motivate customers to buy, and sales managers try to motivate salespeople to perform at a higher level.

The final chapter in Part I, Chapter 5, deals with ethical and legal issues. There is probably no place in an organization that is more susceptible to ethical abuse than sales. By the very nature of the process, there are any number of ethical issues that can arise in the course of a day. Although no code of ethics is foolproof, if sales professionals take the time to examine their personal ethical systems and see how they compare to those of the firms for which they work, they can avoid some major pitfalls.

Part II deals with the personal selling process. Each chapter in this part addresses a particular element in the process. Chapter 6 covers the prospecting, planning, and preparation phases of selling. Without prospecting, new customers are difficult to obtain. Inadequate planning results in a lack of confidence on the part of salespeople, an inability to handle contingencies that arise, and customers' feeling that they are not important. Chapter 7 covers the initiation stage of the sales call and the all-important sales presentation. Because impressions are formed by the way the prospect is approached, this part of the selling process sets the tone for the rest of the sales call. The sales presentation is the part of the sales call in which salespeople get to "tell their stories." Buyers have limited time to listen to salespeople, and, therefore, the salespeople who are able to make clear, concise presentations will generally be the ones who are successful. Chapters 8 and 9 deal with the most difficult parts of the sales process: closing the sale and handling objections. Objections are an inherent part of the selling process, and being able to handle them effectively is often the difference between success and failure. Particularly for new salespeople, it is a challenge to close the sale, that is, to ask for the order. Chapter 10 addresses the follow-up portion of the selling process. The follow-up should not be viewed as an end to one sale but, rather, the beginning of another. Increasingly, good service is essential to long-term customer relations and repeat sales.

Part III deals with managing the sales force. Chapter 11 is concerned with the leadership role of the sales manager. It delves into the characteristics of leadership and what a leader actually does. It also discusses the difference between leadership and supervision. Chapter 12 presents issues in organizing a sales force, both general and specific.

Chapters 13 and 14 are on hiring and training salespeople. The material delves into locating prospective salespeople and the proper screening of those who apply. Chapter 13 looks at the usefulness of the various tools for screening prospects, as well as the legality of these tools. Chapter 14 focuses on approaches to training, presenting principles of learning that are essential to successful training programs.

The final three chapters of Part III discuss forecasting (Chapter 15), developing a reward system (Chapter 16), and evaluating salespeople (Chapter 17). Various approaches to forecasting and their implications are covered. The components of the reward system and how the system can be used to motivate salespeople are presented. Focus is on what needs to be evaluated and the implications of various approaches to evaluating the different aspects of the salesperson's job. The legal aspects of performance evaluations are also addressed.

The final part of the text contains cases. The cases, most of which are multidimensional, are related to the various topics in the book. For the most part, they are based on actual situations in real companies. Additionally, most of the cases have not appeared in print before and thus should provide some fresh material and new insights. Some of these cases are set in the international arena, which can add to the richness of the discussion.

Available with this text is an optional component containing short case scenarios that deal with various issues in the personal selling process. It should enhance the personal selling component of the course.

ACKNOWLEDGMENTS

Many individuals—sales professionals, professors, students, and editorial staff—have contributed to the success of this book. Special thanks for initial editorial assistance go to Sandra Steiner, Wendy Goldner, and Robert Watrous. Don Hull, John Chillingworth, John Larkin, Barbara Bernstein, and Linda Pawelchak provided additional editorial assistance throughout the development and production of the manuscript. The staff of Prentice Hall Business Publishing worked closely with us to include the articles from *SELL!NG* magazine found in each chapter. We especially want to thank Erin Fogarty and Brenda Harris for typing the manuscript in a timely manner, and Erin Fogarty and Catherine Brown for providing research material and editorial assistance.

We are indebted to the following reviewers whose comments, insights, and examples were invaluable: Ramon Avila, Ball State University; S. Bandyodadhyay, Lamar University; Louis Canale, Geneseo Community College; Lyndall Chew,

University of Missouri at St. Louis; Robert Errmeyer, University of Wisconsin at Eau-Claire; Darrell Goudge, University of Central Oklahoma; David Heckenlively, San Francisco State University; Elaine Notorantonio, Bryant College; Cliff Olson, Southern College; John Pepin, Memphis State University; William Ross, University of Pennsylvania; William Seale, Murray State University; Stanley Steinberg; James Strong, University of Akron; and Mike Swenson, Brigham Young University. We would like to acknowledge Barron's for its support and publication of our earlier work, *Selling and Sales Management*, which was written for the trade and in which some material in this new book was initially published.

Finally, this book is dedicated to our families. First, to Tina, Kelly, Kary, and Katy Hisrich for your patience and understanding concerning the time involved in this project. Perhaps the greatest "selling job" of all was to each of you. And also to Gary Jackson and Debra Cain, and your families, because of your words of encouragement and support during the process of researching and writing this book.

_____ Chapter 1 _____

The Selling Process
and Its Management

OPENING SCENARIO

Bob Kelly, the president of Dumas Makt., H.K., was perplexed. How could he develop a good distribution system for one of the company's newest imports—wines from Hungary? He had first learned about the wines and their attributes during a business trip to Germany, Poland, Russia, and Hungary. The wines not only had a good taste but had no chemical additives. This gave the Hungarian wines a competitive advantage over most wines being sold in the United States. And it could be sold at a good retail price point of $4.99 for the three types of white wine, $5.49 for the rosé, and $5.99 for the three types of red wine. Bob was aware that overall U.S. consumption of alcohol had been decreasing the last several years, but that the market for wines in the price range of the Hungarian wines had not decreased at all. Still, Bob was concerned that most people in the United States had limited knowledge about wines, their prices, and their qualities.

He was considering a total marketing plan for the wines' introduction but knew Dumas Makt., H.K., could not afford any significant amount of advertising, as the margins for the wines would not support extensive advertising expenditures. What should he do? Should he market to retail stores or to restaurants? Should he price the wines higher and have a larger margin? Should he have a market resource study done? Should he hire a manufacturer's representative? Should he hire a salesperson?

Chapter Objectives

After reading this chapter, you should be able to

- Discuss the nature of the selling process and its management.
- Explain the relationship between personal selling and marketing.
- Discuss the positions of sales management within an organization.
- Discuss sales as a career.
- Define the emerging issues in selling.

INTRODUCTION

The questions confronting Bob Kelly of Dumas Makt., H.K., confront business-people in the United States and throughout the world on a regular basis. These questions are being considered even by not-for-profit organizations and federal and state governments.

Everyone has ideas about what is involved in sales and selling, but did you know that the state you live in is probably engaged in selling itself? States have been aggressively selling themselves as good locations for new plants, distribution centers, and corporate headquarters. Today this selling task has expanded overseas as the role of international business has taken on increased importance.[1] Europe especially has received a great deal of attention from the American states. Many states actually have offices in the business centers of Europe that assist in the selling task. Georgia has had an office in Europe for nearly 20 years.

These state offices undertake a variety of selling roles. One role is to boost European tourism to the particular state by pointing out the unique attributes of the region. Promoting tourism has become increasingly important due to the valuation of the dollar versus most European currencies and the new interest on the part of Europeans to travel in the United States. The mountains of North Carolina and the beaches of Florida have been successfully promoted as vacation spots for Europeans.

Another role of the state offices in Europe is to promote exports of products made by companies located in the state. This selling task mainly focuses on educating European consumers and businesspeople about the leading industries in the state, the state's supportive business infrastructure, the quality of the state's labor force, and the pro-business attitude of the state's government as reflected in training programs, favorable tax treatment, and business assistance provided by the state. Michigan positioned its positive aspects to attract new business to help offset the downturn in the automotive industry.

A more direct selling role of the state office abroad is to help exporters in the state by organizing trade missions to European and other countries. These trade missions help a business to investigate the viability of opportunities in the foreign country. Some state offices go beyond just organizing the trade mission and act as sales representatives of the company by contacting interested attendees and setting up meetings between U.S. and foreign businesspeople.

State offices also inform foreign manufacturers about joint venture opportunities with U.S. businesses or the benefits of establishing facilities in a particular state. Most European trade delegations of states are organized and coordinated by the state office in that particular country. The purpose of the office is to convince European manufacturers of the many perks of locating in the state. One obvious benefit to the state is that the resulting new facility would create jobs for Americans. Frequently, the task of selling the state is coordinated with the efforts of a particular company. For example, Delta Air Lines and the state of New York cooperated in a joint promotion in Germany with the twin goals of increasing Delta's transatlantic business and New York's tourism.

Regardless of who or what you are, you, as well as everyone else, have done some form of selling. You may have been trying to increase your allowance or attempting to get an extension on a due date for a term paper. Or perhaps it was in obtaining your job or asking for a raise. To varying degrees, each of us employs personal selling in our day-to-day activities both on and outside the job. It is important for us to understand the characteristics and responsibilities of personal selling and how to use it to better our lives and perform more effectively.

NATURE OF THE SELLING TASK

Although we all are involved, at some time or another, in some sort of selling, very few of us know a formal definition of personal selling. **Personal selling** can be defined as a formal, paid-for, personal presentation of some aspects of a company to an individual or group. These personal presentations are one of the most important stimulants for sales and profits of a company. Successful personal selling requires a very professional person, not the stereotypical hail, hearty, well-intentioned fellow with no concern for customers, only for selling as much as possible. The stereotypes of selling and sales people have endured for a long time, as the following results of a survey of college students show:

- Selling benefits only the seller.
- Selling is not a job for a person with talents and brains.
- Salespeople bring out the worst in people.
- Salespeople must lie and be deceitful in order to succeed.[2]

These beliefs notwithstanding, it is no longer possible to be successful at personal selling by being brash, pushy, or making grandiose claims. Personality and other individual characteristics will always be part of successful selling, but these alone will not complete a sale in today's hypercompetitive environment.

A successful sale requires that the salesperson have a thorough understanding of the company's products and how these fulfill the needs of the customer.

The selling task has greatly increased in complexity as the technology of the products and services, consumer knowledge, and competition have increased also. It is further complicated in many instances by shared decision making—that is, companies' buying decisions that require input from many individuals at various levels of the organizations.

In this environment, a salesperson needs training in both the attributes of the product and selling techniques. A successful salesperson must have a combination of innate ability and acquired skills. When queried, many buyers will typically say that the characteristics most liked in a salesperson are reliability, credibility, professionalism, integrity, and knowledge of the product or service being presented.

Product knowledge and the skills necessary to present the product effectively require extensive training and practice. The need for this is so great in today's hypercompetitive environment that many companies have their own corporate schools for sales training and management. Xerox has such a school in Virginia, as do IBM in New York and AT&T in Colorado. This professionalism and training have modified some of the negative stereotypes and attitudes toward salespeople. In more recent surveys, many college students, particularly those in schools of business and management, feel that a sales job is challenging, rewarding, a good use of their college education, and requires a high degree of creativity and professionalism.[3]

Importance of Personal Selling

The fact that companies are willing to establish their own training schools and programs attests to the importance and the extremely high cost of personal selling. More than 10 percent of the labor force in the United States—over 7.5 million people—are in personal selling jobs.[4] Of these, more sales activity is directed toward professional and industrial customers than toward consumers.

To the customer, the salesperson is the personification of the seller's company. Often the salesperson is the only individual the customer ever comes into contact with from the company. As a result, the salesperson's actions and behavior can significantly enhance or detract from the company's image. Although usually blamed for unfilled or inappropriately filled orders, billing errors, late delivery, and faulty products, the salesperson is also given credit for all the good aspects of the company and particularly for all the services provided.

The fact that an increasing number of individuals are taking courses in selling even though they do not plan to have a sales career attests to selling's importance to success in business. They understand that everyone in business uses some of the principles of selling during each workday: The product manager sells a new marketing plan to the sales force; the accountant sells a new cost control system to management; the human resource manager sells the new wage package to the union representatives; and the vice president of products sells a new production process to the senior management committee. They all sell.

The Professional Salesperson

Each year the level of professionalism needed to be a successful salesperson has risen.[5] The increase in customers' knowledge, as well as in their expectation level, has radically changed the selling task. Salespersons may call on customers at all levels of management and need to be able to adjust appropriately. This has caused some companies, such as IBM and Xerox, to call their sales representatives **market representatives.** This change has been accompanied by even more emphasis on the correct training of the market representatives. This new emphasis involves thorough initial and intensive follow-up training to ensure that the proper presentation, product knowledge, and company image are presented to the customer.

Progressive companies increasingly recognize the need to be represented by talented, professional salespeople who can effectively deal with the customers and potential customers who themselves determine whether the company succeeds or fails. The recognition that negative word of mouth can have a significant impact on sales is shaping management philosophy in terms of hiring, selecting, training, and compensating the sales force.

Salespeople's Time

The professionalism of each salesperson is particularly significant in the use of time during a typical week (see Figure 1-1). In an average 47-hour work week, salespeople spend only 50 percent of their time actually selling—30 percent (14.1 hours) selling face-to-face and 20 percent (9.4 hours) selling over the telephone.[6] The rest is spent on traveling and waiting (23 percent, or 10.8 hours), administrative tasks (14 percent, or 6.6 hours), and service calls (13 percent, or 6.1 hours).

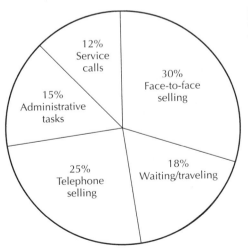

FIGURE 1-1
How Salespeople Spend Their Week (*Source:* 28th Sales Force Compensation Survey 1994–1995 [copyright 1994], The Dartnell Corporation, 4660 N. Ravenswood Ave., Chicago, IL 60640 [800] 621-5463; fax [312] 561-4842.

Given the high cost of a sales call and the amount of time spent in nonselling activities, it is imperative that salespeople be professional in their selling in order to be successful in making sales and profits.

RELATIONSHIP BETWEEN PERSONAL SELLING AND MARKETING

Salespeople are becoming more and more market oriented as their new title "marketing representatives" suggests. Like selling, marketing is a central, integrated part of society, and to some extent affects the lives of everyone. Marketing is not an isolated function within a firm but, rather, begins and ends in the changing external environment, starting with an idea for a product or service and ending only when the consumer has purchased and has had sufficient time to evaluate the product.[7]

Defining objectives is a critical first step in implementing a marketing strategy. This must be done using the going-concern concept—that the firm intends to do business with the same or similar customers continuously over a period of time. This concept implies that repeat business and loyal customers are objectives, and all strategic decisions on marketing activities will be based on the needs and desires of the targeted group of customers. The activities that facilitate exchange are the controllable marketing elements of the marketing mix—product, price, distribution, and promotion.

Marketing and the Marketing Process

Marketing influences everyone in society to some extent. Marketing has an increasing impact on the decisions being made not only by the buyer and seller but by many others—politicians, architects, authors, students, clergy. For example, a state politician may be trying to decide how to allocate the promotional budget during the last two weeks of her election campaign. Should an expensive television advertisement be used? Should there be more radio spots? Or would additional advertisements in various newspapers across the state be a better use of the available money? Other decisions need to be made on where the candidate should spend her limited time. Should she visit precincts that are borderline, or should she put emphasis on those that are only somewhat favorable? These and many more basic marketing decisions are made throughout any local, state, or national political campaign.

Buyers of industrial products are confronted with different factors of marketing. They must carefully weigh many factors in selecting the correct product and supplier to fulfill a particular company need. Should sources of supply be switched because of the superior quality and lower price of a new supplier? Will a new firm be consistently able to supply the quantity needed at this price? Will the new supplier deliver the product on time, thus avoiding costly plant shut-downs caused by an out-of-stock condition?

Finally, consider a consumer—you or me—trying to decide on a hairstylist. Should the number of styling awards, the services offered, or the number of employees be considered? Should the convenience of location take priority? What about switching to a different hairstylist? Are these the factors that also contribute to loyalty for a certain stylist? No one can escape marketing.

Marketing: An Integrated Definition

But what, exactly, is this activity that has such an impact on our lives? The answer to this question depends to some extent on the perspective of the individual. People in law, finance, economics, and operations—and just plain consumers—all view marketing from a somewhat different vantage point. In today's quickly changing, highly competitive environment, the following definition of marketing seems most applicable: **Marketing** is the "process by which decisions are made in a totally interrelated changing business environment on all the activities that facilitate exchange in order that the targeted group of customers are satisfied and the defined objectives of the organization are accomplished."[8]

This definition has four major parts that need to be further explored. First, working backwards, how are the **objectives** established and then accomplished? Although specific objectives vary from firm to firm, as well as from product to product within a single company, it is impossible for strategic marketing decisions to be made without defined objectives. The obvious objective of a profit organization is to make a profit, but this objective may not occur in the short run or for some of the firm's products; overall, each firm must make a profit in the long run in order to continue to exist. Obtaining this objective under the going-concern concept (the organization plans to do business with the same or similar customers year after year) means that any profits realized cannot be at the sacrifice of customers or the environment.

The second part of the definition—the satisfaction of the target group of customers—requires that the customer be the orientation and focus of all the firm's activities. The customer's wants and needs must be constantly analyzed, in order for the firm's offering to be exactly what is desired. This is the essence of the **marketing concept.** Without this focus, the targeted customers could easily choose an alternative offering from a competing firm.

All the activities that "facilitate exchange," the third part of the definition, are the controllable marketing elements of the firm. These elements make up the firm's offering and can be classified into four areas—product, price, distribution, and promotion. As outlined in Figure 1-2, each element has its own mix of strategic decisions that are needed to achieve customer satisfaction.

The **product area** includes all the features that make up the physical product or service being offered for sale. Decisions need to be made on quality, the breadth

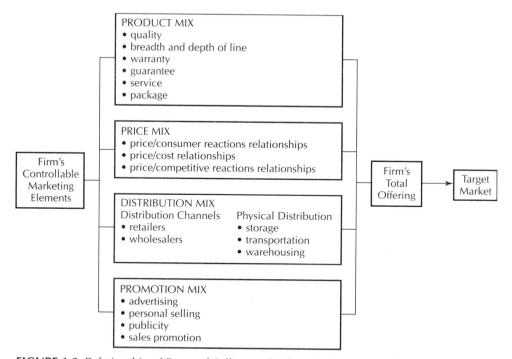

FIGURE 1-2 Relationship of Personal Selling and Other Marketing Activities

and depth of line, warranty, guarantee, service, and the package. All these make the final product or service more, or less, appealing to the target market.

Closely related to the product and its mix is the **price.** Probably the least understood element, the price of the product greatly influences its image, as well as whether it will be purchased. The established price needs to take into consideration the three Cs of the pricing decision—cost, competition, and consumer.

Distribution includes two areas: (1) *channels of distribution*, which deal with the institutions, such as wholesalers and retailers, that handle the product between the firm and the consumer; and (2) *physical distribution*, which deals with actually moving the product from the firm to the consumer, including storage, transportation, and warehousing.

The final element, **promotion,** involves policies and procedures related to four subareas:

1. *Advertising.* Policies and procedures relating to the budget, message, and media of making nonpersonal, paid-for presentations.
2. *Personal selling.* Policies and procedures of making personal presentations.
3. *Publicity.* Policies and procedures relating to a comprehensive program for good media coverage and building a strong company image.
4. *Sales promotions.* Policies and procedures relating to budget and types of consumer and trade promotions and displays; nonrecurring promotional activities.

The fourth part of the definition of marketing—the "totally interrelated changing business environment"—indicates that marketing is done in constantly changing external and internal business environments. Decisions in the other functional areas of the company, as well as those made in competitive firms, affect the company and its need to change, as do other variables.

The Marketing Concept

More than any other functional business area, marketing helps develop the goals and direction of organizations. A firm's basic management philosophy should focus on the satisfaction of the target customer. Under such a philosophy, a marketing concept is developed where the consumer becomes the dominant focal point, with all the resources and activities of the firm directed toward customer satisfaction.

The adoption of this marketing concept by many firms in the United States and throughout the world was precipitated by several factors. First, an increase in the intensity of competition in both the national and international markets has forced organizations to place greater emphasis on consumers and their satisfaction. A second factor is the increased level of consumer knowledge and sophistication. Consumers are more aware of product attributes, alternatives, and prices than ever before. And, as they become increasingly aware of the various options available, consumers will purchase only those products and services that they recognize as satisfying a need.

An increase in production capabilities in conjunction with the development of mass worldwide markets has also led to the adoption of a marketing concept geared toward customer satisfaction. Increased production capacity has led to economies of scale in production—a decrease in per unit production costs as the total number of units increases. The increased number of units produced can only be sold by successfully reaching mass markets and by focusing on customer satisfaction.

Finally, the need to develop innovative products in order to survive has forced firms to place the customer first. Just a simple count of the number of times you have heard the phrase "new and improved" should indicate the size of the consumer appetite for new and supposedly better products. Yet, in spite of this need and the consumer appetite, between 80 and 90 percent of all new products fail. A key ingredient to a successful new product is knowing the needs and buying habits of the target group of consumers.

In no area is customer satisfaction more important than in personal selling and sales management. By adopting the marketing concept a salesperson focuses on ensuring that customers are satisfied and will only be sold the types of goods and services needed in the correct quantities. This in turn helps to establish customer rapport that, in the long run, results in continuous sales of a variety of products.

Under this philosophy of knowing the needs and buying habits of the consumers and wanting to satisfy them, the customer is never blamed for any problems in the sales cycle. Without the marketing concept, a salesperson could believe that customers make objections just to be annoying. With it, a salesperson first asks why customers have these objections. Is it because they do not have enough information? Is it because there are some problems with the product that are not satisfying their needs? Or is it because there is not enough concern about the customer in the selling process?

POSITIONS IN SALES MANAGEMENT

In order to have an effective selling effort, firms must have strategic sales management. In planning, directing, and monitoring personal selling activities, a sales manager can have either a narrow or a broad spectrum of responsibilities: estimating demand and preparing sales forecasts; establishing sales force objectives and quotas; preparing sales plans and budgets; establishing the organization and size of the sales force; recruiting, selecting, and training the sales force; compensating the sales force; evaluating the performance of the sales force. The performance of these activities is crucial to a firm because personal selling is one of the few activities that directly generates the income without which the firm cannot survive.

The exact responsibilities of **sales managers** vary greatly from industry to industry, as well as among firms within a given industry. Responsibilities depend on the nature of the product, the characteristics of the firm itself, and the attitude of top management toward personal selling. Whereas in some firms, sales managers are mainly supervisors of the sales force, in other firms they perform all the activities just listed. The latter case is frequently found in small, growing firms that are opportunity rich and cash poor and have few employees.

The responsibilities of a sales manager also vary depending on the level of that position in the organization. Typically, the two highest level sales executives in a firm are the vice president of sales and the national sales manager. The vice president of sales, the highest level sales executive, usually reports to the vice president of marketing or sometimes to the president of the company. The vice president position involves long-range planning and developing and implementing the sales part of the marketing strategy. In companies with no vice president of marketing, the position often expands to include responsibilities for all the marketing activities.

The national sales manager is the link between upper-level management and the sales force. This position provides the sales force with the necessary guidance and strategic planning to carry out the sales part of the marketing strategy.

Below the national sales manager may be two middle-level supervisory positions: middle-level sales managers and first-level sales managers. Also called regional, divisional, or zone sales managers, middle-level sales managers are responsible for line sales activities in a designated geographic area when all three levels are present. Zone sales managers usually report to divisional sales managers, who in turn report to regional sales managers. Below these middle-level sales managers are the first-level sales managers, frequently called field sales managers or sales supervisors. This position is responsible for the day-to-day activities of the salespeople reporting to them.

The final position in sales management is often the key account or national account manager. This position involves selling to a few key (major) customers, such as the central buying offices of major chains such as Kroger, K-Mart, Walmart, Sears, J. C. Penney, or IGA. Under the key account manager, salespeople are assigned to call on individual stores in the chain.

SALES CAREERS

Sales can be one of the most diverse, challenging, exciting, and financially rewarding careers available. A **sales career** is seldom boring because it involves dealing with different individuals and their changing wants, needs, and behavior patterns. Depending on the compensation method, a sales career provides the security of working for a company and yet the freedom and independence associated with being one's own boss. Given his or her direct impact on sales and profits, a good salesperson usually has a significant amount of job security and often job opportunities as well.

Shortage of Good Salespeople

In spite of the many job opportunities in sales and their frequently high level of compensation, there always seems to be a shortage of good, qualified salespeople. Not counting replacements, about 400,000 new salespeople are needed each year. This shortage is compounded by the relatively low output of many salespeople who quit after a short time. This results in a high turnover rate and causes the majority of actual sales to be made by a small number of salespeople.

Career Path

A sales career can lead to an upper-level management position. Many executives in various management positions in Fortune 500 companies started their business careers in a sales position. This reflects the importance of learning the business from the perspective of the individuals who ultimately determine the success or failure of the business—the final customers.

Benefits

A career in sales offers income possibilities and perquisites as good as those of any other business career. Salespeople are among the best paid in business. Those who work for industrial products companies (generally paid a salary plus commissions) earn more than those who work for consumer products or service companies (generally paid a straight salary base). Many salespeople on a straight commission and bonus earn more than $100,000 a year, and some straight commission salespeople earn more than their sales manager. In some companies, a salesperson is expected to earn at least $50,000 a year after the initial training period.

Because their efforts can be directly measured, salespeople and sales executives are usually objectively evaluated and compensated based on their performance. This performance measurement leads to significant job security and opportunity. Even during times of personnel cutbacks, sales personnel are among the last to be severed because their reduction usually means further loss of sales and revenues.

A salesperson also has good perquisites. The expense account, the benefits of entertaining potential and present customers, a company car, paid membership dues, and an office at home further enhance the high level of income earned.

Sales Careers for Women and Minorities

Sales career opportunities for women have dramatically increased over the past two decades. Old myths about women not being reliable, suitable, or strong enough to deal with customers have been largely laid to rest. Today, more women than even before are in sales, and many have key selling and sales management positions in industries ranging from retailing to steel, life insurance to pharmaceuticals, and brewing to biotechnology.

In many companies, saleswomen have outperformed men in relative sales positions. In fact, saleswomen may have advantages over men in that women seem to be better listeners, more easily remembered with this positive recall being transferred to the product(s), and better able to obtain appointments with buyers. Still, women basically face the same problems as men do in a sales job and career. Saleswomen can get advice and help from such professional organizations as the National Association of Business and Industrial Saleswomen and the National Association for Professional Saleswomen.

Accompanying the increasing number of women in sales careers is an increase in the number of African Americans, Hispanic Americans, Asian Americans, and Native Americans in the sales force. Although strong legal and moral pressures under civil rights legislation have contributed to their presence, recognition of the abilities of minorities by business has also positively affected their numbers in sales positions in a wide variety of industries.

EMERGING ISSUES IN SELLING AND SALES MANAGEMENT

It appears that the importance of salespeople in the overall marketing strategy of the firm will continue to increase in the next decade. In some instances, salespeople have already become the most critical component of successful marketing of

SELL!NG
THE FRONT LINES OF BUSINESS

Peering Through the Glass Ceiling
Cathy Madison

What Paula Morgan brings to work each morning at Schering-Plough, no salesperson should be without: passion.

As vice president-Schering sales, Morgan has reached a level unusual for women in the pharmaceutical industry. In her position, she oversees the efforts of 800 salespeople, 63 district managers, and seven regional directors, leading them through the increasingly complex healthcare business.

Morgan has seen great changes in pharmaceuticals since coming to Schering in 1980, and change is never easy. Yet she remains passionate about her job. "I love my work," she says fervently. "I like to succeed because [at Schering] we've always been able to promote or enhance the success of each other."

Times have been tough for many pharmaceutical makers during the past few years, but Schering-Plough isn't one of them. Earnings have risen steadily for the Madison, N.J., company. One industry analyst projects Schering's annual growth for the next five years at 13 percent—healthy by any standard.

"The bottom line is selling product—that's how we're measured," says Morgan. "But looking at the bottom line doesn't tell you what you need to do. It just tells you whether you did poorly or well, not why."

The "why" behind a winning performance in pharmaceutical sales is what has changed in the business. Basic sales attributes—strong interpersonal skills, influencing ability, and self-discipline—are still necessary. But gone are the days when a successful salesperson's main concern was, "Can I sell you?" Now Morgan and her colleagues in upper management look for a strong business sense in reps. They feel that salespeople must understand the myriad factors that affect not only the decisions they themselves must make but also those made by their prospects.

Another change Morgan has seen during her career in pharmaceuticals is that salespeople move up through the ranks faster than they used to. Still, she has no complaints about her own progress. She joined Schering as a prescription sales rep. In 1984 she became district manager, respiratory and allergy sales. By 1988 she was director of sales operations, prescription products; two years later she was named national director of oncology sales. In 1991 Morgan was promoted to vice president-sales, prescription products, taking on the duties of developing and implementing sales and marketing programs for Schering's three sales forces for prescription products.

Morgan wasn't born with a burning desire to sell. In fact, it was her husband, Mike, a salesman for Stanley-Proto Industrial Tools, who convinced her that she possessed the personality, poise, and drive for the challenge of selling. Morgan had started her career as a physical therapist, and she loved her first job in the field. But when her husband was relocated, she was forced to take a new job, which she hated. At the same time, she could see how much her husband enjoyed sales, and how he could determine his income. So she decided that she would give it a try. Refusing to let her lack of experience get in the way, Morgan persisted until she landed a job at Ayerst in Columbia, S.C.

The way she describes it, "I had that 'Well, I'll show you' attitude."

Ten months later came a wrenching move to Atlanta, and Morgan was forced to decide between returning to physical therapy and sticking with sales. Although her experience in the sales world was limited, she had seen enough to know that this was where she wanted to be, so she signed on with Schering.

Today 40 percent to 50 percent of Schering's sales reps are women. But Morgan says that when she joined the company, she was the only woman in a 10- or 11-person sales group. She handled the situation by staying focused on her job, and says she encountered no "extraordinary difficulties" breaking through the glass ceiling into upper management. At the same time, she acknowledges that politics can have a greater impact as the management pyramid narrows at the top.

The greatest trials of Morgan's career have involved "the orchestration of being a two-career couple" and the necessity of relocating in order to advance—which is equally problematic for both spouses. So far, she and her husband have taken turns. "We laugh in retrospect," she says, "but both times, there were about six months that were extraordinarily difficult."

Morgan credits the support of her husband and her 8-year-old daughter, and says she has no problem switching gears from managing pharmaceutical sales to making dinner or checking homework. Crucial to her success, however, is keeping her energy level high, which she does by working out on a regular basis (when she's on the road, she makes sure to stay at hotels with health clubs). Not paying enough attention to fitness, Morgan adds, "will take its toll on your health or the quality of your work."

Those would seem to be words to heed, since the furious rate of change in pharmaceuticals shows no signs of abating, and salespeople face formidable challenges simply keeping up. Reps must develop an overview. They must satisfy their customers' needs by becoming part of the healthcare team and by understanding the forces buffeting all of its parts. But sales organizations, too, must adapt and evolve.

"We recognize the need to be more customer-focused instead of product-driven," Morgan says. "But as much as everyone talks about it, the way an organization is structured makes it difficult to make that transition."

The rise of managed healthcare has complicated decision-making in the business immeasurably. "No longer does a rep have sole autonomy," Morgan notes. Schering formerly matched one salesperson with one physician, but today's prescribing decisions have become multilayered. "It's not as much of an individual effort as it used to be," she says.

Management has adjusted, becoming more horizontal and working more often in teams. Seniority has become less important, the willingness to take risks more so. Individual competitiveness has taken a backseat.

"Achievement motivation is the most important thing," according to Morgan. "We want people to be successful, but not at the expense of their peers within the company."

Reprinted with the permission of SELL!NG magazine.

the firm's product. This has led to salespeople being given expanded responsibilities and requiring more education and training to compete effectively in today's competitive market. Simultaneously, salespersons will benefit from higher compensation, more prestige and security, and more opportunities for advancement.

Although previously a college degree was not considered necessary for a salesperson, very few people have this view today. With the increase in competition and the technical sophistication of products and customers, a college education helps develop a broader, more confident and capable individual with better skills for analysis, communications, and personal interactions.

Nonetheless, interest in sales positions in sales and sales management will continue to increase. Sales is an excellent entry-level position with a firm. Positions in sales and sales management have significantly expanded in responsibility and professionalism in the past several years and will continue to do so in the foreseeable future, due to several factors. One reason is the continuous increase in customer expectations. Consumers are becoming less tolerant of faulty products and of product or service limitations. Rapport and loyalty can be established by a good salesperson, but a dissatisfied customer can quickly switch to a competing product or service. Firms need to emphasize the need to develop customer-oriented innovations and quality products and services to help ensure customer satisfaction and loyalty. This emphasis will require the sales organization to be even more aware of customers' needs and satisfaction levels, as well as diligent in regularly gathering and reporting complaints.

A second factor involved in the increasing importance of sales is greater buyer expertise. With tighter budgets and profit squeezes, buyers are becoming more adept at obtaining value for their dollars. Buying committees are being used more frequently to ensure that the purchase decision has input from many different perspectives. Many consumers now treat an increasing number of purchase decisions as long-term investments. This places more responsibility on salespeople to develop long-term relationships with their customers by having a thorough understanding of their buying process and needs. Professional salespeople who focus on consulting instead of persuasive selling are increasingly needed.

The effects of these two factors on the future of personal selling and sales management have been compounded by a third factor: international hypercompetition. The large U.S. market with its significant purchasing power attracts quality, cost-competitive products from all over the world. This requires that salespeople and sales managers give a quality performance in this very competitive home-market situation as well as abroad.

One last factor to consider is the electronic revolution in communications and computer technology. Today salespeople and sales managers use personal computers for order entry and customer and sales analyses. Variations in sales performance can be quickly identified and various "what-if" scenarios run to determine the impact of changing sales territories or reassigning salespeople.

Sales presentations are becoming much more vivid and realistic through the use of videotapes. Through videotape presentations, the company's products can take on attributes not possible from catalog pages or product brochures. Videotapes are also useful for sales managers to communicate a message to salespeople in the field. Videoconferencing minimizes travel time and costs; it allows a professional presentation to be made from a single location to customers in other locations.

Mobile and cellular telephones and electronic beepers continue to increase in use, allowing the sales manager to have almost instant contact with salespeople in the field. In turn, these devices allow salespersons to be in close contact with their customers. Notification about changes in a scheduled meeting or delivery of a product can be done in a timely manner, lessening possible inconvenience.

CHAPTER SUMMARY

Personal selling—the formal, paid-for, personal presentation of some aspects of the company to an individual or group—requires a professional person who is willing to take the initiative to satisfy the customer. A successful sale requires a thorough understanding of the company's products and how the products fulfill the needs of the customer. With hard work salespeople can develop successful selling skills and by combining these with their innate characteristics can greatly heighten their selling strengths. Most buyers note reliability, credibility, professionalism, integrity, and product knowledge as the most desirable traits of a salesperson. Because of their position and contacts, salespersons can significantly enhance or detract from the image of their company. Furthermore, with the importance and increasing complexity of the selling task, the high cost of a sales call, and the significant amount of time spent in nonselling activities, salespeople must emphasize time management skills.

A firm's sales strategy must incorporate marketing techniques. In order to develop sales strategies, a firm must first define its objectives. This requires customer data, which often are collected at the sales management level. Additionally, sales management establishes objectives and quotas for the sales force, prepares sales plans and budgets, and determines sales force compensation.

These factors all help ensure that a sales career will continue to be diverse, challenging, exciting, and financially rewarding. More and more women and minorities are taking advantage of these opportunities and are pursuing sales careers. Technical advances, such as videoconferencing and electronic beepers, help to increase sales and performance; and sales presentations are becoming more vivid and realistic through the use of videotapes.

KEY TERMS

distribution, p. 8

marketing, p. 7

marketing concept, p. 7

marketing representative, p. 5

objectives, p. 7

personal selling, p. 3

price, p. 8

product area, p. 7

promotion, p. 8

sales careers, p. 11

sales manager, p. 8

CHAPTER QUESTIONS

1. If selling is such an integral part of our daily lives and business activity, why does it have such a negative reputation and salespeople such a negative image?

2. Is obtaining a college degree useful for a sales career? Why or why not?

3. Comment on the following observations on selling:
   a. "I would not be a good salesperson because I just can't try to make someone buy a product he does not need."
   b. "I could not sell a product that I do not believe in."
   c. "I could not be a good salesperson because I am not an extrovert."

4. Should the marketing manager of a consumer goods company have a basic knowledge of the selling process? What about the marketing director of a company making industrial products?

5. Should everyone in the marketing department of a consumer goods company have personal selling experience? What about in an industrial manufacturing company?

6. Why are some outstanding salespeople poor sales managers? Compare and contrast the skills needed to succeed as a salesperson with those needed as a sales manager.

7. Should you seek a beginning career in sales? Why or why not?

NOTES

1. For more information on this topic, see Allyson L. Stewart, States can be your marketing rep in Europe. *Marketing News,* April 12, 1993, 21.
2. Donald L. Thompson, Stereotype of the salesman. *Harvard Business Review* (January–February 1972), 20–29.
3. Allan J. Dubinsky, Recruiting college students for the sales force. *Industrial Marketing Management* (Winter 1980), 37–45; and Allan J. Dubinsky, On campus, selling is still a tough sale. *Sales and Marketing Management,* August 16, 1982, 58–59.
4. For complete statistics on employment in sales, see *Statistical Abstract of the United States 1994* (Washington, DC: U.S. Government Printing Office).
5. The information in this section as well as some other sections throughout this book has been previously published in Robert D. Hisrich and Ralph W. Jackson, *Selling and Sales Management* (Hauppauge, NY: Barron's, 1993).
6. *Twenty-sixth survey of sales force compensation* (Chicago: Dartnell Corporation, 1990).
7. For a complete presentation on all aspects of marketing, see Robert D. Hisrich, *Marketing* (Hauppauge, NY: Barron's, 1990).
8. Ibid., 3.

SUGGESTED READINGS

Dawson, Leslie M. Will feminization change the ethics of the sales profession? *Journal of Personal Selling and Sales Management* (Winter 1992), 21–32.

> A study was done to measure the ethics and moral reasoning of a group of male and female college students preparing to enter the business world. Part of the survey contained 15 business situations dealing with salespeople and managers in ethical dilemmas. The second part consisted of two longer, more detailed scenarios. The results stated that the increasing feminization of the sales force has a positive effect on moral standards and ethics of sales organizations.

Drefack, Raymond. Income boosters for the success-minded salesperson: The selling edge. *American Salesman* (October 1992), 24–27.

> Computer-controlled time utilization (CCTU) is the key to successful sales, according to its creator, Percy Swift. This program plans the most efficient schedules, sales calls, and upgrades swiftly and easily. Swift has reduced correspondence time up to 50 percent with this program. Additionally, he has two dozen business-related programs and four personal programs on his computer.

Duncan, Ian D. Research the market. *CMA Magazine* (September 1992), 39.

> Once a product is developed, the entrepreneur should define the product's target group. This group should be well defined according to age, gender, geographic location, and economic status. Primary research, such as a questionnaire, and secondary research, a study of existing data, will help to define the target market.

Graham, John R. It's time to stop selling and start making sales. *American Salesman* (November 1992), 3–8.

> Traditionally salesmen have told customers anything that they want to hear in order to make a sale. Customers today will not stand to be deceived in this manner. If cus-

tomers feel they are being manipulated they will look for another company to do business with. With continuous customer emphasis, clients begin to trust their salespeople and are content with the service they receive. Additionally, prospect identification, customer cultivation, and customer commitment are helping to create customer satisfaction.

Melchinger, John H. Rating sales for marketing effectiveness. *Broker World* (October 1992), 118–122.

A profitable sales performance is the only measure of the effectiveness of marketing. Sales and ratio trends are indications of marketing activities employed to increase business. Agents can use the "Sales Rater" as a tool to measure selling skills and selling techniques for each individual case. This device is easy to use and can be self-administered for an increased performance.

Mills, Joseph E. Target market: Single professional businesswomen. *Life Association News* (September 1992), 129–132.

There is a major difference between approaching men and women with insurance packages. Single women often have a limited knowledge of life, health, disability, or overhead expense coverage and no real urge to be educated about them. Therefore, it is necessary for agents to establish a trust with such clients and assure them that their interests are most important. This task can be accomplished through detailed planning before the initial sales meeting and outlining the benefits for the prospective client.

Mulhearn, Cynthia A. Female agents: Separating myth from reality. *LIMRA's Market Facts* (November/December 1992), 15–17.

There are six predominant myths associated with female insurance agents. Most of these myths are unfounded, considering the statistics that have been compiled. For example, it is commonly believed that female agents do not deal with rejection as well as male agents, even though statistics show that males have a 19 percent four-year retention rate and female agents a 17 percent rate.

Smith, Christopher A. Successful selling in a highly competitive environment. *American Salesman* (November 1992), 16–20.

When the selling environment becomes highly competitive, salespeople need to work harder to satisfy their current clients and pursue new ones. Therefore, it is important to maintain a positive relationship with current customers. These customers are an excellent source for new leads. A competent sales force that is able to supply customers with detailed product comparisons and give interesting sales presentations are well prepared to work in a competitive environment.

Chapter 2

The Organizational Buyer and the Buying Process

OPENING SCENARIO

Bob Thompson, the purchasing manager for HOUTEX Industries, was considering adding another supplier to the company's list of approved vendors for electric motors. He had been contacted by Trish Cornwell, of Specific Electric (SE), the week before. He was familiar with the reputation of SE products but was not sure whether they would be a good choice. Their motors had a reputation for high quality and a reasonable price, but he had heard that SE was sometimes late with deliveries.

Additionally, since he had first moved into purchasing, Bob had worked with Jim Johnson, the salesperson for Delta Motors. Delta had generally been a good source of supply; the quality of their motors was high and their price was reasonable. Plus, Bob liked Jim and knew what to expect from Delta. The reason for his considering adding Specific Electric to his approved vendors list was that the comptroller was concerned that HOUTEX might be paying too much for component parts and was asking that Bob's department consider using SE as the supplier for all major components. Also, engineering was considering some changes in the design of their products, which would result in changes in the specifications of the motors HOUTEX used.

Chapter Objectives

After reading this chapter, you should be able to

- Identify the forces that affect the buyer and the buying process.
- Understand the human dimension in organizational buying decisions.

- Recognize how the type of organization affects the buying decision.
- Know the steps in the buying process and how the salesperson must relate to the customer at each step in the process.

INTRODUCTION

One of the characteristics of top salespeople is their ability to understand and empathize with the buyer. Today, emphasis is being placed on developing a relationship with buyers instead of focusing on single transactions. This fact, along with the increasing professionalism in organizational purchasing, means that the ability to empathize is critical for all salespeople.

Sales professionals are faced with a dynamic environment that complicates their job. A major part of this dynamism is related to the buyer and the buying organization. At one time it was assumed that buyers simply made decisions based on a set of guidelines put in place by the organization (the "rational man" model). Because of this, they were seen as little more than pawns in the purchasing process. However, it is more accurate to say that the buying process is a rationalized process—that is, although the buying decision is constrained by organizational guidelines, "buyers are people, too." To be successful today, salespeople must recognize that offering a good product at a good price is not enough. Salespeople cannot assume that all buyers are alike in the way they do their jobs or in what is important to them. Changing these outdated views requires openness on the part of salespeople as well as some fresh thinking.

Barbara Jackson, a marketing and sales consultant, describes the situation this way: "The complexity and variety of behavior of individual accounts make understanding customers' behavior a tall challenge. Inadequate understanding can lead to poor marketing decisions. Successful relationship marketing is difficult."[1] Although **relationship marketing,** also called "partnering," is difficult, it is essential for companies that want to be competitive in today's business environment and in the future.[2] A first step in understanding these complexities is to examine the forces that shape buyers and their decision-making processes.

ORGANIZATIONAL BUYER BEHAVIOR

At any given time, organizational buyers are affected by a number of factors. Figure 2-1 depicts the major internal and external forces that have an impact on organizational buyers. Think of internal forces as those characteristics and traits that make a person unique. External forces, on the other hand, are those situations and events outside the person. The external forces tend to have an effect on the internal forces, which, in turn, directly influence buyer behavior. These internal and external forces are interrelated and dynamic.

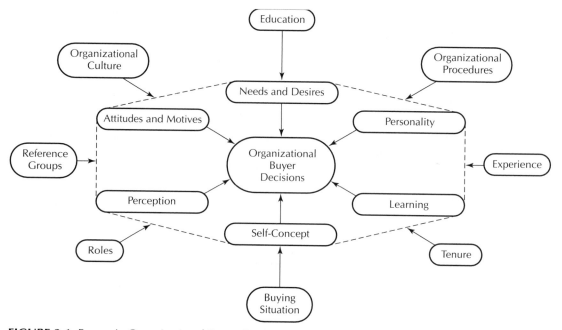

FIGURE 2-1 Forces in Organizational Buyer Decisions

Internal Forces

The internal forces that affect buyer behavior include those things that shape thoughts and actions. They represent the psychological makeup of the buyer and develop over time in response to a number of influences. These internal forces include the following:

Needs and desires
Perception
Personality
Self-concept
Attitudes and motives
Learning

They are dynamic in that they are constantly subject to change and interaction with the person's environment. The salesperson, then, must guard against drawing conclusions too quickly about a particular buyer and then assuming that the buyer is always going to act in a certain way.

Needs and Desires. **Needs and desires** of buyers are the driving force behind any purchasing decision. As with consumers, needs of organizational buyers are complex and multifaceted.[3] One of the more critical lessons for salespeople to learn is that buying decisions are based on meeting a need or set of needs. Needs may be organization specific or person specific. Both are powerful and both have a part to play in the buyer's decision. Whereas the former determines the type of product sought and an approved set of suppliers, the latter will decide which specific vendors will be asked to offer a quote and/or awarded an order. For example, when a buyer is purchasing a new lathe for a manufacturing application, the lathe must meet the needs of the company for doing precise metal fabrication. However, the buyer may decide on a particular supplier with which she has done business in the past. Her decision is based on the need to ensure that the lathe is delivered on time and installed correctly. The personal need in this case is the avoidance of risk.

Salespeople often make the mistake of thinking that it is enough to meet the organization-specific needs. But in many selling situations, the products, the prices, and the terms being offered by the various competitors may not be significantly different. The successful vendor in this case is often the one who better meets the person-specific needs. Another way to think about this is that the only competitive advantage—the difference that makes one company superior to the other in the mind of the customer—is how well the salesperson works with the buyer.

Perception. The second internal force is **perception,** our awareness of the world through the senses. To illustrate the importance of perception, all one has to do is think of the classical case of a car wreck and the four different reports of what happened from the four witnesses who saw it. Each watched what happened, but each saw a different wreck. Why? It could be a matter of where each was standing when witnessing the wreck, and that certainly will play some role. However, the major part of the difference likely arises from each person's individual perception of the situation. W. I. Thomas, a sociologist, stated: "If men define situations as real, they are real in their consequences."[4] In other words, what people perceive becomes reality for them. It becomes "objective truth," in which people believe and on which they act.

For the professional salesperson, forming the right impression, or helping the buyer form the correct perception, is important. Unfortunately, a buyer's perception is sometimes based on factors over which the salesperson has little control.[5] Although this is unfair, it means that the salesperson sometimes must work that much harder to gain the buyer's trust. Salespeople are often tempted to think that doing a good job is enough, and that customers should realize they are doing a good job. However, a "good job" is often not noticed until it is *not* done. The salesperson must always do a "good job," but he should also let the buyer know what a good job he is doing.

This is not to say that the salesperson continually brags about what a wonderful person he is, nor does it mean that he continually reminds the customer how privileged the customer is to have such a wonderful person calling on the account. What the salesperson can do, for example, is, when checking on the progress of an order to call the customer and let her know that he has done so and provide a status update of the order. Or the salesperson could send his customer magazine or newspaper articles that are relevant to her business. Certainly, to form a good impression, the salesperson should show concern for the customer, conduct himself as a professional, consistently do a good job of following up on orders, and pay attention to details.

Personality. Philip Kotler and Gary Armstrong define **personality** as "the unique psychological characteristics that lead to relatively consistent and lasting individual responses to one's own environment."[6] Individuals of different personality types will take in, that is, perceive, information differently. They will use different processes in decision making. Additionally, some buyers will be more extroverted and others will be more introverted. Also, depending on their personality, some people tend to be decisive, whereas others have difficulty making a decision.

The salesperson needs to adapt her sales presentation to the personality of the buyer. For example, the introverted buyer may be hesitant to reveal what real objection he has with the product. In this case the salesperson must "draw the person out" so that the customer's objections can be discussed and overcome. For the buyer who is very logical in decision making, the salesperson needs to present the advantages of her product and show how the purchase makes sense in light of the facts.

Self-Concept. **Self-concept** is that complex combination of impressions a person has shaped about himself or herself. These impressions are formed through feedback the person receives from others, as well as from the person's own reactions to the external environment.[7] As shown in Figure 2-2, a person's self-concept is a complicated combination of four elements.

1. **Ideal self:** who the person would like to be. This would consist of a "model" the person has within his or her mind of what he or she ought to be.
2. **Self-image:** how the person views himself or herself. This is the person's perception of who he or she really is. It would include beliefs about his or her personal strengths and weaknesses, as well as the traits that make the person unique.
3. **Looking-glass self:** how the person thinks others view him or her. This would consist of the sum total of the "messages" received from others over time and is currently receiving from others.
4. **Real self:** who the person actually is. This is the sometimes difficult to know "objective truth" about a person. It is really who the person is behind the outer layers.

These four elements come together to form the "self." The extent to which they are consistent, or, in terms of the figure, the extent to which each area overlaps, can determine how easy the person is to get to know and how consistently the person acts.

The more salespeople can understand each of these elements of self, the better they can work with buyers. Certainly, these elements can change and be af-

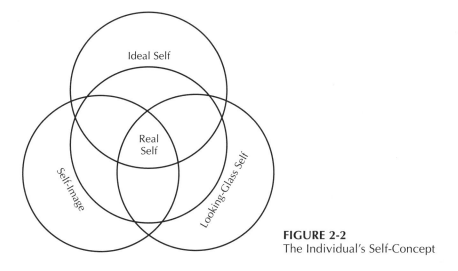

FIGURE 2-2
The Individual's Self-Concept

fected by events in everyday life. Although we readily recognize the power of self-concept to shape personal consumer behavior, we are tempted to assume that it does not have an impact on the behavior of the professional buyer in an organization. However, when the buyer walks through the door of the company for which she works, she does not leave her psychological makeup at the door. In an organizational setting, self-concept may be even more complex and may take on a different meaning than for the consumer making a purchase for personal use. For example, part of a person's organizational self-concept may be his feeling of being a professional or perhaps the feeling of being a center of power within the organization.

Attitudes and Motives. **Attitude** predisposes people to think and act in a particular fashion. In the words of Leon Schiffman and Leslie Kanuk, "attitude is a learned predisposition to behave in a consistently favorable or unfavorable way with respect to a given object."[8] In other words, attitude will guide an individual's reaction to a given object, idea, person, or activity. Attitude could be thought of as preestablishing the boundaries of a person's reaction to something.

Attitudes consist of three elements: affective, cognitive, and behavioral[9] (see Figure 2-3). The affective component includes feelings and emotional reactions. The cognitive component includes the information and knowledge we possess about objects, people, and ideas. The behavioral component directs how we tend to act. All three components come together to shape attitudes.

Just as the other elements of internal influences may change over time, so do attitudes. For the salesperson, this dynamism of attitudes can represent both a threat and an opportunity. It is a threat in the sense that one incident of poor service or product quality can have a negative impact on attitudes toward the salesperson, product, and company, even if the vendor previously had an unblemished

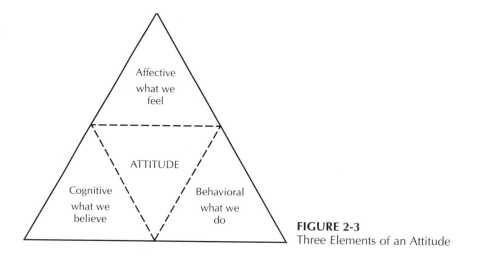

FIGURE 2-3
Three Elements of an Attitude

record. It can be an opportunity in that it allows salespeople a second chance to overcome past mistakes they or their company have made. However, remember that bad attitudes are often more difficult to overcome than good ones.

Whereas attitudes create a predisposition to act or behave in a certain way, **motives** provide the reasons for acting. A motive can be defined as "an internal energizing force that orients a person's activities toward satisfying a need or achieving a goal."[10] In other words, motives are the driving force for action. They can be either internally or externally generated. For example, thirst is an internal motive for buying a soft drink. However, when a supermarket puts soft drinks on sale, that action provides an external motive for people to buy them, whether they are thirsty or not. Normally, for professional buyers, motives are generated by their company, at least insofar as the need to make a purchase is considered. However, from whom the buyer purchases the product is affected by motives that are not company generated, such as the motive to help a salesperson who is a friend.

Salespeople must be aware of the fact that often there are more reasons for not buying from a source than buying from that source. The salesperson, then, must continually provide the buyer with reasons to choose his company rather than a competitor. Simply to feel that because he has established rapport or a good working relationship with a particular buyer does not mean that the buyer will select his company when the decision is made. It is often true, no matter how professional the buyer, that "out of sight, out of mind" is the prevailing rule.

Learning. **Learning,** the last internal force affecting buyer decisions, is the manner in which our thoughts, beliefs, and attitudes are shaped. It is a dynamic process, and there are various avenues through which people learn. According to Frederich Webster and Yorum Wind, two marketing scholars who have written extensively about buyer behavior, "Learning is the process by which behavior is influenced by previous behavior in similar situations. If behavior is successful in moving the individual toward an objective, the attainment of the goal will reinforce the behavior."[11] Individuals are continually learning. In the organizational setting, buyers learn not only from past experience but from other buyers, supervisors, and even salespeople. Learning about a supplier can begin even before the first contact by a salesperson. The reputation of the supplier and other people's experience with that supplier are powerful shapers of the image a buyer holds about a company.

In the rare case that the buyer has no previous knowledge of a particular vendor, the initial contact by the salesperson forms the basis of the learning that takes place. First impressions are important. Often, when a person is faced with a new situation, she goes through an **associative thinking process** to gain some frame of reference for dealing with the situation. That is, the process of linking together similar previous experience or knowledge to understand the new situation. The mind asks itself, "What have I seen or experienced like this before?" When the buyer meets a new salesperson, because he has so little information and is forced to come to some conclusion about the new person, he will, generally in an unconscious manner, associate the new person with some person he already knows. If that association is positive, he tends to have a positive view of the new person, or vice versa. Although people are usually open to learn new information, it is very difficult to displace negative information, to "unlearn" what has already been learned.

External Forces: Person Specific

In addition to internal forces, there are a number of outside forces that have both a direct and an indirect impact on the buyer over time and at any given point in time. These external forces can be divided into person specific forces and organization specific forces. Forces are person specific because individuals are always affected by the sum total of their unique life experiences. Forces are organization specific because people are also affected by the organization in which they work. We will discuss the person-specific forces first.

The major person-specific external forces that directly influence individuals are the following:

Education
Work experience
Tenure
Roles
Reference groups

Education. By **education,** we mean formal education, or what the person has been exposed to in the classroom. Education is obviously important in the sense that it has an impact on the outlook of buyers as well as their ability to gather and evaluate information. Given the increasing professionalism in the purchasing profession, buyers are generally better educated than in the past.[12] This trend means that salespeople will also need to be more educated and to develop their sales message with a higher educated audience in mind. In other words, successful salespeople will need more product knowledge, greater skills for expressing themselves, and a deeper understanding and appreciation of various cultures.

Work Experience. **Work experience,** the sum of all that has happened to individuals in their occupation, affects the buyer in that it provides a base for decision making. Although some buyers enter the field of purchasing as their first job, many buyers move into purchasing from other functional areas in the organization. That background will have an influence on the type of training the buyers have, how they tend to view the purchasing function, and probably even their approach to decision making. For example, if the buyer had previously been in production scheduling, she might be more concerned about delivery dates, whereas the buyer who comes from engineering will be more concerned about the technical aspects of the product, and the buyer who was previously an accountant might look more at price.

Tenure. **Tenure,** that is, the length of time one has worked for the organization, will likely affect the buyer in several ways. For example, one study reported that buyers with longer tenure tended to be more interested in receiving only the facts and less interested in polite conversation.[13] Additionally, buyers with longer tenure are more enculturated into the operations of the organization. Also, they will be aware not only of formal procedures but of the actual latitude they have in making a decision or resolving a problem. Furthermore, longtime employees tend to espouse more completely the values of the organization.

Roles. The different roles the buyer plays have a major effect on the decision process. **Roles** can be thought as the dynamic aspect of a status, that is, what we do in relation to what we are. For instance, the role of "buyer" dictates that the person act in accordance with the rational decision-making model; that is, the person always makes a decision that would give the greatest economic contribution to the organization. In other words, the buyer tries to obtain the right supplies when they are needed at the lowest possible price. But doing so requires that the buyer fill a multiplicity of other roles also.

The buyer may play the role of "technocrat" because she needs to judge whether a product will meet the specifications developed by the engineering group, or if the quality of the materials will meet the specifications established by the merchandise manager. To ensure that items arrive on time, the buyer fills the role of "scheduler." She needs to understand how the production process works and when particular products are needed, or the buying habits of retail customers and the dynamics of the industry producing the goods being purchased. To get the best price means that the buyer becomes a "negotiator." She needs to understand the pricing structures in the industry as well as the profit margin that her company needs to achieve. As a negotiator she also needs to be able to communicate well, to analyze situations, and to compromise.

There are other, not so apparent roles that a buyer may fill. First, most buyers consider themselves professionals and act according to standards set by the profession as well as those of their organizations. If a buyer views herself as a professional and subscribes to the standards set by a professional society, such as the National Association of Purchasing Management (NAPM), she will try to fulfill the role of professional buyer. Interestingly, some upper-level managers have resisted the increasing professionalism in purchasing because they do not want their buyers to follow standards not set by their companies.[14] Another set of roles fulfilled by the buyer revolves around the family. The buyer who is also the main provider for the household might be less willing to take risks and jeopardize her job because of that important role.

The existence of these multiple roles leads to **role conflict,** the situation where the demands of two or more roles are at odds. Role conflict, at a high enough level, causes psychological discomfort and puts pressure on the individual to attempt to resolve the situation quickly. Related to role conflict is **role stress,** the psychological pressure inherent in performing a particular role. It has been suggested that the role stress experienced by organizational buyers arises from their position as boundary spanners.[15] A **boundary spanner** is a person who operates between two or more parties, who make demands on the person. Figure 2-4 depicts the position of a boundary spanner and the sources of role stress that accompany the position.

Although role stress is inherent in purchasing jobs, the amount of role stress is inversely related to **role clarity,** how the nature and conduct of the job

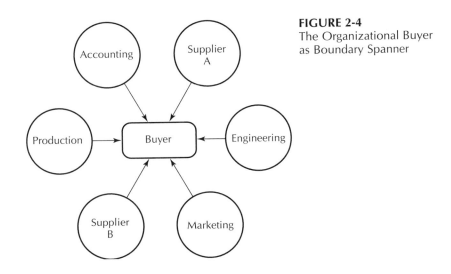

FIGURE 2-4
The Organizational Buyer
as Boundary Spanner

are defined and what is expected of the buyer. Higher levels of role clarity in purchasing jobs have been associated with higher levels of job satisfaction.[16] This may be due to the lessening of role conflict as a result of a greater understanding of job requirements. Although the salesperson can do little to alleviate role stress as such, she can understand the precarious position held by the buyer and attempt to minimize its effect through showing her appreciation for his position and working to help him satisfy his various constituencies.

Then there are the roles within the organization that the buyer must fill as being part of the buying center.[17] The **buying center** is the group of people who have a direct impact on a buying decision. It consists of representatives from six distinct areas:

Initiator. The person who detects the need for a purchase and begins the process, such as a shop foreman.

Influencer. The person who has an impact on the decision-making process through the information he or she possesses, such as an engineer.

Gatekeeper. The person who controls the flow of information and/or access to others in the organization, such as a secretary or a receptionist.

Decider. The person who actually makes the final decision, such as the vice president of purchasing.

Buyer. The person who locates sources of supply and who issues the purchase order.

User. The person who will make use of the item purchased, either using it in the operation of the firm or adding it to the product being produced, such as maintenance personnel or machinists.

For salespeople, the importance of the buying center concept relates to how people in these roles influence the purchase decision-making process. Additionally, salespeople need to remember that the buyer often fills more than one role. In some cases the buyer may also act as a gatekeeper or, in others, as the decider. The importance of each of these roles will vary, of course, depending on the situation. In general, the more important the decision, the greater the likelihood that all of these roles will be involved. For simple rebuying purchases, generally the buyer is the only role of significance.

The implication of the buying center concept is that the salesperson must recognize that each person in the buying center has different factors that he or she is concerned about. The salesperson must not only recognize this but must also address the concerns of each member of the center. In the purchase of a major piece of machining equipment, for instance, not only is the buyer involved but the firm may assign a mechanical engineer to incorporate the machine into their operations and to work with the supplier. During the vendor selection process, this engineer will be interested in the technical aspects of the equipment and in finding a supplier that is able to meet the established specifications. Thus the engineer plays the part of the influencer. Also involved in this purchase, perhaps, is the vice president of finance, who will make the ultimate decision of whether the firm can justify buying the equipment. This person will be interested in having information on the life-cycle cost of the equipment and on the payoff period. The user in this example is the shop foreman, who is interested in how the machine operates, how efficient it is, and how much downtime can reasonably be expected.

In order to gain access to these people, the salesperson must work with the buyer, who in addition to actually issuing the purchase order, may play the part of the gatekeeper. The salesperson should not assume that if she puts together a packet of materials for each member of the buying center that the buyer will deliver the material in such a way as to get the attention it deserves. The problem is that the buyer is not a salesperson. He may be an excellent buyer and may even favor the salesperson's firm over the competition; however, he has not been trained as a salesperson and does not possess the salesperson's knowledge of the product and industry. It is important, then, that the salesperson get direct access to each member of the buying center, if at all possible. And yet, the salesperson should avoid doing an "end run" around the buyer; that is, she should not go directly to each person without consulting the buyer first. Buyers are protective of their "turf," and they have a right to be. When a purchase is made, and something goes wrong with the purchased product, the buyer will likely take the blame, regardless of whether or not he made the final purchase decision.

Reference Groups. The reference groups to which the buyer belongs have an effect on that person's influence in the organization and hence on her buying behavior.[18] By **reference group**, we mean a group of people with whom a person identifies to the extent that his or her behavior is affected by the group. Reference groups can be formal or informal. Note, too, that a person does not necessarily have to belong to a reference group for it to affect how she behaves. She could aspire to membership in a particular group, and that aspiration would affect her actions. For example, if the buyer desires to become a certified purchasing manager (CPM), a designation established by the National Association of Purchasing Management, her actions will more likely conform to the code of conduct of CPMs than will those of someone who has no desire for that designation.[19]

If a buyer is new in the organization, he will often associate with the other buyers to "learn the ropes." This group of buyers would constitute an informal reference group, and the new buyer would tend to espouse the ideals of that group if membership in the group were desired. Informal reference groups can be as powerful in shaping behavior as formal reference groups are. For the salesperson, being familiar with the buyer's reference group is an essential element in understanding the buyer.

External Forces: Organization Specific

The major organization-specific external forces include the following:

Organizational culture
Organizational procedures
Buying situation

SELL!NG
THE FRONT LINES OF BUSINESS

The World's Toughest Customers
Linda Corman

On a May day in 1992, some 150 sales executives packed themselves elbow to elbow into 15 rows of hard-backed chairs in the first-floor conference room of Scott Paper Co.'s world headquarters, hard by Philadelphia International Airport. The executives, representing the company's largest suppliers, had been invited—no, ordered—there by Sharon Robbins, Scott's newly appointed vice president of worldwide procurement. From the tone of the directive ("You be in Philadelphia on Monday at 8 a.m.," by one salesperson's account), it was clear this would be no party. As it turned out, it was judgment day.

Robbins spared her guests an anxious wait. Standing at a podium and backed by slides, she told the suppliers in no uncertain terms, says one attendee, that they had been feeding off of Scott for years, charging the company far more than its competitors. To get a fair shake, Scott meant to slash its number of vendors by more than half. Those who expected to continue selling to the company would have to cut prices and eliminate waste. And they would have to explain every step in their production processes so that Scott could help them cut their costs, and consequently, their prices.

"It was as if she were saying, 'You are guilty and now you're going to pay,'" recalls the supplier. "For five hours we were being beaten about the head and neck.

"The straw that broke the camel's back was the one percent of sales they said each company would have to remit at the end of each quarter," the supplier says. "I'd never heard of that." Neither had most of the others.

What seemed like hours actually lasted 45 minutes, says one who was there. But it was long enough. As the stunned sales chiefs left, many were in shock. They shouldn't have been. As another supplier notes, "This is exactly what's going on in the world. To an extent, I admire the initiative she took. She's eliminating waste. That's the same thing we're doing with our vendors."

Indeed, while Robbins's presentation may have been unconventional, her message is increasingly common. She is a model for the new breed of purchasing agent—hard-driving, uncompromising, and far more powerful than ever before. Today's purchasing agents are enjoying newfound clout and stature in the corporate world. (Witness the drama of Jose Ignacio Lopez de Arriortua, whose reputation for brutal cost-cutting led Volkswagen to steal him away from General Motors last spring.) These tough customers are leading the charge for cost control and improved profitability. No longer relegated to the back room, they have direct access and accountability to the executive offices.

Across the country, purchasing agents are pruning suppliers like so much dead wood. In doing so, they are rewriting the rules of sales. Fishing trips, lavish lunches, and small talk count for precious little these days. No account is solid. To survive, salespeople must remake themselves and their companies into the kind of strategic partners their customers now demand. The reward: long-term relationships and larger orders.

Some purchasing chiefs, such as Robbins or Lopez, come across like Ivan the Terrible. Others disavow off-with-their-heads techniques with talk of win-win relationships. But however they dress it up, they are duty bound to change sales forever. "We can't wait for the revenue side to save us because of the weak economy," explains Rick Gerardo, vice president of materials management for Dow North America. "What do I [as a company] have control over? Obviously, purchasing."

So what do these power purchasers look for in a vendor? Someone who can provide the best-quality products at the lowest prices. Suppliers must pass elaborate qualifying processes that rate their dependability, response time, lead times, and the ability to minimize defective products. What matters most is being capable of building strong business relationships, not personal ones. Salespeople must be in a position to sell their own organizations. "It's not the salesperson who would win our business," explains Lael Nussbaum, a purchaser at Dow North America. "It's the company behind the salesperson who could win our business."

In another shift, salespeople must be ready to answer to more than one decision-maker. Purchasing agents don't just fill orders anymore; they work with different departments to choose what products to buy. Even in this era of strategic partnering, it still comes down to product. And salespeople had better bone up. "If you're not ready to talk to the technical properties of your product, if you say, 'Well, I thought I was just going to see the purchasing agent, so I'm not prepared,' that's the answer—you're not prepared," says Land O' Lakes' head of corporate purchasing, Fred Fezatte.

So be prepared, and be warned. With these tough customers, there will be no second chance. Here are five of the world's most demanding buyers, and their tips for surviving the great shakeout of sales.

SHARON ROBBINS

Scott Paper, Vice President of Worldwide Procurement

Sharon Robbins, who has spent most of her career in marketing and operations, was assigned to her current post in late 1991 with a mandate to revolutionize purchasing. During the past 15 months, she has cut ties with about 5,000 of Scott Paper's 11,000 U.S. suppliers. At the same time, the company slashed its overall costs by $200 million, as much as $60 million of which came from purchasing, according to Morgan Stanley analyst Thomas Clephane. It posted a $220 million pre-tax profit last year, compared with a $120 million pre-tax loss in 1991.

"How much of that can be attributed to Sharon grabbing our ankles and shaking hard is hard to know," says one supplier who made Scott's initial cut. "But a lot of it certainly came from us." The supplier adds that his company reduced its prices to Scott 10 percent last year for one major product.

By the end of 1993 Scott expects to cut its suppliers to fewer than 2,000. To that end, Robbins has been holding a second round of meetings with vendors, urging them to sustain their cost-cutting measures.

"We've merely scratched the surface," says Robbins. In weeding out suppliers, she is looking for those that have the most control over their own cost structures. Low production costs translate into low prices.

"To decide who are the best competitors, we invite suppliers in, engage them in a process to understand their costs, their technical resources," Robbins says. "We allow them to make proposals for our business. We're searching out the best value."

Price is not the only criterion. Scott is changing from "relationship- to fact-based buying," according to Robbins, so salespeople need to become more like technical specialists. They must be able to discuss how their companies can help improve Scott's operations.

Along with cutting costs and suppliers, Robbins has brought sales techniques to the buying side. "We see the buyer shifting to the role of product manager so that before they source a product, we expect them to know more about the marketplace than the product manager who calls upon him," she says.

FRED FEZATTE

Land O' Lakes, Vice President of Corporate Purchasing

Buyers traditionally have relished the game of ducking salespeople's verbal barrages. If a salesperson managed to breach the barricades and get within shouting distance, purchasers did all they could to appear not to listen. Now Fred Fezatte is turning the tables. He urges his staff to solicit an earful from salespeople. In fact, one of the quickest ways to turn him off is by not having enough to say—of substance, that is.

"Salespeople say, 'We have the quality process in our plant.' I say, 'Tell me about it,' and all of a sudden they're stammering and stuttering. If they are involved in the quality process, they should know what it is, what objectives there are, and where the company is in the process. When they get vague, it's a real turnoff," says Fezatte, who has headed purchasing for the Minneapolis company since 1984.

Fezatte is turning the tables literally as well as figuratively, encouraging his staff to take salespeople to lunch. There's nothing better than having reps captive for a while to find out just what they're offering.

That knowledge is crucial for Land O' Lakes, where weeding suppliers is a high priority. In the past three years the company has cut its suppliers by 20 percent, down from several thousand. In the next two years it expects to cut another 20 percent, says Fezatte.

Suppliers make the grade by offering something novel, by making it clear their companies want to sell over the long term, and by showing they are willing to diversify into new products as Land O' Lakes needs them. Fezatte is also after "quality suppliers," the ones who have the lowest rejection rates, who most frequently deliver on time, and who "add value" by automating a plant, achieving faster turnarounds, or providing technical assistance for production lines.

Fezatte does not have much time for salespeople who are only interested in boosting sales 10 percent every month, or in "me-too players." The former, he says, are not likely to be looking to the long term. And the latter are the ones who do not work with Land O' Lakes to find innovations and who are looking only to match whatever anyone else has to offer.

RICK GERARDO

Dow North America, Vice President of Materials Management

For Dow, it's all in the numbers. In the next three years the Midland, Mich., company plans to slash by at least a third the tens of thousands of suppliers from which it buys some $5.5 billion worth of materials and services annually. Says Rick Gerardo, "We're quite focused on reducing numbers. The more we have, the more it costs to have people to interface with them, [the more it costs] in accounts

payable, and the harder it is to aggregate and leverage purchases."

These days, Dow is leveraging purchases by giving big orders to a few companies and then negotiating the most favorable terms. Although it has been cutting vendors for the past year, so far, Gerardo says, fewer than 10 percent have been eliminated overall, and savings have been small. On the other hand, on some products, cuts have been dramatic. For one particular service, he says, 150 suppliers were reduced to only four. Gerardo says that the suppliers who will continue to do business with Dow are the ones most interested in selling in the long term and in developing new products and cost-saving processes.

Gerardo, whose 27 years at Dow include 18 in manufacturing, is especially impatient with the one-hand-feeds-the-other, expense-account comaraderies that in the past so often glued relationships between purchasers and salespeople. Never having listed purchasing management as a goal ("Companies didn't put their top people in it," he says), Gerardo only wants to play that game if it will have a significant effect on the company's bottom line. "We want to translate [new purchasing approaches] into lower costs," he says. "We're not interested in getting together for nice team meetings and golf outings."

Gerardo was named to his newly created position, which has North American operating board status, a year and a half ago. Previously, the director of purchasing was not on the operating board, but reported to an executive who was. Gerardo says the new arrangement has effectively eliminated one management layer between purchasing and Dow's top executives.

JACK ZAVES

American Airlines, Managing Director—Fuels Management and Contract Services

American Airlines chairman Robert Crandall reportedly once said there are "three criteria for buying an airplane: price, price, and price." In all areas, the company has long been one of the industry's leading cost-cutters.

In October 1992 American adopted a comprehensive cost-reduction program that has shaved $55 million from its $4 billion in annual materials and services purchases (excluding aircraft). For his part, Jack Zaves has saved American $9.8 million in fuel costs.

The program features "alternative currencies"—unique options offered to suppliers to break a tie between quotes. They range from buying ads in the airline's *American Way* magazine to sending employees for computer training at American's information services subsidiary, Amris. They are "ways of reducing our costs or increasing our revenues aside from the service or product we are buying," explains Zaves.

American has also shaved costs by negotiating better payment terms, eliminating automatic escalation clauses, and imposing penalties for not meeting contract terms. And since October, it has been intensifying its efforts to scale back on suppliers. With larger orders, the remaining vendors can reduce costs through economies of scale and then pass on the savings.

While it has cut suppliers in such areas as spare parts (down 25 percent), the Fort Worth, Texas-based airline has been trying to increase its number of fuel suppliers. That is because it wants to counteract the trend of refineries shutting down, and keep as much competition in the business as possible. Still, according to Zaves, the airline plans further supplier cuts in other areas.

A former salesman himself, Zaves looks for "innovative salespeople, not those who are just couriers from some pricing department." The ones who get his ear are those who "don't put down canned presentations. If someone came in and said, 'We'd like to renew our contract, what do you want?' I'd [probably want to] kick him out of the office. He should be coming to us with ideas."

GENE RICHTER

Hewlett-Packard, Executive Director of Procurement

For the past five years, Hewlett-Packard has been deciding which 30 percent of its several hundred main suppliers it could do without. In that time, Gene Richter has taken note of salespeople who have become scarce after winning an order. He wants to stick with those who solve production-line problems before Hewlett-Packard gets wind of them. And he wants to lose those who, when asked about a bottleneck threatening to shut down a production line, respond, "Which plant?"

Since becoming the Palo Alto, Calif., company's top purchasing exec in 1988, Richter says he has cut back primary suppliers to fewer than 300. Although the company does not plan additional cuts, it will continue to hold vendors to an exacting standard and "requalify" them every three years. Besides keeping tabs on how products are performing, it is looking to see which salespeople get involved with decision-makers in all departments. At Hewlett-Packard, that means discussing pricing and other business issues with top executives. And it means keeping pace with the technological and design changes in the industry in order to work effectively with the company's engineers.

"It takes a lot of getting to know each other," says Richter. "I don't know what attention-getting letter, joke, or slick multimedia presentation would impress someone who's been around the procurement scene for 32 years, as I have. You've seen it all. It's dogged determination."

Besides cutting suppliers, Hewlett-Packard for the past two years has been reducing its costs through zero-based pricing. That means periodically reviewing every cost of turning out a component and determining whether any part of the process can be done less expensively—instead of reviewing only the portions of a component's cost that are rising. As Richter notes, "When you look at every element of cost, there is more opportunity to keep questioning why."

Reprinted with permission of SELL!NG magazine.

Organizational Culture. Organizational culture is the corporate mind-set that creates the environment in which employees work. It not only sets the boundaries of acceptable actions but establishes the climate in which people interact. *Culture* can be thought of as a system of knowledge, beliefs, and values that result in norms of behavior and a common worldview. Although we think of values as being stable, as they generally are, there is a dynamic aspect to them. For example, our increasing concern about the environment has brought pressures on buyers to make socially responsible buying decisions.[20]

Culture is often imparted to employees directly through codes of conduct. Culture is also indirectly taught through the socialization process. As people enter the organization, they learn what is acceptable and what is not. What they learn can be both "official" values of the firm—what the company says is true and correct—and "latent" values—"the way it really is here in the trenches." Generally, they learn a combination, and both shape their outlook and actions. The salesperson who has a knowledge of the corporate culture of his customers will know better what is expected and how he should proceed in certain situations.

The type of organization is related to organizational culture. By type, we mean not only the general category of the organization but also the specific type of product produced or service performed. There are a number of approaches to classifying organizations by type. A simple approach is to classify them into groups according to their purpose or objective. This method yields three groups, as depicted in Figure 2-5: commercial organizations, government organizations, and institutional organizations. Each of these can be subdivided into more specific groups.

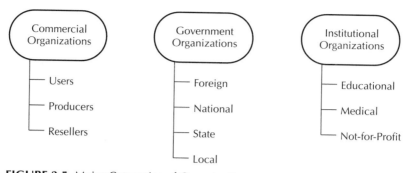

FIGURE 2-5 Major Categories of Organizations

Commercial organizations are defined as those organizations that exist for the purpose of making a profit. The operation of their business depends on achieving a return on their investments. In general, the primary concern of commercial organizations is the allocation of resources to obtain the best possible return, and their guiding principle is the efficient use of funds. This means that for these firms, salespeople must stress getting the greatest value for the expenditure invested.

Although commercial organizations share some common characteristics, they can be subdivided into three types, each of which has unique properties: users, producers, and resellers. *Users* purchase a product for the purpose of using it in the operation of their business. These products become part of overhead, the cost of doing business. When an organization buys the product as a user, the primary concern is cost—not only the money it takes to buy the item but other costs associated with it, such as opportunity costs. The salesperson must be able to justify the cost to the buyer in terms of how this purchase decision will contribute to the efficient operation of the firm.

Producers purchase a product for the purpose of including it in whatever they are producing. For a manufacturer, the product may be a component part or raw material; for a construction firm, it may be building materials. The items producers buy represent direct costs. Although the cost of the item is a concern for the producer, quality is likely to be a more important consideration. This is because customers will blame the producer if the product fails or praise the producer if it works. Customers may acknowledge that the producer did not actually make all the components that are used in their products; however, that is of little comfort if the product fails. The producer, then, recognizes that its product is "only as strong as its weakest part." The job of the salesperson in this case is to help the buyer determine what component part will perform the function needed for the buyer's product to operate as well as how the buyer's product is positioned in the market in terms of quality. Only then can the salesperson offer a product that provides the appropriate quality at the best possible price. Additionally, when the salesperson is selling to a producer, he will need to understand the production process and what approach the producer wishes to take in terms of stocking of that component.

Resellers are organizations that buy items for the purpose of reselling them at a profit. Included in this group are both wholesalers and retailers. There is a popular misconception about resellers and their relationship with manufacturers. Students often have the impression that resellers are simply selling agents for the manufacturer. This view would suggest that manufacturers control the marketing of their products and that the reseller's job is to implement programs of the manufacturer. Once a person recognizes that the manufacturer and the reseller have a different view of the product, the fallacy of this impression is apparent. Think about it this way: Does the purchasing manager for a supermarket chain, such as Albertson's, view Procter & Gamble's Tide detergent the same way the product manager for Tide detergent does? The answer is obviously no. For Albertson's, Tide, though it is a major brand, is only one of a number of brands of detergents that the store carries, and detergent is only one of thousands of other products the store carries. On the other hand, for Procter & Gamble, Tide is a major profit center.

Resellers, rather than seeing themselves as selling agents for manufacturers, view themselves as purchasing agents for their customers, and therefore, their main goal is to provide what their customers need and want. Resellers are concerned with margin and turnover. The salesperson, in this case, must be knowledgeable about the reseller's customers and be able to show that the product will justify the allocation of shelf space in terms of margin and turnover. Additionally, the salesperson must adopt the mind-set of the store manager and thereby assist the manager in selling the product lines she represents.

Governmental organizations are the next major category. Although it might be instructive to discuss the different types of governments, given the limitations on space, our discussion will concern governments in general. Whereas commercial organizations are profit driven, government organizations could be said to be budget driven.[21] Government organizations exist for the purpose of serving the public and, hence, are supported by the public through taxes. Their revenues do not result from the profit created through enterprise but, rather, flow from the public's ability to pay taxes. Because that ability is limited, governments are limited in the amount of revenue to which they have access. The budget, then, becomes the guidance mechanism.

Governments mandate some special programs and provisions that are unique to government contracts.[22] In its **compliance program,** a government requires that affirmative action programs be employed if a contractor is to be eligible to compete for a contract. A government also has a **set-aside program** that requires a certain percentage of their contracts and projects be given to minority and small businesses.

The salesperson's job in selling to governments is somewhat different than selling to commercial organizations. The salesperson must keep abreast of the purchasing procedures of the government and ensure that her organization is in full compliance with those procedures. Governments generally use a formalized bidding process in which price is again a major factor. Perhaps almost as important is ensuring that the product conforms to government specifications and is delivered in the time promised. Failure to deliver on time often results in the cancellation of orders and, sometimes, in the assessment of a penalty.

A number of useful publications are available to companies that wish to sell to the federal government. They are generally available from the Government Printing Office and government depository libraries. Some of these titles are *Doing Business with the Federal Government, Selling to the Military, Selling to the U.S. Air Force,* and *Commerce Business Daily.* Additionally, for small businesses, the Small Business Administration offers assistance in selling to the federal government.

Institutional organizations, like governments, tend to be budget driven. Institutions are educational, medical, or not for profit. They often depend on outside agencies for their funding, and therefore answer to those agencies for their expenditures. Because institutions, like governments, tend to be bureaucratic, they often have strict procedures to follow. So one of the salesperson's responsibilities involves compliance with procedures. Institutions are unique in that purchase decisions are often made by people who would be considered professionals but who are not experts in purchasing. Also, there are more group decisions.[23] This means that the salesperson must be able to communicate with the nonpurchasing professional. The salesperson, however, must not ignore the buyer during the selling process.

The three major categories of organizations vary differently in their buying procedures and therefore require different approaches by salespeople. Figure 2-6 depicts the major concerns of these organizations when they make their buying decisions.

For salespeople, it is often necessary that they get a precise definition of the type of business they are targeting, especially when gathering data for forecasts or for developing prospect lists. Perhaps the most well-known and precise approach to classifying organizations is the **Standard Industrial Classification**

FIGURE 2-6 Major Concerns of Organizations

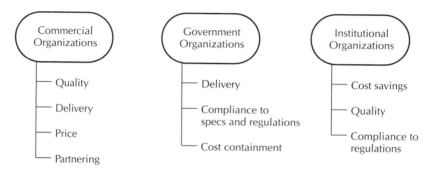

(SIC) system developed by the federal government. The advantage of using the SIC code is that there is a tremendous amount of information readily available that uses SIC code numbers to categorize organizations for the purpose of reporting data. The system classifies companies beginning with major divisions and gradually refines the classification until it gets to the manufactured products level. Table 2-1 shows an example of how the classification works. Although, as shown in the table, the SIC system can refine the classification of a company to the seven-digit level, most reporting agencies do not go beyond four digits. Although this provides a fair amount of specificity, the four-digit level still has fairly wide categories, and often data for the category will include businesses that are somewhat dissimilar. However, in general, they are similar enough that most data are usable.

Organizational Procedures. **Organizational procedures** refers to the standard operating methods used by every purchasing organization. Some of these are formalized, written guidelines, but many are not codified by the firm. These procedures place constraints on how the buyer is to make purchasing decisions and are followed for the purpose of making less risky decisions.[24] Generally, they will spell out how many quotations the buyers should obtain on particular sizes and types of purchases, how they are to go about evaluating the bids, and what major criteria of selection the buyer should use. Given the increase in the number of firms that use approved vendor lists,[25] these procedures also spell out with whom the buyer may do business. Because these procedures vary widely among firms, salespeople must familiarize themselves with their customers' purchasing processes and adapt their strategy accordingly.

Regardless of the category of organization, the salesperson needs to recognize that purchases by organizations are the result of **derived demand,** which

TABLE 2-1 An Example of an SIC Classification

Level	SIC Code	Description
Division	D	Manufacturer
Major group	34	Manufacturer of fabricated metal products
Industry subgroup	344	Manufacturer of fabricated structural metal products
Detailed industry	3441	Manufacturer of fabricated structural steel
Product category	34411	Manufacturer of fabricated structural steel for buildings
Manufactured products	3441121	Manufacturer of fabricated structural steel for buildings—Iron & steel (for sale to companies: industrial)

means that organizations make a purchase as a result of their customers' or clients' purchasing from them. An example of derived demand would be the fact that when the purchase of Ford automobiles increases, the purchase of sheet metal by Ford increases. In other words, the purchase of sheet metal by Ford is derived from the purchase of cars by the consuming public.

This concept is important for a number of reasons. First, if the salesperson is attempting to forecast sales for the coming year, she probably needs to go beyond simply examining the trends in her industry and examine projected buying behavior by her customers' customers. It is not enough to be an expert in one's own industry; the salesperson also needs to become an expert in her customers' industries.

Another aspect of derived demand is that of trying to compete in an industry that sells relatively undifferentiated products. Often there is little difference between the salesperson's product and that of a competitor. The only real difference is the individual salesperson. One way a salesperson can gain a competitive advantage is by helping the customer reach her market. The salesperson who understands the implications of derived demand will work with her customers to help make them more successful in their marketplace.

Buying Situation. The **buying situation** is determined by factors from the environment, from inside the organization, and from within the individual.[26] Specifically, the type of purchase affects the buying situation. Purchases can be divided into three types:[27]

1. **Straight rebuy.** A purchase that is made on a repetitive basis. It involves routinized response behavior because there is no substantive difference in the product since the last time it was purchased.
2. **Modified rebuy.** This purchase situation involves some change in the product that means the buyer must engage in some search behavior and problem solving. Although somewhat familiar with the product, the buyer has to get more involved in making this purchase.
3. **New task purchase.** In this situation the buyer has not bought the product before. It involves extensive decision making in terms of determining the specifications of the product, who to solicit for bids, and who actually to buy from.

The salesperson needs to understand the type of buying situation that is facing the buyer because this can alter the type of information the buyer needs and the number of people involved in the buying decision, as well as a number of other factors.

THE ORGANIZATIONAL PURCHASING PROCESS

The organizational purchasing process is very complex. The process has been broken down in various ways and may have anywhere from three to a large number of major steps.[28] For our purposes, we will view the process as involving six steps:

1. Recognizing a need
2. Developing specifications
3. Selecting vendors
4. Evaluating quotes and selecting suppliers
5. Placing the purchase order
6. Receiving the materials

Figure 2-7 shows our six-step purchasing process model. It presents the steps involved in a more extensive purchasing decision, such as a new task or perhaps a modified rebuy purchase. Obviously, the process will vary, depending on the type of purchase. For example, for a straight rebuy, firms often forgo this multistep process through the use of **blanket purchase orders (BPO),** a preset agreement with a supplier that outlines the price and the terms for the purchase of a given item. When a requisition is received by the buyer, she simply releases it to the BPO supplier, who automatically delivers the goods. BPOs are used by a majority of firms today.[29]

The process begins with the *recognition of a need.* In different organizations and different purchasing situations, the manner in which needs are recognized will vary. Purchasing organizations today make heavy use of computers in the purchasing process.[30] In many manufacturing organizations, the computer keeps track of inventory level and scheduling, and when stock reaches a certain level, the computer notifies the purchasing department. In some cases the need is formally recognized with the signing of a contract for a product or construction project. In this case often a person in the engineering or the drafting department completes a materials takeoff, that is, a list of items needed to complete the product or project. Finally, in other cases the need arises during the normal course of a business, such as a secretary notifying purchasing of a need for typing paper.

The second step in the process is *developing a set of specifications* for the product to be purchased and issuing a requisition. Where the need arises as the result of a stockout, the set of specifications is already completed and do not require redevelopment. However, in the new task or modified rebuy purchase, the development of specifications can be complex, perhaps involving people from

FIGURE 2-7 Steps in the Organizational Buying Process

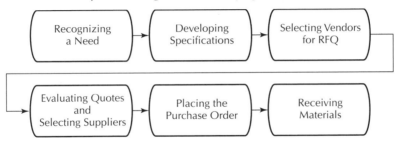

engineering, production, purchasing, and marketing. Once the requisition is drawn up, it is forwarded to the purchasing department.

The third step involves *selecting the vendors* to be sent a **request for quotation (RFQ),** the listing of items with a request for the vendors to bid on them. Just as the process of developing specifications will vary with the type of purchase, so, too, will the extent of search behavior required by the buyer. Increasingly, firms are using formalized **approved vendor lists (AVL)** from which suppliers must be drawn. AVLs are formalized lists of vendors that have been certified by the purchasing department as suppliers for an item. Generally, to be on the list a supplier must go through a screening process by the customer. Such a process often will include consideration of the supplier's financial stability and a visit to the supplier's plant.

When extended search behavior is required by the buyer, suppliers' names must be readily available to the buyer.[31] Buyers make heavy use of such sources as the *Thomas Register.* Professional directories such as *Thomas* and ads in trade publications provide leads for the selling firm and thereby supplement the sales effort. When the buyer does not need to engage in extended search behavior, the task of the selling organization is not only to be included on the AVL but to make sure that the customer associates the firm with a reasonably high level of service.

Evaluating the quotations and selecting suppliers make up the next step. Although price and/or value is probably the main determinant at this point, other factors are also important.[32] The promised delivery date and quality are often equally as critical as the price, and, at times, each of these will serve as the major criterion. Other factors, such as payment and delivery, are evaluated because they represent a cost for the buyer's firm.

During this selection phase, the salesperson's role is extremely critical and takes on a different purpose. Until now, the sales message revolved around the reliability of the supplier and its products, and the object was to convince the buyer that what the salesperson has to offer will fulfill the buyer's needs. At this juncture, however, the selling job becomes one of arriving at mutually acceptable terms. The buyer already has a need for the salesperson's product and knows that the company can be counted on to supply the product, but the buyer must now be convinced that the best possible terms have been offered. Most buyers do want the selling firm to make a profit; however their job is to see that the profit is reasonable and that their own firm is not being overcharged. It is also important to remember that different buyers sometimes have different needs and use different strategies in making the final purchase decision.[33]

Placing the **purchase order** is generally a fairly mechanical process. The ease with which this step is accomplished is in direct relationship to the quality of the quotations supplied by the selected vendor. Errors may often arise at this point because a clause is not properly spelled out in the RFQ and is subject to misinterpretation. Although the buyer should catch any discrepancy, it is typically a buying clerk who actually produces the *purchase order,* and this person may not be familiar enough with the nature of the order to know when mistakes are present. Buyers generally have a tremendous amount of work to do and are subject to missing details that may be important later. So when the salesperson receives the purchase order, he needs to check it carefully to ensure that it complies with the quotation.

The final step involves *receipt of the material.* Although many salespeople consider the sale closed when they receive the purchase, the sale is not closed for the buyer until the product is received in good order and at the right time. Monitoring the order and a follow-up phone call go a long way toward cementing the relationship between the buyer and the seller. Information about conformity to specifications, quality and the condition of the product, and whether the order arrived on schedule provides feedback for the buyer and affects future decisions concerning vendors from which to solicit quotations in the future.

The buying process described here will vary among companies and situations. Certainly, some of the steps can be combined or done away with altogether. With the three types of purchases discussed earlier—straight rebuy, modified rebuy, and new task—all six of these steps may or may not be used for a particular purchase. In general, the less routine the purchase the more of these steps will be involved in the process. Each step requires different action by the salesperson if she is to be successful in working with the customer. Also, the salesperson must remember that this buying process can seldom be speeded up and she therefore must be flexible in working with the demands of the customer and on waiting for decisions to be made.

CHAPTER SUMMARY

This chapter described the major influences on the organizational buyer and the buying process. The factors that influence the organizational buyer are either organization specific or person specific, and both combine to govern the decisions made by the buyer. Often the buyer is influenced by forces of which he is not even aware, and yet these forces have a tremendous impact on his actions. Additionally, the person operates within an organization that places constraints on how he performs his job. Although organizational purchasing does not always strictly involve rational decision making, it does involve a rationalized process.

The major types of organizations and how they vary in their approaches to purchasing was the next major topic discussed. There are major differences in the purchasing approaches of commercial and government organizations, and these differences, in large part, spring from their different purposes, structure, and size. We looked at the Standard Industrial Classification (SIC) system and how it works.

The chapter also outlined the six major steps involved in organizational buying. The process begins with the recognition of a need and does not stop until the fulfillment of that need. The combination and number of the steps in purchasing will vary among organizations and situations, but in general, at some point, the six basic steps are completed.

The astute salesperson, though not needing to be a psychologist or an expert in purchasing, does need to be aware of the complex nature of organizational buying. Furthermore the salesperson needs to be able to relate to and empathize with the buyer and be flexible enough to meet the needs of the buyer as much as possible. In short, the salesperson's principal job is to solve the problems of the buyer. If that is done, the salesperson's problems will, in turn, be solved.

KEY TERMS

approved vendor list (AVL), p. 44

associative thinking process, p. 27

attitude, p. 25

blanket purchase order (BPO), p. 43

boundary spanner, p. 29

buyer, p. 30

buying center, p. 30

buying situation, p. 42

compliance program, p. 39

decider, p. 30

derived demand, p. 41

education, p. 27

gatekeeper, p. 30

ideal self, p. 24

influencer, p. 30

initiator, p. 30

learning, p. 26

looking-glass self, p. 24

modified rebuy, p. 42

motives, p. 26

needs and desires, p. 22

new task purchase, p. 42

organizational culture, p. 37

organizational procedure, p. 41

perception, p. 23

personality, p. 24

purchase order, p. 44

real self, p. 24

reference groups, p. 31

relationship marketing, p. 21

request for quotation (RFQ), p. 44

role, p. 28

role clarity, p. 29

role conflict, p. 29

role stress, p. 29

self-concept, p. 24

self-image, p. 24

set-aside program, p. 39

Standard Industrial Classification (SIC), p. 40

straight rebuy, p. 42

tenure, p. 28

user, p. 30

work experience, p. 28

CHAPTER QUESTIONS

1. Does the organizational buyer fit the "rational man" economic model of decision making? Why or why not?
2. What are the major forces that affect the organizational buyer in his decision making, and how can the salesperson act to influence those forces?

3. What part does the buyer's psychological makeup play in decision making?

4. Why is it that sometimes buyers do not buy the "best" products?

5. Why is derived demand important to salespeople?

6. What are the three major classifications of organizations? How do they vary in purpose, and how does that affect the way they make buying decisions?

7. How does the SIC system work, and how can it be used by salespeople?

8. What is the organizational buying process? What role does the salesperson play at each step in the process?

NOTES

1. Barbara B. Jackson, *Winning & keeping industrial customers* (Lexington, MA: Lexington Books, 1985), 5.

2. F. Robert Dwyer, Paul H. Schurr, and Sejo Oh, Developing buyer-seller relationships. *Journal of Marketing* 51 (April 1987), 11–27; Kate Bertrand, Crafting "win-win relationships" in buyer-seller relationships. *Business Marketing* (June 1986), 42, 43, 46, 50; R. E. Spekman, Strategic supplier selection: Understanding long-term buyer relationships. *Business Horizons* (July–August 1988), 75–81; David Ford, The development of buyer-seller relationships in industrial markets. *European Journal of Marketing* 14 (1982), 339–353; and Paul Matthyssens and Christophe Van den Bulte, Getting closer and nicer: Partnerships in the supply chain. *Long Range Planning* 27 (February 1994), 72–83.

3. John Haywood-Farmer and Michiel R. Leenders, Psychological need profiles of purchasers. *Journal of Purchasing and Materials Management* (Winter 1986), 23–29.

4. W. I. Thomas, The persistence of primary-group norms in present day society. In *Suggestions of modern science concerning education,* ed. Herbert S. Jennings (New York: Macmillan, 1917), 159–197.

5. Tony L. Henthorne, Michael S. LaTour, and Alvin J. Williams, Initial impressions in the organizational buyer-seller dyad: Sales management implications. *Journal of Personal Selling & Sales Management* 12 (Summer 1992), 57–65.

6. Philip Kotler and Gary Armstrong, *Marketing* (Englewood Cliffs, NJ: Prentice Hall, 1990), 153.

7. Arnold M. Rose, *Sociology* (New York: Knopf, 1965), 75.

8. Leon G. Schiffman and Leslie Lazar Kanuk, *Consumer behavior* (Englewood Cliffs, NJ: Prentice Hall, 1991), 227.

9. Henry Assael, *Consumer behavior and marketing action* (Boston: Kent, 1992).

10. William M. Pride and O. C. Ferrel, *Marketing* (Boston: Houghton Mifflin, 1993), 156.

11. Frederich E. Webster and Yorum Wind, *Organizational buying behavior* (Englewood Cliffs, NJ: Prentice Hall, 1972), 98.

12. Larry Giunipero and Gary Zenz, Impact of purchasing trends on industrial marketers. *Industrial Marketing Management* 11 (1982), 17–23.

13. Seymour Fine, Buyer and seller psychographics in industrial purchase decisions. *Journal of Business & Industrial Marketing* 6 (Winter 1991), 49–58.

14. Giunipero and Zenz, Impact of purchasing trends on industrial markets.

15. Ronald E. Michaels, Ralph L. Day, and Erich Joachimsthaler, Role stress among industrial buyers: An integrative model. *Journal of Marketing* (April 1987), 28–45.

16. A. Parasuraman, Role clarity and job satisfaction in purchasing. *Journal of Purchasing and Materials Management* (Fall 1981), 2–7.

17. Webster and Wind, *Organizational buying behavior;* Thomas V. Bonoma, Major sales: Who really does the buying? *Harvard Business Review* (May/June 1982), 111–119.

18. John R. Ronchetto, Michael D. Hutt, and Peter H. Reingen, Embedded influence patterns in organizational buying systems. *Journal of Marketing* 53 (October 1989), 51–62.

19. Giunipero and Zenz, Impact of purchasing trends on industrial markets.

20. Minette E. Drumwright, Socially responsible organizational buying: Environmental concern as a noneconomic buying criterion. *Journal of Marketing* 58 (July 1994), 1–19.

21. J. L. Gibson, J. M. Ivancevich, and J. H. Donnelly, Jr., *Organizations* (Plano, TX: Business Publications, 1985), 43; see also Rose, *Sociology*.

22. Thomas L. Powers, *Modern business marketing* (St. Paul, MN: West, 1991).

23. Michael D. Hutt and Thomas N. Speh, *Business marketing management* (Ft. Worth, TX: Dryden, 1992).

24. Christopher R. Puto, Wesley E. Putton III, and Ronald H. King, Risk handling strategies in the industrial vendor selection. *Journal of Marketing* 49 (Winter 1985), 89–98; Richard N. Cardozo, Modelling organizational buying as a sequence of decisions, *Industrial Marketing Management* 12 (February 1983), 75–81.

25. Ralph W. Jackson and William M. Pride, The use of approved vendor lists. *Industrial Marketing Management* 15 (1986), 165–169; A. Parasuraman, Characteristics of firms with and without formal vendor evaluation systems: Implications for institutional buyers and sellers. *Akron Business & Economic Review* (Spring 1981), 30–34.

26. Frederich E. Webster, A general model of organizational buying behavior. *Journal of Marketing* (April 1972), 12–19; J. N. Sheth, A model of industrial buyer behavior. *Journal of Marketing* (October 1973), 50–56; Allen M. Weiss and Jan B. Heide, The nature of organizational search in high technology markets. *Journal of Marketing Research* 30 (May 1993), 220–233; Ruby Roy Dholakia, Jean L. Johnson, Albert J. Della Bitta, and Nikhilesh Dholakia, Decision-making time in organizational buying behavior: An investigation of its antecedents. *Journal of Academy of Marketing Science* 21 (Fall 1993), 281–292.

27. Patrick J. Robinson, Charles W. Faris, and Yorum Wind, *Industrial buying and creative selling* (Boston: Allyn & Bacon, 1967).

28. Ralph W. Jackson, The effect of approved vendors lists on industrial marketing. In *Advances in business marketing,* vol. 3, ed. Arch G. Woodside (Greenwich, CT: JAI Press, 1988), 79–94; Richard N. Cardozo, Modelling organizational buying as a sequence of decisions. *Industrial Marketing Management* 12 (1983), 75–81.

29. Ralph W. Jackson, How multi-dimensional is the purchasing job? *Journal of Purchasing and Materials Management* 26 (Fall 1990), 27–33.

30. Jackson and Pride, The use of approved vendor lists; A. Parasuraman, Use of computers in purchasing: An empirical study. *Journal of Purchasing and Materials Management* (Spring 1981), 10–14.

31. Jackson and Pride, The use of approved vendor lists.

32. William B. Wagner, Changing industrial buyer-seller pricing concerns. *Industrial Marketing Management* 10 (1981), 109–117; Scott W. Cullen, The role of vendor pricing. *The Office* (June 1990), 14, 19–20; Raydel Tullous and Michael J. Munson, Organizational purchasing analysis for sales management. *Journal of Personal Selling & Sales Management* 12 (Spring 1992), 15–26.

33. Gene Brown, Unal O. Boya, Neil Humphreys, and Robert E. Widing, Attributes and behaviors of salespeople preferred by buyers: High socializing vs. low socializing industrial buyers. *Journal of Personal Selling & Sales Management* 13 (Winter 1993), 25–33.

SUGGESTED READINGS

Cateora, Philip R. *International marketing.* Homewood, IL: Richard D. Irwin, 1983.

To implement the marketing concept in the world marketplace, companies must take a different approach than in the domestic market. Not only is this true for large firms but for smaller ones as well. Presenting a product without understanding the nuances of a particular region of the world will not work.

Hutt, Michael D., and Thomas W. Speh. *Business marketing management*. Ft. Worth, TX: Dryden, 1992.

> When competing for the business customer, companies need a strategic focus. Because the purchasing process and the industrial buyer are different than in the consumer marketplace, strategies must be developed that address that difference. This involves all phases of marketing.

Jackson, Barbara B. *Winning & Keeping Industrial Customers*. Lexington, MA: Lexington Books, 1985.

> In the face of increasing competition, just making that one sale is not enough. To be successful, businesses must build relationships with customers that go beyond a single transaction. Partnering is the key to success, partly because keeping customers is much less costly than making new ones.

Powers, Thomas L. *Modern business marketing*. St. Paul, MN: West, 1991.

> Marketing products to businesses is essentially different than marketing to consumers. Additionally, marketing high-tech products offers unique challenges, especially when much of the competition is from the international arena. These factors call for an in-depth understanding of marketing today.

Schnitzer, Martin C., Marilyn L. Liebrenz, and Konrad W. Kubin. *International business*. Cincinnati, OH: South-Western, 1985.

> American businesses are facing new and different challenges as they compete in the world marketplace. Approaches to conducting business internationally vary considerably and need to be applied according to the constraints of the individual business. Management practices and policies need to be adapted to the country in which the company does business.

_____ Chapter 3 _____

The Place
of Communication
in the Sales Profession

OPENING SCENARIO

Danielle Smart sat down in the office of Anthony Perez, the senior buyer for PetroColombia, a Central American oil company. Smart was the new Latin American Region salesperson for Allied Products, out of Houston. Allied had been supplying PetroColombia with oil-field supplies for more than 20 years. Until this past year, the companies had maintained a good working relationship. Although the management at Allied did not know exactly what had happened between the former salesperson, Howard Tomkins, and the buyers at Petro-Colombia, it was obvious that the relationship had soured quickly after several orders were shipped with incorrect items and, in some cases, with used equipment. PetroColombia had cancelled all orders and had ordered Tomkins off the premises during his last visit. Because of improprieties that had emerged after the incident, Tomkins had "resigned" his position with Allied.

Danielle Smart had been a salesperson with International Tool Company (ITC) for three years prior to taking the Allied job. She had a marketing major in college with a second major in Spanish. At ITC she had successfully worked with several Latin American accounts. After several months, she had obtained an appointment with Anthony Perez. After an initially warm greeting, it seemed that the meeting had taken on a very formal atmosphere. Perez was polite but had an almost aloof demeanor. During the conversation, Smart felt that he was uncomfortable and not open to reconsidering doing business with Allied. She had a number of good points to make but was afraid of losing control of the conversation and not being able to get them across.

Chapter Objectives

After reading this chapter, you should be able to

- Understand the symbolic nature of communication.
- Recognize the different ways people communicate.
- Realize the importance of listening in sales communication.
- Know how all the elements in sales communication work together to give a complete message.
- Understand the importance of communicating benefits and not just features when presenting a product to a customer.

INTRODUCTION

Human beings have always interacted with each other. Thus it would seem that at some point people would have learned how to communicate accurately. However, we all know that to express precisely what it is we want to say to others, and for those others to understand what we are saying, is very difficult. Sales is, essentially, a process of communication. It is purposeful communication that involves informing, persuading, and reminding. Additionally, communication is a two-way process that involves not only speaking but also listening.

It is often assumed that the successful salesperson is a "good talker" who has developed storytelling into a high art. Although it may be true that speaking well certainly helps a person communicate effectively, this is probably not the premier skill in communication; in fact, it may be less important than listening well. Effective observation, that is, gaining meaning from what one sees, is also an essential part of communication.

Good communication is an essential element in relationship marketing. Communication allows the salesperson to understand the needs of the customer, to uncover any underlying problems, to help the customer develop the right solution for a problem, and to persuade the customer that the solution will work. Perhaps more subtle and probably more important, good communication can establish the trust relationship between the salesperson and customer that is essential.[1]

COMMUNICATION IS SYMBOLIC

A wise person once stated: "Words don't mean, people do." **Communication** is the process of conveying a message from one person or group to another. The message can include facts, feelings, beliefs, desires, and fears, as well as a good deal of other information. The message a person wants to give to another first exists as a mental image. It is impossible to convey this raw mental image to the other person directly, so the communicator must translate this message into symbols that he or she believes the other will understand. These symbols can be roughly divided into three classifications:

1. Verbal expressions
2. Nonverbal actions
3. Objects

Communication typically involves some combination of these. When used in conjunction with each other, some often alter or strengthen the message conveyed by the other symbols being used.

Communication is made difficult by the fact that each person enters into it from a different perspective. Even within one's own country, the meanings of symbols will vary across regions and between individuals. Certainly when we move into another country with a different culture, we need to alter our communication approach. Words, of course, need translating into another language, but so do actions and objects.[2] The American hand signal that means "okay" would be considered a vulgar insult in Brazil. The color white in the United States is used for wedding gowns and symbolizes purity, whereas in East Asia it is the color of mourning.

Verbal Expressions

Verbal expressions refer to words and verbal intonations. Verbal intonations, like words, can convey meaning. For example, "uh-huh" (aside from its use in the Pepsi-Cola advertising campaign) generally means the person understands what the other has just said. "Um" may indicate that the person is thinking about what has just been said. A grunt or a groan may convey a particular message depending on the context. Verbal intonations generally serve to embellish speech. In fact, sometimes these intonations are added to words either to enhance or alter the meaning of the words.

Words, however, are the basic means of communicating ideas. According to sociologist Arnold Rose, words increase our ability to communicate in several ways:

1. They allow people to communicate about objects even when the objects are not present.
2. Words can be used to communicate about abstract and nonobservable concepts.
3. Words aid in memory because of their ability to succinctly capture a concept.
4. Words aid in learning and reasoning.
5. Words permit people to relate behavior to each other to a much greater extent than non-verbal symbols.[3]

Words, then, make it possible to communicate more effectively and more efficiently. Words also enable us to communicate more accurately than would be possible through nonverbal methods alone.

People often operate under the implicit assumption that words are a precise means of communicating. Although some words have precise meanings, in most cases words have more than one meaning, and that meaning can vary with use.[4] For example, you can describe a computer screen as blue. Blue is a specific color that is distinguishable from red, but there are a number of shades of blue. So the word blue may mean a number of different color tones, or it may mean nothing to a person who is color-blind. If I were to use the word *blue* to describe a person, it would mean something entirely different than a color, unless of course, the person has held his breath for a long time.

Moreover, the connotations that words may pick up over time can further diminish their preciseness. For example, the simple word *dog* has come to have a number of meanings, both good and bad. It can mean the mammal that is considered everyone's "best friend." However, within our society, it can also mean a car that does not run well, a poorly performing stock, a mechanical device for holding something, or an ugly person. Even when both parties in a conversation know that dog is being used to mean the mammal, the word can still represent something different to each. For the one who likes dogs, the image is positive; however, if the other does not, the image is very negative. When we move into other cultures, again a dog represents something very different. In some cultures, when a person comes in contact with a dog, he or she is ceremonially unclean and must go through a religious ritual to become "clean" again. Thus a dog is something to be avoided.

When one translates from one language into another, the differences between words will be even more pronounced and cause greater problems in communication. Because of this, Yuri Radsievsky points out the necessity of carefully planning for global marketing campaigns.[5] He goes on to state that simply translating a marketing message into another language is not enough. To be effective, the cultural context of the country, along with the local connotations of particular words, needs to be factored into the translation process. Although he indicates that the process is an involved one, careful planning and adequate research will ensure that the same message can be successfully conveyed in the language of another culture.

Words can also vary in meaning according to their use in various regions of a country.[6] For example, a soft drink is referred to as soda water in parts of the South and as pop in the Midwest. If you were to request soda water in the Midwest, you would likely receive just that—soda water, a nonflavored, carbonated water that is mixed with other beverages. If you are invited for dinner in some parts of the country, that means the large, noon meal, whereas in other areas it means the evening meal.

Nonverbal Actions

Another way we communicate is through **nonverbal actions**—gestures, facial expressions, body language, and various others. It has been suggested that nonverbal communication plays a "value-added" role.[7] In other words, nonverbal communication augments or alters the meaning of the words we use in one of three ways:

1. The **amplifier phenomenon.** Supports, modifies, or emphasizes the meanings conveyed by verbal communication.
2. The **unintentional display.** Often give clues to true feelings or beliefs that contradict the words spoken.
3. The **consistency phenomenon.** Often serves to confirm the verbal message.

An example of the amplifier phenomenon would be a person hugging another person when he says, "I've missed you!" Or a firm handshake to accompany the words "Its nice to meet you!" An example of an unintentional display might be a person frowning when he says, "Congratulations, you deserved to win." And an example of the consistency phenomenon might be when a salesperson nods her head when she says, "I think we have a solution to your problem."

The power of such actions as facial expressions, posture, and gestures in creating meaning is tremendous. They not only serve to enhance or alter the meaning of words, but they provide cues to the general demeanor of the person speaking. The buyer who seems to be fidgeting with her watch or is not maintaining eye contact is most likely uninvolved in the conversation. Likewise, the salesperson who appears nervous or who gives a weak handshake may be showing a lack of confidence.

Objects

Objects have always been used to convey meaning. The ruler's scepter conveyed authority and the peasant's garments conveyed poverty. Even the automobile, which was developed as a more effective means of transportation, denotes status. Businesspeople read books about how to dress well, because they recognize the power of clothes to communicate status. Often, by observing the trappings of a person's office, we can learn a great deal about that individual, because people tend to surround themselves with items that give them a sense of identity. This tendency may or may not be conscious but, nonetheless, if understood, can give a clue to what is important to that person.

The salesperson needs to recognize the power of symbolic communication. Not only what salespeople say but how they say it communicates a message to customers. The more salespeople become sensitized to the various messages being conveyed, the better they will understand the needs of the customer. For example, in any organization there are both formal and informal channels of communication, and the latter is often the most critical.[8] Being sensitive to the customer is a skill. Like any other skill, it can be learned, and the ability to perform it improves with practice. Likewise, when the skill is not used, it steadily deteriorates.

COMMUNICATION IS PROCESS

The classic model of communication is shown in Figure 3-1. In this model, the **source** has some piece of information that he wants to convey. He must **encode** that information, or put it into a form that is transmittable. The appropriate **medium** is selected to convey the encoded information. The **receiver** must then **decode** that information, or translate it into something meaningful to her. The information, once decoded by the receiver, has the potential of rendering some effect on that person.

The classic model includes a feedback loop whereby the receiver conveys some reaction to the source. This feedback serves either to confirm that the information is being received as intended or that it is not being understood correctly. The feedback can be either direct, such as a statement, or it can be as subtle as a nod or a smile.

Noise can interfere with the process at any point along the way and will tend to cause a distortion in the message if the noise level is high enough. Noise can be early in the process, causing the source to formulate an unclear message. It can also occur due to some malfunction in the medium of transmission, such as the source using words that the receiver does not understand. It can even come at the receiving end, if, for example, the recipient is distracted or is preoccupied.

This model does a good job of breaking down the communication process into discrete steps that can be more closely examined and understood. It also portrays the idea that communication is complex and has the potential for distortion. The major drawback with this model, when we attempt to apply it to personal selling, is that it tends to convey the idea that communication is really a one-way process, with the receiver's only active part being to provide feedback. Although this may be true in many instances of mass communication—for example, television and print advertising—it represents an inaccurate view of the personal selling situation. Personal selling is a dynamic, interactive process affected by the actions of both parties, and not a one-way process that relies on occasional feedback.

In addition, the model makes the implicit assumption that the receiver has the information necessary to decode the message. In other words, the model

FIGURE 3-1 The Classic Communication Model

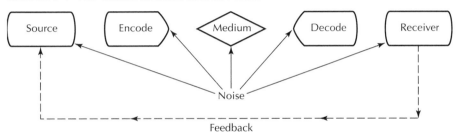

assumes that the receiver can "relate" to the source. This assumption may be flawed. Certainly the more common ground that the source and the receiver share, the better each will be able to understand the other; however, that common ground is often smaller than we assume.

The Personal Selling Communication Model

To get a more accurate picture of communication in personal selling, we must modify the classic model. Figure 3-2 illustrates our modified model, the personal selling communication model. Although the process is similar to that in the classic model, it more clearly presents the idea that communication is a two-way process. It shows that while one person is speaking, the other is not simply passively receiving information but, rather, is conveying information at the same time. This is very different from simply providing feedback. While the salesperson is speaking, he must be aware of what the other person is communicating at the same time. Therefore, this two-way model requires a different approach on the part of the salesperson than does the typical one-way model.

Another feature of this model is its inclusion of the field of experience and the common field. The **field of experience** is defined by the psychological, social, and cultural backgrounds of both individuals. That background is unique for every individual and forms the basis of personality and outlook on life. Philip Harris and Robert Moran, experts in global business, refer to this as the person's "psychologi-

FIGURE 3-2 The Personal Selling Communication Model

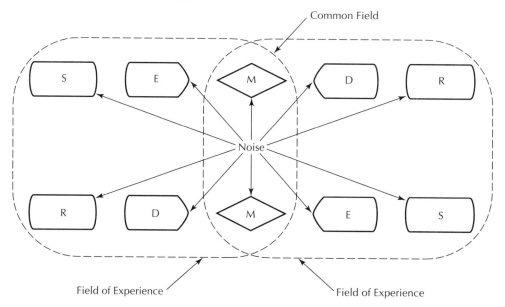

cal environment" and propose that it is axiomatic that each person operates in his or her own private world or perceptual field.[9] They further argue that understanding this concept is a key to communicating with people from other cultures.

The development of one's field of experience through socialization begins in earliest childhood and generally continues, in some form, throughout one's life. In other words, a person is at least somewhat a product of his or her environment. Both the source and the receiver in the communication model have been through this socialization and culturalization process and carry into any interaction the baggage from that process. A **common field**—where these fields of experience overlap—exists, and that is where effective communication takes place. The greater this overlap or the larger the common field, the more easily two persons or groups can communicate. The smaller this common field, the greater the potential for misunderstanding. Developing a "relationship edge," that is, finding this common field, is an important element in a salesperson's being competitive.[10]

Noise, however, is not the only external variable that can hinder the communication process. Following are some additional factors that can affect the process:[11]

> The *context* of the communication. This includes the time and place of the communication. A discussion in the office is likely going to be very different than one that takes place on the golf course.
>
> The *purpose* of each party. This refers to what each hopes to accomplish in the communication. The purpose as it is perceived by the other person in the interaction will affect how that person responds to a statement or question.
>
> The *feelings and beliefs* each party holds. This certainly will have a major impact on how each reacts to the other and on how each interprets the meaning of what is said and done.

These three factors are important because they convey the idea that anytime people communicate they do so on two levels—the cognitive and the affective. That is to say, a person communicates informational content on the cognitive level and at the same time communicates feelings on the affective level.

A problem arises when a sender is not consciously aware of these two sets of messages and is then surprised when a receiver responds in what the sender would consider an inappropriate way. For example, a sales manager calls in a recently hired salesperson who graduated from his alma mater, of which he is a faithful booster. The salesperson is turning an average performance for a new hiree. As the manager begins the "coaching" session, he begins by saying he is disappointed by her performance because he feels that she is not achieving her potential. As they discuss this, the hiree states that although she too wants to improve, she has been doing as well as the other new employees and so is a bit confused by his disappointment. At this point in the conversation, the sales manager becomes agitated and says, "Salespeople who don't achieve their potential probably won't last long in this company." The hiree goes away from the conversation bewildered and a bit angry herself. What happened?

At the outset, we need to remember that the sales manager was communicating on two levels. On the cognitive level, he wanted to let the person know that although she was doing as well as the other new hirees, with her potential she could be promoted quickly through the ranks in the company and that he would like to see her do so. On the affective level, the sales manager felt some embarrassment that the person recruited from his alma mater was not leading the group of new hirees in sales. He felt that somehow his school's reputation was on the line. Although he may not have been aware of this or may not have wanted to admit that this was the case, it was the source of his agitation. Had he paused long enough to become aware of that fact, he probably would have seen the fallacy of that feeling and the meeting would have had a very different tone and level of effectiveness. Furthermore, had he handled the communication properly, it would have served to increase his influence with the new salesperson.[12]

THE ELEMENTS IN SALES COMMUNICATION

Sales communication has five elements:

1. Active listening
2. Observation
3. Open-ended questions
4. Clearly stated messages
5. Effective presentations

Each of these elements has its place in the sales process. They are all important; however, those that help the salesperson better understand and relate to the customer are often the most neglected and perhaps the most critical in successful selling.

Active Listening

Often we make the mistake of thinking that active communication takes place only when we are speaking and that listening is passive. However, if communication is a two-way process, then listening should also be considered an active part of it. Although this may, at first glance, seem like arguing semantics, the point is that if salespeople are to communicate effectively, they must be at least as good at listening as they are at speaking. Typically, people assume that speaking is the more difficult of the two skills to master, and often people erroneously believe that they listen effectively because it is something they do naturally.

There are several types of listening behavior:[13]

Hearing: the physiological process whereby sound waves are received by the ear and transmitted to the brain

SELL!NG

THE FRONT LINES OF BUSINESS

She Said, He Said

Robert Sharoff

Ask top salespeople for their single most important selling tip and chances are it will be, "Listen to what your client has to say." Sounds easy. What they probably won't tell you is that men and women use distinctly different styles and patterns of speech to deliver the same message. Cracking this code can be anything but easy.

An edgy female middle manager who asks to "see more data" and her overly gregarious male counterpart who gushes, "Super!" "Excellent!" "Extraordinarily promising!" are essentially saying the same thing: "Looks good. Let me think about the best way to present it." A salesperson who's tuned in to the nuances of gender-speak knows to give her tight, well-researched information, and to present him with an opportunity to be perceived as a hero by his superiors (that string of superlatives pertained more to his career than it did to yours). Similarly, the female prospect who says, "Let me tell you what the people upstairs are looking for," and the male prospect who invites you to join him for a round of golf next Saturday are delivering the same message in different ways. Translation: "I like your style, and I'm interested in working with you. I'll do what I can to make the deal come through."

After you've completed your pitch, a woman might say, "I am going to show this to a few of my colleagues, see what they think about it, and get back to you." A man might say, "You've given me a lot of interesting information. I'd like to take some time to go through it again and analyze it further." What they both mean: "Your proposal looks promising, but I'm not yet ready to commit myself to it."

Before we go any further, we should issue a proviso: Gender differences are only *tendencies*. The best salespeople understand that the key to selling well hinges on responding to both the stated and unstated needs of each individual customer—be it male or female. Human beings have a way of evading neat psychological categories. "I've seen women who are absolute sharks, and I've seen men who are pussycats," says Anne Miller, president of Chiron Associates Inc., a New York sales training company. "A certain homogenization takes place when people do the same jobs. They begin to act in similar ways." So don't bet the farm on a stereotype. Still, remember that salespeople *can* benefit from a closer reading of what he said, what she said—and what both really mean.

In recent years gender issues have become a major focus in business. In 1993 more than half of all U.S. companies with more than 100 employees—including some of the biggest names in corporate America—sponsored some form of "diversity training." The reason, say experts, is simple: There are far more women in the work force than ever before, and many are starting to move into areas—such as sales—that were formerly dominated by men. "It's an enormous anthropological shift," says Susan Van Vleet, president of Susan Van Vleet Consultants Inc. in Englewood, Colo., which advises Fortune 500 companies on gender issues. And it's a shift that many men find threatening.

The transition can be rocky. What makes this particular situation especially tricky is that it relates to one of the oldest and most emotional issues in society—namely, how we relate to members of the opposite sex. At the very least, both sides are having to make some adjustments and rethink some attitudes. In her best-selling book *You Just Don't Understand*, linguist Deborah Tannen maintains that "the risk of ignoring differences between the ways in which men and women communicate is greater than the danger of acknowledging them. Denying real differences can only compound the confusion."

How do men and women differ in sales situations? It starts from the very first meeting. "When two men meet, after they've said hello, they'll often cut directly to something like sports," says sales trainer Miller. "Women don't bond that way. Women often bond with stories and personal information."

"Men build rapport by doing things together—rafting, fishing, going to a ball game—but not necessarily saying more than a dozen words to one another," says Mike Zaruba, a Baltimore-based sales and sales management consultant with the Burkhardt Group Inc., an affiliate of the Sandler Sales Institute. "They are much less accustomed to discussing their feelings and explaining themselves."

What this means is that when men and women find themselves sitting across the bargaining table, they have to adjust their styles. "If I'm chit-chatting with men, I talk about something that's happening in the city or with the Green Bay Packers," says Lori Kasten, an account executive for DCI Marketing in Milwaukee.

Bruce Bolger, director of the People Performance division of Miller Freeman Inc. in New York, has an approach that works as well with women as it does with men. "I look at what's on their desk or on the walls," he says. "If there are photos of children, that's a great place to start."

As the sales process continues, men and women each exhibit some unique strengths. And they each face some stumbling blocks. One commonly noted difference is that women are more patient than men. "Women are often raised to be accommodating and are frequently better than men at questioning and listening," says Miller. "Men may be stronger at going for the close, but sometimes they lack some people sensitivities."

She tells the story of a company that changed its product mix, then informed the sales force of the change by memo after the decision had already been made. "I don't think a woman would have done that," says Miller. "A woman—or a man with greater people sensitivities—would know intuitively that you just don't lay this kind of huge change on somebody without any preparation."

Many also believe that men have more of a "lone wolf" attitude toward working. "Many times you want to sell men in middle management in terms of what the implementation will do specifically for them," says Alan Asman, who leases and sells commercial real estate with the Carey Winston Agency in Vienna, Va.

"Women are often more concerned with the ramifications a program will have on the company itself. The company's well-being concerns them as much as their own," he says.

The upside of male aggression is that men tend to accept—even enjoy—the more rough-and-tumble aspects of the business world. "Men play hardball a little harder," says Miller. Adds Asman, "Men respond better to the hard sell. Women don't appreciate being pressured. If that's what you're doing, both will think, 'Boy, is this guy pushy.' The man, though, will probably add, 'But that's what he's hired for.'"

Which is why, conversely, some men are wary of dealing with women. A male client who has no qualms about "playing hardball" with other men may feel awkward—because of cultural conditioning—using the same tactics on women. Holly Craig, an advertising salesperson for Condé Nast Publishing in New York, recalls a problem she had with an advertiser who pulled back on an agreement.

"He never said anything hostile to me, but then he called my boss and carried on about how I hadn't been servicing the account in a satisfactory way," she says. "Then afterward, he got on the phone and tried to make nice."

In such situations, it becomes critical for salespeople to draw the prospect out and get to the real issue, even if it's not one that the prospect feels comfortable discussing. "Listening is very critical right here," says L. Clinton Eason, who recently retired after 25 years in the sales trenches for BASF and is now a management and sales consultant in Dalton, Ga.

"You have to hear the subtleties, the little things that are adding up to a big problem for him," he says. "You talk about the technical qualities and servicing and competitive advantages. That will force him to tell you the problems he's having with your product."

Another time women have to tread carefully is when they are pioneering formerly all-male territory. "In the past, in many traditional industries like machine tools, the only women you saw were on calendars," says management consultant Darlene Orlov, president of Orlov Resources for Business Inc. in New York, who often speaks on gender issues.

"So now it's hard for some men to imagine women jumping off the calendar and selling the product," she says.

Paradoxically, for all the exaggerated concern many men show for women's feelings, they also say women are harder to sell than men. "I've had women bust my chops," says Bolger. "They watch everything I say and make sure I keep my promises. Their attitude is, don't use your male guile with me and don't think for a moment you're going to get away with anything." Adds Van

Vleet, "Women are very bottom-line. They don't care how you look in your three-piece suit."

Or do they? We now come to one of the touchier aspects of gender awareness. But it's one that most salespeople admit is at least an unconscious factor in the selling process. "I think each sex is generally a bit vulnerable to the other," says Orlov. Miller recalls one of her first jobs as an ad salesperson at a financial magazine. "My boss was very clever," she says. "He hired all women. Think about it. If you were an investment banker on Wall Street, would you rather talk to some guy from *Fortune* or an informed, attractive woman? We weren't bimbos. We knew our business. And men liked talking to us."

This kind of talk, of course, is heresy today, and in truth, very few sales are based on sex appeal. "There's just so much that goes into a sale that I can't believe a chromosome would be the deter-mining factor," says Orlov. "I'm doing too much hard work for that to be true."

While gender differences are real, many salespeople say the realities of the marketplace are working to minimize them. "It's a very unforgiving world out there today," says Miller. "To succeed you must be gender-neutral. You must be good on the relationships and good at getting the business."

As Kasten notes, "People are buying on the basis of price and quality today, not good-old-boy relationships. The relationship-building I do isn't so much based on my being their best friend as on whether they count on me to deliver the program. And on my side, I've never walked into a meeting and said, 'Oh, darn, there are more women here than men.' My feeling is, I'm thrilled there's a body sitting there. I don't care what sex it is. It's somebody who wants to hear what I have to say."—*with contributions from Michael Kaplan.*

Reprinted with the permission of SELL!NG magazine.

Information gathering: The absorption of stated facts.

Cynical listening: Defensive listening that assumes all communication is designed to take advantage of the listener.

Offensive listening: An attempt to trap or trip up a speaker with his own words.

Polite listening: Meeting minimum social requirements while waiting for the opportunity to speak.

Active listening: Involves the listener with the responsibility to obtain a complete and accurate understanding of what the speaker is trying to convey.

Of these, active listening should be the receiver's goal if he is to communicate effectively. It is the only form of listening that facilitates good communication, because it attempts to understand the *entire* message and not just what is being spoken.

Why do people not listen better than they do? First, listening is hard work. Research has shown that when a person actively listens, his or her metabolic processes increase slightly, causing a slight rise in body temperature, and the pupils tend to dilate slightly. This indicates that real listening is anything but passive. A person who is truly listening is paying close attention to what is being conveyed and is providing the speaker with affirmation that he or she is tuned in to what is being said.

Often people use the time when they are not speaking to "rest" and will simply act as though they are listening. They will look at the person, nod their head, and may even utter some indication that they understand, when in reality their mind is rehearsing what they are going to say next, thinking about the discussion they had with their spouse that morning, or is at the lake. Active listening means concentrating, and concentrating is hard work.

A second reason that salespeople fail to listen well is that they feel uncomfortable when not talking. This is especially true for new salespeople. They often make the excuse that they do not want to "lose control of the interview." They fear that if they are not in control, they will not be able to get a fair hearing for their message. More often than not, however, they feel that if they are not speaking they are not selling, and that they need to provide the buyer with as much information as they possibly can. Certainly the need for providing adequate information is paramount, but salespeople, particularly new ones, often attempt to do a "core dump," that is, give the customer all the information that they possess about the product. They fear that if they fail to do so, they will leave out the one important factor that will make the sale.

In discussing what attributes distinguish good salespeople from average and poor ones, a recent study found that sales managers from a variety of companies overwhelmingly indicated that listening is the key skill in selling. To quote one: "I have sold more merchandise by listening than I ever did by talking."[14] William Brooks, an author and sales trainer, states: "Listening means paying attention to what the prospect is saying and that is the most important task of the salesperson."[15] Sales managers, then, need to train their salespeople to be better listeners.

Because people who enter sales carry certain stereotypical images of salespeople,[16] this need for training in effective listening cannot be overemphasized. A review of three of the major sales training courses in the United States, Xerox, Forum, Inc., and Wilson Learning, found that listening skills are a primary part of their training.[17] Conrad Elnes, sales consultant, defines four goals that listening accomplishes in the selling process:

1. It ensures the customer that he is important.
2. As the customer talks, he will provide clues as to what is important and what he wants and needs.
3. As the customer talks and reasons things through, he often talks himself into buying.
4. As the customer talks, he is able to get thoughts "off his chest" and becomes more willing to allow the salesperson a fair chance to talk.[18]

Some salespeople do not listen well because they are more interested in their own message than in what the customer has to say. Elnes refers to this phenomenon as the "telling tension." He believes that because we all have a desire to express what is on our mind, this desire detracts from our ability to listen.[19] One reason this attitude is so destructive is that, like selling, purchasing is becoming more professional and this has led to higher expectations of salespeople on the part of buyers. More and more, salespeople with this attitude will become the exception rather than the rule and, hence, will stand out from the crowd of poor listeners.

In the same study of managers that dealt with what sets good salespeople apart, these managers also stated that one of the more important characteristics of good salespeople is that they possess an ability to empathize; that is, they are able to understand the other person and relate to him or her.[20] The attitude that what the customer has to say cannot be as important as what the salesperson has to say is the antithesis of empathy. Although this attitude is slowly waning in today's era of more professional selling, it is a vestige of an earlier time that still persists.

Active listening is an important way to bring about change in people.[21] A major part of the salesperson's job is to change how the customer views a product or to discover what changes in the company's product or service are needed to serve the customer better. And that requires active listening. There are two basic elements in active listening that help a salesperson accomplish these changes:

> **Paraphrasing.** Summarizing the speaker's expressed thoughts as they were understood by the listener; putting what the speaker has said into the listener's own words. Often begins with phrases like: "I hear you saying that . . ." or "So, in your opinion . . ."
>
> **Perception checking.** Describing what the listener perceives to be the unspoken feelings (emotions) or wants of the speaker. This description is offered tentatively and nonevaluatively. Often begins with phrases like: "I get the impression that . . ." or "It sounds like you felt . . ."

Paraphrasing and perception checking enable the salesperson to understand what the buyer is really attempting to convey. They provide the salesperson with new information or with confirmation of information already developed in the preparation of the sales process. Paraphrasing is a reality check for the salesperson. When the listener restates the speaker's words in his own language, the speaker can confirm the information the listener just received. If the listener summarizes the information incorrectly, the speaker will be able to correct him. Perception checking helps the listener go beyond the words being said and understand what he believes the speaker is feeling. Sometimes the speaker either is hesitant to say what she is really feeling or has been unable to put those feelings into words. When both parties in the conversation engage in active listening, they provide feedback to each other, thus facilitating communication.

Active listening lets the speaker know that she or he is being listened to. This gives the one talking added incentive to be open with the listener. In conveying the listener's empathy, active listening thereby helps to develop the trust between the listener and the speaker that is necessary for a satisfactory relationship.

Active listening facilitates communication in still another way: When one person listens to another, the listener then has earned the right to speak. Although this may sound a bit idealistic, it is true that a person who feels that he has been heard will feel more inclined to hear what the other has to say. This may be based on a feeling of implicit obligation or on the fact that the speaker feels closer to the person who has heard and understood his beliefs and feelings. This is referred as the **norm of reciprocity.** It is the idea that when a person does something for another person, that other person is willing to return the favor in kind.

Observation

As stated earlier, a majority of the information we receive about others comes from nonverbal sources. The surroundings in which a person works and the clothes he or she wears provide messages about that person and his or her company. Some are very clear, such as a diploma on a wall; others, such as the way a person's desk is arranged or the kind of artwork that decorates the office are subject to interpretation. Regardless of the clarity of these messages, they are important pieces of the puzzle the salesperson has to construct about the customer. Often that puzzle has to be constructed in a short amount of time and under adverse conditions.

There is no magic formula for effective observation. However, we can get a better grasp of the process of observation by thinking of the selling environment as consisting of three zones: the outer zone, the immediate zone, and the personal zone.

The **outer zone** consists of what the salesperson sees in the outer surroundings, such as a company's buildings and grounds, the workers, and the manufacturing space and equipment. The salesperson should look for such things as the age and the style of the office building and plant, the relative modernity of the equipment that is being used, and the dynamics of the interaction of employees. These pieces of information can provide clues to the corporate culture and even the financial prowess of the company. For example, if the salesperson notices that the plant is operating at only half capacity, this may be a signal that the company is experiencing a downturn in sales and, possibly, financial difficulties.

The **immediate zone** consists of the office surroundings of the customer. In this zone such things as the way the office is arranged, the decoration used in the office, and whether any themes seem to predominate are important points to consider. For example, if a buyer has her degree hanging on the wall and has some memorabilia about her university in the office, it may be a signal that the university is an important source of identification for her. Another buyer might have a number of framed, exotic photographs hanging on the wall; this may well mean that the person has photography as a hobby or likes to travel.

The **personal zone** consists of the customer herself. The clues that are important here are such things as how she tends to dress, her personal mannerisms, and even her demeanor on a given day. If the customer appears agitated, it may indicate that she is running up against a deadline and needs to get some other work finished instead of taking that time to look at the latest product in the salesperson's line. Perhaps a particular buyer always wears starched shirts and nice ties and tends to be formal in his approach to the salesperson. This may indicate that he is very concerned about appearing professional and wants to be considered a professional.

Certainly, **observation** as a way of gathering information is much more an art than a science. However, treating it in a systematic way makes it a powerful tool for the salesperson. Notice that as one moves through the outer zone and the immediate zone to the personal zone, the nature of the information changes. It becomes more specific, both about the person and about the circumstances prevailing at the time of the sales interview. Obviously, the information gathered through observation needs to be treated as evidence and not concrete fact. All observational information should be confirmed over time and through other means, such as asking questions.

Open-Ended Questions

One of the avenues of communication between salespeople and customers is the **open-ended question**—a question that cannot be answered with a simple yes or no. The salesperson should draw up a list of questions during the preparation phase of the sale.

According to Elnes:

> A carefully prepared list of written questions can help you guide the direction of your interviews. Considerable evidence demonstrates that a person who uses prepared questions throughout an interview is less likely to overlook key pieces of information regarding a prospect's needs, attitudes, and problems.[22]

The open-ended question is better than a yes-no question because the customer is forced to provide more complete information in answering the open-ended question. Additionally, this type of question makes the sales call much more conversational. Yes-no questions make the interview sound like an interrogation and can often lead to the customer prematurely ending the interview. Table 3-1 gives some examples of yes-no versus open-ended questions.

Often salespeople will ask yes-no questions thinking that they are open-ended. Some buyers take great delight in answering such a question with a simple yes or no, knowing full well that the salesperson intended it to be open-

TABLE 3-1 Open-Ended Versus Yes-No Questions

Yes-No Question	Open-Ended Question
"Do your secretaries have difficulty with your current word processing system?"	"What difficulties are your secretaries having with your current word processing system?"
"Do you feel financially secure?"	"What plans have you made for your financial security?"
"Is your communication system up to date?"	"What are the changes you have made in your communication system to ensure that it is state of the art?"

ended. They particularly seem to enjoy engaging in this sport with new sales-people.

Clearly Stated Messages

Although we have discussed at length the importance of listening and understanding the customer, being able to present material in a cogent, concise manner is also a critical factor in successful selling. Doing so requires thoughtful preparation before the interview. For instance, the salesperson should

- Know beforehand what information is important to the buyer.
- Determine the most effective order of presentation.
- Devise an approach to which the buyer can relate.
- Speak to the buyer, not over or around him or her.
- Know how to tie the elements of the message together.

It is important to remember that the buyer is bombarded by sales and promotional messages every day. Furthermore, the buyer faces the same story from just about every salesperson: "Our company is the best; our products are the finest; our prices are the lowest; and we love you the most!" Obviously, it is important for the salesperson to think about what she can do to stand out from the rest and still deliver the right message to the customer. This is where the element of creativity comes into play. The salesperson who can paint "word pictures" for the buyer will be able to convey information much more effectively than the person who is simply able to state the facts. This does not mean that the salesperson's goal should be to "turn a phrase" but, rather, it means that the salesperson should recognize that there are various ways to say something and find an interesting and fresh way of giving her message. The salesperson should always avoid getting into a rut with a sales message and should continuously update her information and message.

Effective Presentations

Confucius is believed to have said: "I hear and I forget, I see and I remember, I do and I understand." That truth certainly applies to a selling situation. It represents what can be termed an **awareness progression.** As a person moves from hearing to seeing to doing, he or she moves to a greater level of awareness than was possessed at the previous stage. The effective sales presentation that incorporates this progression will

- State the sales message in an effective and appropriate manner.
- Utilize sales aids, such as pictures of the product, written testimonials, charts detailing the benefits of a product, or dealing with a company.
- Include, where possible, a demonstration of the product, benefit, and/or concept.

Presentations represent the time allotted for the salesperson to build his case. The best way to obtain and hold the buyer's interest is to get her involved in the process. In a sense, the buyer becomes part of the presentation. It is no longer the salesperson's words but, rather, the buyer's own experience that is part of the persuasive content of the presentation. The buyer is no longer simply relying on the words of the salesperson but, rather, on her personal experience. This adds to the strength of the presentation.

In planning for the presentation, the best approach to selling is to take the strategic view and pull all the elements together to form a cohesive whole. The salesperson must realize that different approaches and influence tactics will be needed with each firm.[23] Presentations should be thought of as trying to tell a story, and the telling of that story will be enhanced by using a variety of methods.

CHAPTER SUMMARY

This chapter discussed various aspects of communication as it relates to the sales profession. Because sales is principally a communication process, a thorough understanding of the process is essential for salespeople. In communicating, we use symbols that have certain meanings for us, but they can vary in meaning for each person or in different regions of the country or the world. These symbols can take the form of verbal expressions, nonverbal actions, and objects.

The two models of communication we discussed are the classic communication model, which better applies to mass communications, and the personal selling communication model, which describes a two-way process. This model includes the idea that both parties in the communication bring to it a field of experience, the psychological, social, and cultural factors that shape the individual. When these fields overlap in the common field of shared references, effective communication can take place. The salesperson must understand the buyer's frame of reference in order to find that common field and facilitate the communication process. This means understanding the background of the customer as well as the cultural nuances of the region or foreign country.

Often, people only consider the speaking side of the communication process but, in reality, the most important part of the process is effective listening.

The chapter also discussed the elements of sales communication—active listening, understanding the entire message; observation, gaining understanding by seeing clues in the environment; open-ended questions, keeping a dialogue going with a customer; clearly stated messages, presenting material in a concise, cogent manner; and effective presentation, using the awareness progression method.

When the salesperson engages the buyer in a sales presentation, she must remember that the product is more than what is picked up off the shelf. To communicate so that the buyer will listen, the salesperson must speak in terms of the needs that her company and products will meet. She should cultivate all the elements of communication so that she may provide the customer with the information needed to make the decision to buy.

KEY TERMS

active listening, p. 62

amplifier phenomenon, p. 54

awareness progression, p. 68

common field, p. 57

communication, p. 51

consistency phenomenon, p. 54

cynical listening, p. 62

decode, p. 55

encode, p. 55

field of experience, p. 56

hearing, p. 58

immediate zone, p. 65

information gathering, p. 62

medium, p. 55

noise, p. 55

nonverbal actions, p. 53

norm of reciprocity, p. 65

objects, p. 54

observation, p. 66

offensive listening, p. 62

open-ended questions, p. 66

outer zone, p. 65

paraphrasing, p. 64

perception checking, p. 64

polite listening, p. 62

personal zone, p. 66

receiver, p. 55

source, p. 55

unintentional display, p. 54

verbal expressions, p. 52

CHAPTER QUESTIONS

1. Are words the most precise form of communication? Why or why not?
2. How do the three elements of communication—verbal expressions, nonverbal actions, and objects—work together to form a cohesive message?

3. Give some examples of nonverbal actions and objects and explain how they affect communication.

4. Why is the mass communication model not appropriate for personal selling?

5. How is a field of experience developed, and how does it affect communication?

6. What are the five elements in sales communication, and why is each important to the salesperson?

7. What are the different types of listening?

NOTES

1. Mary Ann Oberhaus, Sharon A. Ratliffe, and Vernon R. Stauble, *Professional selling: A relationship process* (Ft. Worth, TX: Dryden, 1993).

2. Philip R. Harris and Robert T. Moran, *Managing cultural differences* (Houston, TX: Gulf, 1991); Yuri Radzievsky, Multilingual marketing campaigns: How to speak your customers' language. *Financier* (May 1991), 26–27.

3. Arnold M. Rose, *Sociology* (New York: Knopf, 1965).

4. William V. Haney, *Communication and interpersonal relations* (Homewood, IL: Richard D. Irwin, 1986).

5. Radzievsky, *Managing cultural differences.*

6. Haney, *Communication and interpersonal relations.*

7. Thomas V. Bonoma and Leonard C. Felder, Nonverbal communication in marketing: Toward a communicational analysis. *Journal of Marketing Research* 14 (May 1977), 169–180.

8. J. David Johnson, William A. Donohue, Charles K. Atkin, and Sally Johnson, Differences between formal and informal communication channels. *Journal of Business Communication* 31 (April 1994), 111–122.

9. Harris and Moran, *Managing cultural differences.*

10. Oberhaus et al., *Professional selling.*

11. Ibid.

12. Nancie Fimbel, Communicating realistically: Taking account of politics in internal business communications. *Journal of Business Communication* 31 (January 1994), 7–26.

13. Harris and Moran, *Managing cultural differences.*

14. Conrad N. Jackson and Ralph W. Jackson, What sets good salespeople apart from average and poor ones? working paper, 1993.

15. William T. Brooks, *High impact selling* (Englewood Cliffs, NJ: Prentice Hall, 1988).

16. Donald L. Thompson, Stereotype of the salesman. *Harvard Business Review* (January–February 1972), 20–25, 28, 29, 159–161.

17. Jeremy Main, How to sell by listening. *Fortune,* February 4, 1985, 52–54.

18. Conrad C. Elnes, *Inside secrets of outstanding salespeople* (Englewood Cliffs, NJ: Prentice Hall, 1988).

19. Ibid.

20. Jackson and Jackson, What sets good salespeople apart?

21. Haney, *Communication and interpersonal relationships..*

22. Elnes, *Inside Secrets,* 12.

23. Hakan Hakansson, Jan Johanson, and Bjorn Wootz, Influence tactics in buyer-seller processes. *Industrial Marketing Management* 5 (1977), 319–332.

SUGGESTED READINGS

Elnes, C. Conrad. *Inside secrets of outstanding salespeople.* Englewood Cliffs, NJ: Prentice Hall, 1988.

> Increasing sales performance requires greater knowledge and skill rather than simply working harder. Salespeople who are the high achievers rely on coaching that helps them refine their skills. They then work to improve those skills continuously and adapt them to their personal style.

Harris, Philip R., and Robert T. Moran. *Managing cultural differences.* Houston, TX: Gulf, 1991.

> Every region of the world has particular cultural characteristics that shape the way people act. To be successful, a business must learn the cultures of the regions where it operates and adapt its approach to those cultures. This requires rethinking how the business operates.

Mackay, H. B. *Swim with the sharks.* New York: Ivy Press, 1988.

> Both the world of business in general and the world of selling in particular are intensely competitive. Creating and maintaining a competitive edge does not just happen. It requires specific approaches and actions that must be used if one is to survive.

Terpstra, Vern, and Kenneth David. *The cultural environment of international business.* Cincinnati, OH: South-Western, 1985.

> Cultural systems in different regions of the world are based on, among other things, language, values, religion, and education. These cultural systems shape the way politics are played out, the way people interact, and the way businesses operate. A basic understanding of the cultural system is essential for businesses competing in the international marketplace.

_____ Chapter 4 _____

Motivation in Selling and Sales Management

OPENING SCENARIO

Jeff Baker was in the process of reviewing sales figures for the 23 salespeople in his region. He had been going over the data for two days and was nearing the end of his task. Although sales were generally trending upward compared to the same period the year before, he noticed several problems. First, his salespeople seemed to be pushing the easier-to-sell, lower-profit items and ignoring the higher-profit products in their line. Second, though the regional sales were higher than the year before, his region's sales were not growing at the same rate the other regions were. Finally, of the 23 people in his region, 4 seemed to be carrying the region.

Baker's company, Midwest Medical Supply, was a wholesale distributor of pharmaceuticals, medical equipment, and medical supplies. Midwest had been in business since 1948 and had earned a good reputation for service and quality products. This reputation was due in large part to the fact that the company recruited only the brightest and the best candidates and paid them very well. The company put its people through extensive initial training and gave them refresher training twice a year. The turnover rate was just about right for the industry. Baker's territory consisted of a good mix of experienced salespeople. Six had been with the company less than three years, ten between three and ten years, and seven more than ten years.

Baker felt that his salespeople were working hard but needed an extra push to get sales figures in line with what they should be. He needed to come up with an overall plan to motivate his region as well as a plan for dealing with those who were performing below average. The plan had to be in the hands of the national sales manager in ten days.

Chapter Objectives

After reading this chapter, you should be able to

- Understand the major theories of motivation and how they apply to selling and sales management.
- Recognize the place of extrinsic and intrinsic rewards in motivating salespeople.
- Realize the importance of having a motivational program that is fair to all salespeople and yet caters to individual needs.
- Appreciate the effect of career stage on a salesperson's motivation level.
- Get salespeople involved in the motivational program.

INTRODUCTION

An ongoing challenge for both salespeople and sales managers is how to motivate people. For the salesperson, the challenge is motivating buyers and customers to make a favorable decision. For the sales manager, the task involves motivating members of the sales force to perform well. Some salespeople believe that customers are motivated only by lower prices. Likewise, some sales managers believe that salespeople are motivated only by money. Others argue that though good prices are important to customers and good salaries are important in retaining salespeople, money is just one of many motivational forces that affect people. Still others hold that a person cannot be motivated by any external force—that a person must be internally moved to act—and thus the sales manager has little or no effect on salespeople's level of motivation. Rather they must concentrate on recruiting people who are internally driven. It is likely that the truth about motivation, as in so many other cases, is to be found somewhere in the middle.

Although it is true that salespeople have an impact on customers and sales managers can have an effect on their salespeople, in reality, no one can "motivate" anyone else. One person cannot bring about an effective change in the behavior of another human being unless that person accepts the influence of the other. One might coerce a person into altering his or her actions, but that is not motivation. If it were, the person who robs a convenience store is an expert at motivation. Motivation only results when a person voluntarily alters his or her action or opinion. In the words of organizational theorist Wendell French, motivation is the desire and willingness of a person to expend effort to reach a particular goal or outcome. Individual motivation is a consequence of many forces operating simultaneously in the person and the person's environment.[1]

Motivation, then, is the attempt to influence another person to do something that we think is worthwhile or helps us to accomplish a goal that we desire. However, motivation is the process not only of obtaining conformity of action but of bringing about a change in the person so that the action will be ongoing. Motivational approaches may address the outward circumstances, but their purpose is to affect the inner person. In this chapter we discuss the background material pertinent to developing an effective motivational program.

THEORIES OF MOTIVATION

It has been said that there is nothing as useful as a good theory. Although we might not agree that every theory of motivation is useful, we would hold that it is necessary for the sales manager to understand some of the basic theories of motivation in order to design effective motivational programs. Otherwise, a discussion of motivational programs becomes largely anecdotal without providing any clear-cut understanding of why certain programs seem to work and others do not.

We will discuss some theories of motivation that will help to build a framework for understanding those things that move people to do what we want them to. An underlying concept in motivation is the **law of effect.** According to this law, people tend to repeat behavior for which they are rewarded. The law of effect can be described this way: "The tendency of a person to repeat behavior that is accompanied by favorable consequences and not to repeat behavior that is accompanied by unfavorable consequences."[2]

When we seek to motivate a person, we need to spell out specifically and explicitly what it is that we wish her to do and give her a reward when she does it. Furthermore, we should not reward the person when she does something contrary to what we stipulated. So, implicit in the law of effect are the need to communicate accurately what it is that we wish another person to do and the need to establish a system that rewards "good" behavior and does not reward "bad" behavior. For the salesperson, when a customer makes a concession, that customer needs to be rewarded in some way. For the sales manager, when the salesperson is performing well, an appropriate reward should follow.

Obviously, the law of effect is related to reinforcement theory. When a person is rewarded for performance, he will tend to repeat that performance. At this point in our discussion, it is instructive to note that satisfaction and performance are not necessarily related, even though reinforcement and performance are.[3] Some managers seem to believe that if they can make their salespeople happy, performance will improve. The way to make people happy is to reward them, but if their performance is not related to that reward, they will not be moved to improve their performance. They will be happy as a result of the reward, but they will not work harder. For example, a sales manager might decide to give a poorly performing salesperson the same raise as a good performer because he thinks she has a great deal of potential and he believes it will improve her satisfaction. In doing so, he has rewarded poor performance, and she will likely repeat that poor performance.

Needs-Based Theories

It goes without saying that people act or react to meet particular needs that are important to them. However, just how they do so has been the subject of speculation. Perhaps the most well-known need-based theory of motivation is Abraham Maslow's **hierarchy of needs theory,**[4] as illustrated in Figure 4-1.

According to Maslow, people attempt to fulfill their needs in a hierarchical fashion. In other words, people begin by meeting their most basic needs, and, as those basic needs are met, new ones emerge that they will seek to fulfill. According to Maslow, these needs are universal and people will tend to follow the hierarchical chain in somewhat lockstep fashion. **Physiological needs** include such basic things as water and food, that is, the essentials for life. Once those needs are met, people will then seek to take care of **safety needs,** such as clothing, shelter, and self-defense. The next level of needs are **social needs,** the need to associate with other people, to form communities that engender relationships with others. Next are **esteem needs,** the need to feel a sense of self-worth and prestige. Finally, **self-actualization needs** emerge; these are the highest-order needs of personal growth and self-fulfillment.

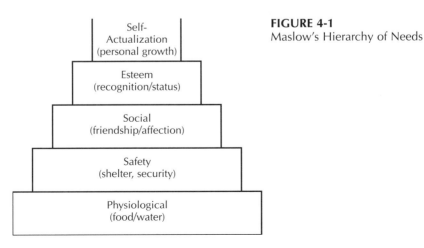

FIGURE 4-1
Maslow's Hierarchy of Needs

The problem with Maslow's scheme is that he seems to propose that these needs and their fulfillment must follow in an ordered fashion, probably an overly simplistic assumption. However, this theory suggests that, generally, needs are hierarchical and that, unless a person has taken care of basic needs, attempting to motivate him or her to meet other needs will have limited effectiveness.

Clayton Alderfer, another social scientist, took a slightly different approach and yet developed the same basic idea.[5] Alderfer proposed that needs could be divided into three categories:

1. *Existence needs.* Those having to do with the essentials of life, such as food, clothing, and shelter.
2. *Relatedness needs.* Those related to human relationships, such as family, peer groups, fellow workers, and friends.
3. *Growth needs.* Needs relating to achievement, self-fulfillment, and personal growth.

Alderfer's theory holds that a person will attempt to move through the needs as a progression, beginning with existing needs and ending with growth needs. However, contrary to Maslow, Alderfer would say that a person may also revert to meeting lower-order needs under certain circumstances.

As an example, for the salesperson, the buyer's needs are paramount, and as discussed in Chapter 2, those needs are both organizational and personal. When the buyer makes a decision to purchase a product, he does so because the organization needs the product. However, when he makes that decision, he is also meeting certain personal needs. The buyer might have a high need for security (existence need to keep his job), and as a result, he will be inclined to purchase only from proven sources. Another buyer might be meeting a self-esteem need (growth need) when she negotiates very hard for a price reduction because, in doing so, she feels she has done a good job. Generally, then, the decision to buy a particular product meets an organizational need, whereas the decision from whom to buy may meet a personal need.

For sales managers, the needs of their sales force form the basis for any motivational program. A salesperson early in his career may be in the process of accumulating possessions, and so the need for money is paramount (existence need). Another salesperson, who is more established in her career, may have a need for self-esteem or self-actualization (growth need). Thus she may be more motivated by an award for achievement or by being given more responsibility in the company.

Equity Theory

Another theory of motivation relevant to salespeople is *equity theory*. According to this theory, people seek fair treatment in the way they are rewarded for job performance. It can be described this way: "We compare the ratio of our outcomes to inputs with the ratio of outcomes to inputs for some 'comparison person.' The comparison person may be a co-worker or a group average (such as prevailing standards in a department, organization, community, or industry)."[6] In other words, we take the amount of effort we put into an endeavor versus the results we get and compare that with the amount of effort versus results of another. This amounts to comparing a set of ratios:

$$\frac{\text{Our outcomes}}{\text{Our inputs}} \quad \text{compared to} \quad \frac{\text{Others' outcomes}}{\text{Others' inputs}}$$

A situation will be deemed equitable if those two ratios are equal, regardless of whether or not the person actually receives more rewards.[7] If, for instance, a salesperson knows that another salesperson earns one and a half times what he does but she also puts in 50 percent more hours working, the situation will be considered equitable. If, however, that other salesperson earns one and a half times the salary while putting in roughly the same hours, the situation will be considered inequitable and will act as a demotivator for both parties. For the one who feels shortchanged, the situation will be deemed unfair and he will feel that there is no way to get ahead. For the other, the fact that she is inequitably rewarded means that there is no reason to increase her effort. For either party in an inequitable reward situation, when there is an inequitable distribution, the significance of rewards is lessened.[8] In other words, both the person receiving a more than equitable reward and the person receiving a less than equitable reward will tend to view those awards as insignificant.

The same situation can occur between salespeople and customers and between management and salespeople. Salespeople need to give equal treatment to customers because every industry has its rumor mill and buyers from different companies talk to each other. If one customer is being given favored treatment, eventually the word will get out and create hostility. Nor should a sales manager show favoritism to certain salespeople. Once that rumor gets started, any attempt at motivation is undermined.

Attribution Theory

Attribution theory is concerned with how people mentally assign the causes for their successes or failures. The way they do so can strongly affect their motivation. Figure 4-2 depicts the contingency table related to this assignment process.

Very simplistically, we can categorize a person's performance as good or poor, and we can categorize attributions regarding causes for that performance as personal or environmental. The reason for relative success or failure will be viewed either as a function of what the individual did or did not do or as a function of some factor outside the individual. Often, as a defense mechanism, when a person performs poorly she will have a tendency to ascribe those results to something external and when that person performs well, she will assign that to

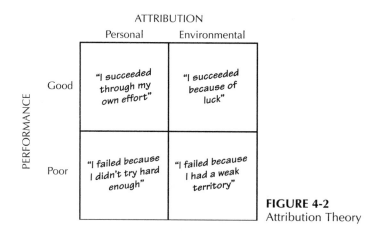

FIGURE 4-2
Attribution Theory

personal reasons. For example, students will almost always say: "That so and so gave me a D, but I made an A in Professor Smith's class." Salespeople will likewise say, "I didn't make quota because of the lousy territory they gave me" or "I exceeded quota because I know how to sell!" Both examples illustrate the fact that individuals will attempt to assign causality because there seems to be an element in human nature that wants to make sense out of an event.

In addition, people make attributions not only for their own behavior but for the behavior of others. If a friend has a success, we tend to make personal attributions for that success. But if a person we do not like succeeds, we tend to attribute it to environmental causes.

The attribution that a person makes regarding her performance has a direct impact on her ability to perform the next time.[9] This is especially true when the person performs poorly.[10] If the attribution for a successful sale is external ("It was luck."), the salesperson may begin to rely on luck rather than hard work. The importance of attribution theory for a sales manager is that part of the process of motivation involves providing feedback. If the person has not performed up to par, she needs to understand what caused the poor performance. By the same token, if the person has done well, she needs to understand that the performance was based on her own actions and not on luck or other external forces. The sales manager must guide salespeople to make the correct attribution. Anything else shortcircuits the motivational program.

Attribution theory is important for salespeople because buyers also make attributions for successes and failures. If an urgently needed order arrives on time because of the special effort of the salesperson and his staff, it is important for the buyer to know that. The salesperson should not boast about his accomplishments, but on his next contact he should subtly let the buyer know the extra effort that went into that success.

Herzberg's Two-Factor Theory

One of the major debates in sales management revolves around whether money is the only truly motivational incentive for salespeople. Some sales managers take the position that if their salespeople are not motivated by money, there is no way to motivate them. Others think that salespeople are motivated by both money, which is an extrinsic reward, and by various intrinsic rewards, such as recognition. Herzberg addressed the power of extrinsic and intrinsic rewards in his *two-factor theory* and found they both have their place in motivating people.[11] Although his theory has been debated, it has much support.[12]

In his research, Herzberg found that satisfaction and dissatisfaction are not the opposite ends of a single continuum but, rather, two separate influencing factors. Figure 4-3 illustrates his concept. At any one time, a person has feelings of motivation and satisfaction as well as feelings of dissatisfaction and demotivation. In examining this phenomenon, Herzberg found two separate sets of variables that are related to those two different factors. Variables related to satisfaction and motivation he termed **motivators.** These consist of intrinsic rewards of the job, such as recognition of achievement, experienced responsibility, advancement, and the challenging nature of the work itself. The presence of these tend to be associated with increased levels of satisfaction. For sales managers to obtain optimal performance or to have salespeople perform better on a particular aspect of the job, they need to provide intrinsic rewards.

The other factors Herzberg labeled **hygienes,** and these are related to dissatisfaction and demotivation. These factors consist of extrinsic rewards, such as salary, work conditions, and company policy. If these are positive, the person experiences lower levels of dissatisfaction; however, their presence alone does not ensure satisfaction. In other words, hygienes do not necessarily serve to motivate but help keep people from being demotivated.

High levels of dissatisfaction tend to be related to higher turnover rates and absenteeism. To cut down the level of dissatisfaction, a sales manager needs to structure a system of motivation that provides salespeople with a reasonable level of extrinsic rewards. Salespeople generally have a good idea of the average salary of people in their industry and company. If their salary is not approaching that average, the tendency to move elsewhere is higher. If changing jobs is not feasible, salespeople may well have higher rates of absenteeism. This does not

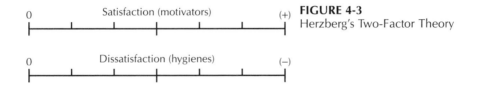

FIGURE 4-3
Herzberg's Two-Factor Theory

mean that they necessarily will call in sick, but, rather, they will simply spend fewer hours on the job. Obviously, this tendency would compound the problem, creating a vicious cycle. To prevent this problem, extrinsic rewards must be adequate and equitable.

Although Herzberg's findings have been challenged and have not been adequately tested with salespeople, they do indicate that a good salary is not enough to motivate people to perform at their optimal level. One study found that pay raises were ranked higher than fringe benefits, incentive rewards, and recognition.[13] This finding, however, rather than negating the importance of intrinsic rewards, may in fact be evidence of their importance. The reason we say this is that the raise itself was viewed as important because it served to recognize achievement. As part of the reward system, sales managers must include a variety of incentives that make the selling job more meaningful and enjoyable, as William Keenan, an editor for *Sales & Marketing Management*, points out.[14]

Expectancy Theory

To understand more fully the process of motivation, it is necessary to break down that process into smaller elements, as expectancy theory does.[15] (See Figure 4-4.) According to *expectancy theory*, a person must believe that he is able to perform whatever it is that is asked and he must believe that the promised outcome will take place. Finally, the person must feel that the net gain is valuable to him personally. These elements are essential if a person is to be motivated by a particular program.

Whenever an individual is asked to perform a specific task, he goes through a mental assessment of the likelihood that a given level of effort will lead to a particular performance. That mental assessment is referred to as the person's **expectancy.** Research has shown that expectancy is related to the person's self-esteem and to the nature of the job.[16] Other researchers have indicated that higher expectancies are related to higher established goals.[17] Additionally, there is some indication that expectancy levels are related to gender, with one study reporting that female salespeople have significantly higher expectancy estimates than their male counterparts.[18]

A person also goes through a mental assessment of the likelihood that a given performance will lead to the desired outcome. This is the person's **instrumentality.** Finally, the person assesses the net gain or value of the outcome, which is his **valence.**

To illustrate expectancy theory, we will use an example from a sales setting:

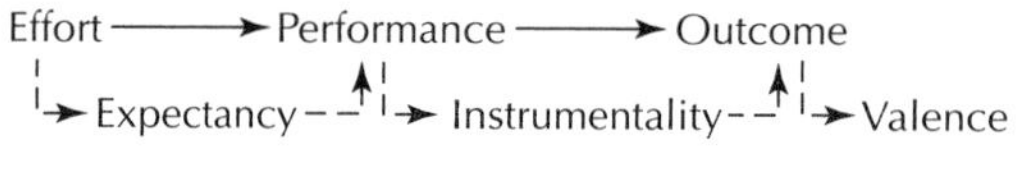

Effort ──────▶ Performance ──────▶ Outcome

└─▶ Expectancy ──┘└─▶ Instrumentality ──┘└─▶ Valence

FIGURE 4-4
Components of Expectancy Theory

A sales manager decides that her company needs to increase sales volume in the next quarter. Currently, she has 50 salespeople working for her. She develops a sales contest whereby any salesperson who increases sales volume by fifty percent in the next quarter will win a one-week, all-expense-paid trip for two to Hawaii. However, in this company, salespeople are expected to render a high level of service to existing accounts and are currently averaging 60 hours per week to simply keep up with current volume.

Effort is the work necessary to increase volume

Performance is increasing volume by 50 percent

Outcomes are the trip to Hawaii (positive valence), feelings of accomplishment (positive valence), more time on the job (negative valence)

In this case, the salesperson's instrumentality (the link between performance and outcome) should be relatively high in that he knows that if sales volume is increased by 50 percent in his territory over the next quarter, he will go to Hawaii. The salesperson's valence (the net value of the outcomes) could be high or low. If we assume the salesperson really wants to go to Hawaii and would feel good about himself, and is not bothered by the extra time on the job, he should have a positive valence. The expectancy (the linkage between effort and performance) will likely be extremely low, because the salespeople are already "stretched to the limit" at existing levels of performance. In all likelihood, this person will conclude that he cannot put forth enough effort to increase volume by 50 percent—he views it as simply impossible. In this case he will not be motivated by the contest even if he has a very high valence (really wants to go to Hawaii), because of the low level of expectancy.

Let's change our example a bit. Say, for instance, the sales manager designs the contest so that only the first person to increase sales volume by 10 percent over the next quarter will win an all-expense-paid trip for two to Hawaii. In this case, the expectancy (the linkage between effort and performance) will be much higher than in the first case because increasing volume by 10 percent is much more doable. However, the instrumentality (the linkage between performance and outcome) will be considerably lower because only one person will win and the chance of going to Hawaii is significantly lessened. The valence would still be high if the person really wanted to go.

Finally, assume that the sales manager designs the contest so that the first 15 salespeople who increase volume by 10 percent will win the trip. Again the expectancy will be reasonably high, as will the instrumentality, given that roughly one third of the sales force will go to Hawaii. However, suppose the vast majority of the sales force have families with small children and they place extremely high value on spending time with their families. The increased workload will mean more time away from home (an average of 60 hours per week) than they are currently spending. Additionally, because the trip is only for two, this means that either the salespeople must pay their children's way on the trip or must find a place for them to stay while they are gone. These represent negative valences; the net effect may be that the Hawaii trip is seen as more trouble than it's worth. In this case, the contest may have little motivational power.

Among Peers, A Shared Experience

Thomas Forbes

The wisdom of many mentors blends into a person's life, just as streams join a river at different places, swirling and roiling and changing its character at first, then becoming an integral part of the current as the river gathers force. But there is always a primary source, of course, as sure as a four-foot-wide Mississippi River flows out of Lake Itasca.

Initially, a mentor might be your parent or older sibling. Next, perhaps, a boss. Then, as you reach your prime, there emerges a "superpeer," which computer software executive John Wyatt defines as a person who is doing something similar to what you're doing and whom you can call in the middle of the night and say, "Hey, Randy, I'm in San Francisco and I just had dinner with so and so, and this is what happened. What do you think?"

That, at any rate, has been the progression for Wyatt, 49, who himself is a mentor to young software developers through the Council for Entrepreneurial Development in the Research Triangle area of North Carolina. He has worked in the industry for 27 years, starting out as a computer operator at a bank after college. He learned programming from hackers at Bell Labs, then moved to Digital Equipment Corp. in 1967. He joined DEC at an opportune time. Customers were no longer dazzled by the fact that computers could perform mathematical functions with blazing speed. They wanted to know how the computer—be it DEC's, IBM's or Data General's—could solve their particular problems. Software was becoming as important as the hardware that ran it.

"When I got to DEC, the normal salesmen were guys that were electrical engineers who didn't know anything about programming," Wyatt says. As a political science and history major with a background in hands-on programming, Wyatt recalls that he "was almost an experiment" when he made the transition from product support to sales.

The skills he needed to succeed at DEC matched Wyatt's personality; he says he would have failed miserably as a slick huckster. "People that don't do well around me are what I call blue-suede-shoes salesmen. The Dapper Dans. I'd rather have someone who knows the product intimately and teach him how to dress well than a Dapper Dan who is never going to know anything about the product but has a great personality."

That's not to say Wyatt doesn't get along with people; in fact he told an acquaintance that he's a "heat-seeking missile" when it comes to networking.

"I once saw him connect with a stranger in an elevator based on each of them knowing someone in Florida 10 years before," the acquaintance relates.

One of the things that helped Wyatt during his DEC career, he admits, was the number of people he got to know at the company. A dozen years after he left DEC for entrepreneurial ventures, Wyatt says his local DEC sales rep "gets a big kick out of the fact that I know more people at DEC than he does."

Wyatt's father, also named John, had been a vice president at Hinde & Dauch, a leading manufacturer of corrugated packaging that was bought out in the 1950s by Westvaco, where the senior Wyatt became a strategic sales executive. Wyatt has vivid memories of meeting his father's regional sales managers at various locales, including the family living room in Morristown, N.J.

"Two of the people whom my dad mentored live within a half-hour of me, and I still see them," says Wyatt. "My dad is 87, and they're in their 70s. One of them calls my father every month. So the concept of long-term business relationships isn't foreign to me."

Even more ingrained is his father's belief that salespeople cannot effectively sell a technical product unless they know how it's made.

"Dad had a tricky little game that he played," recalls Wyatt. "He used to carry a half-dollar and a penknife that was razor-sharp. And with a flat piece of kraft board, he could take a phone on a purchasing agent's desk and design a package for the phone in real time, with the half-dollar and the penknife.

"It was a little bit of an act, but there was a real strong message there: You have to know how to design the packaging. And that was what he and his salesmen brought to the table."

Wyatt found mentors in some of his superiors at DEC. John Jones, his boss when he was still an applications programmer addressing customers' technical concerns, allowed him to make the kinds of mistakes that are essential to professional growth. One such blunder—he couldn't get the benchmarks that a prospect had given him to run properly—probably cost the company a $200,000 sale. But Jones didn't fire him or demote him or even get angry. He just told Wyatt what he had done wrong.

"I didn't ask for help from someone who was more experienced, who could have saved my bacon," recalls Wyatt. "I just didn't know, at that time, how to escalate the problem. That kind of episode is probably why I'm very, very big on problem escalation. If you're not capable of solving the problem, find someone in the organization to help you."

There is a second point that Wyatt believes is crucial to successful selling: Don't ever hide a lost sale.

"Come forward and let's figure out why you lost it, and let's make sure that it doesn't happen again," he says. "That's a lesson I learned from Mr. Kiesewetter."

Bill Kiesewetter, who today runs an air-freight shipping business in Providence, R.I., was the DEC manager who agreed to let Wyatt move from product support and join his sales team on the condition that he take a Dale Carnegie course.

"Bill redirected career paths when you didn't come clean," Wyatt says.

Wyatt still taps into Kiesewetter's keen business insight and candor. Kiesewetter regularly reviews Wyatt's plans for his two enterprises: EasyEntry Software, which markets a cross-platform data-entry application, and Wyatt Associates, a business development and strategic marketing consultancy.

But the person Wyatt leans on most heavily for selling advice these days is "superpeer" Randall Pinato.

"Randy is the person I most want to be like," he says simply.

Pinato, who is about the same age as Wyatt and who left DEC in the same year, is one of the founders of Telechips, where he is vice president of sales and marketing. The two-year-old firm is marketing a screen-based, multimedia telephone. Wyatt admired Pinato's work at DEC, where he turned a laggard Philadelphia sales office into a top performer. He says he finds Pinato's advice particularly valuable today because "Randy's out here doing the same thing I am."

"Out here" is the striving, scrambling world of entrepreneurship, a world that would seem to be vastly different from selling for a billion-dollar sales organization like DEC. It isn't really, though, says Pinato, because top performers in any sales situation share one quality: "They have mastered the ability to get people to move with them. If you make other people successful with you, if you make them feel good and you put money in their pockets, that's a win-win situation."

"We're a team" is a hackneyed phrase that few people really understand, Pinato believes, and one, he says, that many follow up with a self-aggrandizing variation of "And by the way, I did it."

Pinato himself offers a roster of people who have helped his career. Wyatt ("a true performer") is right at the top. "If there are any people who believe they are the sole persons who bring a piece of business home, they're blowing smoke rings," Pinato says. "An entrepreneurial venture still requires the leveraging of other players, whether they work for you, with you, or outside the company."

Pinato worries that being singled out as a "superpeer" by Wyatt might lead others to believe that he is "capturing the glory." So we won't give him any credit at all for the following circumstances. We'll just state the facts: Pinato's wife, Karla, has a best friend named Debbie. Debbie is now Wyatt's wife.

Reprinted with the permission of SELL!NG magazine.

Expectancy theory deals with the concept that anytime a person is called to take a particular action, he or she goes through a multifaceted evaluative process. The results of this evaluation will determine whether any motivational program will be effective. To be sure, in many cases the person may not even be conscious that this process is taking place, but it does nonetheless.

Thomas Quick presented some practical applications of expectancy theory in motivating salespeople.[19] In his discussion Quick provided some guidelines for its application:

- Tell your subordinates what you expect of them.
- Make the work valuable.
- Make the work doable.
- Give them feedback.
- Reward your salespeople when they've been successful.

Each of these guidelines relates to an element in the theory. Communicating what is expected and making the work doable influence salespeople's level of expectancy. Providing feedback and rewarding salespeople when they perform well relate to instrumentality. Finally, making the work valuable, extrinsically and/or intrinsically, affects their level of valence. If any of these elements is deficient, salespeople probably will not be motivated.

For the salesperson, expectancy theory applies to her relationship with the customer. The customer will be motivated to buy if he believes that when he makes the decision to buy, there is a high likelihood that the product will be delivered in good condition and on time (expectancy). Additionally, he must believe that the product will perform as promised (instrumentality) and that he is getting an appropriate level of value for the investment (positive valence).

In Sum

Each of these theories of motivation speaks to a different aspect of the psychology of the individual. Each must be considered and woven into the fabric of any motivational approach. Both the salesperson and the sales manager must remember that a person has, at any given time, a complex set of needs that seek fulfillment. This fact also speaks to the necessity of building some flexibility into a motivational program so that the needs of different individuals can be met.

Certainly any motivational system must be equitable, and it must be perceived as such by the members of the sales force. If not, it will be robbed of its power and become ineffective. When a sales manager provides feedback to the salesperson, that individual may or may not correctly ascribe the reasons for her success or failure. The sales manager must guide the person to make an attribution that accurately reflects the facts. Additionally, the sales manager must be aware that, depending on his feelings about an individual, the way he attributes that person's performance will be affected. Furthermore, the sales manager needs to be aware that the success of a motivational program is entirely dependent on whether the individuals in the sales force believe they can accomplish a particular task, perceive that they have a reasonable chance to be rewarded for that performance, and know the net value of that reward.

For salespersons, motivation is an inherent part of what they do; however, customers also attempt to meet a complex set of needs and solve problems. They must be given a reason to act, and that reason must be much stronger than their reason for not acting. Also, customers must be shown why one company can do a better job of meeting their needs than all the other companies in the marketplace. Salespersons who view their job as partly being a motivator are well on their way to being successful.

ISSUES IN MOTIVATION

The Career Cycle

It is generally accepted that individuals progress through various stages in their careers. It has been proposed that a person passes through six distinct stages during a lifetime, four of which take place during a career.[20] This concept of a career life cycle has been applied to the sales force.[21] Salespeople progress through four stages during their careers: exploration, establishment, maintenance, and disengagement.[22]

In the **exploration stage,** individuals (typically in their twenties) are concerned with finding an occupation in which they can feel comfortable and succeed. The fundamental question addressed during this period is: "What do I want to do for the rest of my life?" Personal commitment to an occupation usually is low, and several changes in occupation are likely.

Establishment-stage people (usually in their late twenties) seek stabilization within an occupation and a secure place in the working world. Concern focuses on adding structure and stability to one's career, often about the same time that other important life commitments (getting married, buying a home, establishing roots in a community) are being made. Achieving professional success is of utmost importance and frequently involves a desire for promotion.

The **maintenance stage** usually extends from the mid-thirties to mid-forties. Concern during this stage is with retaining one's present position, status, and performance level, which are likely to be relatively high. Desire and opportunity for future organizational and job movement diminish. Greater commitment to an organization is likely because people in this stage are less prone to switch organizations. However, they must adapt to changes, keep current with new developments, and acquire special knowledge and new skills to improve job performance.

In the early development of career stages theory, **disengagement** was associated with preparation for imminent retirement and sometimes loss of identity. Recent empirical research suggests that some people become frustrated long before retirement age and may psychologically disengage themselves from their work rather than search for a new job or occupation. Lower performance generally is associated with disengagement.

Research has supported the theory that salespeople do go through these stages and make significant changes in their goals and their emphasis in both life and career.[23] In an empirical examination of the relationship between career stages and motivation of salespeople, researchers found that salespeople in the exploration stage had lower instrumentality related to achieving sales quotas than did those at other stages.[24] They also found that salespeople in the establishment stage considered promotion a major part of being successful and were more motivated by the opportunity for that than for some other types of rewards. Salespeople in the maintenance stage were found not to be as interested in working harder to receive greater extrinsic rewards as they were in learning how to maintain their current rewards by working smarter and achieving a greater per call success rate. Those who had moved into the disengagement stage indicated they had the lowest instrumentality. Typically these people had a low desire for a pay increase and were more content to perform at minimally acceptable levels. They also tended to indicate a shift of their interests to things outside work, such as hobbies.

It is critical that sales managers recognize that salespeople go through a career life cycle and that what motivated a salesperson at one stage will not do so at another. Two stages seem to present some particular motivational problems. For the person in the exploration stage, the sales manager must be able to provide feedback and encouragement in view of the fact that the person may not be convinced that he or she will be able to perform the job at the level expected. A person in this stage is much more likely to quit when faced with the "normal" frustrations in selling. Not all people who leave the selling profession at this stage should do so, and so the sales manager may need to pay particular attention to struggling salespeople in order to "bring them along." For salespeople who have entered the disengagement stage, the challenge for the sales manager is to move that person to continue achieving his or her potential in light of the fact that he or she is preparing for a transition into a new life phase. Taking into account the various career stages of the salespeople in a company will help make a motivational program more successful.

Buyers also may go through a career cycle that affects how they relate to their job.[25] Just as salespeople are motivated by different factors as they move along this career cycle, so too are buyers. For example, the level of risk buyers are willing to take may be dependent on their career stage. A buyer who is in the establishment stage may be less willing to take a risk than one who is in the maintenance stage. Furthermore, the stage of the career cycle may affect the amount of power the buyer wields in a company and hence his ability to make an independent decision.

The Plateaued Salesperson

A persistent problem that is often related, although not necessarily so, to career stage is that of the plateaued salesperson. When we speak of a **career plateau,** we mean a point in the person's career where the likelihood of advancement or promotion is low. William Keenan estimated that as many as 15 percent of salespeople are plateaued.[26] He states that plateauing can be the result of several factors.

First, it may result from a lack of a clear-cut view of the career path. The person progresses satisfactorily until he or she begins to feel that career growth is coming to an end. Obviously, the sales manager in this case needs to work with her salespeople to assist them in developing new goals as current ones are met. A second major reason for plateauing is inadequate management, according to Keenan. Sales managers usually have so many things to do that unless there is a major problem they will simply take no action. Also the sales manager may be tempted to view a down quarter for a salesperson as a temporary anomaly. Although that is often the case, it can be a signal that the person has plateaued and needs some guidance.

The other reasons mentioned by Keenan can be classified into two categories: personal issues and career-related issues. In terms of personal issues, salespeople plateau because they may be bored, may be burned out, may have met their economic needs, may have personal problems, or may lack ability. Career-related issues include being discouraged with the company, being overlooked for promotion, avoiding the risk of moving into a management position, and being reluctant to be transferred. Dealing with these reasons involves counseling the salespeople, first to isolate the problem and then to help the person arrive at a workable solution.

Plateauing has been tied to a number of problems that sales managers must deal with. One study found that plateaued managers had higher absentee rates and reported more health-related problems. The same study also found that plateaued managers had lower job satisfaction scores and lower motivation levels.[27] Another study found that plateaued employees tended to make personal attributions for their stagnation and indicated a lower aspiration level than other employees.[28] A longitudinal study of salespeople reported that plateaued salespeople were much less committed to their organizations, reported significant attitude differences, and were less concerned with career issues than their non-plateaued counterparts.[29]

Some warning signals can tip off the manager that a salesperson has plateaued:[30]

- The salesperson does not prospect thoroughly enough.
- The salesperson starts failing to follow through.
- The salesperson begins to work fewer hours.
- The person becomes resistant to management suggestion.
- The salesperson lives in "the good old days."
- The person does not keep up to date on new products.
- The person's paperwork is late and/or poorly done.
- The number of customer complaints begins to increase.
- The person begins to manipulate commissions and quotas.
- The rate of absenteeism increases.

The sales manager needs to heed these early warning signs and view them as a cry for help from the salesperson rather than as behavior to be punished. In addition to paying increased attention to the individual, the manager might give the salesperson a new assignment or get the person involved in a leadership role. In short, the sales manager must recognize the plateauing problem for what it is, determine the real cause of the problem, and take concerted, specific action to overcome it.

Cultural Differences

Given the increasingly global character of competition and the pluralistic nature of American society, sales managers will need to be more aware of the effect of cultural differences on motivating salespeople. As mentioned in Chapter 3, cultures vary widely in the meaning of words, actions, and objects. When developing a motivational or sales program to be used in another country, the sales manager must adapt the program to that country. Not only do the nuances of the language need to be taken into account but the orientation of the culture as well. To begin to understand a foreign culture, sales managers need to answer five basic questions:[31]

1. What is the character of innate human nature?
   Humankind is evil.
   Humankind is a mixture of good and evil.
   Humankind is good.
2. What is the relationship of humans to nature?
   Humankind is subject to nature.
   Humankind is in harmony with nature.
   Humankind is master of nature.
3. What is the temporal focus of life?
   It is the past.
   It is the present.
   It is the future.
4. What is the modality of the people's activity?
   It is spontaneous expression of desires.
   It is the development of all aspects of the self.
   It is accomplishing measurable results.
5. What is the relationship of person to person?
   It is lineal: group goals are primary, as is the continuity of the group over time.
   It is collateral: group goals are primary, but continuity over time is not critical.
   It is individual: the individual's goals are important.

How managers answer these five essential questions affects how they approach a culture. For a motivational program to be effective, it must take into account those cultural values and norms that make the society unique. Salespeople and sales managers cannot assume that people in other cultures will respond to motivational techniques in the same way they do in their own culture.

Regina Eisman presented some of the difficulties experienced by Japanese managers in American plants.[32] Trying to utilize the same approach to managing workers in U.S. plants as they did in Japan, Japanese managers found that not only did workers not respond but in some cases were hostile to their efforts. Additionally, some Japanese workers in the U.S. plants were insulted when offered incentives for harder work because they felt that it was their duty to work as hard as possible anyway.

Central to developing any motivational program for use in another culture is an understanding of the differences between it and the U.S. culture. For example, the American business organization places great emphasis on individual decision making, individual rewards, and individual responsibility. Therefore American managers use motivational techniques that work explicitly to control their people. In certain European and East Asian cultures, such is not the case. In Japan and Germany, managers use the so-called "Theory Z" approach to management. Theory Z management places more emphasis on group consensus and participative decision making.[33] Their approach to motivating their people is more implicit in that it does not rely on short-term, specific rewards for performance but, rather, on a long-term payoff for the entire group.

To implement an effective motivational program for another culture requires that sales managers rethink their assumptions. They also need to think in terms of rewarding the group for its overall performance rather than the individual. Additionally, motivational programs should probably have a longer window of performance, with the major reward coming at the end but employing intermittent encouragement during the course of the program.

Getting Involvement in Motivational Programs

Generally, motivational programs comprise both intrinsic and extrinsic rewards. The major form of motivation is salary (discussed in Chapter 16). Too often sales managers, when they develop a program, assume that salespeople will gladly participate in the program. Even if such programs do not violate the tenets of the major theories, the sales manager cannot assume that salespeople will be interested in or motivated by a particular program. Sales managers need to investigate fresh approaches to gain involvement by the sales force.[34] For sales contests, for instance, sales managers need to get people involved along the way using "teasers" to attract the attention and interest of the sales force.

Jack Falvey, a contributing editor for *Sales & Marketing Management*, believes that managers should view salespeople as "internal customers" when developing a plan to market programs effectively to members of the sales force.[35] He goes on to note that, as with customers, flexibility with salespeople is necessary if the sales manager's programs are to be successful. Suffice it to say that the manager needs to be cognizant of the fact that simply developing a program and presenting it will not ensure participation. The manager must work to get the program accepted and to motivate the sales force to participate in it.

Designing Incentive Programs

Based on our discussion, sales managers can develop effective incentive programs. Certainly, such programs should be kept simple. The way the program works as well as the objectives necessary to receive the incentive should be spelled out clearly. Also, the program should be short in order to have reinforcement value.[36] Sales managers often think only of their salespeople when developing incentive programs. However, given the increasing pressure for good service and the vital part that sales support people play, the program should also include some kind of incentive program for those support people.[37]

Of course, the major incentive that salespeople receive is their paycheck. Rewards are discussed more fully in Chapter 16, so we will only touch on a few basic ideas here. According to Herzberg's theory, incentives can be either intrinsic or extrinsic. Certainly extrinsic rewards, especially money, are the most powerful incentives according to a number of recent reports. However, other extrinsic rewards such as trips and vacations to exotic places also have been found to be effective.[38] Even things as simple as premiums and merchandise can be effective motivators. In fact, it has been argued that merchandise can be more effective than cash because it is something that salespeople keep for a time and is a distinct reminder of an accomplishment, whereas cash is often put into a bank account or used to pay bills.[39] A benefit of using premiums is the wide variety of choices that are available.[40] This means that the sales manager can fit the gift to a particular person.

Intrinsic rewards, however, play a powerful role in motivating salespeople. Remember that there is an element of intrinsic motivation even with extrinsic rewards; in fact, if that intrinsic element is absent, the extrinsic reward will not be as effective. Recognition can also be an effective motivator, as can having the person participate in additional training.[41]

Certainly, regardless of the incentives selected, the program should be equitable and rewards should be clearly tied to the person's performance. The program must be doable, and the rewards should be meaningful.

CHAPTER SUMMARY

In this chapter we discussed the background material pertinent to motivating others. We covered several theories of motivation because no one theory can address all aspects of motivation, but each theory has its place in understanding how to motivate. Used in conjunction, these theories can form the basis of meaningful and successful motivational programs.

Both Maslow's and Alderfer's needs-based theories see motivation as fulfilling a variety of personal needs. Maslow suggests that people fulfill basic needs in a hierarchical manner. Alderfer proposes three categories of needs that people try to fulfull in progression. They may have to revert to meeting lower-order needs in certain circumstances. Equity theory addresses the issue of fairness in the reward system. Actually, equity theory is probably more of a theory of demotivation than motivation in that no one will be motivated because a system is equitable, but almost everyone will be demotivated if the system lacks equity. Attribution theory addresses the issue of where a person places credit for success and blame for failure. Causes can be either personal or environmental.

Herzberg's two-factor theory deals with the place of intrinsic and extrinsic rewards in the overall system, as well as the factors related to satisfaction and motivation and those related to dissatisfaction and demotivation. Expectancy theory, perhaps the central theory in the set, views motivation as involving several aspects that interact to develop a particular level of motivation. This is a complex process that involves a series of mental evaluations of the ability to do what is asked, the likelihood of being rewarded, and the overall value of the reward versus the costs involved in carrying out the tasks. This process was related to salespeople, sales managers, and customers.

We moved from these theories to a discussion of some of the major motivational issues facing managers. The stage of salespeople's career cycle will have an impact on how they respond to certain motivational programs. Related is the problem of the plateaued salesperson, the person who has peaked in performance and seems to have stagnated. The fact that a person has reached a plateau in performance does not mean that he or she must stay there. Sales managers can help the person overcome this problem by giving the person a new assignment or a leadership role.

Finally, sales managers and salespeople alike increasingly deal with individuals from a variety of backgrounds and cultures who relate to their career and to others differently.

In short, motivation is a complex issue. Sales professionals have the task of attempting to tap into the internal motivation of each individual and be able to reach that person in a meaningful way.

KEY TERMS

career plateau, p. 87

disengagement stage, p. 86

establishment stage, p. 86

esteem needs, p. 75

expectancy, p. 80

exploration stage, p. 86

hierarchy of needs theory, p. 75

hygienes, p. 79

instrumentality, p. 80

law of effect, p. 74

maintenance stage, p. 86

motivation, p. 74

motivators, p. 79   self-actualization needs, p. 75

physiological needs, p. 75   social needs, p. 75

safety needs, p. 75   valence, p. 80

CHAPTER QUESTIONS

1. If a salesperson were not performing well and the sales manager decided to give him a raise anyway to "encourage" him, how would the salesperson respond according to the law of effect?

2. What are the differences between Maslow's and Alderfer's theories of need?

3. Why might equity theory actually be considered a theory of demotivation?

4. If a salesperson were to perform well and make an external attribution, how would that affect her motivation level?

5. Are salespeople motivated only by money? Discuss your answer in light of Herzberg's theory.

6. Describe in your own words the concepts of expectancy, instrumentality, and valence. Give examples of each.

7. Do the factors that motivate salespeople change over their career cycle? Explain your answer.

8. If a salesperson were to make an external attribution for his performance, how would that affect his expectancy level?

NOTES

1. Wendell L. French, *Human resources management* (Boston: Houghton Mifflin, 1990), 122.

2. Keith Davis and John W. Newstrom, *Human behavior at work: Organizational behavior* (New York: McGraw-Hill, 1985), 78.

3. D. L. Cherrington, H. J. Reitz, and W. E. Scott, Effects of reward and contingent reinforcement on satisfaction and task performance. *Journal of Applied Psychology* 55 (1971), 531–536.

4. Abraham H. Maslow, *Motivation and personality* (New York: Harper & Row, 1970); Douglas T. Hall and K. E. Nougaim, An examination of Maslow's need hierarchy in an organization setting. *Organizational Behavior and Human Performance* (1968), 12–35; M. A. Wahba and L. G. Birdwell, Maslow reconsideration: A review of research on the need hierarchy theory. *Organizational Behavior and Human Performance* (1976), 212–240.

5. Clayton P. Alderfer, *Existence, relatedness, and growth: Human needs in organizational settings* (New York: Free Press, 1972).

6. Dennis W. Organ and Thomas Bateman, *Organizational behavior* (Homewood, IL: Richard D. Irwin, 1986), 125.

7. M. R. Carrell and J. E. Dettrech, Equity theory: The recent literature, methodological considerations and new directions. *Academy of Management Review* (April 1978), 202–210.

8. Pradeep K. Tyagi, Organizational climate, inequities, and attractiveness of salesperson rewards. *Journal of Personal Selling & Sales Management* (November 1985), 31–36.

9. R. K. Teas and J. C. McElroy, Causal attributions and expectancy estimates: A framework for understanding the dynamics of salesforce motivation. *Journal of Marketing* 50 (January 1986), 70–81.

10. Gordon J. Badovick, Farrand J. Hadaway, and Peter F. Kaminki, Attributions and emotions: The effects on salesperson motivation after successful vs. unsuccessful quota performance. *Journal of Personal Selling & Sales Management* 12 (Summer 1992), 1–11.

11. Frederick Herzberg, *Work and the nature of man* (Cleveland, OH: World, 1966).

12. Lawrence B. Chonko, John F. Tanner, Jr., and William A. Weeks, Selling and sales management in action: Reward preferences of salespeople. *Journal of Personal Selling & Sales Management* 12 (Summer 1992), 67–75.

13. D. A. Whitsett and E. K. Winslow, An analysis of studies and articles of the motivation-hygiene theory. *Personnel Psychology* (1967), 391–416.

14. William Keenan, Jr., The nagging problem of the plateaued salesperson. *Sales & Marketing Management* (March 1989), 36–41.

15. For a more complete explanation of expectancy theory, see Edward E. Lawler III, *Motivation in work organizations* (Belmont, CA: Wadsworth, 1973); O. C. Walker, Jr., G. A. Churchill, Jr., and N. M. Ford, Motivation and performance in industrial selling: Present knowledge and needed research. *Journal of Marketing Research* 14 (May 1977), 156–168; G. A. Churchill, Jr., N. M. Ford, and O. C. Walker, Jr., Personal characteristics of salespeople and the attractiveness of alternative rewards. *Journal of Business Research* (1979), 25–50.

16. Kenneth R. Teas, An empirical test of models of salespersons' job expectancy and instrumentality perceptions. *Journal of Marketing Research* 18 (May 1981), 209–226; Jhinuk Chowdhury, The motivational impact of sales quotas on effort. *Journal of Marketing Research* 30 (February 1993), 28–41.

17. Howard Garland, Relation of effort-performance expectancy to performance in goal-setting experiments. *Journal of Applied Psychology* 69 (1984), 79–84.

18. Alan J. Dubinsky, Marvin A. Jolson, Ronald E. Michaels, Masaak Kotabe, and Chae Un Lim, Perceptions of motivational components: Salesmen and saleswomen revisited. *Journal of Personal Selling & Sales Management* 13 (Fall 1993), 25–37.

19. Thomas L. Quick, The best-kept secret for increasing productivity. *Sales & Marketing Management* (July 1989), 34–38.

20. Donald Super, *The psychology of careers* (New York: Harper & Row, 1957).

21. Marvin A. Jolson, The salesman's career cycle. *Journal of Marketing* 38 (July 1974), 39–46.

22. William L. Cron, Industrial salesperson development: A career stages perspective. *Journal of Marketing* 48 (Fall 1984), 41–52.

23. John W. Slocum, Jr., and William L. Cron, Job attitudes and performance during three career stages. *Journal of Vocational Behavior* 26 (1985), 126–145; William L. Cron and John W. Slocum, Jr., The influence of career stages on salespeople's job attitudes, work perceptions, and performance. *Journal of Marketing Research* 23 (May 1987), 119–129.

24. William L. Cron, Alan J. Dubinsky, and Ronald E. Michaels, The influence of career stages on components of salesperson motivation. *Journal of Marketing* 52 (January 1988), 78–92.

25. Ralph W. Jackson and T. Bettina Cornwell, The effect of the buyer life cycle on purchase decisions. In *Proceedings of Southwestern Marketing Association,* ed. Peter J. Gordon, Dallas, TX, 1991.

26. William Keenan, Jr., Shopping for motivators? *Sales & Marketing Management* (April 1990), 112–114.

27. J. Near, A discriminant analysis of plateaued versus non-plateaued managers. *Journal of Vocational Behavior* 26 (1983), 177–188.

28. M. G. Evans and E. Gilbert, Plateaued managers: Their need gratifications and their effort-performance expectations. *Journal of Management Studies* 21 (1984), 99–108.

29. Suzanne K. Stout, John W. Slocum, Jr., and William L. Cron, Dynamics of the career plateauing process. *Journal of Vocational Behavior* 32 (1988), 74–91.

30. Keenan, Shopping for motivators.

31. Philip R. Harris and Robert T. Moran, *Managing cultural differences* (Houston, TX: Gulf, 1991).

32. Regina Eisman, When cultures clash. *Incentive* (May 1991), 65–70.

33. For a more complete discussion of this, see Martin C. Schnitzer, Marilyn L. Liebrenz, and Konrad W. Kubin, *International business* (Cincinnati, OH: South-Western, 1985).

34. Al Urbanski, Motivational masterpieces. *Sales & Marketing Management* (September 1987), 60–62.

35. Jack Falvey, Selling to the sales force. *Sales & Marketing Management* (April 1992), 12–13.

36. What incentives really work? *Sales & Marketing Management* (November 1989), 10–11.

37. Tim Harris, Sales support: No longer those left behind. *Sales & Marketing Management* (April 1990), 102–108.

38. What incentives really work?; Christina Lovio-George, What motivates best? *Sales & Marketing Management* (April 1992), 113–114.

39. Richard Szathmary, Better than cash! *Sales & Marketing Management* (April 1992), 110–112.

40. Keenan, Shopping for motivators?

41. "What incentives really work?"; Lovio-George, What motivates best?

SUGGESTED READINGS

Davis, Kenneth, and John W. Newstrom. *Human behavior at work: Organizational behavior.* New York: McGraw-Hill, 1985.

> Organizations are social systems. Given that, social science principles can be brought to bear on problems that arise in organizations. Issues such as motivating members of the organization and bringing about changes in the organization are critical for managers to understand and address.

French, Wendell L. *Human resource management.* Boston: Houghton Mifflin, 1990.

> Organizations today need to strive not only to be effective but also to have a high quality of life within the organization. This means going beyond simply motivating people to achieve the goals of the organization but also enhancing the quality of their own lives. By doing so, organizations will realize tangible benefits.

Harris, Philip R., and Robert T. Moran. *Managing cultural differences.* Houston, TX: Gulf, 1991.

> Every region of the world has particular cultural characteristics that shape the way people act. To be successful, a business must learn the cultures of the regions where it operates and adapt its approach to those cultures. This requires rethinking how the business operates.

Organ, Dennis W. and Thomas Bateman. *Organizational behavior.* Homewood, IL: Richard D. Irwin, 1986.

> Organizations are dynamic organisms composed of individuals. The organizational climate, organizational structure, and organizational dynamics all impact the performance of those individuals. This means that hiring, socializing, and motivating those individuals are critical in facilitating their performance and the overall performance of the organization.

Randolph, W. Alan. *Understanding and managing organizational behavior.* Homewood, IL: Richard D. Irwin, 1985.

> Knowing the various theories in organizational behavior is certainly useful for managers as well as students of the subject. However, these theories need to be placed in perspective and in a framework so that they can be applied by the manager. Effective management goes beyond simply knowing; it involves understanding.

Schnitzer, Martin C., Marilyn L. Liebrenz, and Konrad W. Kubin. *International business.* Cincinnati, OH: South-Western, 1985.

American businesses are facing new and different challenges as they compete in the world marketplace. Approaches to conducting business internationally vary considerably and need to be applied according to the constraints of the individual business. Management practices and policies need to be adapted to the country in which the company does business.

Chapter 5

Ethical and Legal Issues in the Sales Profession

OPENING SCENARIO

Christi Martin, of the FloDrive Company, had just left the buying office of her largest customer, Atlantic Industries, Ltd., and was going over in her mind the rather unsettling feelings she had about the meeting. The meeting had been with Nigel Jacobs, the Atlantic buyer for bearings and other related items. Christi had been with FloDrive for two years and she had just been transferred to the London office. The previous salesperson in this territory was Al Johnson, whose promotion to manager of European operations had made this prize territory available.

The feelings she was having arose from several sources. First, although Nigel had not said so directly, he intimated that he and Al had enjoyed a "mutually beneficial" arrangement whereby Nigel received certain "gifts and considerations" in exchange for the assurance that FloDrive was Atlantic's major bearings supplier. Christi knew that such an arrangement would be counter to company policies on undue influence, but Nigel had described the situation in such vague terms that she was not sure if the arrangement constituted a violation. She also knew that she was expected to continue the level of sales that Al Johnson had achieved.

There were a couple of other complicating factors. First, Christi was only the third female salesperson hired by FloDrive. The first one had left in frustration after only six months, and the second had met with marginal success. Christi had been very successful in her first two years and had been indirectly informed that future hiring decisions would be based in part on her success. She was clearly a test case in the company's view. Another problem was what, if anything, she should do about Al Johnson. If he were exercising undue influence, this violated company policy, was unfair to salespeople who conformed to policy, and had resulted in his promotion. She knew that whistle-blowers were not viewed favorably by the management at FloDrive.

Chapter Objectives

After reading this chapter, you should be able to

- Understand the various approaches to ethics.
- Recognize the ethical conflicts inherent in corporations.
- Know the major ethical and legal issues facing salespeople and sales managers.
- Determine specific actions that sales managers can take to help salespeople establish appropriate ethical standards.
- Appreciate the ethical issues that arise when doing business in the global arena.

INTRODUCTION

Probably no single issue plagues people in the sales profession more than ethics. In the world of business, the pressures to attain a high level of performance are great. Often there is not a great deal of difference among the various product offerings in the marketplace, and as a result, salespeople are constantly looking for ways to gain a competitive edge. Coupled with the effects of an economic downturn, this striving for a competitive edge carries with it the temptation to compromise one's ethical standards. The situation has been described this way:

> The result has been an eruption of questionable and sometimes plainly criminal behavior throughout corporate America. We are not dealing here so much with the personal greed that propelled Wall Street operators of the Eighties into federal prisons. Today's miscreants are more often motivated by the most basic instincts—fear of losing their jobs or the necessity to eke out some benefit for their companies. If that means fudging a few sales figures, abusing a competitor, or shortchanging the occasional customer, so be it.[1]

Among the reasons that ethics is such a hot issue today is that ethical standards appear to be breaking down. Businesses are becoming more "people businesses" with more sophisticated employees and customers, and some of the primary sources of ethical values have diminished in importance, while at the same time social responsibility is increasingly viewed as an integral part of business.[2] Whereas the vast majority of people in sales act in an ethical and morally responsible way, there are, nevertheless, countless stories of unethical and sometimes illegal behavior on the part of salespeople and their managers. These stories serve to bolster the stereotype of salespeople being "sleazeballs" who are willing do anything to make a sale. In the popular media salespeople are portrayed as being inept and willing to cut corners when necessary. Such fictional creations as Herb Tarlick of *WKRP in Cincinnati* and the characters in movies like *Used Cars* and *The Tin Men* provide humorous characters but also subtle support for popular misconceptions.

One reason ethics are so difficult to deal with is that they are subjective and qualitative. With the pressure to perform, salespeople and sales managers often find it difficult to know how to apply ethical standards. Generally speaking, most people have no problem in determining what is right and wrong on major issues. Selling a product that is clearly defective or inadequate to do the job, or that is inherently unsafe, is blatantly wrong and would be considered unethical by the majority. Most ethical problems arise in "gray zones," where right and wrong are not so clearly determined.[3]

An additional concern are the legal liabilities associated with making claims about products. There is often a fine line between boasting about a product and misrepresenting a product to the customer. Sales managers cannot afford to take a laissez-faire attitude regarding the ethics of their salespeople.[4]

THE FOUNDATION OF ETHICAL DECISION MAKING

Two major schools of ethical thought in modern ethics are **teleological ethics,** which emphasizes the consequences resulting from making a choice—the ends, and **deontological ethics,** which emphasizes the means by which an end is accomplished.[5] The two schools have been described this way:

> The fundamental difference is that deontological theories focus on the specific actions or behaviors of an individual, whereas teleological theories focus on the consequences of the actions or behaviors. In other words, the key issue in deontological theories is the inherent righteousness of a behavior, whereas the key issue in teleological theories is the amount of good or bad embodied in the consequences of the behaviors.[6]

The teleological school of thought would take the view that "the ends justify the means." The deontological approach says, "It doesn't matter whether you win or lose, it's how you play the game." For instance, two salespeople are vying for a major order. One takes the teleological approach. He would reason that getting the order is essential because if not, his company will lose business and thus have to lay off employees. Therefore, any action that helps him get the order is probably acceptable. The other salesperson follows the deontological approach. His view would be that, although it is important to get the order, he has certain rules that he adheres to, and he will not violate those, even if it means losing the order.

These two main schools are broken down into several specific ethical approaches in Table 5-1. Knowing these different approaches provides the salesperson and sales manager with some insight into the philosophical bases on which people make decisions about ethical problems and an understanding of how different people arrive at different conclusions regarding an issue.[7]

ETHICAL CONFLICTS

One of the problems facing today's sales managers is how to deal with ethical inconsistencies and moral dilemmas that lead to ethical conflicts.[8] For example, when a salesperson goes to work for a new company, she is entering an organization with an existing ethical system that is part of the corporate culture and has both formal and informal components. It is likely that her personal ethical standards will not exactly match those of the company. To the extent that they do not match, there will be an ethical conflict. Additionally, she may be joining a company that has a different set of ethical standards for different groups within the

TABLE 5-1 The Major Schools of Ethical Thought

Teleological Ethics

Ethical egoism:	The dominant rule is that a person should act in such a way that will maximize his or her own long-term interests.
Utilitarianism:	The dominant rule is that a person should act in a way that will maximize the good for the greatest number of people.
Machiavellianism:	The guiding rule is expediency: Do whatever is necessary to get the job done. Denies the relevance of morality in making a choice.
Pragmatic ethics:	The approach considers how each party will be affected by a decision and takes the course that will satisfy the largest group of people.

Deontological Ethics

Spencer's social evolution:	This approach holds that ethical standards either do not exist or are irrelevant. The important thing is not to interfere with the natural evolution of society and that survival of the fittest is the dominant rule.
Kant's categorical imperative:	This approach holds that people should act in such a way that their actions will become the guideline for universal law.
Situation ethics:	Whatever society says is right in a particular circumstance is the correct choice; social approval is the ultimate test of right and wrong.

Sources: William Frankena, *Ethics* (Englewood Cliffs, NJ: Prentice Hall, 1963); W. D. Hudson, *New studies in ethics,* vols. 1 and 2 (New York: St. Martin's Press, 1974); and W. T. Jones, Frederick Sontag, Morton O. Beckner, and Robert J. Fogelin, *Approaches to ethics* (New York: McGraw-Hill, 1977).

company. The sales manager may take the view "Don't do as I do, do as I say" in regard to expense reports. That will tend to undermine the overall ethical standard of the organization because salespeople would be aware that they are held to a different standard than those adhered to by upper management. Finally, the salesperson, like all people, likely possesses certain stated standards but sometimes actually operates, often unconsciously, under another standard.

What we have described here are the three major types of ethical conflicts with which salespeople must cope: macro-micro conflicts, macro-internal conflicts, and micro-internal conflicts.[9]

Macro-Micro Conflicts

The process of ethical decision making is complicated by the fact that the individual exists within a corporation whose cultural climate provides a framework for behavior and ethical decision making.[10] However, the individual comes into any corporation or group setting with a value system unique to that person.[11]

There are two possible areas of conflict between the personal and corporate ethical systems. First, the corporate ethic might not be in agreement with that of the individual. The person's standards might be higher or lower than those of the corporation. Second, in any corporate setting there is often a dissipation of individual responsibility for a decision or action. When a group makes a decision, no one person takes total responsibility for that decision.[12] In the first area the person must become familiar with corporate standards and determine what changes are needed to bring her standards in line with those of the corporation and whether she is able or willing to do so. In the second, the person must become aware of this tendency toward no one individual taking responsibility and must act as a catalyst in the group to ensure that the decision or action is the result of the group or corporate standard. One more complicating factor is that corporate culture is dynamic and is subject to change with new leadership.

This inherent conflict between group and individual ethical standards is called the **macro-micro conflict.** Either of the situations described would constitute such a conflict. Both serve to complicate the overall corporate ethical standard and undermine its implementation. The written corporate ethical standard can be a powerful tool in shaping behavior, but simply writing and presenting it to employees is not enough. One way that has proven effective in exposing all employees to the corporate ethical standard and sensitizing them to ethical issues involves formal training.[13] Through subsequent written and verbal communication, the sales manager should reinforce that standard.

The informal culture of organizations is often as powerful a force in the shaping of employees as is the formal one. Informal culture is learned through a process of socialization. This may result in an individual "hearing" about a different ethical standard than the official, stated company standard. The sales manager, then, needs to be realistic enough to recognize the power of this informal socialization process and must be sensitive enough to determine whether the informal ethical atmosphere is in line with what is acceptable to the company.

Macro-Internal Conflicts

Another ethical dilemma concerns the inconsistent application of ethical standards within the company. Having different sets of ethical standards for different groups is referred to as a **macro-internal conflict.** The corporation may have a strong sense of ethics built into its corporate culture and may support it with a clear and concise code of conduct. However, no matter how formalized the ethical position or how well worded the document on ethics, the standard must be adapted for the different groups in the organization. Those groups can consist of different functional areas or of different levels in the organization.

The problem arises when the ethical standard is applied inconsistently across the corporation. This leads to individuals either questioning the ethical standards or dismissing them altogether. For example, when upper management fudges expenses or spends more on entertainment than the company guidelines allow and yet demands that subordinates strictly adhere to those same guidelines, the entire ethical system of that firm is undermined. Management may dismiss this as a "rank has its privileges" excuse, but the message being communicated is that the standards are not really that important.

As another example, the purchasing department is given very restrictive guidelines about the gifts buyers may accept, but the sales department is given license to buy gifts as well as provide entertainment and meals for buyers of customers' organizations. According to an article in *Purchasing* magazine, this practice is all too common and undermines the overall corporate ethical standard.[14] Sales managers have the responsibility to make sure that their behavior is consistent with the ethical standard established by the company. As part of the management team in the company, sales managers need to work with other functional areas to ensure that the standard is applied equally across the firm.

Micro-Internal Conflicts

Chris Argyris, a scholar in organizational psychology, presented the idea that individuals often operate under two differing models—one that they verbalize and one that actually guides their behavior.[15] People assume that their espoused beliefs direct their behavior, when, in fact, their behavior may, either consciously or unconsciously, not align with those espoused beliefs. This tendency to operate from two distinct standards leads to a **micro-internal conflict.**

When an individual arrives at a decision regarding an ethical question, some factor not taken into account may constrain what the person actually does. Shelby Hunt and Scott Vitell, who have conducted extensive research in marketing ethics, propose what they call "situational constraints" that face the person and affect the person's decision making; and O.C. Ferrell and Larry Gresham, two other marketing ethics scholars, speak of the "opportunity" that enters into the decision process.[16] For instance, a salesperson might know that giving the buyer a kickback will result in winning a large order. She might believe that this would be morally wrong and decide that she will not do such a thing. However, if immediately prior to visiting the customer, she finds out that a large sale to another customer has fallen through, she might become willing to split her commission with the buyer as a "bonus" for receiving the order. The loss of the order to the other customer constitutes the situational constraint necessary to alter her intended actions.

Generally speaking, salespeople are not significantly different from other marketing professionals in their espoused ethical standards. However, they do tend to place more importance on their personal interests than do other marketing professionals.[17] This greater emphasis on personal interests can be a factor in the salesperson's taking actions contrary to her stated ethics. She would likely continue to take the ethical position that giving a kickback is wrong and might not even be aware of the violation of her ethical position. However, if she were to realize the inconsistency between her actions and beliefs, and this awareness created anxiety, she would likely be forced to adjust her stated position or make a greater effort to be consistent when the dilemma arises again.

The sales manager needs to sensitize salespeople to the fact that the tendency exists to operate from two separate, often inconsistent, frameworks. A heightened awareness on the part of salespeople would mean that they will be more circumspect in their actions and decisions. Often the ethical problems that arise for salespeople begin as insignificant events to which they may give little attention or thought, but which snowball into a major problem. The sooner the person recognizes what is happening, the less likely that the event will turn into such a problem.

ETHICAL AND LEGAL ISSUES
FOR SALES PROFESSIONALS

Before we consider some specific ethical and legal dilemmas facing salespeople and sales management, remember that often a fine line distinguishes unethical from illegal behavior. People often take the view that ethical codes of conduct should be based on what is legal. However, generally speaking, whereas most illegal behaviors are unethical, many unethical behaviors are not illegal. Consider the following observation:

> Proper ethical behavior exists on a plane above the law. The law merely specifies the lowest common denominator of acceptable behavior. This proposition undercuts the argument that legality is the only criterion for judging acceptable behavior. If this proposition does not hold, the study of ethics is extraneous. While some members of the legal profession may challenge this postulate, the entire field of moral philosophy

rests on its inherent truth. This proposition provides a rationale for examining the compelling argument that ethical propriety and legality do not necessarily coincide. For example, it is not illegal to exhort children to ask their parents to buy a product promoted via a commercial on a children's television show. Whether such a practice is unethical, because it exploits the gullibility of children, can be vigorously debated.[18]

So, as we move into considering specific ethical and legal issues, keep in mind that we do this not to determine "how close to the edge you can walk" but to learn what those issues are and, possibly, how to avoid being trapped by them.

Too many situations that have possible ethical and legal implications exist to discuss even a majority of them in this chapter. However, some seem to be particularly troublesome for salespeople. In general, the difference between what is unethical and what is illegal concerns not only a person's intent but also a person's action.

Gifts and Entertainment

Although giving gifts to customers and entertaining them are, in and of themselves, not ethical problems, they have the potential for abuse that may lead to such problems. In all likelihood, this is the area in which more problems arise than any other. A decade ago, according to Walter Keichel, more than 50 million business gifts with an estimated value of over $1 billion were given annually.[19] Certainly, those figures have risen steadily since that time and represent a major expenditure by business.

Sales managers are tempted to downplay the importance of gifts. Many say that they are not trying to buy customers with gifts but are simply rewarding faithful customers. Although a buyer may not be bought with a gift, he may feel a certain level of obligation to the salesperson because of it.[20] The problem, according to Keichel, is that the gift has the potential to alter the relationship and make it more complex. Once the relationship moves away from being based on providing the customer a good value for the right price, it moves onto shaky ground.[21]

In terms of gift giving, no hard-and-fast rule exists for when and if a gift is ethical. A study of purchasing professionals found two major factors that are important in making this determination:

1. The value of the gift—the larger the value, the less ethical the gift is considered to be
2. Whether the recipient is a current customer—gifts given to current customers are considered more ethical than those given to potential customers.[22]

One reason companies give gifts is that they feel that customers expect gifts. However, buying organizations are increasingly beginning to regulate the acceptance of gifts. Some organizations, such as Wal-Mart, will not allow their buyers to accept any gifts. One study reported that 66 percent of the respondent companies had a formal policy on accepting gifts.[23] In fact, in some cases giving a gift to a buyer may place the buyer in violation of company policy and, in turn, subject to disciplinary actions. On one occasion, when a vendor firm was found to have violated his firm's gift policy, all orders with that vendor were cancelled and the firm was removed from the approved vendors list. Such an action can have a tremendous impact on a company. Therefore, salespeople should be familiar with the policies of their customers' buying departments.

The major issue for salespeople concerning gifts and entertainment is how to decide where to draw the line and know at what point a gift becomes a bribe. What might be considered a harmless gift by one buyer or company could be considered a major one by another. Generally speaking, much of the input for deciding where that line is comes from the industry. For most industries, informal standards of practice have developed and provide some insight into this issue. Giving gifts above and beyond those standards, in all probability, constitutes unethical behavior. However, those standards cannot become the final determination of what the individual should do because they are often poorly defined and are subject to change. The sales manager can set the standard for individual salespeople. In setting that standard, the manager needs to consider the following issues:

- What is the purpose of the gift or entertainment?
- What part does it play in the overall approach to sales?
- How should gifts and entertainment be dispensed?
- How is the gift or entertainment likely to affect the buyer and his or her decision process?
- What, if any, are the customer's policies on acceptance of gratuities?
- Does the gift or entertainment have the potential of compromising the professional image and behavior of customers?

Sales Puffery or Misrepresentation?

Sales is basically a process of communication about the reasons why the customer should buy one product versus another or buy from one company versus buying from a competitor. During the course of the sales presentation, the salesperson generally makes a number of statements and claims. The question arises as to when these claims become legally binding. What is the difference between "sales talk" and misrepresentation? According to the book *Law for Business*, "The elements of misrepresentation are ordinarily given as: misrepresentation of a material fact justifiably relied upon to the detriment (causing harm to) of the person relying."[24]

The authors go on to point out that the person making the claim is not excused because he or she did not know the statement was false. A salesperson's statement must be of material fact—that is, it must be a major reason for the buyer's decision to buy, if it is to be legally binding. Whether it is a major element in the decision depends on the circumstances. Another major element in determining misrepresentation is whether the statement is one of fact or opinion. A fact is something that is "knowable." Statements predicting the future ("The value of this property is bound to increase.") or opinions ("This is the nicest home in the neighborhood.") do not fall into the category of being knowable. They would be classified as "puffery" or "sales talk" and as such are not legally binding.

The difference between puffery and misrepresentation is generally not very clear-cut. For example, if the salesperson were to say, "This would be a great car to own," the statement would be puffery. If the salesperson, however, said, "This car was owned by an elderly widow who only drove it to church on Sundays," he would be guilty of misrepresentation if the car had been owned by anyone else.

There are several rules salespeople should follow regarding what they say during a presentation:

1. Salespeople should be thoroughly knowledgeable about the performance and limitations of the product.
2. Salespeople need to stress the criteria that are important and guide customers to a better understanding of how to make a reasonable choice.
3. Salespeople must be careful to state accurately the product's capabilities and performance parameters.
4. Salespeople must recognize the difference between statements of fact and opinion about the products, and when offering praise about the product do so in general terms.
5. Salespeople need to be familiar with local, state, and federal laws regarding price discrimination, warranties, and so forth.
6. Salespeople must recognize that they are agents of the company and that statements made during the sales process can legally bind the company.

Anticompetitive Practices

In a number of instances salespeople face such strong competition that in the push to perform they may engage in patently illegal acts. One common occurrence is **price discrimination.** According to the Robinson-Patman Act of 1936, charging different prices to similar customers is illegal. This sounds simple enough, but a number of exceptions complicate the issue. For example, a company is allowed to offer discounts to customers buying large quantities of a product if the lower price is the result of cost savings brought about by selling in larger quantities. A firm is also allowed to offer a lower price to a particular customer if it is doing so to meet competition. A company may also charge different prices to different classifications of customers, for example, one price for contractors and another for the general public. Generally, the courts decide if an act constitutes price discrimination.

Another action that may be illegal is a **tying arrangement,** a situation in which a company refuses to sell one product line unless the customer also buys another line of products. This is illegal if there are two distinct and separate product lines involved and the situation represents a restraint of trade. **Exclusive dealerships** can be considered illegal if they are deemed in restraint of trade. By exclusive dealerships, is meant a situation in which a manufacturer requires that resellers carry only its brand. **Exclusive territories,** or guaranteeing that a particular firm will be the only one with the right to sell a product within a given territory, can be illegal under certain circumstances. Generally speaking, this would be illegal if it can be proven that establishing exclusive territories lessens competition and restrains trade.

Tying arrangements, exclusive dealerships, and exclusive territories are potential violations of the Clayton Act. The courts will generally apply the "rule of reason" in cases related to these issues. This approach is positive in that it gives a fair amount of latitude to the courts but is negative in that it establishes no hard-and-fast rule to guide salespeople.

Sabotaging Competitors

All too often, the pressure to perform leads to a dismissal of ethical standards. One practice that occurs too often is interfering with competitors. An example is in sales of consumer products to food stores. Store managers will often allow the salesperson for a consumer products firm to have access to store shelves. That salesperson will suggest a shelving plan for his products and also will check the shelves and replenish any stock for the store manager. A common but ethically questionable practice is for the salesperson to reduce the shelf facings of competitors' products and replace them with his own products without the store manager's permission. Another instance of sabotage is when a salesperson spreads a false, damaging rumor about a competitor to customers.

Some would defend both of these practices as being no big deal, but they do constitute unethical behavior. The acid test of whether a practice is unethical is to answer this question: "What would be the consequence to me of my competitors doing the same thing?" If everyone engaged in the same behavior, no one would achieve an advantage.

Expense Reports

Selling is an expensive process. However, the expense is justified because selling is the most productive process in persuading customers to buy products. The salesperson is entrusted with assets of the company in the form of an expense account and often a company automobile. The policy on company expenses must follow a fine line between being overly costly and ensuring that the salesperson is fairly reimbursed. Being overly costly results in high sales costs becoming even higher. If the salesperson isn't fairly reimbursed, the company is inviting sales-people to become dishonest about expenses. Although filling out expense reports is often viewed as "creative writing," the vast majority of salespeople make a concerted effort to give an accurate accounting of their expenses. In striving to hold down overhead costs, companies have forced their salespeople to more ac-curately account for expenses through an increased amount of paperwork.

Probably the best way to ensure that salespeople do not inflate expenses is for a firm to instill in them a strong company ethic against such practices. Also, the company should provide a simple to use expense ledger. The ledger would have a place for mileage, lodging, meals, and entertainment, as well as other ex-penses that should be covered. It might be simpler, especially for meals, to pro-vide a per diem amount based on the average cost of restaurant meals in an area. The company should strive to reimburse salespeople promptly so that they are not tempted to inflate one month's expenses in order to "float" the next month's. Additionally, the company should make some provision for recouping an ex-pense that might have been missed on an earlier report.

"Green River Ordinances"

A number of cities and towns place restrictions on salespeople operating in their communities. Generally the ordinances (named after Green River, Wyoming, where one of the first such regulations was enacted) require that a salesperson have a local permit or license to sell in the area. The stated purpose of these laws is to regulate companies outside the areas that sell within them, and by doing so, guard against unethical sales practices. Often, however, they have been used to protect local business by restricting trade and/or to generate revenue for the city.

ETHICAL AND LEGAL ISSUES FOR SALES MANAGERS

In the final analysis, the ethical tone and standards of a corporation are estab-lished by managers. To the extent that they hold healthy values and exhibit those values in their decisions, an ethical system and a code of conduct will be effective in their companies.[25] Concerning ethics in the corporation, the buck stops at the manager's desk.

Decisions about Territories

A major portion of a sales manager's responsibilities revolves around developing and revising sales territories. This is particularly burdensome in regions that are experiencing drastic changes in the composition of the population. Although ter-ritory decisions may not seem like ethical issues at first, they do have a major impact on salespeople. In addition, the way the decisions are made and how they are communicated have ethical overtones.

Consider the following example. Bert has done a good job of developing his sales territory, but without being consulted, he was told that it was being given to another salesperson, Erna. Furthermore, Bert was informed that he must relocate to another territory. In this situation, Bert may feel that the company is simply using him and has no conscience where employees are concerned.

Often this feeling is aggravated by the way in which the decision is communicated to the salesperson. For example, Maria, a salesperson, received a cryptic call from the regional office and was told to bring all her files into the office on Friday. No further explanation was provided. Upon arrival at the office, she was instructed to leave the files with the receptionist, and in the privacy of the manager's office was told to report to a new territory in two weeks. This situation is all too common for salespeople.

Certainly the company may have the right to make such decisions, but the fact that the person is not consulted on the decision and is not given some forewarning in effect means that the company views the salesperson simply as a tool, not as an individual with needs, wants, and desires that go beyond the workplace. This approach is probably indicative of an underlying attitude within management, and, regardless of how much that management gives lip service to caring about employees, such actions communicate a very different message. Stories of such incidents spread quickly within a company and within an industry and, eventually, will have a negative impact on the quality of people attracted to the organization.

Sales managers can do much to soften the impact of territory decisions on their salespeople. They can

1. Have a stated policy regarding the decision to change territories and to reassign major accounts, and communicate that policy to salespeople when they are hired.
2. Involve the salesperson in the decision process when such actions are considered initially.
3. On decisions that will involve relocation, plan such changes to correspond with the school year.
4. As much as possible, ensure that the person's territory will have as much potential after the change is made as before. After taking away a key account, this may involve altering the person's territory.
5. Do not reduce the decision to make such a change to a matter of formulas or numbers. Other factors are as important as the bottom line.
6. Make only the changes that are necessary. This may go without saying, but it is amazing how many times such changes are made with very little rhyme or reason.

The Dysfunctional Salesperson

The salesperson who is going through a prolonged illness, is having a problem with alcohol or drugs, or may be experiencing severe personal or emotional problems presents a particularly difficult situation for sales managers. Often managers do not understand the causes of drug and alcohol problems and how to deal with them. Some fail to understand that alcohol is the most commonly used drug and needs to be dealt with seriously.[26] Some managers take the view that they are not social workers and therefore do not want to get involved with the problem. Their feeling is that if the person can't cut it, then the best thing to do is let him or her go. As a result, managers often do not take action until the problem has become exacerbated. In fact, ignoring substance abuse problems in the workplace is costly.[27] Certainly, losing a salesperson who has been a valuable asset is an additional cost for a firm. Most studies indicate that it is cheaper to rehabilitate someone than to hire and train a new person.[28] The sales manager generally has the best chance of taking early preventive action because of his or her close contact with salespeople. Managers who fail to do so are costing their company money.

Following is a list of actions that sales managers can take to help members of their sales force who are going through severe problems:

1. Get to know the salespeople and how they tend to act and react in different situations.
2. Take notice of sudden changes in behavior and performance, especially if they involve a sharp increase in absenteeism.
3. Practice good listening skills.
4. Spend some time with those persons who are exhibiting changes in behavior and attempt to determine the cause.
5. If the behavior continues over time and drug or alcohol abuse is suspected, confront the person and demand he or she start a treatment program.
6. For a salesperson who is ill or experiencing serious personal problems, attempt to lighten his or her load temporarily during the recovery process.
7. As much as possible, keep the matter confidential.
8. In general, show emotional support for the person involved.

Sexual Harassment

A major change in the sales profession has been the increased entry of women into the sales forces and sales management. This will result in new, positive approaches and fresh ideas being introduced into personal selling. Additionally, evidence indicates that this should result in a higher overall ethical standard in sales.[29] However, anytime a major change takes place in an organization, confusion and misunderstandings are likely. To foster the assimilation of women into the workplace, companies often have resorted to superficial measures without examining why the measures were being taken. Rather than encourage women to develop a management style consistent with their personalities, organizations have either overtly or covertly encouraged women to adopt the style favored by their male counterparts. This has resulted in frustration on both sides and a relatively high turnover rate among some female professional groups.[30]

Another result of the misunderstanding caused by more women entering previously male-dominated professions has been an increase in sexual harassment. At one time, sexual harassment was thought to involve only the boss's trying to physically force himself on a female subordinate. Whereas this certainly constitutes harassment, we now recognize that sexual harassment also involves many actions that used to be considered innocuous, including verbal suggestions and innuendos dealing with sex. Also, sex-related jokes that are repeated over time, as well as offensive and suggestive remarks, may constitute harassment. Certainly, repeated and unwanted advances by one person upon another are considered sexual harassment.

Sexual harassment generally falls into one of three categories:

1. *Verbal*—sexual innuendos, comments, threats, jokes, or insults
2. *Nonverbal*—suggestive or insulting noises, obscene gestures, whistling, or leering
3. *Physical*—touching, assault, or coercing sexual intercourse

Conduct of a sexual nature constitutes sexual harassment when submission is either explicitly or implicitly made a condition of employment, submission or rejection of sexual advances is used as a basis for employment decisions affecting a person, and such conduct interferes with the person's performance of duties or creates a hostile working environment.[31] In general, any nonprofessional behavior of a sexual nature toward a fellow employee may fall under the purview of sexual harassment. Action by the company in response to allegations of harassment is the basis on which court decisions have been made.[32]

Sexual harassment especially can present problems for sales managers because selling has traditionally been a male-dominated profession. As a result, patterns of behavior have developed over the years that are difficult to alter. Many managers are not aware of the fact that a company can be liable for third-party harassment.[33] For example, a female salesperson calls on a buyer who persists in making unwanted sexual advances. If she complains to her sales manager, and that manager takes the attitude that it is her problem or that it "is the cost of doing business," he and the company can be legally liable for the harassment.

The sales manager can address the issue of sexual harassment by taking the following actions:

1. Provide subordinates with written standards of behavior.
2. Set a positive example of professional behavior.
3. If a salesperson engages in questionable behavior, approach him or her, outline the specific behavior in question, and remind the person that he or she is expected to comply with company policy.
4. Have a system in place whereby complaints of sexual harassment can be made in a confidential, nonthreatening manner.
5. If allegations of sexual harassment arise, investigate them thoroughly and immediately.

SELL!NG

THE FRONT LINES OF BUSINESS

Flirting, and Skirting the Issue

Robert Nylen

You've heard this harassment story before. Or have you? Two attractive young people worked closely together in a five-person sales office. The boss was athletic and tough, a 32-year-old go-getter with 10 solid years of sales experience. The junior salesperson, an ash-blond 23-year-old, had recently arrived, fresh out of college, with hopes high and energy aplenty. Together they plotted calls, sweated over budgets, and threw darts at target lists. They did all those cozy things that salespeople do together in offices, cheering one another's victories, lambasting their rivals, and lamenting unreturned calls.

It was probably natural that some attraction would develop between them. Propinquity, you know, and hormones. Perhaps it was also natural that the attraction wasn't entirely reciprocal; after all, unrequited affection is the way of the world, and if romance was always exactly mutual, there would be no brokenhearted blues or country songs, and life would be boring.

In the office, one-sided affection is always worse when the boss likes the salesperson more than the other way around. (Otherwise, what you have is just a case of blushing and stammering.) Here it was indeed the boss whose desires got out of control. The boss offered casual invitations—let's go out together, let's have a drink after work—which the junior rebuffed with gentle excuses, deflecting the proposals as if they hadn't really been meant as, well, dates. But some people can't take a hint, you know, and the suggestions grew more insistent. Still, the salesperson gamely resisted.

Though unencouraged, the boss's flirtations deepened, and turned to unreciprocated passion. Flirtation ended. Bullying began. Still the junior salesperson resisted, though now more nervously. Finally, a couple of months into this unfair courtship, the obsessive boss called the young salesperson into the office, closed the door, and asked for a favor that wasn't entirely unreasonable—and wasn't at all sexual either.

The office was stuffy. The boss asked the junior salesperson to let in some fresh air. That meant that the salesperson had to climb a chair and stretch awkwardly to reach an upper window. While standing on tiptoe, the salesperson felt the unmistakable touch of the boss's hand at a delicate point between the waist and the knee.

Ah. Um. Er.

What to do?

Slap? Quit? Scream? Plead? Or just quiver?

And acquiesce?

It says a lot about our priorities and insecurities that we even need to ask. The scrupulous response? Stand up and cry, "Foul!" or at the very least, "Cut it out!" Sexual harassment is bad business—and against the law. But in the real world, the reactions often are denial, embarrassment, fear, and flight. If dealing with the problem is hard, admitting it in the first place is even harder.

Sales is seduction, isn't it? Many words in the selling lexicon are also part of the vocabulary of love songs. We woo, wine, and dine, and we push, charm, and tempt—but not literally! When we sell passionately, when we pitch ardently, even when we're using the language of courtship in business, it is understood that we aren't giving an invitation of pure, naked sex. Sure, some of us flirt a bit when we sell, but we rationalize that we're just playing the game. In the modern workplace, though, there is often ambiguity about what's permitted, what's symbolic, and what's illusion, and some folks choose to interpret the code of innocent flirtation more liberally than they should.

Every business relationship offers the authentic possibility of degenerating into genuinely unpredictable human behavior at any moment, including—let's not be prudes—good old sex. The intimacy of working closely together as buyer and seller (or boss and salesperson) can lead to other intimacies. The big problem occurs when the affection, or worse, the groping, isn't requited.

When a boss—or a buyer—sees a sexual invitation when none has been of-fered, that's hardly romance. That's a problem. When an employer—or a customer—tries to take advantage of the disparity in power by turning an innocent relationship into a tryst (or worse), that's trouble. Sex is great, unless it's exploitive. And when trouble happens, there's nothing wrong with blowing the whistle really, really loudly.

Let's pick up our story again. The kid is up on the chair, and the boss is fully engaged in what might be called either a caress or a full-blown act of sexual harassment, depending upon whether you were giving or getting it. What to do?

Well, would your answer change if you learned that the boss was a woman and the salesperson was a man? Maybe. But should it? Probably not.

Harassment is almost always male on female. But as it happens, this real-life story is one in which an unusual modern-day role reversal was at work. The blond chair-climber was a man, and a very cute one, the women who worked with him assured me. And the vigorous, tough-minded, athletic boss was a lovely—if insensitive—young woman.

How did the victim handle the situation? Secretively. Terminally embarrassed, he left the room, and then he left the office itself without a word. When he returned, not only did he avoid telling another soul, but he began a clandestine search for different employment. He found a new job within a month, and didn't tell his story to anybody for years.

Now please don't misunderstand. Overwhelmingly, women, not men, are the victims of sexual harassment, just as they are the victims of all sorts of nonsexual exploitation, too. That's the way the species works. Men tend to be aggressors in the war of the genders. Still, there are no ironclad rules.

What do you do when you're in this predicament? Although we like to think we live in an enlightened age, complaining about harassment still takes more nerve than most of us, male or female, can muster. Although harassment complaints have doubled in the past decade, it's excruciatingly unpleasant to be the target of unwanted advances, and it's hard to talk frankly about them. We feel weak. No one wants to admit weakness. And we don't like to tattle.

When you are aware of bad behavior, muster the guts to blow the whistle. Don't shrink away—unless you have good job prospects elsewhere, and just don't want the aggravation. There are laws that protect workers from harassment. Before you threaten to use them, though, talk to the offender frankly, once. Talk to a trusted co-worker, too; it's possible that you aren't alone. Then make a record: Describe your experience in writing or on tape to be filed away at home. If you have a recurrence, attack your nemesis. Go to the boss's boss. If you have no boss, go to the law. Here's the hard part: You must be prepared for a counterassault on your own character. But whatever you do, don't just keep on working, shrinking away from a confrontation, and accepting the unacceptable.

Reprinted with the permission of SELL!NG magazine.

6. During the course of the investigation, keep the information confidential and respect the individual's right to privacy.
7. Deal with the facts of the case and avoid the reliance on third-party information when drawing conclusions.
8. Take the immediate, corrective action needed to halt harassment but avoid a knee-jerk decision to fire an alleged harasser before the facts are clear.
9. If a customer, client, or supplier has engaged in sexually harassing an employee, inform that person or organization that such behavior is unacceptable and that the repeat of such incidents could have serious consequences.

ETHICAL AND LEGAL ISSUES IN THE INTERNATIONAL ARENA

It is impossible within the scope of this book to outline all the variations in ethical standards throughout the world. What is ethical and acceptable varies from culture to culture. In the words of Philip Cateora, an expert in international marketing:

> The moral question of what is right and appropriate poses many dilemmas for domestic marketers. Even within a country, ethical standards are defined, and there is no common frame of reference. The problem of business ethics is infinitely more complex in the international marketplace because opinions of what is right are spread more widely because of basic cultural diversity.[34]

This fact frustrates many marketing and sales professionals to the point that they believe that they are powerless to cope with it. However, sales professionals can begin by being sensitive to the variations in ethical standards and beliefs and by trying to determine what adaptations they can make in their current way of doing business. Additionally, they must be sufficiently comfortable with their personal ethical standard to make an appropriate response to the standards of others and to explain to a customer from another background why they are responding in a certain way. What sales professionals should not do is attempt to convert the customer to standards.

A starting point in understanding any ethical system is a familiarity with the values of the culture. Businesspeople working abroad often have problems with determining what is acceptable behavior. Many have suffered embarrassment and have encountered hostility when they have taken inappropriate action. The situation can be summed up this way:

> Social life is not programmed like a computer game, where discretely different, unambiguous actions must be performed in different circumstances. People in society often face moral dilemmas, ambiguous circumstances where several choices of proper norms and behavior are possible. Values are priorities for sorting out and, when one has the will and the resources to do so, implementing one code for behavior rather than others. . . . Put another way, values direct people in a society to selectively attend to some goals and to subordinate others.[35]

As in the United States, codes of conduct elsewhere are not often precisely defined. Even when they are, they are stated in such general terms that they provide little guidance. However, by studying the underlying values of a culture and a country, a person can begin to grasp the ethical standard used there. Certainly, whatever conclusions she may draw should be presented to a person from that culture with whom she is working and adjusted according to his comments.

Understanding an ethical standard, though, does not necessarily mean that one should conform to it. For example, one major issue that American businesspeople constantly face is the payoff or the bribe. The reason is that the selective use of bribes is not considered an ethical problem for some foreign companies and governments.[36] However, U.S. businesses are constrained by the Foreign Corrupt Practices Act from offering bribes and payoffs. The act does three things:

1. It establishes accounting standards that require accurate records of expenditures and a system of accounting controls.
2. It prohibits the corrupt use of the mail service or other means of commerce to offer, pay, or promise to pay a gift to any foreign official, foreign political party, officer, candidate, or third party who might wield influence with foreign officials to make a favorable business decision for the company giving payment.
3. It provides sanctions for violation: fines of up to $1 million for companies and of up to $10,000 and imprisonment for up to five years for individuals.[37]

The problem with this act is that it often makes for an uneven competitive playing field, because companies from other countries do not have to comply with it. That is the reason American businesspeople are tempted to violate it even though they believe giving a bribe is unethical and know it has legal ramifications.

CHAPTER SUMMARY

In this chapter we discussed the legal and ethical problems facing salespeople and sales managers. The discussion began with a consideration of the deontological and teleological schools of ethics. These two approaches to ethical decision making follow different lines of reasoning and thus can lead to very different courses of actions. The teleological school might be characterized by "the ends justify the means," whereas the deontological school might be captured by "it doesn't matter whether you win or lose, it's how you play the game." Within each of these schools are a number of approaches to ethics, each of which could lead to a unique decision. Understanding these frameworks of ethical decision making will help sales professionals decide on an appropriate approach.

Three major types of ethical conflicts face individuals in an organization: macro-micro conflicts, which arise when differences exist between the standards of the organization and those of the individual; macro-internal conflicts, when an organization has different standards for different functional areas in an organization; and micro-internal conflicts, differences in what a person espouses as his or her position and what that person actually does.

In discussing some of the major ethical and legal issues facing salespeople and sales managers, we say that there is often a major difference between what is legal and what is ethical. Taking the law as the standard of ethics will lead to ethical problems; the law merely represents a baseline from which ethics begin.

In general, the difference between what is unethical and what is illegal concerns not only a person's intent but a person's actions also. Giving gifts and entertaining have a great potential for abuse that may lead to ethical problems. Whether a gift is ethical depends on its value and whether the recipient is a current customer. Although salespeople often use sales puffery (a statement of opinion about a product), only misrepresentation (an untrue statement presented as fact about a product) can be legally binding on a company. Anticompetitive practices, such as price discrimination (charging different prices to similar customers), is illegal, but a number of exceptions exist. Other practices—tying arrangements, exclusive dealerships, and exclusive territories—may or may not be illegal, depending on how the court rules in a particular case. Another issue of ethics important to salespeople especially is the fair reporting of expenses.

Issues of importance to sales managers include reassigning sales territories, dysfunctional salespeople, and sexual harassment, a major problem that is not well understood by many in management. Sexual harassment falls into three categories: verbal, nonverbal, and physical.

Finally, ethical and legal issues in the global marketplace were discussed. Understanding the different ethical standards of other cultures depends on being familiar with the value systems of those cultures. The payoff or bribe, which is perhaps the paramount issue facing American sales professionals in the international arena, is illegal for U.S. businesses under the Foreign Corrupt Practices Act, but companies from other countries do not have to comply with the act.

KEY TERMS

deontological ethics, p. 99

ethical egoism, p. 100

exclusive dealerships, p. 107

exclusive territories, p. 107

Kant's categorical imperative, p. 100

Machiavellianism, p. 100

macro-internal conflict, p. 102

macro-micro conflict, p. 101

micro-internal conflict, p. 102

pragmatic ethics, p. 100

price discrimination, p. 106

bituation ethics, p. 100

Spencer's social evolution, p. 100

teleological ethics, p. 99

tying arrangement, p. 107

utilitarianism, p. 100

CHAPTER QUESTIONS

1. How might a person who uses a teleological approach to ethics differ from one who employs the deontological approach regarding the giving of a large gift to a foreign government official in order to obtain a major sale?

2. Describe and give an example of a macro-micro conflict, a macro-internal conflict, and a micro-internal conflict.

3. If it is false, does the statement "This is a one-owner car with only 40,000 miles on it." constitute sales puffery or misrepresentation? Explain your answer.

4. Would a shoe company that requires the retailers that sell its shoes also to carry its line of belts be guilty of an illegal tying arrangement? Explain your answer.

5. Why is the dysfunctional salesperson an ethical problem for sales managers?

6. Why is sexual harassment a potential problem in sales?

7. Give examples of behaviors that would constitute sexual harassment.

8. What is the relationship between what is ethical and what is legal?

9. What place do values play in a culture's ethical system?

10. Why is bribery such an important issue in international marketing?

NOTES

1. Kenneth Labich, The new crisis in business ethics. *Fortune,* April 20, 1992, 167.

2. Alan Weiss, Seven reasons to examine workplace ethics. *HRMagazine* 36 (March 1991), 71–72; Elizabeth K. LaFleur, and P. Forrest, A social responsibility framework to guide sales management. *Journal of Personal Selling & Sales Management* 11 (Fall 1991), 27–38; Kenneth C. Schneider and James C. Johnson, Professionalism and ethical standards among salespeople in a deregulated environment: A case study of the trucking industry. *Journal of Personal Selling & Sales Management* 12 (Winter 1992), 33–43.

3. Ronald R. Sims, The challenge of ethical behavior in organizations. *Journal of Business Ethics* (July 1992), 505–513.

4. O. C. Ferrell and John Fraedrich, Understanding pressures that cause unethical behavior in business. *Business Insights* (Spring/Summer 1990), 1–4; Do good ethics make good profits? The "prisoner's dilemma." *Ethikos* (January/February 1990), 6–8; Kenneth R. Andrews, Ethics in practice. *Harvard Business Review* (September/October 1990), 99–104; David Vogel, Ethics and profits don't always go hand in hand. *Los Angeles Times,* December 28 1988, 7; Gregory T. Gundlach and Patrick E. Murphy, Ethical and legal foundations of relational marketing exchanges. *Journal of Marketing* 57 (October 1993), 35–46; Rosemary R. Lagace, Robert Dahlstrom, and Jule B. Gassenheimer, The relevance of ethical salesperson behavior on relationship quality: The pharmaceutical industry. *Journal of Personal Selling & Sales Management* 11 (Fall 1991), 39–47.

5. William K. Frankena, *Ethics* (Englewood Cliffs, NJ: Prentice Hall, 1963); W. D. Hudson, *New studies in ethics,* vols. 1 and 2 (New York: St. Martin's Press, 1974); W. T. Jones, Frederick Sontag, Morton O. Beckner, and Robert J. Fogelin, *Approaches to ethics* (New York: McGraw-Hill, 1977); Donald P. Robin and R. Eric Reidenbach, Social responsibility, ethics, and marketing strategy: Closing the gap between concept and application. *Journal of Marketing* (January 1987), 44–58; Geoffrey P. Lantos, An ethical base for decision making. *Journal of Business & Industrial Marketing* (Spring 1987), 11–16.

6. Shelby D. Hunt and Scott J. Vitell, A general theory of marketing ethics. *Journal of Macromarketing* (Spring 1986), 5–16.

7. John Fraedrich and O. C. Ferrell, Cognitive consistency of marketing managers in ethical situations. *Journal of the Academy of Marketing Science* 20 (Summer 1992), 245–252; Shelby D. Hunt and Arturo Z. Vasquez-Parraga, Organizational consequences, marketing ethic, and salesforce supervision. *Journal of Marketing Research* 30 (February 1993), 78–90; Richard Tansey, Gene Brown, Michael R. Hyman, and Lyndon E. Dawson, Jr., Personal moral philosophies and the moral judgments of salespeople. *Journal of Personal Selling & Sales Management* 14 (Winter 1994), 59–75.

8. Gene Laczniak, Business ethics: A manager's primer. *Business* (January/February/March 1983), 23–29; Sherry Baker, "ethical judgment." *Executive Excellence* (March 1992), 7–8.

9. Ralph W. Jackson and Steve Cashon, The inherent conflicts in the corporate setting. *Proceedings of the American Marketing Association Winter Educators' Conference,* Newport Beach, CA, 1993.

10. Anusorn Singhapakdi and Scott J. Vitell, Analyzing the ethical decision making of sales professionals. *Journal of Personal Selling & Sales Management* 11 (Fall 1991), 1–12.

11. Ferrell and Fraedrich, Understanding pressures that cause unethical behavior in business.

12. For an interesting discussion of the dilemma caused by this dissipation of responsibility, see Bowen H. McCoy, The parable of the Sadhu. *Harvard Business Review* (September/October 1983), 103–108.

13. Patrick E. Murphy, Creating ethical corporate standards. *Sloan Management Review* (Winter 1989), 81–87; Douglas K. Hoffman, Vince Howe, and Donald W. Hardigree, Ethical dilemmas faced in the selling of complex services: Significant others and competitive pressures. *Journal of Personal Selling & Sales Management* 11 (Fall 1991), 13–25.

14. Gifts: One issue that puts purchasing on the hot seat. *Purchasing,* February 13, 1989, 18–19.

15. Chris Argyris, The executive mind and double-loop learning. *Organizational Dynamics* 11 (Autumn 1982), 5–22.

16. Hunt and Vitell, A general theory of marketing ethics; O. C. Ferrell and Larry G. Gresham, A contingency framework for understanding ethical decision making in marketing. *Journal of Marketing* (Summer 1985), 87–96.

17. Anusorn Singhapakdi and Scott J. Vitell, Marketing ethics: Sales professionals versus other marketing professionals. *Journal of Personal Selling & Sales Management* 12 (Spring 1992), 27–38.

18. Laczniak, Business ethics, 24.

19. Walter Keichel, Business gift-giving. *Fortune,* January 7, 1985, 123–124.

20. Scott W. Kelley and Michael J. Dorsch, Ethical climate, organizational commitment, and indebtedness among purchasing executives. *Journal of Personal Selling & Sales Management* 11 (Fall 1991), 55–66.

21. Ibid; Alan J. Dubinsky, Marvin A. Jolson, Ronald E. Michaels, Masaaki Kotabe, and Chae Un Lim, Ethical perceptions of field sales personnel: An empirical assessment. *Journal of Personal Selling & Sales Management* 12 (Fall 1992), 9–21.

22. I. Frederick Trawick, John E. Swan, and David Rink, Industrial buyer evaluation of the ethics of salesperson gift giving: Value of the gift and customer vs. prospect status. *Journal of Personal Selling and Sales Management* (Spring 1989), 31–38.

23. Gifts.

24. James A. Barnes, Terry M. Dworkin, and Eric L. Richards, *Law for business* (Homewood, IL: Richard D. Irwin, 1991), 175.

25. Archie B. Carroll, In search of the moral manager. *Business Horizons* (March/April 1987), 7–15; Lee R. Ginsburg and Neil Miller, Value-driven management. *Business Horizons* (May/June 1992), 23–27.

26. Minda Zetlin, Combating drugs in the workplace. *Management Review* (August 1991), 17–24.

27. William C. Symonds, James E. Ellis, Julia Flynn Siler, Wendy Zellner, and Susan B. Garland, Is business bungling its battle with booze? *Business Week,* March 25, 1991, 76–78.

28. Zetlin, Combating drugs.

29. Shay Sayre, Mary L. Joyce, and David R. Lambert, Gender and sales ethics: Are women penalized less severely than their male counterparts? *Journal of Personal Selling & Sales Management* 11 (Fall 1991), 49–54; Leslie M. Dawson, Will feminization change the ethics of the sales profession? *Journal of Personal Selling & Sales Management* 12 (Winter 1992), 21–32.

30. Laura L. Castro, More firms 'Gender train' to bridge the chasms that still divide the sexes. *Wall Street Journal,* January 2, 1992, 11, 14; Amy Saltzman, Trouble at the top. *U.S. News & World Report,* June 17, 1991, 40–42, 44, 46–48.

31. Janet Harris-Lange, Everybody's problem. *Entrepreneurial Woman* (May 1992), 77.

32. Robert K. McCalla, Stopping sexual harassment before it begins. *Management Review* (April 1991), 44–46.

33. L. A. Winokur, Harassment of workers by 'third parties' can lead into maze of legal, moral issues. *Wall Street Journal,* October 26, 1992, B1, B8.

34. Philip R. Cateora, *International marketing* (Homewood, IL: Richard D. Irwin, 1983), 138.

35. Vern Terpstra and Kenneth David, *The cultural environment of international business* (Cincinnati, OH: South-Western, 1985), 117.

36. Cateora, *International marketing.*

37. Martin C. Schnitzer, Marilyn L. Liebrenz, and Konrad W. Kubin, *International business* (Cincinnati, OH: South-Western, 1985).

SUGGESTED READINGS

Burgunder, Lee B. *Legal aspects of managing technology.* Cincinnati, OH: South-Western, 1995.

The management of technology is of growing concern to businesses today. With the rapid changes in technology and the application of it to various aspects of the organization, there are some major pitfalls that must be avoided. Managers need an understanding of the process of protecting mental property and to ensure that such property is used in the manner intended.

Ferrell, O. C., and John Fraedrich. *Business ethics.* Boston: Houghton Mifflin, 1994.

Ethical issues are an inherent part of business life, and increasingly, issues of ethics and socially responsibility are making headlines. Businesspeople must come to grips with these issues, develop a personal ethic, and apply that personal ethic to decision making.

Terpstra, Vern, and Kenneth David. *The cultural environment of international business.* Cincinnati, OH: South-Western, 1985.

Cultural systems in different regions of the world are based on, among other things, language, values, religion, and education. These cultural systems shape the way politics are played out, the way people interact, and the way businesses operate. A basic understanding of the cultural system is essential for businesses competing in the international marketplace.

_____ Chapter 6 _____

The Selling Process—
Preparation

OPENING SCENARIO

"It was going to be a long week," thought Phil Kary, sales manager of Dumas Makt., H.K., a leading distributor of wines and specialized food products, as he drove to work. This week he was preparing for the company's strategic meeting where the final decision would be made concerning the best method for introducing a new brand of Hungarian wines into the Georgia market. Phil knew that one of the pivotal points in a successful introduction would be the ability of the sales force to locate customers through prospecting and then thoroughly preparing for the sales call to follow. Phil knew that he had to decide which of the prospecting methods would yield the best results in this particular selling situation. Was there an appropriate directory available, or could he find a good mailing list? This afternoon he was going to review the company's internal records to see what prospects turned up. He hoped a method could be found that would yield better results than would cold canvassing, as it was very important for Dumas Makt. to achieve good distribution the first month the wines were introduced.

A second question concerned him even more. The sales force of the company was probably in the habit of doing minimal preparation before each sales call. The company had not added any new products recently and the people on the sales force were content with their present customer and product knowledge. Phil knew that these new wines with no chemical additives would require some sales call preparation if good initial distribution was to be achieved. He would like to find enough information from which his salespeople could develop customer profiles, particularly on the key accounts for the new wine. Maybe he would stop at the business library at the university before he went into work. He remembered from undergraduate days that the librarian could be extremely helpful.

Chapter Objectives

After reading this chapter, you should be able to

- Identify a prospect.
- Use different prospecting methods and strategies.
- Find information about prospects.
- Turn a lead into a prospect.
- Discuss the importance of planning a sales call.
- Plan sales calls for individual prospects.

INTRODUCTION

Phil Kary's concerns are justified, for many salespeople do not pay enough attention to two important parts of the selling process—prospecting and planning. In planning sales presentations, more and more salespeople, with companies making everything from shoes to spaghetti sauce, are developing strong demonstrations to make their products more credible. For example, Rockport shows a man wearing the company's shoes while running in the New York City Marathon to illustrate that its shoes are lightweight and able to stand up even in tough conditions.[1] The message in the advertisement is "Some might be surprised to learn that a man actually ran a grueling 26-mile marathon in dress shoes, it will come as no surprise that they were Rockports." Similarly, Spirit's demonstration is a team of women playing basketball in the company's pump shoes with a catchy slogan: "It looks like a pump, feels like a sneaker."

Demonstrations are important in the luxury car business. Wanting to focus on its superior construction, Lexus demonstrates a pyramid of wine goblets being built on the hood of one of its cars while it is traveling on a dynamiter simulating travel at more than 100 miles per hour. Nissan counters with a similar demonstration with the slogan, "While you have seen many luxury cars show how smooth a ride is given, have you ever seen that smooth a ride at $13,000?"

Whether in an advertisement or a sales presentation, demonstrations are very effective in building recall and getting the customer to buy a product. The easiest way for a salesperson to use a demonstration effectively is to create one that illustrates a proven product advantage. Another way is for the salesperson to demonstrate something in the product that makes the product unique and preempts any competitive product even when every competing product has a similar attribute.

The selling process is a series of seven steps: prospecting, planning, approach, sales presentation, handling objections, closing the sale, and after-sale service (see Figure 6-1). Selling requires that a salesperson develop a systematic ap-

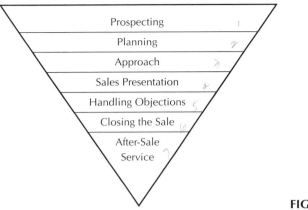

FIGURE 6-1

proach adapted to each type of customer and situation. This chapter deals with two of the most important, yet less glamorous, parts of this selling process— prospecting and planning the sales call. If salespeople want to increase or at least maintain their sales volume, they must find new customers continually. Once prospects are identified, salespeople must use all the information obtained about the prospect in developing the best approach and presentation for their sales calls.

GENERAL ROLE OF PROSPECTING

Of the seven steps in the selling process, the first, prospecting, often receives too little attention. **Prospecting** is the act of obtaining the names of potential customers. Although prospecting does not result in immediate sales, without it salespeople cannot locate new customers efficiently. And, without making sales to new customers, salespeople won't be able to replace lost sales or counter a decrease in sales from present customers.

How are good prospects found? By qualifying leads from a variety of sources into good potential prospects on the basis of their needs and wants, their authority to purchase, and their ability to purchase. **Qualifiers** include the type and size of company, its financial condition and creditworthiness, and the company's potential application of the product or service being offered. A salesperson should group prospects into clusters based on relevant demographic information in terms of their potential to buy. **Demographic information** is the factual data about a particular customer—buying patterns, specific buying characteristics, history of prior purchases—that is helpful in developing appropriate objectives, preparing the best sales presentation, and composing the most accurate customer profile.

Needs and Wants

Sometimes salespeople become so involved with the products they offer and with meeting sales quotas that they forget that the product must fulfill a particular customer's needs. Good salespeople constantly evaluate the products being offered and the sales presentation from the customer's viewpoint. Salespeople must remember the cardinal rule of the going-concern concept: Selling needed products and services to a customer will keep the customer satisfied and willing to buy again and again. In order to identify prospects who can become these satisfied customers, salespeople need information. One way to obtain this information in a selected target group, and thereby identify the best prospects for receiving a sales call, is through telemarketing. **Telemarketing** is the process of obtaining or providing information, setting up appointments, and whenever possible, making the sale by telephone. Given the increasingly high costs of a personal sales call, telemarketing is often used to provide good prospect information as well as to support other parts of the selling process. For some products, it can also be used to obtain the sale.

Authority to Purchase

Particularly in industrial sales, it is important for the salesperson to identify as early as possible the person (or persons) in the organization who will make the purchasing decision. Salespeople should avoid making presentations to people who do not have the authority or the influence to purchase. High-priced industrial sales are usually decided by a committee of representatives from several different disciplines and opinions. The salesperson must make sure everyone involved in the decision process has the necessary information.

For example, when trying to sell a piece of machinery, such as a bumper welder, the salesperson should be aware that the machine operator needs to know the characteristics of operating the machine, its outputs, and ease of operation. At the same time, the plant manager needs to know the relationship of the output of the machine to other aspects of production, the rate of output, the efficiency of the machine, and the way the machine fits into the layout of the assembly area. The vice president of production needs to know the efficiency rate and cost per unit of output versus those of other machines. All three people need specific information tailored to their area of responsibility before making the decision to buy.

Even at the consumer goods level, such as the purchase of a durable good like carpeting, the purchasing decision can involve several individuals. One spouse may decide the color and texture of the carpet and the other the brand to be purchased. Sometimes children may have a say in the carpet choice for their room.

Ability to Purchase

When loans and credit are difficult or costly to obtain, or when the economy is in a recession, it is particularly important that the prospect, whether a company or an individual, has the resources to make the purchase. Salespeople should determine their prospects' financial status. Banks, the Better Business Bureau, other customers, and local credit agencies can provide information on a prospect's financial condition and any problems experienced with payments. For most corporations, Dun & Bradstreet can provide information at a reasonable cost on their financial condition. Knowing this information will allow the salesperson to prepare beforehand alternative means of purchase, to meet any eventuality.

PROSPECTING METHODS

Several different strategies for prospecting are listed in Table 6-1, and each is discussed in this section. Although all the sources listed can have good results, the most commonly used strategies are centers of influence, information exchange, trade shows, contests, directories, and mailing lists.

Inquiries from Advertising. Amazingly, some companies do not follow up on inquiries received by telephone or letter from those who have learned about the company or its products and services from its advertising. Every inquiry should receive immediate follow-up because these inquiries usually come from the best prospects. Because not responding to an inquiry amounts to ignoring a potential customer, a company needs to establish a systematic approach to handling inquiries. One approach is to have the telemarketing staff respond to each inquiry and immediately pass the information on to a salesperson handling that territory.

Centers of Influence. One of the best methods for obtaining leads and prospects is through contacts at various clubs and organizations. Membership in centers of influence—country clubs, fraternal organizations, service organizations, and

TABLE 6-1 Prospecting Strategies

- Inquiries from advertising
- Centers of influence
- Chain of leads
- Cold canvassing
- Contests
- Directories and mailing lists
- Group meetings and parties
- Information exchange
- Internal records
- Observation
- Service personnel
- Spotters
- Trade shows and exhibits

professional groups—provide the opportunity to meet people who, if not prospects themselves, might be able to identify people who are. One professional group every salesperson should join is the local chapter of the American Marketing Association. In most areas of the United States, "tips clubs" are popular. The objective of a tip club, which meets once a month, is to get business leads (tips) from others in the club who are in other areas of business.

Chain of Leads. Current satisfied customers, particularly new customers, are excellent sources of leads. New customers may be able to provide names of people in previously uncontacted companies or departments. One lead can provide another lead and so on in a continual chain. Sometimes satisfied customers will agree to provide testimonial letters of referral. By using such referrals, salespeople can continuously update and lengthen the chain of leads. Sometimes salespeople give rewards if a referral becomes a customer of the company.

Cold Canvassing. Cold canvassing in person is seldom cost-effective unless the physical product needs to be seen, as in the case of vacuum cleaners or cosmetics, and will be purchased at the time of the presentation. Because such consumer products are sold on a door-to-door basis, cold calls are expected. For most products, telephone cold calling is much more cost-effective. A telephone canvassing plan is outlined in Table 6-2.

The first step in the plan is to establish the criteria for qualifying the prospects. Next, develop a list of prospects using the established criteria. This step involves using such sources as the Yellow Pages, business directories, local chamber of commerce directories, trade journals, and membership lists of various clubs and organizations such as Rotary, the Kiwanis Club, and the Elks Club.

Once a list has been made, determine the financial condition and creditworthiness of each prospect. This third step can be accomplished with the help of Dun & Bradstreet, a local credit organization, the company's credit department, or other people supplying the company. The fourth step—establishing objectives

---

TABLE 6-2 Plan for Telephone Cold Canvassing

---

1. Establish criteria for qualifying the prospects.
2. Develop a list of prospects using the established criteria.
3. Determine each prospect's financial condition and creditworthiness
4. Establish call objectives.
5. Prepare an opening statement and sales message.
6. Prepare various closes for the sale.
7. Prepare a wrap-up if a sale is made, or a request for an early appointment if a sale is not made.

---

for each call—is often overlooked. Basic sales call objectives can include gathering prospect information and trying to sell a small order over the telephone. By selling a small order over the telephone, the prospect can be given a company account number, and necessary background checks can be done to facilitate the ordering process once a personal sales call is made. Answers to some basic questions are useful in obtaining important prospect information. Product use and interest can be ascertained by asking, "How would your company use a product like this?" and "Do you currently use the product or a similar one?" In-depth purchasing criteria can also be obtained by asking, "What questions come to mind when thinking about a product like this?" "What benefits do you think you would obtain from using a product like this?" and "What is your usual decision time in purchasing this type of product?"

The fifth step involves preparing the opening statement, the actual sales message, and the close. The opening statement is probably the most difficult and most critical part of the presentation, particularly in telephone prospecting. Without a good opening, further communication with the prospect usually does not occur.

A good opening statement has three basic parts. First, the salesperson should identify himself or herself and the company: "Good afternoon, Mr. Johnson. I hope you are having a good day today. This is Kelly Hanks of H&B Associates." Then the salesperson should make an interest-creating comment: "I understand that Dumas Makt., H.K., has just had a record year and is interested in expanding its sales base overseas. I am calling because H&B Associates can assist you and your company in accomplishing this objective." Finally, the salesperson should establish customer rapport: "Given the wide variety of quality products your company is known for throughout the United States. I'm sure you want to continue this image overseas by launching the correct product in the best possible market. H&B Associates has helped companies like yours face just such a problem in Europe, both East and West, and the former U.S.S.R. I know you are an extremely busy person and I don't want to waste your time, but I would like to take a few minutes to explain our international program."

A good opening statement needs to be followed by a strong, succinct sales message that stresses product or service *benefits*, not features. The benefits are best described using positive, vivid words that paint upbeat mental pictures; these can be personal words, such as *you, me, we,* or *I,* or action-oriented, emotion-creating adjectives. The sales message should contain information that will offset any anticipated objections.

Following the sales message is the close. The close attempts to persuade the prospect to order at least a trial amount, making it easier to sell larger orders in the future. The final step depends on whether the close was successful in obtaining a sale. If so, the salesperson should discuss the details of order processing and establish a time for the next call to take place. If no sale is made, the salesperson should set up an appointment. A good method for setting up an appointment uses a strong lead and gives the prospect a choice. "Mr. Johnson, I would like to meet with you for a short time to show you how our program here at H&B Associates can help you and Dumas Makt., H.K., achieve profitable sales overseas in a short period of time. Would 10:00 Wednesday morning or 2:00 Thursday afternoon be good for you?"

Contests. Companies or salespeople can use contests to obtain inquiries from people who might be interested in the company's product or service. For a contest to be successful, the prize must have value to the type of prospect being solicited. The contest must also be easy for the potential prospect to enter. This is a particularly good method for obtaining the names of prospects by mail for such things as real estate investments, vacation homes, and travel vacations.

Directories and Mailing Lists. In developed countries like the United States, a mailing list can be compiled for just about any group of people. Mailing lists can be further developed by various breakdowns, but the cost per name and address increases with each breakdown. The list can be printed on gummed labels at a slightly higher cost for ease in mailing. For example, a list of the ministers who preside over Methodist churches with more than 1,000 members or a list of firms in Massachusetts that employ more than 100 people can be obtained.

Most popular and trade magazines sell their subscription lists. Also, sometimes a mailing list is already compiled in a published directory. Professional groups, such as those for architects, doctors, and lawyers, and specialty subgroups, such as cardiologists, often publish directories. Most associations, such as the American Marketing Association, the International Small Business Association, the American Management Association, the Chamber of Commerce, the Association of Women Entrepreneurs, the Association of Chemical Engineers, and the Association of Certified Financial Planners, have membership directories.

There are also directories of individuals with distinctions. For example, those just graduating from high schools in a particular city, those listed in *Who's Who in America,* and those receiving the Freedom Foundation Award.

Group Meetings and Parties. Some companies use groups or parties to show and demonstrate their products or services. These are usually done for consumer products, such as Tupperware or vitamins. This approach can also be used when the product is unique or has a technological advantage over competing products.

Information Exchange. Given the continuous interactions between companies and the salespeople representing these companies, a good way to obtain the names of potential customers is to exchange information with other salespeople from noncompeting firms. This can be done on a regular basis with a short initial meeting established between the individuals. For example, a salesperson selling cake mixes to large retail stores notices that the store has a limited assortment of frostings, and informs the sales representative of a company that sells frostings.

Internal Records. An overlooked method for obtaining a mailing list is the internal records of the company. This is particularly fruitful in companies with multiple divisions selling different products to similar target markets. Often customers of one division are good prospects for the products of another division. This referral system can be even more effective by establishing a system for referrals among divisions.

Observation. Prospects can be obtained by a salesperson who is observant and who has a systematic method for recording the names of potential leads. A good method is to systematically scan local newspapers for information on real estate transactions, marriages, new residential and commercial construction permits, divorces, fires, accidents, company stories, births, and job promotions. Noting any changes seen while driving to a sales call may also produce a prospect.

Service Personnel. Service and repair personnel are a valuable source of prospects. They visit companies regularly and know of their equipment needs. For example, automobile mechanics may know who will soon or already needs a new car.

Spotters. A spotter is an individual who is close to potential prospects and provides information on good potential prospects to salespeople for a fee. Retail clerks are close to customers making purchases, and can be good spotters. Secretaries are excellent spotters because they know what is taking place in a company or division. These people can be the eyes and ears of the salesperson in markets with good potential. The best of all spotters are satisfied customers who can provide referrals on potential prospects.

Trade Shows and Exhibits. The most popular method for obtaining a list of prospects is from exhibits or demonstrations at trade shows. This is a particularly good method because a trade show attracts individuals who already have interest in the area. In fact, one purpose of exhibiting at a trade show—or even attending one—is to obtain a list of attendees for follow-up sales calls or mailings. For example, the annual computer show is an excellent way to introduce the company's latest software. The annual consumer electronics show provides the names of attending retailers or wholesalers to a company that might be interested in these products.

GATHERING PROSPECT INFORMATION

Once prospects have been identified, it is important to obtain as much information about them as possible. Amazingly, almost all the information available about a prospect is useful at some point during the selling process. Salespeople should find out the name, position, title, authority to buy products, educational background, buying behavior, and important personality traits of their prospects. Personal information—hobbies, interests, political views, lifestyle—is also helpful.

SELL!NG

THE FRONT LINES OF BUSINESS

The SELL!NG Guide
to Getting the Inside Story

Linda Corman

If salespeople want to spend their time in the library instead of in the field, they should think about becoming librarians, right? Not at all. In fact, if they're *not* cracking the books, they might want to rethink their sales careers. Researching prospects has become as vital a step in the selling process as writing proposals or making presentations. More so, perhaps. Because in today's competitive climate, if you don't know your prospect and your prospect's business *before* you make your first move, you may never get to make the second one.

"The biggest problem is that salespeople don't want to prepare. They want to 'ready, fire, aim!' " says Steve Franklin, president of Global Access Learning in Atlanta, a management consulting and training firm that teaches salespeople how to research prospects prior to approaching them.

In this age of partnering, research is critical. "To develop an alliance to save both companies money, you've got to know that guy's business," says John Peeling, director, national accounts for the Olin Corp. of Stamford, Conn. "To come up with a clever proposal, you need to know what you're talking about."

There are numerous resources available to help you get the inside line on prospects—many of which cost nothing more than a little time and effort. The first order of business is knowing what questions you should be asking. The second is knowing where to find the answers. Now go out and get the facts. They just might help you get the sale.

What Industry Is the Company In? What Is Its Sales Volume? What Are Its Major Product Lines?

Start with the obvious. If you don't know what business a company is in, how do you know what to sell it? Or even if you should try. A prospect's sales volume can give you an idea of what kind of a selling effort you should make. For the answers, Bill Long, national account manager for Ryder Commercial Leasing and Services in Miami, says, "Go to the companies first and foremost. If they are publicly held, call investor relations and they will commonly send you quarterly reports, newsletters, and annual reports. It's amazing what they'll send you."

If this doesn't work, you can get annual reports on-line from Disclosure, an information-services company in Bethesda, Md. (800-638-8241). The full text of annual reports and other Securities and Exchange Commission (SEC) filings can be called up on Disclosure's **EdgarPlus** database, which eventually will be on more than 40 services (right now use LEXIS-NEXIS). The cost of calling up and printing out an annual report runs between $50 and $60. Or call Disclosure's **Demand Service** to have annual reports or the other company filings faxed or overnighted to you. To get an annual report this way costs about $35.

Next try **Standard & Poor's Register of Corporations, Directors and Executives,** published yearly by Standard & Poor's, a division of McGraw-Hill in New York (800-221-5277). The three-volume register includes information on more than 55,000 of the largest U.S. companies, both publicly traded and privately held.

Volume 1 includes basic information on each company: location; top officers; sales; number of employees; primary banking, law, and accounting firms; and a description of its business. Volume 2 includes biographies of some 70,000 company directors and executives. Information usually includes work affiliation, home address, fraternal and professional affiliations, date of birth, and educational history. Volume 3 indexes companies by location and industry. Other features include a corporate family tree of parent companies and their subsidiaries. S&P's Register is a yearly service; for $625 you can lease the three volumes along with quarterly supplements, although you are required to return the materials if you don't renew. Directories are also available

on-line through DIALOG and LEXIS-NEXIS.

For private companies, try **Enhanced Dun's Market Identifiers,** published by Dun & Bradstreet Information Services of Murray Hill, N.J., a subsidiary of Dun & Bradstreet Corp. Through this customized service, you can get listings of 10.2 million companies within categories that you determine. For example, you can ask for listings of companies in a certain industry in a given geographical area with at least $1 million in sales.

Each company listing contains 18 pieces of information, including address, lines of business, sales, number of employees, and names of top executives (you identify the titles, the service provides the names). The cost for a 1,000-company search is $675. To order searches, call 800-624-5669. This information is also available on-line through DIALOG, Dow Jones News/Retrieval, Prodigy, Compu-Serve and Data-Star.

What Is the Financial Condition of the Company?

You want to make sure they're not on the verge of bankruptcy," says Jack Caldwell, manager, national accounts, North American operations at Otis Elevator in Woodcliff Lake, N.J. "You want to make sure they have the assets to pay."

The best source of this information? Annual reports, says Kelly Stanyon, manager of Olin Corp.'s Business Information Center. "Then you're getting it straight from the horse's mouth." Second best: 10-K annual filings with the SEC. Both documents are available directly from companies or through Disclosure.

Investext, published by The Investext Group of Thomson Financial Services in Boston, provides full texts of analysts' research reports on publicly traded companies and industries. Hard copies of reports may be obtained by calling 800-662-7878. After an initial fee of $95, Investext is a pay-as-you-go service; cost is $7.30 per page, plus handling and shipping costs. Reports run from one to 30-plus pages; they're also available on-line on Investext's own service—I/PLUS DIRECT—or through DIALOG, LEXIS-NEXIS, Dow Jones News/Retrieval, and other major services. Or you can get the reports for free from the individual investment houses if you know which ones to ask for.

Another option: **Moody's Corporate Profiles,** published by Moody's Investors Service, New York. This reference covers 8,000 of the largest U.S. public companies. For each company there's a general business description, a history, a detailed financial profile (including much of the information found in annual reports), names of officers and directors, phone numbers, addresses, and dividend and earnings-per-share information. It's available on-line only through DIALOG.

Moody's puts more extensive information in print in a set of eight annual directories, including the **Industrial Manual,** the **OTC** [over-the-counter] **Industrial Manual,** the **OTC Unlisted Manual,** and the **Bank and Finance Manual.** The average price is $1,500, for which you also get weekly news updates. For information, call 800-342-5647, ext. 0435. (You can also read the manuals for free at the library.)

For private companies, it's tougher to get inside information, and "some you just won't get," warns John Guerin, regional account manager of Swift Adhesives in Raleigh-Durham, N.C. The first place to look is **Dun & Bradstreet Credit Reports,** published by Dun & Bradstreet Information Services. The company provides credit information on about 10 million public and private U.S. companies, including how quickly they pay their bills. A full company report for subscribers, who contract to buy 100 reports or more annually, costs $22. For non-subscribers, the same report costs $60. Abbreviated, customized versions of the reports are available to non-subscribers for about $20 (less for subscribers). Call 800-879-1362. These reports are not available on-line.

Your next option should be to check out the **American Manufacturers Directory,** published by American Business Directories, Omaha (402-593-4600). This reference covers more than 500,000 public and private manufacturers with at least 25 employees, and includes addresses and telephone numbers, sales, credit ratings, number of employees, years in business, and top executives at each plant location. For $1,295 a year, you can lease the printed directory along with the CD-ROM version. Or you can access it on-line through DIALOG, CompuServe, LEXIS-NEXIS, or Online Computer Library Center. And again, there's always the library.

What Is the Company's Strategic Imperative? Is It Focused on Reducing Costs, Improving Quality, or What?

We need to know what our customers are trying to do," says Greg Hawes, national account district manager for ADP of

Roseland, N.J. "For example, if they're downsizing, how can I help them cut costs?"

For public companies, read the annual reports—especially the chairman's or president's report to shareholders. Also, check Investext.

Private companies take more digging. Try business journals and local papers, many of which are on LEXIS-NEXIS and DIALOG. Another source: industry newsletters, which can be found on-line through the **NewsNet** and **PTS Newsletters** databases.

What Is the Organizational Structure? Who's in Charge?

A salesperson must know the company's formal structure "so he can do things that are politically correct," says Lee Blackstone, a former salesperson and a principal at Blackstone & Cullen of Atlanta, makers of software for salespeople. "You need to understand so you don't jump three levels above someone, or below. You need to work through the structure."

To get the structure, simply ask the company for its organizational chart, suggests Blackstone. If that doesn't work, try the **Directory of Corporate Affiliations,** published by Reed Reference Publishing Co. of New Providence, N.J. (800-521-8110). This five-volume set includes listings on more than 100,000 of the world's leading companies. There's a volume on U.S. private companies, one on U.S. public companies, one on international companies, and two volumes of indexes. Information includes addresses of corporations and subsidiaries; descriptions of company busi-

nesses; key personnel and directors; sales and other financial information (for public companies), including assets, earnings, liabilities, and net worth; legal, accounting, and other service providers; and the reporting structure of subsidiaries. The full hardbound five-volume set sells for $950; it's commonly available in libraries, and can be accessed on-line through DIALOG.

Also look at annual reports and at Enhanced Dun's Market Identifiers.

Who Is Really in Charge?

Organizational charts might tell you who *not* to call, but they don't always reveal who *to* call. "You need inside contacts," maintains Guerin of Swift Adhesives. "You need to understand the corporate purchasing philosophy. Are decisions made on the site level, the corporate level? I don't want to be spending time with people who aren't making decisions—say, with the plant engineer—if the decision to buy commodities is made at the corporate level."

If you already have access to high-level executives, just ask them. If not, check out the general business press—*The Wall Street Journal, The New York Times, Business Week, Forbes,* and *Fortune*—as well as smaller business journals and local newspapers. Look for these publications on such on-line services as DIALOG, Dow Jones News/Retrieval, and LEXIS-NEXIS.

What Products Is the Company Developing? What Products Is It Planning to Develop?

You want to know in what divisions or products the company is investing its research dollars, says Peeling of Olin Corp.

"That will give you a clue as to where the company is investing its dollars overall. If the company is walking away from your area, then you ought to think about your approach."

Start with **The Wall Street Transcript,** published by Wall Street Transcript Corp. of New York (212-952-7400). Weekly issues often contain so-called Special Reports, which are discussions by analysts of specific industries and interviews with chief executives. These reports include new-product information and investment assessments of companies and industries overall. Printed copies of the Special Reports cost $85. Single issues of the complete Transcript are $175. Individual interviews are $35. The service is also available on-line through Dow Jones News/Retrieval.

Then there's **PROMT,** a database produced by Information Access Co. of Foster City, Calif. (800-321-6388). This includes abstracts of new-product announcements; market research studies and reports; and abstracts or full texts of general and business newspapers, trade journals, and other business publications. PROMPT is available through 10 on-line vendors, including DIALOG, Data-Star, LEXIS-NEXIS and FT Profile. A subset of the information is also available in a hard-bound directory, **The PROMPT Directory.** You can read it in the library or shell out $1,100 for your own copy.

Where Are the Company's Plants?

The easiest place to locate this information is in the lobby of prospects' offices, says Bill Bushing, sales director/national

accounts for IMRS, a software company in Stamford, Conn. "You don't need high-level contacts for some of this information."

Or get a list of subsidiaries from the prospect's purchasing department, suggests Blackstone.

If by now you prefer the library, look at Enhanced Dun's Market Identifiers or the American Manufacturers Directory. Also, try the buyer's guides put out by trade associations or trade publications. Trade associations are indexed in the **Encyclopedia of Associations,** from Gale Research of Detroit (800-877-4253), which is priced at $415 per volume. Trade publications are indexed in **Ulrich's International Periodicals Directory,** published annually by Reed Reference Publishing of New Providence, N.J. (800-521-8110). The five-volume set will cost you $415. Ulrich's is also available on-line through DIALOG or CDP Online Support.

What Has Been Going On at the Company in the Past Year?

Read, read, read. Blackstone's top suggestion for brushing up on current events is the company newsletter. In general, read the business press, local newspapers, and trade publications. Keep up to date on-line through LEXIS-NEXIS or DIALOG.

Who Are Your Company's Major Competitors? Where Do You Stand in Relation to Your Competition?

Caldwell of Otis Elevator says his clients give him copies of contracts from competitors with the pricing crossed out. "They just want us to see what they're offering," he says. If it doesn't come that easily for you, peruse trade publications, industry newsletters, and PROMPT.

Who Is Already Selling to the Prospect?

This is 10-karat-gold information because if you have sold against those vendors before, "they become predictable," says Blackstone. "If you've competed against them seven times, you know exactly what he's going to do every time."

You can best get these nuggets through the grapevine and by asking the company straight out, says Guerin of Swift Adhesives. Or read press releases, available on **PR Newswire** (800-832-5522) and **Business Wire** (800-227-0845).

PR Newswire, which puts out releases on 17,000 public and private companies, is on-line through some 90 services, including DIALOG, LEXIS-NEXIS, and Dow Jones News/Retrieval. Business Wire, with releases from some 12,000 organizations, including public and some private companies, trade groups, and government organizations, is on 80-odd services, including Dow Jones News/Retrieval, CompuServe, LEXIS-NEXIS, and DIALOG.

Who Are Their Customers?

If you and your prospect share customers, you may be able to feed your prospect nonproprietary information about those common customers, says Blackstone. Further, you may be able to team up with your prospect to offer your mutual customer products that stand out from the competition's because of your collaboration. For these tidbits, ask the company's sales manager. Annual reports and a com-

pany's sales literature often show pictures of customers, says Blackstone. Other possible sources of this information: press releases, trade publications, and on-line databases such as **Trade & Industry** and **ABI/INFORM.**

What Are Some of the Major Marketplace Factors—Regulatory, Competitive, or Economic—That Are Affecting the Company?

These are very important to keep up on, says Hawes of ADP. For example, new government regulations that require more reporting and paperwork mean more business for ADP, which sells data processing services.

Blackstone says the best sources for this information are SEC filings, including 10-Ks, which discuss regulatory issues, and 10-Qs, quarterly reports that discuss market conditions.

Read the business press and newswire reports on LEXIS-NEXIS, DIALOG, CompuServe, and Dow Jones News/Retrieval. Newsletters are especially good for the regulatory area.

Where Did the Prospect Go to College? How Many Kids Does He Have? What Are Their Names?

With this kind of information, "you can talk more about [the prospect's] interests," says Jim Brown of The Ardmore Group, a marketing and consulting firm in Ho-Ho-Kus, N.J. "You used to have to look at the pictures on the office wall."

Bob Gleason of Bowen & Associates, the Dale Carnegie representative in the Chicago area, suggests starting with the company receptionist. His approach? "I'll say, 'I'm going to meet with the president. May I please ask some questions?' Usually they say yes."

If they don't, head for the library and take out **Who's Who in America,** published annually by Marquis Who's Who, a division of Reed Reference Publishing (800-521-8110). This provides biographical information on some 90,000 people in business, government, education, and more. Included is date of birth, date of marriage, names of children, occupation, education, professional certifications, career-related activities, creative works, professional memberships, awards, and—if available—religion, political affiliation, avocations, and mailing address. It's available in hardcover for $450 or on-line through DIALOG.

Reprinted with the permission of SELL!NG magazine.

Additionally, salespeople must understand the buying situation of the company and the industrial environment of the prospect. Understanding the buying situation involves knowing the competitive position of the firm in the industry, the objectives and goals of the company, the company's major customers, and any current problems and opportunities. If the company is publicly held, most of this information is available from the annual report or 10K. The 10K is the report a publicly traded company files with the Securities and Exchange Commission. Other sources of company information include business guides, government publications, indexes of published information, and trade association directories. These are described in detail below.

Business Guides. A wide variety of business guides are available to salespeople for finding valuable information on an industry and specific companies in that industry. Probably the most complete and fastest source is CD-ROM on-line references. *Dun & Bradstreet's Reference Book of Corporate Managements* provides information on more than 30,000 executives who are directors and officers for more than 2,000 large corporations. *Moody's Industrial Manual* gives detailed information, such as principal officers and directors, major plants, merger and acquisition activity, and products of a company, as well as seven years of statistical records and financial statements.

Standard & Poor's publishes several books that provide valuable information on prospects. One of these, *Standard & Poor's Corporation Services,* has several services, including industry surveys providing weekly stock market information; a stock guide providing data on 5,000 stocks on a monthly basis; and a trade and securities book providing statistics on business, finance, foreign trade, productivity, and employment. *Standard & Poor's Register of Corporations* lists the names and titles of top executives of 36,000 U.S. companies, as well as 75,000 directors and executives in the United States and Canada. Finally, the *Directory of Corporate Affiliations* provides information on the 16,000 divisions, subsidiaries, and affiliates of more than 3,000 parent corporations, and it cross-references all of them.

Government Publications. Many government publications provide useful information on potential customers. Most of this information can be found in two publications: *Monthly Catalogue of United States Government Publications* and *Monthly Checklist of State Publications*. The first provides a monthly comprehensive list of federal publications by issuing agency. The second does the same for state publications. *Survey of Current Business* provides monthly statistics on more than 2,500 different statistical series, such as gross national product, national income, employment, construction, real estate, domestic and foreign trade, and balance of payments.

Other extensive data compiled by the government are *Census of Retail Trade*, which provides information on the sales, payroll, and personnel of a large number of retail operations by Standard Metropolitan Statistical Area (SMSA); *Census of Selected Services*, which provides information on various service operations, such as hotels, motels, and beauty parlors; *Census of Wholesale Trade*, which provides information on a large number of wholesale outlets, such as sales, payroll, and personnel by SMSA; *Census of Housing*, which provides detailed information on various housing characteristics; and *Census of Manufactures*, which provides information on employment, payroll, new capital expenditures, cost of materials, and value of shipments of manufacturers.

Indexes. A wide variety of indexes can help salespeople become familiar with potential customers. One of the most used is *Business Periodicals Index*, a cumulative subject index listing business articles found in more than 175 periodicals. Two Fúnk & Scott indexes are also popular. The *F&S Index of Corporations* indexes company, product, and company information on U.S. companies from more than 800 business-oriented newspapers, financial publications, and trade magazines. The *F&S Index of International Industries* provides information on foreign companies classified by the Standard Industrial Classification (SIC) code. Another useful reference, *Applied Science and Technology Index*, is a cumulative subject index of articles in various science periodicals.

Trade Association Directories. A final source are trade association directories. The most widely used directory is the *Encyclopedia of Associations*. This reference book has three volumes that list trade association executives. Another, the *National Trade and Professional Associations of the United States and Labor Unions*, provides information on more than 50,000 trade associations, professional associations, and labor unions.

IMPORTANCE OF PLANNING THE SALES CALL

In addition to prospecting, an often overlooked but extremely important step in the selling process is planning the sales call. Although it is especially important when calling on prospects to know as much about them as possible, planning is also important when calling on established accounts. There is nothing more damaging to a salesperson's or the company's reputation than being unprepared. Lack of preparation is all too obvious to even a novice buyer, as indicated in the four most important reasons for planning, which follow.

Planning Reflects Professionalism.   Selling is a process that requires good business relationships, relationships that are built on the concern of salespeople for their customers and their knowledge of the industry, company, competitive products, and company needs. The professionalism of planning the sales call allows the specialized knowledge of the salespeople to solve the customers' problems and fulfill their needs. A useful tool for assessing a salesperson's product knowledge is given in Table 6-3.

TABLE 6-3 Product Knowledge Checksheet

Salesperson's Name _____

Date _____   Product Category _____

	Excellent	Good	Fair	Poor
• Overall product characteristics				
• How products are manufactured				
• Customers in the market for our products				
• Major competitors of our products				
• Competitive activities affecting our products				
• Important uses for our products				
• Company programs designed to promote products				
• Basic product facts most frequently asked by prospects and customers				
• FEATURES and functions of products				
• BENEFITS of products				
• Importance of giving BENEFITS a dollar-and-cent value whenever possible				

Strengths of the salesperson: _____

_____

Weaknesses of the salesperson: _____

_____

Planning Develops Goodwill. Customers appreciate and welcome salespeople who understand their problems and needs and who are prepared to present a product or service that helps to fulfill their needs. This can best be accomplished through the salesperson using an account sales plan (see Table 6-4). Having the knowledge of the company's product and service and the buyer's needs at the heart of the sales plan develops goodwill between the salesperson and buyer. Over time, this leads to trust and goodwill.

Planning Builds the Confidence of the Salesperson. The ability to be professional and build goodwill depends to some extent on the confidence of the salesperson. This confidence level significantly increases when the sales call is carefully planned, as the salesperson has already focused on the customer's needs. Because self-confidence is often a prerequisite for obtaining an order from a buyer, this reason alone is enough for the salesperson to plan the call. A sales planning checksheet, useful for assessing a salesperson's ability to plan, is presented in Table 6-5.

Planning Increases Sales Probability. A self-confident, well-prepared salesperson who can illustrate how a particular product or service can best meet the customer's needs has better sales results than an unprepared salesperson. Planning ensures that the right match between the customer's needs and the company's product and service mix is well thought out and developed into a succinct presentation that maintains the customer's interest and spurs willingness to buy.

PLANNING THE SALES CALL

There are three basic aspects in planning a sales call: establishing the sales call objective; developing a customer profile and benefits; and preparing the sales presentation.

TABLE 6-4 Account Sales Plan

Date: _____   Salesperson: _____

Customer/Prospect: _____   Address: _____

Telephone: _____   Fax: _____

Objective	Primary Contact	Particular Buyer Characteristics	Benefits Desired	Specific Actions	Achievement Date

TABLE 6-5 Planning Checksheet

Salesperson's Name _____

Date _____

	Excellent	Good	Fair	Poor
• Knowledge of products and their attributes				
• Knowledge of application of products				
• Knowledge of prospecting techniques				
• Knowing about the preparation and use of weekly schedules				
• Knowing call planning procedures				
• Knowing information sources useful in planning calls				
• Knowing the Feature-Function-Benefits technique				
• Knowing how to develop specific sales points of prime concern to customers				
• Knowing the techniques for involving customers in sales interviews with questions				
• Knowing the necessity to pinpoint decision makers				

Strengths of the salesperson: _____

_____

Weaknesses of the salesperson: _____

_____

Establishing Objectives

Every sales call should be based on one or more objectives. Objectives guide the preparation of the specific sales presentation and allow the salesperson to evaluate the results. Objectives must, first, be quantifiable—that is, stated in specific numbers—so that specific activities can be developed to accomplish the objectives. Examples of quantifiable objectives follow:

- Sell three cases of 16-ounce ketchup.
- Sell a new binding machine.
- Establish a cooperative advertising agreement.
- Increase the number of shelf facings by one.

Second, the objective must be measurable. A salesperson develops skills when each sales call is carefully evaluated and the results achieved are compared to the objectives. This can only be accomplished when the objectives are measurable. Measurable means that the results of the effort to achieve the objective might be to increase the number of new customers by eight during the next month can be evaluated by comparing the actual number of new customers with the benchmark objective of eight.

Finally, objectives must be understandable and beneficial to the customer. If the customer does not clearly understand how the purchase is a benefit, the salesperson will have difficulty making the sale. A useful aid in developing an appropriate objective is a call sheet, as illustrated in Table 6-6.

TABLE 6-6 Example Call Sheet

Firm Name: _____

Address: _____
       Street   City, State, Zip

Telephone: _____

Telefax: _____

Firm Characteristics

Type of Business: _____

Size of Business: _____

Usual Buying Pattern: _____

Products Purchased	Annual Purchase	Company Purchase	Brand Preferred	Other Suppliers
1.				
2.				
3.				
4.				
5.				

Key Customer Contacts:

Calling Hours	Department	Name of Buyer	Buyer's Responsibility

Other Key Customer Information:

    Desired Terms of Sale: _____

    Past Purchasing Activity: _____

    Competitive Products Purchased: _____

The past purchase history helps to determine which customers need to re-order and indicates the company products not yet purchased.

Developing a Customer Profile and Benefits

Once the sales objectives have been established, the next step is to determine the customer's profile. A customer profile includes all available information on the firm, the buyer, and any individuals in the firm who influence the buying decision. This information should be reviewed to develop the best customized presentation possible. A good customer profile includes the following information:

1. Who makes the buying decision
2. The background of this individual (or individuals), as well as the background of the company
3. The probable terms of sale, such as delivery, payment period, and service
4. Past purchasing activity
5. Competitive products purchased

This information, as well as specific actions to be taken, can be recorded on the example call sheet in Table 6-6.

The main reason that a product will be purchased is that it meets the needs or solves a particular problem of the customer. Salespeople can determine what those benefits are by answering the question, "Why should this customer purchase this particular product?" The answer helps determine what product features and advantages the salesperson should present.

The features, advantages, and benefits of a product become the basis for developing a marketing plan. The **marketing plan** shows how the particular product meets the needs of the customer, explains the anticipated returns to the company, and indicates the payment plan. This process is often called delineating the benefits. The marketing plan assists the salesperson in developing a suggested purchase order for the customer. The analysis in the market plan can justify the proposed amount to be purchased by the customer. The suggested purchase order should be complete in terms of the kinds and quantities of each product the customer should purchase.

Preparing the Sales Presentation

The sales call objectives and the customer profile and benefits are the basis for the final step in sales call planning: preparing the actual presentation. The sales presentation (discussed in detail in Chapter 7) consists of a series of steps—approval, presentation, trial close, and close—that move the buyer from interest to action. In planning the sales presentation, salespeople should keep in mind the mental process a customer goes through in making a purchasing decision. The steps in this mental process are attention, interest, desire, conviction, action (purchase), and after-purchase evaluation. An effective sales presentation helps to move the buyer through this mental process.

Attention. From the moment contact is made with a buyer, a salesperson should obtain and hold the buyer's attention. This can be difficult at times because the salesperson is calling on the buyer in the buyer's own territory. The buyer is often distracted by other responsibilities or by events going on in the firm, and may be interrupted by personnel about problems that need immediate attention. The situation is even more difficult when the buyer has little interest in the product being offered. The goal of the salesperson is to attract the buyer's initial attention and move the buyer to the next stage, interest, as quickly as possible.

Interest. In the interest stage of the buyer's mental process, the salesperson can determine buying motives. A salesperson must link the purpose of the call and the products being offered with the buyer's needs and interest. Once this link has been made, it is easier to move the buyer through the mental process to a satisfactory conclusion—a sale. If the salesperson has not been able to determine the buyer's motives, questions can help pinpoint those motives. A buyer who enters into a discussion, and becomes involved, is more likely to maintain a high interest level than one who does not.

Desire. This stage in the mental process occurs when the buyer moves from interest in the product to expressing a wish or want for a particular product. The potential buyer questions the salesperson and presents objections to determine whether a particular product should be purchased. A salesperson should anticipate the major objections that may be raised and be ready with answers. Whenever possible, the objections should be dealt with in the actual sales presentation and references made to the presentation when the objections are raised. Sometimes objections can be used successfully in the sales presentation as a series of questions most buyers ask.

Conviction. Even though the buyer may want or desire the product being offered, this is frequently not enough to make a purchase decision. A buyer's concerns about the purchase must be reduced by convincing the buyer that the product is the right one and that the salesperson's company is the best supplier. The buyer is convinced when he or she has no doubts that the product should be purchased from the particular company. The more this belief can be developed and supported, the easier it is to close the sale.

Action (Purchase). Once the stage of conviction is reached, it is important for the salesperson to determine the most appropriate way to ask for action—make the sale. This is perhaps one of the most difficult stages, as many salespeople make good presentations but fail to close because they fail to ask for the sale. The more skillfully the buyer has been guided through the mental stages, the easier it is for the purchase to occur.

Postpurchase evaluation. The last stage in the mental process is critical for future sales and is often overlooked—the postpurchase evaluation. A customer tends to analyze a purchase after it is made to help ensure that the decision was the correct one. This concern, called cognitive dissonance, needs to be eliminated in order for future, repeat sales to occur (discussed in Chapter 10).

CHAPTER SUMMARY

The selling process is a series of seven steps: prospecting, preapproach, sales presentation, handling objections, closing the sale, and servicing. Of these, prospecting is frequently overshadowed by the pressures of making immediate sales. Yet salespeople must obtain information on the needs and wants, ability to purchase, and resources available to purchase of each prospect. This can be done through the use of several prospecting strategies: inquiries from advertising, centers of influence, chain of leads, cold canvassing, contests, directories of mailing lists, group plans, information exchange, internal records, observation, service personnel, spotters, and trade shows. Information on prospects can also be found through a wide variety of information sources, such as business guides, government publications, indexes of published information, and trade association directories.

The preparation stage of the selling process begins with planning the sales call. The four most important reasons for planning the sales call are indicating professionalism, building goodwill, building the salesperson's confidence, and increasing the likelihood of a purchase. The three basic steps of planning a sales call are establishing a concrete sales objective, developing a customer profile and benefits, and preparing the sales presentation. Both prospecting and planning the sales call are important to make the best possible sales presentation.

KEY TERMS

cold canvassing, p. 126   prospecting, p. 123
demographic information, p. 123   qualifiers, p. 123
marketing plan, p. 142   telemarketing, p. 124

CHAPTER QUESTIONS

1. As a salesperson, develop a prospect list for each of the following companies:
   a. A manufacturer of plastic extrusion equipment
   b. A distributor of low-priced imported wines from Hungary

c. A travel agency specializing in group tours to Eastern and Central Europe, Russia, and Ukraine

d. A manufacturer of a new high-priced spread for bread

2. You are a salesperson for a company that carries a complete line of equip-

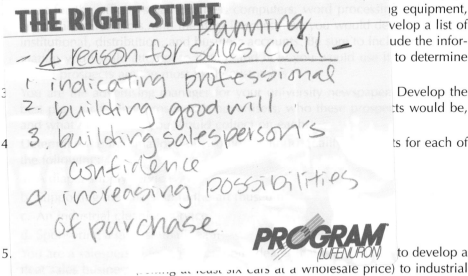

companies in the area. First, develop a plan to establish a prospect list and the information you would obtain. Second, develop a screening plan. Finally, plan a sales script you would use when calling on your first prospect.

6. Discuss the importance of making an appointment before visiting a prospect and a customer. Describe some circumstances when an appointment might not be necessary.

7. You have just received your undergraduate degree and are starting your career as a stockbroker. Develop a plan for obtaining a list of prospects and a rating system for each one. Do the same for starting your career as a life insurance salesperson.

8. As a salesperson for an industrial products company, you are attempting to set up an appointment for a personal interview. In response to your comment: "Mr. Salipante, please. John Kory calling," the secretary responds, "What do you want to talk to Mr. Salipante about?" How would you respond? Assume the secretary responds to your answer by saying: "Mr. Salipante is too busy to talk to you. May I help?" How would you then respond?

NOTE

1. This and other demonstrations are discussed in Cyndee Miller, Demonstrating your point. *Marketing News,* September 13, 1993, 2.

SUGGESTED READINGS

Arnold, Bob. How to establish and maintain your TSA market. *Broker World* (February 1991), 74–78.

> The importance of prospecting in selling tax sheltered annuities is discussed.

Berman, Helen. Pre-call planning: Finding the facts. *Folio,* December 1, 1991, 92–94.

> The various sources available to a salesperson for selling a prospect are the focus of this article. The best source is the information the prospect will provide once a working relationship has been established.

Fox, Dennis. Ringing up prospects. *Sales and Marketing Management* (March 1993), 75–77.

> This article discusses the new paradigm that has emerged in today's competitive environment: The relationship with the customer begins not with the first face-to-face appointment but, rather, with the first contact, which is often the prospecting telephone call. To maximize the benefits of this first telephone call, and to avoid wasteful appointments with non-decision makers, a three-step telephone approach is discussed. This approach focuses on the right place, the right person, and the right purpose.

Ingram, Thomas N. Improving sales force productivity: A critical examination. *Review of Business* (Summer 1990), 7–12, 40.

> Since the estimate of an average sales cost is $200, all the money spent on personal selling must be carefully evaluated according to this article. Seven highly interrelated steps in the selling process are discussed, as well as the importance of developing a more professional, productive sales force.

Kitzing, Fred. Exhibiting by objectives. *Agri Marketing (AGJ)* (July/August 1992), 52–53.

> Trade shows as a cost-effective method for reaching potential customers are discussed. To be cost-effective, all aspects of the trade show (strategies, exhibit architecture, graphics, and the selection and training of the exhibit staff) must be determined by the objectives established.

Livingston, Tom. Data base prospects don't go stale at Tyson Foods. *Business Marketing* (May 1992), 36–37.

> The method Tyson Foods uses to make sure its database of food service operators and managers do not become dated is the topic of this article. The method uses an audiotex-based give-away program that asks callers a few key questions before informing them of what prize they won.

Stern, Aimee L. Telemarketing polishes its image. *Sales and Marketing Management* (June 1991), 107–110.

> Telemarketing is becoming a sophisticated, complex technique used by many Fortune 500 firms according to this article. The American Telemarketing Association indicates that over 481,000 companies sell by telephone, many employing well-trained operators to handle the incoming calls.

Use your sales techniques when you ask for an appointment. *Profit-Building Strategies for Business Owners* (October 1991), 17–18.

> This article discusses the value of selling the prospect on the importance of seeing a salesperson. Ten tips for doing this are presented.

Wimialski, George G. Sell to the masses, not the classes. *Life Association News* (September, 1992), 68–74.

> By targeting the best potential prospects—the individuals who earn between $18,000 and $35,000 each year, an agent can provide for the prospect's needs and make a profit. Small firms that employ these individuals are particularly good prospects.

Chapter 7

The Selling Process—
The Sales Presentation

OPENING SCENARIO

Phil Kary, sales manager of Dumas Makt., H.K., knew that tomorrow was a critical day for the company. He was going to make a sales presentation to one of the largest wine wholesalers in Georgia about the wines from Hungary that Dumas Makt. was importing. How should he approach Jim Dalton, the buyer for the wholesaler? Would the product approach or question approach be more effective, given both the product and the personality of Dalton? How could he make the sales presentation a successful one? Phil was particularly concerned about getting Jim's attention, as he was always very busy. During the last presentation, Dalton was interrupted two times by managers of his company. Phil was also considering the presentation itself, trying to decide whether the needs satisfaction presentation or the problem resolution presentation would be more effective. Phil thought, "Little did I know 12 years ago before I got into sales that there were so many decisions involved in making a good sales presentation."

Chapter Objectives

After reading this chapter, you should be able to

- Define the various selling approaches.
- Discuss the basic characteristics of a sales presentation.
- Present the basic principles of effective communication.

- Discuss the best approach for a selling situation.
- Describe the most appropriate type of sales presentation for a particular selling situation.

INTRODUCTION

Phil Kary's dilemma occurs in business, not-for-profit organizations, and governments everyday. It routinely confronts Ray Ackerman, representative of so many successful executives, being one-part salesman, one-part leader, and one-part dreamer. In the 1950s Ackerman dreamed of building a large advertising agency. He used his leadership ability and particularly his sales skills to build Ackerman and McQueen, an advertising agency headquartered in Oklahoma City, into a $35 million operation. His dream started to be fulfilled with the purchase of the George Knox agency in 1952. Ackerman then used his sales ability again to expand the agency to a national level. Then a merger with a Tulsa advertising agency in 1988, Hood, Hope and Associates, led to the Ackerman McQueen agency with current earnings of $80 million.

Ray Ackerman uses his abilities to sell, lead, and dream in his civic life as well. As the chairman of the Oklahoma City Chamber of Commerce, he envisioned the development of the city's economy. Through his leadership and salesmanship, the image of the city has been enhanced and companies have expanded or relocated there, such as Ameis in telemarketing with 400 jobs; API Enterprises, Inc., in plastics manufacturing with 200 jobs; and Gilandi and Sons, Inc., in food processing with 200 jobs. Ackerman acknowledges the importance that being a practical salesman played in his successful career.[1]

An effective sales approach and presentation are at the heart of all personal selling. Once the sales call has been planned, it is important that the prospect be approached correctly and given the most appropriate presentation. This occurs when a salesperson understands the prospect's needs, motives, and habits. Each presentation needs to be developed so that it informs, persuades, and convinces the prospect that the product or service should be purchased.

APPROACHING THE PROSPECT

The first few minutes of the sales presentation may be the most critical as they establish a buyer's attitude toward the salesperson. This critical period, called the **approach,** is so important that it is treated as a separate feature of the sales presentation. In approaching the potential buyer, it is important for the salesperson to initially plan the sales call, have the right attitude, understand the situation, and use the appropriate technique(s).

Planning the Sales Call (The Preapproach)

In order to make maximum use of the time allocated by the prospect for the sales presentation, as well as making the correct approach, it is most important that the salesperson carefully plan the sales call. This planning, or preapproach, stage, best done before the sales call, involves reviewing the plan before approaching the prospect. Good planning also requires strategic information about the prospect. This is best facilitated through the use of a call sheet, discussed in Chapter 6.

All information about the prospect and his or her company can be strategically useful, but at a minimum the salesperson must know the potential buyer's name, position, buying pattern, responsibilities, and typical products purchased. It is also helpful for the salesperson to know something about the prospective buyer's personality traits, hobbies, interests, political views, family, and lifestyle. Any unusual traits or characteristics should be noted in the section on key customer information on the call sheet.

Such background information is necessary to customize a sales plan for each prospective customer. This sales plan will assist the salesperson in developing the best approach/presentation as specific objectives and actions for particular customers are developed. Although there may be changes during the presentation, a well-thought-out sales plan shows the customer that the salesperson has given much care to the presentation and helps to establish the right atmosphere for a successful sales call.

Attitude During Approach

The appearance and attitude of the salesperson create the first impression for the prospect. As in most things, this first impression is critical to a successful presentation. Several factors help to create a good first impression: wearing appropriate clothing; being neat in dress and grooming; not smoking or chewing gum; standing tall and confident; being enthusiastic and positive; maintaining eye contact; learning and pronouncing the prospect's name correctly; and using the prospect's name several times throughout the presentation.[2]

It is an unusual salesperson who does not experience some tension in the first dealings with a prospect. This tension can be greatly increased when the salesperson has preconceived ideas about the negative characteristics of the prospect and all that may go wrong during the sales call. Successful salespeople have learned to reduce the degree of stress and focus on the positive rather than the negative aspects of the situation. Some use **creative imagery.** First, the salesperson envisions the worst that can possibly happen, followed by how he or she will react to the situation if it occurs. Then the salesperson envisions the best that can possibly happen. He or she prepares contingency plans just in case the selected sales presentation needs to be abandoned. Finally, the salesperson focuses on the slim chance (less than 1 percent) that things really do go wrong, even with all the careful planning—remembering, though, that this means there is a greater than 99 percent probability that the presentation will go smoothly.

The Situation of the Approach

The situation confronting the salesperson will determine the actual approach technique that should be used. Several variables affect the situation, including the type of product(s) being sold; the degree of knowledge about the customer's needs; the time available for making the presentation; whether the call is the first one or a repeat; the sales call objective and customer benefits; and the number of approaches available.

Types of Approaches

Depending on the situation, eight methods can be used to effectively approach the prospect. These approaches are described below.

Compliment Approach. When done subtly and sincerely, a **compliment approach** can illicit a very positive reaction and establish a pleasant atmosphere for the sales presentation. Almost all businesspeople are receptive to receiving positive feedback about themselves and their company. This usually is best accomplished through an indirect complimentary approach rather than a direct one, which might be viewed as flattery. Some good compliment approaches include the following:

> Kary, your office has such lovely decor and your staff so helpful that it is always a pleasure to make this call.
> Kary, you have a wonderful secretary. He not only switched my appointment due to a problem that came up, but he called me to reconfirm the new date.
> Kary, I understand congratulations are in order on your recent promotion.
> Kary, it's a great pleasure dealing with a company such as yours that is on the cutting edge of technology.

Reference Approach. This approach includes mentioning several satisfied customers who are known and respected by the prospect. The **reference approach** is made even stronger when the reference is an industry leader known for being dynamic and innovative. An example of this approach is: "Your colleague, Barra O'Cinneide, the sales manager at Dumas Makt., H.K., has just started buying this product, as have three other leading companies in the area." A testimonial letter from a satisfied customer can be very helpful not only in the approach but in the presentation itself. A salesperson needs to be careful that any names mentioned are indeed satisfied customers because the prospect may actually contact the individual. Some salespeople have used this approach to obtain good leads by asking each new customer for the names of others who might be interested in the product.

Sample Approach. The **sample approach** has had a long history of establishing goodwill while positively approaching a prospect. Offering a trial size of the product, a luncheon invitation, a free seminar, or a sample of the services is an excellent way to approach a prospect. When introducing a new cake mix to the trade, one consumer goods salesperson took a piece of cake as a sample of the product. It is much easier to consummate a sale when the prospect has already tried the product or service being offered and found it satisfactory.

Customer-Benefit Approach. Because part of all buyers' jobs is to solve problems or provide some benefit, this approach starts with this most important area—describing the customer's benefits.[3] Usually just one or two buying motives significantly affect the purchasing decision. These need to be identified and appealed to whenever possible. Some examples of **customer-benefit approaches** are

> Kelly, are you aware that our control product reduces the amount of energy lost by 25 percent in just one year?
>
> Kelly, did you see in the paper yesterday that an independent research company determined more consumers preferred our product than any other on the market?
>
> Kelly, did you know that your company can ship and deliver your products through Liverpool to London faster through our service than any other?

Dramatic Approach. A **dramatic approach** can be used to gain attention should all other approaches fail, or when a novel way is needed to make the presentation.[4] One salesperson put $5 on a buyer's desk, announcing that the buyer could keep the $5 if the salesperson was not able to show all the benefits of the product within 25 minutes. Vacuum cleaner salespeople often throw dirt on the carpet of the buyer and then demonstrate the efficient way their product picks up the dirt. One salesperson even set fire to a $1 bill while saying: "Katy, let me show you how you and your company can stop burning up your profits by using our product in your production process."

Product Approach. Another good approach, the **product approach,** shows the prospect a sample of the product right at the start. This approach allows the prospect to see what is being sold and provides for a smooth transition into the sales presentation. Since a picture is worth a thousand words, an example printout of the new computer program for sale with the name of the prospect's company prominently displayed, or a taste of the new food product being presented, can significantly affect the prospect's reception of the sales presentation to follow.

Question Approach. The **question approach** gets the prospect involved in two-way communication early in the sales presentation. This is important, as it is very beneficial to have the prospect involved in the presentation as soon as possible.

Asking thought-provoking questions provides this involvement because the prospect is required to give a response. This approach also has the advantage of providing additional prospect information, such as the level of interest in the product or service being offered.

Questions that qualify a prospect by eliciting a degree of interest are particularly good, such as: "If I can show you how using our product in your production process will provide your company with 5 percent fewer defects per 100 products, would you give me an hour of your time?" This type of question requires some thoughtful consideration on the part of the prospect and can provide an opportunity for an early close on those prospects who clearly indicate an interest. Prospects with a low degree of interest can be given a different presentation, perhaps shorter, if time is a pressing issue. A question that helps identify the prospect's desired benefits is especially good: "What features or benefits are of primary importance when you purchase a product such as this?"

Regardless of the question used, it should be one that elicits a positive, not a negative, response. However, simple yes-no questions should be avoided. It is all too easy for a prospect to quickly answer "no" and end the conversation.

Introductory Approach. One of the weakest approaches is the **introductory approach.** There is only one chance to start the presentation positively, so a salesperson should make sure the introductory approach used is interesting and flows smoothly into the presentation. An initial bad approach should not be followed with another one. A friendly, smiling greeting and a sincere, firm handshake are critical starting points in a good introductory approach. In the introductory approach, a salesperson should use the person's name and company such as: "Good afternoon, Katy. I am Troy Bradley from the Food Division of Imperial Products, here for our 3:00 appointment."

FEATURES OF A SALES PRESENTATION

Following the approach, the nature of the sales presentation depends on the type of selling, the product, and the disposition of the prospect. Although each prospect has a unique personality, all prospects generally fall into one of the following basic types: procrastinator, silent, skeptical, opinionated, impulsive, methodical, talkative, or grouch. By understanding the particular mood and personality of the prospect, a salesperson can quickly develop the most appropriate sales presentation. Some basic aspects needed for a successful sales presentation for each of these types are detailed in Table 7-1.

By taking the personality and mood of the prospect into account, a good sales presentation moves the prospect from approach to action smoothly and logically. No matter what the objective, each sales presentation must meet five basic requirements: (1) obtain the attention of the prospect; (2) arouse the prospect's interest; (3) stimulate desire for the product's benefit; (4) secure the prospect's

TABLE 7-1 Aspects of Sales Presentation for Certain Personality Types

Personality Type	Sales Presentation
Procrastinator	Emphasize benefits that will not be obtained if immediate action is not taken. Emphasize their ability and position of decision making.
Silent	Continually ask questions to get prospects to talk. Try to get them to share some things that are personal. Be very personal during the entire presentation.
Skeptical	Present a conservative presentation filled with facts.
Opinionated	Listen attentively to what they say and never directly disagree with the views expressed. Use features of the product that are in line with their opinions whenever possible.
Impulsive	Give a short presentation highlighting most important points and omit lengthy details. Close early.
Methodical	Make the tempo of the sales presentation fit their tempo. Include many details and backup facts for key points.
Talkative	Be careful that continuous small talk does not affect your sales presentation. Listen attentively, but get the presentation back on track as soon as possible.
Grouch	Do not argue or become defensive. Ask questions to try to understand the nature of their underlying problems and the story behind the disposition. Agree with them as much as possible.

conviction; and (5) motivate the prospect to take action and buy. Not every presentation will require the same amount of concentration on each step; nevertheless, each step needs to be briefly incorporated into the sales presentation. The steps are modified to fit the particular selling situation.[5]

Obtain Instant Attention. The first few seconds in any sales presentation are the most important. The salesperson needs to get the prospect to focus on what is being said as quickly as possible. This is sometimes difficult because a prospect is usually thinking about things that must get done and other responsibilities.

Each prospect has one overriding thought: "What's in it for me?" This question needs to be addressed not only at the start of the presentation but throughout the presentation as well. One of the best ways to gain a prospect's attention is to relate your product or service to the prospect's need or problem: "Sara, did you know that almost every firm in the industry uses our product?"

Creating Interest. Once the prospect's attention is obtained, it must be quickly converted into interest. The salesperson can help the prospect become interested by writing down key selling points built around benefits for the prospect. This requires that the salesperson thoroughly understand the product and the prospect and be able to communicate the product's benefits clearly. An illustration of this approach, called the **feature-advantage-benefit approach,** follows:

FAB

Feature	A characteristic of the product (or service) that produces a benefit
Advantage	What the feature will do or how it works
Benefit	The advantage to the prospect of the feature backed by evidence of confirmation

This approach requires that the salesperson identify those benefits that will have the most appeal to the prospect. This identification can be made by determining what the prospect needs and what he or she wants most; relating these desires to the product or service being offered; and selecting the benefits of the product or service that should be of most interest to the prospect; and then building appeal around these identified benefits.

Stimulating Desire. As the salesperson is making the presentation and linking the prospect's interests to the benefits of the product, the prospect is usually thinking: "Why should I believe you? What you're saying sounds good, but how do I know that you are telling the truth?" The sales presentation must facilitate the prospect's understanding that the product or service will provide the benefits sought and solve any problems mentioned.

Securing Conviction. As the prospect starts desiring the product or service, it is important for the salesperson to transfer this desire to a conviction that the offering is the best possible alternative. This requires the salesperson to develop both rapport and credibility with the prospect. The body language of the salesperson can play a role here. For example, a salesperson will want to appear relaxed and not tense. Body language can give the impression of being relaxed. The relaxed impression reflects the national culture and is, therefore, different depending on the country. This is evident in the difference in leg crossings of salespeople in Europe and the United States. In Europe male and female salespeople cross their legs the same way—one leg over the other, crossing at the knee. In the United States, women cross their legs similarly, whereas men cross their legs by putting an ankle over the knee.

Besides questioning the credibility of the statements of the salesperson, the prospect is also asking: "How do I know that there is not some alternative that will provide this same benefit more cost-effectively?" This question can be answered and conviction obtained by presenting facts about the product or service being offered; offering expert evidence in the form of reports of authorities or results of a market test; or offering a guarantee (or warranty) that the product will perform just as indicated. Any questions or objections of the prospect must be thoroughly and accurately dealt with.

Motivate to Action (Purchase). Motivating the prospect to action (or what is commonly called closing the sale) is the ultimate purpose of the sales presentation. It is very difficult for some salespeople, especially beginners, to ask the prospect to buy or obtain the order. Because a prospect will seldom indicate outright that he

SELL!NG
THE FRONT LINES OF BUSINESS

How to Sell in Japan
Paula Champa

Vince Matal was somewhere in the middle of the Tokyo leg of his tour of duty as a program manager for IBM's Asia-Pacific Group when the *gomen nasai* letter arrived from Domino's Pizza. "*Gomen nasai* means 'I'm sorry,'" he explains—sorry, in this case, for failing earlier in the week to deliver dinner to the Matal household within the advertised 30-minute time frame.

When the steaming pizza showed up 10 minutes late, the delivery man (or "rep," as Matal automatically refers to him) apologized profusely and extended the guaranteed price discount on the order. That reparation was good enough for the customer but not, apparently, for Domino's. Matal still chuckles when he talks about the "parchmentlike" letter that came four days later offering him a free pizza and a six-pack of Coke for his troubles. "'We know we already said you would get 1,000 yen off—and you got that—but that's not good enough,'" he intones, recalling the letter's polite, if stilted, English. "'We're so heartily sorry we ever did this, and we want to swear it will never happen again. So please—get another pizza free.'"

Welcome to selling in Japan. Selling in the purest and most refined sense of the word. Selling so subtle, so faint in its resemblance to the Western idea of sales, we can't even bring ourselves to call it sales.

As Matal puts it, the Japanese "don't sell. They service." The distinction is an important one, for servicing includes, within its gentle name, the extravagant entertaining, the marathon meetings, and the constant gift-giving that Westerners have come to look upon with awe. And it's hard work. Aside from the sheer number of hours the Japanese put behind their sales endeavors (while things are changing, the typical Japanese work week is still six days—or about six hours per week longer than the U.S. average), consider the effort involved simply in conducting daily business in Japan, where life is full of formality and rituals.

First there's all the bowing. "It was amazing how people would bow [even when talking] on the telephone," says Sarah Rowland, a free-lance graphic designer from Richmond, Va., who spent a year in Tokyo assisting on a book project. During the morning rush hour, she adds, Shinjuku Station ("like Grand Central magnified a hundred times") is filled with businessmen—ears pressed to pay telephone receivers—bowing to clients who can't see them. "It's such a normal thing to do. For me to say hello to you, I would be bowing." After a while, Rowland couldn't help but adopt the habit herself.

Then there's the tricky business of what Matal describes as the "gift-giving thing": the highly ritualized practice of exchanging presents that establishes the tenor of a professional relationship. The custom is one way in which relationships are built, not only between companies doing business together, but also between employees and superiors within Japanese companies. In all cases, the decorative wrappings and even the stores where the items are purchased are as important as the gifts themselves.

As for presents, "the more lavish the better," says Rowland, who learned her lesson after returning from a few buying missions with "totally inappropriate" items, such as books, which are generally deemed too practical or unimpressive for the gift swap. More on target, she says, are luxuries: French chocolates or fine wine or hard-to-come-by treats, such as the honeydew melon she once presented to a client. "It was a $55 melon," Rowland says. "It was an imported melon from—possibly California—I don't know. But they sure don't grow them in Japan. It came in a beautiful wooden crate. And then we gave them a beautiful bottle of very nice sake. Another $90. So we gave a $150 gift, easily, and that was regular."

And, of course, there are meetings. In a country where decisions are made by consensus (and consequently are carried out without debate), time-consuming group encounters are the norm. "Nobody does a one-on-one," sighs Matal. "Everything is mass meetings. It's always three, four, five people or more at every one of these things, and all within the pecking order. Then [you] typically go to eating establishments and then, depending on your relative rank or the relative rank of the people that you were with, [the place you ended up] could be anything from a local noodle house to a very fancy sushi bar or one of the very, very expensive entertaining clubs."

Listen closely—these are examples of servicing. To understand the concept, keep in mind some of the "us-versus-them" comparisons that crop up when Americans try to get a handle on the Japanese—most reflecting more favorably on "them." We are talkers. They are listeners. We are primarily interested in the deal. They are interested in building relationships. We win the business by making shrewd presentations. They win with patience. Years' worth, sometimes.

"We tend to sell rationally, or at least have the rational part as an underpinning for some kind of emotional connection," says Jack Sansolo, marketing adviser and president of Point A Consulting in Los Angeles. Sansolo was president/U.S. of Hill, Holliday Advertising in 1988, when the agency won Nissan's Infiniti U.S. automobile business, and then helped import the Japanese sensibility to American consumers.

"We, as Americans, are very pragmatic. They are very sensory," he adds. "They tend to be more conceptual than we are. They tend to be more long-term than we are. For example, we tend to worry about the quarterly results—or even the monthly results—of something.

They will have a 10-year time frame, or a 20-year time frame."

Chuck Laughlin is co-founder of Corporate Visions, a sales training firm in Lake Tahoe, Nev., and co-author with Karen Sage and Marc Bockmon of *Samurai Selling: The Ancient Art of Service in Sales*, which uses the traditional Japanese warrior as an inspirational metaphor. Laughlin says the way he understands the modern sales process in Japan, "a salesperson will spend a lot of time in the very early stages developing a relationship and not even mentioning a company or product, [while] in the U.S., the company and product come out from the very first call."

Since it's customary in Japanese companies for a sales representative to be formally introduced to a prospect, the purpose of the initial calls are understood but not discussed. The decision to do business together, if it occurs, results from the subtlety and patience of relationship-building. "We may be into the middle of the sales process within days, hours," Laughlin notes, "where a Japanese selling person can spend a year building the relationship before he begins to introduce his product."

"It's all a matter of time," Matal agrees, then thinks again. "Proportion, I guess, is what I'm saying. Where we might be 20 percent relationship, rapport, that kind of thing, and 80 percent selling the product, they're the opposite."

Now back in the U.S. as a consulting marketing representative for IBM in Raleigh, N.C., Matal remembers the rules from his early days in sales. "You always try to develop a relationship and service your customers," he says, "but [the Japanese] do it to the exclusion—in my opinion—of actually trying to sell the product."

With years of relationship-building before any deals get done, how do salespeople earn a living? The answer—a flat salary—unusual in the U.S., is standard procedure in Japan. This compensation arrangement, which goes hand-in-hand with the tradition of lifetime employment, was the inspiration for the term "salarymen," the unglamorous description of employees in a work force that was once predominantly male.

Given the amount of servicing expected and the time it takes to close deals, the reliance on salaries makes some sense—at least to the Western mind, which typically demands grounding theory in logic. However, as the Japanese economy continues to stall in a recession and some employers abandon "womb-to-tomb" employment (take Pioneer Electronic Corp., which last January gave 35 managers the choice between retiring or being fired), the idea of commissions is gathering some steam.

Granted, the steam seems to be gathering primarily at foreign-owned companies in Tokyo, and even there, it is a recent phenomenon. Says Matal, "It was only in the last several years that [IBM's Japanese] salespeople went on commission plans. They were always salaried because the assumption was you would work as hard as you possibly could, and therefore you didn't need the commission incentives."

At Japan Database—founded five years ago by 18-year IBM veteran Masanori Suzuki—account executive Daniel Wong is the only salesperson on a commission system, and that's because he specifically negotiated for it in his contract when he signed up. "My president is a very forward-thinking guy," Wong says of the entrepreneurial Suzuki, whose company was the first to introduce UTP cabling in Japan. (This "data-graded" cable replaced coaxial cable and is now an international standard.)

"He's very open-minded and he has very clear ideas. He wanted to implement a commission system in this company, but he came up against resistance . . . from the salespeople."

Wong, who also had a commission deal in a previous sales position at a foreign-owned concern in Japan, is the only foreigner at Japan Database. (His nationality, he says, is "English out of Hong Kong.") He sells the company's data cabling services for networks and computer systems to foreign multinational companies in Tokyo. "The rest of my colleagues are, of course, Japanese," he says, "and they service the Japanese clients." Being the one executive hired specifically to cater to customers in the English language, Wong is a living, breathing example of the Japanese concept of service in sales.

He points out that when the commission proposal didn't fly throughout the rest of Japan Database, it wasn't a case of "the salespeople in my company wanting a commission system and being turned down by the management."

Indeed, abandoning salaries is not exactly a worker movement that's sweeping the nation. Wong, who has lived in Japan for only two years, is cautious about overgeneralizing, but comments, "In a Japanese company, it's stability which is more important than actually having huge rewards if you close a deal."

The commission system, like many other symbols of change in Japan these days, has its proponents among the young. Tomoko Zenman, who works in direct sales for Austin, Tex.-based Dell Computer Corp., spent three years as a buyer in Tokyo before interviewing with a dozen companies, ranging from medical equipment suppliers to real estate agencies, in search of a sales position with a commission deal. (Understand, with Japan's unemployment rate only about 2.1 percent and with about 150 jobs available for every 100 college graduates, candidates are as likely to be interviewing employers as the other way around.) "From my experience," Zenman says, "about 50 percent were offering commission-based pay," with the real estate companies being most likely to offer commission and small firms least likely. In the end, she took another job in procurement—buying computer notebook parts at Dell—and moved over to the sales department at the beginning of 1993. She has never worked at a Japanese company.

She? Yes, she. Major accounts are still handled by men (and there is no change in sight), but Zenman is among the growing number of Japanese women who have entered sales in a variety of retail, telemarketing, or direct-sales positions. Zenman's accounts—all handled over the telephone—tend to be individuals as well as smaller companies that respond to magazine advertisements, or bigger firms that are just beginning to purchase computer equipment from Dell. When an account becomes large enough, it is moved out of her department and into "major accounts."

When asked the Japanese words for "salesman" and "saleswoman," Zenman says no special terms come to mind, then consults with another rep. She finally reports back that a Japanese person would use the English words, "salesman" and "saleswoman" (or perhaps even "saleslady," depending on the connotation). The adoption of an English phrase is common enough in Japanese business parlance; it's surprising to hear that a term like "saleswoman" is not, particularly in a professional context.

Asked why not, Zenman explains graciously, if indirectly: "The society has changed, but before, there were not very many saleswomen, so we didn't need a title for them." But since her situation proves a need for such a term, she is pressed when she's asked how she would respond to a question about what she does for a living. She opts for the clever answer, and says with a laugh, "I'd say, 'I'm selling computers.' "

This explanation is more revealing about the Japanese concept of servicing than anything else. Zenman expresses her profession not as a formal description or a title but as an ongoing activity: "I'm selling computers." It's a mind-set. Where U.S. salespeople might consider themselves to be representing a company, their Japanese counterparts are their employer and are their product. "And they *are* their account," Matal adds. "In other words, they must represent that account to all extents. And if anything goes wrong, they will do anything to fix it."

The tendency to fix problems with entertainment, Matal admits, is certainly not unique to the Japanese, but he gives them credit for doing it "as an art form." It accounts not only for Domino's *gomen nasai* letters but also for at least some of the more extravagant expenditures racked up. (It's the kind of entertaining that might require two or three separate credit-card receipts.) "We had a quality problem with some product or another at a major account [in Tokyo]," Matal remembers, "and the manager was bemoaning to me the fact that this was really going to cost him a big piece of his entertainment budget that month. That's the way they view it."

Obviously, all the businessmen out in the entertainment districts, night after night, are not just fixing business problems—at least not specifically. But even when they aren't taking clients to expensive restaurants and hostess clubs a few nights a week, the ritual of going out for drinks, dinner, and karaoke addresses some important needs of the salarymen themselves. "They entertain one another because they can't speak their minds during the workday," Matal explains. "That's when they talk—that's when they really communicate about whether they think something's a bad idea or a good idea or whatever, because during the business day they don't do that.

"In the hierarchy," he continues, "a junior would never say something negative to a senior in the workplace, but when they're out, it's okay." This agreement to disagree, Matal has observed, derives from a conflict inside the workplace between two uniquely Japanese needs:

saving face and saving space. It's a small country with tight quarters. On a crowded office floor with very few real walls and little privacy, it would be disruptive to create any conflict.

So while salarymen are on the job, it's "heads down." After work, it's bottoms up.

"I personally think [the cycle] is very inefficient, and it's one of the reasons why they work so many hours," Matal says. Wong concurs: "If you go to any Japanese office, you would be surprised by how inefficiently everything is run. But somehow, things get done anyway."

They sure do. Whether the details of selling ever change in Japan, the basic approach to service likely won't. It's too ingrained. More to the point, it's been hugely successful. And, in various ways, it's being emulated in the West. "What's so interesting," Jack Sansolo notes, "is that we're finally rediscovering [the idea of service] to some degree. That's the latest thing: customer service, the customer is right, lifetime customers. Those are all the buzzwords now, because for so many years that wasn't the case.

"The reason it wasn't the case," he adds, "was that it was an expanding economy—you could sell anything you made and people would buy it. But now that there's more competition and it's a battle for market share, what is your value added for your brand? And one value-added area is customer service and customer respect."

In Sansolo's view, the Japanese concepts of service and respect go far beyond the superficial examples of the customer being entertained or "patted on the back all the time . . the way a lot of American companies interpret it. I would rather forgo [a *gomen nasai*] letter and make sure that the product costs less, works better, [and] never breaks down," he says, "and I think that's where the Japanese have beat us, and we're finally starting to learn that lesson. It's a different interpretation of customer service."

Citing automaker Infiniti's promise to deliver the "total ownership experience" (including roadside assistance, ease in servicing, loaner cars, etc.) as an example of a substantial commitment to service, Sansolo continues, "People are looking for what happens in the sales process—in being treated with respect, and being treated like an adult. People are looking for the kind of care and support after they buy, as well as before."

Is this a Japanese concept? "I believe it is," he says. "Because we're still naming it in America. And when you ask people which are the best consumer-service companies, the fact that people can actually name them tells you how new and unusual the concept is in America. Everybody says L.L. Bean, because they've always treated customers well. Yes, it's true, but that's a little product like a shirt, so if the button breaks, they can give you a new one. That's not like spending $40,000 to $50,000 on a car."

It's a strong argument, but the last word on service goes to Matal, who remembers how his wife would come home from Tokyo department stores feeling completely frustrated by the Japanese salespeople's inability to say "no." She found that when she inquired about whether a particular appliance was in stock, "They would say, 'We only have the demonstration unit,' " he remembers. "Or, 'We only have the blue one,' if you're looking for green. They never come out and say, 'No, we don't have it.' "

Clearly, there are many ways to experience selling Japanese style. At least one of them, Matal knows, "can make you nuts."

Reprinted with the permission of SELL!NG magazine.

or she wants to buy the product or service, a salesperson must be able to recognize when the prospect is ready to buy the product and act upon it immediately with a trial close anytime in the sales presentation. This aspect of the selling process is the focus of Chapter 8.

TYPES OF SALES PRESENTATIONS

A sales presentation is a persuasive vocal or visual explanation of a business proposal. Among the many ways to make a sales presentation, the four most commonly used methods, in order of the degree of structure, are the following:

1. Memorized (or canned) presentation
2. Planned (or formula) presentation
3. Needs satisfaction presentation
4. Problem-solution (or survey-proposal) presentation

Memorized (Canned) Presentation

Some companies require their salespeople to memorize and follow a well-prepared, well-tested canned presentation. These presentations are especially beneficial when the same product is sold over and over again and there is little variation among the prospects. They are particularly useful when the sales force is inexperienced and the company is not going to expend time and energy in extensive training. Canned presentations are often used in telemarketing sales. These presentations are so worded that a high percentage of closings result from the canned words that still can come alive for each prospect by a well-trained salesperson.

A memorized sales presentation is based on stimulus-response theory (that certain words and actions—the stimulus—will bring about certain reactions—the response—from the prospect) and one of the following assumptions: (1) that a prospect's needs can be stimulated by direct exposure to the product through the sales presentation, or (2) that the prospect has already been at least partially stimulated and now needs to be moved into an affirmative response and a purchase request.

In this type of presentation, the salesperson does most of the talking and the prospect only occasionally responds, usually to a predetermined question. Because there is no attempt to determine the prospect's needs or understand exactly what the prospect is thinking, the salesperson concentrates on discussing the product and its benefits and then asking for the purchase. This presentation method relies on a convincing presentation of the benefits of the product—the stimulus—that will cause the prospect to buy—the response.

The memorized presentation is most used in selling nontechnical items in door-to-door sales or in telemarketing. It requires limited training and ensures that all prospects will receive the same basic message. Sometimes a company has several standardized sales presentations that can be interchanged as options or as a part of the main presentation. In this circumstance, salespeople can develop their own individualized sentences and phrases in their presentations.

There are several major disadvantages to the memorized sales presentation. First, it allows little, if any, prospect participation. Second, it can be viewed by the prospect as high-pressure selling as the salesperson moves directly through the presentation and asks for the order at preestablished times. It does not take the circumstances of the sales call into consideration and may not coincide with the time the prospect is ready to consider purchasing. Finally, this type of presentation does not consider the individuality of the prospect and may present features and benefits that have little or no meaning to the prospect.

Despite its impersonal nature, the memorized presentation does have some advantages. First, it makes sure that each prospect receives a similar well-planned presentation. Second, it requires very little training. Finally, it can be successfully used by very inexperienced salespeople to sell nontechnical products.

Planned (Formula) Presentation

In situations where a more personal touch is needed along with a very structured approach, the planned (formula) presentation may be most appropriate. This type of presentation is by far the most widely used, because it presents a carefully planned, personalized sales message. The salesperson, knowing something about the prospect, uses a less structured, general outline within which the presentation is made. The presentation is based on the assumption that similar prospects in similar situations can be approached with similar presentations. The salesperson follows a general outline with parts of the script memorized, while maintaining constant prospect involvement and interaction. The salesperson maintains control of the conversation particularly at the beginning and follows the attention, interest, desire, conviction, action procedure.

Most consumer goods, particularly those that are sold on a repurchase basis, are sold by this method. When the buyer is already aware of the quality of the company and is presently purchasing (or has previously purchased) some of the company's products, a flexible, customized sales presentation is not necessary. This is the situation for such consumer goods companies as Colgate, Palmolive, Quaker Oats, General Foods, H. J. Heinz, Procter & Gamble, Pepsi-Cola/Fritolay, Gillette, Revlon, and Beecham.

A typical formula presentation for a typical retail buyer in a food, drug, or discount store has the following series of steps:

Step 1   Plan the call.
  • Review the situation.
  • Check the sales plan.
  • Establish objectives and modify the plan if needed.

Step 2   Check stock.
  • Check shelf facings and note the appearance on the shelf.
  • Note out-of-stocks.
  • Straighten shelf stock.
  • Check back room for stock.
  • Revise the sales plan if needed.

Step 3   Approach the buyer.

Step 4   Make the presentation.
  • Use sales tools.
  • Make the presentation clear and interesting.
  • Tailor the presentation to the specific situation.

Step 5   Close.
  • Present and ask for a suggested order.
  • Answer questions and handle objections.
  • Get the order.

Step 6   Do merchandising and keep records.
  • Give the terms of sales.
  • Provide a delivery date.
  • Build displays.

Step 7   Prepare reports and analyze the call.
  • Complete a report immediately after the call.
  • Review the call to improve the next presentation.

Formula selling has a number of advantages. First, it ensures that all information is presented in a clear, logical manner, allowing for a reasonable amount of buyer interaction. Second, it handles anticipated questions and objections smoothly. There are no major disadvantages to the formula presentation as long as the prospect's needs and wants have been correctly identified. However, in more complex selling situations, the formula presentation method may not be the best choice.

The Needs Satisfaction Presentation

The needs satisfaction presentation is a relatively flexible, interactive presentation that is very challenging and creative. This type of presentation frequently starts with a question, such as "What are you looking for when you purchase this particular type of product?" or "What needs or problems does your company have that I may be able to assist in solving?" This type of question elicits the prospect's needs while providing the salesperson with the opportunity to determine the products that meet those needs or solve the problem identified. Usually, the first 50 to 60 percent of the sales call is devoted to determining and discussing the prospect's needs. The last part of the presentation illustrates how the product will satisfy those needs. The buyer's response to the final part of the presentation dictates what follows. If an objection is raised, for example, the salesperson can handle it through one of the ways discussed in Chapter 8.

Care must be taken not to use too many questions in determining the prospect's needs in the first part of the presentation. Too many questions can alienate the prospect. Many prospects do not want to discuss needs or problems with a salesperson right away. Similarly, many salespeople do not feel comfortable using this sales approach because it is more personal and does not provide strong control of the presentation situation.

Problem-Solution (Survey-Proposal) Presentation

The two-step problem-solving presentation approach is frequently used in selling systems or highly complex technical products. For success, the approach often requires a survey to obtain original data and then several sales calls to develop a detailed analysis of the prospect's needs. The prospect must be convinced that an in-depth study of the present situation and any problems or needs will be beneficial. A carefully written proposal is then developed that solves those needs and problems. This flexible, customized approach often proceeds as follows:

1. Propose the analysis to the prospect.
2. Conduct the analysis.
3. Mutually agree on problems and needs identified with the prospect.
4. Prepare and present proposal for solving prospect's problems and needs.

The proposal is usually presented to a group of managers and can require a selling team, particularly when a technical, high-dollar investment is involved. Successful team selling requires good interaction and planning and effective communication among team members.

PRINCIPLES OF EFFECTIVE COMMUNICATION

A basic requirement of making an effective presentation is understanding two-way communication. A salesperson must not only know what a prospect is saying and thinking but also be able to communicate in the language and interest level of the prospect.

Communication involves learning to be a good listener and deciding on the appropriate content and length of the presentation. One way to discover a prospect's needs is to ask good questions. The questions, however, have little value if their answers are not carefully listened to. Often careful listening is more important to professional selling than talking. To establish rapport with a prospect, a salesperson should be sincerely interested in what the prospect is saying. This is particularly important in successfully handling objections. An effective sales presentation explains what a prospect is hearing, seeing, smelling, tasting, or feeling about the product or service being offered.

The best presentation gives the prospect total understanding in the shortest period of time. While the exact length of the presentation depends to a large extent on what is being sold, a good salesperson can effectively present some products or services in two or three minutes using 200 to 300 carefully chosen words. The average sales presentation lasts from 10 to 15 minutes, and those of a technical nature usually last longer. Rarely should even a technical sales presentation last longer than 30 to 40 minutes. Here are some basic steps for any sales presentation: give your presentation; listen, listen, listen; obtain the order; and leave. All this should be done in the shortest time possible.

Communication Involves Clear Writing. Because it takes a well-organized, smooth-flowing presentation to obtain a sale, it is often effective for the salesperson to write out the presentation using a detailed outline in either chart or graph form. An effective written communication uses words that create images. A presentation is most effective when image-producing words are used that give a prospect a clear mental picture of the selling points and how the product will be of benefit. These selling points need to be organized logically so that the salesperson can remember them and present them smoothly.

Communication Involves Clear Speaking. No matter how carefully planned the presentation, an oral presentation is usually only 30 percent effective in conveying an idea accurately. Both the salesperson and the prospect communicate using words. However, this is problematic because meaning does not exist in the specific words; rather, meaning comes from the significance assigned to the word based on each individual's experience, attitudes, and beliefs. It takes two people—a sender and a receiver—to communicate an idea. When there is no mutual understanding between the sender and the receiver, the message cannot usually be understood. The responsibility for facilitating mutual understanding lies with the salesperson (the sender), not the buyer (the receiver). A salesperson can ascertain whether a prospect clearly understands the message by communicating it and then asking that it to be repeated. Effective communication uses words, voice, body, face, and eyes. The best words are action words and illustrations that create images. A salesperson should speak clearly and positively at a steady pace, varying the pitch, tone, and speed while always conveying confidence and interest. A salesperson should always smile, letting his or her face exude happiness, confidence, and warmth. Maintaining eye contact transmits enthusiasm, interest, and sincerity.

Communication Involves Using Tools. Various communication tools can help stimulate the prospect's senses. These tools are particularly effective when the prospect participates in the presentation, such as in the demonstration of the product or service. Although the traditional sales aids, such as product samples or models, sales manuals, posters, handouts, and flip charts, should not be overlooked, a multitude of newer visual aids are available—VCRs, slide projectors, and portable computers are just a few. Regardless of the communication tool used, the most effective ones get the prospect involved to the greatest extent possible in the presentation itself.

CHAPTER SUMMARY

In order to improve the chances of making a sale, it is important to know how to approach a prospect and make an effective sales presentation. Before making the sales call, plan the sell by finding out pertinent information about the prospect and company; make a good first impression through your attitude and appearance; and determine the best approach to use. The approach methods include compliment, reference, sample, customer-benefit, dramatic, product, question, and introductory. A particular method should be selected based on the presentation method and needs of the buyer. Four common presentation methods are memorized, planned, needs satisfaction, and problem-solution. The presentation should move the prospect logically through the stages of attention, interest, desire, conviction, and action. Good approaches and presentations require effective communication skills, which require careful listening, clear writing, and clear speaking. Using communication tools to involve the prospect in the presentation can only enhance a sales presentation.

KEY TERMS

approach, p. 149

compliment approach, p. 151

creative imagery, p. 150

customer-benefit approach, p. 152

dramatic approach, p. 152

feature-advantage-benefit
approach, p. 154

introductory approach, p. 158

product approach, p. 152

question approach, p. 152

reference approach, p. 151

sample approach, p. 152

CHAPTER QUESTIONS

1. Under what conditions is it desirable to make an appointment before visiting a customer? When is it unnecessary to make this appointment?

2. Discuss why the first few seconds of the salesperson's contact with the prospect is so important.

3. Respond to a salesperson who dresses the way he or she wants to on a sales call because the salesperson believes that no one has the right to mandate what to wear.

4. Is it important for a salesperson to make a good impression on the prospect's subordinates? Discuss.

5. Studies have shown the need to increase the listening quotient of a prospect particularly when prospects tend to hear only about one-fourth of what is said. What can a salesperson do to increase the listening of the prospect so that more of the presentation is heard?

6. In many industrial sales, several individuals influence the purchase decision. You have just completed your sales presentation with an industrial prospect and believe you should contact other people in the company. Discuss how you would save the prospect and find out who else should be called on.

7. You are a sales representative of a nationally known maker of office supplies and have an appointment for your first call on the office manager of a large, very successful firm in the car industry. After a 15-minute wait, you are brought into the office where she appears businesslike and pressed for time. Discuss how you would approach this prospect and begin your presentation of your company's new writing implement.

8. You have just telephoned a prospect to make an appointment and have said to the secretary answering the telephone: "Mr. Bryce, please, Kelly Hughes calling." How would you respond to the secretary's question: "What do you wish to talk to Mr. Bryce about?" Then the secretary answers your response by saying, "Mr. Bryce is too busy to see you." How would you respond?

9. You are a sales representative for one of the major airlines. You have been given the responsibility of calling on business firms in Cleveland to get them to use your company's airfreight service to ship their goods. Outline the major selling points and benefits you would use in building your sales presentation.

10. Prepare a list of features and benefits to use in a presentation to high school students encouraging them to enroll in your college or university.

11. Some companies use a two-person selling team to present their products. Discuss the advantages and disadvantages of this selling approach and identify some selling situations where this approach would be particularly effective.

12. Develop a good stimulus statement for the following products and identify the expected response:

    a. A life insurance policy

    b. A $700 custom-made suit

    c. A new, energy-efficient foreign-made washing machine costing $1,000

    d. A $150,000 condominium in Orlando, Florida

NOTES

1. For further information, see Max Nichols, Family eclipses hall of fame honors for Ackerman. *Journal Record,* July 31, 1993, 1, 5.

2. For a discussion on the importance and characteristics of good appearance, see John T. Molloy, *Dress for success* (New York: Peter H. Weyden, 1975); John T. Molloy, *The women's dress for success* (Chicago: Follett, 1977); Suit may not be best way to top. *New York Times,* November 4, 1985, 1, D-4; and Dressing for success isn't what it used to be. *Business Week,* October 27, 1986, 142–143.

3. This approach is discussed in more detail in Robert F. Gwinner, Base theories in the formulation of sales strategies. *MSU Business Topics* (Autumn 1976), 37–44.

4. A discussion of dramatizing the approach and presentation can be found in Sherle Adams, Liven up that presentation. *Sales and Marketing Management,* August 16, 1982, 40–42.

5. For a discussion of some of the aspects of these steps, see Barton Weitz, Relationship between salesperson performance and understanding of customer decision process. *Journal of Marketing Research* (November 1978), 501–516.

SUGGESTED READINGS

Berman, Helen. Overcoming your fear. *Folio: The Magazine for Magazine Management,* October 1, 1991, 147–152.

> Salespeople must learn to overcome fears in order to present a more effective sales presentation. By taking small risks, they are able to achieve a higher gain. It is important for salespeople to know themselves and recognize their limitations. They do not have to go through this process alone, however; directors and publishers are available to assist them.

Epstein, David L. Developing sensitivity to ethnic/cultural distinctions. *Telemarketing* (July 1991), 76–79.

> Telemarketing has become an effective, cost-efficient approach to sales. Epstein examines the ethnic and cultural differences that can cause problems in telemarketing and provides training mechanisms to aid in sales presentations. Role playing, classroom study, on the job training, and support training through a mentor or buddy

system are a few methods that can help sales personnel to overcome miscommunication due to cultural differences.

Garner, Kenneth P. A proper sales pitch. *Graphic Arts Monthly* (July 1991), 95–97.

Sales presentations should follow an outlined approach. The purpose of the presentation is to interest the prospect in the proposed information. The sales representative should be confident that the information being presented applies directly to the customers' needs.

Kaplan, Michael. The secrets of super salespeople (that everyone can use). *Working Woman* (May 1990), 92–95, 129.

Developing a persuasive sales strategy is crucial in any form of sales presentation. Effective sales pitches are customized to their audience. The sales call should be informative rather than argumentative. Salespeople should be capable of change.

Lukaszlwski, James E., and Paul Ridgeway. To put your best foot forward, start by taking these 21 simple steps. *Sales and Marketing Management* (June 1990), 84–86.

An outline is given of 21 easy steps to successful sales calls. The key to an effective sales presentation is preparation. It is important to keep a quick pace and speak in specific terms. Sales representatives should attempt to make the presentation as exciting to the customer as possible.

LuPillot, Patricia. Touch the customer's bases—and sell. *American Salesman* (August 1991), 10–12.

Sales calls should be completed as quickly as possible, so as not to take added time away for the customer's job responsibilities. Salespeople should help their customers be more effective on the job, or no sales will be made. Salespeople can touch base with their clients most effectively by making their visits brief, leaving data behind for examination, and returning later to discuss any new information, if necessary.

Sherlin, Jack, and John Hanc. Board games. *Folio: The Magazine for Magazine Management* (January 1, 1992), 90–92.

Board presentation can be a useful tool to aid salespeople in promoting a weekly magazine. They can enhance the sales presentation without the use of slide projectors, VCRs, or any other electronic visual equipment. There are a few guidelines to remember when preparing a board presentation. The presentation should be clearly organized with a beginning, middle, and an end. The salesperson should use board presentations only when presenting a novel idea.

Stevens, Michael. Personal presence. *Marketing* (August 27, 1992), 24.

There are many programs available to help people learn to make more effective presentations. Most of these courses are available through business schools, management training centers, general training organizations, and specialist companies. These programs range from one-day basic courses to specific courses in radio and television techniques.

Chapter 8

The Selling Process—
Closing the Sale

OPENING SCENARIO

Sitting in her car outside a large retail liquor store, Katy Ksiezyk, salesperson for Dumas Makt., H.K., was considering the sales call on Jim Brown, the manager. She wanted this store to purchase and display 15 cases of the company's imported Hungarian wines. Several questions were bothering her: Would she be able to recognize any buying signals from Jim Brown? What form of trial close should she use? Should she have Jim try some of the red wine to taste the quality? Will her close be effective? If not, what close would be effective? What specific terms should be recorded on the advantages to purchase side of the T-account close? What problems will Jim pose that will make it difficult to close the sale?

Chapter Objectives

After reading this chapter, you should be able to

- Understand the essential points in closing the sale.
- Know how to determine when to ask for an order.
- Understand several closing techniques.

INTRODUCTION

Katy Ksiezyk should keep in mind that in concluding a presentation and closing a sale, it is important that her personality be a part of the selling process. According to Anita Roddick, founder and managing director (president) of the

Body Shop, "Passion persuades, more than intellectual debate, more than reasoning, more than strategy plans."[1] This passion has propelled the Body Shop into a highly successful international cosmetics company with a most unusual company philosophy. Anita Roddick believes that every company has the responsibility of giving something back not only to the stockholder and customers but to the community as well.

The passion and maverick outlook, which includes social change and antimaterialism, came naturally to Anita Roddick. As the third of four children of Italian immigrants who settled in West Sussex County, England, Anita soon learned what it meant to be different. After studying English and history at Bath College of Education, she took a job in the library at *the International Herald Tribune* in Paris. Following a job at the United States embassy in Geneva and traveling to exotic places, she returned to England and met her husband, Gordan Roddick, a Scottish poet with a kindred spirit. Following the couple's successful joint venture in a bed-and-breakfast and then a restaurant, Anita Roddick borrowed $6,000 and opened her first Body Shop in 1976 while her husband was exploring the Americas on horseback. In just 17 years, the Body Shop has grown to more than 900 stores worldwide with annual sales of $574 million and $34 million profit by selling natural products, opposing animal testing, and not spending any money on advertising.

The passion of the founder carries over to the company's many philanthropic programs. The best known is its Trade Not Aid Program where local communities around the globe grow ingredients and produce finished goods for the Body Shop; in return, the company provides employment and a source of income. All these benefits to society provided by the Body Shop make people feel good when buying products at the store.

As Katy Ksiezyk and Anita Roddick know, one of the most difficult tasks in the selling process is knowing when and how to ask for the order, or **closing the sale.** One successful salesperson commented, "I was making wonderful presentations for my previous company, but I was never able to ask for the order. In my new position, I learned how to close the sale and it has made me the leading salesperson in the district." Successful salespeople develop a basic instinct that aids them in sensing when and how to close and ask for an order with each prospect.

Unless a salesperson uses an effective and timely close, a sale rarely happens. Indeed, there are few individuals in any sales force who close effectively in every situation. It is usually the close that separates great salespeople from good ones. Salespeople who are good at closing spend significant time in preparing a sales call; have a strong desire to make the sale; are good listeners; do not accept "no" right away, and know to ask for the sale and then stop talking.

Preparation for the sales call enables salespeople to be good at closing.[2] These good-closing, high-performance salespeople take time to understand the industry, find out the characteristics of their customers, and pinpoint each customer's needs and benefits. With this understanding and a thorough knowledge of how the company's products produce the benefits the customer desires, good salespeople carefully plan several closing strategies for making a sale and look for opportunities to use the most appropriate one.

Individuals good at closing have a *desire* to close each and every sale. They are not satisfied with just giving a good presentation. They need the close to feel that they have done their job well. Each customer becomes a challenge. These high-performance salespeople understand that situations may occur when a sale in the future can be made but not during the present sales call.

Individuals good at closing are also good at **listening.** Perhaps one of the biggest problems in not being able to close well is not being able to listen well. Unless salespeople can listen carefully and hear opposing views and the strengths of various objections, it is almost impossible to develop the best answers for the objections and choose the best time and method to close.

Individuals good at closing *never accept the first "no."* When a customer says "no," good salespeople evaluate the objection behind the "no," and provide more information relevant to that objection. They will use a trial close (when appropriate) to ascertain whether the objection has been overcome and determine if there are any more objections. With each trial close, a salesperson is one step closer to a sale.

Finally, individuals good at closing know the importance of **asking for the sale** *and* then *being quiet* while waiting for an answer. After asking for the order, salespeople should say absolutely nothing. They know that every word spoken decreases the probability of making the sale. The prospect in turn realizes that he or she has to make a decision and respond to the close before the salesperson says anything else. While this time may seem interminable, particularly to the salesperson, rarely does the silence last more than 25 to 30 seconds. Every salesperson has the urge to talk to relieve the uncomfortable situation that becomes stronger the longer silence remains, but good salespeople overcome this urge. Talking to the prospect destroys the closing moment and does not allow the prospect to make a decision.

During this silent period, good salespeople say nothing, but they do project **positive nonverbal signs** to the prospect. They also mentally prepare responses to possible objections the customer might make. Then after the buyer says, "yes," good salespeople do not talk too much. Continuing the presentation at that time may provide information to change the prospect's decision. Once the prospect decides to buy, good salespeople finalize the details of the sale and leave.

CLOSING A SALE

In developing a good close, it is helpful to follow an individualized version of the following series of steps. Because a salesperson usually cannot be successful by just adopting another person's closing techniques, each salesperson should develop a customized procedure that is based on the customer's reaction. This helps a salesperson perfect a personal routine procedure, resulting in a better closing technique. The nine steps in this procedure are

1. Plan the sales call.
2. Understand and confirm the prospect's needs and desired benefits.
3. Make a clear presentation.
4. Listen and ascertain any underlying objection.
5. Try a trial close whenever warranted.
6. Ask for the order and then say nothing.
7. Always leave the door open for a future sale.
8. Be positive and confident.
9. Always be professional.

By following a customized version of these nine steps, a salesperson does not succumb to the temptation of thinking that closing is just one giant step. Following this method helps remove any seemingly mystical quality about closing. Closing is not tricky, nor is it a case of being able to employ just the right clever words. Closing results from knowing useful selling techniques and understanding the customer and the nature of the selling process.

By following this method, the close becomes a part of the presentation. Sometimes the prospect may actually provide a salesperson with the close by saying: "That sounds all right; I'll try your product." Although it seems obvious, some salespeople forget that prospects know the salesperson is there to sell them something. Depending on his or her level of interest and knowledge, the prospect may be well beyond the stage of the presentation and actually ready to make a decision very early in the selling process. Salespeople must realize this and capitalize on the opportunity when it arises.

TIMING THE CLOSE

One of the most frequently asked questions by a sales trainee is: "How do I know it's time to close? When should I attempt to close a sale?" This question is very difficult to answer because a prospect can be ready to buy at any point in the selling process. One prospect can be ready to buy early, at the approach stage; another will be ready only the day after the presentation. This wide variation requires that salespeople listen carefully and be very attentive to visual and verbal clues from the prospect. Remember, however, 80 percent of the time the close will logically follow the presentation as planned.

Buying Signals

During the selling process, prospects frequently give some sign of where they are in the mental process of deciding whether to buy. This **buying signal** refers to any visual or verbal cue indicating a readiness to buy. There are many buying signals that indicate a prospect is near the conviction stage of the buying process (see Table 8-1).

TABLE 8-1 Buying Signals Made by the Prospect

- Making a positive statement about the product
- Asking about the use, price, installation, or delivery of the product
- Asking the names of others who use the product
- Playing with a pen and order form
- Physically handling the product
- Changing voice tone to a more positive one
- Changing from a worried, defensive expression to a more happy, relaxed one
- Testing or trying the product

One of the best buying signals is when the prospect asks questions about price, installation, delivery, buying incentives, or others who use the product. This can take the form of such questions as: "How much is it?" "What is the earliest date of delivery for the first order?" "What support services do you provide?" "What is your company's return goods policy?" Questions such as these indicate that a trial close should be attempted.

In order to better understand a prospect's thoughts about the product as well as the prospect's needs, a salesperson can respond to a question with another question. If a prospect asks, "What is the price of the product?" the salesperson can respond, "In what quantity are you considering a purchase?" If a prospect asks, "How many would you suggest I order?" the salesperson can respond, "What is your average weekly purchase of a similar product?" or "What is your usual production run?" If a buyer asks, "When can you make delivery?" the salesperson can respond "When is the earliest delivery needed?" By answering a question with a question, a salesperson obtains additional information while measuring the interest level of the prospect. The more positive the response of the prospect, the higher his or her interest level in purchasing the product.

A second frequent buying signal is that the prospect relaxes and becomes more friendly. Once a prospect makes the internal decision to purchase the product, the pressure involved regarding purchasing is eliminated. This can become physically apparent before it is verbally expressed. The visible anxiety or concern on a prospect's face can change to a more happy, relaxed expression.

A third buying signal is that the prospect either asks who else is buying the product or asks for another person's opinion. When a prospect calls a colleague into the office for an opinion concerning the purchase, the buyer's interest level is high enough to attempt a trial close.

A fourth buying signal is that the prospect starts handling and carefully scrutinizing the product. This indicates that the prospect has more than a passing interest in the product and is indirectly asking for more information and reasons for purchasing the product. This warrants the salesperson to attempt a trial close, such as asking the prospect, "What do you think about . . . ?" Upon receiving a positive response to this question, the salesperson would move to close the sale.

TRIAL CLOSE

Verbal or nonverbal buying signals may be sent by the prospect anytime during the selling process. Once a buying signal is given, a salesperson should attempt a trial close. A **trial close** attempts to discover if the prospect is ready to buy and if the salesperson should attempt to close the sale. In beginning a trial close, a salesperson should emphasize the major selling points that address the prospect's needs. If a positive response to the trial close is received, then the salesperson can proceed directly to the close. If a negative response is received, then the salesperson must determine what the objections are, meet those objections, and attempt another trial close. This process is repeated until the prospect gives a positive response and the salesperson can move on to the close or until it is obvious that more trial closes will not bring about a positive response.

When no more trial closes are warranted, the salesperson should be professional and ask for another appointment in the future and leave. Regardless of whether a trial close is successful, at the very least it provides the salesperson with an assessment of the selling situation.

Forms of Trial Close

Trial closes can take on many forms. Here are some examples:

- "Would you be interested in comparing the lease versus buy options?"
- "Which model do you like best, Model 4000 or Model 8000?"
- "Would you be interested in purchasing the maintenance contract that goes with the product?"
- "Would you like to inspect the product more closely?"
- "Do you feel the product will do the job?"
- "In what quantities would you generally purchase the product?"

These and other trial closes will elicit various responses from the prospect. While some signs to attempt to close may emerge, signs of caution could also emerge. Signs of caution include

- The prospect requests more information.
- The prospect refuses to communicate with the salesperson.
- No positive response occurs.
- An interruption occurs that affects the prospect's positive state of mind.

If a more positive response occurs from a trial close, then the salesperson should move to the closing part of the selling process, using one of a variety of techniques.

CLOSING TECHNIQUES

A good salesperson knows that in order to close successfully, it is essential that the prospect's overall attitude is understood, as well as his or her responses to the presentation and trial close. This allows the salesperson to use the most appropriate closing technique.[3] Instead of asking prospects if they want to purchase the product, good salespeople select the appropriate closing technique for the prospect from the many available. Table 8-2 presents a list of alternative closing techniques, a few of which we elaborate on below.

TABLE 8-2 Alternative Closing Techniques

Closing Technique	Explanation
Asking for order	Make a direct or indirect request for the order.
Assumption close	Assume the decision to purchase has already been made to help compel the prospect to buy.
Attachment close	Leave the product for the prospect to use for a short time so that he or she can become familiar with it.
Compliment close	Close using compliments and praise of the prospect.
Contingent close	Have the prospect agree to buy if benefits promised can be demonstrated satisfactorily.
Continuous-yes close	Use a series of benefit questions the prospect must answer.
Last sale close	When nothing is working, ask prospect what it would take for a sale to occur right then, and if possible offer that.
Minor-points close	Obtain positive decisions from the prospect on minor points leading to acceptance and purchase of the product.
No-risk close	Agree to take the product back with total refund if it is not satisfactory.
Resistance close	Answer the objection by turning the problem into a benefit and then asking for the order.
Special deal close	Offer the prospect a one-time special offer to purchase.
Stimulus-response close	Ask a series of leading questions that require a yes answer, making it easier to say yes when asked for a purchase.
Success story close	Tell about a customer with a similar problem or need who had good results by purchasing the product.
Summary-of-benefits close	Summarize advantages and disadvantages of product before asking for order.
Supply close	Imply that supply is limited and opportunity to buy will not be available for much longer.
T-account close	Put advantages of purchasing and not purchasing side by side in a T-account format.
Turnover close	Turn the prospect over to another salesperson for closing.

Assumption Close

In the **assumption close,** the salesperson assumes that the prospect will purchase and indicates this feeling through comments and nonverbal actions: "Do you want the order delivered this Wednesday or Friday?" or "Will that be cash or charge?" or "Do you need any more than the amount indicated on the sales plan?" Nonverbal actions include getting out the credit-card machine, handing the prospect a pen and order form, or starting to wrap the product.

Although useful in any selling situation, the assumption close is particularly good for repeat orders where the salesperson has earned the confidence of the buyer to such an extent that the buyer almost always approves the salesperson's suggested order. When this situation exists, a closing comment could be, "This is the amount I believe you need to order this month."

Compliment Close

The **compliment close** is particularly useful for a prospect who is a self-named expert, has a big ego, or is in a bad mood. This type of prospect responds very favorably to compliments. Compliments help make the prospect listen and respond favorably.

All prospects appreciate a sincere appreciation of their better points. A salesperson needs to find out what is important to a prospect and then look for a way to make a compliment in that area as the sale is being closed. Most people can detect insincerity or an undeserved compliment, so it is important that only genuine compliments be used.

Choice Close

In the **choice close,** the prospect is asked to choose between two versions of the product, not whether to buy a single product. The prospect is not given the choice of buying or not buying but, rather, the choice of the product type or the amount. Examples of a choice close include: "Do you want the 4000 or 8000 version?" "Do you want three cases or four?" "Which do you prefer, the blue and yellow shirts or the blue pinstripe and red pinstripe shirts?"

If the prospect responds to this type of close by saying, "I'm not sure," then the salesperson knows the prospect is in the desire not the conviction stage and needs to hear about more product benefits. If the prospect likes both options but cannot make a decision, the salesperson can ask, "Is there something you're not quite sure about, Mr. Hughes?"

The choice close is one of the most effective and easy to use closing techniques. It provides a choice between two things, not a choice between something and nothing. When a choice is presented, the salesperson receives either an order or some objections that, if met successfully, can result in an order.

SELL!NG
THE FRONT LINES OF BUSINESS

Of Renovations and Revelations

Thomas Forbes

Gail B. Goodman, a graduate of Tufts University and a registered occupational therapist, was running the activities department at a prestigious rehabilitation facility. She had organized and been president of a chapter of her professional organization, published a paper, and spoken at a national conference of her peers. Then in 1980, at the age of 28, she found herself bored and fed up with the medical establishment. So she literally walked out on five years of career accomplishments.

To make ends meet, Goodman tended bar through the summer. Then she met Sam, an installer for an outfit that remodeled kitchens and refaced cabinets in Rockland County, N.Y. Sam told Goodman that she was a natural salesperson, and convinced her to apply for an open position at the FaceLifters Ltd. dealership where he worked. The owner of the dealership saw the same qualities Sam had and hired Goodman, despite her utter lack of selling experience. From October through December, Goodman went out on 25 calls, trying to convince people to spend up to $5,000 to reface their kitchens. She didn't make a single sale.

Goodman's husband, from whom she's now divorced, was a graduate student at the time, and Goodman was the family's sole breadwinner. But despite the support of her family and in-laws, she says, she became frustrated, even desperate, as sale after sale slipped away.

"Sam would come up to me and say, 'Gail, my kids can't eat,'" Goodman recalls. "I started to realize that the life of the salesperson is to have total responsibility for everybody's security. That if I wasn't selling kitchens, Sam wasn't getting paid to install them."

Goodman had always been an achiever, but for all her raw ability, she couldn't get prospects to sign contracts. And worst of all, she didn't have a clue about how to turn things around.

"My leads were perfect, and I was blowing every one of them," she says.

Goodman's boss brought in a local sales trainer (who happened to be a rabbi, too) to figure out what Goodman was doing wrong. Whatever advice the rabbi gave Goodman pales before the sage recommendation he provided her employer. "You're making a big mistake," he said, "by not sending her to Maurice."

Maurice F. Linden owned a successful FaceLifters Ltd. dealership in Pittsburgh. Whenever fellow dealers across the U.S. needed to break in a new salesman—and the sales force was entirely male except for Goodman—they would ship him to Linden, who conducted an intensive boot camp in a number of sales methods, including the one-call close (which Goodman defines as "beat 'em until they give you the order or you're thrown out").

Goodman went out on calls with different members of Linden's sales force from 9:00 in the morning until 9:00 at night. After that, she would return to the showroom for one-on-one sessions with the master. The first night, Linden handed Goodman a presentation book and asked her what she thought she should do from the moment she entered a prospect's house.

"After about three minutes he took the book away from me and he slammed it down," Goodman says. "He said, 'Okay, look, you've got to empty your head of everything you've been doing. You've got to be a blank slate and let me write on it.' "

If she asked Linden a question, says Goodman, she was told to shut up. Today, when she recalls those sessions, Goodman is quick to point out that Linden was a gentle and an entirely supportive teacher. But make no mistake: His schooling was rigorous. The program continued each day and night for four days. "I'd come back to the showroom at about 10:00 or 11:00, and he'd sit me down and start teaching me what I had watched all day," Goodman says.

Linden broke everything down, step by basic step. The first thing to say when the prospect answers the door, he told Goodman, is "hello." He then moved on to describe everything from when you

should walk over to the cabinets to how you should hold your hands when you turn toward your prospects.

"He staged me like an actor being directed in a play. He denied me everything but air and cigarettes. I felt sleep-deprived. I barely got enough to eat," Goodman says. She did not have a moment alone with her thoughts until she arrived at the airport for the trip home. Then, she says, all of a sudden, the information Linden had been stuffing into her gelled.

"It was the biggest 'aha!' of my life. It coagulated in my head like a sonic boom," she says. "All of the verbiage went away, and I got the essence of what a sale is." Linden's sales message seemed clear. "It's human interaction," Goodman says. "It's a purchase for a need to be fulfilled."

She had already intellectually understood the dynamics of a sale. Now, after her grueling training sessions with Linden, she intuitively understood the key principle of selling, which she now knows is called "need satisfaction."

"It stops being words. It starts to be an energy sensation," she says. "As a New Age person, you could say that you get to a new vibratory level. I don't know how else to describe it because it's non-verbal."

But this enlightenment was practical as well as mystical, and the payback was immediate. Goodman says that as soon as she returned home, she began to convert one in three kitchen leads into orders. In fact, she says, she has always made money selling since her airport epiphany.

Goodman went on to become Face-Lifters' first director of dealer operations, and later was promoted to vice president of training. In 1987 she left to start a company that marketed photographic business cards and postcards. Then, the following year, she made a career move that drew on all she had learned from Linden, and from her own years in sales.

Goodman opened Consul-Tel, a Rye, N.Y., telemarketing consulting company that trains direct-sales people in the financial-services industry. Goodman says she's selling her program constantly—although much of her business is by referral—which keeps her sharp and gives her credibility with the agents she trains. Her client list reads like a round-up of top insurance companies.

Linden remained a valued mentor in Goodman's early career. And she still uses his best advice with her trainees: Know your presentation backward and forward; practice it in front of a mirror without cracking up; and sell to your parents, keeping a straight face throughout.

There are some things that she does differently, however. "I became a very, very hard closer because that's what I was taught to do," Goodman says. "Only over the past few years, with the confidence of my experience, have I developed something more feminine."

"She has come quite a long way," says Linden, who is now developing sales and marketing systems for an insurance company that sells long-term-care health insurance. "I think the last few times that I've spoken to Gail, I've asked her questions."

In fact, the relationship has been one of give and take since Goodman's first trip to Pittsburgh. The night before she was to return home, even before the light bulb went off in her head, Goodman knew that she wanted to repay Linden. As an occupational therapist, Goodman says, she was trained to interpret people's personalities by watching them performing their routine activities. She had just spent four intense days with Linden's sales staff.

"She sat down and she gave me an overall view of every employee I had," Linden recalls. "Just picked up on their good points and their bad points. She was pretty much right on everybody."

For her part, Goodman credits her successful sales career to the "brutal" four days she spent with Linden in Pittsburgh more than a decade ago The reason is as basic as sheer survival.

"He was my lifeline," she says. "If I listened to this man, I made money; if I didn't listen, I didn't make money."

Reprinted with the permission of SELL!NG magazine.

Minor-Points Close

This closing technique has the prospect agreeing on progressively larger decisions by starting with minor points. For some buyers, a big purchase decision is difficult to make; it is much easier for this type of buyer to concede and agree on minor points. This closing technique is also useful for a prospect who is not in the mood to buy. In the **minor-points close,** the prospect is asked to make a decision concerning the product features, size, color, delivery date, warranty terms, payment terms, or size of order before being asked for the order itself. Some questions for the minor-points close include "Are you interested in the installment plan?" "Would you like your car to have a sun roof?" "Would you prefer the deluxe or regular model?" "Would you prefer delivery this week or next?"

The minor-points close can also be successfully used as a second close if the first one failed. In this case, the salesperson can get the prospect to agree first on minor points and then on the purchase.

Summary-of-Benefits Close

The most frequently used close is the **summary-of-benefits close,** where the salesperson concludes the presentation by summarizing the major advantages of the product's features and the benefits to the prospect. The summary-of-benefits close is particularly useful when the salesperson needs a straightforward close that does not need to take into account any unique characteristics of the prospect, as for consumer products and industrial products.

If a salesperson knows that the buyer likes the profit margin, 90-day payment terms, and two-day delivery schedule, the close could be: "Ms. Hernandez, you have indicated that you like the profit margin, the 90-day payment terms, and the prompt delivery schedule of this product. These features have allowed other customers just like you to make a lot of money from selling this product. I can have an initial order of 10 cases here by next Monday so you can start making money for your store."

Continuous-Yes Close

The **continuous-yes close** uses benefit questions that the prospect answers instead of summarizing product benefits, as in the summary close. In this close, the salesperson has identified the benefits important to the customer and puts these in question form before asking for the order. For example, if a prospect likes the quality, profit margin, and merchandising offer, a salesperson can develop the following scenario:

Salesperson:	Ms. Kelly, you said you really like the quality of the product, correct?
Kelly:	Yes that's true.
Salesperson:	And you like the high profit margin on the product?
Kelly:	Yes, I do indeed.
Salesperson:	You also said you like the merchandising allowance offer that is now in place?
Kelly:	That's right.

Salesperson: Ms. Kelly, since you like the quality of the product, the profit margin, and the merchandising allowance offer that will only be in effect for the next few weeks, you should be ordering . . .

Using a series of questions to have the respondent continuously respond favorably to the benefits of the product puts the prospect in a positive frame of mind for also responding positively to the request for purchasing the product.

Supply Close

The **supply close** applies some pressure on the prospect to buy now and not delay. The salesperson indicates that so many people are buying the product that it may not be available at a later date or, if it is available, it will be only in a smaller quantity than the prospect needs. The salesperson should take great care to use this closing technique only when supply problems are almost sure to occur. Although this approach can reflect the realities of the buying situation, it can bring about questionable feelings in the prospect, particularly when the sincerity of the salesperson and the supply problems are not apparent. And, if the supply problems do not occur, the ethics of the salesperson can be questioned by the prospect, making it very difficult to establish a relationship and make future sales. This closing technique is particularly good when extraneous factors such as a strike, bad weather, transportation problems, price increase, or government-imposed quotas are known to the prospect. Some examples of this closing technique are

- "Mr. Donaldson, this machine will increase in price by 10 percent next week. Can I place the order today, so you can avoid this announced price increase?"
- "This has really been a fast-moving item this month, and I'm not sure there is any left to sell you, Chris. I'll have to check availability once I have your order."
- "Since it appears a rail strike is going to occur next week, Dave, I suggest you order today to ensure delivery before the strike starts."
- "Unless something unusual happens, Ms. Kale, it looks like the union will go on strike next week, causing some severe problems in supply as well as delivery."

T-Account Close

The **T-account close** is based on the mental process each prospect goes through in making a purchasing decision. In this technique the advantages and disadvantages of buying the product are enumerated on either side of a line drawn down the center of a piece of paper—a T-account. All the pros for buying the product are put on one side of the line and all the cons are put on the other side. This simulates the process the prospect actually goes through in making a purchase decision—weighing the pros against the cons.

A salesperson can draw a large T on a sheet of paper placing a "To Buy" on the left-hand side and "Not to Buy" on the right-hand side. The salesperson then reviews the presentation with the prospect, listing the preferred product features, advantages, and benefits on the left-hand side of the T and all the negative points on the right-hand side. With such an individualized list, the salesperson helps the prospect to see more easily how the benefits of purchasing the product outweigh the negative aspects.

For example, if during the presentation the prospect found that the quality of the product, the speed of delivery, and the profit margin were good but the terms of payment not favorable, the T-account developed by the salesperson would be

To Buy	Not to Buy
Quality product Fast delivery Good margins	Poor payment terms

Some salespeople prefer to discuss the reasons not to buy first and prefer that the "Not to Buy" column is on the left and the "To Buy" column is on the right, allowing the presentation to end on the positive side. Other salespeople modify the T-account approach to only one column. Feeling that it is better not to remind the prospect about any negative reasons for not buying, they use only one column, to list the reasons to buy. The T-account or modified T-account is a very good closing technique because it closes along the same lines as the prospect is thinking—weighing the positive and negative points of the purchase.

This technique is also very useful as a backup close if an earlier closing technique did not end in a sale. There is nothing better than letting the prospect air the negative aspects and even record them on paper, as in the T-account. This allows the objections to be put in proper perspective in light of the benefits: in some cases, the objections may even disappear.

CLOSING DIFFICULTIES

Even though closing a sale should be one of the easier steps in the selling process, it can be the most difficult for many salespeople. Instead of viewing the close as a method for solidifying the details of the purchase agreement, these salespeople see the close as something the prospect views negatively. They forget that for a product that meets the needs of the prospect, the close establishes the method whereby the prospect can obtain this needed product. Several difficulties are encountered in closing the sale, however.

First, salespeople often make their own determination, sometimes before the selling process even begins, that the prospect does not need the product being offered. Guided by this feeling, they find it difficult to ask the prospect to make a purchase. These salespeople should remember that they are not in a position to make such a decision; it is the prospect's decision, not theirs, and the prospect's responsibility to purchase or not to purchase the product.[4]

Second, some salespeople fail to do their homework on the prospect's profile and benefits. This lack of effort usually results in a very poor sales presentation; when this occurs, the salesperson rarely has a good opportunity to easily close the sale by asking for a purchase.

Finally, some salespeople fail to close because of a lack of self-confidence. Sometimes this reflects previous failures in closing.

Number of Times to Close

A question that frequently arises when difficulties in closing are discussed is, "How many times should I close?" While there is no magic number for the upper limit, each salesperson should remember that he or she was hired to call on customers and prospects and sell the company's products. In order to accomplish this objective, multiple closes are in order. Once a trial close is made, salespeople need to determine and meet objections and attempt another trial close until a positive response occurs and a close can be done. Whereas courtesy and common sense should be used to determine the appropriate number of closes in a particular situation, usually three to five well-executed closes can be considered a minimum. This number usually will not offend the buyer if they are professionally done.

Closing After "No"

Closing after being rejected on the first attempt is one of the most difficult parts of closing.[5] But it is a very rare situation that a salesperson should stop closing after the first no. A salesperson must be able to ask a prospect to place an order even if the prospect has already said no, is hostile, or is in a bad mood. The job of the salesperson is to sell the company's products to established customers and to prospective customers.

CHAPTER SUMMARY

One of the most difficult stages in the selling process is closing the sale. Salespeople who are good at closing spend significant time in preparing a sales call; have a strong desire to make the sale; are good listeners; do not accept "no" right away; and know when to stop talking. There are nine steps in the closing procedure that salespeople should individualize to suit a particular situation. The time to make the close is when the salesperson recognizes buying signals from the prospect. Such signals include asking about price or delivery, becoming more relaxed and friendly, or asking for another person's opinion. A trial close attempts to discover if the prospect is ready to buy. Many closing techniques can be used, depending on the salesperson's assessment of the selling situation. These closing techniques include assumption, compliment, continuous-yes, choice, minor-points, summary-of-benefits, supply, and T-account. The chapter concludes with a discussion of the reasons for the difficulties in asking for the purchase, as well as the number of time this should be done with a particular prospect.

KEY TERMS

asking for the sale, p. 173
assumption close, p. 178
buying signal, p. 174
choice close, p. 178
closing the sale, p. 172
compliment close, p. 178
continuous-yes close, p. 182

listening, p. 173
minor-points close, p. 181
positive nonverbal sign, p. 173
summary-of-benefits close, p. 182
supply close, p. 183
T-account close, p. 183
trial close, p. 176

CHAPTER QUESTIONS

1. Comment on the following statement: The most successful salespeople are those who close sales long after they have heard "no" several times.

2. A sales representative for a large industrial machine that controls the output of plastic extrusion feels that he always needs to concentrate on timing the request for the prospect's signature on the order throughout the sales presentation. Comment on whether this is good selling, as well as on the strengths and weaknesses of the approach.

3. If the sale cannot be made, a good salesperson at least attempts to leave the door open for a future sales call. Discuss ways a salesperson can do this.

4. You are selling office duplicating equipment and receive the following comment after making what you believe was a good presentation: "This does sound interesting and I'll probably buy your product. I just need some time to think it over." Develop two to three responses to this comment in order to close the sale.

5. Comment on the following statement and its importance in sales: When prospects say no, they are saying no to the proposal, not to the salesperson personally.

6. Comment on the appropriateness of the following close: "Bob, our notepads are the best-selling ones in the world. With the present display and advertising allowances, you really can't go wrong. Let's place an order now."

7. You are a retail clerk selling a very nice twelve-gauge shotgun. After your great presentation, the prospect says, "I would like to buy it, but I need to be able to pay for it in 60 days without paying any interest or carrying charges." Your company policy prohibits this, so what would you say in return?

8. Comment on the importance of a trial close and its use. Are there times when it is better not to use a trial close but, instead, wait until the prospect seems ready to make a decision before attempting to close? Illustrate with a specific example.

9. One salesperson always follows the rule: "Tell prospects what you are going to tell them; tell them; and then tell them what you told them." Comment on the validity of this rule and the reasons for your thinking. Illustrate your answer.

10. You are going to sell vitamins and supplements door to door while attending college. The company asks that you prepare six different closing routines. Develop the routines and select the two you think would work best.

NOTES

1. Francis Lear, Lunch—Francis Lear meets with entrepreneur Anita Roddick. *Lear's*, August 1993, 14.
2. See Mark Hanan, The trick is to close by opening. *Sales and Marketing Management*, September 9, 1985, 157–158.
3. See Alan N. Schoonmaker and Dougles B. Lind, One custom-made close coming up. *Sales and Marketing Management*, June 13, 1977, 6.
4. See Mark Hanan, When your salespeople get a shot at the top man, don't let them get shot down. *Sales and Marketing Management*, July 5, 1982, 102–114.
5. See E. Roy Bond, What to do about that lost sale. *Sales and Marketing Management*, April 2, 1984, 19.

SUGGESTED READINGS

Ballow, James A. Closing and handling objections. *Life and Health Insurance Sales* (October 1990), 42–44.

> Insurance agents find that the assumed consent close and the medical close are effective closing techniques. In the assumed consent close, the agent begins filling out the application before the client has given a definite answer. The medical close is one in which the agent refers to the client's medical files.

Bermen, Helen. Basic closing techniques. *Folio: The Magazine for Magazine Management* (May 1990), 131–133.

> An overview of eight of the most effective advertising sales closes. The direct request close is the easiest of all techniques. The assumptive close is one in which the agent assumes the client has agreed to do business. In the physical action close, the agent initiates the close by having the prospect complete the sale through a physical action, such as signing the contract.

Eight steps to close more sales. *Folio: The Magazine for Magazine Management* (November 1988), 227–232.

> The three initial steps of the sales call are the introduction, opening statement of benefits, and qualification and fact finding. These steps should create interest in prospects and prepare them for the closing techniques. The final step is a strong follow-through, in which the agent reinforces the sale and lays the ground for future business.

Tadjer, Rivka. Closing when you open: Clinching sales from the start. *Life Association News* (December 1989), 78–83.

> Life insurance agents rely on a trust relationship with clients. This relationship should develop from the initial visit. The confidence that clients feel in their agents will make closing sales simple and fast.

Test, Alan. The old ways still work. *American Salesman* (September 1992), 18–19, 22.

> The two most important factors that contribute to a successful sale are sales technique and the ability to close. The number of sales made have gone down in recent years due to the lack of motivation of salespeople. Company salaries are high and, therefore, salespeople have no incentive to make sales. Companies should set minimum goals for their salespeople to encourage them to succeed. They should make their salespeople learn sales techniques, in order to increase sales performance.

Timing the close. *Folio: The Magazine for Magazine Management* (November 1989), 197–200.

> The key to an effective advertising salesperson is timing the close. The agent should get the prospect in a buying mood. The most important point to keep in mind when making the close is the client's interest. A close should be made only when the prospect is ready. Clients' interest can be measured by the questions they ask and their enthusiasm or interest during the presentation.

Training agency salespeople #8—Closing: Techniques that get the orders. *Agency Sales Magazine* (January 1992), 38–41.

> Effective salespeople do not make only one close at the end of the presentation, but they attempt trial closes throughout. A negative response to a trial close is not the final answer, and the salesperson should continue with the presentation. There are several good points during the presentation to attempt a trial close. After an important point has been made or after an agent has overcome an objection are key times to attempt a trial close. If a closing techniques does not seem to be particularly effective with a customer, then another method should be developed to fit the individual case.

Chapter 9

The Selling Process—
Handling Objections

OPENING SCENARIO

Katy Ksiezyk pushed the can of root beer aside. She had better stop daydreaming and start planning for her sales calls tomorrow. She was calling on some of her most important, yet most difficult, customers. On a previous call two weeks ago, Tom Curly, owner/manager of Ranch Acres, one of her largest customers, was particularly hard to deal with. He had raised some objections to carrying Dumas Makt., H.K.'s new line of Hungarian rosé wines, and she had not been able to handle them successfully. This sales call would be different, as Katy was considering which method she would use to overcome the anticipated objections. Given Ranch Acres' customer base and reputation, Katy knew that once she overcame Tom's objections, the rosé wine would sell. If she could only remember the various techniques for handling objections taught by her college professor of personal selling and sales management just two years ago. Why hadn't she paid more attention that day? Sometimes her daydreaming caused problems.

Chapter Objectives

After reading this chapter, you should be able to

- Discuss general guidelines for dealing with objections.
- Use questions to obtain a better understanding of the objections being raised.
- Know how to use various methods for dealing with objections.

INTRODUCTION

Handling objections is nothing new for Dan and Tim Price, the inventors and entrepreneurs operating the radically new, yet relatively simple concept of sending digitized popular tunes over telephone lines as gifts for all occasions.[1] The Send-A-Song Corporation was born from the brothers' enjoying the musical messages left on their answering machine by their younger sister, Eileen, whenever there was something to commiserate or celebrate. The lyrics expressed their feelings so adequately that Tim Price, a computer engineer with Westinghouse, decided to computerize the singing-message concept by converging computers with new voice-processing technology.

In early 1990, Tim began developing the software to digitize and store popular recordings. By Christmas of that year, a prototype had been developed that allowed his friends to send songs to their friends. The automated network had an inventory of 125 songs, such as Bing Crosby's "Happy Birthday to You" and Billy Joel's "Just the Way You Are." While the initial sound was good, evoking an almost visceral response, particularly if a strong emotional tie was present, the sound became even sharper with further refinement, and a company was born in spite of all the obstacles and objections.

Rarely does a selling situation not involve handling some questions and objections from the prospect regardless of the quality of the product or service being offered or the capability of the salesperson. The fourth stage in the selling process, handling objections, is one of the most difficult tasks in sales.

GENERAL GUIDELINES

Regardless of what method a salesperson uses to deal with objections, rarely can a salesperson ignore any objection raised.[2] In dealing with **objections,** some general guidelines should be followed.

1. The salesperson should never respond to an objection quickly. Certainly the objection needs to be addressed, but the salesperson should always pause and reflect in order to make sure the objection is clearly understood before responding. Also, if a response is too quick, the prospect may feel pressured.

2. The salesperson should never provide too much information or overanswer. Some salespeople have a tendency to attach too much meaning to an objection; in responding to an objection, the salesperson can confuse the prospect by providing too much information. This can have a negative effect by giving the prospect information overload. After handling an objection, the salesperson should move on to other positive elements in the sales presentation and not dwell on the objection. Always remember that a prospect buys because of the benefits of the product, not because of the salesperson's skills in handling objections.

3. A salesperson should actually welcome a prospect's objections, as often only a major objection stands between the salesperson and a successful close. Prospects who don't say anything during a presentation and those who always seem to agree with the salesperson may be hiding their true feelings and be very difficult sales. This does not mean that a salesperson should try to create an objection that would cause a sale to be lost. Rather, a salesperson should learn to welcome and be able to deal satisfactorily with a valid objection.

4. A salesperson should never guess or present wrong information in response to an objection. If a salesperson does not know the answer to the objection, he or she should promise to get back with the correct information in a specified period and then do so.

5. The salesperson should not argue about a prospect's objection, and an endless discussion of an objection should always be avoided. A salesperson should not set the stage for an argument by responding to an objection with "no." Also, the word "objection" should never be used by a salesperson; instead, the objection should be referred to as an "interesting point" or a "question." The salesperson should also remember that some objections are not answerable. Even the best product may not have all the advantages desired by the prospect, and even the best answer to an objection may not be enough. When an objection cannot be answered satisfactorily, the salesperson should move on to another positive point about the product by saying, "I perfectly understand your point Ms. Skyrmes and I have tried to explain it the best I can. There is something else I have not had the opportunity to mention about the product."

6. The salesperson should never display doubts about his or her response to an objection by acting as if the objection has not been completely answered. At all costs, the salesperson should avoid saying, "Does that answer your objection completely?" This comment casts further doubt and may even elicit a "no" response or more objections. If the objection has not been completely satisfied, a genuinely interested prospect will say so.

THE USE OF QUESTIONS

The proper questioning of a prospect is usually necessary in selling. By asking questions, a salesperson develops two-way communication with the prospect, thereby increasing the prospect's participation while obtaining valuable information. The only questions that should be asked are those that will help make the sale and that a prospect is willing and able to answer. Questions should be carefully worded and used sparingly.[3] Questions are very useful in ascertaining the relative importance of objections and even the most important objection being raised. This allows the salesperson to focus on the most important areas. There are four basic categories of questions that can be used: direct, open-ended, rephrasing, and redirected.

Direct (Close-Ended) Questions

The *direct,* or *close-ended, question* can be answered with very few words, frequently a simple yes or no. This type of question is particularly useful in moving a prospect forward in a specific, well-defined area. Some examples of this use are "Mr. Bryee, are you interested in making extra money on some vacant floor space in your store?" or "Making additional revenues is very important today in a retail store, isn't it?" A yes answer can be anticipated from both these questions, helping the salesperson to focus on the topic desired—the use of floor space to make additional revenues.

A salesperson must be careful not to use a direct negative question; that is, a question which completely cuts off the conversation. The classic negative question is one used far too often in retail selling: "May I help you?" The usual reply of "No, I am just looking," cuts the salesperson off from easily and logically continuing the conversation.

Besides yes-no direct questions, other types of direct questions ask such things as "how many?" or "what kind?" These types of direct questions ask for a short, limited answer from the prospect: "How many 12-ounce packages does your store sell in an average week?" or "What kind of delivery schedule do you prefer?"

Even though valuable, direct questions give very little feedback because the answers do not provide a great deal of information. In determining the needs and problems of the prospect, more information is usually needed. This information can often be best obtained through the use of open-ended questions.

Open-Ended Questions

More information and two-way communication can be obtained through *open-ended questions.* These can take the form of one-word questions, such as "Oh?" or "Really?" with the tone of voice being raised so that the prospect is prompted to continue talking. Other useful open-end questions can be created by beginning the question with one of six words: who, what, where, when, why, and how. Here are some examples:

- Who usually purchases this product?
- What features are you looking for in a product in this category?
- Where will you display the product?
- When will you need the product delivered?
- Why don't you like to use promotional allowances?
- How frequently will you purchase this product?

Through the use of open-ended questions, a salesperson can obtain more information, leave the situation open for more discussion of what is really on the prospect's mind, and give the prospect the sense of participating in the sales call.

Rephrasing Questions

Rephrasing questions are particularly helpful in getting a clearer understanding of what the prospect means. Care must be taken to ask rephrasing questions in a sincere, nonaggressive way. When a prospect objects to the price of an item, a salesperson could say: "Mr. Dalton, are you saying that price is the only thing you are interested in?"

In another situation the salesperson could use the following rephrasing question: "Then, Ms. O'Cinneida, what you are saying is if I can provide some introductory promotional allowance you would be interested in purchasing 10 cases of this product?" If the prospect answers yes to this question, the salesperson can work out the specifics of the introductory promotional allowance and close the sale. If the prospect answers no, then the salesperson should ask further questions to try to determine the prospect's real reason for not wanting to buy.

Redirected Questions

The final type of question, the *redirected question,* is used to redirect the prospect's attention to some previous area of agreement. By focusing attention on areas of mutual agreement, this approach facilitates handling objections by emphasizing some positive aspects of the meeting. The objection can then be dealt with from a more favorable positive perspective.

For example, when the prospect says, "There is really no reason for us to further discuss my purchasing this product. We are very satisfied with our present supplier," a salesperson could use redirected questions by saying: "Mr. Szirmai, we agreed that it is important to you and your company to have suppliers that can help reduce your costs and increase your sales. Would you not agree that you continually need to find new ways to reduce your costs and increase your company's sales in this particular market?" This redirected question moves the conversation from a negative dead-end position to a positive or neutral position and reestablishes the possibility for positive communication.

In order to use successfully a redirect or any of the other three types of questions, the salesperson must listen carefully to the prospect. Partly because of the nature of their profession, many salespeople are so used to talking and presenting that they forget to listen to what the prospect says. In fact, many salespeople do not know how to listen. And, anyone, particularly a prospect, appreciates a good listener. A salesperson who is a good listener is viewed as being interested in the prospect and his or her situation and being an individual who truly wants to help. Always remember when using questions to handle objections that a salesperson needs to know the answer before developing the question that should be asked to obtain that answer.

DEALING WITH OBJECTIONS

Even though objections can make selling more difficult, they should also be viewed as a sign of interest. In one sense, objections are an indirect way of asking for more information.[4] To avoid the risk of making a mistake or reducing his or her "purchase dissonance," the prospect raises different objections. **Purchase dissonance**—the concern a prospect has about making the purchase—can often be lessened or eliminated by providing more information and increasing the confidence level of the prospect. An example of this type of objection is "This packaging does not appear to be very strong. The product will probably leak in a very short time and cause me even more problems in having to clean the display case." This question indicates that the prospect is looking for more information and assurance from the salesperson that the product's packaging is strong. The salesperson should be able to overcome this purchase dissonance by describing the strength, quality, and sealing capability of the packaging.

Very often an objection is a stalling device or a way for the prospect to get out of the situation and not have to make a decision. When a prospect says that he or she wants to talk it over with others in the company or that the company cannot afford to buy now, this may be a valid reason. Often, however, this indicates that the prospect is experiencing too much dissonance or purchase anxiety to make the purchase decision right then. When this is the case, the salesperson must offer risk-reducing benefits or lose the sale. **Risk-reducing benefits** are those features of the product that help assure the prospect that he or she is making the right decision in buying the product.

Several successful methods for reducing the purchase risk and handling objections are the boomerang method, counterbalance method, denial method, indirect denial method, failure-to-hear method, and the question method.

Boomerang Method

When using the **boomerang method,** the salesperson attempts to turn the objection into a reason for buying, being careful to avoid making the prospect look foolish or ignorant for having raised the objection. If a prospect says, "It is not worth taking the space from the aisle for your point of purchase display," the salesperson can respond, "Ms. Kitchin, you said you were concerned about not obtaining enough sales and profits from your existing store. This is an opportunity for you to earn $24.00 for just displaying 12 cases of the product for three days using only a space of 2 feet by 4 feet. This will impact your profit per square foot and still leave ample room for shoppers." As in this example, the prospect must never be made to feel stupid. Neither should the salesperson seem to be condescending.

SELL!NG

THE FRONT LINES OF BUSINESS

Revving Up for Rejection

Francy Blackwood

In the normal scheme of things, a sales call is an effort to move a prospect from apathy to purchase. But John Fuhrman has an even longer haul—all the way from *aversion* to purchase. In his line of sales, apathy would be progress. "We're *shooting* for apathy," he quips. Fuhrman, 37, works for Universal Underwriters, an Overland Park, Kan., firm that sells a broad range of insurance products for cars, including vehicle service contracts (better known as extended warranties). Problem is, most consumers think such prepaid plans are bad news. The press has panned them as overpriced and overrated. Worse yet, says Fuhrman, "any product associated with an auto dealership is looked at by the media as a rip-off."

Fuhrman's dealer customers know extended warranties are a tough sell, which tends to dampen their enthusiasm for his product. Plus, Fuhrman competes with automakers, who also offer service contracts, and, in many cases, dealers "are under pressure to give the factory their business," he says. In other words, a Ford dealer feels obliged to buy extended warranties from Ford. Indeed, the typical prospect dismisses Fuhrman's plan because "it's not from the factory." His response: "If we could prove our coverage is as good or better than the factory's and that we will pay you more per repair, then would you see the benefit?"

Sometimes the real objection is rooted in a bad experience. "We had a plan from another company, and we had problems with claims," the prospect says. Fuhrman counters that one with testimonials. But he doesn't make sales calls armed with a lengthy client list. Instead, he contacts a well-respected local dealer who's a satisfied Universal customer and asks him to call the reluctant prospect.

Fuhrman's trump card is Universal's training program. "We're willing to come in and pay for sales training for the dealership, and no other company will do that," he says. In the face of entrenched consumer resistance to extended warranties, sales training is a big draw—and a big part of Fuhrman's job. As a regional administrator based in Bedford, N.H., he helps Universal account executives sell plans to car dealers in Maine, New Hampshire, and Vermont. But he also spends a good deal of time training the dealers to sell extended warranties to customers who are downright disinclined to buy. "I teach people to fall in love with rejection. The quicker you get the customer to say no, the closer you are to the sale."

With this product, it doesn't take long to get a prospect to say no. The "call" begins immediately after the sale of a new car, when the customer is already frazzled. "He's tired," says Fuhrman. "The last thing he wants is to get sold again."

The salesperson broaches the subject gently by reviewing the factory warranty and pointing out what it doesn't cover. Why not purchase an extended warranty, he suggests. The classic customer response is, "No. *Consumer Reports* says they're a bad idea."

Instinct might dictate a point-by-point rebuttal of *Consumer Reports,* and Fuhrman has plenty of ammunition to counter negative press. But first, he says, the salesperson should come back with, "Suppose *Consumer Reports* said it was a good idea. Then could you see the benefit?" The point is to test the veracity of the objection. "Salespeople often make a mistake by spending an hour defending their position against a bogus objection," Fuhrman says.

If the customer says an endorsement by *Consumer Reports* would indeed sway him, the salesperson knows the objection is real. Even then, it's better not to challenge the merits of the consumer bible.

"This is nonconfrontational selling," says Fuhrman. "You can't put customers on the defensive, because they're very good at defending. If you try to defend your position, and the customer tries to defend his, you'll lose in the tie. Anything that involves defense is a conflict, and you don't want conflict."

Instead, he advises, make an ally of the media authority. "Say, '*Consumer Reports* made some very good points, and that's why we picked this company to provide our service contracts. For example, *Consumer Reports* said there's no wear-and-tear coverage in extended warranties, but this contract covers wear and tear.'"

If the customer says even glowing press reviews wouldn't sell him on the benefits of a service contract, the salesperson should ask why. "I had one and it never covered anything," the prospect might respond. That's a pretty sweeping indictment, says Fuhrman. "You have to find out exactly what it didn't cover." Often it's something minor, like a fan belt. That's an easy one, says Fuhrman: "Say, 'I'll give you an extra fan belt to keep in your car.'"

The point is to determine the precise objection, so you can establish the value of the product in terms that are meaningful to that customer. In the case of an extended warranty, Fuhrman might point out that the contract is transferable with the sale of the car, that it's good throughout the U.S. and Canada, or that the customer qualifies for a rental car while his vehicle is in the shop.

Extended warranties cost anywhere from several hundred to several thousand dollars, depending on the plan and the car. Success rates vary, but the average dealer sells the contracts to 45 percent to 50 percent of his customers. Dealerships commonly pay a commission on service contracts, but the value of selling the plans goes beyond dollars and cents, according to Fuhrman. "People who buy service contracts report the highest dealer-satisfaction ratings in the country," an important factor in generating the repeat business and referrals that are the bread and butter of auto sales.

Even when a prospect is averse rather than apathetic, "there are only two reasons somebody doesn't want something," says Fuhrman. "They think it doesn't solve their problem, or they don't realize they have a problem." Either way, the sooner they say no, the closer you are to pinpointing the objection—and responding with appropriate features and benefits.

"If you handle objections deftly," he adds, "the customer will always tell you what you need to close the deal." His advice: "Throw the first objection away. If the customer goes to the trash and brings it back, it's real." If the first objection isn't valid, the second will be. "Customers can't lie twice. The next objection out of their mouths is the real one."

Fuhrman learned the value of "no" in the trenches. Before joining Universal Underwriters last year, he was a salesman and sales manager at auto dealerships. As a manager, he noticed that his salespeople had far too many prospects in limbo. "If customers didn't say no, they became 'pending,'" says Fuhrman. So he made an offbeat proposal, offering $50 to the salesperson who got a firm no from the greatest number of pending prospects. His sales force ended up making 12 appointments and selling eight cars.

Asks Fuhrman, "What makes the difference between earning $25,000 and $100,000 per year? If you surveyed the most successful salespeople, you would discover the extra $75,000 comes from a passion for rejection and a love of the word 'no.'"

Reprinted with the permission of SELL!NG magazine.

Counterbalance Method

In the **counterbalance method,** an objection that cannot be denied is countered by citing an even more important benefit in making the purchase. One of the most difficult problems for a salesperson is trying to overcome a valid objection. When a valid objection is raised, a salesperson should counter it by developing a positive benefit that the objected feature has. It is usually a good idea (unless the objection raised is blatantly baseless, when the denial method should be used) to try to reduce the size of an objection for the prospect rather than overcome it totally. Some prospect's objections are a result of deeply rooted convictions, and trying to overcome these objections entirely could antagonize the prospect and make the salesperson lose credibility. If a prospect says, "This computer clone is very difficult to access for repair," the salesperson could comment: "You're right, Mr. Dalton, it is difficult to access. The company designed it that way to keep unauthorized and untrained personnel from tampering with the machine. Other companies such as yours have found that this feature has significantly reduced repairs by making it difficult for unauthorized people to attempt to repair or modify the computer."

Denial Method

There may be times when a prospect has incorrect information about the company or its products that are hindering the sale. This is the time to use the **denial method.** When the salesperson is absolutely sure that the prospect's idea is completely wrong and that without this being stated no sale would occur, then there is no alternative but to deny the wrong idea politely and firmly. Whenever possible, supportive data should be furnished, then or at a later date, to confirm the accuracy of the denial. If a prospect says, "I would consider buying something from your company but I understand your company is near bankruptcy," the salesperson could respond by stating: "Yes, Mr. Donaldson, I have heard that rumor too, and the company is trying to find out how the rumor got started. It is definitely not true. Our company had one of its best years ever last year, and I would be glad to show you the company's year-end and last quarter reports."

Indirect Denial Method

The **indirect denial method** is useful when the comment of the prospect cannot be directly refuted. This method, also called the *"yes, but"* method, has the salesperson agreeing with the prospect's comments and then immediately following with a disclaimer. When a prospect comments, "I understand your company's cars are known for having a high recall rate," the salesperson could respond using the indirect method by saying, "Yes, Mr. Lopez, we did have the problem for several years in earlier models, but in the last few years our company has spent over $500 million to correct the situation. The result has been that we have had virtually no car recalls in the last two model years."

Failure-to-Hear Method

While a salesperson should rarely ignore any objection, situations may occur when that may be the best course of action—the **failure-to-hear method.** If an objection is so absurd that it is apparent the prospect really does not believe it or that it is such a low-priority objection that it will not hinder the sale, sometimes it is better just to pretend not to hear the objection than to create the possibility of a direct confrontation. This method should rarely be employed and only by salespeople who are good at carefully listening to everything a prospect mentions, including the prospect's tone of voice, as well as observing the prospects' body language.[5] Even a very minor objection not addressed can hinder a sale.

Question Method

As discussed earlier in this chapter, asking a question is particularly useful in clarifying or handling a prospect's objection. By using the **question method** in response to an objection, a salesperson puts the ball back in the prospect's court, causing the prospect to at least restate, but hopefully rethink, the objection. In the best case, this questioning will cause the prospect to rethink the objection and minimize its significance. At least, the question method gives the salesperson more time to think about the response to the particular objection. The restatement of the objection usually takes a form different from the original statement, which can help to clarify the objection for the salesperson. If a prospect says: "I do not like the design of this keyboard," the salesperson could ask: "Ms. Marsale, what, specifically, don't you like about the design?"

CHAPTER SUMMARY

Handling objections in a professional manner is one of the most difficult aspects of the selling process. This chapter listed several general guidelines for dealing with objections. It also discussed using direct, open-ended, and rephrasing questions to understand what objections the prospect has to buying the offered product. The six basic methods of handling objections were discussed—the boomerang method, the counterbalance method, the denial method, the indirect denial method, the failure-to-hear method, and the question method. No matter what methods or guidelines are used, a salesperson should deal with every objection raised even if it is merely saying: "I will get you more information." The slightest unanswered objection may cause a lost sale, as happened in the previous sales call of Katy Ksiezyk.

KEY TERMS

boomerang method, p. 194
counterbalance method, p. 197
denial method, p. 198
failure-to-hear method, p. 198
indirect denial method, p. 198

objection, p. 190
purchase dissonance, p. 194
question method, p. 198
risk-reducing benefits, p. 194

CHAPTER QUESTIONS

1. Discuss a controversial, timely topic with another student in the class. Each should use a variety of techniques to disagree with each other's statements. Record those techniques most effective and those techniques not effective.

2. Often the most difficult task of a salesperson is to get through the screen of a secretary, receptionist, or assistant to make the presentation to the decision maker. Develop responses to the following objections initiated by a screen:

   a. "I am sorry, but Ms. Kelly is too busy right now to see you."

   b. "We are in the process of doing our budget for next year, so you will need to come back after it is finished."

c. "The company is in an austerity program, cutting back on all expenditures."

d. "A salesperson from your company was here recently."

e. "The company has a new directive that prohibits any new purchases or any new company suppliers."

f. "Your products are too expensive for us."

3. A general rule is to try to anticipate all objections and turn them into sales points. Determine how you would turn the following anticipated objection into a sales point: You are showing a potential buyer a new home and you anticipate the prospect will say that the kitchen and dining areas are too small.

4. You are planning to work part time during the summer selling door-to-door vitamins and health-food supplements. The company you represent guarantees its products, requires regular customer contact, and offers premiums for special purchases. Make a list of objections you expect to encounter and provide at least one way to meet each objection effectively.

5. A salesperson must decide whether to take a prospect's objection seriously. If a prospect makes an objection first to make a response to a presentation or to stall for more time, what action should be taken and what should be avoided?

6. If the salesperson believes the prospect is not giving the real objection, what should the salesperson say?

7. A salesperson is frequently given many reasons for not purchasing the product. Because it is important to determine the exact reason in order to close the sale, if a customer gives reasons for not buying your product, how can you identify whether the real reason has actually been stated? What techniques would you employ to identify the real objection?

8. Give at least one way to handle each of the following objections:

a. After the sales presentation, the prospect says: "You have a good product. I appreciate your showing it to me. If we decide to purchase it, I'll give you a call."

b. After the sales presentation, the prospect says: "It appears that your product is good, but we just don't need it right now."

c. After the sales presentation, the prospect says: "I'm sorry but we just cannot afford it at this time. Call on us again in about six months."

d. After the sales presentation, the prospect says: "While your product is good, I like your competitor's product better."

9. Develop the appropriate response to the following negative customer attitudes:

a. "Your company's reputation is not good. I've had many problems with your products."

b. "Your machine has so many different outputs, it's hard to believe it will continuously function reliably."

c. "While your machine has some good points, I like my present machine better."

10. You have been showing new end tables to a young married couple. She is interested in a particular style. The husband says, "If that's what you want, it's fine. How much is it?" You respond, "It's $199.00." The husband says, "For that little thing?" What would you say and do?

NOTES

1. Jay Finegan, Sing to me, Baby. *Inc.* (August 1993), 90–98.
2. Handling objections. In *The Paper Mate selling process.* Boston: Gillette Co., Paper Mate Division, 1983), V1–37.
3. Don Meisel, Add salespower! Ask questions. *Industrial Distribution* (November 1976), 64.
4. See Daniel K. Weadcock, Your troops can keep control—Close the sale—By anticipating any objections. *Sales and Marketing Management*, March 17, 1980, 102–106.
5. Gerhard Geschwondtner and Pat Garnett, *Non-verbal selling power* (Englewood Cliffs, NJ: Prentice Hall, 1985).

SUGGESTED READINGS

Ballow, James A. Closing and handling objections. *Life and Health Insurance Sales* (October 1990), 25–29.

An insurance agent must show sincerity when handling objections while trying to maintain an air of authority. It is important for a salesperson to be able to anticipate a client's objections and be prepared to respond with an intelligent answer. A response should be straightforward and positive.

The benefits way to profit from objections. *American Salesman* (March 1989), 21–23.

A salesperson must realize that objections are a natural part of the sales process and that not every objection needs to be answered. The eight-step benefits approach is a helpful guideline to follow in handling objections. A salesman should be attentive to the clients and evaluate their objections. Most importantly, the salesperson should respond directly and convincingly and then close the sale and probe the client for any unanswered objections.

Booten, Terry L. Go to the top: Five crucial insights that will help you land big accounts. *Success* (May 1992), 34–35.

A company can begin to achieve maximum performance by assigning salespeople jobs that best fit their sales personality. During the sale, some "smoke-screen" objections may be sent out by the client. These are not true objections but simply concerns about whether or not they are a valued customer, or they just need reassurance about the company's capabilities.

Cimberg, Alan. Overcoming price objections. *Small Business Reports* (July 1990), 25–29.

A salesperson should not respond to a price objection by lowering the price. This will only lower profits and eventually the quality of the product produced. A salesperson must have an extensive knowledge of the product in order to discuss the way in which it will benefit the client. A good salesperson is able to foresee a customer's objection and respond intelligently.

Elnes, C. Conrad. To close: Read the client's lips and mind. *National Underwriter,* June 8, 1992, 13.

> An agent may overcome an unstated objection by questioning the clients to discover their concerns. Agents must learn techniques that will aid them in establishing trust between themselves and their clients. It is necessary for an agent to be aware of all their clients' needs.

Eusebro, Thomas C. Health insurance marketing: Good news/bad news. *Life and Health Insurance Sales* (April 1991), 63–64.

> The good news concerned with objections is the fact that they usually come near the close of the sales presentation. The bad news is that objections can slow down the closing of the sale. A salesperson must be able to show a genuine concern for the customer when handling objections in order to make the sale.

Overcoming "not-now" sales objections. *American Salesman* (March 1990), 13–15.

> A competent salesperson has the ability to recognize that a client's "not-now" objection is sincere and not just a stalling tactic. Another technique for handling the "not-now" objection is setting up a future appointment to continue the presentation. A salesperson may choose to use the "why be the last to own this" approach. There are other methods of handling "not-now" objections that can also save a sale.

Palmroth, Bill. Techniques for handling objections. *American Salesman* (May 1991), 8–10.

> There are a variety of reasons why clients pose objections. They may be hesitant to change or have a need for additional information. Two of the most common objections are price objections and lack of need objections. Objections can be handled by being familiar with the product's benefits, changing each objection into a question, or simply answering each question one at a time.

Swaab, Barbara. How to handle objections. *Cellular Business* (February 1989), 46, 48.

> A salesperson can gain a greater sense of confidence and increase sales productivity by learning how to handle objections. Salespeople must keep in mind that clients' objections are part of the natural order in the sales process. A salesperson may want to change the direction of the presentation or rephrase the objection to provide the response needed.

Chapter 10

The Selling Process—
The Follow-Up After the Sale

OPENING SCENARIO

It was a difficult decision that Phil Kary, sales manager for Dumas Makt., H.K., had to make. Phil always believed that everything in marketing, including sales, should be customer-oriented, but this complaint was a most unusual one. One of the company's retail stores was claiming that the wine it had purchased was vinegary. This was the only case in the entire batch that had been distributed and sold throughout the state of Georgia that had resulted in any complaints. Three hundred and forty-nine other cases of the Hungarian wines had been delivered, with the majority being sold throughout the state without any complaints. This particular wine had no chemical additives and traveled well (had no problems in shipping) in the many previous shipments.

Was the problem of Delaney's, the distributor lodging the complaint, actually the result of something that had nothing to do with the original quality of the wine? The company's customer complaint form did not indicate anything unusual. But perhaps it should be revised so that more pertinent information would be provided. Delaney's was a first-time customer, so there was no sales and complaint history available. Because the distributor might eventually become a good account, Phil thought he would probably issue credit toward the purchase of a new case of wine once he verified the vinegar taste problem. Phil always preferred to err on the side of the customer, as he was attempting to establish a strong distributor network for the company's wine in the state.

Chapter Objectives

After reading this chapter, you should be able to

- Know how to leave after making the close.
- Implement the appropriate follow-up steps.
- Understand the importance and types of customer service.
- Handle customer complaints.
- Use suggestion selling.
- Develop goodwill.

INTRODUCTION

Today's hypercompetitive environment has forced companies to be more concerned than ever before about servicing the customer after the sale. Gone are the days when the major concern was simply selling. In fact, a good product at a fair price backed by customer service is not outstanding in today's competitive market. Companies are concentrating more and more on servicing the customer, particularly after the sale, as is illustrated in the following two company situations.[1]

Manco, Inc., located in Westlake, Ohio, grew from $4 million sales in 1977 to $76 million in 1992 by helping customers cut costs. This has transformed the company from a distributor of industrial tape to a major supplier of tapes, weather stripping, and mailing supplies to retail stores. According to the company's president, Tom Corbo, "Retailers are pushing inventory management off on us. It is a burden we like, as it gives us more control. It (the new selling) requires teamwork, a different kind of salesperson, and investing the time where it is worth it." This approach has now developed into one of Manco's distinguishing services—managing the inventory of its 30 products for such large customers as K-Mart and Wal-Mart.

A similar concern with service has impacted G&F, a small manufacturer of molded-plastic parts in Sturbridge, Massachusetts. In 1987, the company was asked by Boise, a $500 million acoustic-speaker manufacturer in Framingham, Massachusetts, to assign a G&F employee to work full time at Boise's plant. Even though this move would eliminate the need for a G&F salesperson to call on Boise and would, in turn, help Boise decrease the costs of buyers and planners, it was a radical move for a small company with only $3 million in sales. The decision to put a G&F salesperson at Boise started the company implementing a new type of selling. According to President John Argitis, "Instead of spending time trying to get new accounts, we concentrate solely on servicing and pricing. This has changed our whole way of doing business, but I never thought it would work this well. You don't really sell, you look for opportunities." This new philosophy has stimulated the company to grow 25 to 40 percent each year despite a depressed plastics industry, and in 1992, sales reached about $15 million.

After making even the smallest sale, a good salesperson always thanks the customer for the business and follows up to ensure that the customer is satisfied. A good salesperson realizes that the best customers in the future are satisfied customers. Because many buyers get after-purchase anxiety (concern that they made the wrong decision in buying the product), a follow-up sales call can alleviate or at least minimize this dissonance and result in additional sales being made immediately. At the very least, the follow-up will result in developing a satisfied customer who will make additional purchases in the future.

LEAVING THE CLOSE

For many salespeople the period immediately following the close when a sale is made or not made is very awkward. If the closure has ended successfully, the time can be used for referrals or reorder periods. However, even if the sale has been lost, the situation can be made more positive, thereby increasing the probability of a future sale.

Departure Following Success

Upon making a sale, salespeople feel two emotions. They usually feel the excitement of victory and success, followed by a second emotion—the fear that the customer may change his or her mind and cancel the order. Both feelings need to be controlled to allow the proper closure and departure that can lead to future sales. This is the time for salespeople to thank the customer sincerely for his or her time and business. The words and attitude of salespeople during this time can help reduce any cognitive dissonance felt by the buyer. **Cognitive dissonance** is the feeling on the part of the buyer that the decision to purchase the product was perhaps not correct.

Dissonance can best be reduced when the salesperson, in a relaxed, natural manner, thanks the customer for the order, handles any questions regarding delivery and payment, assures the customer of being available to answer any future questions, and makes sure the order is delivered in a timely manner. The biggest error salespeople can make during this time is to prolong the stay and continue talking. Their goal should be to leave as quickly and naturally as possible.

Departure Following Failure

Perhaps more than at any other time, the true professionalism of salespeople becomes apparent when a good departure occurs following the failure to obtain a sale. The key is that professional salespeople do not let the loss of the sale cause them to acknowledge defeat or intimidation. Instead, they make sure the prospect does not feel that the time has been wasted but that he or she has obtained worthwhile information. Professional salespeople attempt to leave the prospect with a favorable image of themselves as well as their company. This lays the groundwork for a future sale or a good referral. Salespeople need to remember that every product will not meet the needs of every customer everytime. Sometimes sales are just not made.

Even when turned down in a harsh, negative manner, salespeople should continue to maintain a courteous, friendly attitude. The prospect, secretary, and receptionist should all be left with the feeling that the salesperson is confident and courteous regardless of the situation. The words and actions of salespeople at this difficult time can be the first steps in achieving a sale on the next time the prospect is given a presentation.

If the prospect has the potential to purchase products in the future, salespeople need to make sure the prospect knows that they are interested in the prospect as well as the organization and want to build a continuing business relationship. The first step in this process is to call or send a note thanking the prospect for his or her time. The second step is to determine why the sale was not made by asking the prospect for the real reasons for not purchasing. Sincere, honest questions usually elicit honest answers, as well as the opportunity for a callback at a later date.

This final step can be painful because it requires the salesperson to analyze carefully the entire selling process to determine what went wrong. This critical self-analysis often uncovers some things that, upon correction, will lead to a successful sales call in the future. Questions that need to be asked are: Did I prepare for the sales call properly? Was I awkward in approaching and greeting the prospect? Did I quickly arouse and hold the prospect's interest? Did I give all the key points in my presentation? Did I use all the sales aids effectively? Was I successful in understanding all the objections and handling them effectively? Did I use the prepared trial close? Did I use the proper closing techniques? Did I have the proper attitude throughout the selling process? Did I leave pleasantly? The answers to these and other self-evaluation questions will allow salespeople to modify any present problems, thereby making better, more successful sales presentations in the future. Although no salesperson can close every sale, through self-evaluation and application of sound selling principles and techniques, the percentages of successful closings will increase.

FOLLOW-THROUGH TECHNIQUES

In order to develop a group of satisfied customers, salespeople must always follow up after making a sale.[2] This part of the selling process is often overlooked in favor of making more sales to other customers. Yet, if a proper follow-up does not occur, there is a chance that a satisfied customer will become a disgruntled one. Although the exact nature of the follow-up depends on the particular product/market situation, there are some general techniques salespeople can use to ensure customer satisfaction. A list of positive and negative actions that affect salespeople's relationships with their customers is found in Table 10-1.

TABLE 10-1 Salesperson Actions Affecting Customer Relationships

Positive Actions	Negative Actions
• Initiate positive phone calls	• Make only callbacks
• Make recommendations	• Make justifications
• Use candid language	• Wait for service requests
• Show appreciation	• Use "owe us" legal language
• Make service suggestions	• Respond only to problems
• Use "we" problem-solving language	• Use long-winded communications
• Indicate any personality problems	• Hide personality problems
• Talk of "our future together"	• Talk about the past
• Routinize responses	• Do emergency responsiveness
• Accept responsibility	• Shift blame
• Plan the future	

Source: Adapted from Theodore Levitt, "After the sale is over. *Harvard Business Review* (September–October 1983), 87–93.

Good follow-up techniques begin with a sincere, written expression of appreciation, in addition to the thank-you given after the successful closing. About two days after the sale, a formal letter on company stationery, an informal note, or just a postcard thanking the customer makes sure that the salesperson's appreciation is clearly evident to the customer. An example letter is reproduced in Figure 10-1.

The second follow-up activity is to check delivery. On the day of delivery the salesperson should telephone the buyer not only to ensure that delivery was made but to indicate that the salesperson cares about servicing the customer. If problems arise either in the delivery not being made or damage occurring to the products received, the salesperson can take the appropriate, prompt action. When there is a problem, the customer should be informed by the salesperson, not by someone else.

Third, the salesperson should check to make sure that the employees of the buying organization are knowledgeable about the product and its operation or use. Proper knowledge and training in the buying organization can often eliminate many complaints before they have a chance to occur.

Finally, for products requiring installation, the salesperson should visit the buying organization soon after delivery to ensure that the product is properly installed and no problems are occurring. Even if there are no problems, this call indicates to the company that the salesperson is sincerely interested in building a long-term relationship. This visit, probably more than any other, shows the sincerity and reliability of the salesperson and the selling organization.

By providing good follow-up, salespeople can ensure that their customers are satisfied. This is important for future sales because it is easier to sell satisfied

Ms. Katerina Ross
H&P Associates
171 Chagrin Boulevard
Cleveland, OH 44112

Dear Ms. Ross:

Your continuous purchases are greatly appreciated. Good customers like you are wonderful to deal with. As a token of our appreciation I have enclosed a certificate of appreciation and a credit certification that gives you and your company the highest credit rating we offer.

This rating is only given to selected, special customers entitled to maximum credit and buying privileges. We hope you will find it useful in doing future business with us.

Thanks again for your support.

Sincerely,

Kelly Frik
Sales Manager

FIGURE 10-1 An Example Follow-Up Appreciation Letter

customers more of the same product or new products than to locate and sell to new prospects. Although it is sometimes difficult for buyers to find salespeople willing to give prompt, efficient service, follow-up service often results in establishing a relationship of trust and confidence between a buyer and a salesperson. This trust and confidence in turn lead to repeat business and further cementing of the relationship.

Good follow-up service also provides prospect referrals, for satisfied customers are usually the best source for information about potential new customers.[3] Some satisfied buyers believe that one way they can "repay" salespeople for their follow-up interest and service is to provide them with names of others who are likely to have an interest in their product or service. The relaxed relationship between customers and salespeople who provide follow-up service is very conducive to the customers' giving leads and referrals. Sometimes this can take the form of an introductory letter or telephone call from the customer to a prospect. There is, of course, no better support of the claims in a sales presentation than the testimony of a satisfied customer.

FOLLOW-UP PROCEDURE

Given the importance of good follow-up for building customer rapport, salespeople should develop and implement follow-up procedures for their territories. This procedure requires several initiatives:

- Develop a system within the company to ensure that all requests for information, complaints, or problems from customers or prospects are handled promptly and efficiently.
- Develop a system for regularly checking on the customers' views of products they have purchased.
- Make sure you are informed of any customer complaints or problems and personally try to handle as many as possible.
- Meet with key persons in each customer's company on a regular basis, making sure that each of them is on your company's mailing list to receive all announcements and promotional materials. The frequency of this contact should be based on the sales potential to the customer.
- Make yourself as available as possible to each customer, leaving evening and weekend telephone numbers where you can be reached. Feel comfortable that these numbers will be used only in extreme emergency.
- Make your customers feel a part of your network by sharing with them names and information that may be helpful and contacting them on a regular basis.

By establishing and implementing a sound follow-up procedure, each salesperson can develop the type of relationship with each customer that results in repeat sales and customer loyalty.

OVERALL CUSTOMER SERVICE

Although often not frequently considered in the selling process, personal selling involves two actions: making the sale and then servicing the sale. Servicing the customer must be a major part of the selling process because a satisfied customer is the key to repeat sales. Good customer service keeps present accounts satisfied and helps attract new accounts through direct referrals and a good company reputation.[4]

Each customer has needs that make a well-planned customer service program essential—feeling good during the purchase and feeling comfortable after the purchase. You can understand the importance of these two concepts by reflecting on your own major purchases. Did you feel good while making the purchase? Did the salesperson contribute to this good feeling? What factors other than the product and the price affected your purchase decision? What went through your mind several days after the purchase? Did you reflect on whether the purchase decision was correct? Were you concerned that a better alternative product might be available at a better price? Answering these questions can help you understand the reactions most buyers have during and following a sale.

Creating a comfortable feeling in the customer during the sale requires that the salesperson focus on the buyer's need for compliments and recognition. Everyone responds positively to sincere affirmation and recognition and negatively to insincerity and indifference. A handwritten note thanking the buyer for the order or a follow-up telephone call inquiring about the customer's satisfaction indicates to the customer that he or she is important and the business is valued.

Feeling comfortable after the sale focuses on the insecurity people feel after making a decision. Regardless of whether this insecurity is based on facts, such as late delivery or faulty installation or just on concerns and feelings, it is still very real to the individual. The salesperson and company who are able to minimize or even eliminate this feeling through good customer service is far ahead of competitors in developing customer loyalty and repeat purchasing. Customers feel good knowing they are in caring hands of the salesperson and the selling company.

COMMON AFTER-SALE PROBLEMS

A good customer service program needs to address after-sale problems. Although many problems are specific to a particular company, some common problems exist: price changes, late delivery, poor installation, credit denial, lack of promotional information, and insufficient training.

Price Changes. Price changes, particularly price increases, can cause problems if they are not handled correctly. Any price changes that occur should be immediately recorded on the company's price list if a new one is not issued. Nothing generates more distrust and irritation on the part of the customer than when the price of the product or service is not correctly stated the first time. When prices have changed or, even more important, are about to increase, salespeople should notify customers so that they can take any appropriate action.

Late Delivery. No after-sale problem occurs more frequently and causes more buyer negativity than late deliveries. A late delivery can affect the buyer's plans and can eliminate sales for a period of time if the delay results in an out-of-stock situation. While a late delivery may be out of the salesperson's control, salespeople should minimize their potential for occurring by accurately quoting delivery dates and promptly keeping the customer informed of any delays and the reasons for the delay. Salespeople can help prevent some delays by making sure the submitted order is accurate, contains all the necessary information, and is processed correctly by the company.

Poor Installation. For certain products, the satisfaction of the buyer is related to whether the product is properly installed. Usually the installation of the product is not the responsibility of the salesperson, but it is good policy for him or her to do everything possible to ensure that installation is properly completed. This can be accomplished by getting the best installers and/or directly supervising the installation. At the very least, each salesperson should contact the customer to be sure no problems have occurred during installation.

Lack of Promotional Information. A salesperson must be sure that each customer is aware of any promotional monies or allowances that might be available. Most companies give customers promotional allowances in the form of money or products. These allowances can be in the form of cooperative advertising, product purchase quantity, promotional display, or new product trial. Whatever the form, the salesperson needs to make each customer aware of the allowance and how the customer can take advantage of it.

Credit Denial. One problem that directly affects a customer's good feeling is being denied credit or given limited credit. Salespeople need to become acquainted with people in the credit department of their company and make sure that those responsible for their accounts maintain a good business relationship with their customers. Salespeople should find out about potential credit problems with a particular customer and give the customer a carefully detailed explanation to avoid any problems and hurt feelings.

Insufficient Training. For certain products, it is important that personnel in the buyer's company are well trained in the use of the product. In some instances, the technology is so complex that training is an integral part of the follow-up. Without such training little customer satisfaction will occur. When training is not sufficient, the product may not be used properly and customer dissatisfaction will result.

HANDLING COMPLAINTS

No part of service after the sale is more important than proper handling of customer complaints. A firm should not spend millions of dollars on advertising and promotion to make a sale and build customer loyalty and then be unresponsive to legitimate customer complaints. One important way to handle complaints effectively is to use a good complaint handling form and have an effective complaint handling system in place. An example form is illustrated in Table 10-2.

When handling complaints, salespeople should remember that better sales and profits can be obtained from the repeat purchases of satisfied customers than from initial sales. The cost of making the first sale to a customer is almost always higher than the cost of repeat sales. Handling complaints correctly can provide

TABLE 10-2 Dumas Markt., H.K., Inc. Customer Complaint Form

Taken By: _____ Complaint Date: _____ Ship Date: _____

Customer Number: _____ Invoice Number: _____

Customer Name: _____ Telephone: _____

Address: _____ Fax: _____

_____

Salesperson Name: _____

Account Manager Name: _____

Details of Complaint: _____

_____

_____

_____

First Corrective Action: _____

_____

_____

_____

Second Corrective Action: _____

_____

_____

_____

Corrective Action Personnel: _____

_____

_____

Complaint Close: Date: _____ Authorization: _____

the salesperson with the opportunity to resell the customer on the company and its products. Because very few customers are chronic complainers, when a customer does make a complaint, the salesperson and company should make every effort to handle it to the customer's satisfaction. An excellent way to adjust customer complaints is through a personal visit by the salesperson.

There are several ways to deal with complaints in typical selling situations.

SELL!NG
THE FRONT LINES OF BUSINESS

For Service, Send in the Troops
Robert Sharoff

It was Gary Fleshman's first great selling lesson. "I was 10 years old, and there was a contest in our community for who could sell the most newspaper subscriptions," he recalls. "The prize was a new bike. I wanted that bike more than anything in the world. And I lost by something like three or four subscriptions. Later I found out that the winner—I still remember that her name was Susan—had her mother and her sister helping her. They were all out there selling subscriptions.

"I was crushed. Then and there, I realized two things. First, you rarely get a level playing field in selling. And second, if you want to win the bike, you have to work hard and work smart."

Fleshman, 42, now does both at Nike Inc. in Beaverton, Ore., where he oversees the athletic-footwear maker's accounts with the five branches of the armed forces—Army-Air Force, Navy, Marines, Coast Guard, and Veterans. His job has taught him another lesson: Selling is a long-term game. "We are very focused on results," he says. "We don't just make deals. We try to get involved in all aspects of the business that affect us. We don't wait around for circumstances to dictate actions. We make changes before they have to be made."

It may come as a surprise that the military, with its worldwide network of base exchange stores, qualifies as one of the country's largest retailers. The biggest branch—the Army-Air Force—has 233 stores around the globe. The Veterans have 172 stores, followed by the Navy with 138 stores, the Coast Guard with 46, and the Marines with 19.

The individual stores vary in size from the relatively small to near departmentstore size. "They strive to offer the same range of products as Penney's or Dillard's but at 15 percent to 20 percent less," says Fleshman. All of the branches do their own buying, and there is a wide variance in the degree of sophistication they bring to the process. The bottom line, however, isn't much different than in civilian retailing. "You deal with buyers who set up product assortments to serve their customers," says Fleshman.

Fleshman has been on the military beat since 1984, when he left a job in Nike's promotions department to join a sales unit devoted to straightening out troubled accounts. At that time, he says, "we were doing $10 million a year with the military, but no one had a clue what the business was all about." Today Nike's military business has grown to $72 million and serves as a model for customer service for the entire company.

So what *is* it all about? The basics are easy enough to grasp. All of the branches do their own buying and have different policies. The Army-Air Force, for example, buys centrally out of an office in Dallas. The Marines stores buy individually. ("Like dealing with a local sporting goods store," says Fleshman.) The branches have buyers and general merchandise managers, most of whom are civilians.

When Fleshman took over the account, there were two main problems. The first was product assortment. "It was too narrow," he says. "They were ordering the same 20 items every season, and they weren't meeting the needs of their customers. We had to convince them to carry more styles and to tailor assortments to individual bases. If it's a training facility, you need more men's shoes and more running shoes. If it's a regular base, you need merchandise for families."

Distribution was the other trouble spot. "It was extremely inefficient," says Fleshman. "The orders were being shipped to warehouses where they sat for days. Sometimes it would take a store 35 or 40 days to get an order." After studying the problem, Fleshman's solution was to bypass the warehouses entirely and ship all orders directly to the stores. Today, according to Fleshman, the stores receive their orders in 10 days or less.

His success in troubleshooting convinced Fleshman that salespeople need to redefine their roles. "We have to be partners and help customers plan their business," he says. "Instead of just identifying problems, we have to propose solutions and then make sure the solutions get executed. I mean, we have a lot of great ideas, but they don't mean anything unless they reach the selling floor."

To make sure they do, Fleshman has totally revamped the way his salespeople operate. "If anything related to Nike product needs to be done, we do it," he says. "I don't care if it's crawling all over the back room looking for a lost box of product, tracking down a fixture, holding a training session, or stocking a display. Our salespeople visit each store every month, and the average sales call is six hours. If it's a large store and there's a lot to do, they may spend two days."

The results are hard to deny. In addition to the steady growth of sales (at a time when the military generally has been downsizing), Nike recently won a Partnership Award as one of the Army-Air Force's top vendors. What's more, Fleshman's group, Nike Military, was recently named Nike's top agency for the 1994 fiscal year, and Fleshman himself was named Nike's sales manager of the year.

Just as gratifying from Fleshman's standpoint is the trust that exists between client and vendor. "They listen to us, and my commitment to them is that we're in this for the long haul and we're not going to do something unless it's right," he says.

Even if it means turning down business. Says Fleshman, "I'm not an arm-twister, and I will not sell people something they don't need. If it's not right, I'll say, 'I don't want you to buy this. It's not a good deal for you at any price.' "

Fleshman sees Nike's military relationship as a model for achieving customer satisfaction. "It's the difference between being good and wanting to be the very best," he says. "I once read that the biggest threat to being great is being good. Most people are content to be good. They don't push themselves to be the very best."

Fleshman says his biggest challenge as a salesperson is overcoming negativity. "You have retailers who plan to be down for the year, and then they go out and make it happen. Or you have a salesperson who always finds the negative in everything. If 10 things are right, they talk about the one thing that's wrong. I don't understand why people plan to fail."

The key, he adds, is seizing the moment. "You have to take responsibility for the future. I believe you can do that. If you want certain things, you can make them happen. You just have to be willing to make the tough decisions to make them happen." And don't underestimate the competitive instinct. Says Fleshman, "Hey, I'd love to go up against Susan and her mom and sister today. I'd blow them away."

Reprinted with the permission of SELL!NG magazine.

Encourage Customers to Explain the Problem

Customers feel much better after having the opportunity to talk about their irritation or anger. It is important that salespeople let the customers explain the problem fully, without interruption. Interruptions only add to any existing anger and hostility and make handling the complaint even more difficult. When anger and hostility are present, reason rarely prevails, and it becomes almost impossible to arrive at an equitable settlement for both parties. The salesperson must be equally open in dealing with less emotional customers who may give little vocal evidence of their irritation but may have the same underlying hostility.

The ease in handling complaints is significantly affected by the atmosphere created by the salesperson at the start of the discussion. A dissatisfied customer wants salespeople to be sympathetic and friendly. After listening very carefully and attentively without interrupting, the salesperson should then express concern and regret for any inconvenience experienced by the buyer. Based on all the information obtained, the salesperson should attempt to discuss those points of mutual agreement. Agreeing with the customer on whatever points possible is a sincere way to get the process off to a good start.

Obtain and Determine the Facts

Because it is easy to be influenced by a customer who is sincerely trying to make a case for his or her claim as strong as possible, the salesperson must be careful to determine the true facts of the situation. The buyer will emphasize the facts that strengthen his or her position, so the salesperson has the responsibility to the company to make sure a satisfactory solution is obtained based on all the facts of the case.

It is important to have the customer thoroughly explain the problem and show exactly what is wrong with the product. The customer and salesperson should physically examine the product together unless the defect or problem is such that a physical examination is neither possible nor necessary. When this is the case, the salesperson should be very sure that the complaint is fully understood.

It is important for salespeople to be familiar with any reasons for a product to appear defective when actually it is not. In some cases, the defect may have occurred because the product has not been used properly. Leather may become defective if placed on a radiator; fresh food can be harmed if frozen; or a duplicating machine may become jammed if improper paper is used. Upon examination of the facts the salesperson may find that the customer is at fault. Sometimes neither the customer nor the company is at fault, as when the product is damaged in shipping.

The most difficult situation arises when the facts do not indicate the reason for the problem or when both the customer and the company are at fault. In such situations, the customer needs to be made aware of the difficulty in obtaining an equitable solution but that, nonetheless, the object is to obtain a fair, equitable solution.

Provide a Solution

After listening to the customer and examining everything available at the customer's place of business, it is the responsibility of the salesperson to take some action and eventually come up with an equitable solution. Whereas some companies assign the responsibility for settling problems to the salesperson, other companies have the salesperson investigate the problem and make recommendations while the actual settlement is made by the claims department at the home office. Companies allowing salespeople to make settlements feel that because they are closest to the customer they are best suited to make fair, satisfactory adjustments in a prompt manner. Companies using the opposite approach feel that the customer will be more likely to accept the offered settlement if it comes from a higher level of management than the salesperson.

Regardless of company policy, remember that the customer is interested in a prompt response. The salesperson must avoid the temptation to blame the shipping department, installation crew, or someone else in the company. Disgruntled customers do not appreciate passing the buck. The salesperson has the responsibility for resolving the problem without making any negative remarks about the company. Because nothing is so perplexing to a customer as having an action postponed for a long period of time or indefinitely, the salesperson should do everything possible to expedite the response and obtain action from the company. If the response time is too long, there may be little opportunity to resell the customer.

Most customers are reasonable and satisfied when they receive fair timely treatment. The salesperson must be sure the customer understands that the proposed settlement is fair. In some cases this may require some explanation and convincing. Settlements fair to both the company and the customer do more to bring about goodwill than any other action on the part of the company. To convince the customer of the fairness of the settlement sometimes requires a detailed explanation, reviewing the terms of the warranty or guarantee with the customer, or discussing the company's settlement process and the reasons it was established. Under no circumstances should the salesperson agree with the customer so that a customer/management confrontation occurs. Merely agreeing with the customer does not lead to the development of a friendship and can cause the customer to lose faith in the company and the salesperson. Any problems involved in the settlement should be handled between the company and the salesperson without the customer being directly involved. The action decided upon should then be presented to the customer in a decisive, convincing manner by the salesperson.

REACHING A FAIR SETTLEMENT

In order to help the company provide a fair settlement, salespeople must obtain the following information: dollar amount of the claim, frequency of customer claims, size of customer account, importance of customer, extent to which action taken may affect customer and other accounts, experience of salesperson in dealing with other claims, and specific claim information. After examination of the provided information, the company's settlement may take any one of the following forms:

- Full product replacement, without any cost
- Full product replacement, only charging for labor and transportation
- Full product replacement, with joint customer/company sharing of costs
- Full product replacement, with the customer paying a reduced price
- Product repaired at customer cost
- Product sent to company factory for a decision
- Customer proceeding with a claim against a third party

Although it is very unusual for a customer to willfully file a false claim, when the salesperson is convinced that neither the company nor a third-party agent of the company, such as the transportation agent, is at fault, the salesperson should give the buyer an opportunity to save face and drop an illegitimate claim by suggesting that another party may be to blame. Salespeople could say:

"Perhaps the maintenance crew failed to . . ." Customers who have been found out making false claims usually take this opportunity to drop the claim. If this occurs, the salesperson should note this in the customer's file and attempt to keep the account.

Another approach the salesperson can take, which is far more risky, is to call the customer on the fraudulent claim and attempt to appeal to the individual's sense of fair play. More than likely this action will lose the customer, but that may not be bad for the company. This approach requires great care, as every company wants to avoid any bad will that could be spread by a disgruntled customer.

A fair settlement provides the salesperson with an excellent opportunity to resell the company's products and services. Because the customer has just had a positive experience with the company and knows that the company is interested in keeping a satisfied customer, he or she should be receptive to consider purchasing other products from the company.

In handling any complaint, the salesperson should take care to ensure that, whenever possible, "The customer is always right." This requires that the salesperson, when making a settlement, should act like a public relations representative. Good service and complaint handling lead to good customer relations and satisfied loyal customers. A checklist to evaluate a salesperson's follow-up after the sale is provided in Table 10-3.

SUGGESTION SELLING

One form of customer service often overlooked is **suggestion selling**—the process of suggesting other products or services related to the main product purchased. Suggestion selling should only be done when salespeople feel the additional items will significantly enhance the satisfaction level of the customer. Some salespeople believe that suggestion selling is not a service but a bother to the customer. However, when handled properly, it does help to improve relations with most customers.

Suggesting Related Items

Frequently, salespeople represent a broad line with complementary products. At times, related products or services will enhance the customer's satisfaction with the item already chosen, and together the package of products will better meet the customer's needs. This is similar to the experience many have had after buying a new suit when the salesperson suggests they look at a new tie or shirt to complement the suit.

A related item that adds to the purchased product's versatility is an especially good selling suggestion. For example, a company that buys a photocopy

TABLE 10-3 Checklist: Follow-Up After the Sale

Salesperson: _____

Date: _____

Question	Excellent	Good	Fair	Poor
1. Knowledge of all company services available to prospects and customers				
2. Understanding what servicing is as far as this company is concerned				
3. Knowing what services are to be performed regularly by the salesperson and how they are to be performed				
4. Knowing the personnel to contact within the company for servicing assistance when necessary				
5. Understanding servicing policies				
6. Understanding servicing procedures				
7. Knowing methods for seeking out opportunities in which to perform services that contribute to immediate or future sales				

Major Strengths to Reinforce: _____

_____

Weaknesses to Overcome: _____

_____

How? _____

_____

machine may want to consider an automatic sorting option. For an individual just purchasing a new quality camera, an additional lens that would significantly increase the camera's versatility might be suggested. A service contract might be an important option to a customer purchasing a major piece of equipment in order to reduce the worry of downtime and the potential high costs of repair.

Suggesting Large Quantities

Salespeople should always be ready to suggest larger quantities of an item if it would be beneficial to the customer. The most common benefit is economy, as most companies offer a discount on larger orders. If the customer buys a few more items, the price per item of all the purchases might be significantly reduced.

Another common benefit of a larger order is to beat a forthcoming price increase. If a salesperson is almost certain that prices will rise in the not too distant future, at the very least, customers should be informed so that they can take advantage of the lower prices. Good salespeople take great care to ensure that when suggesting larger quantities the customer will benefit and not just their own sales quotas. Salespeople should remember the **going-concern concept** when suggesting a larger quantity—they will call on the customer again and again. The next sales call following one when too much was ordered will be very difficult.

Suggesting Better Items

Because most companies offer a range of products in a given category that vary in quality and price, allowing customers choice in the purchase decision, salespeople must carefully assist the customer in selecting the most appropriate price/quality product. Sometimes a customer needs to have a higher-priced, better-quality product than the one first selected. This process of moving a customer to a better grade of merchandise, called **trading up,** should be used only when there are benefits to the customer. Sometimes the better-quality product has a better warranty, greater trade value, more comfort, or better durability. Salespeople decide whether it is best to show the higher-priced product first or last in the presentation. Salespeople need to do what fits the particular product/customer context, remembering that the highest-quality product, whenever presented, becomes the benchmark for evaluating all other products presented.

Trading up, as well as other forms of suggestion selling, should be viewed as just one more way to provide service to the customer. When used correctly to benefit the customer, suggestion selling can build sales and increase customer rapport.

DEVELOPING GOODWILL

The entire thrust of the selling process, particularly the after-sales service, should be oriented toward developing **goodwill**—the positive feelings and attitudes an individual has about salespeople, a company, and its products. Customers who are satisfied and have confidence in the company and its products, have a strong feeling of goodwill. When customers lose confidence, their goodwill can be quickly eliminated.

Goodwill not only helps make the first sale but also secures repeat sales. It helps a customer choose the company's products over several competitive products of like grade and quality. It can help attract new customers and lead to referrals. This positive word-of-mouth more than anything else is the best advertising a company can have.

CHAPTER SUMMARY

This chapter dealt with an often overlooked yet very important area, after-sale service. After-sale service covers a wide variety of areas, from proper departure after the presentation to developing goodwill. Salespeople must maintain their professionalism when leaving the sales call, even if a sale was not made. A friendly departure can help build the bridge to future sales. Follow-through techniques include sending the customer a letter thanking him or her, checking that delivery was made, providing training and information about the product to the buying organization's employees, and being sure the installation is done properly. Salespeople must develop follow-up procedures within their own company to aid their ability to perform good follow-up. Being aware of the most common sales problems, such as price changes, late delivery, or poor installation, and effectively handling complaints are two of the more important areas after the sale. When appropriate, suggestion selling can increase the benefits to the customer and in turn the customer's satisfaction. This, as well as the other types of customer service, will lead to the establishment of goodwill and the development of a strong relationship that will result in increased sales and referrals to potential new customers.

KEY TERMS

cognitive dissonance, p. 205
going-concern concept, p. 220
goodwill, p. 220

suggestion selling, p. 218
trading up, p. 220

CHAPTER QUESTIONS

1. Discuss how the art of listening can be used in handling customer complaints.
2. Reflect on a recent major purchase you have made, such as an appliance, automobile, or suit of clothes. Rate the salesperson you dealt with in terms of post-sale activities and attempts to develop goodwill. What, if any, services were provided? What was your level of cognitive dissonance after the purchase? What specifically could the salesperson have done to reduce this dissonance?
3. Today, more than ever before, consumers in the United States have high expectations regarding the products and services they purchase. What has caused this phenomenon, and what implications does it have for developing goodwill and repeat purchases?

4. Discuss with specific examples the following statement: "Salespeople should handle all complaints so that customers are completely satisfied."

5. As salespeople for a major consumer goods company selling food products to wholesalers and retail grocery stores, develop six things that you could do to develop goodwill that costs little or nothing.

6. Select another person in the class and each of you interview one or two purchasing agents in the community concerning the types of gifts (if any) received from companies they do business with and their reaction to the gifts. Develop conclusions based on this research and design an appropriate gift program for building customer goodwill.

7. Discuss what action you would take as a salesperson once you found that your company was not able to deliver the product until 60 days after the date you promised the buyer. Be specific.

8. As a consultant, you have been assigned the task of identifying common customer complaints that are the major sources of customer irritation that could destroy the goodwill and reputation already established by

   a. A large commercial bank with branches throughout the city

   b. A well-known quality conscious department store

   c. A specialty store renting videos

9. You are the sales manager for a large car dealer who is concerned about customers becoming irritated when they take their cars to the garage for servicing. Develop a list of suggestions for the manager of the service department and the manager of the parts department that will build goodwill and good customer relations.

NOTES

1. Susan Greco, The art of sellings. *Inc.* (June 1993), 72–80.
2. See, for example, Josef Adams, The newcomer's page: Follow-through on new sales. *American Salesman* (February 1989), 6–8; and Training agency salespeople #9: Follow-up before and after the sale. *Agency Sales Magazine* (May 1992), 54–57.
3. See How to make effective and profitable service calls. *Agency Sales Magazine* (June 1990), 39–44.
4. See Nancy Friedman, Follow-up or foul-up: Service after the sale. *Agency Sales Magazine* (October 1992), 21–22.

SUGGESTED READINGS

Adams, Josef. The newcomer's page: Follow-through on new sales. *American Salesman* (February 1989), 6–8.

It is important for a salesman to keep in mind that every new sale opens the door for future business. A follow-up leaves customers with the assurance that their salesperson is personally interested in their needs. If a product is not appropriate for the client, then a follow-up from the sales representative can salvage the situation and reinforce his or her interest in the client's needs.

Friedman, Nancy. Follow-up or foul-up: Service after the sale. *Agency Sales Magazine* (October 1992), 21–22.

A consulting company reports that attaining a new customer costs five times more than keeping a current one. In 1992, the average U.S. company will lose 10 to 30 percent of its customers because they were not treated with the attention they deserve. Following up with an unhappy customer through such inexpensive means as notes, cards, or telephone calls can help avoid future problems.

Hostetler, James G., Jr. The high cost of one-shot calls. *Insurance Sales* (December 1988), 24–26.

The failure to follow up a call is a waste of time and money because a sales call is expensive. There are certain aspects of the sales call that the sales representative should keep in mind in the follow-up. Timing is crucial, and factors that applied during the initial sales call may no longer apply. Clients feel that the agent has a personal interest in them if a follow-up is made.

How to make effective and profitable service calls. *Agency Sales Magazine* (June 1990), 39–44.

A follow-up can be as rewarding to salespeople as a new sales call. A satisfied customer is a doorway to many more successful sales. Due to the importance of the follow-up, it should be planned as carefully as an initial call. A follow-up must not always be made in person; a telephone call or a thank-you note can sometimes be as effective.

McClure, Deborah. The close never stops, even at policy delivery. *National Underwriter,* January 29, 1992, 17, 24–25.

It is important for insurance agents to keep their current customers happy. Planning an annual review of client coverage and talking with them at least twice a year help maintain good relations. Another effective follow-up technique is a call on a client's birthday. Service after a sale is just as important as the initial sales call in maintaining customer satisfaction.

Nemec, John. Salvage junk time to make it work for you. *American Salesman* (August 1990), 11–14.

Follow-up times should be organized in a file in order to maintain an open line of communication with the client. It is to salespeople's advantage to organize their time in order to decrease stress and better serve their clientele. "Junk time" is a short period, 5 to 10 minutes, in which salespeople are able to work on their presentation and review client information.

Shiffman, Stephan. Taking control of the sale. *American Salesman* (February 1990), 22–24.

Salespeople lose business by failing to guide prospects through the proper stages necessary to make the sale. Prospects must be able to understand the advantages of participating in the sales process. Salespeople should ask questions to familiarize themselves with their prospects' company history in order to suggest the appropriate product to meet their needs. The final step in the selling process is to build a lasting relationship with the prospect. When salespeople are making the sales presentation, they should remember to use ability, sincerity, and knowledge.

Training agency salespeople #9: Follow-up before and after the sale. *Agency Sales Magazine* (May 1992), 54–57.

Following up after the sale is an important part of the sales process. Customer satisfaction is a valuable sales tool. A timely, organized follow-up may lead to more profitable sales in the future.

_____ Chapter 11 _____

Leading the Sales Force

OPENING SCENARIO

Margaret Kahla had just been promoted to the position of regional manager for Mid-Continent Chemicals. She would be in charge of the northwestern United States, which includes Washington, Oregon, Idaho, Montana, and Wyoming. She had been with Mid-Continent for six years and had served as the district manager for the Washington district for the last three years.

Kahla's first job was to get settled in her new home office in Helena, Montana. She was looking forward to the challenge of being regional manager. Kahla knew that she would need to adapt to the new position because of the different mind-set required and the additional duties associated with the job. She also knew that this adaptation would require that she cultivate some new talents and abilities. She was concerned because she wasn't sure yet what all those talents needed to be, and it probably would take some months to find out.

Kahla's second job, and perhaps of equal importance as the first, was selecting her successor in the Washington district. This was probably the most critical district in the region, and the person who would fill that position would need to be an extremely capable manager. She had several good choices to fill the position. She also knew that several people were extremely interested in being promoted into the position, and at least two of them would likely take jobs with competitors if they were passed over. All the viable candidates had been successful salespeople, but some seemed to have additional qualities that could lead to their being fine leaders.

Chapter Objectives

After reading this chapter, you should be able to

- Identify the characteristics that good sales managers possess.
- Comprehend the major theories of leadership and how they relate to the job of the sales manager.
- Understand how the different approaches to decision making affect the operation of a sales organization.
- Know the major roles the sales manager plays in the organization.
- Recognize the place of the sales force in the overall organization and the part the sales manager plays in the sales force.
- See how the job of sales manager changes when a company enters the global arena.

INTRODUCTION

Any career transition requires a degree of reorientation both in thought and action. It can be major, requiring extensive changes in behavior and approaches to the job, or it can be relatively minor. For all successful salespeople, the opportunity usually arises for them to move into sales management and it often comes early in their careers. Although there are additional skills needed to be successful as sales managers, the transition, by and large, does not require a whole new set of skills as much as it does the transformation of existing skills. Sometimes this is a more difficult process than learning new ones, and often this difficulty is not really appreciated and understood by prospective sales managers.

The job of sales manager is even more multifaceted than that of salesperson. It involves interacting with a different set of people as well as performing a different set of tasks. Sales managers are more than supervisors—they are leaders. As such, their primary responsibility is "empowering" salespeople—that is, equipping them to achieve the goals of the company as well as their own goals. Empowerment begins with planning and organizing the selling function. It also involves hiring the right people, training them sufficiently to perform their job, motivating them to achieve short-term and long-term goals, and giving them feedback.

Before looking at the sales manager's job in detail, let's consider some of the differences in the levels of sales managers.

THE NATURE OF SALES MANAGEMENT

What makes the job of sales manager so attractive is also what makes it very unattractive for many salespeople: the increase in responsibility. The person who is a high achiever is attracted to the opportunity for greater challenges, precisely what the job of sales management holds. Those challenges tend to increase and vary the further the person moves up the management ladder. Figure 11-1 depicts the management ladder as an inverted pyramid. Lower levels of management require some specific but limited decisions, whereas the upper-management positions are not so specific and are much less limited in scope and power. In other words, as individuals move up the sales management ladder, they will be required to make very different types of decisions because of the nature of the job. This means that these individuals must make a fundamental change in their outlook. The first-line managers deal with many more of the day-to-day operational issues. Their decisions are much more tactical. Their job requires much more person-to-person interaction with salespeople.

As individuals move from being first-line managers to regional managers, the job changes. Although regional managers must be concerned with the performance of individual salespeople, they must look at things from a wider perspective and learn how to manage managers—a talent that is unique unto itself. The decisions the regional managers make are much less tactical and begin to take on a strategic viewpoint.

Finally, as people move into the upper reaches of sales management, they are required to shift focus once again. In the upper level, individuals must be able to view the operation strictly from a strategic standpoint and be able to establish programs and policies that are appropriate for the different business units under their authority.[1] As managers move to the upper levels of the organizational structure, they must allow operational decisions to be made by those under them. This requires placing a great deal of faith in their lower-level managers. It also requires, however, being able to provide specific enough direction for those managers to be able to make operational decisions that are in line with company goals. In general, moving up the sales management ladder is a process of growth—to be willing and able to learn new things and implement what one learns.

FIGURE 11-1 The Levels of Sales Management

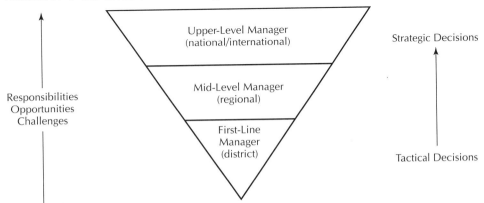

Upper-Level Manager (national/international)

Mid-Level Manager (regional)

First-Line Manager (district)

Responsibilities Opportunities Challenges

Strategic Decisions

Tactical Decisions

Regardless of which level on the sales management ladder people occupy, they perform seven basic functions:

1. Planning
2. Organizing
3. Staffing
4. Training
5. Leading
6. Monitoring
7. Administering

These seven functions are interrelated, and therefore, each needs to be considered as part of the sales manager's position. The specifics of these functions will change, but the functions themselves will not. Interwoven throughout is perhaps the most critical part of the sales manager's job—leadership.

CHARACTERISTICS OF SUCCESSFUL SALES MANAGERS

Just as certain personality attributes, skills, and knowledge distinguish good salespeople from average and poor ones, so, too, certain personality attributes, skills, and knowledge make for good sales managers. As we mentioned earlier, many of the characteristics necessary for successful sales managers are simply extensions and transformations of the characteristics needed by salespersons, some, though, are unique to the position of sales manager.

Some companies make the mistake of believing that good salespeople will always make good sales managers. According to Bill Kelley, senior editor for *Sales & Marketing Management,* being good at sales does not always lead to being good at management and, ironically, a major reason is exactly why the person is good at sales. For example, salespeople who are successful because they are intuitive and independent would have a more difficult transition into management than salespeople who are successful because they are well grounded in basic selling skills.[2]

Personality Attributes

Some characteristics necessary for good sales managers are shared with successful salespeople, such as empathy, ego drive, ego strength, flexibility, and integrity. **Empathy,** the ability to view a situation from the other's standpoint, is a prominent characteristic of successful salespeople. For the sales manager, or for any good manager, empathy is critical because it allows the manager to deal with people as individuals. Each person has a unique set of needs, desires, and goals that managers and salespeople must address. Empathy allows sales managers to treat each of their salespeople as individuals, just as salespeople treat each customer as an individual.

We know that **ego drive,** the concept that success in selling is tied directly to the salesperson's self-image, is another critical personality trait for salespeople. And ego drive is just as critical for sales managers. Sales managers succeed when their sales team is successful and when individuals within their unit achieve their potential. Sales managers with ego drive establish an atmosphere where success is not only possible but probable.

Ego strength or **resilience,** the ability to bounce back after a letdown, is another necessary attribute of good sales managers. Although sales managers do not face the same kind of rejection as do the people who sell, they still need the ability to rebound from defeats. For managers, these defeats often come in the form of failing to redeem a salesperson who is foundering. Although it is extremely defeating for a person in whom the sales manager has invested time to fail, failures happen despite the manager's best efforts. A lack of ego strength may result in the manager becoming discouraged when a salesperson does fail and, because of that, may tend to write off salespeople in the future who show signs of failure.

Flexibility is another of the necessary attributes shared by both. Sales managers need tremendous flexibility in dealing with their sales staff. And because of the multifaceted nature of the sales managers' job, flexibility permits them to deal with unforeseen problems that arise almost daily. Another aspect of flexibility is keeping an open mind when listening to new approaches offered by salespeople. The need for flexibility is characterized by these words:

> Keeping an open mind is crucial to the success of your marketing/sales partnership. Someone may suggest a way of dealing with a certain marketing issue that's radically different from what has been done in the past. Don't fear innovation! Take advantage of such creative thought to revamp your marketing where needed.[3]

The attribute of **integrity,** so necessary for the development of trust in the buyer/seller relationship, is doubly critical for sales managers. The old adage "Don't do as I do, do as I say" is the reason for the downfall of many salespeople and managers. Integrity is the basis for building trust without which sales managers won't succeed.[4] Sales managers must decide early in their tenure what their limits of acceptability will be.

A reputation for integrity grows out of personal ethics. It is earned, and if ever lost, almost impossible to reclaim. For example, Acme Industries has a policy that restricts the amount of money that can be spent to entertain clients and forbids the purchase of alcoholic beverages with company money due to liability concerns. Herb Tinkly, the sales manager, strictly enforces this policy, and stresses the importance of accurately reporting expenses. In trying to win a major new account for Acme, Herb had a party at his house with live music, lavish food, and an open bar. He invited the principals of the account as the guests of honor, as well as the Acme sales force. Other guests included some of Herb's friends and relatives. The next Monday, Henryetta Blodgett, one of Herb's salespeople, told him what a nice party it was, and mentioned that she was impressed that he was willing to spend that much of his own money to win a client. Herb's response was, "Oh, the company's gonna pay for it! I just need to figure out a way to include it on next quarter's expense report. I guess that course in creative writing I took in college will come in handy." Certainly, word of this episode would spread quickly in the sales force, and it would serve to undermine both company policy and Herb's reputation among his salespeople.

Although the attributes discussed here are necessary for success as a sales manager, remember that having these attributes does not guarantee manager success. Like outstanding athletes, sales managers must develop their attributes through practicing the skills related to their job.

Skills

Just as is the case with attributes, the skills required to be a successful sales manager often are the same skills required of a salesperson. Skills are the abilities that an individual possesses. They can be learned and tend to improve with practice. Sales management skills, like other kinds of skills, are usually complex combinations of actions that come together to form the skill. Generally, learning a skill involves practicing each of its components independently of the others and then joining them together. Skills important to both managers and salespeople include listening, speaking, and organizing. More applicable to sales managers are leadership skills, strategic thinking skills, political skills, and diagnostic skills.

Listening may be the premier skill in the selling profession: It provides information, it creates the basis for developing trust, and it lets the person who is speaking know that he or she is important. Good listening provides a greater depth of information and allows the development of rapport and trust between sales managers and subordinates. Listening also communicates a depth of concern for the speaker as an individual.

Often salespeople who are having difficulty have at least a rudimentary understanding of what the root cause of the problem may be. Active listening by the sales manager can help the speaker hear what he or she is really saying. (For more information on active listening, see Chapter 3.) It enables the speaker to arrive at some conclusion about the problem; and when the speaker "owns" the solution, he or she will be much more likely to act on it. On the other hand, a sales manager who is more ready to speak and tell the salesperson what to do will often find that effort thwarted, even when correctly diagnosing the problem. In such a case, the sales manager will be frustrated because the answer is "as plain as the nose on your face" and will often conclude that the salesperson either does not care enough or is too lazy or stubborn to take corrective action. There is something in human nature that makes us respond better when we have arrived at a conclusion ourselves instead of having someone tell us what the correct solution is.

Effective speaking is a skill necessary not only in sales but also in sales management. Effective speaking does not mean delivering a speech but, rather, being able to communicate accurately and efficiently. It is not as easy as it sounds. First, the speaker needs to speak on a level with and in a way that will be understood by the person being spoken to. This involves having at least some understanding of that person.

Often, how a thing is said is at least as important as what is said. People sometimes get their motives confused when they begin talking. As pointed out in Chapter 3, people almost always communicate two sets of messages—one informational and the other emotional. When a person is upset, the individual may state some truism not for the purpose of correction and providing feedback but simply to "vent steam." This interaction may give the appearance of providing direction, but the real motive is to let the other person know that the speaker is angry, and the results will be different than if the speaker were simply providing information and feedback. The problem is that the person is often not even conscious of the actual motive and is surprised when the individual being spoken to does not respond in a positive way.

Often people, especially when they are upset, revert to particular patterns of communications that involve making generalized, sometime derogatory statements about the behavior of others. For instance, a manager might say, "You're always wasting time at the office instead of being out selling!" A better approach might be to say, "I've noticed you have been spending more time than usual in the office lately." Both statements are saying the same thing; however, the former is a condemning statement that conveys anger, and the latter is an observation that invites dialogue. Similar examples abound; suffice it to say that sales managers should examine their speech patterns, be mindful of their motives when speaking, and avoid condemning statements.

Organizing is another skill that is important to both managers and staff. For salespeople, it is crucial that they be able to organize time, presentations, and accounts efficiently. Poor organization is one of the great wasters, and it contributes to poor overall performance. Sales managers must not only be able to organize their own jobs and work but also be able to assist salespeople in organizing theirs. Additionally, the scope of organizational skills must be expanded for sales managers so that they can organize the sales force as a unit. This means that they must have a good grasp of territorial management and a good understanding of the strengths and weaknesses of the sales force and their company and products.

Organizing the sales unit means that sales managers need to be able to coordinate the efforts of the company sales force with any manufacturer's representatives that the company uses. This requires thinking strategically, in terms of mission, objectives, strategies, and tactics. Given that sales managers are often called on to travel more than when they were in sales, it is essential that in making travel plans the byword is efficiency. Time is the one commodity that cannot be replaced.

Some skills are probably more applicable to sales managers than to salespeople. Among these are the ability to think strategically, political skills, diagnostic (problem-solving) skills, and leadership skills. Leadership skills are so important that they will be discussed separately in a later section. Strategic thinking skills involve going beyond the immediate situation and being able to consider the long-term impact of decisions. The specific objectives of the sales force must follow from the overall mission and objectives of the organization. The sales force objectives lead to the sales force strategy, the general plan for accomplishing the objectives. Tactics, the short-term operational actions, flow from the sales force strategy.

The discipline of planning is difficult, and often sales managers who are action-oriented will attempt to get ahead of themselves in the planning process. Doing so will result in approaches that are loaded with inefficient operation and even with actions that are contradictory. When sales managers include tactics in their strategic plans, they find that the two do not meld together well. The sales force strategy is the "grand plan." If it is well thought out, the tactics will be reasonably easy to develop.

Political skills include the ability to operate within the organization. This means garnering necessary support and working with other functional areas of the company. Sometimes it can also mean being able to smooth the ruffled feathers of a customer or a salesperson. Political skills can be thought of as "diplomacy," which is an essential part of the sales manager's job.[5] This "skill" likely comes more naturally to the pragmatist, a person who is oriented toward practical solutions. It involves the ability to analyze situations and organizations and, from that analysis, to develop effective courses of action. It recognizes that while, in the purest sense, the political nature of organizations may not be commendable or desirable, company politics are a fact of life and to prosper within the company, a person must adapt. It also involves the ability to "read people" and be flexible enough to work with a variety of people. Additionally, political skills involve the ability to focus on things that are important and not get sidetracked by minutia.

Problem solving is a **diagnostic skill.** It involves the ability to break a problem down into its component parts and develop a plan of attack to address those components, thereby solving the problem. Problem solving is really an extension of analytical skills. The effective sales manager must be able to look beyond the easy answer. Too often an easy answer simply addresses symptoms rather than the root problem. Problem solving also involves patience—the ability to search long enough to find the right answer. In most cases, a well-defined problem is three-fourths solved. Being able to diagnose problems properly involves having a good understanding of all the issues and components in the problem and bringing those to bear on the solution.

Knowledge

Sales managers must possess certain knowledge in the same way that salespeople do. Perhaps for sales managers, "people knowledge" is the most important to possess, for sales managers must be able to work with individuals both subordinate and superior in the organization. Understanding human nature enables managers to work with those various people and to create programs tailored to the needs of individual salespeople to get maximum effectiveness.

Certainly, customer knowledge is critical for sales managers as well as for the salesperson.[6] For sales managers, customer knowledge will help them assist individual salespeople who might be having trouble with customers. It is also important to the sales manager in making forecasts and establishing quotas. Company knowledge, knowing how things operate within their own organization, is critical in working with other departments or divisions in the company. Sales managers are called on to pass along the corporate ethic and must truly understand it in order to effectively apply it to the sales force.

In a study of Fortune 500 companies and the criteria they use for selecting salespeople to promote to first-level sales managers, 11 crucial traits were uncovered: intellectual ability, motivation, human relations skills, perception of threshold social cues, higher than average energy level, persuasiveness, personal impact, human interaction, behavior flexibility, ambition, and tolerance of uncertainty.[7] In another article that took a different approach to the issue, the characteristics that make for poor sales management were outlined:[8]

1. *The office as enemy.* Having an antagonistic relationship between salespeople and others in the organization, often subtly encouraged by the actions of sales managers.
2. *Failure to respect personal time.* Having a tendency to intrude into the personal time of their salespeople and expect them to respond positively.
3. *Withholding information.* Not divulging crucial information they feel might make salespeople quit selling.
4. *Robotizing the sales force.* Having a tendency constantly to check up on salespeople to ensure they are out in the field.
5. *Who got the order?* Rewarding only the salesperson who actually wrote up the order and not giving credit to salespeople who assisted in getting the order.
6. *Meetings abuse.* Using meetings to browbeat or preach to salespeople.
7. *Puffing the plan.* Exaggerating the benefits of a sales promotion program.
8. *Counterfeit management.* Having salespeople do reports that the manager never gets around to reviewing.

Some of these practices result from a failure to exhibit certain critical attributes, from a lack of training, or from a poor attitude. All work against the effectiveness of sales managers.

THE PLACE OF LEADERSHIP IN SALES MANAGEMENT

Leadership is one of those topics that is probably discussed more often than it is understood. From our perspective, leadership can be defined as the following: affecting a person or a group by imparting a sense of purpose through providing direction and guidance to achieve objectives considered worthwhile by the leader. To be useful, this definition needs to be broken down:

Four elements of effective leadership are

1. A vision of what should be, a vision that takes into account the legitimate interests of all the people involved.
2. A strategy for achieving that vision, a strategy that recognizes all the broadly relevant environmental forces and organizational factors.
3. A cooperative network of resources, a coalition powerful enough to implement the strategy.
4. A highly motivated group of key people in that network, a group committed to making that vision a reality.[9]

Theories of Leadership

Corporate managers are often plagued with the gnawing question of whether they are really a "good" leader. Often they try to get a definitive answer by looking for a list of characteristics that identify good leaders. This approach arises from the trait theory of leadership, the idea that leaders possess specific attributes that nonleaders do not. Although this is a popularly held belief, the list of characteristics uncovered in various research studies ranges from the sublime to the ridiculous, contains traits that are contradictory, and fails to provide a clear-cut picture of a good leader.

Another theory of leadership that takes into account the impact of situational variables on leadership effectiveness is the path-goal theory.[10] Borrowing from the expectancy theory of motivation, it was proposed that the leader's effectiveness rests in his or her ability to provide both intrinsic and extrinsic rewards as well as enabling subordinates to complete a task by providing guidance and direction in certain situations. The original theory was later enhanced by breaking leadership down into four categories, each of which is appropriate in various situations:[11]

1. **Supportive leadership.** Provides subordinates a supportive climate in which to work by showing concern for them personally.
2. **Directive leadership.** Provides subordinates with specific guidelines for performance.
3. **Participative leadership.** Allows subordinates to have input into the decision-making process.
4. **Achievement-oriented leadership.** Sets challenging standards of performance and elicits response through conveying high expectations that subordinates will succeed.

The modified path-goal theory draws its strength from the fact that it factors in not only the characteristics of the task and work environment but also those of the subordinates. Additionally it considers the role that rewards play in the leader's ability to affect subordinates.

Another theory of leadership we discuss was proposed by Gary Yukl.[12] In his model, Yukl included the effect of characteristics of the individual subordinates

SELL!NG
THE FRONT LINES OF BUSINESS

Top Guns

Thomas Forbes

Cathie Black, the president and chief executive officer of the Newspaper Association of America, swears she has never left voice-mail messages for her staff at 4:30 a.m. In fact, she insists, she *never* makes calls before 5:30 a.m., and then only when she's on the West Coast. Still, she will admit that there was that one call to Nelson Mandela at 4:00 a.m.

Nelson Mandela? Four a.m.?

The consummate salesperson—she began her career by selling restaurant ads in the back of *Holiday* magazine and went on to become the president of *USA Today*—Black will go to almost any length to close a deal. In this case, she had hoped to convince the South African leader to speak at the Reston, Va.-based NAA's annual convention. She had been asked to call him at 2:00 p.m. South African time—or 7:00 a.m. Eastern time. But on this particular day, Black happened to be in Los Angeles, which added three hours to the time difference. She left instructions with the hotel switchboard for a very early wake-up; her call to Mandela was on schedule.

That kind of diligence is the stuff of legends, the little-engine-that-could determination that sets the standard for the business of sales. "Unfortunately," says Black, "I didn't get the order." But that won't keep her from trying again. And again.

Cathie Black's tale illustrates one of the new realities of '90s business: You can't be an effective CEO without being a willing and able salesperson—and without having a salesperson's capacity to recover from setbacks and rejections. Chief execs of the 1980s undoubtedly were better versed in the practices of downsizing and divesting than in the arts of cold calling and follow-through. But now Corporate America has gotten back to the business of doing business, making people with selling skills ripe for leadership.

"Sales and marketing are more in the forefront today for one underlying reason, and that is competition," says Tom Ingram, professor of marketing at Memphis State University. "When things are tough, it puts a premium on those who can bring in the dollars."

Two mandates are reverberating through top management: Get close to the customer, and bring fresh ideas to market. For the first time in a long time, the lessons learned in sales have real value and a new appreciation in the front office. Just ask some chief executives who have been in the sales trenches themselves.

"Somebody coming up on the sales side has a leg up in that he or she is customer-driven, usually is persuasive, and is able to build a consensus," says Patrick Dinley, president of Norelco Consumer Products Co. of Stamford, Conn., who began his career as a sales rep for Xerox in the early '60s. "These are all important to today's management style of empowerment and team-building."

Even those corporate leaders who didn't start out in sales end up selling on a daily basis. "We can have the greatest ideas in the world, but until we sell them to somebody, and get somebody to do something about them, the ideas don't have any particular value," says Raymond E. "Gene" Cartledge, chairman and CEO of Union Camp Corp., a $3 billion paper, packaging, and chemicals company in Wayne, N.J.

"Most of the CEOs I know, regardless of what their discipline was, are pretty good salesmen," adds Cartledge, who started in sales at Procter & Gamble. "Good salesmen do much more than talk to customers. One of the toughest jobs salespeople have is to sell their own companies. It's their job to articulate customers' needs in a way that their own company can satisfy them."

But as much as great CEOs are necessarily great salespeople, the converse is not always true, according to Herbert Greenberg, a clinical psychologist and a principal at Caliper Corp., a Princeton, N.J., management consultancy. "The great salespersons tend to not have great tolerance for detail," he says. "They would rather be out dealing with people, while the CEO is often bogged down with a lot of administrative details."

The biggest mistake top salespeople can make is to become managers when they are not temperamentally suited to the role. In addition to being harmful to the company, such a move can be unfulfilling to salespeople, both personally and financially. As Greenberg puts it, "For the good ones, sales is still the most lucrative profession going."

Yet there are aspects of being CEO that even the most committed salespeople say are uniquely gratifying. Black finds the broad challenge of running an organization much more stimulating than straight sales. Harvey Mackay, the author of three best-selling business books and the chairman and CEO of Mackay Envelope Corp. in Minneapolis, points to the enormous power and influence that heads of major corporations can wield. While the road to the top is as varied as individual luck and pluck, three recurring themes run through the stories and counsel of salespeople who are now running the store.

To Thine Own Self Be True

There's a reason this axiom struck a chord even in Shakespeare's day—it's sound advice. Before deciding that you want to become a manager, take a hard look at both your motivation and ability. Your sales talent is irrelevant to your management potential. "Avoid the Peter Principle of rising to the level of your own incompetence," warns Greenberg. "Don't assume success in selling is automatically going to mean success in management. It's not."

That's not to say that a super salesperson can't be a super manager. "You have to know what your strengths are, and decide what area is going to maximize that," says Black. "I've always loved selling, but I was determined to be—and be viewed as—more than just a sales executive."

Branch Out

"The discipline of sales is a good, honorable place to start a career," says Cartledge. "But as you go forward, you have to take the time to understand the rest of the business: finance, production, service, employees, customers, investors. Learn what their interests are and, not unlike selling, find out what you need to do to satisfy those interests."

Dick Holder, chairman and CEO of Reynolds Metals Co., Richmond, Va., believes salespeople in major corporations are too seldom exposed to other disciplines, particularly finance. "Take any opportunity you can to broaden your knowledge, whether it be through formal training or things that you can do on your own," he advises.

Mackay recommends that salespeople get an MBA, or at least take courses in accounting and economics at a local college. He also suggests they join Toastmasters International to improve their public speaking skills, and spend six to eight hours reading the Sunday *New York Times* each week. "Most salespeople only know their own little world, and have their focus on their accounts," he says.

It is no accident that most CEOs at major corporations have banking or financial backgrounds. "Anybody who is aspiring to become more than a sales executive must really steep themselves in the business side of the operation and be-

come very familiar with the whole bottom-line orientation," says Black.

Think Long-Term

"A salesman has to have goals. It's every week, every month, every year, year after year. There's always charts, there's always measurements," says Mackay. "So you do get into that mentality of, 'How did I do this quarter?' " Short-term thinking, he adds, is the single biggest mistake of American management. And it is drilled into salespeople.

Chief executives with sales backgrounds are acutely aware that the system forces salespeople to sacrifice long-term strategy to meet short-term goals. "Hit those numbers and earn X," says Norelco's Dinley, "and then we roll all the numbers back to zero on Jan. 1."

Not only is that mind-set bad for management, he says, it has become detrimental for salespeople as well. "If Kmart is a customer today, don't we want them to be a customer tomorrow?" Dinley asks rhetorically. "It takes more today than calling on the buyer or senior buyer. You've got to penetrate the account vertically and horizontally to be a good, effective salesperson. We're starting to look at that as a measurement of performance and not, 'Gee whiz, did they get the sales quota number or not?' "

Dinley is experimenting with compensation structures at Norelco that are designed to overcome the built-in incentive for salespeople to be volume-driven instead of profit-driven. Such foresight comes from years of experience in the field. So it is with a touch of irony that Dinley notes, "Sales has been perceived as a necessary evil. In other words, 'We got to hire these bright, glib people, and we seem to have to pay them a lot, but by god, don't ever put them in charge of anything.'" But as far as Dinley and other chief executive salespeople are concerned, that perception couldn't be further from the truth.

Reprinted with the permission of SELL!NG magazine.

along with the characteristics of the group as a whole. He also included situational variables, such as the task structure and the degree of role formalization, as well as the nature of the leader-subordinate relationship. Yukl proposed that a leader's effectiveness is determined in large part by how skillfully he or she is able to correct any weaknesses within the group, either of the individual members or of the group as a whole. A leader can enhance his or her leadership through a proactive approach by doing such things as initiating long-term development programs, changing the structure of the organization, and gaining more control over the amount and quality of resources used to support the sales effort.

Autocratic vs. Democratic Leadership

A major decision facing sales managers is how much input to seek from subordinates in carrying out their role as leader. There are at least four levels of subordinate input:[13]

1. **Autocratic decision.** The leader decides on courses of action without seeking input from subordinates.
2. **Consultation.** The leader seeks opinions and suggestions from subordinates but makes the decision himself or herself.
3. **Joint decision.** The leader meets with subordinates or a representative group and they make decisions together.
4. **Delegation.** The leader parcels out various decisions to subordinates, who have the responsibility for making decisions regarding a particular aspect of the operation.

Yukl's approach is similar to the one suggested by Victor Vroom, who examined the extent to which leaders were people-oriented or task-oriented and went on to suggest four leadership styles:[14]

1. Tells. Emphasis placed is on the task performed rather than on person performing it. The manager makes the decision.
2. Persuades. Heavy emphasis is placed on both the task and the person. The manager makes the decision and then "sells" the idea to subordinates.
3. Participates. Heavy emphasis is placed on the person and little emphasis is placed on the task. The decision is made jointly between the manager and the subordinate.
4. Delegates. Little emphasis is placed on either the task or the person. The decision is left to subordinates who are responsible for carrying through with appropriate action.

Autocratic versus democratic leadership styles, rather than being two distinct typologies, could better be viewed as the opposite ends of a continuum, as illustrated in Figure 11-2. As the figure indicates, democratic leaders tend to utilize information from subordinates and relegate more personal responsibility for making decisions to those individuals than do leaders who are more autocratic. In effect, democratic leaders rely more on subordinates than do autocratic leaders and, therefore, will probably need to hire people who merit such reliance. Additionally, democratic leaders tend to be more people-oriented and less task-oriented than do those who are more autocratic.

Given the increasing professionalization of sales, the autocratic style likely will not work well today. Actually, that approach has probably never worked well with field sales representatives because they are seldom in the office, where they can be monitored, and they themselves must make independent decisions everyday. Based on these studies and given the nature of a sales career, we can make several conclusions about leading the sales force:

1. Decision participation by subordinates is consistent with the personality characteristics of successful salespeople.
2. Participation in decisions leads to a greater acceptance of and commitment to sales goals and more well-defined action plans for achieving them.
3. Participation in decisions will tend to increase understanding of the reward system and how rewards can be obtained.
4. Participation in decisions tends to increase cooperation in solving problems, which is an essential part of the sales job.
5. Participation in decisions can result in better decisions because both the salesperson and the sales manager are party to pertinent information that the other may not possess.

What Leaders Really Do

What do leaders actually do? In other words, what functions do they perform in their organizations? In an excellent presentation on this issue, William Hitt proposes that leaders perform eight major functions related to their role as predominant change agents in their organizations.[15] These eight major functions are

> **Creating the vision.** The leader is the person who imparts to the people a sense of direction and purpose. This involves helping the organization define what it is about and what should be achieved. The sense of vision forms a bond for members of the organization and provides them a point of reference.

FIGURE 11-2 The Leadership Style Continuum

DEMOCRATIC   Delegates   Participates   Persuades   Tells   AUTOCRATIC

(Subordinate Centered)   (Boss Centered)

Developing the team. It is people who accomplish the task. No leader, regardless of how talented and driven he or she is can bring about an effect without support. This function not only involves bringing together the right people, but also forging them into a team that is greater than the sum of its parts. Through open communication and assimilating common goals, teams can accomplish the goals of the organization when an unincorporated group of individuals is destined to fail miserably.

Clarifying the values. Any organization needs a set of values that clarify what is important to that group. This set of values forms the core of the "corporate culture." Values also form the basis of the code of ethics. The leader cannot make all decisions related to the ethical conduct of the organization, however, he or she must work to ensure that all decisions made related to it are in line with the proper value system.

Positioning. Regardless of how well the vision and system of values is delineated in the organization, without an effective strategy the organization is destined not to perform to par. The leader must present a plan for prioritizing the goals of the organization and for the effective use of resources. The different functional areas of the organization must act in accord and yet still perform their individual tasks.

Communicating. The effective leader must be able to communicate well. He or she must be able to do so on the individual level as well as the corporate level and must be able to do so in the spoken and the written word. The leader needs to recognize that "words don't mean, people do" and so will be aware that not only what he or she says is important in communication, but also what he or she does is equally critical.

Empowering. Leaders are constantly involved in moving people toward goals. This involves providing specific direction, but more especially providing motivation to move. Empowerment means developing the forum whereby people can meet their needs through accomplishing the goals of the organization.

Coaching. Leadership is an ongoing process that involves providing guidance to those being led. This means giving feedback to the person so that he or she can develop to his or her full potential. It also involves encouraging people to "stretch themselves" to reach those heights that have not been reached in the past.

Measuring. Leaders need to "keep their finger on the pulse of the organization." This means that they need information about how the organization is performing relative to the goals it has established. This information is obtained from the Management Information System and by the leader walking around the organization to find what is happening in the trenches.

Each of these eight functions is important, but particular ones can be more important than others at certain times.

POWER AND INFLUENCE IN LEADERSHIP

Effective leadership means that a person possesses the ability to wield power. Although authority does provide a source of power, to be effective, leaders must go beyond vested authority if they are to exert influence on subordinates. Power arises from several sources within the organization. Here are five:[16]

1. **Legitimate power.** Rests on the fact that the leader has the right to request/demand an action and the subordinate has an obligation to comply.

2. **Reward power.** Rests on the ability to mete out rewards. Although this often corresponds to a legitimate position in the organization, the extent of this base of power will vary considerably.

3. **Coercive power.** Resides in the person's capability of issuing punishment or negative sanctions. This may involve a loss of something covert such as money or position, or it could mean the loss of something more personal such as psychological support and friendship.

4. **Expert power.** Based on the knowledge possessed by the person and the willingness to share that knowledge.

5. **Referent power.** Rests on the fact that a person is admired and others want to emulate him or her or at least be identified with the person.

Sales managers who are truly leaders use the latter two as their main bases of power. We say this because salespeople in the field generally have a fair amount of autonomy in the execution of their jobs. They are constantly making decisions that have an effect on their firms. For these decisions to be consistent with the policies and culture of the organization, the salespeople must have internalized those policies and that culture. The salesperson who performs a task only for the reward will ultimately require bigger and bigger rewards to do the right thing. The salesperson who complies with a request only because of the threat of punishment will ultimately lose the fear of punishment. And the salesperson who takes a particular action because she was told that "I'm the boss and that's all you need to know!" will soon lose respect for that boss. Only expert power and referent power will sustain a good leader.

THE ROLES OF THE SALES MANAGER

The Sales Manager as Filter

As shown in Figure 11-3, sales managers act as a boundary spanner between internal and external forces and the sales force. A boundary spanner occupies a place between two entities and acts as a go-between. Just as the salespeople are boundary spanners between their company and their customers, the sales managers are boundary spanners between three groups—the company, the sales force, and the customers. This boundary spanner position requires that the person understand the needs and desires of all the groups involved, know how to accommodate each party within reason, and have the skill to carry it out. The boundary spanner position can lead to **role stress.** However, the leader's ability to develop mutually satisfying exchange relationships with all the parties involved will reduce that role stress.[17]

In reality, this boundary spanner position means that sales managers are **filters.** That is, they implement the marketing plans within the confines of the internal and external forces. They are expected to play the role of interpreter and refiner of the plans and decide on the priorities that will be conveyed to the sales

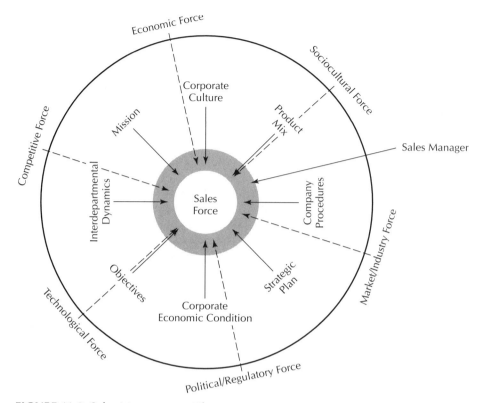

FIGURE 11-3 Sales Manager as a Filter

force. Sales managers receive feedback from salespeople, and this information will not only affect their decisions but will also be transmitted by the managers to upper management. This role as a filter, then, is critical in carrying out the plans of upper management while taking into account the pertinent factors within the organization. It is instructive to note that because both the internal forces of the organization and external forces of the environment are dynamic, sales managers must be flexible and creative to deal with them successfully.

The **external environment** consists of factors outside the organization that have an effect on how it operates. These environmental forces interact to create both threats and opportunities for the organization and thus have a direct impact on strategic planning. However, the impact on the sales force is indirect. A major part of the planning process consists of analyzing this external environment. From this analysis, the organization is able to examine its mission statement, its objectives, its strategies, and its tactics. The process of examining the external environment is called **environmental scanning.** True environmental scanning consists of a continuous, systematic gathering of information from relevant sources, summarizing this information by a collection center, and dispensing the information to the appropriate functional areas in the organization. This not only provides a flow of fresh information for the planning process; it also reveals the presence of **strategic windows,** unique opportunities that arise in the marketplace and are limited as to time and the number of competitors that will have a viable opportunity to take advantage of.[18]

Within any organization there exists an **internal environment,** a set of interactive forces that affect its operation. These forces establish the dynamic within the organization, which affects the magnitude and use of resources, the strategic planning process, and specific strategies employed. The internal forces also directly affect the management of the sales force. They come together to form not only a social system but also the "atmosphere" in the workplace. These internal forces are affected by the external ones and will be altered as a result of a change in one of those external forces.

The Sales Manager as Intrapreneur

One of the attractions about the job of sales managers is that they are, in effect, building a business that will be an extension of themselves. If managed correctly, it will be a healthy, going concern long after the manager has moved on to other things. This is really the essence of "entrepreneurship," "the process of creating something different with value by devoting the necessary time and effort, assuming the accompanying financial, psychic, and social risks, and receiving the resulting rewards of monetary and personal satisfaction."[19]

However, given that sales managers exist within a larger organization and are not entrepreneurs as such, they more closely fit the definition of **intrapreneur,** "entrepreneurship within an existing business structure."[20] Intrapreneurs need to possess a vision for what they wish to accomplish, be able to address problems creatively, decide on an appropriate course of action, and carry the project to completion. Those elements certainly are present in successful sales managers. Another aspect of intrapreneurship involves being able to marshal people and resources to accomplish the strategic plans of the organization. In short, the sales manager needs to treat the job as a business to be managed and not simply as a position to be filled.

The Sales Manager as Goal Setter

It is generally a given that the establishment of goals is a critical element in success. We hear phrases like "If you aim at nothing, you will hit it" and so forth. Certainly, goals provide a sense of direction and help establish a set of priorities. Goals are also important when we attempt to determine the best allocation of resources. Obviously, sales managers play a critical role in goal setting. They not only need to establish both personal goals and goals for their sales units, they also play a major role in helping salespeople establish goals for themselves. Thus sales managers help salespeople to set **performance goals** (goals related to their output), as well as **learning goals** (goals related to improving their abilities).[21]

The Sales Manager as Change Agent

Sales managers are change agents. By **change agent,** we mean a person who, through correct diagnosis of problems within the organization, is able to develop solutions and facilitate the adoption of those solutions.[22] Sometimes the change agent can be a person from outside the organization who acts as a consultant. However, sales managers often do not have the luxury of hiring such a person and must become proficient at intervening in problems within the sales force.

Being a change agent begins with taking an objective look at what is going on by conducting a systematic analysis of the problem. This is very difficult for sales managers because they likely have been living with the problem for a period of time and have developed some preconceived notions as to what needs to be done. Taking an objective look at the problem means that sales managers will need to distinguish the apparent symptom from the underlying problem. Probably the simplest way to do so is actually to list all the symptoms of the problem in a column on the left-hand side of a piece of paper, and across the page, list the corresponding problem that has led to the symptom. The next step involves listing the various tenable alternatives for each aspect of the problem and then delineate the strengths and weaknesses of each alternative. Once a solution is developed that adequately addresses the problem, sales managers must then implement the necessary corrective action or, in other words, facilitate the necessary changes.

Kurt Lewin proposed that change is essentially a modification of those forces that keep behavior stable within an organization.[23] He stated that in any organization there are forces that attempt to maintain the status quo and another set of forces that are striving to bring about change. To facilitate change, the change agent may either decrease the forces supporting the status quo or increase the forces that strive for change. Lewin proposed three steps in the process of facilitating change:

1. **Unfreezing.** Lessening the forces that maintain the status quo. This can be done through providing new information about the discrepancy between current behavior and what is acceptable, or perhaps showing how the person or group can better achieve their goals through a new approach.
2. **Moving.** Creating new behaviors on the part of the person. This is done by providing a cognitive map of where the change will take the person or group and the steps necessary to make the change. It often involves facilitating new attitudes as well as new actions.
3. **Refreezing.** Stabilizing the person or group in the new position. This is done through developing a support framework for the new behavior. The use of motivation, feedback, and compensation is an essential part of such a framework.

Sales managers sometimes must work not only to change organizations but also to change individuals. Often managers are tempted to view this idea with skepticism; their view is that people don't change and the sales manager who tries to do so is wasting time. Sterling Livingston counters this notion with the idea that managers do in fact have a major impact not only on how people perform but also on what people become. He states that the key to that impact is the expectations managers hold for subordinates, and he calls this concept the **Pygmalion effect.**[24] This effect of personal involvement works between the sales manager and the salesperson, as well as between upper management and a sales manager.[25]

The Difficulty in Bringing About Change

Even when the need for change is apparent to all concerned, change still creates dissonance and will likely meet with resistance. There are a number of reasons for this. First, human nature is such that the present reality represents a form of security. Even though that reality may be detrimental to a person and/or the organization, it is a known quantity, and generally people have adapted to it. Change means that a whole new set of rules must be learned and that a person faces many unknowns.

Another reason people might resist change is that they may have an investment in the status quo. The system, despite its flaws, may have been a good one for them, and any change means that their circumstances may not be improved appreciably and may even deteriorate. Some individuals may have devoted a great deal to bring their positions within the organization to a particular point and will be hesitant to see that work "go down the drain."

Any change may result in the loss of autonomy for some people. Even though this may not seem significant, one of the factors that makes a job attractive is the degree of autonomy individuals enjoy. A change may mean that someone may be called on to turn over "his accounts" to another and face some scrutiny as to how those accounts have been handled. Additionally, people may be shifted around in the organization and be placed under a new supervisor who may necessarily exercise more control over them than they have been accustomed to.

For salespeople, changes often represent a more direct threat—a threat to their livelihood. Anytime salespeople are called on to change territories, it means that their sales will suffer at least a temporary slump as they try to get established in the new area. A change in territory means they will need to learn about new customers, new geographic areas, and new competitors. At the same time, they may feel that all their work to build up their old territory has been for naught. It may also mean relocation, and that can create a whole other series of problems.

THE SALES FORCE AS A SYSTEM

The sales manager's job depends to a large extent on how the sales force fits with the corporate strategic marketing plan. Figure 11-4 illustrates how the sales force can be viewed as a system within the corporate organization.[26]

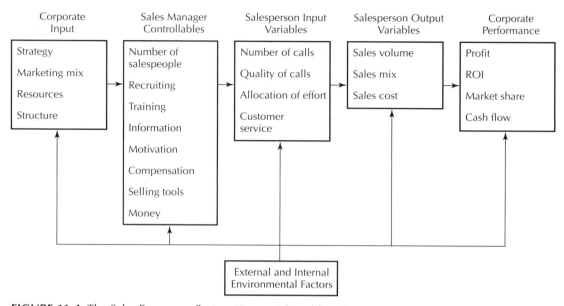

FIGURE 11-4 The Sales Force as a System (*Source:* Adapted from Porter Henry, Manage your salesforce as a system. *Harvard Business Review* [March–April 1975], 89–95.)

Corporate input represents elements of the strategic plan—strategy, marketing mix, resources, and structure. These represent the resources made available to the sales manager, whose responsibility is to manipulate them to achieve maximum results. **Sales manager controllables** are those factors over which the sales manager exercises control—number of salespeople, recruiting, training, information, motivation, compensation, selling tools, and money. Because each of these affects the others, these elements must be treated as a whole. All are important, and a failure in one means a breakdown of the system. Certainly, we know that such things as the recruitment and training of salespeople and the establishment of motivational and compensational packages are critical, but the other controllables cannot be ignored. For example, information is an extremely critical variable in an organization's ability to be competitive, and most successful sales forces are those that have ready access to information.[27] It is extremely unusual for any individual to achieve mastery in all aspects of the job; therefore sales managers must examine those areas where they are weak and attempt to develop them further.

In one sense, the sales manager's realm of control does not extend beyond this set of controllables. In other words, the sales manager has the ability to affect directly those controllables; however, the sales manager has only an indirect effect over salesperson variables. If the manager does a good job with those things over which he or she has control, in the long run, salesperson input and output variables should be in line with performance guidelines. This is perhaps one of the most difficult truths for sales managers to accept, because they may be tempted to "ride herd" on salespeople to ensure that they are doing their jobs "right."

Salesperson input variables are those things over which a salesperson exercises direct control—number of calls, quality of calls, allocation of effort, and customer service. The salesperson has to be depended on to make the right number of high-quality calls and to allocate his or her effort correctly. Simply viewing sales as a "numbers game"—if enough calls are made, sales will be high—is a shortsighted view. The calls need to be planned and executed well, especially in light of the increasing pressure toward a problem-solving approach to selling. Additionally, the salesperson needs to balance his or her effort so as to spend the most time with the best prospects while nurturing accounts that have promise.

Salesperson output variables—sales volume, sales mix, and sales cost—flow from the inputs. At one time, sales volume would have been much more heavily emphasized than the other two output variables. However, more and more sales organizations are accepting the reality that the sales mix and the sales costs are at least as important in determining profitability as is volume. Sales volume can be increased through a number of means other than good salesmanship. Salespeople can "buy" business with cheaper prices and/or wining and dining customers, but in doing so, they are sacrificing margin. Generally the customer won over in this fashion stays around until someone else "buys" their business.

Corporate output is the net result of all the former elements in the system—profit, return on investment, market share, and cash flow. It is the "bottom line." This is the way in which businesses measure success, obtain feedback as to the quality of the overall program, and fuel the machinery for future achievements. Unsatisfactory performance in this area indicates some problem in the system. Such problems are not easily diagnosed, and unless the system is carefully examined to determine the flaw, corrective actions may be inappropriate or too late.

SALES MANAGEMENT IN THE INTERNATIONAL ARENA

When sales managers move into the international arena, the complications they face increase dramatically. Whether stationed abroad or based in the United States, they must not only be knowledgeable about the country in which they are working but adaptable in their approach to the job. Additionally, they must extend their communication skills to be effective in a foreign setting. The importance of the sales manager in creating a high-performance atmosphere does not diminish as she or he moves into the international arena.[28]

Home versus Host Country Sales Managers

When a company moves into the international arena, one important issue has to do with whether to use sales managers who are from the country where the company is based, from the country where the firm wishes to do business, or another, third country. If the company chooses to use a manager from its home office, it has to decide whether he or she will be based in the home or host country. If the company bases the person in the home country, this saves the costs and risks of relocation. Additionally, it does keep the manager closer to what is going on in the company. Obviously, the drawback is the cost of time and travel associated with the manager's being based at the home office. For the company with small segments of business in different parts of the globe, having the manager based at the home office is probably preferred.

If the company chooses to have the sales manager be from the home country, it may choose to locate him or her abroad. Although this gets the manager closer to the markets, it also presents some special problems. According to international business experts George Taoka and Don Beeman:

> Multinational enterprises regularly transfer personnel across national and cultural boundaries for short durations to meet a particular need, as a part of the career development program or for a permanent assignment. Those involved are likely to encounter problems in the new culture. They must deal with different languages, customs, beliefs, superstitions, attitudes, values, and religions. Social adaptation for the manager and family is usually more difficult than job adaptation. Language barriers will limit social interactions. To add to the problems, the spouse may have too much free time because servants are hired. Boredom and loneliness can lead to serious problems. Excessive drinking and money-spending are not uncommon under such conditions. The expatriate manager's satisfaction and performance is to a great extent determined by the family's ability to adjust to the new environment.[29]

The best thing a company can do when relocating a manager abroad is to give both the manager and his or her family adequate indoctrination to the culture of the foreign country along with some personal counseling. If a counselor detects friction between the spouses concerning the move, the company would be well advised not to relocate that manager.

The advantage of choosing a manager from the host country is that the person is already familiar with the culture of the country. Additionally, there may be political and social pressures to use a host-country manager. For example, in many cultures, "outsiders" are looked on with suspicion, especially if they are from a culture that is very different from that of the host country. Using host-country managers seems to be the trend today.[30] However, the host country may not have an abundance of people qualified to manage the sales force, and the people they do have, because the culture is so engrained, may not be able to adapt to the norms of the company.

Another alternative is to select a manager from another country. For example, a company may employ a German manager for its sales operations in South America if that person is familiar with both the company and the country. The advantage is that this person might possess the managerial skills that may not be readily available in the host country and yet would not have the cultural bias of a U.S. manager.[31]

A related issue is how to mix nationalities recruited for the overseas sales force. Regarding employees in general, that mix depends on five factors:[32]

1. The type of business and the company's strategy
2. Laws and regulations requiring the hiring of nationals
3. Laws and regulations regarding bringing in employees from outside the country
4. The availability of personnel within the host country
5. Cost considerations

Certainly the importance of each of these factors will vary from country to country. In terms of the sales force, an additional factor is the nature of the market in the host country, as well as the strategies used by local competitors.

Characteristics of the International Sales Manager

Given the special nature of marketing internationally, sales managers need certain characteristics to be successful. For example, not only should the manager have language skills and be adaptable but, as Philip Harris and Robert Moran suggest, he or she should possess a good sense of humor.[33] Harris and Moran list some other specific skills that international managers need:

Having respect. The person must be able to demonstrate respect for people and customs in other countries.

Tolerating ambiguity. The person must react to different and sometimes unpredictable situations without showing discomfort and/or irritation.

Relating to people. The person must be able to get the job done in such a way that people feel a part of the project and feel that they have profited from being involved.

Being nonjudgmental. The person must maintain objectivity and refrain from being ethnocentric.

Personalizing one's observations. The person must realize that one's view is culturally bound and offer suggestions or commentary tentatively.

Having empathy. The person must understand the frame of reference of the other person and relate to that person on that basis.

Being persistent. The person may not be successful with the first attempt at something, but must be willing to pursue goals even in the face of initial rejection.

Obviously these characteristics are related and represent some of the same qualities necessary for success as a sales manager in the United States.

Approaches to Management

One issue that is important when moving into the international arena is the management approach employed. Based on his study of managers and workers in 50 countries, Geert Hofstede suggests that the American style of participative leadership and management by objectives is not readily transferable overseas.[34] For example, in studying American versus Japanese management approaches, it has been argued that the two predominant styles historically favored in the

United States have been "Theory X" and "Theory Y," whereas the one employed in Japan is "Theory Z."[35]

Managers who employ **Theory X** believe that workers are unmotivated and lazy and need constant supervision. For example, if Roger Tey, the sales manager for Midwest Industries, were a Theory X manager, he would have his salespeople fill out a number of reports to ensure that they were doing their jobs. Additionally, he would constantly check up on them by either riding with them or calling customers to make sure that his salespeople were making their calls. Managers who use **Theory Y** believe that workers are willing, responsible, and simply need support and encouragement. For example, if Thelma Frump, the vice president of sales for Northwest Industrial Supply, used a Theory Y approach, her main interaction with her salespeople would involve coaching and providing support rather than monitoring their activities. Theory Y is the predominant model in use today in the United States. In countries such as France and Germany, a Theory Y approach is not considered authoritarian enough.[36] The **Theory Z** approach, favored in Japan, involves achieving group consensus of workers and is participative in nature. For example, if Bud Lot, the sales manager for Big Sky Chemicals, were using a Theory Z management style, he would leave the majority of decisions to his salespeople. Bud would spend much of his time providing information to his salespeople and ensuring that they had adequate resources to be competitive in their territories.

CHAPTER SUMMARY

In this chapter we examined the job of the sales manager, beginning with a discussion of the characteristics important for sales managers to possess, such as personality attributes, skills, and knowledge. Many of these characteristics are the same ones that salespeople need to be successful; however, some are unique to the sales manager position. For example, just as with salespeople, sales managers should also possess a good deal of empathy, listening skills, and customer knowledge. However, the sales manager additionally must possess political skills and diagnostic (problem-solving) skills that are not necessarily as critical for salespeople. In reality, many of the characteristics that sales managers need are simply characteristics they needed in selling that they adapted to the management role.

Perhaps the most critical aspect of the sales manager's job is leadership. Specifically, some major theories of leadership were presented and applied to the sales manager position. In the final analysis, being a good leader is as much a function of the situation as it is of the person. Because the requirements of leadership vary considerably between situations there are no "born leaders."

Next, styles of leadership were discussed. Specifically, the democratic leadership style was contrasted with the autocratic style. They can be seen as the opposite ends of a continuum. We next considered what leaders really do—specific aspects of leading people. Also, the concept of power and influence in the organization was examined.

Sales managers occupy the position of a boundary spanner as they play the role of a filter. They are called on to channel and adapt the internal and external forces that have impact on the sales force. The sales manager in reality must function as an intrapreneur within the company. They also play a crucial part in goal setting for the sales organization, both in terms of the overall goals of the sales force and of individual goals. Additionally, sales managers are change agents in that they work to bring about changes in the organization and within individuals. We also considered the concept of the sales force as a system and the implications of that for sales managers.

The chapter closed with a discussion of global aspects of sales management. The move into the global arena necessitates some changes in the approach to sales management and requires that managers have some characteristics that may not be necessary for managing a domestic sales force. An important consideration for companies when moving into international marketing is whether to use managers and salespeople from the host country, the company's home country, or from elsewhere.

KEY TERMS

achievement-oriented
    leadership, p. 234
autocratic decision, p. 238
coercive power, p. 241
change agent, p. 244
consultation, p. 238
corporate input, p. 246
corporate output, p. 247
delegation, p. 238
diagnostic skill, p. 232
directive leadership, p. 234
ego drive, p. 229
ego strength (resilience), p. 229
empathy, p. 228
environmental scanning, p. 242
expert power, p. 241
external environment, p. 242
filters, p. 241
flexibility, p. 229

integrity, p. 229
internal environment, p. 243
intrapreneurship, p. 243
joint decision, p. 238
leadership, p. 233
learning goal, p. 244
legitimate power, p. 240
"moving," p. 244
participative leadership, p. 234
performance goal, p. 244
political skills, p. 232
Pygmalion effect, p. 245
referent power, p. 241
"refreezing," p. 244
reward power, p. 241
role stress, p. 241
salesperson input variables, p. 247
salesperson output variables, p. 247
sales manager controllables, p. 246

strategic windows, p. 243
supportive leadership, p. 234
Theory X, p. 250

Theory Y, p. 250
Theory Z, p. 250
"unfreezing," p. 244

CHAPTER QUESTIONS

1. How do the types of decisions made by managers change as they progress up the management ladder?
2. Which characteristics are required for being successful sales managers as well as being successful salespeople?
3. Which characteristics are needed by sales managers that are not necessarily needed by salespeople?
4. Are there born leaders? Defend your answer.
5. When dealing with a sales force, is an autocratic or democratic approach the better one to employ? Why?
6. What are the five different types of power, and which one is probably the best for the sales manager to use? Explain your answer.
7. What does it mean when we say that the sales manager acts as a filter for the sales force?
8. Explain the idea that in viewing the sales force as a system, the sales manager cannot control salesperson input variables.
9. Why does the sales manager as change agent have a tough job?
10. What additional requirements do sales managers need in the global arena?
11. What are the implications of using home-country versus host-country managers in the international marketplace?

NOTES

1. Madhubalan Viswanathan and Eric M. Olson, Implementation of business strategies: Implications for the sales functions. *Journal of Personal Selling & Sales Management* 12 (Winter 1992), 45–57.
2. Bill Kelley, Transition and travail. *Sales & Marketing Management* (February 1992), 32–36.
3. Philip Carpenter, Bridging the gap between marketing and sales. *Sales & Marketing Management* (March 1992), 29–31.
4. Ibid.
5. Ibid.
6. Cynthia A. Christie, Managing the managers. *Sales & Marketing Management* (June 1992), 63–66; and Carpenter, Bridging the gap.
7. Donald B. Guest and Havva J. Meric, The Fortune 500 companies' selection criteria for promotion to first level sales management: An empirical study. *Journal of Personal Selling & Sales Management* 9 (Fall 1989), 47–52.
8. George J. Schenk, Are you abusing your salespeople? *Sales & Marketing Management* (April 1990), 32–40.
9. John P. Kotter, *The leadership factor* (New York: Free Press, 1988).

10. Robert J. House, A path goal theory of leader effectiveness. *Administrative Science Quarterly* 16 (1971), 321–339.
11. Robert J. House and T. R. Mitchell, Path-goal theory of leadership. *Journal of Contemporary Business* 3 (Autumn 1974), 81–97.
12. Gary A. Yukl, *Leadership in organizations* (Englewood Cliffs, NJ: Prentice Hall, 1981).
13. Ibid.
14. Victor H. Vroom, Leadership. In *Handbook of industrial and organizational psychology,* ed. Marvin D. Dunnette (Chicago: Rand McNally, 1986).
15. William D. Hitt, *The leader-manager* (Columbus, OH: Battelle, 1988).
16. J. R. P. French, Jr., and Bertram Raven, The bases of social power. In *Studies in social power,* ed. D. Cartwright (Ann Arbor, MI: Institute for Social Research, 1959).
17. John F. Tanner, Jr., Mark G. Dunn, and Lawrence B. Chonko, Vertical exchange and salesperson stress. *Journal of Personal Selling & Sales Management* 13 (Spring 1993), 27–36.
18. Derek F. Abell, Strategic windows. *Journal of Marketing* 42 (July 1978), 21–26.
19. Robert D. Hisrich and Candida G. Brush, *The woman entrepreneur* (Lexington, MA: Lexington Books, 1986).
20. Robert D. Hisrich and Michael P. Peters, *Entrepreneurship* (Homewood, IL: BPI/Irwin, 1989).
21. Harish Sujan, Barton A. Weitz, and Mirmalya Kumar, Learning, orientation, working smart, and effective selling. *Journal of Marketing* 58 (July 1994), 39–52.
22. Chris Argyris, *Intervention theory and method* (Reading, MA: Addison-Wesley, 1970).
23. Kurt Lewin, *Field theory in social sciences* (New York: Harper & Row, 1951).
24. Sterling Livingston, Pygmalion in management. *Harvard Business Review* (July–August 1969), 81–89.
25. Jack Falvey, A study of strengths. *Sales & Marketing Management* (June 1992), 12–14; Christie, Managing the managers.
26. Porter Henry, Manage your salesforce as a system. *Harvard Business Review* (March–April 1975), 85–95.
27. Dayle E. Zatlin, How well connected is your sales force? *Sales & Marketing Management* (January 1992), 25–31.
28. David W. Cravens, Ken Grant, and Thomas N. Ingram, In search of excellent sales organizations. *European Journal of Marketing* 26 (1992), 6–23.
29. George M. Taoka and Don R. Beeman, *International business* (New York: HarperCollins, 1991), 526.
30. Martin C. Schnitzer, Marilyn L. Liebrenz, and Konrad W. Kubin, *International business* (Cincinnati: South-Western, 1985).
31. Ibid.
32. Simcha Ronen, *Comparative and multinational management* (New York: Wiley, 1986).
33. Philip R. Harris and Robert T. Moran, *Managing cultural differences* (Houston, TX: Gulf, 1991).
34. Geert Hofstede, "Do American Theories Apply Abroad?," *Organizational Dynamics,* 10 (Summer 1981), 63–80.
35. Schnitzer et al., *International business.*
36. Vern Terpstra and Kenneth David, *The cultural environment of international business* (Cincinnati: South-Western, 1985).

SUGGESTED READINGS

Drucker, Peter. *The frontiers of management.* New York: Harper & Row, 1982.

Today's leaders are dealing with the consequences of decisions made by their predecessors and, at the same time, are making decisions that will impact future generations. Businesses exist in a dynamic environment where change is an inherent element. Change, if it is based on good information and sound principles, serves to make businesses more competitive and prepares them for the future.

Harris, Philip R., and Robert T. Moran. *Managing cultural differences.* Houston, TX: Gulf, 1991.

Every region of the world has particular cultural characteristics that shape the way people act. To be successful, a business must learn the cultures of the regions where it does business and adapt its approach to those cultures. It requires rethinking how the business operates.

Hickman, Craig R. *Mind of a manager—soul of a leader.* New York: Wiley, 1990.

Managers today are faced with a number of conflicting demands, some that require a careful manager, others that demand a dynamic leader. This creates a tension that is often not fully appreciated but, if unresolved, can lead to major difficulties. Bridging the gap requires that the manager come to have a good self-awareness as well as an understanding of those with whom he or she interacts.

Patton, Forrest H. *Force of persuasion.* Englewood Cliffs, NJ: Prentice Hall, 1986.

The ability to influence others is critical to being a successful manager. Being successful requires that the manager recognize the connection between mind-set and actions. People react to a number of influences, many of which they are not even aware.

Taoka, George M., and Don R. Beeman. *International business.* New York: HarperCollins, 1991.

In the global marketplace, businesses face challenges that are unique in every region of the globe. Additionally, they face both international and intranational environmental factors. Business must constantly adapt and change to compete in such a dynamic marketplace.

Yukl, Gary A. *Leadership in organizations.* Englewood Cliffs, NJ: Prentice Hall, 1994.

Leadership effectiveness has a number of different aspects. The effective leader is one who not only helps the organization achieve its goals but also creates an environment in which members of that organization willingly follow. The effects of leaders can be short term or long term and direct or indirect.

Chapter 12

Organizing the Sales Force

OPENING SCENARIO

Suzanne Hite had just taken over as vice president of sales for Wheaton Tools U.S. (WTUS). Established in 1927, WTUS was a producer of high-quality machine tools used mainly in the auto industry. The machine tool industry was undergoing rapid change both in the design and operation of the machine tools and in the way business was conducted. WTUS originally produced machine tools for small machine shop applications. Although machine tools for the auto industry was now its major line, the original line for small shops was still a viable part of the business. Both machine tool lines were sold directly to end users. WTUS also produced high-quality hand tools for metal fabrication. These were sold through distributors.

Because of its high-quality products and high level of service, WTUS's sales had been increasing despite tough economic times in the industry. While some competitors attempted to compete with imports on the basis of price, WTUS stayed the course by offering high quality with a high level of service support, but it charged a higher price. Most of those domestic competitors that had attempted to compete on price had vanished from the marketplace. They had begun to compete for some international business in the past five years, and this accounted for about 10 percent of their sales.

The machine tool business had grown rather stodgy in its outlook, and many companies had failed to keep up with the times. Although WTUS had been a leader in the technological end of the business, its management practices and the organization of its operation were coming under fire. WTUS organized its sales force geographically, with each salesperson selling the products in all three lines. There were four regional managers in the United States, with each responsible for roughly a quadrant of the country. There were two district managers under each of the regional managers. The northeast region, which included Michigan, had 23 salespeople, the southeast region, had 15 salespeople, the northwest 19 salespeople; and the southwest 13. WTUS also had an international sales manager who had two salespeople working for him. It expected its salespeople to follow a rigid set of guidelines and required prior approval from the home office before agreeing to anything out of the ordinary.

Recently, WTUS had not been able to respond quickly enough to some customer requests, and as a result, had lost some business. Suzanne was also concerned that the needs of its different customer groups were so different that its current structure was not appropriate. Finally, she was unsure how to approach the international market in terms of the organization of the sales force.

Chapter Objectives

After reading this chapter, you should be able to

- Recognize the inherent dilemmas sales managers face as they organize their sales forces.
- Know the principles of organizational structure.
- Appreciate how organizational structure affects the functioning of the organization.
- Understand the roles that manufacturer's representatives and telemarketing play in carrying out the sales mission.
- Delineate the different approaches to organizing a sales force.
- Recognize the issues involved in organizing for global marketing.

INTRODUCTION

The development of business structures within a given industry is generally evolutionary because it involves a gradual adaptation to the pressures of a changing environment. Those firms that successfully adapt tend to succeed, and those that do not often fail. The structure of organizations, however, affects the ability of firms to adapt to this changing environment.

Organizational structure has some impact on the ability of the firm to meet the needs of its customers. Additionally, design of the organization affects operating expenses. So, in the two areas that primarily affect profitability, revenues and costs, structure plays a key role. Organizational design also has implications for how individuals within a firm relate to each other. Often decisions about organizational design are made without enough thought given to the assumptions being made about the individuals within the organization or about the role of communication in it. The correct organizational structure does *not* ensure success; however, an inappropriate structure will certainly impede success.

In this chapter we will examine the factors that should be considered in the design of an organization. We will also discuss what makes for an excellent organization. The chapter will use these concepts as a basis for considering specific issues related to organizing the sales force.

ISSUES IN ORGANIZATIONAL DESIGN

Efficiency versus Effectiveness

Managers often proffer the idea that their particular organization is striving to be the "most effective and efficient" firm in the marketplace. Although this certainly sounds like a reasonable and perhaps even noble goal for any organization, it presents something of a dilemma. Organizational theorists Peter Blau and Richard Scott suggest that operating *efficiency* is the main problem of business concerns. They define operating efficiency as "the achievement of maximum gain at minimum cost in order to further survival and growth in competition with other organizations."[1]

In business, the overriding goal is to make and keep customers. This sounds simple enough, but it means that the company must be tuned in to customers' needs—entailing not just having a department that monitors and reports on customers' demands and buying habits but viewing the market as the center of the company's activities which is what we mean by the term **effectiveness.** This is also termed the **marketing concept.** Although the marketing concept has often been misunderstood and misapplied, it does call attention to the fact that the successful firm keeps in mind the importance of considering what customers' needs are and attempts to design the product around those needs.[2]

When sales managers begin the process of designing a sales organization, they must remember that **efficiency** and effectiveness represent trade-offs. The salespeople who are truly effective work to meet the needs of customers, particularly those of the major accounts. However, efficiency demands that they cover as much of their territory as possible at the lowest possible cost. Somewhere between those two extremes lies the right approach. Sales managers are largely responsible for helping salespeople find that approach.

Bureaucracy and Professionalism

Certainly, sales is becoming more of a profession rather than just an occupation. This "professionalization" of sales has developed from pressures within and outside the sales profession. From within, sales managers are attempting to legitimize selling as a profession that is a viable career choice for new college graduates—a career track that, in itself, has all the challenges and rewards necessary to make it attractive. It also is a way of getting on the "fast track" in the corporate world.

Additionally, given the current costs per sales call (see Figure 12-1), sales managers recognize that they cannot afford to keep salespeople who act in a non-professional manner. Upper management pressures sales managers to have the sales force yield results that are profit-oriented for the long term instead of simply being oriented toward sales volume. Also, with the growing professionalism in the purchasing profession, buyers are much less willing to work with salespeople who do not act as professionals.

FIGURE 12-1 Median Cost per Call, by Industry Type, 1987–91 (*Source: 1992 sales manager's planner. Sales & Marketing Management,* June 22, 1992, 73. Reprinted by permission of Sales & Marketing Management; June 1992.)

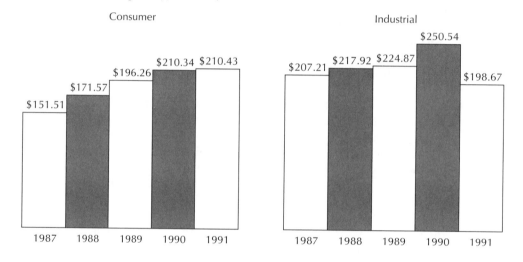

The approach to managing professionals is fundamentally different from that used in managing nonprofessionals. It requires not only a different mind-set but also a different organizational structure. Some organizational structures used with salespeople more closely resemble ones appropriate for managing bureaucrats rather than for managing professionals. Although a **bureaucracy** and a professional organization are similar in a number of ways, they are fundamentally different in the way they assign responsibility, manage people, make decisions, and relate to the client group. Table 12-1 lists the contrasts between these two orientations.

The differences between the professional and the bureaucratic orientation have the potential of creating some difficulties for management. For sales managers, these difficulties typically arise when a bureaucratic organization

TABLE 12-1 A Comparison of Professional and Bureaucratic Orientations

Professional	Bureaucratic
Similarities	
The trained professional is a specialized expert who enjoys no authority outside his or her area of expertise.	The bureaucrat has specialized knowledge restricted to a given area or expertise; he or she has circumscribed authority.
Relationship with clients is characterized with affective neutrality. Professional codes forbid emotional involvement with the client.	Relations with clients is marked by impersonal detachment.
Differences	
Decisions are based on the judgment of the professional, predicated on his or her training and the standards of the profession.	Decisions are based on the rules and procedures of the organization; not subject to the judgment of the individual.
Decisions are governed by universal standards, objective criteria, independent of the particular case.	Decisions are governed by abstract principles applied to particular cases.
Allowed to practice self-control through voluntary associations; the norms are established by the colleague group.	Control is imposed through the directives of the organization.
Performance is judged by the standards of the profession, independent of the organization.	Performance is judged by compliance with the rules of the organization.
Practitioner's decisions are predicated on furthering the good of the client.	Decisions are predicated on furthering the good of the organization.

Source: Peter M. Blau and W. Richard Scott, *Formal organizations* (San Francisco: Chandler, 1962). For a more in-depth discussion of bureaucracies, see Hans H. Gerth and C. Wright Mills, *From Max Weber: Essays in sociology* (New York: Oxford University Press, 1968).

exists in the company while, at the same, sales managers expect salespeople to act as professionals. This situation typically results not only in frustration for the sales force and sales managers, but also in hostilities. Often sales managers are not even aware that a bureaucratic structure is in place in the company. They may only become aware of its existence after several confrontations. Often the structure and standard operating procedures are handed down from one administration to the other, and, unless they are forced to do so, new managers will not examine their effectiveness.

Treating salespeople as professionals by granting them the latitude and power to manage their territories is the key to a more effective sales force. Specifically, in terms of organizing the sales force, the major issues are

- Whether the salesperson is given latitude to make decisions based on professional judgment
- Whether the welfare of the customer should be sacrificed for the "bottom line" of the company
- Whether the salesperson is judged primarily on the ability to make good decisions and service accounts or on whether he or she conforms to the specific standard operating procedures
- Whether the corporate culture encourages personal professional development or whether the norm is that attending company-sponsored sales training is sufficient.

Principles of Organizational Structure

Whenever one examines the structure of an organization, certain characteristics seem to stand out as facilitating a smooth running operation. Although there is a tremendous variation in organizations, some principles can be applied to the organization:[3]

Scalar principle. From the bottom of the organization up, each position or level in the organization is subordinate to another position above it.

Unity of command. No person in the organization should be responsible to more than one superior. The **matrix organization** is an exception to this rule but can be applied only in certain circumstances.[4]

Span of control. The number of subordinates reporting to one superior should be limited. The number is determined by the complexity of the job and the market, the ability of the supervisor, and other factors. Also, the number is related to the culture of the country in which the company is operating.

Distinction between line and staff. Line performs the major functions of the organization, and staff provides support, advice, and service to line. These two are separated so that duties can be more efficiently assigned and to ensure that the main thrust of the organization is not bogged down in paperwork.

Specialization. Jobs are designed so that there is little or no overlap in work. The idea behind the concept is that as workers perform a particular job, they become more proficient in carrying it out. This approach increases the overall operating efficiency of the organization. Classic theorists suggested four approaches to dividing work: major purpose served, process performed, type of clientele, and location.

THE "EXCELLENT" ORGANIZATION

In just about any discussion of business today, the themes of excellence and quality prevail. Quality assurance programs and quality circles are rapidly becoming central to the operation of organizations. Quality and excellence represent a kind of ideal for an organization and, as such, are difficult concepts to implement. It is not an easy process, and how a firm is organized has a direct impact on implementation. At one time, the ideal organization was centrally organized and stressed efficiency of operation. However, with the dynamic nature of business today, a centralized structure is often a hindrance to making the necessary adaptations to serving the market.

The Peters and Waterman Approach

The importance of the organizational structure on the successful operation of a firm was demonstrated by Thomas Peters and Robert Waterman in their classic *In Search of Excellence*.[5] Their book examined the dynamics of a set of "excellent" companies, those that seemed to demonstrate a successful approach to meeting the needs of the marketplace while coordinating the efforts of a large organization. The emphasis in these organizations was on excellence as opposed to efficiency. Peters and Waterman found that each of their chosen companies had eight distinguishing traits in common:

1. A bias for action. The atmosphere promotes decisive action.
2. Closeness to the customer. The individual customer is of utmost importance.
3. Atmosphere of autonomy and entrepreneurship. Companies sponsor leaders and innovators.
4. Productivity through people. Trust of the employee and the importance of the employee's contribution are stressed.
5. Hands-on, value-driven management. Management is involved with the operations and is a role model.
6. Stick to the knitting. The companies stay reasonably close to the business they know.
7. Simple form, lean staff. The organizations are not overly complex and stress structural flexibility.
8. Simultaneous loose-tight properties. The organization grants autonomy to the workers while maintaining its core values.

Since its publication, the Peters and Waterman book has come under fire from a number of quarters. The crux of the criticism has been that the authors were too simplistic in their analysis. The fact that some of the companies they labeled as excellent have fallen on hard times since the book's publication calls into question the long-term viability of the P&W formula. Also, some have suggested that these companies were in industries with similar dynamics and that the formula may not be applicable to other situations. Others have indicated that the P&W approach will not apply to organizations outside the United States. Generally speaking, however, the lessons that we can draw from the book outweigh its weaknesses.

The suggestion that one particular approach to designing organizations will apply equally well in all situations is absurd. If one approach would work equally well for all situations, the Model T would still be the predominant automobile. The Model T met its demise precisely because the thing that made it successful ultimately led to its downfall—the design of the organization. When the bureaucratically structured, assembly-line approach was instituted by Ford to produce the Model T, the marketplace was crying out for an affordable automobile, and the competition could not respond to the challenge posed by the Ford organization. That is what made the Model T so successful. However, the situation changed. Namely, the marketplace began to clamor for something other than the old, standard, black Model T. Because of the structure necessary to make the assembly line work, Ford could not adapt to the needs of the marketplace, nor could Ford respond to the competition's challenge. The result was that General Motors replaced Ford as the market share leader.

A particular organizational structure that ensures success in all situations does not exist. The appropriate structure is dictated by the demands of the marketplace, the dynamics of the industry, and the nature of the competition. George Lucas and Larry Gresham presented an argument that the appropriate structure for the design of a channel is based on the industry dynamics and the nature of the market.[6] They employed contingency theory to suggest which organization structures are appropriate in a given set of circumstances. Although this was applied to channel design, their approach can be applied to the overall organization.

The idea behind **contingency theory** is that one set answer does not exist for all situations, and that to arrive at the correct answer, situational variables must be considered.[7] In applying contingency theory to organizational structure, two major factors need to be considered; the environment in which the organization operates and the market that the organization is attempting to serve. Figure 12-2 depicts a four-cell matrix that compares these two factors. Although the matrix is extremely simplified, that simplicity adds to its usefulness.

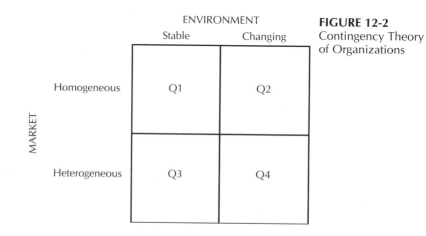

FIGURE 12-2
Contingency Theory
of Organizations

In the figure the environment consists of those forces that shape the industry: the technology of production, the type of material used in the product, the type of customer in the customer base, the manner in which the product is used, and the type of competitors. This environment is either stable or changing. By market, we mean the particular market being served by the industry. The market is classified as either heterogeneous, comprising a number of segments that are essentially different insofar as their use of the product is concerned, or is homogeneous, in the sense that the product is basically the same for the entire contingent of users in terms of how they shop for and consume the product.

All businesses can be roughly classified by the quadrants in this contingency table. Business types will fit into four groups:

> Quadrant 1 Business. The business operates in a stable environment and homogeneous market. The organizational structure does not need to be very adaptive to the environment given that it does not change dramatically from year to year. Also, the organization does not need to design a separate marketing mix for the different segments. Therefore, the structure for this organization should be more or less bureaucratic. Management knows generally what the environment and the market will be like and can centrally control how the firm will respond.
>
> Quadrant 2 Business. This business operates in a changing environment and homogeneous market. The organization must be adaptive to the changes in the market, but still works with only one basic marketing mix because the market is the same in terms of the product. The structure can be somewhat centralized in the sense of only needing one organizational unit to manage the mix, but must be adaptive to the changes in the environment. The system of communication within this somewhat centralized organization will need to be very open.
>
> Quadrant 3 Business. This business operates in a stable environment and heterogeneous market. It will need to be structured so that it can meet the needs of the different segments it serves, but does not need to allow for drastic changes in the environment. Within the overall organization, the separate units that serve the segments will need to have autonomy, but within each unit the decisions can be made by the management of the unit.
>
> Quadrant 4 Business. This business operates in a changing environment and serves a heterogenous market. Therefore, this organization must have an "open" structure. It should be decentralized without a rigid structure and encourage open communication. This type of organization must be highly adaptive.

Each of the four types of business works toward a different aim with its structure. Although in any business optimal efficiency is the goal, in quadrant 1 business, efficiency is a primary goal. The reason for this is that both the market and the environment are relatively predictable, and competition exists between companies that do not have a high degree of product differentiation. Therefore, competition centers on price. Price competition demands as much efficiency as possible. The Q1 business, then, needs to structure itself in a relatively rigid format and limit the actions of its employees to a prescribed set of standards. This creates a learning curve effect.

An example of such a business is the cement industry. On the consumer side, an example is a fast-food restaurant such as McDonald's. McDonald's has built its reputation around consistency. For it, quality is represented by a consistent operation. The benefit for customers is the fact that they know what to expect at a McDonald's. For the franchisee, this consistent and rigid way of doing business lowers costs, resulting in a higher profit.

Quadrant 2 and quadrant 3 businesses represent a compromise between the very rigid bureaucratic structure and the very open, loosely organized structure. The Q2 business has a high need for a structure that allows for the flow of information without being required to respond to different segments of the market. An example of such a business would be found in the fashion industry. The market for fashion garments is similar across the board. People that tend to buy designer clothes are fairly similar, in their motivation for shopping, in their shopping habits, and in their demographic characteristics. This market is somewhat singular and predictable. However, in the fashion industry, changes come on an annual basis or possibly more frequently. The types of fabrics, the styles, and the suppliers change. Management in that industry must keep its finger on the pulse of the industry and be able to react to the trends. The structure cannot be bureaucratic because bureaucracy tends to thwart creative communication. However, it does not need to be structured to account for differences in the market because those differences essentially do not exist.

A Q3 business needs a structure that adapts to the differing needs of the various market segments. Given their stable environment, they do not need to adapt to abrupt changes. Their structure would have a decentralized group of units, each with a fair amount of internal centralization. Each unit must be able to meet the needs of its market segment without being severely constrained by a centralized corporate management. However, the structure within each unit does not need to have the open flow of communication that is necessary in Q2 and Q4 businesses.

An example of a Q3 business would be the automobile industry. Although that industry has undergone a high degree of competitive restructuring, the basic technology, types of materials, supplier bases, and so forth have remained essentially the same.

A Q4 business requires a noncentralized structure with an open flow of communication. This is, in reality, the type of structure that Peters and Waterman spoke of in their book. Whereas Q1 businesses stress efficiency, Q4 businesses stress effectiveness, that is, they must work to be extremely adaptive to the changing, complex marketplace. A bureaucratic structure would choke such a business because it would not be able to react.

An example of such a business is in the personal computer industry. Technologies are changing at an incredible rate and the supplier base is highly volatile. At the same time, the market is fragmented with a number of user types, each needing different types of computers for different purposes.

Sales managers need to examine their organizational structure and practices in light of contingency theory. An inappropriate structure can be harmful to the organization. Although sales managers may be able to do little to change the organizational charts of their companies, they need to look at the current management practices. If they are reminiscent of a bureaucratic structure in an industry that is highly fragmented with a rapidly changing environment, the potential exists for being left behind by the competition.

THE DESIGN OF THE SALES ORGANIZATION

When sales managers are called on to design or redesign the structure of the sales force, they must consider a number of issues in addition to general organizational design factors. Generally, the design represents a compromise between efficiency and effectiveness, and revolves around the best deployment of resources given existing market, competitive, and environmental conditions.

The Manufacturer's Representative

Often it is expedient for a producer to use **manufacturer's representatives** (agents) in place of a company sales force.[8] The reps are independent business-people who will act as the sales force for the company. They are paid on a commission basis and will typically also represent producers of similar products, although generally they will not carry competing lines. For organizational buyers, the manufacturer's rep is viewed as the salesperson for a particular producer, and yet the rep offers the convenience of being able to offer quotations on a related set of products. For producers, the rep provides coverage of a territory similar to that of a company salesperson. Reps generally are trained by the company about the features and advantages of its products, and have a knowledge of the industry and the particular geographic market in which they operate.

Table 12-2 outlines the advantages and disadvantages of using a manufacturer's rep as compared to using a company sales force. Particularly when the company is moving into a new territory, the manufacturer's rep provides an advantage. Because new territory is relatively undeveloped vis-à-vis the particular brand, entry into the territory could be financially prohibitive. A rep is generally already familiar with that territory and has established contacts. Additionally, the company will not be forced to go to the expense of opening an office in the region with all its associated overhead costs. In a similar vein, if a territory has gotten to the point of no longer being able to support a company sales office, the company can contract with a representative to provide coverage in the area.

For small companies, the manufacturer's rep provides a way to have a sales force in the field that costs something only when the product is sold. This reduction in overhead makes it possible for smaller companies to be in areas that would be impossible otherwise. For the small company, also, the rep can be a major source of market intelligence that would otherwise be difficult to access.

A major issue facing companies that use manufacturer's reps is when sales have climbed to the point of making it profitable to have coverage by the company

TABLE 12-2 Advantages and Disadvantages of Using Manufacturer's Representatives

Advantages	Disadvantages
Reps have local expertise in that they know the companies and buyers in their region.	Reps may have mixed loyalties in that they already have a relationship with buyers in a region.
There are virtually no fixed costs when using reps, only minor administrative costs.	The company exercises less direct control over the actions of reps than a sales force.
Reps allow a company entering or exiting a region to have a presence without committing the resources for a sales force in the area.	Because reps work on commission, they may be tempted to push other product lines they represent if these lines are easier to sell and/or have a higher commission structure.
Reps allow a small company to have adequate sales coverage without spending precious resources.	Because the buyer associates a company's product with a particular rep, the company may lose sales if it changes reps or begins using a company sales force in the region.
Reps carry a complementary set of product lines so that buying from them represents a convenience for a buyer.	Because they work on a commission, reps will generally place more emphasis on sales volume and may not provide the level of service that a company might desire.
Reps generally do not carry competing brands within a given product line.	

salesperson. In Figure 12-3, we see the decision from an economic point of view. According to the figure, although the company sales force begins with a much higher set of fixed costs than does the manufacturer's rep, the variable cost of the company sales force is lower. Prior to some point x on the graph, using a manufacturer's rep has a lower marginal cost than using a company sales force; however, beyond point x, the marginal cost of using a manufacturer's rep exceeds that of the company sales force. Theoretically, at least, point x on the graph is where the company should substitute the company sales force for the rep.

The graph depicts a situation that ignores many of the considerations pertinent to the decision to disengage a rep and institute a company salesperson in an area. For instance, companies that get the reputation for "pulling the plug" on reps once they have reached a sales milestone soon find it difficult to obtain the best reps when they seek to enter new territories. Also, if reps get the idea that the milestone is being reached, they may curtail selling efforts somewhat to forestall being cut off.

Although we will not argue the ethics of doing this, from the reps' point of view, they have labored long and hard to build up a territory, and about the time it becomes a lucrative, they are dismissed. Even though reps may understand the logic that "some MBA" is using to make the decision, such a decision will cause ill-feelings. Those ill-feelings will often result in the reps informing buyers in their territory that after all their hard work they are being cut off. However, they will often pick up a new line to substitute for the old one, and the buyer, having developed a good working relationship with the rep, may be willing to switch products. Additionally, when the new company salesperson enters the territory,

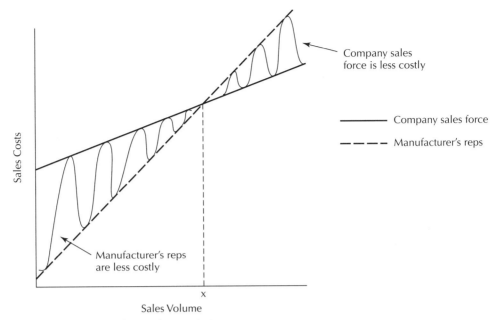

FIGURE 12-3 Use of Manufacturer's Reps

he or she must take some time to learn the ropes. This means a loss in sales momentum, so that point *x* on the graph may move significantly to the right.

Although there is no one way of dealing with manufacturer's representatives, some generalizations are helpful to keep in mind:

1. When a firm contracts with a representative, it should insist on a clause that allows for termination of the relationship by either party with 60 days' notice.
2. If the firm has a policy of replacing the rep with a company sales force when a certain sales milestone is reached, this should be spelled out in the initial agreement.
3. Rather than automatically replacing the rep when a preset milestone is reached, the manufacturer should consider some "phase-in" approach whereby the rep will receive a reduced commission for a period with the understanding that the rep will assist the manufacturer's salespeople in getting established in the new territory.
4. The firm should view reps as an extension of the company and, as such, pay attention to training them and involving them in any special incentive programs.

The Place of Telemarketing

With the ever-increasing cost of personally contacting a customer, sales managers are looking to the telephone as a way to increase the efficiency of their overall selling effort. In reality, telephone selling has been in practice just about as long as the phone itself has. The term **telemarketing** generally applies to more recent efforts by sales forces to incorporate the phone as a strategic weapon in sales. If telemarketing were simply a way to increase efficiency without being of any benefit to the customer, it likely would not be receiving the attention it is currently getting. Apparently, buyers find that telemarketing is actually more efficient for them as well and have readily accepted it as a business practice.[9]

Among the benefits of telemarketing are the following:[10]

1. It can be used to locate and qualify prospects. Some firms include an information request form in their ads that a prospective customer can clip and send in. The prospect can then be contacted, and, if warranted, a field salesperson can be assigned to call.
2. It can be used to handle the sales of lower-value, standardized items that are bought on a repeat basis.
3. It can be used for follow-up after a sale to ensure that the customer is satisfied and to answer any questions that might have arisen.
4. It can be used to sell additional goods and services related to a major purchase.
5. It can be used to handle customer service, such as dealing with problems the customer is having with a product or to provide information on shipment.
6. It can be used to handle smaller customers or those who are currently outside the areas being covered by the outside sales force.
7. It can be used as a screening tool and for training potential outside salespeople. It provides the chance to observe the person's work habits and abilities, and it gives the individual a chance to learn about the industry, products, and customers.

Just as with manufacturer's reps, sales managers may need to take a different approach with telephone salespeople than they do with premise salespeople.[11] For example, they may need to recruit individuals with different types of skills than would be necessary for the outside sales personnel. Additionally, inside salespeople will need to undergo a different type of training. Inside salespeople are more likely to use a formula-based selling approach (for example, a sales presentation script), whereas the outside salespeople are more likely to use more of a problem-solving, consultative selling approach.

Servicing Key Accounts

In selling, the 80–20 principle applies to the customers of a firm. That is, 80 percent of the business comes from 20 percent of the customers—**key accounts.** Because this is true, many sales managers recognize the need to give special attention to those few major customers that constitute the bulk of their business. In other words, they segment their accounts according to sales volume. Companies that have employed a major account program have experienced an increase in sales through

- Greater ability to retain large customers
- Increased sales to current customers
- Enhanced working relationships with large customers[12]

There are several viable approaches to handling key accounts. We discuss a few of them here.

Separate Key Accounts Division. A separate key accounts division would entail an entire division of the company devoted specifically to the needs of the major accounts. The justification is that they are important and their needs merit a division-level approach. However, this would mean a great deal of added expense for the company to bear.

Separate Sales Force. A separate sales force is dedicated to service only the key accounts. This would have the advantage of being able to meet the sales and service needs of these accounts without incurring the expense of a separate division. It has the benefit of providing a track for the better salespeople if they do not desire to enter management.

Sales Managers. Assigning key accounts to sales managers has the advantage of giving special attention to the key accounts and being able to use the manager's power to take action when needed. It also lets the accounts know that they warrant special attention. This can, however, place an added burden on the sales managers.

Regular Sales Force. The benefit here is principally for the company and the sales force. It saves the company money and lets the salespeople keep the most lucrative accounts. However, it may result in those accounts not receiving the attention they need.

All these options, save the last one, represent some added costs for the company. However, key accounts, due to their size and special needs, usually warrant the extra expense.

APPROACHES TO ORGANIZING THE SALES FORCE

A major decision that sales managers must make is the way in which they will organize the salespeople. This is critical because it affects both the efficiency and the effectiveness of the sales force. A number of factors enter into this decision. The complexity and the location/dispersion of the market and the complexity and complementariness of the product line are perhaps the most critical.[13] Other factors, however, such as the nature of tasks involved in a particular sales job, are also important because of their effect on the motivation and degree of commitment of salespeople.[14] Although we discuss these different approaches separately, generally two or three are used in combination to suit the particular situation.

Geographic Organization

Organizing the sales force by geographic location is the approach most used. Even though a sales force may be divided in other ways, the need for efficiency often forces some limitation as to the geographic area an individual can serve.

About the only times some type of geographic organization will not be found is either when the company serves only one area of a country or when the customer base is very limited. The benefits of using **geographic organization** are:

- The salesperson is able to become an "expert" on a given region.
- It generally means lower travel costs and fewer nights away from home for the salesperson.
- Customers know exactly who they need to speak with about a question or problem.
- This approach is generally easier to administer.
- A company can feasibly better ensure that a region is being adequately covered.
- This approach lends itself better to conducting a limited test market.

The drawbacks of geographic organization are

- If the company has a wide spectrum of products, it is very difficult for one person to know the full line.
- If there are very different types of customers, a salesperson may not be able to provide proper service for each.
- It may be difficult to get the necessary "push" that may be needed or desired for a given product.
- Salespeople may not be willing to relocate when they are assigned a new territory because they have put down roots where they are.
- Salespeople must be generalists instead of specialists, and that can create difficulties in certain circumstances.

Product Organization

For companies that have a wide variety of product lines or for ones that have several, very different and complex lines, the **product organization** can provide the most effective approach to covering their products. In the case of companies with complex products, the sales force's workload is geometrically increased because of the need to understand not only the company's own product line but those of the competition as well. This increased complexity means that the sales force will be stretched too thin if salespeople are expected to cover a wide spectrum of products. Also, generally with more complex products comes a higher level of customer service. It would not take too long for the average salesperson to get overburdened if he or she were not given fewer products to carry.

The advantages of using product organization are

- The approach allows the salesperson to become a specialist in a particular product or product line.
- The salesperson can better serve the more specific and complex needs of customers.
- The approach provides the ability to better control and monitor the marketing of a particular product.

The disadvantages of this approach are

- There is duplication of effort. More than one salesperson will be covering a given geographic area, which leads to an increase in costs.
- Customers may be confused about which salesperson to talk to.
- Salespeople's travel time and travel costs increase.
- The administration of this approach is more difficult than others.
- Sometimes this approach can lead to parochialism in that each product group will tend to protect its turf.

Customer Organization

With an increasing emphasis on the marketing concept, firms are looking for more effective ways to serve the specific needs of the different market segments. Especially in the situation where products are not standardized, customer needs may vary greatly and salespeople must become experts at dealing with the needs of a particular type of customer. Additionally, even when customer needs do not vary much, their approach to the purchasing process may be so different that it presents difficulties for salespeople attempting to serve a wide variety of customers. Finally, there are certain types of customers who require a much greater investment in time. A salesperson cannot effectively handle those customers who require a large chunk of their time and serve a large number of customers at the same time.

The advantages of a **customer organization** are

- It lets the sales force meet the specific needs of the different customer segments.
- Salespeople are closer to the customer—knowing what is happening in their industry and how they are changing.
- The company can better allocate resources to the different segments that are vying for them.
- Salespeople can work more closely with customers to develop new technologies and products.

The disadvantages of this type of organization are

- There is less efficiency due to having more than one salesperson in a geographic area.
- Provincialism among salespeople covering the different types of customers may occur.
- Salespeople have to know the entire product line.
- Administering and coordinating the efforts of the different groups are more difficult than for other approaches.

One company that switched to a customer organization is Novell, Inc.[15] This marketer of computer network software markets its products through systems integrators and through resellers, including some national chains. Prior to the reorganization, Novell used a geographic organization. According to the executive vice president of sales, each manager focused only on his or her region and dealt with OEMs (original equipment manufacturers), distributors, major accounts, and resellers. As network computing became a standard in the 1980s, the geographic approach became less effective. Each of the different types of customers had unique needs that could not be effectively met by a salesperson.

Novell reorganized along market segment lines. With the new plan, its salespeople call on OEMs, major users, and resellers. The OEM group calls on customers such as NCR, Wang, and Electronic Data Systems and helps them to incorporate the Novell software into their hardware. The major-user account group calls on national accounts (Fortune 500 companies) and federal, state, and local governments. The reseller group calls on distributors and retailers such as ComputerLand Corporation and BusinessLand, Inc. By dividing its customer segments into groups, Novell was able to put specialists in place who were better able to meet the increasingly sophisticated needs of their customers.

Functional Organization

The sales job includes a variety of different skills and tasks that must be performed. Often these are in conflict—performing one well may mean not doing an adequate job on the other. For example, a salesperson in charge of a geographic territory must spend the vast majority of time servicing the major accounts in that territory. However, there may be a number of potentially good customers in that region who are not being prospected and developed. The time constraints, plus the fact that prospecting and developing accounts require a different set of skills than servicing existing ones, mean that the salesperson will not be able to prospect the territory adequately.

As another example, when a company sells technical products through distributors, the distributor's salespeople are probably handling a large variety of items. It is not possible for any one salesperson to know all the technical details of the company's product. The company could use **sales engineers** (sales professionals with an engineering degree) to assist distributor salespeople in their sales calls. The sales engineer would not try to close the sales but, rather, would provide the technical expertise in how to use the product and answer technical questions.

The answer to the problem of needing specialized selling expertise is to organize the sales force by the tasks that need performing. This approach is particularly useful when there are a wide variety of such tasks and the tasks require different skills and knowledge. The advantages of the **functional organization** are

- The strengths of individual salespeople can be leveraged in the company.
- The firm can concentrate on certain critical tasks.
- Allocation of resources can be more defined.

The drawbacks of the functional organization are

- There are increased costs of having more salespeople to perform specialized functions.

- Customers may become confused.
- There may be difficulty in finding the right salespeople to be specialists.
- It is a complex system to administer.

An interesting approach to a functional selling organization involves the use of temporary salespeople, hired for a short period of time, generally for a special promotional program, to provide support for the regular sales force. The use of temporary salespeople is a phenomenon that is growing according to Arthur Bragg in an article in *Sales & Marketing Management*.[16] For example, Kimberly-Clark uses temporary salespeople as merchandisers in retail outlets. They service the accounts by ensuring that customers have an adequate supply of products and that their products are displayed properly. Using temps saves Kimberly-Clark money because the overhead costs associated with hiring and employing a full-time person are greatly reduced. Additionally, greater flexibility is gained because temps can be added quickly and are used only for the period of time they are needed.

ORGANIZING FOR TEAM SELLING

Team selling is an increasingly popular approach to competing in today's marketplace. It involves putting together a group of professionals, such as salespeople, engineers, and production managers, to work with a group from the customer's organization. Each person in the selling team complements the talents of the other members. Among the reasons for the interest in team selling is the fact that **buying centers,** the group of people in the customer's company who take part in the buying process, are much more the rule than the exception today, and this requires a different strategic orientation on the part of sales managers.[17] Buying centers represent a diverse group of people that require different information and support. One person will have a difficult time providing all the information and support necessary. Thus the team selling approach allows a company to match the expertise of individual sales and sales support people with the various individuals involved in the buying decision. This results in a quicker and more precise resolution of problems.

Team selling is certainly not applicable in all situations and with all companies. Three major criteria should be used in determining if sales managers should consider a team selling approach:[18]

- The company sells complex or customized products.
- The company's products require extensive after-sales support.
- The company's prospects use buying teams.

Sales managers must keep in mind that although team selling may be a viable option for the company, it does require a high degree of coordination and a different set of management skills, and thus it can cause some major headaches if it is not well planned and implemented. For example, often managers assume

Team Selling: Four in One

Francy Blackwood

It was one of those bleak moments in selling. Elliot Holtz and a sales team from the Metropolitan Life Insurance Co. had spent weeks developing and hours rehearsing a group presentation to a major prospect. Despite all their preparation, the pitch was chaotic. Thrown off course by the unpredictable dynamics of team selling, "We walked out of the presentation saying, 'We blew it,'" Holtz recalls.

Their brush with disaster is a classic example of how team sales can go awry. As team selling catches on—especially with complex industries and bigticket sales—a growing number of salespeople face new and pointed challenges. Among them: the loss of individual control in a sales call, the uncertainties of group dynamics, the considerable effort and skill required to engage an entire group of customers in a presentation, and the tough job of forging a cohesive sales team when team members may not know each other well.

Holtz is a regional director at MetLife in Philadelphia, where he and five salespeople sell a full range of benefit programs to large companies with anywhere from 200 to 30,000 employees. Team selling has become the norm in Holtz's business. Employee benefits have

become so complex and so costly that the average company has a host of experts on the case. Even the CFO gets involved. "It's the nature of the industry," Holtz says. "There are lots of different specializations, and the customer has become very sophisticated." Thus a sales presentation attracts a bevy of specialists and executives on the client side, and MetLife has to come in with an equal team.

This particular call was to pitch a major investment banking firm on a $750,000 package of disability benefits—a large program by disability standards. MetLife had recently landed two other big-name investment banking houses. ("I can't even put a price on the value of those references," Holtz says.) Before the team call took shape, MetLife used a broker to present the prospect with a proposal. Based on the feedback, "we knew what the issues were, so we were able to prepare a presentation geared to their needs." At the top of the list was the issue of defining earnings. "That was their entire focus," he says. Employee earnings—which establish a benchmark for disability benefits—tend to fluctuate wildly in investment banking, so the issue was a logical concern. No problem, Holtz thought; he simply put the subject of earnings front and center on his agenda for the call. (Little did he know that the all-important point would be lost when the presentation derailed.)

MetLife assembled a sales team, choosing people based on rank and subject expertise. The final four: Holtz; a senior group rep in his sales force; Holtz's boss, a regional vice president; and a Chicago-based vice president in charge of all disability programs, who brought extra know-how and decision-making power to the team. The customer "wanted someone who could make decisions and commitments on the spot," Holtz explains. The investment banker's team, meanwhile, would include a vice president of the firm, the director of benefits, and a financial manager.

With a team in place, the nitty-gritty work at MetLife began. The team members detailed the agenda, outlining the points they wanted to cover. They prepared an opening that combined ice-breaking small talk and a preview. A brief outline of what's to come is important at the start of a team presentation, Holtz explains. "We want to make sure we're going to cover what they want to discuss, so we don't go off on our speech without addressing their concerns." (Ultimately, that's what happened, but not for lack of guarding against the pitfall.)

The group assigned a role to each team member. The sales rep, for example, would handle the opening. Holtz would share the closing, asking for the business. He also would watchdog the entire process, making sure the team covered all the salient issues and throwing in pointed questions if the presentation seemed to get off track. (A good strategy that unfortunately didn't work.)

These particular MetLife people had never made a presentation together, so the three in Philadelphia spent five hours rehearsing. They practiced questions and answers, vital components in team selling. "You want to encourage give-and-take, you don't want to have a lecture," Holtz points out. "Sometimes that's difficult, because you have a lot of people involved and you don't necessarily know them all. There's a different dynamic in team selling. People are more careful about what they say in front of peers and superiors." Still, Holtz pushes hard for customer participation in a team call, stopping at regular intervals to ask, "Do you have any questions about that point, or can we move on?"

A team presentation can fall prey to personal agendas, Holtz says. In one case, Holtz was on a team presenting to 15 people, including one who had been a MetLife customer in a former job. He kept raising points rooted in his previous experience that weren't relevant. "His very specific questions were derailing us. If we had addressed them, we might have lost the other 14 people." To keep personal agendas in check, "you really have to be able to control a room," says Holtz. One technique: "Know who the decision-maker is. Play to that person."

The day of their call on the investment bankers, the Philadelphia MetLife team took a morning train to New York. There they huddled over lunch to run through the presentation with the vice president from Chicago. At 2:30 p.m. sharp they filed into the investment banker's conference room. Right off the bat, the prospect put MetLife on the clock. "They let us know they only had an hour before they had to move on to an important meeting." The presentation actually went well, for the most part. The senior group rep delivered a compelling opening. "This guy is a great salesperson," Holtz says. "He talked about why the client was looking for someone new [to provide disability benefits], which addressed their needs. He used references to our advantage, covering all the things we'd done for other investment banking customers, which really got their attention." The tone of the call was promising. "There was good chemistry and comfortable rapport." And the MetLife team kept the presentation from turning into a lecture. "It was very interactive, with questions and answers throughout."

There was only one near-fatal glitch. A member of the selling team went off on a tangent that missed the point of the client's primary concern with earnings. As a result, "we didn't show a clear understanding" of a major issue, says Holtz. The other sellers tried to refocus, but to no avail. "There's really no way you can cut someone off," Holtz says, explaining that you risk appearing rude to one of your own people. Moreover, at that point, "the client was so thrown off, he probably wasn't even listening," Holtz says. "We had lost the chief decision-maker. Once you lose someone, it's hard to bring them back."

It was an unhappy MetLife foursome that filed out of the conference room. But they regrouped immediately; during their return to Philadelphia, they drafted a letter to the decision-maker. Their message: "We heard you, we know what you need, and we're going to deliver." The letter was short, precise, and effective. Soon thereafter, MetLife landed the account.

Despite the close call, Holtz says team selling has advantages. "You can pool so much knowledge from presenters and clients. The interaction can be terrific. Good group dynamics can really make a presentation feel good." Moreover, at MetLife, the team stays together after the pitch—a fact Holtz emphasizes in every team presentation. "What you see," he tells prospects, "is what you'll get."

Reprinted with the permission of SELL!NG magazine.

that if they pick professionals with good track records for the team, it will be a success. However, unless the manager engages in some team building at the outset of the project, the group is not likely to work together as a cohesive unit. Selling teams, no matter how talented their members, do not automatically work smoothly. Sales managers must facilitate the team building.

ORGANIZING IN THE INTERNATIONAL ARENA

Culture has a major impact on how organizations operate. This is true in the United States as well as abroad. For example, here we generally place a higher value on change than do other parts of the world. So, when some experts suggest that we need to develop organizational structures that promote change, many readily accept such suggestions. However, such ideas may not be met with wide-spread acceptance in places such as East Asia, where change is not necessarily viewed as a positive. The important thing to remember is that when organizational structure is developed for use in one country, it may not work at all in other countries. Management must adapt that structure to the culture and characteristics of the country in which it is to be used.

Centralization of Authority

One of the primary ways in which countries vary in their organizational structures is in the centralization of authority. According to Vern Terpstra and Kenneth David, there is a tendency to use a bureaucratic style of management in many parts of Asia, Latin America, and Africa that results in an unwillingness to delegate authority.[19] In other parts of the world, this is not the case. For example, they point out that in many European countries, a decentralized structure is favored and a hierarchical structure would not work. Japan, though, is unique in that there is both centralization of authority and decentralization in decision making, at the same time. It is centralized in that traditional authority rests in those who are at the top of the organization. However, those people at the top rely on those at the bottom of the organizational chart for input to make decisions, and even allow them to make operational decisions on their own.

The International Organizational Structure

In general, a firm moving into the international marketplace has three basic approaches to selling from which to choose: exporting, making contractual arrangements overseas, or investing directly abroad. These three approaches can be broken down into seven basic organizational arrangements:[20]

1. **Export department.** This is the simplest approach. It consists of a department within the company that ships goods overseas. It depends on other areas in the organization to take care of the advertising, sales, production, and financial functions.
2. **Export division.** This approach involves using separate groups for different geographic locations. It differs from the export department in that within the division will be the functional areas of sales, advertising, and sometimes the financial group. Typically, the export division will not include the production function.
3. **International division.** In this approach, when it is economically feasible, all the functional areas will be handled overseas. However, whether these are handled directly by the company or are contracted out depends on the situation. The corporation will typically have a vice president of the division, who will answer directly to the president.
4. **International headquarters company (IHC).** The IHC structure truly moves the company into the global arena. This approach does not view international operations as extensions of domestic operations. In this structure, the corporation uses a

board of directors, a president, and a set of vice presidents who are separate from those of the parent company. How the functional areas of the IHC are organized will depend on the circumstances.

5. **Joint venture.** Two companies contribute resources such as capital to a partnership arrangement that results in the creation of a separate entity. Each holds a certain percentage of ownership which is determined by its amount of contribution to the venture. Some countries will not allow a foreign company to have greater than a 49 percent ownership of the venture.

6. **Strategic alliance.** A fairly new phenomenon whereby companies directly combine their resources in a way that each brings a particular strength into a cooperative effort. This varies from a joint venture in that the two firms do not simply contribute a set amount to a new venture. Instead, they each contribute a variety of resources, including people and facilities. This pooling of resources may or may not result in a separate entity being formed.

7. **Global company (GC).** The GC is the firm in which the distinction between domestic and international trade has no meaning. This is the organization where each area of the globe is of equal importance to the firm. The operations in the various countries represent separate profit centers with their own set of competitors and products.

Each of these approaches represents a different level of commitment of resources and level of risk. The export department represents the lowest commitment and the GC the highest. That increasing level of resource commitment and risk is accompanied by increasing level of profitability. In other words, each of these approaches represents a trade-off of risk and return. A company in the international arena must decide on an appropriate approach considering that trade-off.

When deciding on the right approach for operating internationally, a company should consider four factors: corporate strategy, management style, external forces, and internal forces.[21] These factors are depicted in Figure 12-4.

Corporate Strategy

The strategic plan has four elements: the mission statement, the statement of objectives, the strategy, and the tactics. The **mission** is a description of why the organization exists. It defines the organization and, hence, who its competitors are. The **objectives** are what the organization is trying to accomplish. These should, as much as possible, be measurable, contain a benchmark, and include a time frame. The **strategy** is the grand, relatively long-term, comprehensive plan of how the objectives are going to be achieved. The **tactics** are the short-term, operational decisions to make the strategy work. In sum these elements can be thought of as follows:

Mission: the definition of the firm
Objectives: the direction in which the firm wants to go
Strategy: the description of how to proceed
Tactics: the deployment of resources

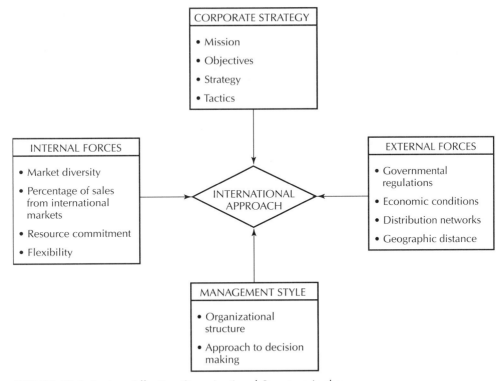

FIGURE 12-4 Factors Affecting Organizational Structure in the International Arena (*Source:* Adapted from Jean-Pierre Jeannet and Hubert D. Hennessey, *Global marketing strategies* [Boston: Houghton Mifflin, 1992], 547.)

Management Style

Management style refers to both the organization's structure and the approach to decision making that is employed. As pointed out earlier in the chapter, the structure of the organization is determined largely by environmental and market forces. This holds true in the international arena as well. The style of decision making employed needs to vary according to the culture of the country. The major mistake made by many U.S. companies when they move into the international arena is that they fail to take into account the cultural anomalies of the various countries in which they do business.

Internal and External Forces

Both the internal and external forces that a firm encounters influence its approach to the international marketplace. Internal forces refer to characteristics of the organization that make it what it is. For example, the percentage of sales the organization derives from its various operations, the diversity of markets it serves, and the amount of resources it can allot are all internal forces that shape the organization. Additionally, the degree of coordination within the sales force that is required for the company to serve its customers has an effect on the way it should be organized and how well its salespeople perform.[22] When a firm moves into the international arena, it encounters a new set of governmental regulations and a different type of customer. These factors along with such others as geographic distance, economic conditions, and distribution networks make up the external forces that affect the company's global strategy. Taken together, the internal and external forces set the parameters within which the company operates.

CHAPTER SUMMARY

In this chapter we examined the various considerations in designing the sales organization. Organizing and coordinating selling efforts is a complex process. Any decision regarding organizational structure, regardless of how simple or seemingly worthwhile, may have potentially negative consequences. In considering some issues about organizations in general, we discussed the differences between bureaucratic and professional organizations and presented the implications for sales managers. Additionally, organizational principles such as the scalar principle, span of control, specialization, and unity of command were defined.

We also discussed the concept of designing for excellence. Although there are some guidelines that can prove worthwhile if used properly, the structural design that is appropriate for an organization is dependent on the environment and the market in which the company operates. For some companies, a hierarchical structure is appropriate; for others, the relatively flat corporate structure works best.

We then considered some specific issues facing sales managers when designing their sales organizations—for example, the place of manufacturer's representatives in the overall marketing of the firm and how telemarketing increases the efficiency of the sales force by allowing a company to reach otherwise unreachable prospects. An issue of great concern to sales managers is how to handle key accounts. Various approaches include using a separate division or sales force or assigning sales managers.

The different ways in which we can divide the work of the sales force include a geographic organization, a customer organization, a product organization, and a functional organization. Generally, some combination of these approaches is used. Again, the approach is contingent on a number of factors, each of which can impact the operation of the firm. Choosing the appropriate approach is a matter of trading off advantages and disadvantages.

The chapter closed with a discussion of issues related to organizing an international selling effort. Obviously, a firm that wishes to compete effectively in the global arena must adapt its approach to organizing individuals in other countries. When the company manages salespeople from different cultural backgrounds, it needs to take those cultural differences into consideration, for instance, how a culture views centralization of authority. Firms have three basic approaches to selling: exporting, making contractual arrangements, or direct investment. An additional consideration when moving into the international arena is what form of international operation the firm will use. Also, the firm must decide on its strategy, management style, and how to deal with the internal and external forces it will encounter in the international marketplace.

KEY TERMS

bureaucracy, p. 259

buying center, p. 273

contingency theory, p. 262

customer organization, p. 271

effectiveness, p. 257

efficiency, p. 257

export department, p. 277

export division, p. 277

functional organization, p. 272

geographic organization, p. 270

global company (GC), p. 278

international division, p. 277

international headquarters
   company (IHC), p. 277

joint venture, p. 278

key accounts, p. 268

line vs. staff, p. 260

manufacturer's representative
   (rep), p. 265

marketing concept, p. 257

matrix organization, p. 260

mission, p. 278

objectives, p. 278

product organization, p. 270

sales engineer, p. 272

scalar principle, p. 260

span of control, p. 260

specialization, p. 260

strategic alliance, p. 278

strategy, p. 278

tactics, p. 278

team selling, p. 273

telemarketing, p. 267

unity of command, p. 260

CHAPTER QUESTIONS

1. How do efficiency and effectiveness work against each other?
2. How would a manager treat subordinates who are professionals differently than subordinates who are bureaucrats?
3. Why would a single type of organizational structure not work well for all firms?
4. What are some of the characteristics of "excellent organizations" according to Peters and Waterman?
5. How can the span of control be increased?

6. Why is telemarketing a more important tool for the sales manager today than in the past?

7. Why is team selling more critical today than in the past?

8. Explain why a geographic organization might be considered more efficient while a customer organization might be considered more effective.

9. How does a strategic alliance vary from a joint venture?

10. Why does the degree of risk and the potential return increase as a company moves from an export department form of international involvement to an international division form?

NOTES

1. Peter M. Blau and W. Richard Scott, *Formal organizations* (San Francisco: Chandler, 1962).

2. Theodore Levitt, *Marketing for business growth* (New York: McGraw-Hill, 1974).

3. Dennis W. Organ and Thomas Bateman, *Organizational behavior* (Homewood, IL: BPI/Irwin, 1986).

4. In the matrix organization, specialists are accountable to both a superior from their area of expertise (such as engineering or production) and a coordinating manager (such as a project manager).

5. Thomas J. Peters and Robert H. Waterman, *In search of excellence* (New York: Harper & Row, 1982).

6. George H. Lucas, Jr., and Larry G. Gresham, Power, conflict, control and the application of contingency theory in marketing channels. *Journal of Academy of Marketing Science* 13 (Summer 1985), 25–38.

7. Robert W. Ruekert, Orville C. Walker, and Kenneth J. Roering, The organization of marketing activities: A contingency theory of structure and performance. *Journal of Marketing* (Winter 1985), 13–25.

8. For more information on the use of manufacturer's reps, see Harold J. Novick, The case for reps vs. direct selling: Can reps do it better? *Industrial Marketing* (March 1982), 90–98; Lois C. DuBois and Roger H. Grace, Master reps: Value-added distribution. *Business Marketing* (December 1987), 62–63.

9. Rebirth of a salesman: Willy Loman goes electronic. *Business Week*, February 27, 1984, 104.

10. For a more complete discussion of the benefits of telemarketing, see Merrill Tutton, Segmenting a national account. *Business Horizons* (January–February 1987), 61–67.

11. William C. Moncrief, Charles W. Lamb, Jr., and Terry Dielman, Developing telemarketing support systems. *Journal of Personal Selling & Sales Management* (August 1986), 43–49.

12. Jerome A. Colletti and Gary S. Tubridy, Effective major account sales management. *Journal of Personal Selling & Sales Management* (August 1987), 1–10.

13. Ram C. Rao and Ronald E. Turner, Organization and effectiveness of the multiple-product salesforce. *Journal of Personal Selling & Sales Management* (May 1984), 24–30.

14. Sanjeev Agarwal and Sridhar N. Ramaswami, Affective organizational commitment of salespeople: An expanded model. *Journal of Personal Selling & Sales Management* 13 (Spring 1993), 49–70; Sridhar N. Ramaswami, Sanjeev Agarwal, and Mukesh Bhargava, Work alienation of marketing employees: Influence of task, supervisory, and organizational structure factors. *Journal of the Academy of Marketing Science* 21 (Summer 1993), 179–193.

15. Kate Bertrand, Reorganizing for sales. *Business Marketing* (February 1990), 30.

16. Arthur Bragg, Temporaries: The new look in sales. *Sales & Marketing Management* (August 1987), 39–41.

17. Michael D. Hutt, Wesley J. Johnston, and John R. Ronchetto, Jr., Selling centers and buying centers: Formulating strategic exchange patterns. *Journal of Personal Selling & Sales Management* (May 1985), 33–39.

18. Cathy Hyatt Hills, Making the TEAM. *Sales & Marketing Management* (February 1992), 54–57.

19. Vern Terpstra and Kenneth David, *The cultural environment of business* (Cincinnati, OH: South-Western, 1985).

20. For a more complete discussion, see George M. Taoka and Don R. Beeman, *International business* (New York: HarperCollins, 1991); and Jean-Pierre Jeannet and Hubert D. Hennessey, *Global marketing strategies* (Boston: Houghton Mifflin, 1992).

21. Jeannet and Hennessey, *Global marketing strategies.*

22. Frank V. Cespedes, Sales coordination: An exploratory study. *Journal of Personal Selling & Sales Management* 12 (Summer 1992), 13–29.

SUGGESTED READINGS

Blau, Peter M., and W. Richard Scott. *Formal organizations.* San Francisco: Chandler, 1962.

> Often organizational structures are established that actually are counter to the goals of the organization. The organization can either be structured in such a way as to maximize coordination and control or to maximize communication and problem solving. Additionally, the organization cannot simultaneously maximize both efficiency and effectiveness but, rather, some compromise between the two.

Drucker, Peter. *The frontiers of management.* New York: Harper & Row, 1982.

> Today's leaders are dealing with the consequences of decisions made by their predecessors and, at the same time, are making decisions that will impact future generations. Businesses exist in a dynamic environment where change is an inherent element. Change, if it is based on good information and sound principles, serves to make businesses more competitive and prepares them for the future.

Levitt, Theodore. *The marketing imagination.* New York: Free Press, 1986.

> Global competition is something facing all businesses today, regardless of size. Companies that are successful will be those that are able to differentiate their products in consumers' minds and that are able to build ongoing relationships. Companies need to maintain their focus on the business that they are in.

Peters, Thomas J., and Robert H. Waterman, Jr. *In search of excellence.* New York: Harper & Row, 1982.

> Organizational structure can either enhance or impede the organization's ability to achieve its goals. Among "excellent" organizations there seem to be some common characteristics. Organizations should be structured in such a way as to adapt to changes in the marketplace.

Womack, James P., Daniel T. Jones, and Daniel Roos. *The machine that changed the world.* New York: HarperPerennial, 1991.

> Many of the problems that American car makers have faced in recent times are of their own making. The failure to adapt made them vulnerable to attack by car companies from overseas. The American car makers that are competing effectively have changed their approach to business.

Chapter 13

Recruiting and Selecting Salespeople

OPENING SCENARIO

Jay Sager was in the process of developing a new sales territory in the southeastern part of the United States for NORDAIR, Inc. NORDAIR produces spare parts for aircraft and reconditions aircraft parts. The company's customers include the major airlines, regional carriers, and private fleet owners, as well as fixed-base operators who are licensed to repair aircraft. Jay had been with NORDAIR for seven years, and for the past three years, he had been the sales manager for the northwest region. Prior to working for NORDAIR, Jay worked for McDonnell Douglas in the parts division.

NORDAIR had previously been distributing through manufacturer's reps in the southeast region, which consists of Florida, the Carolinas, Georgia, Kentucky, Alabama, and Mississippi. At NORDAIR's annual strategic planning meeting, Caryn Tripp, company president, had suggested that, due to the volume of sales, now was the time to put a company sales force in place in the southeast. She had asked Jay to establish the new southeast region and be its first manager. This new position was going to be a challenge, and Jay knew that upper management was grooming him for a v.p.-level job.

He had determined that he needed 21 salespeople for the new territory. Although he wanted to hire some veteran salespeople from the aircraft industry, he also wanted to hire some recent college graduates and have them grow with the company. He was willing to hire salespeople who had been working in other technology-based industries. Whomever he hired, they would be expected to go through NORDAIR's training program, which covered product and industry knowledge, as well as selling skills. They did not need to have an aeronautical engineering background, but they certainly would need to be comfortable in dealing with a technical product. They would also need to be dedicated to providing a high level of customer service and be willing to work hard enough to "get the job done," especially when a part was urgently needed, such as an A.O.G. (aircraft on ground) situation (an instance in which an aircraft is out of service due to the need for the part and which carries a federal mandate for highest priority service).

Jay was attempting to outline his recruitment strategy. He had a thousand possibilities in mind and wanted to prioritize his approach and systematize the search process.

Chapter Objectives

After reading this chapter, you should be able to

- Understand what sales managers look for when trying to hire successful salespeople.
- Recognize the importance of matching the requirements of the sales job with the type of person you recruit.
- Know the advantages and disadvantages of the various sources of sales candidates.
- Appreciate the use of the various tools for selecting recruits.
- Be aware of the legal implications of recruiting and hiring decisions.
- Appreciate the special issues involved in international recruitment.

INTRODUCTION

A major part of the job of the sales manager is building a sales force that will provide the type of representation the company needs in the marketplace. This means locating and successfully recruiting salespeople who can relate to customers and provide the level of service they need, who have the intelligence to learn about the product line as well as the desire to continue learning about changes in technology, and who possess those attributes, skills, and knowledge necessary to ensure a reasonable chance of success. With as many people as there are in the job market today, it would seem that this might be one of the easier tasks confronting sales managers. However, given the number of salespeople who fail or are marginal performers and the relative dearth of "successful" salespeople, the process of building the sales force is more difficult than it appears on the surface.

The difficulties in recruiting begin with the problems of precisely defining what characterizes successful salespeople and then attracting recruits who possess those characteristics. The latter problem is made more difficult by the all too common negative and unfair stereotype of salespeople, referred to by Donald Thompson as the "traveling salesman stereotype."[1] This negative image ranges from viewing the salesperson simply as an incompetent to the even more negative view as a "licensed thief." This inaccurate stereotype sees a good salesperson as anyone who is talkative and has a firm handshake and a ready smile.

Related to this is the view that a successful salesperson is one who possesses some ephemeral quality whereby he goes through life without making any real contribution to anyone or anything. His job consists chiefly of cajoling customers and moving on before customers have time to think logically about the purchase decision and change their minds. In the play *Death of a Salesman*, Arthur Miller provides this description of the rather pitiable character, Willy Loman:

> Willy was a salesman. And for a salesman, there is no rock bottom to his life. He don't put a bolt to a nut, he don't tell you the law or give you medicine. He's a man way out there in the blue, riding on a smile and a shoeshine. And then you get a couple of spots on your hat, and you're finished. Nobody dast blame this man. A salesman is got to dream, boy. It comes with the territory.

On one level we know this view of the successful salesperson is very inaccurate. However, there persists in the back of the minds of many sales managers "the myth of the perfect salesperson," in other words, a type of person who possesses a particular set of characteristics, who looks and acts a certain way, and who is always successful. The myth goes on to suggest that "if I had some kind of device that would measure every applicant who comes through the door and indicate if he or she is that perfect type, my problems would be solved."

A major part of the recruiting and selecting process consists of determining where and how to locate that set of prospects who fit the profile for the "right" salesperson. The sales manager needs to examine current methods of screening prospects and determine which is effective. This may mean that new approaches may have to be employed and new instruments devised that more clearly highlight the best candidates for a position.

In this chapter we will explore the set of characteristics that successful salespeople possess. These fall into three broad categories: attributes, skills, and knowledge. Although there are some distinct differences between successful and unsuccessful salespeople, there is no one, single set of characteristics that ensures success. Each company and selling environment is different, and so different people are needed.

CHARACTERISTICS OF SUCCESSFUL SALESPEOPLE

Although we cannot say that successful salespeople possess a certain specific set of characteristics and that those who are unsuccessful do not, we can say that there are some things successful salespeople have in common. A number of research studies have addressed the issue of what it is that sets good salespeople apart from average and poor ones. Although some variance exists in the findings, there is some agreement on the traits that characterize good salespeople.

These traits can be roughly divided into three major categories:

1. Attributes: specific personality characteristics
2. Skills: specific abilities
3. Knowledge: specific information

Attributes

The number of **attributes** that have been found consistently in studies of successful salespeople is relatively small. Among the most commonly mentioned is **empathy**[2]—the ability to understand a situation from another person's perspective. Mark Redmond reports that empathy enhances a person's ability to make predictions about others and helps to create a supportive/confirming atmosphere.[3] The former aspect of empathy enables the salesperson to anticipate and prepare for customer actions. The latter is critical in that the salesperson is attempting to build a relationship with the buyer. If buyers feel that the salesperson does not understand their problems, this relationship building will be thwarted.

Probably the second most commonly found attribute is ego drive.[4] **Ego drive** is the determination brought about by the fact that the salesperson's self-image is inextricably tied to success in making a sale. In other words, the person who possesses this attribute wants to succeed at selling because of identification with the job. Although many believe that salespeople are "only in it for the money," better salespeople enjoy making a sale. Certainly, good salespeople earn a relatively high income, but that income is the result rather than the driving force.

Ego strength or **resilience** is the ability to bounce back from defeat. For the salesperson, defeat comes in the form of being turned down in a sales call. Obviously, salespeople generally hear "no" more than they hear "yes." According to Saul Gellerman

> An unsuccessful call batters the seller's ego; it bluntly questions one's competence. A typical seller runs into more rejection in the course of a day than most of us have to absorb in weeks, if not months. From an emotional perspective, selling is a rough way to make a living. Self-respect is on the line every time you walk through a customer's door.[5]

He goes on to say that better salespeople do not let such refusals shake them. They stay with the fundamentals of selling and are able to put such setbacks behind them.

In a recent study that asked sales managers about the attributes of good salespeople, honesty or integrity was ranked first.[6] This attribute is perhaps the most critical in today's marketplace because it is essential for building trust.[7]

Sales managers recognize that honesty and integrity are the cornerstones of trust. If a salesperson's word cannot be relied upon, the buyer will quickly seek out someone whose word is trustworthy.

There are a number of other attributes that have been discussed in various studies as being important.[8] Among them are the following:

- Self-discipline
- Intelligence
- Creativity
- Flexibility
- Adaptability
- Self-motivated
- Persistent
- Personable
- Dependable

Although the necessary attributes may vary, empathy, ego drive, ego strength, and honesty are essential and are the basis of a successful sales career.

Skills

Possessing certain attributes, however, is not enough. Successful salespeople use particular **skills** more effectively than those who are unsuccessful. A number of studies have found certain skills that seem to predominate in successful salespeople. Some of the most commonly reported skills in recent studies are[9]

- Communication skills
- Analytical skills
- Organizational skills
- Time management skills

Generally, the idea that **communication skills** are important derives from the belief that salespeople need to be "good talkers." However, communication, as mentioned in Chapter 3, is a two-way street involving both listening and talking. According to sales managers from various types of companies, listening is perhaps the paramount skill of good salespeople. To quote one manager: "Over the years, I have sold more products by listening than I ever did by talking." Alan Korschun also characterized listening as a critical skill in selling.[10] **Active listening** is the process of gaining an understanding of the entire message and not simply hearing words being spoken. It provides insight into underlying feelings of the speaker in addition to comprehending the spoken message.

Analytical skills, the ability to break down a problem into its component parts and determine the best solution, are important in today's selling climate with its emphasis on consultative selling. One familiar phrase is "A problem well defined is half solved." Good salespeople have the ability to go beyond the symptoms and get to the heart of the matter—the real problem. Part of this ability is the result of being able to listen, but it also involves the ability to ask the right questions. Additionally, good analysis means that the salesperson possesses an adequate understanding of the customer's business and needs.

Organizational skills and time management skills are related because the latter are really the ability to organize one's time. **Organizational skills,** the ability to prioritize and place elements in a logical order, are important because of the tremendous amount of information that the typical salesperson is called on to handle. He or she must deal with information about each customer, about the product line, about the general economy, about the industry, about the company. Each must be organized into some usable format. There is, after all, a difference between data and information. Each time the salesperson makes a sales call, he or she must be able to organize that presentation into one that is meaningful to the customer. Simply loading the customer with an endless array of information is not the same thing as informing the customer. Unfortunately, too many salespeople believe that "if I can't dazzle them with my footwork, I'll baffle them with my . . ."—well, you know the rest.

Time management skills, the ability to make an accurate assessment of time requirements and prioritize one's daily activities, are critical for two reasons. First, the typical salesperson spends only about one third of the time in face-to-face selling.[11] Anything the person can do to spend more time with the customer should increase sales. Additionally, as we noted in Chapter 12, there is the 80–20 principle: about 80 percent of a person's sales come from 20 percent of the customers. The better salespeople allocate their time so that they can spend most of it with that 20 percent. However, successful salespeople do not forsake those smaller customers because they represent future earning potential. Thus the only way salespeople can handle the needs of their customers is through good time management.

Skills can be developed over time, and generally speaking, skill development is the actualization of the attributes the person possesses. Many new hires view the challenge of personal selling as formidable, and some do not enter the sales field because they do not believe they can learn the skills necessary to succeed. This misconception is caused by looking at the sales job as a whole rather than viewing it as a compilation of a number of skills and actions. By breaking down the sales job into its components, an individual can begin to work on each skill necessary to succeed.

In the same way, skill development is a process that involves breaking down each skill into its component parts and practicing each component separately before combining them again to perform the skill. Basketball players may spend an hour a day practicing nothing but jump shots and then another hour working on ball handling. However, basketball is not only jump shots and good ball handling. The players may be great at these two components, but unless they possess the other skills necessary, they will never succeed at basketball. However, to play basketball well, players must practice each of these components separately.

Sales works the same way. Each of the selling skills needs to be developed and practiced independently and then put together to use in selling. Over time, the skill becomes almost second nature. In other words, salespeople perform the skills without thinking about them. However, just as the basketball player who makes it to the pros will continue to practice the individual basic skills, veteran salespeople also must continue to practice those skills that have become second nature.

Knowledge

The third category of traits that set good salespeople apart is **knowledge.** The major types of knowledge most often mentioned as needed by salespeople are

- Product knowledge
- Customer knowledge
- Knowledge of the industry
- Knowledge of the competition
- Knowledge of their company

Of these, the first two are generally considered the most important. One study reported that product and customer knowledge ranked second and fourth, respectively, in their importance.[12]

Training is the forum for providing new hirees with a foundation of information on which they can build. However, if the acquisition of knowledge stops there, the salesperson will soon become outdated. Given that no one can expect to possess all the knowledge or information necessary for all situations, successful salespeople are the ones who are able to garner information when needed—they need to know where to get the necessary information. Additionally, salespeople must be able to examine information sources critically, glean pertinent material from them, and then be able to assimilate and organize that material.

In sum, to recruit the best salespeople, sales managers must keep in mind those characteristics that make for success in selling. However, they also must recognize that the choice cannot be based on one or two criteria but on an overall evaluation that considers the strengths and weaknesses of each candidate.[13] Certainly there are particular attributes that are important for the salesperson to possess. However, without the skills necessary to demonstrate those attributes and to relate to customers, the potential that a candidate possesses will not be realized. Finally, good salespeople continually keep abreast of developments in their industry and with their customers. The knowledge that comes from doing so gives them a competitive edge.

SELL!NG

THE FRONT LINES OF BUSINESS

Send in the Marine

Linda Corman

In football, they call it the end-around play. In warfare, it's known as a flanking maneuver. The crowds that gather around the chess masters of the world are watching for what's referred to as a wing attack.

But no matter what it's called, it's about striking off into uncharted territory while the competition trudges along the straight, narrow, and predictable path. And in the business of selling, it's the point of operating style that sets Rick Conrad apart from his peers.

The executive vice president/chief operating officer of Bell Atlantic Mobile (BAM) in Bedminster, N.J., attributes his success to his listening skills. "Your prospects will tell you what you need to do to sell them in the first few minutes— if you'll just shut up and listen," says Conrad. "The fatal mistake is to assume you know what your customer wants. People get frustrated with salespeople when they talk too much."

Listening, he adds, helps a salesperson decide whether a prospect is asking a question or airing an objection. "Someone asks, 'What does it cost?'" Conrad hypothesizes. "What did that person just ask you? He doesn't want a dollar figure.

What they really want to know is, 'Is there value in it?'"

While Conrad has been in management for 20 years (the last nine at BAM), he says he has never stopped listening. Or selling. In fact, it's his ability to listen, evaluate, communicate, and, finally, ask for the order—no matter where he happened to be on the corporate ladder—that has brought him the professional acclaim that culminated in his being named the National Account Management Association's 1995 Executive of the Year.

Conrad has ears for everyone: engineers who tell him why a product won't work, store managers who tell him his product packaging is too cumbersome, and members of an in-house committee studying consumer fraud. He hears the different message from each constituency. "Many managers assume that their employees have the same motivations," Conrad explains. "You have to read people, work with whatever their motivation is, and develop a common purpose."

"What I've learned from him is enthusiasm and the sheer joy in beating up the competition—and the way he does that, by assessing the situation and finding nontraditional ways to respond," says

Lonnie Lauer, BAM's vice president for Northern New Jersey. "He doesn't cut the price 10 percent if the competitor does. His way is not to be led by the competition but to create his own statement in the marketplace, because his statement is louder and clearer."

This determination to be different is at the heart of a no-nonsense style that dates to Conrad's first days in sales, in 1974, when he left the Marines to join Dictaphone. Daniel Hilbert, a colleague from that time and now the chief executive of Breg International, an environmental products company in Fredericksburg, Va., was an early witness to Conrad's selling success.

As Hilbert tells the story, Conrad was trying to sell a new line of desktop dictation machines. Dictaphone's product cost $675; a prospect told him the competition was charging $500 for a comparable model. Conrad replied, "If you want me to compare apples to apples, then tell me what features you want me to take off this machine." The prospect wrote out a check for the full $675.

"Most people would have said, 'I'll sell it to you for $500,'" says Hilbert. But Conrad closed the deal by forcefully communicating his product's superiority.

"When you start you're on equal footing," Conrad says about this kind of selling challenge. "I know our products are best, but the customer doesn't know that. The person who is best at listening and communicating wins."

Since becoming chief operating officer 11 months ago, Conrad has listened to the marketplace and demonstrated his propensity for original solutions time and time again. As the individual responsible for the marketing and distribution of BAM's cellular telephones, data services, and equipment, Conrad must distinguish his company from its rivals in both the consumer and business markets. More visibility at retail, he reasoned, would build a stronger identity. So he announced the goal last June of completing, by year's end, an ongoing plan to more than double BAM's retail outlets, from 31 to 72.

Naturally, many company employees were skeptical. "He set a very aggressive target," says Laura Knoop, BAM's director of channel marketing. "Everyone said, 'This is impossible.'"

The difficulty of the task notwithstanding, Conrad and his team dug in. Within the proposed period, the expansion was complete. More important, reports Conrad, retail sales in 1994 were up 300 percent from 1993.

On another front, Conrad oversaw a test market in Annapolis, Md., that was designed to enhance the company's consumer service. BAM kept prices for consumers well below those for business users by limiting the area in which consumers could use their cellular service. The intention was to entice prospects who otherwise would eschew cellular phones as unnecessary, pricey gadgets. At the same time, to attract the business market, Conrad threw his support behind a test in Northern New Jersey that allowed callers to reach BAM subscribers through one number that connected not only to cellular phones but to home and office landline phones, too.

The ex-Marine is able to operate on several fronts at once, say his colleagues, because he has the vision and leadership skills to bring together disparate players to work as a team. His ability to sell through his program is grounded in the respect he shows for his co-workers and, again, his willingness to listen.

Thomas Bartlett, a BAM vice president in the Philadelphia area, vividly remembers a conference call that demonstrated Conrad's consensus-building skills. The topic was business-plan development, and Bartlett had taken a position that was somewhat counter to the one favored by the rest of the team. Moreover, he admits, he was "coming at it like a bull in a china shop. I didn't want to budge." As Bartlett defended his position, Conrad took control. " 'Let's hang up,' he told us all. 'I want to talk with Tom,' " recalls Bartlett. "He could have put me on the spot." Instead, Conrad allowed his colleague to voice his concerns and then gave him the opportunity to buy into the more popular agenda on his own terms. That kind of one-on-one professional courtesy, according to Bartlett and others, is a major source of the loyalty and respect Conrad commands.

Conrad, who grew up in Virginia, joined the Marines in 1971 after graduating from Old Dominion University with a history degree. It was while he was in the service that he decided on a business career. While he did not set out for sales, Conrad carefully studied a number of Fortune 500 companies and concluded that selling was the best place to begin a business career. He chose Dictaphone because of its training program and its opportunities for advancement.

After only a year and a half as a rep, Conrad was on his way up. Frank McCarthy, a Dictaphone vice president of sales who occasionally served as a talent scout in the early '70s, spotted Conrad as someone who should, he says, "move along quickly" at the company. "He was a player right from the beginning, when he was about 25 years old," says McCarthy.

From the field, Conrad moved to headquarters, where he managed the special markets of medical, legal, and government. Two years later he became a sales manager in Washington, then a district manager for a new product line. Next came stints as a product general manager, and, finally, a national vice presidency with direct responsibility for federal government operations. "Of course, his numbers were outstanding," says McCarthy, now retired. "But great numbers are just an entree to getting noticed. Then you have to show other characteristics."

In Conrad's case, those other qualities included seriousness, intelligence, intensity, and an ability to motivate others. As to the effectiveness of his selling style, McCarthy points to one simple truth: Several of the young Dictaphone salespeople made Conrad, just a few years their senior, their role model.

In 1983 Conrad left Dictaphone and followed developing technology to AES, a word processing company in Gaithersburg, Md., where he was director of federal government operations. The company folded, but Conrad kept moving ahead, joining Fairchild's Cardkey company in Centerville, Va., again as director of federal government operations. Two years later, in 1986, he signed on with BAM as a regional director charged with creating, then managing, a sales force in the Washington area. BAM was appealing to Conrad because it was a new company in a new field with wide-open potential. And, not so incidentally, it offered him a return to sales management.

This, too, proved to be a good career move. Conrad soon became director of sales operations, then president of Bell Atlantic Paging in 1990. In 1992 he was named regional vice president for BAM's Southwest division. Two years later he took on the executive vice presidency, adding the chief operating title last June. While his rise has been rapid, he has not lost his perspective on the transition from the active sales force to the front office.

Conrad's best tip for salespeople with management aspirations is to learn everything there is to know about their current jobs, the business their company is in, and their company's organization. For a rep at BAM, this means soaking up as much as possible about the industry's fast-changing technology. "You need to study, to read all you can, to access everything you can about the technology," says Conrad. "That separates the successful from the less-successful salesperson, and it inspires confidence in the customer."

Other tips for would-be managers include learning to manage people and to succinctly define your goals so that as a manager, you can convey to your employees where their efforts should lead. "You can learn from everyone," says Conrad. "Often people who report to you know how to do things better."

The secrets to Conrad's success, say those who know his work habits, are ambition, determination, and smarts—not to mention the fierce competitiveness you would expect from a former Marine. McCarthy says his former protege scored career points by being able to channel his competitiveness toward rivals outside Dictaphone. Inside company walls, he was—and remains—the model of cooperation.

Early on, McCarthy recalls, Conrad also demonstrated the patience of a consummate team player. When Dictaphone selected another salesperson for a district sales managership, Conrad was upset. And while he didn't hesitate to express that chagrin, he burned no bridges. As it turned out, his response all but assured him of the next promotion. "His stock went up 100 percent in my mind," says McCarthy. "He first said that he and his family were very disappointed. Then he said that his job was now to prove that he was the person for the next job, and that he had to redouble his efforts to prove it. He's a guy not easily defeated. He'll take a defeat, and you'll never beat him on that same ground again."

Which suggests another tactic that Conrad says every businessperson—from sales rep to COO—should cultivate: to keep on learning. "If you win," he instructs, "always ask the vendor why you won. And if you lose, ask why. Customers often surprise you."

In that absolute need to be open to change, Conrad finds his continuing challenge at Bell Atlantic Mobile. Given his corporate growth expectation of about 50 percent, he explains, "I've got to service two times as many customers every 24 months, to build a network, to double the organization every 24 months. That's an incredible challenge."

And, notes Conrad, "you will fail unless you are looking to improve all the time. The beauty of it is your competition is faced with the same thing. If I'm the person who handles it best, I win."

Reprinted with the permission of SELL!NG magazine.

THE RECRUITMENT AND SELECTION PROCESS

Job Analysis and Description

The discussion of the characteristics of successful salespeople provided a general overview. However, every company and sales job is different, and sales managers need to examine those factors specifically related to the particular job before hiring a person to fill that slot. Beginning the search process by developing a candidate profile will guide the entire process of selection and help ensure that the right person is hired.[14] Herbert and Jeanne Greenburg of Personality Dynamics, Inc., a New Jersey–based consulting firm, found that the match between the person and the job was the key to hiring high-performance salespeople.[15] In other words, a complete understanding of the particular sales job is an essential beginning point in the recruitment process.

The **job description** is the formal mechanism for detailing the requirements of a job. It is instructive to examine an existing job description to determine if it is up to date, accurate, and adequate. One important reason is that often the sales manager is not the only person involved in the hiring process. Others in the sales division will take part in the process, as will people from the human resources department. Human resource personnel may not realize that a job description is out of date, and as a result, the people they consider may not be qualified for the position.

The **job analysis** needs to consider a number of factors:

The market. Who does the salesperson call on? Does the market consist of wholesalers or end users? Will the salesperson call only on buyers, or will other people have an impact on the buying decision, such as engineers who need information?

The product line. How technical is the product line? How many different products will one person be responsible for? Is the product standardized, or does it need to meet the specifications of each customer?

Tasks and responsibilities. Does the job require any special skills and does it have physical requirements beyond the typical white-collar job? What kind of travel is involved? Does the salesperson perform certain service tasks that require a particular skill? How often and with whom does the person interact in the company?

Degree of autonomy. How much freedom does the person have in making decisions? How often does the person interact with superiors?

When recruiting on a college campus, sales managers should consider not only applicants' amount and type of education but also such things as involvement in outside activities in school and whether or not they supported themselves while in school. When recruiting veteran salespeople, issues such as the type of selling they have been doing, the industries in which they have worked, and the nature of the organizations for which they have sold are all important considerations.

Sources of Candidates

Once the set of requirements of the job are determined and the job description is complete, the next issue is where to recruit qualified candidates. Certainly the job description has some impact on where to find the best recruits. In general, there are several viable sources for prospective salespeople. For example, sales managers can recruit from within the company, from university campuses, from competitors, and from outside the industry. Table 13-1 presents the positive and negative aspects of recruiting from the various sources.

Each of these sources has its advantages and disadvantages. At times, company personnel from nonselling areas offer distinct advantages.[16] However, if the company has a critical vacancy, does not have the time to train new salespeople, and would prefer not to shuffle its current salespeople, recruiting from competitors can be the most expedient and effective approach. For example, in 1985, when Wilkinson Sword USA was switching from manufacturer's reps to its own sales force, it had to put people in place quickly who had sales experience and who could "hit the ground running." They did not have the time or the resources to train inexperienced salespeople.[17]

Reaching Recruits

A related issue in finding the best source of candidates is how to reach those candidates. Several issues need to be considered when determining which medium to use to reach prospective candidates. One is the amount of time sales managers have to get a salesperson in place and to devote to the task of recruiting. Another is the question of how many people can be spared from their usual duties to do the recruiting. Also, there is the issue of the amount of money available for recruiting.

Advertising. Advertising is commonly used for reaching candidates. The obvious advantage is the wide exposure received. When using advertisements, sales managers must address three major questions: First, will the company advertise in newspapers, magazines, and/or trade journals? Second, and related to the first, is which specific publications will be used?

The advantage of magazines and trade journals is that they are targeted media that reach a specific audience and eliminate unnecessary responses. With newspapers, the advantage is the wider audience that is reached. However, with that wider audience will come a number of responses from less than qualified candidates. Another advantage of newspapers is that people have become accustomed to seeking job opportunities in newspapers and therefore will often peruse them first when looking for a job. Newspapers give wide coverage in a specific geographic area.

TABLE 13-1 Sources for Recruiting Salespeople

Source	Positive Aspects	Negative Aspects
Within the company	Candidates are familiar with the product line. They are familiar with company procedures. They tend to be more loyal to the company. It is less expensive than external recruiting. It provides the chance for advancement within the company. There is already some information on candidates' abilities and work habits.	There may not be candidates who are qualified for the position. Candidates who are considered and then turned down for the position may become dissatisfied. Candidates may have a mistaken perception of the sales job. Candidates may have a difficult time making the transition to the sales job.
Colleges and universities	There is a large pool of qualified candidates in one place. Candidates are in a learning mode and hence will be more trainable. They are eager to get their career started and the enthusiasm carries over into the job. They have demonstrated the ability to establish and accomplish a goal. Usually the pay scale is lower for new graduates than for veteran salespeople. Generally, they are younger and will have more physical energy to devote to the job. New graduates are usually more mobile and willing to relocate. New graduates usually enjoy the travel involved in a job more than do veteran salespeople.	Candidates tend to lack experience and may not fully understand the requirements of the sales career. Candidates may be somewhat immature. There tends to be a higher turnover rate for younger salespeople than for veterans. Candidates may "shop" companies that recruit, that is, they may interview with companies they have no intention to work for.
Competitors	Candidates are veterans and know their industry. They understand the type of customers that buy from the firm. They have a realistic understanding of the sales job. They have established accounts and may bring some of their customers with them. They have a track record that can be evaluated. They are likely to have some knowledge of your product line.	Candidates will be more expensive to hire. They may not be loyal to one company; if you hired them, someone else can. They may have certain ways of doing things and may be difficult to "untrain." If they leave, they may take your customers. They will likely be less mobile than younger salespeople.
Other industries	These prospects are veterans who require less training on how to sell. They may bring a fresh perspective. They have an established record that can be evaluated.	These candidates will be relatively expensive to hire compared to college students. They may find that they do not like selling in your industry.

(table continues)

TABLE 13-1 (*continued*)

Source	Positive Aspects	Negative Aspects
Other industries	They have a good understanding of the sales career. Generally they will bring a certain enthusiasm given their willingness to change industries.	They may have certain ways of doing things and will need to be "untrained." They may have a "prima donna" attitude.
Professionals from a nonsales background	These candidates will have some knowledge of the business world. They will tend to have a mature outlook. They will likely be enthusiastic and willing to learn. They may introduce a fresh perspective to the sales job. Generally, they are willing to work hard to get established in a sales career.	They may be impatient with the process of building a sales career. They may not have a realistic view of the sales profession. They may experience a good deal of stress brought about by a career change. They may be expensive to hire.

With national magazines a company can also restrict the geographic coverage to a certain extent. If a firm wants to hire salespeople for its southwest region, it can run an ad only in the southwest region of national magazines. If it wants to hire a sales engineer, it can run an ad in trade publications aimed at engineers. Generally, any magazine will provide a profile of its audience upon request. Additionally, a firm can refer to *Standard Rate & Data* (available in public libraries) for a synopsis of the audiences for the various magazines.

The third question is will the company use open or blind ads? **Open ads** are those that identify the company doing the recruiting. **Blind ads** provide a post office box number to which candidates are to send résumés. By identifying the company, open ads may attract people who are interested in a specific company and eliminate some who are not. However, they do result in more "drop-in" applicants. Blind ads eliminate the problem of drop-ins, but they may discourage some people who are very particular about where they wish to work or those who might be afraid that their current employer is doing the advertising and would not want their firm to know they are looking.

Employment Agencies. Another avenue for reaching prospective candidates is **employment agencies.** A major advantage of using "headhunters" is that they will screen candidates for a company, which saves a tremendous amount of time and effort. Additionally, these agencies specialize in the recruiting process and thus possess an expertise that sales managers often do not have. They know what questions to ask and generally what to look for in selecting a pool of applicants.

However, the use of agencies also has a couple of disadvantages. First, most professional positions are "fee paid." In other words, the recruiting company pays the agency a percentage of the position's salary, and these fees can be quite expensive. This outlay, however, is offset by the fact that the company uses fewer of its internal resources in the recruiting process. The second major drawback is the complaint that they are mainly interested in earning their fee, and, hence, will send out applicants that are less than satisfactory. However, if a company does a good job of specifying exactly what it is looking for in candidates, is careful in selecting which agency to use, and develops a long-term relationship with an agency, this second problem can be largely avoided.

When selecting an agency, the company needs to decide if it will use a general-line agency, one that recruits for a number of types of jobs, or an agency that specializes in a particular profession, such as sales. The advantage of the latter is that this type of agency possesses a greater understanding of the specifics of a particular profession and has extensive contacts within that area. The advantage of the former is that a wider array of prospects use it.

Campuses. As already pointed out, recruiting recent college graduates has some advantages. Certainly, which schools a company recruits from is important, because the needs of the company will determine the type of person it wishes to recruit.[18]

When recruiting on a campus, a company can use three major avenues. Probably the most common is the *placement center.* Placement centers specialize in matching students with interested organizations. Generally, they are widely used on campuses and often offer students additional services such as career counseling. The main advantage of going through the placement center to reach candidates is because it is so widely used by the student body. That, also, is perhaps its major disadvantage: The recruiter may interview a number of students who do not fit the profile the company is looking for. Another disadvantage of placement centers arises from the magnitude of demands placed on them by students. One more advantage of using placement centers, though, is that they often provide a place for interviewing.

Typically, placement centers are forced to use some kind of **bid system** to match students with recruiting companies. Given that one company can only allocate so many slots for interviewing, the center will select students for those slots by giving each student a specific number of points. The students then "bid" for the chance to interview with a particular company. The students with the highest bids for the company will get the time slots. The problem for recruiters and students, too, is that they can miss interviewing some candidates who might be qualified for the job.

Another way to reach students is by contacting *faculty members.* Despite the difficulties in establishing contact with the proper faculty member, once the relationship is developed, faculty members can provide not only names of prospective students but also some in-depth information about them. Jon Hawes points out that when a recruiting company contacts faculty members ahead of time, they can encourage students to sign up with a particular company.[19] If a university offers a sales or sales management course, the company should attempt to establish contact with the instructors teaching that course. Also, through a faculty contact, a recruiter may get the chance to speak to a class or marketing club and thus expose students to their company's philosophy and recruiting needs. In general, recruiters should use placement centers and faculty members in conjunction with each other for best results.

The third avenue to recruit college students is the **job fair.** This typically is a forum for companies to set up information booths on campus. In a job fair the company can see a wider range of students than is possible through the placement center. In turn, many students, after having had such a chance to find out about a company, discover they might enjoy working there. Additionally, often students who are interested in a particular company can make contact with that company and start the recruitment process at the fair. Sometimes, in conjunction with a fair, individual companies will hold a reception for interested candidates. This provides an opportunity for more personal contact and for candidates to get more in-depth information about the company.

Regardless of the route chosen, sales managers should keep in mind that recruiting is an ongoing process. In an interview reported in *Sales & Marketing Management,* consultant and author Harvey Mackay stated that recruiting is something sales managers engage in 52 weeks of the year.[20] In other words, recruiting is an everyday part of the sales manager's job. Sales managers should have a ready source of qualified applicants whenever an opening occurs, in order to minimize needless and costly delays in filling positions. J. Doug Clopton of Hershey Chocolate U.S.A. advocates a rethinking of the whole recruitment process whereby the sales manager takes advantage of opportunities such as trade shows to meet potential applicants.[21] He suggests that the sales manager should regard people who inquire about sales jobs not as nuisances but as potential customers. An up-to-date file of qualified applicants is a rich source of potential salespeople.

Who Should Recruit. One critical factor when recruiting on campuses is the person doing the recruiting. Several studies have dealt with the issue of what characteristics are necessary for college recruiters to be effective.[22] Following are some of these characteristics:

1. They need to demonstrate an interest in and appreciation for the students as individuals.
2. They need to show enthusiasm and make the job sound inviting.
3. Students seem to prefer recruiters who are between 35 and 55 years of age. Ones younger than that lack credibility in the eyes of students and ones older than 55 are not perceived as understanding students.
4. Effective recruiters take time to both talk and listen. Students want the opportunity to tell the recruiter what they have to offer and want the chance to find out about the firm.
5. Effective recruiters build rapport with students. They do not use stress interviews, nor do they try to put students on the spot.

Recruiting involves balancing the process of "selling" the company with that of screening applicants. Especially for college students, who are generally a bit intimidated with the process to begin with, recruiting is a major event in their careers.

TOOLS OF RECRUITMENT AND SELECTION

The process of recruiting and selecting the right salespeople is one of the more difficult tasks facing sales managers. Before they use the various tools at their disposal for recruiting, managers should remember that no tool, regardless of how sophisticated or elegant it is, is a substitute for their own good judgment. As Jack Falvey, a contributing editor for *Sales & Marketing Management*, points out, each of these tools can provide a "good surface read" of an individual applicant but does not provide the depth that managers need to make a decision.[23] That depth comes from having an understanding of people and the requirements of the job. Sales managers then should continually upgrade their skills in recruiting and selecting salespeople and should use skills and tools together, allowing each to fill in a piece of the puzzle.

From the outset, the recruiting process can be rendered more difficult or less so, depending on the quality of the instruments and the processes that managers employ. In general, these tools must possess three characteristics if they are to be useful:[24]

1. **Validity.** Does the device measure what it is supposed to measure, and how well does it relate to the requirements of the job? For example, does ranking high on an interview mean that the person is a good fit and will perform well?
2. **Reliability.** Are the results consistent and stable? In other words, does the device yield similar results with similar people? Also, do two people who are objectively equal receive a similar evaluation in terms of desirability for hiring?
3. **Job relatedness.** Is the instrument or process relevant to the job? For example, a typing test has job relatedness for a secretarial position but not for a sales position.

It is not enough that these characteristics were present when these tools were first devised, because organizations and jobs change over time. With each change the possibility exists that the validity, reliability, and job relatedness of these tools will be undermined. Sales managers must ensure that tools like application forms, tests, and interviews are current in terms of these three characteristics.

LEGAL ISSUES

It is impossible for any one person to understand all the legal ramifications involved in hiring decisions. Not only are the requirements of the **Equal Employment Opportunity Commission (EEOC)** complicated, but other issues are involved in the hiring process, such as the legality of promises made to potential employees.[25] For sales managers, who have so many other concerns, keeping abreast of the changing world of EEOC requirements is out of the question. However, it is the responsibility of the sales manager to take a proactive stance related to legal issues in recruiting.[26]

Because of the formidable task of keeping abreast of EEOC requirements, companies involve people with legal expertise from the human resources department in the hiring process. However, there are two basic rules the sales manager must understand when recruiting. These rules are based on the Civil Rights Act of 1964 and subsequent legislation. First, when a plaintiff brings a discrimination charge against a company, he or she is not required to show intention to discriminate, only that the practice has a disproportionate impact on a protected group. In other words, for a sales manager to plead that she did not mean to discriminate is not a defense in court. Second, once the impact is demonstrated, the burden of proof shifts from the plaintiff to the defendant (the company). In other words, the plaintiff does not need to establish how the discrimination was carried out or who exactly was involved, only that it took place. After this is done, the defendant must show that, in fact, discrimination did not take place.

Generally speaking, discrimination based on age, sex, race, national origin, religion, ethnic background, handicap, and so forth is strictly forbidden. The exception is if the discrimination is justified by business necessity. This exception is referred to as a **bona fide occupational qualification (BFOQ).**[27] In other words, if the requirements of the job necessitate that certain limitations be placed on the type of person who fills it, this would constitute a BFOQ. Until now, in no case has race been found to be a BFOQ, but both age and sex have been. For example, if clothing designers were looking for models to appear in their spring dress line, they could specify that they needed female models. The designers could not, however, specify that the models be a particular race or religion. Another example would be if the job required that skill and dexterity levels be maintained for purposes of safety, the employer may specify that applicants be below a certain age level. An airline company may refuse to hire a pilot who is 60 years of age as a trainee, given the number of years required to become a first officer and the issue of passenger safety. However, the same airline company could not refuse to hire a person who is female or who is Asian. In short, a BFOQ is a very restrictive classification, and there must be a clear-cut relationship between it and the performance of the particular job in question.

There almost seems to be more questions that cannot be asked on an application or in an interview than can be asked. Basically, any question regarding the demographic background of the individual, unless it is related to a BFOQ, is legally suspect. Following is a list of subjects that are forbidden areas:

- Sex
- Religion
- Race

- Ethnic background
- National origin
- Type of military discharge
- Arrest record
- Weight and/or height
- Credit history
- Marital status
- Children
- Handicaps

If unsure of the legality of a particular issue, a sales manager should seek the advice of an expert in EEOC regulations.

Although discrimination is repugnant to most people, it still exists. Some have attempted to circumvent the law by asking for certain information indirectly. Also, others have asked discriminatory questions very innocently. However, it must be remembered that the intention to discriminate is not a requisite to being guilty of discrimination. The idea behind this is that if individuals are not directly asking for the information concerning forbidden subjects, they are not in violation of the law. However, any attempt to ascertain this information is considered discriminatory. Following are examples of indirect questions or requests for information that would likely be considered illegal:

> Please enclose a photo with the application.
> When did you graduate from high school?
> What is your hometown?
> How old are your kids?
> Would your minister mind providing a reference?
> Are you planning on getting married anytime soon?
> Are you looking forward to Christmas?
> What are some of your hobbies?
> Do you own or rent your home?
> When did you get your honorable discharge?
> Please list any arrests you have had along with the reason.
> How long have you been in this country?
> Will you provide a credit history?

Even though this list has some questions that seem innocuous, each is related to some aspect of discrimination. For example, because arrest rates are higher among black youths than white ones, questions about arrests indirectly concern race. Questions about hobbies might be a way of getting at national origin or religion. Certainly, asking about whether someone is looking forward to Christmas is a way of finding out about a person's religious preference. In short, discriminatory practices, regardless of which form they take, are illegal. The exceptions related to BFOQ are relatively few.

Application Forms

Application forms are utilized in the vast majority of organizations. Given their pervasiveness, and the fact that generally once they are devised they are rarely changed, the forms are often either inappropriate, illegal, or both. Therefore, they should be reviewed periodically to ensure that the questions are valid, reliable, job related, and legal. Although application forms provide information similar to that found in the résumé, having the information in a standardized format that covers areas of concern to the company makes them useful.

Application forms generally address four basic areas:

1. Personal data, such as name, address, phone number where the person can be reached, and social security number
2. Education
3. Experience, including where the applicant has worked and the types of jobs
4. General health questions

Typically, the applicant is asked to sign the form. By signing, the applicant attests to the accuracy of the information and gives the company permission to conduct a background check. Some companies use a weighted application form in which different pieces of information are given more importance than others and an overall numerical score is computed to indicate the relative qualifications of the applicant. This is an attempt to make the selection process more "objective," to ensure the minimization of interviewer bias. The usefulness of the weighted form in accomplishing this end is, however, limited.

A well-designed application not only can provide information useful in the selection process but also useful in the interview. It will help keep the interviewer on track and provide insights into the areas that may need to be probed more deeply. Additionally, it can assist the interviewer in making the applicant feel more relaxed during the interview. The interviewer can begin by going over basic background information to get the candidate talking and then branch out into more in-depth questions, such as those dealing with goals, accomplishments, and reasons for applying.

Interviews

The interview is an integral part of the recruitment and selection process. The interview not only verifies the information in the application form or résumé but also provides meaningful insight into the candidate as a person. For instance, the interviewer can ask about the goals of the person or, perhaps, what the person has accomplished that he or she is proud of. This will give a clue to what is important to the individual and thereby provide information as to whether the company or the job can become a major part of accomplishing goals important to that person. Often the recruiting process involves several interviews. The initial one is a screening interview, and as the process continues, the interviews become more detailed and progressively deal with issues that are more pertinent to the job.

There are four general types of interviews. The **structured interview** uses a questionnaire with a specific set of questions. The interviewer simply goes through the questionnaire checking the responses of the candidate. Here is an example of a question:

> Of the following answers, which one describes the major reason that you are attracted to sales?
> I like to work with people.
> I enjoy persuading others to do what I want them to.
> The job involves knowing and doing several things.
> A person can make a lot of money in sales.
> There are always new challenges in sales.

The candidate is read the question and must choose which of the five answers best tells about him or her.

Structured interviews do ensure consistency more than the other types of interviews and do not require that the interviewer have the higher skill level needed for the other approaches. However, it does restrict the information that is received and does not allow for any variation in the questions. This approach is probably not well suited for recruiting salespeople, given that often the determination of suitability of candidates rest as much or more on how they responded as on the response itself.

The **semistructured interview** consists of the interviewer using an interview schedule with specific questions to ask. The questions are often open-ended, and the interviewer has the option of probing deeper, depending on the response of the candidate. Examples of such questions include "What is it about sales that attracts you?" and "How does a career in sales fit with your overall goals?" This type of question allows the candidate to give more detailed answers than the structured interview but guides the direction of how he or she answers. The interviewer has to be adept at picking up on information that needs further clarification, even though he or she does have a framework from which to work. This is probably the most common type of interview used.

The **unstructured interview** consists of the interviewer asking open-ended questions and allowing the candidate to talk extensively. The interviewer encourages the candidate through the use of active listening and providing occasional feedback. This approach provides insight into the candidate's ability to "think on her feet." The unstructured interview often causes some discomfort on the part of candidates because it calls for them to be able to determine what information is pertinent and be able to present it in a clear fashion.

This approach also calls for a high level of expertise on the part of the interviewer. Some examples of questions used in this approach include "Tell me about yourself" and "Where do you want to be five years from now?" Obviously, the questions have the potential to yield answers that are fairly far afield of anything to do with sales. However, a skilled interviewer has the ability to focus and direct the interview without taking it over. This approach probably requires more of the interviewer than it does of the candidates, but it also has the potential to give a great deal of insight into the person being interviewed.

The fourth type is the **problem-solving interview,** and it consists of presenting the candidate with an issue or a problem to solve. The candidate goes through the process of resolving the problem and answers questions by the interviewer. In sales, this approach often involves role playing when the candidate is asked to sell a particular item. At times, this approach takes the form of a stress interview in which the candidate is put into a problem-solving situation, must devise a solution to the problem, and then defend that solution. Although the stress interview has been criticized because of creating unproductive stress for the candidate, in general, the problem-solving interview has been shown to be useful.

Unfortunately, interviewing is often the weakest part of the recruitment and selection process, because the person conducting the interview is not always trained in interviewing. Interviewing requires both training and practice. The process is more than simply asking a series of questions and getting a "gut feel" for the candidate. It also means understanding what to look for in candidates, knowing how to frame questions to obtain the most open and honest response, actively listening, and observing to glean all the information that is possible. Additionally, the interviewer must be able to draw all this together to form some kind of solution to the problem.

Harvey MacKay presents some questions and topics that should prove useful in the interview and that the applicant should be prepared to answer:[28]

1. Describe your ideal job—the position you would most like to have (include title, responsibilities, who you would report to, who would report to you).
2. Describe your ideal company (size, industry, culture, location, structure).
3. Where do you want to be in your career in three to five years?
4. What do you want your next job to do for you that your last job didn't do?
5. What kinds of growth should a new job offer (promotions, training, challenges)?
6. What skills will you be able to add to your résumé while you have this job?
7. Why should a company want to hire you? What's special about you as a candidate?
8. What personal and professional accomplishments are you the most proud of?
9. What do you least want to be asked in an interview—what are the questions you dread the most?
10. How will you handle the tough questions?
11. What compensation, including salary and benefits, do you want to earn and can you legitimately ask for?
12. What are the most important benefits other than salary that would prompt you to go to work for a new company?
13. What tools and resources can you draw on to help you through your job transition?
14. What can you say in an interview that would really set you apart from other candidates for your ideal position?

15. What could your current employer do for you that would prevent you from looking for another job in the first place? (Have you asked?)
16. How will you know when you've become a success?

Tests

A number of tests can be used to screen and select candidates, including the following:

Aptitude tests. Examine the capacity of one to perform a particular type of job and/or to learn how to perform that job.

Intelligence tests. Measure the overall mental capacity of the person. These deal with the person's ability at logic and reasoning, use of language and math, and the ability to understand spatial relationships.

Knowledge or proficiency tests. Measure the amount of information possessed about a subject.

Personality tests. Attempt to categorize people into a personality profile, measuring the inherent traits the person possesses.

Honesty tests. Attempt to assess the inherent honesty of the individual. These tests attempt to uncover the person's ethical value system and judgment of situations where honesty is an issue.

There is no shortage of tests or scales available, and new ones are being introduced all the time, such as a scale that measures the value system of candidates.[29] Although these tests are generally useful, they are not without their problems. They should be used with caution because of their quality and limitations. With any test, the issue of validity is critical.[30]

Finally, there is always an underlying legal issue involved with tests. The company must be able to show that performing in a particular fashion on these tests is related to performing well on the job. If that cannot be statistically proven, the test should not be used. Also, a number of court cases have found certain of these tests, particularly intelligence and personality tests, to be discriminatory.

A company can find a number of tests that have been validated and are available in the public domain, or it can purchase validated tests from commercial sources. Another solution is for companies to hire a testing service that specializes in administering, scoring, and validating tests. Generally, they have developed the database necessary to demonstrate the validity and reliability of any test they use.

It is worthwhile to note that the use of **polygraph tests** was outlawed by the Employee Polygraph Protection Act of 1988. This law prohibits the use of such tests for the purposes of hiring except for government employees, employees of security firms, and employees of pharmaceutical companies. If the firm suspects economic loss due to the actions of its employees, the use of a polygraph is generally acceptable. Some firms attempt to use honesty tests to replace the polygraph. Again, however, the validity of such tests is suspect.

Also, the use of tests is limited by the process itself. Candidates, particularly ones with a behavioral science education, can often "knock off" employment tests; that is, they can determine answers acceptable to the company and simply give those responses rather than their "true" responses. Additionally, a candidate may feel uncomfortable giving an honest response to a test and will provide a "socially acceptable" one.

Reference Checks

It has historically been the practice of companies to perform reference checks on perspective employees. This is done either through requesting letters of reference from people who are familiar with the candidate or through contacting former employers and teachers. It is generally a given that letters of reference will only come from persons who are predisposed to give a favorable report of the candidate, and, therefore, their usefulness has been questioned. However, references will often provide insights into just why others think a particular candidate is worthwhile to consider. Such information can be useful in the decision process.

Although reference checks are sometimes viewed as "an exercise in futility," it is estimated that between 20 and 25 percent of all résumés contain fabrications.[31] Reference checks are useful for spotting these inconsistencies. Increasingly, former employees are successfully suing companies that give out negative information about them, so many firms will only verify dates of employment and job titles. The information to be gleaned from reference checks is, therefore, limited. However, a background check can serve to verify basic information, such as length of employment, the position occupied at a former company, and salary.

Because of the growing number of cases in which applicants indicate they earned a degree when, in fact, they have not, companies should request official transcripts from the applicant's university. The reason we specify "official" transcripts is that they are stamped by the registrar's office and are less likely to be forged. It is also advisable to obtain a written release from the candidate prior to checking references.

Physical Examinations

Typically, the final step in the hiring process is the physical examination by a qualified physician. Physical exams serve the purpose of screening out employees with health problems that might lead to a high rate of absenteeism. Also, such exams generally can negate insurance company claims of preexisting conditions if the person has medical problems later. Physical exams, however, are not very good predictors of future health.[32] As with the other tools of recruitment and selection, physical exams must pass the test of job relatedness.

RECRUITING IN THE INTERNATIONAL ARENA

One of the emerging challenges facing sales managers is helping their sales force to become truly global. Certainly, part of the process is training salespeople and enculturating them in the global perspective. However, in many cases, using salespeople from the company's home country is not as effective as recruiting salespeople who are native to the country in which a company does business. There are two main reasons that host-country salespeople seem to work better in the long run:

1. Local salespeople have a better understanding of the local culture, and they often already have established contacts.
2. The costs of relocating salespeople and their families from the company's country are high, and often they have problems adapting to the new culture.[33]

Although employing salespeople from the host country is generally preferable, recruiting in another country has a number of pitfalls. Managers who are accustomed to finding a number of qualified prospects for sales positions in the United States will find that, in other countries, there will be fewer qualified candidates, and it will likely take longer to recruit. This is partly due to the image of the sales career overseas. In Europe, a sales career is held in lower esteem than it is in the United States.[34] This means that it will be more difficult attracting talented individuals who have the qualifications needed. A company who is recruiting in that setting will need to emphasize the benefits of a sales career.

Also, international recruiting involves adapting the tools used in screening candidates. For example, reaching the right applicants is also difficult because of the differences in the media of the countries. Not only do applications need to be translated, but they often need to be completely redesigned.

Interviewing will also be different due to the differences in culture and language. Many of the subtleties in communication that give sales managers valuable information during the interview can be extremely different in a foreign country. A gesture or facial expression may mean one thing in the United States and something very different elsewhere. Also, the interviewees' approach to the interview will likely be very different. For example, college seniors in the United States who are interviewing for jobs are fairly aggressive in their approach, and that aggressiveness helps convince the interviewer that they are interested in the job. However, in some other cultures, such aggressiveness would be considered impolite. Unless the interviewer is aware of this cultural difference, he or she may interpret this politeness and seeming passiveness as a lack of interest.

Many intelligence and aptitude tests have been criticized as being culturally biased, even for use in the United States. Certainly, when they are used in a foreign country, cultural bias is magnified. These tests would not only need to be rewritten; they would also need to go through a new process of validation if they are to be used in a foreign country.

Most of the difficulties mentioned here can be alleviated by working with an employment agency in the country where the company wants to recruit, or by working with individuals in the company who are natives of the country. Either approach can provide guidance in the hiring practices in the country, as well as in the legal issues involved in recruiting and hiring. Additionally, it has been suggested that the use of assessment centers is particularly useful in recruiting salespeople in the international arena.[35] Assessment centers are agencies that for a fee screen potential employees. They do so through using validated tests and scales, interviews, and so forth. They generally provide a report on each candidate, detailing strengths and weaknesses.

Foreign employment agencies can give advice on hiring decisions born out of experience in interacting with persons from the country in which the firm wants to do business. Additionally, there are some major employment agencies in the United States that have a division that specializes in foreign recruitment, and some agencies specialize only in foreign recruitment. Given the pitfalls, sales managers need to rely on persons with greater expertise when recruiting a global sales force.

CHAPTER SUMMARY

This chapter presented various factors that are important in the recruitment and selection process of salespeople. Traits that seem to separate good salespeople from average and poor ones include ego drive, empathy, resilience, and integrity, along with listening and organizing skills and product and market knowledge.

We then discussed the recruitment process for reaching potential candidates. The recruitment process begins with an assessment of the requirements of the particular sales job. The type of person and the best approach to reaching him or her follow from this assessment. Certainly successful salespeople share some common characteristics; however, each sales job is unique and requires a particular individual.

The avenues and tools of recruiting and hiring salespeople were also examined. A company can hire salespeople directly out of college, from within its own organization, from competitors, or from other industries. Each of these approaches has positive and negative points. The tools used in deciding on candidates are a critical element in the hiring process. Application forms, interviews, various kinds of tests, and background and reference checks provide information critical to the hiring decision.

The recruiting and hiring process is a legal minefield. The chapter presented some basic Equal Employment Opportunity Commission regulations that are involved. If a company violates EEOC guidelines, whether the violation was intentional or not, it is subject to penalties. These guidelines apply not only to the application and the interview process but also to testing procedures and background checks. Once it has been shown that hiring practices have a disproportionate impact on a protected group, the burden of proof shifts to the employer to show that there was no discrimination.

The chapter closed with a discussion of recruiting and hiring salespeople from foreign countries in which the firm does business. Given the differences in language and culture, this process is much more difficult than domestic recruitment. Probably the best approach is to engage the services of an agency or consultant who understands the hiring practices in the country where a firm does business. These people not only can help with developing the proper tools of recruitment but also can give advice in the hiring decision.

KEY TERMS

active listening, p. 288

analytical skills, p. 288

aptitude tests, p. 307

attributes, p. 287

bid system, p. 299

bona fide occupational qualification (BFOQ), p. 302

blind ads, p. 298

communication skills, p. 288

Equal Employment Opportunity Commission (EEOC), p. 301

ego drive, p. 287

ego strength, p. 287

empathy, p. 287

employment agencies, p. 298

honesty tests, p. 307

intelligence tests, p. 307

job analysis, p. 295

job description, p. 295

job fair, p. 300

job relatedness, p. 301

knowledge, p. 290

knowledge or proficiency tests, p. 307

open ads, p. 298

organizational skills, p. 289

personality tests, p. 307

polygraph tests, p. 307

problem-solving interview, p. 306

reliability, p. 301

resilience, p. 287

semistructured interview, p. 305

skills, p. 288

structured interview, p. 305

time management skills, p. 289

unstructured interview, p. 305

validity, p. 301

CHAPTER QUESTIONS

1. Why are empathy and ego drive necessary for successful salespeople?
2. What part does honesty play in sales?
3. Why is job analysis an integral part of the recruiting process?
4. What are the positive and negative aspects of college recruiting? How about recruiting from competitors?

5. What is the value of the application blank in the hiring process?

6. What information does the unstructured interview provide that the structured interview does not?

7. Why would a firm go to the trouble of checking references?

8. What is a BFOQ and why is it rare?

9. Why are some aptitude tests not suitable for use in another country?

NOTES

1. Donald L. Thompson, Stereotype of the salesman. *Harvard Business Review* (January–February 1972), 20–25, 28, 29, 159–161.

2. Lawrence M. Lamont and William J. Lundstrom, Identifying successful industrial salesmen by personality and personal characteristics. *Journal of Marketing Research* 14 (November 1977), 517–529; Herbert M. Greenberg and Jeanne Greenberg, Job matching for better performance. *Harvard Business Review* 58 (September–October 1983), 128–133; Bruce K. Pilling and Sevo Eroglu, An empirical examination of the impact of salesperson empathy and professionalism and merchandise salability on retail buyers' evaluations. *Journal of Personal Selling & Sales Management* 14 (Winter 1994), 45–58.

3. Mark V. Redmond, The functions of empathy (decentering) in human relations. *Human Relations* 42 (July 1989), 593–605.

4. Greenberg and Greenberg, Job matching.

5. Saul W. Gellerman, The tests of a good salesperson. *Harvard Business Review* 68 (May–June 1990), 64–71.

6. Conrad N. Jackson and Ralph W. Jackson, Characteristics that distinguish successful salespeople. Working paper, 1993.

7. For example, see Harris M. Plotkin, Taking the guesswork out of hiring successful salespeople. *Sales & Marketing Management* (December 1986), 72–73; William Keenan, Jr., Mack attack! *Sales & Marketing Management* (June 1993), 52–58.

8. Barton H. Weitz, H. Sujan, and M. Sujan, Knowledge, motivation, and adaptive behavior: A framework for improving selling effectiveness. *Journal of Marketing* 50 (1986), 175–191; Jerry R. Goolsby, Rosemary R. Lagace, and Michael L. Boorom, Psychological adaptiveness and sales performance. *Journal of Personal Selling & Sales Management* 12 (Spring 1992), 51–66.

9. Rose V. McCollough, Evaluate your sales personality. *Rough Notes* 122 (June 1979), 80–86; Murray Raphel, Ten characteristics of top salesmen. *Direct Marketing* (November–December 1981), 102–103, 121; Fran Smith, The profile of a successful salesperson. *Sales & Marketing Management in Canada* (July–August 1979), 14–15; Alan M. Korschun, Success is only one degree away. *American Salesman* 27 (1982), 13–16.

10. Korschun, Success.

11. Alvin J. Williams and John Seminerio, What buyers like from salesmen. *Industrial Marketing Management* 14 (1985), 75–78.

12. *26th survey of sales force compensation* (Chicago: Dartnell Corp., 1990).

13. W. E. Patton III and Ronald H. King, The use of human judgment models in sales force selection decisions. *Journal of Personal Selling & Sales Management* 12 (Spring 1992), 1–14.

14. Robert G. Head, Systematizing salesperson selection. *Sales & Marketing Management* (February 1992), 65–68.

15. Greenberg and Greenberg, Job matching.

16. Rene Y. Darmon, Where do the best sales force profit producers come from? *Journal of Personal Selling & Sales Management* 13 (Summer 1993), 17–29.

17. Rayna Skolnik, The birth of a sales force. *Sales & Marketing Management*, March 10, 1986, 42–44.

18. Bob Wood, Recruiting the best and the brightest. *Sales & Marketing Management,* August 16, 1982, 51–55; Jon M. Hawes, How to improve your college recruiting program. *Journal of Personal Selling & Sales Management* 9 (Summer 1989), 47–52.

19. Hawes, College recruiting.

20. Keenan, Mack attack!

21. J. Doug Clopton, Becoming proactive about recruitment. *Sales & Marketing Management* (September 1992), 93–97.

22. David J. Cherrington, *Personnel management* (Dubuque, IA: William C. Brown, 1987); Dan C. Weilbaker and Nancy J. Merritt, Attracting graduates to sales positions: The role of recruiter knowledge. *Journal of Personal Selling & Sales Management* 12 (Fall 1992), 49–58.

23. Jack Falvey, The manager as a lightning rod. *Sales & Marketing Management* (January 1992), 8–10.

24. For a more complete discussion, see Wendell L. French, *Human resources management* (Boston: Houghton Mifflin, 1990).

25. Steven A. Meyerowitz, The legal side of hiring salespeople. *Business Marketing* (June 1989), 77–80.

26. David C. Shepherd and James C. Heartfield, Discrimination issues in the selection of salespeople: A review and managerial suggestions. *Journal of Personal Selling & Sales Management* 11 (Fall 1991), 67–75.

27. For a further explanation, see Lawrence S. Clark and Peter D. Kinder, *Law and business* (New York: McGraw-Hill, 1986).

28. Harvey MacKay, "The MacKay Sweet Sixteen" from *Sharkproof: Get the job you want, keep the job you love . . . in today's frenzied job market* (New York: HarperCollins, 1993). Copyright © 1993 by Harvey B. MacKay. Reprinted by permission of HarperCollins Publishers, Inc.

29. Michael J. Swenson and Joel Herche, Social values and salesperson performance: An empirical examination. *Journal of Personal Selling & Sales Management* 22 (Summer 1994), 283–289.

30. Kate Bertrand, Hiring test: Sales managers' dream or nightmare? *Business Marketing* (July 1990), 34–41.

31. French, *Human resource management.*

32. Cherrington, *Personnel management.*

33. Brian Toyne and Peter G. P. Walters, *Global marketing management* (Needham, MA: Allyn & Bacon, 1989).

34. Jean-Pierre Jeannet and Hubert D. Hennessey, *Global marketing strategies* (Boston: Houghton Mifflin, 1992).

35. Roy A. Cook and Joel Herche, Assessment centers: An untapped resource for global salesforce management. *Journal of Personal Selling & Sales Management* 12 (Summer 1992), 31–38.

SUGGESTED READINGS

Butler, James E., Gerald R. Ferris, and Nancy K. Napier. *Strategy and human resources management.* Cincinnati, OH: South-Western, 1991.

> Human resource management cannot be effectively approached as a separate entity within an organization. To be effective, the human resource function needs to be viewed strategically as part of the "big picture." Taking this approach completely changes the way decisions are made, and even the decisions themselves.

Elnes, C. Conrad. *Inside secrets of outstanding salespeople.* Englewood Cliffs, NJ: Prentice Hall, 1988.

> Increasing performance as a salesperson requires greater knowledge and skill rather than simply working harder. Salespeople who are the high achievers rely on coach-

ing that helps them refine their skills. They then work to improve continuously those skills and adapt them to their personal style.

Mackay, Harvey. *Sharkproof: Get the job you want, keep the job you love . . . in today's frenzied job market*. New York: HarperCollins, 1993.

Good jobs don't just happen. Finding and keeping the right job is a matter of preparing yourself. Honest self-assessment, asking the right questions, and being prepared to make reasonable decisions are all part of the process.

Chapter 14

Training the Sales Force

OPENING SCENARIO

Mike Johnston, president of Advanced Technologies, Inc. (ATI), a producer of graphic imaging equipment, is considering developing an in-house training program for all ATI salespeople. ATI had been using an assortment of "canned" training programs; and although some of them were good, none fit ATI's needs very well. Mike was frustrated that the programs treated all ATI's salespeople alike. In fact, they had very different training needs and were at different stages in their careers.

Mike had been told by his vice president of finance, Diana Legg, that whatever program ATI introduced it should minimize the amount of time salespeople spent in training, because when they were in training they were not selling. Additionally, Diana felt that the company could pull together any necessary materials and equipment needed for training and should not spend money on such things. Although she did not like the idea of ATI salespeople being pulled off the street, Diana felt as Mike did, that their current training was seriously inadequate and threatened to make ATI's sales force ineffective relative to other sales forces in the industry.

Chapter Objectives

After reading this chapter, you should be able to

- Recognize the part that training plays in the socialization of salespeople.
- Understand the issue involved in the training process and the importance of training objectives.
- Relate the principles of learning to a training program.

315

- Gain awareness of the nuances of skills training and how it differs from knowledge training.
- Relate the important topics in sales training to approaches to training.

INTRODUCTION

As noted in Chapter 13, hiring good people is critical. However, hiring is just the first step in building a successful sales team. Two other processes are involved in a person's becoming a part of the sales organization—socialization and training. Generally speaking, socialization is an informal process and training is the formal way of introducing a person to the aims and expectations of the firm. Although this idea has some merit, it might be more instructive to view training as a specialized form of socialization. Training has specific, overt goals and, therefore, tends to be very specific in its approach. Informal "socialization" extends beyond the initial training of new salespeople; it is an ongoing process of enculturating them into the organization.

Training represents a major expenditure as evidenced by the fact that organizations spend in the neighborhood of $30 billion annually and dedicate more than 15 billion work hours on training programs.[1] It is interesting, though, to note that top performing sales forces do not significantly outspend sales forces that do not perform as well; thus they must be spending their money more effectively.[2]

Training is the process of helping people learn the materials and skills the company thinks is important. Through training, salespeople are introduced to the overall goals of the organization, the procedures used to accomplish specific tasks, and the skills and knowledge necessary to succeed in selling the company's products. Newly hired salespeople must not only be shown what they need to learn but must be approached in such a way as to help them get the most out of the learning process. Veteran salespeople must be motivated to involve themselves in the training process so that they can learn new information and can regenerate their selling skills for new products and changing environments.

Training is increasingly being viewed as a basic part of the sales job. For example, recruits from college campuses have come to expect a training program that will get them started on their career track, and some are even using the adequacy of a training program as a criterion in deciding where to work.[3] If for no other reason than being able to attract the brightest and the best, training is something that a company needs to do well.

THE SOCIALIZATION PROCESS

Whenever an individual joins a new organization, he or she needs to assimilate the beliefs and practices of the organization. Such an assimilation process is called **socialization.** Socialization can be defined as "the process of communicating the culture to the [newcomer] so that he/she understands it and uses it in his/her behavior."[4] Thus the process of socialization involves not only learning the corporate culture but also incorporating that learning into one's behavior. In other words, it is learning that affects change in the person.

Some might dismiss the concept of socialization as relatively unimportant if a strong training program exists. The thinking behind this idea is that a well-developed training program will bring in people and teach them precisely what they need to know. Also, this training will forestall any appreciable effect of socialization that is contrary to the information covered in training. However, socialization has a direct impact on the outlook of salespeople, their level of motivation, and their commitment to the organization.[5]

Why is socialization so important? In reality, what happens generally is that new people usually want to "fit in." That is the reason why new hirees are generally more trainable than veteran salespeople. The moment those new people walk in the front door, they are subjected to a host of influences and messages about what is and what is not acceptable in the organization. At first, they will closely conform to the "party line" and tend to reject those influences that are contrary to it. However, as they become more comfortable in the setting and begin to feel more secure, they may tend to assimilate the more contrary norms that every organization contains within it.

This process can take place faster if what they are taught in training is out of line with what really happens within the organization or if they are given an unrealistic picture of what life is like in the field. Often the first words heard by new salespeople after they complete the initial training program and arrive in the field is "Okay, now forget all that stuff you learned in training. This is how it is really done!" The new salespeople, unless they feel a high need for acceptance by the veteran salespeople, will often initially reject such advice until they meet with failure. Then they will reevaluate the training and may reject it—the training has been compromised.

Sales managers need to be aware of the **informal culture** operating in the company, admit to newly hired salespeople that it exists, and address it in training. Second, sales managers need to ensure that what is taught in training is as close to reality as possible. An approach to training that rejects the real world and proposes something like a "sure-fire approach to selling" is a waste of time and resources, because there is no one approach to selling that works every time.

It is probably ethically questionable for a company to provide an unrealistic picture for sales trainees. If the company does so, when these salespeople arrive in the field, they are not prepared for what they will face. Often as a result, they get their careers started off on the wrong foot and do not recover. They may even reject a sales career altogether, when in fact, they were quite well suited but simply were ill prepared for one.

One important issue in socialization is of women in the sales force. Until relatively recently, women in the sales force were much more the exception than the rule. Also, some men still adhere to the concept of traditional roles of women and are uncomfortable with the new roles that women now fill. Based on a study of salespeople for over-the-counter pharamaceuticals, it has been pointed out there is a need for special programs to facilitate the socialization of women into the sales force.[6] For example, men need to be sensitized to the issue of sexual harassment, and women need to be aware of how to deal with buyers who tend to be more domineering with women. One researcher suggests that female salespeople can avoid harassment by taking a few basic steps:[7]

1. Do not listen to sob stories about customers' relationships.
2. Maintain independent transportation.
3. Avoid being alone with male customers for prolonged periods.
4. Do not drink at business functions.
5. Do not become too friendly with customers, particularly after business hours.
6. Trust your instincts.

Although nothing can ensure that sexual harassment will not occur, salespeople and managers need to be aware of the possibility that it will happen eventually and take steps to prepare for it.

ESTABLISHING TRAINING OBJECTIVES

For many sales managers, training is similar to advertising: They know it is important, but they are not quite sure how and why it works, and they view it in generally the same way—as a waste of money. But if it is done with care, understanding, and knowledge, a well-constructed training program can be the most rewarding part of building a sales force, for both the salespeople and the company.

At the outset of designing a training program, sales managers must develop a set of objectives that the program should meet. They need to ask themselves what it is they want to accomplish. Those objectives should be related directly to the nature of the group that is being trained and should affect the topics to be covered. For example, if a company is training newly hired salespeople recruited from colleges, a number of topics must be covered, such as selling skills, customer knowledge, product knowledge, company knowledge, industry knowledge, and competitor knowledge.

In other words, this group would need training in just about every area. New recruits from business schools may have taken a course in sales/sales management, however; in such a course, it is likely that they have been exposed only to the rudiments of selling, and only for a grade, not for employment.

In establishing training objectives, sales managers must decide what knowledge or skills their salespeople do not know or are not able to do well. Obviously, such a decision will yield a rather lengthy list of things sales managers would ideally like to have their people know or be able to do. However, given that salespeople can never know everything about every product and that training cannot possibly supply all the knowledge and skills they will need, managers must prioritize the list—and those priorities must be related to the needs of the group being trained.

Obviously, it is impossible to customize the training to fit every individual's needs. However, to use that as an excuse for offering "one size fits all" training is not justifiable. Perhaps the optimal approach involves using a modular system of training whereby different topics are arranged into groups, or modules. Managers can then select the module that best fits an individual's needs. At the outset sales managers must establish what they want to accomplish with the particular training program. All else follows from that.

LEARNING

Learning is so basic to life that we tend to take it for granted. Training is really the process of facilitating directed learning. Dennis Organ and Thomas Bateman define learning as "some change within the person that makes behavior change possible."[8] We use this definition for several reasons. First, the change brought about by training (that is, directed learning) deals with the potential to perform. In other words, good training enhances a person's capacity to perform. It does not necessarily mean that the individual will perform better. Better performance is not only a function of training but also a function of such things as motivation and compensation. Organ and Bateman go on to state that learning generally takes place through experience, either through life experiences or experiences in a formal classroom setting. Also, people learn through reinforced practice, that is, through the opportunity to apply material in a lab or actual setting with feedback from the trainer.

Principles of Learning

For a training program to be effective, several principles of learning must be taken into consideration when designing the program. Generally, when a training program is found to be less than effective, one or more of these principles have been violated. The principles that are particularly pertinent to sales training are purpose, motivation, reinforcement, participation, practice, repetition, plateaus, productivity, realism, and customization. Let's look at each separately.[9]

Purpose. The trainer must understand the objectives of the training program and needs to include training material and exercises that are relevant to accomplishing those objectives. Additionally, during the training, the relevance of these objectives must be explained to trainees.

Motivation. Many managers assume that salespeople should be willing to become involved enough in a training program for it to be effective. But that is not always the case. For newly hired salespeople, particularly those just beginning their career, the motivation level is generally high. However, training that is perceived to be irrelevant or boring can lower this level quickly. For veteran salespeople, training is often viewed as something of an intrusion. They often possess an intuitive assumption that training does not yield results proportionate to effort. Also, the time spent in training means time they are not selling. Hence training takes money out of their pockets. Sales managers should make provision for continuance of income during training for veteran salespeople, and should be able to show that training will yield positive results for the person.

Reinforcement. The law of relative effect states: "People tend to repeat those behaviors for which they are rewarded." In training, when people learn material and/or perform well on an exercise, they need to be rewarded with affirmation. By the same token, if people fail to perform a particular skill or learn some material well, they need to receive feedback as to what the problem is and not be rewarded for doing poorly. Feedback, in this case, serves as a type of reinforcement in that it lets trainees know that the problem can be corrected and affirms that they are able to do the job.

Participation. Learning is a two-way process. Trainees should not be viewed as passive recipients of the wisdom of the trainer. Rather, they need to be involved in the program. First, they can experience the concept firsthand and, second, participation tends to alleviate boredom.

Practice. Similar to the idea of participation, practice involves the trainee in the training experience. Particularly when we are talking about learning skills, the more that people are able to perform those repetitively the more that skill becomes ingrained. Listening, for instance, is a skill that improves with practice.

Repetition. As new material is introduced, the trainer should attempt to relate it to past material. In that way, the material is reinforced. Also, reviewing material tends to drive it home.

Plateaus. Generally speaking, learning is not a process that takes place consistently over time. Particularly when learning a skill, people often acquire the basics very quickly but then reach a point where they cannot seem to learn at the earlier rate. This is similar to the way a tree grows. Trees grow in spurts, and then growth subsides for a time. During this time of no-growth, the recent growth matures and gains strength. In training people, the trainer must be aware of these plateaus and let trainees know to expect them. Otherwise when trainees hit such a period, they will likely become frustrated.

Productivity. People learn better at different times of the day, and for a limited amount of time each day. Generally, people learn best around midmorning and midafternoon. Given that a training program cannot possibly be contained only within those times, the trainer can use different approaches in training to break up the monotony and get people involved in the process during those "off times." In this way, effective learning can be facilitated during a longer period of the day. Then there is the amount of time that a person should be in training each day. Especially when training new salespeople, managers want to impart as much information as is possible. As a result, they will often schedule more that eight classroom hours each day when six to seven is probably optimal, and will then have trainees do workbooks or view tapes at night, all interspersed with meetings of various kinds. While the desire to provide employees with as much ammunition as possible is praise-worthy, we would say it is probably more critical that a person learn the important things well and not a lot of things poorly. The trainer should keep in mind the adage: "We teach people and not things!"

Realism. Sales training, perhaps more than any other kind of training, must reflect the real world. Often trainees go through sales training only to find that they have been given unrealistic expectations. This tends to negate the effectiveness of the entire training program. Sales managers must themselves be realistic about what can be accomplished through training and include those things that will best result in achieving that. Additionally, training should accurately reflect the corporate credo. For example, if salespeople are told in training that "the customer is first" but upon arriving in the field are told by their manager that sales volume is first, they will tend to discard the training program as "pie in the sky" and, perhaps in doing so, reject some very solid concepts conveyed during the program. (If, by the way, the corporate credo is something that the company is ashamed to convey in training, then likely the credo needs to be changed.) Again, whether sales managers like it or not, people will go through a process of socialization and will be confronted with any number of "truths." If, in training they are given a realistic picture of what it is like in the field, they can better sort through those influences.

Customization. Sales training needs to be designed to meet the needs of the trainees and to accomplish the goals the company is trying to achieve in conducting the training. Although an entire training program cannot be customized for every individual, as we said before, a modular system of dividing topics into groups can best fit an individual's needs.

To sum up, training helps people learn and develop skills. It also gives trainees information about what is important and where they need to focus attention. To maximize the effectiveness of training, the material should be meaningful and trainees should be actively involved and given encouragement and feedback. Additionally, the training program must allow sufficient time for absorption of information and should cover a reasonable amount of material.

SALES TRAINING TOPICS

The number of topics to be covered in a sales training program will vary with the makeup of the sales force, the type of industry, and various environmental factors. In a study reported by *Sales & Marketing Management*, a variety of training topics were employed by subject firms (see Figure 14-1).[10] Some of the topics shown in the figure apply to managers and some to salespeople; others, such as ethics, could be used with anyone in the organization. Our discussion will focus on those topics that apply more directly to salespeople.

Interestingly, the figure shows that after the first two topics, which deal with orienting the trainee, the top five topics are concerned with personal development as opposed to product or customer knowledge. This reinforces the idea that salespeople are not conveyers of information as much as they are developers of relationships. Another possible reason for this emphasis on personal development is the fact that simply having salespeople acquire knowledge (pieces of information) is useless unless they incorporate what they acquire into their selling efforts.[11]

FIGURE 14-1 Training Topics Covered by Companies (*Source:* Reprinted with permission from the October 1991 issue of *Training* magazine. ©1991, Lakewood Publications Inc., Minneapolis, MN [612-333-0471]. All rights reserved. Not for resale.)

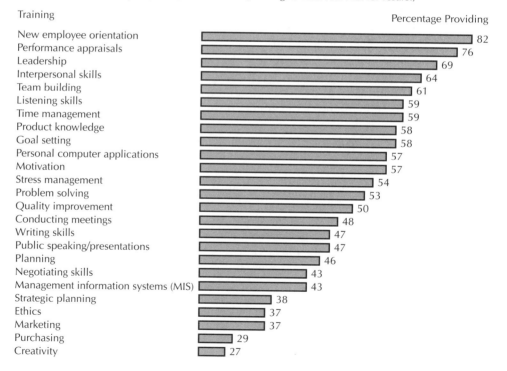

Note: Responses were gathered from a number of different industries and job types, including training, human resources, sales and marketing, and customer service.

Selling Skills

Particularly with new salespeople, training in selling skills is important. As part of a recent study, sales managers were asked to rate the importance of various sales training topics.[12] Interestingly, the two highest rated topics dealt with selling skills. In the study, the topic of sales follow-up and customer service was rated the highest of the various topics presented. The next highest topic was listening skills. These two areas are related to the concept of relationship marketing, the idea that selling is not so much involved in bringing about a transaction as it is in building an ongoing relationship with the customer. Although not rated as highly by the sales managers in the study, other aspects of selling skills were still important components in sales training.

Selling skills, like any other skill, can best be learned through an interactive process. The more the person is given the chance to employ the concept in the training setting, the better he or she will be able to employ it in the field. Among the topics covered under selling skills are

- Listening skills
- Presentation skills
- Time management
- Probing/fact finding
- Customer service
- Prospecting/qualifying
- Handling objections
- Organization skills
- Closing the sale

Dennis Fox, president of Client Development Institute, a training firm, suggests that the ideal training program should include four elements:

1. An assessment tool to detect the presence of call reluctance, and a corrective program to deal with it.
2. A comprehensive, client-centered "hello-to-thank you" model for learning skills.
3. A tracking system for salespeople and managers to measure their posttraining increases.
4. A follow-up program for managers and trainers to monitor progress and provide additional counseling.

Fox states:

Sales training that omits any of these ingredients overlooks a crucial part of the package and takes a major chance that could have a significant impact on the ultimate success both of individual salespeople and companies. Sales training that includes all of them closes the gap and ensures that there are no missing links.[13]

Product Knowledge

Especially for products that are highly technical and/or in industries that are very dynamic, training in product knowledge is an inherent part of the training program. Product knowledge is important in helping the customer solve problems. Often this type of training can be part of a self-paced program, given the need for trainees to be able to absorb the information adequately.

Customer Knowledge

Customer knowledge deals not so much with "reading" the customer as with the nature of the market the company serves. Given the variation in customers, salespeople must have a well-rounded view of people and organizations. For instance, they need to know how the customer uses the product and how the product fits in with the overall operation of the customer. Additionally, sales managers need to be aware of the purchasing process used by their typical customers.

Another, often ignored aspect of customer knowledge is the concept of **derived demand,** the idea that the demand by a producer's customers arises indirectly from the end-user's demand for the customer's products. For example, the demand for robotic welders and sheet metal used in automaking arises from consumers' demand for automobiles. In today's competitive environment where product differentiation is often difficult to achieve, a company is forced to differentiate itself through customer service. The customers' main problem in doing business is not where and how to buy the products they need but, rather, how and where to sell the products they make. Salespeople who understand the customers' customers can better assist their customers in solving this main problem, and as a result, salespeople will be rewarded with more business in the long run.

Competitor/Industry Knowledge

In most cases it is probably almost as important to have a knowledge of your competitors and their products as it is to have a thorough knowledge of your own. Knowing your own products and company provides salespeople with a knowledge of their company's **distinctive competencies**—those things the company does well, or, in other words, the company's strengths. This information is important for salespeople when they attempt to convince buyers to buy. However, simply knowing what a company does well is not enough in most cases. Salespeople also need to know what it is that their company does better than other companies—in other words, what unique advantage the company possesses relative to its competition. This is referred to as **competitive advantage.**

To illustrate the difference between a distinctive competence and a competitive advantage, we can draw an example from the copier business. A salesperson may point out that her copier produces excellent quality copies, and the machine sells at a competitive price. These would be distinctive competencies. However, if the other major competitors had copy machines that were competitively priced and produced excellent copies also, these two factors would not be competitive advantages. However, if the salesperson could point out that her machine used less toner and offered certain automated features not available in the other machines at that price range, those qualities would be competitive advantages. Peter Drucker said it well when he stated: "The essence of competition is doing those things well that are the most difficult to emulate." Salespeople need to understand their own company's competitive advantages, not so they can put down competition but so they can highlight the benefits and advantages unique to their products.

When we speak of industry knowledge, we are not talking so much about competitors as about the dynamic forces that shape the industry. Salespeople who have an understanding of the supply and demand characteristics of their industry have an advantage over those who do not. Certainly, training regarding the competition and the industry is more critical for new salespeople than it is for veteran salespeople. However, it is useful to update veterans on what is happening with competition and in the industry. This not only provides them with new information but also renews their sensitivity to being aware of such information and thereby increases the likelihood that they will obtain it on their own.

Company Knowledge

A final topic in sales training deals with the company itself. Especially for new hirees, company knowledge is critical information. New salespeople need to know not only about the operations of their company and how the sales force fits in the whole scheme of things, but also about the **corporate culture.** Corporate culture is defined as follows:

> Organizational culture, then, is the pattern of basic assumptions that a given group has invented, discovered, or developed in learning to cope with its problems of external adaptation and integration—a pattern of assumptions that has worked well enough to be considered valid and, therefore, to be taught to new members as the correct way to perceive, think, and feel in relation to those problems.[14]

Subsumed under the concept of corporate culture are such things as the corporate credo (the set of values that guide decision making in the company), corporate ethical standards, interdepartmental relations, and the outlook of the company regarding the place of the customer in the whole scheme.

As we mentioned at the beginning of the chapter, training is essentially the formalized part of the socialization process. A major portion of the process involves introducing new people to the norms of behavior and thinking in the company. In any organization there is a set of norms that are overt and part of the stated standards of operation. However, concurrent with those stated norms are others that are unstated and typically operate below the surface. For example, in training, salespeople are told that the "customer is king in our company" and that the needs of the customer should come first. When these salespeople arrive in the field, though, they observe that the company rewards sales volume and moving product, and that salespeople regularly push extra, unneeded products on customers to achieve quota.

Although the company's stated norms say one thing, the actual company practices, although unstated in the training program, say something very different. The latter set of norms can be equally as powerful in shaping behavior as the former, and in some cases, even more so. New individuals will soon learn both and will go through the process of selecting which elements will become part of their own unique view of accepted behavior. In training, these people need to be introduced to the professed standards of the company while at the same time sensitized to what to expect in terms of informal standards. Obviously, the more these two things are in congruence the less conflict people will face.

APPROACHES TO TRAINING

Good training involves a variety of approaches and methodologies. With the expansion of technology, the spectrum of choices of training tools is increasing rapidly. This allows not only for a more interesting training program but also a more effective one. The use of videotapes, for instance, brought about by the proliferation of the VCR, is widespread, and results in cost savings, time savings, and being able to communicate up-to-date information effectively.[15] Additionally, with the greater availability of personal computers, more interactive training programs can be used on an individual basis. Figure 14-2 illustrates a survey reported in *Sales & Marketing Management* that provides some idea of the variety and the pervasiveness of various training methods.[16]

Training is a progression, a process of building up layers on foundations. A person might obtain the information through lectures, observe a variety of meth-

FIGURE 14-2 Training Methods Employed by Companies (*Source:* Reprinted with permission from the October 1991 issue of *Training* magazine. ©1991, Lakewood Publications Inc., Minneapolis, MN [612-333-0471]. All rights reserved. Not for resale.)

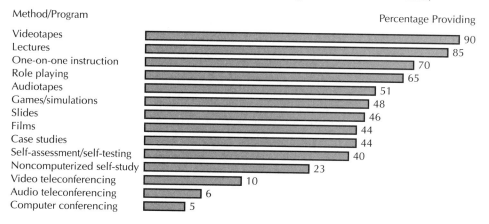

Method/Program   Percentage Providing

Method/Program	Percentage Providing
Videotapes	90
Lectures	85
One-on-one instruction	70
Role playing	65
Audiotapes	51
Games/simulations	48
Slides	46
Films	44
Case studies	44
Self-assessment/self-testing	40
Noncomputerized self-study	23
Video teleconferencing	10
Audio teleconferencing	6
Computer conferencing	5

Note: Responses were gathered from a number of different industries and job types, including training, human resources, sales and marketing, and customer service.

SELL!NG

THE FRONT LINES OF BUSINESS

Up Against It

John Anderson

Seventy feet up in the air, her legs dangling stiffly in the wind, Gail von Rueden of Norwest Banks is perched on a narrow wooden platform, staring out at the unknown. With only the cables of a zip line and the emptiness of air and sky before her, she ponders firsthand the prospect of leaping into space, then racing at breakneck speed down the cables. She blinks, swallows, closes her eyes, looks again, tries to check her fears. She knows she cannot. From a distance she resembles nothing so much as a small child, her body tiny, her limbs thin, her head immense, swollen as it is by a protective helmet.

For eight grueling hours now, von Rueden, a commercial banking representative who sells in new and often hostile territories far from the home office, has subjected herself to increasingly heightened forms of controlled terror. She has fallen backward off a ladder; walked with a partner, hand-in-hand, along the wires of an ever-widening V-shape; climbed a 48-foot vertical "Wall;" and walked across two 15-foot tightropes stretched 60 feet above a grassy hill. Now it has all come down to this: the Zip. To push or not to push. To fly or not to fly. Alone, she thinks, "I would never do this." But von Rueden is not alone.

"Go, Gail!"

"You can do it, Gail!"

"Come on, Gail! We're here for you!"

The voices are not taunting. They are, instead, full of encouragement, and the notes that are struck are genuine. And felt. Both on the ground and high, high up in the air.

The words are those of her teammates, a group of 11 salespeople, come, like von Rueden, to see what outdoor adventure has to say to them, to find out if stretching it here can help them sell back home.

This, in a nutshell, is the premise behind the Pecos River Learning Center's partnering program, Creating Customers for Life, a state-of-the-art course that combines sales training with outdoor (and indoor) adventure. One of several dozen imitators spawned by the success of Outward Bound—an outdoor-adventure training program originally designed for British soldiers in WWII—Pecos has in little more than a decade established its own very lucrative niche. With 1994 sales of $17 million, the company is the leading adventure trainer to corporate America. The figures bear out the claim. Since its beginning in 1983,

Pecos has served its blend of training and adventure to some 500 companies and close to 100,000 individuals, most of them salespeople.

Pecos's message—both to corporate executives and to their salespeople—is simple, according to executive vice president Hersch Wilson. "Our clients know that they're up against massive change," Wilson explains. "They know that today's sales climate is stressful. They know it emphasizes risk-taking. We're here to help their salespeople learn to take those risks—and live to talk about it."

Talk about risks . . .

Up on the platform, von Rueden fidgets, pushes forward, inches back, pushes forward again. Her hands strain at the leather harnesses that tie her to the zip line. There's the trace of a smile on her tightly compressed face. Suddenly she lets out a scream as her body plunges into nothingness.

The cables sing as von Rueden flies down the incline and toward a telephone pole that marks the other end of the zip line. Halfway to the pole, gravity and a sagging line slow her progress. The zip has lost its zap, and three-quarters of the way to the pole, the adventure comes to an end. Von Rueden's body slows into a gently rocking, swinging motion. She kicks her legs wildly. Waves her arms. Shouts. "Yeah, yeah, yeah! I can't *believe* I did this!"

Her teammates feel otherwise.

"*We* knew you could, Gail!"

"We *knew* you could!"

Von Rueden's face, pale and finely textured, glows behind thick tortoise-shell glasses. No jock, she has nevertheless conquered all during this one day of vigorous outdoor activities. From that first backward fall into the waiting arms of her fellow salespeople to this ultimate test, she has pushed herself to the limits, overcoming some of her deepest fears.

And why? Still swaying in the air, waiting to be unharnessed, she looks around at the faces beneath her and begins a litany of thanks. "I was *so* scared, but I thought about you, Edie. And I thought, if you could, *I* could. Then I heard Bruce cheering me on. And I thought about Rita wanting to go even though she was seven months pregnant. And then I heard Alan yell, 'Don't stop now!' And, oh, God, I don't know, I just let go." Normally cerebral and articulate, von Rueden can barely contain herself. She practically babbles. "Now I can't believe how much fun it was. It was thrilling."

If von Rueden is in ecstasy, her companions aren't far behind on the curve. "The reason," says their guide, outdoor trainer John Foster, "is that when one succeeds, they all succeed. Everyone's a winner here today—even if they didn't walk the Monster, climb the Wall, or do the Zip. They were all part of the team. The guy in the glasses who belayed Gail, he didn't even *try* to do the Zip. But he was there for Gail when she needed him. He was her backup. He was an essential part of the team."

The experiences that von Rueden and the others have shared today, explains Foster, "are about pushing you to know your limits, not pushing you past those limits." The Pecos experience is also about partnering. For example, Foster notes, there's the vital act of belaying—holding the safety line that is attached to a climber. "The guy who belayed Gail was her partner," says Foster. "The guys on the ground who encouraged her were her partners. They each had a job, and together they made it happen."

When they return to the everyday reality of selling, Foster continues, "these folks are going to carry with them what they learned here. And there is no better kind of self-knowledge than that which teaches you your limits while showing you how, as a team, you can go far beyond those limits. *You* go as far as *you* can go—and not one step farther. But there's no reason why your team can't go the whole distance. That's the essence of partnering, both out here and back home in sales."

A gentle, earnest man, razor-thin and strong, Foster has had experience in sales as well as in action-adventure training. The two disciplines, he says, "are really just like one. And that's what *this* is all about."

What it's *not* all about is the Pecos River. Although the company's origins do, in fact, lie along the Pecos River at founder Larry Wilson's celebrated former ranch near Santa Fe, Pecos now has a new owner, and its nearly two dozen active "learning centers" are scattered throughout the U.S. and Canada (see sidebars). Typical of these is the Oak Ridge Conference Center in Chaska, Minn., a set of low-strung, utilitarian beige-brick buildings. The outdoor setting more or less lives up to Pecos's billing: "serene," "isolated," "quiet," as one company executive described it. There's a lake—where swimming isn't allowed—behind the complex, and an expanse of acreage in front. Tall trees and rolling hills surround the lake. It's here that the outdoor training takes place.

For six long days, participants not only learn to manage—if not exactly control—their fear of heights, they are also taught how to apply those lessons to the art of sales. Along the way, they're given an intense catch-up course in "reading financials," like corporate reports, and taught the hows, whys, and why-nots of partnering, both internal and external. "It's a lot to swallow in six days," admits veteran Pecos trainer Jim Moore, the chief pathfinder for this week's activities. "But, hey, it's good medicine. Fruit juicy-flavored for sales." A typical Moore-ism, the line is spoken—and accepted—with grins all around at Sunday night's opening session.

It's a varied lot of salespeople who have come here, not to the wilds of New Mexico but to the suburbs of Minneapolis, to imbibe the Pecos experience. Most are relatively young—in their 30s—but there's leavening in the form of Edie Davis, a sales training director at the American Chicle Group of Warner-Lambert. Davis is of a comfortable middle age, 42, with a teenaged son and an aging father at home. She's also comfortable with herself. "I'm just going to do what I feel like doing," she announces at the opening night's session. "And if that's watching someone else climb ladders, that's fine." Davis doesn't mince words, though as her companions soon learn, there's strength and gentleness beneath her directness. She's here with two of her key people, senior sales training manager Judy Degady and salesperson Rita Berger. Like most of those here today, they've come to test the program, to help decide if their company should put hundreds of salespeople through it later.

The same is true of Lynn Schreder and Lori Purves of AT&T, both of whom are sales managers in the company's small-business accounts division in Bloomington, Minn. "You can think of us as guinea pigs," says Schreder. "The company does. I can just imagine someone there saying, 'If we've got to lose somebody up there on the high wire, it had better be Lynn." Then she laughs, while Purves rolls her eyes in mock horror.

Steve Bennett, Alan Bishop, Doug Little, and Steve Murray make for an arresting quartet. To the man, they are big, beefy, and burly. They're also highly informal, to say the least, and jolly and shrewd at the same time. Their business? "We sell to tree, nut, and vine growers through distributors," says Bishop. Then he adds in a pseudo-whisper, "We're Monsanto agricultural chemical salespeople."

"Crop protection—that's what we're supposed to call the business now," Bennett pipes up. "But nobody does," Murray and Little immediately interject. "It's more environmentally friendly-sounding," adds Bishop. Immediately, all four are in stitches. Based in California's Central Valley—Little has since relocated to Michigan—the men know each other so well that their talk often seems a sort of shorthand.

Gail von Rueden and Bruce Christiansen have come by themselves. So, of course, they're paired, and the pairing works. Both are serious sorts, quietly intelligent. For a banker, von Rueden has a finely honed sense of quiet humor, while Christiansen is a quintessential Jimmy Stewart character, the handsome young salesman who is full of solid, old-fashioned virtues.

Christiansen, a printing company account representative for Central Florida Press in Tampa, is typical of the lot. At 36, he's already a veteran salesperson, having been in sales since his sophomore year in college. Moreover, he likes what he does. "I did a lot of cold calling early on, and I found out that I was good at it," he says. Having mastered that skill, Christiansen is hoping now to learn the Pecos way of partnering—even if it means climbing the 60-foot Monster.

"Partnering is the buzzword of the '90s," Christiansen explains, "and any extra edge that I can get to help me increase my sales—I'll do what it takes to get it."

Also here to "do what it takes" are two new Pecos River employees, Tracy Eliason and Bob Carpenter. Eliason's in sales, but at Pecos, everyone is expected to be intimately familiar with the outdoor experiences. "Intimately," adds trainer Moore, "means up there on the high wires."

"Oh, what you mean is that he's here to take your job," says Doug Little, eyeing Carpenter. "Yeah," says Alan Bishop, "and what you also mean is that you're going to get rid of him right off the bat." The Monsanto quartet cracks up.

Grinning, Moore goes, "Riiiight." Then he gets down to the meat of the matter. "But *you're* here because sales today is in a state of permanent whitewater, and you can't get out of the boat. And here's the kicker: There ain't no choice. Your management doesn't know what's coming round the next corner, so you've got to paddle like hell. And you better be prepared for it. Which is where we come in."

Now imagine, says Moore, a competitor that in the next three to five years will put your company out of business. "Imagine a competitor that knows the finances of your company. A competitor that will be viewed by *your* clients as a business adviser rather than a transactional opponent." Then he pauses. "Scary, huh?" Heads nod as one. "Then you better become that company before someone else does."

A preacher preaching to the converted, Moore drives his lesson home with his description of life at the top of the Monster, the 60-foot high-wire act that, he says, will be "a very real part of everyone's world tomorrow.

"Oh, it's high up there," he adds. "Real high. And I'll tell you a secret: I *hate* heights. My hands get clammy. I remember the time I got caught up on the Monster in the middle of a windstorm, and I was hanging on to that sucker for dear life.

"But you know why I'm going back up there tomorrow? Well, it sure as heck ain't because I like the Monster. I don't like him one bit. I go because that Monster's with me every day, and he's with you. Every time you go cold calling, every time you make a pitch or try to seal the deal, that Monster's there, singing, 'I can't. I can't. I can't.' But you can, and a lot of you are going to be surprised tomorrow at how far you go." Moore stops and chuckles: "Sky's the limit, guys." Grinning, he slaps his hands together and gives a thumbs-up.

Rita Berger, seven months pregnant, looks down at her swollen belly and strokes it softly.

D day," as Monsanto's Bennett calls it, begins at sunrise with a hearty break-fast, heavy in cholesterol and fat. The Monsanto boys eat with gusto. "Damn, that's good," says Little. "Gourmet's delight," agrees Murray. "Best food I've eaten in ages," offers Bennett. "Makes a man feel like climbing a mountain," adds Bishop. An hour later the entire gang finds itself facing not a mountain but the Monster. "Gaw-dooow," says Bennett. "Tall, ain't it," agrees Murray.

"Don't worry," says trainer John Foster, "We're going to start with something a little less tall." That something is an 8-foot ladder perched alongside the back of the Wall. The goal, Foster explains, is to climb the ladder, "cross your arms, and as stiff as you can make yourself," fall backward into the waiting arms of teammates. Lynn Schreder takes the first turn, does as she's instructed, and comes up smiling. "Felt like falling into a feather bed," she says.

No problem here, nor is there much of one at the next exercise, low wires slung in a V-shape The object here is for partners to stand on the wires, facing each other and holding hands, while moving out along the V. As the wires get increasingly further apart, the partners inevitably lose their grip or fall off the wires. But the contortions are something to behold, especially when one of the contortionists happens to be the 6 feet 3 inch, 200 pound-plus Murray. When he comes crashing down, it's all his teammates can do to catch him. Yet they do. "Which is the lesson here," says Foster. "They don't, and Steve busts up his face or his knee or worse."

Business starts to get serious when the group is confronted with the Wall. A wooden structure with pegs and ledges fashioned into it, the Wall is meant to simulate the side of a mountain. The object of this exercise is for teams of three to get to the top and deliver the goods. "The goods" consists of a small cup full of water, which is to be emptied into a jar. The teams "contract" to deliver so much water, without spilling it, in so much time. Shackled to one another, they *have* to function as a team—especially since one member makes the ascent blindfolded. Suffice it to say that water is spilled, contracts voided, and new and novel arrangements thought up. By the time the exercise is over, team members have begun to get the hang of it. The blindfolded man or woman carries the water and is in the middle. The most aggressive member climbs the section of the Wall nearest the jar; the least aggressive pulls up the rear. But pull it up they must, for no one gets anywhere unless all get at least near the top. Again, the message is the necessity of teamwork. Though "there's room for the daring eagle," explains Jim Moore, "it's as team leader— not as team loner."

Whether eagle or robin, team members know that John Foster isn't kidding them when he begs their pardon and says, "Sorry about that, guys. I know that seemed like fun. But you ain't seen nothing yet." He's right, too. The backward free-fall, the V, and even the Wall pale before the Monster. Here, there is not one hurdle but many: first a 60-foot climb up a wooden ladder to a small perch, then a walk across 15 feet of high-wire to another small perch, then another high walk, this time across a 15-foot wooden beam to yet another perch, followed by a rappel down. "Of course, you're not alone," says Moore. "There will be four of you, and when you get to the wooden beams, you'll notice that there are four of them—in the shape of a V. Good luck."

As Edie Davis ("I'm too old for this kind of stuff. Plus, I'd probably put somebody else in danger") and the pregnant Rita Berger belay, Lynn Schreder and Alan Bishop ("A pair of pack mules," as one person sums them up. "There's nothing that scares those two") lead Bob Carpenter and Lori Purves up the ladder and into the clear blue Minnesota sky. Their ascent is rapid, the tightwire walk slow and agonizing, the V a semi-disaster. Belayed as they are and further protected by clips and wires, there is no real risk. No one, after all, is going to fall to earth. What's to fear?

And then Lori Purves slips off the beam. Gasps all around on the ground. Phrases like, "Oh, my God," on all lips. Safe, Purves nevertheless dangles for what seems like minutes as Bishop slowly pulls her back up onto the beam. Unsteadily, she rights herself, stands, completes the walk. The four of them then rappel downward. From the ground there is loud clapping, cheers. Most of it is for Purves.

Purves is shaking as she pulls her gear off. She knows she has done it. She has overcome her fears—and survived. But it doesn't keep her from shaking. "After that," she says to no one in particular, "even the Zip looks pretty good."

So Lori Purves survived the Monster, and Gail von Rueden the Zip. True to his word, Jim Moore and his fellow instructor Ron Lehmann, both of them middle-aged and, Lehmann at least, slightly out of shape, did the whole routine. The day done, by nightfall there isn't a fresh-looking face among the lot, old vets and neophytes alike.

At the next day's "debrief," a recharged Moore asks the obvious questions of his refreshed troops: "What are the implications for your business? How are you going to apply what you learned on the ropes and the wires to selling?"

Alan Bishop has his hand up first. "I learned how important the belayers were in my office. Someone on our support staff wrote a letter to one of my customers explaining the chemical analysis of one of our products, and it really helped me make the sale. Well, I owe that person a letter of thanks."

Doug Little puts it more succinctly: "I learned that you need the support of the whole chain to keep you up there."

"Right," says Moore. "There's no lessening of accountability, but once you've got that support, you're so much stronger than when you're alone."

Gail von Rueden sees it as a metaphor for her work as a banker. "My territory consists of several states, so I have to travel a lot. And it's scary being out there on your own. But I learned that I have a terrific team behind me, belaying me, coaching me, offering me support. So

I can afford to take some risks now and then. It's like when I was waiting to do the Zip. I froze. Now I'm a very rational person, and I knew, rationally, that I was going to be all right if I did the Zip. But I wasn't thinking rationally."

Steve Murray interjects: "You were like me on the Monster. I kept hearing those little voices up in my head."

"Exactly," says von Rueden. "But my coach was telling me, 'It's okay.' And she was explaining how the backup system worked. She was countering the bad vibes with really good, detailed knowledge."

"And that did it?" asks Moore.

"Uh, well," von Rueden stammers.

"Tell the truth, Gail," a chorus of voices says.

"No, it didn't. Judy was behind me, and I knew she was scared to death to do the Zip."

"I sure was," Judy Degady affirms. "I was shaking."

"So, well, uh," von Rueden manages. "I knew Judy wouldn't go if I didn't, and the truth is, I didn't want to fail Judy. I didn't want to fail my friend."

"Gail," Moore says gently. "You wouldn't have failed Judy. But what you did succeed in doing was finding your own limit. There *are* no losers at Pecos."

Reprinted with the permission of SELL!NG magazine.

Training is a progression, a process of building up layers on foundations. A person might obtain the information through lectures, observe a variety of methods, and incorporate it through personal involvement.

On-the-Job Training (OJT)

Perhaps the most widely used approach to training is **on-the-job training (OJT).** When used correctly, OJT has the potential to be a very effective training tool. When used incorrectly, it really is not training. Often managers justify a heavy reliance on OJT by saying that "experience is the best teacher" or that "I learned to sell in the school of hard knocks." To those ideas we would respond with a couple of other old adages: "Experience is indeed the best teacher, but it is a fool who will learn by no other." And "The school of hard knocks has tuition higher than most wish to pay."

OJT has the advantage of being able to introduce trainees to real-world experience. Additionally, it provides the trainer with the chance to critique the trainee's performance in an actual setting. OJT also provides candidates a "reality check" prior to being turned out on their own in the field.

For OJT to be useful, the person doing the training needs to establish a forum for it to be a learning experience. There are several things the trainer/sales manager can do:

1. Discuss each sales call with the trainee prior to entering the business to help the trainee in organizing the call and point out any difficulties he or she might face.
2. Go on the call with the trainee but do not get directly involved in trying to make the sale. Instead, observe and mentally critique the sales presentation. Not getting involved in trying to make the sale is probably the most difficult thing for a sales manager during the process; however, the trainee will generally learn as much or more from failure as from success.
3. After the call is completed, give feedback to the trainee, pointing out specific things that he or she did correctly as well as problems with the presentation.

Especially in the early stages of OJT, the trainer/sales manager needs to be directly involved in this process.

Classroom Training

Classroom training lends itself well to the presentation of certain types of information, especially that having to do with product or industry knowledge. In being a structured forum for conveying information, the classroom enables the company to frame what it wants to convey to trainees in a precise manner. Additionally, it is efficient because a good deal of information can be provided in a relatively short time. The classroom also lends itself to the use of videotapes, which can be extremely useful in helping trainees model behavior.

Obviously, classroom training has its drawbacks, such as the "boredom factor"—trainees will tend to grow weary of this approach quicker than with other approaches. Additionally, on average, trainees retain little of what they hear and just a bit more of what they see. This is the reason that in developing a training program, managers should incorporate a number of approaches, such as those suggested in Figure 14-2. Finally, the classroom does require excellent implementers who have the knowledge and skills to present the program well if it is to be effective.

In terms of classroom training, businesses are increasingly calling on universities to provide their students with courses on selling. Although no one can learn all there is to know about personal selling in a classroom, students who have had some exposure to selling during their college careers have an advantage over those who do not.[17]

Electronic Training

Training with computers and with the use of interactive videos has been growing at a rapid rate.[18] Especially with **interactive video (IAV)** programs, where students get instant feedback, this approach provides the opportunity for students to be more involved in the process. Especially for new recruits, instantaneous feedback is important. The concept is similar to the flight simulator for airlines in that mistakes can be made with no cost involved and with the opportunity for corrective action to be taken before costs are incurred. The major drawback of the IAV is the cost.[19] Because the system interacts with trainees, it must be quite sophisticated and, therefore, costly. One additional side benefit of this approach is that becoming familiar with what computers can do will reduce trainees' fear of using computers in their selling.

Experiential Training

The rigidly structured, lecture format of the classroom is appealing to sales managers because they can control the information to which trainees are exposed. Perhaps, however, what Confucius is purported to have said applies here: "I hear and I forget; I see and I remember; I do and I understand." Trainees often learn best when they are allowed to apply concepts, even when they fail in the attempt.[20] One way for this to take place, without risking sales and with minimal risk to the trainee's ego, is through **experiential training** exercises. Among the ones that have been successfully applied are

- Role playing
- Case studies
- Games
- Group projects
- Human relations training

Although training should not consist exclusively of these methodologies, they can be interjected in the training process at appropriate places. They do have the advantage of giving trainees a type of hands-on experience, where they learn by doing and receiving instant feedback on their understanding and retention of concepts. The drawback of these exercises is that the trainer must be able to draw truths from the experience and guide the trainees into understanding the dynamics of what took place.

Thomas Leigh suggests an approach to training that is a modification of role playing and involves the use of "cognitive selling scripts."[21] The selling script provides an appropriate sequence of events or actions/reactions in a given setting. It is almost like an if-then statement in that trainees are given a written script that describes what they are to say or do in response to an action or statement. This approach is particularly useful in training in selling skills with new salespeople. Table 14-1 shows an example of such a script.

Mentoring

Another approach to training that is gaining popularity is **mentoring**.[22] Mentoring enables new salespeople both to obtain assistance in their week areas and to have a role model in the company. It is a useful approach for both small and large firms. Generally, in mentoring programs, new salespeople are each assigned to veterans who work with them on their selling or on a special marketing project. The trainees have access to the accumulated expertise of the veterans, and the veterans gain a number of intrinsic rewards from working with new people, often at a time in their careers when those intrinsic rewards are particularly important.

Certainly, mentors need to be salespeople who have a track record of success and who have an interest in being involved in such a program. Additionally, mentors must be at a stage in their careers where they can take time from their primary responsibilities to become fully involved. Mentors must have the ability to coach others and help them work through mistakes and problems.

Curbside Training

Curbside training involves sales managers acting in the capacity of a coach. Curbside training is different from OJT in that it involves active, ongoing involvement on the part of sales managers. It allows sales managers to monitor the progress of their salespeople and provide feedback to them in a timely manner. Additionally, it helps sales managers to do evaluations of individuals reporting to them. Especially with new salespeople, the manager's involvement in such training is critical for their development into effective, self-directed sales professionals.[23]

When designing a training program, sales managers should use a combination of approaches. They need to keep in mind those principles of learning as the training program is planned. Interspersing the various approaches avoids violating those principles. Additionally, with sales becoming increasingly a consultative process, the approach to training needs to address how to develop that partnering relationship.[24] This involves the ability to work with people, and that means that training needs to develop that ability.

TABLE 14-1 Cognitive Selling Script

Initial Industrial Sales Call

Actions or Behaviors

PA	Looks up and notices you
SP	Smile
SP	Extend greeting
SP	Extend handshake
SP	Introduce myself
SP	Offer business card
PA	Extends invitation to sit
SP	Sit
SP	State my understanding of purpose of meeting
SP	Ask buyer if my understanding is correct
PA	Expands purpose
SP	Ask what brought about need
PA	States cost, bid, quantity
SP	Ask how long the situation has existed
PA	Offers time frame
SP	Ask what departments are involved
PA	States departments
SP	Ask what impact between situations and people
PA	Is evasive
SP	Ask what prior situation was
PA	Offers history
SP	Determine problems
SP	Formulate action
SP	Restate situation
SP	Ask buyer what he perceives as best mode of action
PA	States his plan
SP	Agree with him
SP	Stress his plan as positive
SP	Offer him additional actions
SP	Suggest he contact persons involved
PA	He contacts department heads
PA	He arranges for two immediate meetings with them
PA	He notifies one person that I will contact
SP	Ask for names, titles and telephone extensions of these people to set up meeting
SP	Copy down exact information
SP	Restate my actions with time frame
SP	Ask if I can be of additional assistance
SP	State when my actions will be completed and what results I expect
SP	Stand
SP/PA	Shakes hands
SP	Thank him
SP	Say good-bye
PA	Says good-bye
PA	Walks you back to the reception room

Note: PA = purchasing agent; SP = salesperson.
Source: Thomas W. Leigh, Scripts and stories in professional selling: Mapping the procedural knowledge of exceptional producers. In *Marketing Education: Knowledge development, dissemination, and utilization,* ed. Joseph Guiltinan and Dale Achabal (American Marketing Association, 1986). Reproduced with permission.

OTHER ISSUES IN TRAINING

Who Does the Training

Sales managers are faced with the question of who should conduct training sessions. The choices in general are to use

- Outside consultants
- Inside training specialists
- Company salespeople
- Company sales manager

The advantage of using outside consultants is that they are experts in training salespeople and generally specialize in sales training programs. Additionally, outside trainers may be perceived as having more credibility than people within the company. The drawback is, of course, the high cost. Although some inexpensive training programs do exist, generally there is a strong price/quality relationship in hiring training experts and programs.

Using company training specialists gives the advantage of having someone who is an expert in training and at a lower cost than an outside person. However, such people generally do not specialize in only sales training and therefore may not be able to meet the needs of salespeople as well as outside experts. Using company salespeople does guarantee that a person who has experience in selling a particular product in a given industry will do the training and thus will be familiar with specific issues and problems. Also, this approach can provide intrinsic rewards to the salespeople chosen to do the training. Obviously, the salespeople chosen to conduct these training sessions should be volunteers and should be among the best performers. The major drawbacks include the problem of taking veteran salespeople out of the field to do training. Also, they are not training specialists and may be tempted to grandstand, and they may not be perceived as having the credibility as trainers.

When sales managers do the training themselves, they have the advantage of knowing the weaknesses of their salespeople and of knowing the industry and products well. Andrew S. Grove, president of Intel Corporation, advocates that managers do the training themselves.[25] He suggests that sales managers are in the best position to understand the dynamics of the company and to convey that to salespeople. He also cites the fact that managers can then better serve as role models. The chief drawback with managers doing the training is that salespeople, particularly new ones, may be intimidated with the prospect of "the boss" doing the training. Additionally, sales managers are not professional trainers and generally have enough things to do without also trying to conduct training sessions.

Where to Do Training

Training can be done in various regions or at a central location. Holding training sessions in the regions enables the salespeople to learn in an environment that is comfortable. Also, if part of the training consists of familiarizing salespeople with their territories, regional training is particularly useful. Obviously, regional training saves the company the money of sending salespeople to a central location and providing housing for them. A major drawback is that salespeople will have the distractions that are part of training in the home environment.

Centralized training provides the chance for the company to monitor the progress of the training more closely and ensures a greater degree of standardization in the training. It also enables the company to employ approaches that might be too expensive for use in several locations, but when used at one place with a larger number of people is reasonably efficient. Centralized training does make the training seem to be more "special" to salespeople, and, perhaps because of this, they will take it more seriously.

Training for the Selling of Services

It is well established that the marketing of services is essentially different from the marketing of goods.[26] The major difference is that services are intangible, whereas goods are tangible. Another difference is that the production of services is inseparable from their consumption, and this fact has two implications. First, the quality of some service is dependent on the customer's ability to describe the needed service. Second, the quality of the service is judged at least in part on how the service is produced. Another major difference is that services are heterogeneous; that is, they have a higher variability in quality than do goods. Finally, services are perishable in that they cannot be stored and sold as needed.

According to Paula Kringle, a business communications consultant, services are more difficult to sell than are goods because of their intangibility.[27] She goes on to point out that because of this, salespeople who sell services need to be trained more to communicate value that do sellers of goods. With a good, the quality and features can be readily demonstrated. With a service, this is not so. The salesperson must be able to "capture the customer's reality," that is, determine the mind-set of that customer and relate to it. Thus listening skills are even more crucial in selling services than goods. Additionally, salespeople must be able to add the quality of tangibility to services in order to help the buyer grasp what the product represents in terms of benefits.

How Much Money and Time to Spend on Training

Certainly at the heart of any training program is the issue of value received. By this we mean the amount of cost incurred relative to the benefit received. This issue is made more complex by the fact that there are any number of training programs available; some are very good and others are not.[28] Certainly, companies can do their own training, but even then certain costs arise that are not present with buying commercially available programs. In the final analysis, the basic question always is, "Is it worth it?" This holds true for training perhaps more than for other issues because of the visibility of the costs.

Certainly the direct costs of training are high. In a survey of 1554 companies, *Sales & Marketing Management* found that the average spent on training was $3737 per salesperson per year, with a median of $1767 per salesperson per year.[29] That amount varied with size, with larger companies spending more. A second issue is the amount of time spent training salespeople, an indirect cost of training. The median amount of training time reported in the *S&MM* study was 1.7 weeks (8.5 days) per year. Again, this figure varies considerably. For example, Hercules, Inc., a chemical company, requires that salespeople new to the industry spend 26 weeks in training the first year, but, after that, they receive about one week of training per year.[30] The keys to determining how much time and money to spend are what the company is trying to accomplish with its training and what the trainees need to learn.

TRAINING IN THE INTERNATIONAL ARENA

There are two important issues when training in the international arena. First, the company needs to train its people on how to relate to and operate in another culture. Second, the company that employs natives of the countries in which it operates needs to train them. That training is likely to be different than what is used in the company's home country.

There is increasing pressure on companies to conduct cross-cultural training for its employees, particularly those directly involved in international operations. Philip Harris and Robert Moran point out that companies need to conduct cross-cultural training to help their employees engage in more appropriate, sensitive, and consistent behavior in their interactions with people from other cultures and backgrounds.[31] They believe that there are specific skills and approaches people need to learn in such training. They include

- Communicating respect to others
- Being nonjudgmental
- Recognizing one's own cultural biases
- Being able to display empathy
- Practicing flexibility in carrying out one's duties
- Facilitating communication
- Tolerating ambiguity.

In dealing with these topics, the training program should include language training, cultural information, and awareness training. The cross-cultural training program needs to begin before a person leaves for the assignment and continue after he or she arrives. The material covered will change as the person progresses through the program.

As a firm designs a training program for engaging in global marketing, it needs to address cultural differences, both minor and major. An example of a major difference is in Japan, where there is a certain order to follow in business transactions and certain "rules" for interacting with businesspeople. Other differences are a bit more subtle, such as in Mexico, where a greater emphasis on service is required. According to Geoffrey Brewer, senior editor for *Sales & Marketing Management*

> Doing business in Mexico might require learning a new language and culture. But the formula for success is written in plain English. In fact, it's spelled out in just about any textbook on total quality management. "If you want to win in Mexico, you've got to get the service edge," says Brian Brisson, an assistant commercial attaché with the U.S. Embassy in Mexico. "Mexicans tend to rank service, the personal touch, right up there with price. They want attention before, during, and after the sale."[32]

Regardless of whether the differences are major or minor, the training program should draw trainees' attention to those differences and provide a framework for coping with them.

In educating company employees from other countries to do business in their own country, Vern Terpstra and Kenneth David suggest that two major issues need to be considered: (1) The company should take into account the previous socialization experienced by the individuals in the program; and (2) the company needs to decide if its goals are simply to impart technical knowledge and skills or if it also wants to socialize the employees into the corporate culture.[33] They also point out that multinational corporations may face nationalism that is, emphasizing a country's national interests, and national requirements for employee training.

CHAPTER SUMMARY

In this chapter, we have discussed some of the problems inherent in helping salespeople realize their potential and be good producers on a continuous basis. Specifically, the chapter considered training as a socialization process. Well-defined objectives are essential to developing any training program, for unless objectives are clearly defined, sales managers cannot design programs that meet company and salespeople's needs. We also discussed 10 learning principles related to sales training. Regardless how much information needs to be covered and how limited the time available for training, sales managers who cut corners by violating one or more of these principles will undermine the effectiveness of the entire training program.

The chapter also explored various approaches to sales training, as well as the material that should be included in the training program. The two factors are related. The type of material to be covered will help determine the approach that should be used. Sales managers realize that training includes more than just providing information about products. Skill development is also an integral part of training.

The chapter closed with a discussion of sales training in the international setting. Part of this discussion dealt with cross-cultural training for domestic employees who will have direct contact with customers in other countries. That training involves sensitizing them to the differences in customs and values of people in the other country. Another issue of international training deals with training employees who are natives of the country in which the company is doing business. To be effective, the firm must adapt its training to the customs of the country for which it is targeted.

KEY TERMS

competitive advantage, p. 324

corporate culture, p. 325

curbside training, p. 336

customization, p. 321

derived demand, p. 324

distinctive competency, p. 324

experiential training, p. 335

informal culture, p. 317

interactive video (IAV), p. 335

learning, p. 319

mentoring, p. 336

motivation, p. 319

on-the-job training (OJT), p. 333

participation, p. 320

plateau, p. 320

practice, p. 320

productivity, p. 320

purpose, p. 319

realism, p. 321

reinforcement, p. 320

repetition, p. 320

socialization, p. 316

CHAPTER QUESTIONS

1. Why is training said to be a specialized form of socialization?
2. Why is it critical that a firm develop specific objectives for training?
3. Describe why each of the 10 principles of learning are important.
4. Discuss the idea that the lecture method is not sufficient for training skills.
5. What parts do mentoring and curbside training play in the development of salespeople?
6. Is it true that "a salesperson is born and not made"? Explain your answer.
7. What are some similarities between training salespeople for employment in the United States and training them for an overseas assignment? What are the differences?
8. What are two major issues a company faces when training employees who are nationals of the country in which the firm is operating?

NOTES

1. Lawrence Chonko, John F. Tanner, Jr., and William A. Weeks, Sales training: Status and needs. *Journal of Personal Selling & Sales Management* 13 (Fall 1993), 81–86.
2. Adel I. El-Ansary, Selling and sales management in action: Sales force effectiveness research reveals new insights and reward-penalty patterns in sales force training. *Journal of Personal Selling & Sales Management* 13 (Spring 1993), 83–90.
3. Marc Hequet, No more Willy Loman. *Sales Training* (May 1989), 11–13.
4. Arnold M. Rose, *Sociology* (New York: Knopf, 1965), 731.
5. Scott W. Kelley, Developing customer orientation among service employees. *Journal of the Academy of Marketing Science* 20 (Winter 1992), 27–36.
6. Patrick L. Schul and Brent M. Wren, The emerging role of women in industrial selling: A decade of change. *Journal of Marketing* 56 (July 1992), 38–54.
7. Linda Lynton, The dilemma of sexual harassment. *Sales & Marketing Management* (October 1989), 67–71.
8. Dennis W. Organ and Thomas Bateman, *Organizational behavior* (Homewood, IL: BPI/Irwin, 1986).
9. Compiled from Dennis A. Miller, A successful sales-training program. *Training and Development Journal* (November 1980), 46–49; Bill Kelley, Training, "just plain lousy" or "too important to ignore." *Sales & Marketing Management* (March 1993), 66–70; Organ and Bateman, *Organizational behavior.*
10. Compensation & expenses. *Sales & Marketing Management,* June 22, 1992, 72.
11. David M. Szymanski, Determinants of selling effectiveness: The importance of declarative knowledge to the personal selling concept. *Journal of Marketing* 52 (January 1988), 64–77.
12. Conrad N. Jackson and Ralph W. Jackson, The attributes of successful salespeople, working paper, 1993.
13. Dennis Fox, The fear factor: Why traditional sales training doesn't always work. *Sales & Marketing Management* (February 1992), 64.
14. Edgar H. Schein, The role of the founder in creating organizational structure. *Organizational Dynamics* 12 (Summer 1983), 14.
15. Earl D. Honeycutt, Jr., Tom McCarty, and Vince Howe, Sales technology applications: Self-paced video enhanced training: A case study. *Journal of Personal Selling & Sales Management* 13 (Winter 1993), 73–79.
16. Compensation & expenses, 72.
17. Al Urbanski, Electronic training may be in your future. *Sales & Marketing Management* (March 1988), 46, 48.
18. Arthur Bragg, Personal selling goes to college. *Sales & Marketing Management* (March 1988), 35–37.
19. Urbanski, Electronic training.
20. James T. Strong, Leaders in selling and sales management: John Cameron Aspley and the Dartnell Corporation. *Journal of Personal Selling & Sales Management* 12 (Winter 1992), 65–67.
21. Thomas W. Leigh, Cognitive selling scripts and sales training. *Journal of Personal Selling & Sales Management* 7 (August 1987), 39–48.
22. Arthur Bragg, Is a mentor program in your future? *Sales & Marketing Management* (September 1989), 54–63.
23. Stephen X. Doyle and George Thomas Roth, Selling and sales management in action: The use of insight coaching to improve relationship selling. *Journal of Personal Selling & Sales Management* 12 (Winter 1992), 59–64.
24. Harvey Blustain, Selling and sales management in action—from hot boxes to open systems: The changing world of computer salespeople. *Journal of Personal Selling & Sales Management* 12 (Spring 1992), 67–72; Ray A. DeCormier and David Jobber, The counselor selling method: Concepts and constructs. *Journal of Personal Selling & Sales Management* 13 (Fall 1993), 39–59.
25. Andrew S. Grove, Why training is the boss's job. *Fortune,* January 23, 1984, 93–96.

26. For more information, see Leonard L. Berry, Services marketing is different. *Business* (May–June 1980), 24–29; A. Parasuraman, Valerie A. Zeithaml, and Leonard L. Berry, A conceptual model of service quality and its implications for future research. *Journal of Marketing* 59 (Fall 1985), 41–50; G. Lynn Shostack, Breaking free from product marketing. *Journal of Marketing* (April 1977), 73–80.

27. Paula C. Kringle, Training salespeople to sell services. *Sales Training* (May 1989), 14–18.

28. Kelley, Training.

29. William Keenan, Jr., Are you overspending on training. *Sales & Marketing Management* (January 1990), 56–60.

30. Ibid.

31. Philip R. Harris and Robert T. Moran, *Managing cultural differences* (Houston, TX: Gulf, 1991).

32. Geoffrey Brewer, New world orders. *Sales & Marketing Management* (January 1994), p. 62.

33. Vern Terpstra and Kenneth David, *The cultural environment of international business* (Cincinnati, OH: South-Western, 1985).

SUGGESTED READINGS

Butler, James E., Gerald R. Ferris, and Nancy K. Napier. *Strategy and human resources management.* Cincinnati, OH: South-Western, 1991.

> Human resource management cannot be effectively approached as a separate entity within an organization. To be effective, the human resource function needs to be viewed strategically as part of the "big picture." Taking this approach completely changes the way decisions are made, and even the decisions themselves.

French, Wendell L., and Cecil H. Bell, Jr. *Organizational development.* Englewood Cliffs, NJ: Prentice Hall, 1978.

> Organizations have unique cultures that shape behavior of the individuals within them. By creating an environment of collaboration between managers and subordinates, both organizational and individual goals can be more easily attained. This environment creates and is created by developing satisfying interpersonal relationships within the organization, empowering individuals to act on their own, and enabling individuals to personally grow.

Goffman Erving. *Stigma.* Englewood Cliffs, NJ: Prentice Hall, 1963.

> Socialization is a process that takes place in all organizations. That process both defines the rules that the individual is to follow and becomes part of that person's self-concept. The label a person is given by the organization can either facilitate a healthy climate within the organization or create one of disenfranchisement.

Randolph, W. Alan. *Understanding and managing organizational behavior.* Homewood, IL: Irwin, 1985.

> Knowing the various theories in organizational behavior is certainly useful for managers as well as students of the subject. However, these theories need to be placed in perspective and in a framework so that they can be applied by the manager. Effective management goes beyond simply knowing; it involves understanding.

Chapter 15

Forecasting Sales and Establishing Goals and Budgets

OPENING SCENARIO

Phil Kary, sales manager of Dumas Makt., H.K., reached for his cup of coffee. It was going to be a long night, and he needed to stay sharp. The president, Bob Kelly, had asked for a detailed review of the company's forecasting and budgeting procedures. His request was the result of severe overestimates of sales of two main products, causing considerable excess inventory the company was now going to have to sell below cost. "What caused this?" Kary asked himself. Was it the quantitative techniques the company was using? Perhaps they weren't sensitive enough to predict the turning points and the sharp drop in sales that occurred. Was it the 30 percent growth the company had achieved each year over the last three years that caused the qualitative product forecasts obtained from the jury of executive opinion method to be too high due to the executives feeling that the company was invincible? Was it his fault in not paying enough attention to the forecasting and budgeting part of his job?

Even if he never determined the reason, Kary knew that forecasting and budgeting were going to be extremely important to the company in the next few years. He would have to remember all those techniques he had learned in his class on personal selling and sales management and see if any of the techniques or new ones were appropriate for Dumas Makt. "I am glad Professor Cowen was so insistent on our learning all the possible techniques," Kary thought, even though he recalled not having the same feeling when studying for his exams.

Chapter Objectives

After reading this chapter, you should be able to

- Understand the relationship between planning, forecasting, and budgeting.
- Estimate market potentials for consumer and industrial products.
- Select the most appropriate qualitative and quantitative forecasting techniques.
- Understand and implement procedures for establishing sales quotas.

INTRODUCTION

Budgeting is an extremely important task for sales managers. Developing incentive awards that work must be part of the budgeting process. Sales managers can keep expenses of incentive awards down by arranging trips that require less time away from the selling task. A budget-stretching incentive concept that is growing in popularity is houseboating.[1]

Seven Crown Resorts, in Irvine, California, which claims to be the largest houseboat resort company, organizes houseboat excursions. According to Catherine Heishoj, sales director for Seven Crown Resorts, "Houseboating offers an excellent alternative to the typical resort incentive. While giving sales winners an opportunity to get some rest and relaxation, it also gives them a chance to see some of North America's most precious national parks."[2] Perhaps even more important to the sales manager, this incentive package is good for the budget. With everything included, a week of houseboating costs about $300 per person.

This lower price, cost-effective sales incentive has been used by such companies as Molson Brewers, U.S.A. In May 1992, Molson brought 325 people from 80 distributors across the United States to a houseboating excursion in Overton, Nevada. Each distributor was awarded a houseboat, and could send anyone they desired, depending on how they wanted to award their people. Some distributors wanted to promote camaraderie among the sales force; other distributors wanted to reward the selling effort of an individual and his or her family; still others, the achievement of the sales force. Regardless of the way the distributor used the reward, the houseboating excursion allowed Molson Breweries to reward everyone in its distributor organization at a reasonable cost.

Successful selling requires well-thought-out plans such as this incentive program. Budgets and sales quotas are an important part of this planning because they assist in the planning, evaluation, and control of the selling activities.

SALES FORECASTING AND PLANNING

Central to any planning in a company is the **sales forecast.** Regardless of the size of the company or the sales force, the sales forecast influences all aspects of sales management: planning, budgeting, and establishing quotas.[3] Despite its importance, developing a good sales forecast is not an easy task. Before developing the forecast and selecting the most appropriate sales forecasting method(s), it is important that all the factors affecting the forecast be examined. These factors can be classified into two groups—controllable and uncontrollable.

Controllable factors are those that are under the control of the firm, such as pricing policies, distribution channels, promotion activities, new products, product characteristics, account receivable policies, and the firm's own financial capability. Controllable factors are elements of the internal business environment that affect future sales. **Uncontrollable factors** are environmental elements over which the firm has little, if any, control. These include the state of the world and the national economy, inflation, interest rates, shifts in population, changing consumer tastes, other demographic data, competitive activities, and industry trends. Uncontrollable factors have an impact, to varying extents, on the sales and performance of the firm. It is important that factors having the greatest impact be carefully monitored and taken into account when developing the sales forecast.

One important factor influencing sales is the general economic situation. A company should determine the indices of general economic conditions most relevant to its product category. Three general categories of indices are listed in Table 15-1. **Leading indicators,** indices that lead general business activity, must be

TABLE 15-1 Principal Business Indicators for Use in Sales Forecasting

Leading Indicators

Average workweek of production workers
Construction contracts awarded to commercial and industrial buildings
Contracts and orders for plant and equipment
Newly approved capital appropriations
Net change in the business population (new businesses incorporations and failures)
Corporate profits after taxes
Index of stock prices
Change in business inventories
Value of manufacturers' new orders

Coincident (simultaneous) Indicators

Unemployment rate
Index of help-wanted advertising in newspaper
Index of industrial production
Gross national product
Personal income
Sales of retail stores
Index of wholesale prices

Lagging Indicators

Business expenditures on new plant and equipment
Book value of manufacturers' inventories
Consumer installment debt
Index of labor cost per unit of output

closely examined because the movement of these indices (upward or downward) precedes the sales of the product. Unfortunately, this movement does not consistently mean an upswing or downturn in specific product sales.

Coincident (simultaneous) indicators are those that are in harmony with fluctuations in product sales and are useful in establishing marketing strategies in various stages of the product life cycle. For example, a firm that must borrow funds should be aware that interest rates usually go up sometime after a coincident series peak has been reached.

Lagging indicators are those that lag behind fluctuations in the market. Simultaneous and lagging indicators are less important in making the sales forecast.

Forecasting Concepts

Generally, sales managers are concerned with four items when developing a forecast: market size, market potential, sales potential, and sales forecast. **Market size** is the total number of units a particular market could consume in a specific time period (usually one year) without taking into account such marketing activities as price and competitive activity. The part of this specific market size that is the highest possible total industry sales of a product in a given time period is **market potential. Sales potential** is a subset of market potential that represents the maximum market share a particular company could obtain in the specific time period. Finally, the sales forecast, a subset of the sales potential, is the amount of sales in the specific market that the company may obtain during a particular period of time.

Estimating Consumer Demand

For companies marketing consumer goods, some excellent basic economic data are presented annually in "Survey of Buying Power," a feature of *Sales and Marketing Management*. Particularly helpful to the sales manager in estimating future sales is the **buying power index (BPI),** which is calculated from a weighted combination of population, income, and retail sales expressed as a percentage of national potential. BPIs forecast the purchasing ability in a particular market and are listed in the magazine for the larger standard metropolitan statistical areas.

In the United States, the sales manager can compare the percentage in a particular city with the percentage of total company sales in that city, evaluating the degree of market penetration and whether present company sales results are adequate. If this initial analysis indicates an untapped potential in the city, the sales manager can conduct further research and obtain more information about the market and the amount of competition. This further investigation may indicate that increased selling effort and/or selling expenditures is warranted.

Estimating Industrial Demand Approach

An approach for estimating industrial sales is the **Standard Industrial Classification (SIC) code** approach. The SIC code is a uniform numbering system that classifies all companies according to the type of product produced or operation performed. All products are assigned to a category, with each major industrial group identified by a two-digit number (see Table 15-2). Within each two-digit SIC code, there are specific product classifications. Within SIC codes 20–39, indicating a manufacturing company, SIC code 34 indicates a manufacturer of metal products and SIC code of 3441121 indicates a manufacturer of fabricated metal products and SIC code of 3441122, a manufacturer of fabricated structural iron and steel for buildings. The SIC code numbers can help the sales manager locate potential customers, determine market potential for an area, and assist in making accurate sales forecasts.

To complete a list of potential customers in a market area in a particular SIC code, sales managers can use a state's industrial directory or a more general directory such as *Thomas Register of American Manufacturers, Moody's Industrial Manual,* or *Standard & Poor's Register.* Each of these references provides current information on corporate officers, company name, address and telephone numbers, products or services offered, annual sales, and number of employees of companies having products in a specific SIC code. These data can also be purchased by SIC code classification from a variety of firms, such as Dun & Bradstreet. The SIC code provides sales managers with a procedure for evaluating present sales and forecasting future sales. It also is the basis for uncovering other relevant information in such reference sources as *U.S. Census of Manufacturers, U.S. Industrial Outlook, Country Business Patterns,* and "Survey of Industrial Purchasing Power" in *Sales & Marketing Management.*

TABLE 15-2 Standard Industrial Classification (SIC) System

Two-Digit SIC Number	Major Industry Classification
01–09	Agriculture, forestry, fishing
10–14	Mining
15–17	Construction
20–39	Manufacturing
40–49	Transportation and other public utilities
50–51	Wholesale trade
52–59	Retail trade
60–67	Finance, insurance, and real estate
70–89	Services
91–97	Government
99	Nonclassifiable establishments

NONQUANTITATIVE FORECASTING METHODS

There are many quantitative and nonquantitative ways to forecast sales. Because no single method always results in a consistently accurate sales forecast, it is better to use several methods simultaneously to make forecasts. The results from one method can serve as a check on the results from another method. The method used depends on such things as the length of time of the forecast, the importance of the forecast, the amount of time available, and the amount of data available. Common nonquantitative methods used to forecast sales include the jury of executive opinion, sales force composite, buyers' expectation, the Delphi technique, and the scenario technique. The advantages and disadvantages of the first four methods are summarized in Table 15-3.

Jury of Executive Opinion

The **jury of executive opinion,** one of the oldest and simplest techniques, asks top executives of the firm to forecast sales for a specified time period. By averaging these forecasts, a broad-based forecast is obtained, which is usually more accurate than a forecast based on a single estimate from one executive. Estimates of sales are generally obtained from executives in such diverse areas as marketing, finance, production, and purchasing.[4]

The advantage of the jury of executive opinion is that it is quick and easy. The major disadvantage is that it relies on the opinions of executives who may not be closely associated with the company's products and may inaccurately predict sales.

Sales Force Composite

The **sales force composite** method compiles estimates of future sales from salespeople. Sometimes salespeople make these estimates alone, and sometimes the sales estimates are made in consultation with the sales manager. The results are totaled for the district or region. The district or regional manager then evaluates the estimate by comparing it with the accuracy of past sales estimates. This allows the manager to correct each salesperson's estimate by an appropriate deviation factor and use his or her own experience in developing the final district estimate. This estimate is forwarded to the home office, where a total sales estimate is compiled for the company.

A common bias in using this approach is that the forecasted sales are usually lower than the actual sales. These lower estimates can be compensated for by establishing an index of pessimism for each salesperson. This index is derived by comparing each previous sales estimate with the actual sales that resulted for each salesperson. The difference, when divided by the estimate, becomes the salesperson's index. In one company, the sales estimates for the majority of the

TABLE 15-3 Advantages and Problems of Four Forecasting Techniques

Advantages

Buyers' Expectation Method	Delphi Method	Jury of Executive Opinion	Sales Force Composite Method
Forecast is based on opinions of individuals whose buying activities will determine the actual sales results achieved. Forecasting process reveals general attitudes and feelings about product from potential users. Technique is a very effective method for determining demand for a new industrial product.	Forecast is based on opinion of experts in the field. Technique is a very effective method for forecasting sales of new high-technology products.	Forecast is based on different specializations, judgments, experience, and viewpoints. Method is easily and quickly implemented. Forecast is based on opinions of individuals who can make and implement decisions that will affect the actual sales results achieved.	Forecast is based on specialized knowledge of individuals closest to the market where the sales occur. Forecast is based on opinions of individuals who are directly responsible for the actual sales results achieved. Forecast is easily broken down on a customer, product, or territory bases.

Problems

Buyers' Expectation Method	Delphi Method	Jury of Executive Opinion	Sales Force Composite Method
Forecast is based on expected future actions and events that are subject to change. Forecast is based on opinions of buyers who are at various stages of knowledge and interest. Forecast is based on primary research and data collection with the associated time and costs.	Forecast requires a great deal of time and some money to implement. Accuracy depends on participants' knowledge and level of initial and continued participation. Forecast requires an able, experienced coordinator.	Accuracy of forecast depends on the quality of the opinions solicited. Forecast is based on primary research and original data collection with the associated time and cost. Forecast is often difficult to break down by product or geographic delineations.	Forecast is based on estimates of salesperson, who is often unaware of broad economic patterns and future company plans. Salespeople are evaluated primarily on sales, not on subsidiary activities such as forecasting. Forecast is based on primary research and original data collection with its associated time and costs. Procedures are needed to ensure accuracy of the forecast. When forecast is used in establishing quotas, sales estimates are understated.

Source: Robert D. Hisrich and Michael P. Peters, *Marketing decisions for new and mature products,* 2nd ed. (New York: Macmillan, 1991), 307.

salespeople were within 10 percent of actual sales when the calculated indices of pessimism were applied to the forecasts of each salesperson.

Although the sales force composite method involves sales estimates by knowledgeable people who are closest to the market, there are two problems in producing accurate forecasts. First, the structure of the market often affects the ability of the sales force to forecast sales accurately. When salespeople call on relatively few accounts or when relatively few accounts are the predominant proportion of their business, then the forecasts produced through this method tend to be more accurate. The second problem with the sales force composite method is that salespeople's evaluation, compensation, and promotion are based on sales, not on forecasting accuracy. Therefore, salespeople tend to spend as little time as possible in making forecasts.

Accuracy is greatly improved when a salesperson takes the past sales as a reference point through the use of the form indicated in Table 15-4. This form obtains sales estimates for a particular product on a customer-by-customer basis. Note that the estimates are obtained on a unit, not on dollar, basis to avoid the problem of price increases.

Buyers' Expectation Method

Many companies frequently ask present, past, and potential customers about their future purchase intentions. This approach, the **buyers' expectation method,** works most effectively when relatively few important customers account for the majority of the company's sales. While potential customers can be queried about

TABLE 15-4 Form for Obtaining Salesperson's Estimates on Future Sales Product _____

(Name of Product)

Customer	Sales Last Time Period (week, month, year) in Units	Sales Next Time Period (week, month, year) in Units	Reason for Change

purchase plans by mail, telephone, or in person, an in-person interview provides more accurate and detailed estimates. A problem can occur if potential buyers overstate their buying intentions. One way to correct for this overstatement is to reduce the higher estimates by creating an index of optimism similar to the index established in the sales force composite method. This index is based on past purchases versus forecasts of each industrial buyer. Once determined, it can be used to decrease the estimate of each buyer to reflect more accurately previous estimate/actual sales in the past.

Delphi Method

The **Delphi method** can be used to forecast product sales as well as predict the future direction of an entire industry.[5] The method often involves a controlled succession of brainstorming sessions among a panel of experts. Responses to the first round of questions are summarized and form the basis of the next round of questions. The judgments, insights, and expectations of the experts are evaluated by the entire group, resulting in a shared, more structured, and less biased estimate of the future.

A Delphi sales forecast involves forming a panel composed of 10 to 1,000 persons knowledgeable in the field and having various backgrounds, training, and organizational positions. A letter is mailed to selected panel members, asking them to provide estimates of general industry sales and product sales. Panel members are also asked to indicate their knowledge of the field. The answers are edited and a list of items or statements developed. This list is then mailed to each panel member, who is asked to provide an opinion about when any change will occur and the probability of various sales estimates. The answers are tabulated and further steps implemented as needed. Because the quality of the forecast resulting from the Delphi method is dependent on the expertise of panel members, it is important to select the best possible sample of experts and combine their answers carefully.

Scenario Method

The **scenario method** provides broad pictures of future product sales based on alternative sets of assumptions. By outlining internally consistent yet qualitatively different pictures of the future in terms of their important events and their end points, the sequence of events from the present to the future is developed.

The first step in using the scenario method is to choose a number of sectors of industrial activity and describe all possible ranges of variations and alternatives within each sector. The factors and sectors are then combined in a number of schematic configurations that may exist in the future. The relevant reference scenarios are then selected using the criterion of internal consistency to explore differing scenarios. Finally, the scenarios are outlined so that they are coherent when viewed one at a time. This enables the future sales of each scenario to be more easily determined.

QUANTITATIVE FORECASTING METHODS

The different types of quantitative methods used to make sales forecasts can be classified into three general groups: time series analysis, regression and correlation analysis, and the Box-Jenkins method.

Time Series Analysis

Time series analysis involves the examination of past data as the basis for projections into the future and attempts to relate variables with time. A time series is "a set of ordered observations of a quantitative variable taken at successive points in time."[5]

In assessing past patterns in the data for projection into the future, a typical approach consists of breaking the pattern into four basic components, as indicated in Figure 15-1. The first of these components, trend, consists of an overall pattern of growth or decline. On a macrobasis, it is a long-run pattern basically resulting from technological developments, capital formations, and population growth. Seasonal variation, the second component, reflects the pattern of sales movements within the year and, as such, is a basis for short-term sales forecasting. The seasonal variation often reflects the effects of seasonal buying patterns. For example, the sale of ski goggles is greater in the late fall than in the spring or summer.

Cyclical effects, the third component, are a series of repeated sequences of a different period of time than the seasonal variation. Although few if any business sales have a constant cyclical behavior, when it occurs, it is useful in making in-

FIGURE 15-1 The Four Time Series Components

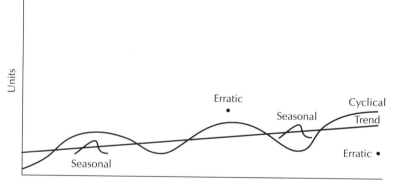

termediate forecasts. The final component is erratic—the random fluctuations in past sales data caused by strikes, raw materials shortages, energy shortages, fires, blizzards, and so on. Because they are nonsystematic and usually cancel out in the long run, erratic components are not used in making the final forecast.

In performing time series analysis, two useful techniques are available: trend analysis and exponential smoothing. The economic indicators previously discussed are often used in time series analysis.

Trend Analysis. **Trend analysis** evaluates past sales to determine if any consistent pattern or trend is evident. The past sales history is then projected into the future. Three basic methods are used to determine the existence of a long-term trend: percentage change, moving average, and curve fitting.

As its name implies, the **percentage-change method** evaluates the change in past sales data on a unit basis between successive periods of time. An example is indicated in Table 15-5. The computed percentage increase (decrease) is then examined to determine whether a sales pattern is evident, either by using an average of all percent changes or the most recent year's percent change. For example, if the average change of all years is used, 13.6 percent, the resulting forecast for 1995 would be

$$947 \times 1.136 = 1076 \text{ (000) units}$$

Despite its frequent use among businesses, trend analysis can yield inaccurate results. Often a trend or turning point in the data can be overlooked, resulting in the forecast being over- or understated, depending on the trend.

A method that helps to overcome a major limitation of the percentage-change method is the **moving-average method.** This method emphasizes more recent time periods in the sales forecast by using a specified number of time periods and dropping the oldest sales value each time a new sales figure occurs.

TABLE 15-5 Sales of Katy's Inc.

Year	Sales (000 units)	Percentage Increase/ (Decrease)
1987	364	—
1988	547	50.2
1989	632	15.5
1990	596	(5.7)
1991	787	15.0
1992	749	9.0
1993	838	11.9
1994	947	13.0

An example of the method for Kelly's Corporation is seen in Table 15-6. Because a seven-month moving average has been selected, the percentage changes (column 2 of Table 15-6) are averaged seven months at a time (column 3). For example, the seven-month moving average for March of 11.8 was determined by averaging the actual percentage change in sales of September, October, November, December, January, February, and March.[7]

$$\frac{14.1 + 5.30 + 20.3 + 8.52 + 14.1 + 11.8 + 8.61}{7} = 11.8$$

The forecast for March is then found by multiplying the seven-month moving average times the sales for the previous month, February. In this case, the estimate of 992.8 is a product of 1.118 × 894. The forecast for August is similarly obtained: 7.25 × 1143 = 1213.

A final method used in trend analysis, **curve fitting,** analyzes any trends in the sales data that express the relationship between the dependent variables, sales and time. The curves vary from linear to more complex ones, such as the Gompertz curve. The selection of the particular curve type to be used depends on which one best "fits" the past sales data, that is, which has the least error occurring between the actual sales during the time period and the estimate of those sales that would have resulted using the curve type. This difference or error can be esti-

TABLE 15-6 Sales of Kelly's Corporation

Month	Sales (000 units)	Percentage Change	Moving Average Percentage Change	Forecast
February	168			
March	179	6.5		
April	253	41.3		
May	353	39.5		
June	467	32.2		
July	531	13.7		
August	446	(16.0)		
September	509	14.1	18.8	526.2
October	536	5.3	18.6	600.6
November	645	20.3	15.6	616.4
December	700	8.5	11.2	715.9
January	799	14.1	8.57	756.0
February	894	11.8	8.30	862.9
March	971	8.6	11.8	992.3
April	1059	9.1	11.1	1077.8
May	1190	12.3	12.1	1186.0
June	1196	.08	9.21	1297.1
July	1134	(5.2)	7.25	1279.7

mated by graphing the past sales data and matching the attributes of the sales data with the attributes of the mathematical types being considered. For example, a second-degree trend with the mathematical form $Y_c = a + bx + cx^2$ has its trend increasing (or decreasing) absolutely. However, the absolute change from time period to time period is not constant but is increasing at an increasing or decreasing rate. Each of the various curve types has different characteristics that make it more applicable when certain data patterns occur.

Once the best curve type has been selected, then the fitting formulas are employed to determine the forecast. The accuracy of this forecast is estimated by using the selected equation to forecast the sales for previous years and then comparing the estimates with actual sales. This measure, the standard error of the estimate, projects the degree of accuracy that will occur in the forecast for the forthcoming year as well.

Exponential Smoothing. Several limitations of the moving-average and other trend analysis methods have promoted the use of **exponential smoothing** to forecast sales.[8] A forecast using exponential smoothing is derived using the following equation:

$$\overline{S}_t + 1 = \alpha S_t + (1 - B)\overline{S}_t$$

where: $\overline{S}_{t+1}$ = the exponentially smoothed sales forecast
  for the next time period ($t + 1$)
  α = the smoothing constant (where $0 \le \alpha \ge 1$)
  S_t = the actual sales
  $\overline{S}_t$ = the exponentially smoothed sales value

Thus, if a company had actual sales of $80,000, and smoothed sales of $60,000, sales could be forecast once an appropriate smoothing constant were determined. If a small smoothing constant of .3 were used, the sales forecast would be

$$S_{t+1} = .3\ (\$80,000) + .7\ (\$60,000) = \$66,000$$

Regression and Correlation Analysis

When sales can be related to something other than time, **regression and correlation analyses** are useful sales forecasting techniques. These widely used statistical methods examine possible mathematical relationships between sales and one or more variables. In this way, a functional relationship is established indicating that a change in one variable accompanies specified changes in another variable or variables. For example, changes in car expenditures can be related to changes in income. If a statistically significant relationship can be established, then income levels can be used to predict car expenditures and car sales.

Correlation analysis is also useful in determining whether sales are related to (correlated with) some variable or variables. The degree of this relationship is measured by the correlation coefficient (r).[9]

The correlation coefficient ranges on a scale from –1 to +1. The sign indicates the direction of the relationship between sales and another variable and the strength of the relationship. A negative correlation coefficient indicates that sales and the associated variable move in opposite directions. For example, if new housing starts were inversely related to interest rates, a negative correlation coefficient would be present. As interest rates increase, new housing starts would decrease. A positive correlation coefficient indicates that the two variables move in the same direction. As income increases, the purchase of furniture also increases, and thus these two variables would have a positive correlation coefficient.

The strength of the relationship is indicated by the numeric value of the correlation coefficient. The closer the calculated correlation coefficient is to 1, the stronger is the relationship between the variables. A coefficient of 0 is the weakest indicator of a relationship and indicates that no relationship exists.

Regression analysis attempts to determine if any causal relationship exists between the dependent variable (sales) and one or more independent variables. If a relationship is found, then the value of the dependent variable (sales) can be predicted based on specific values of the independent variable(s). There are many forms of regression analysis, but the least complex is simple linear regression.[10] Here, the relationship between the dependent variable (sales which is denoted by y) and an independent variable (x) is assumed to be represented by a straight line.

As is the case for correlation analysis, regression analysis can be a powerful forecasting method. Care must be taken to ensure that the underlying relationships being analyzed are in force and will remain so for the time period being forecasted.

Box-Jenkins Method

The **Box-Jenkins method** is becoming one of the more widely used sales forecasting techniques. Although the method is still unfamiliar to some companies, many firms that try it use it on an ongoing basis. The Box-Jenkins method provides information allowing for the particular model to be selected that best approximates the data of the particular company. This approach differs from the other forecasting techniques in that it does not pick a mathematical model on an a priori basis. Rather, a model is tentatively identified, checked for adequacy, and then used to generate the sales forecast.

The Box-Jenkins method uses three general models to analyze past sales and then provide the sales forecast: autoregressive, moving average, and autoregressive-moving average.[11] As their names imply, each of the models is similar to the forecasting techniques previously discussed. Their use in the Box-Jenkins

SELL!NG

THE FRONT LINES OF BUSINESS

Stretched Thin in Textiles

Linda Corman

Consolidations have cut deeply into the home textiles business. But if you're creative, there's still room to grow.

Salespeople wanted. No cold calling. No prospecting. New business not a priority. That's how the want ad would read for a sales job in home textiles—if there were any jobs available. Doesn't sound much like sales? Well, in the shrinking world of sheets, towels, and bedding, the job of selling has become one of servicing. Of keeping old clients, not signing new ones. Consolidation and cutbacks among manufacturers and retailers alike have left fewer and fewer salespeople handling fewer and fewer accounts. And the people who have held on to their jobs long enough to make the adjustment to this new world either love it or hate it.

Mergers and acquisitions have put many textiles salespeople out of work and have heaped more responsibility on those who have survived. When Fieldcrest bought Cannon in 1986 and WestPoint Pepperell bought J.P. Stevens in 1989, both companies cut their sales forces in half. At the same time, retailers have merged or gone out of business, forcing other manufacturers to reduce their forces. To top it off, consumer sales of towels, sheets, and comforters have leveled off. The end result? Job opportunities are few and far between, with the largest companies hiring one or two inexperienced salespeople a year. Training programs have fallen by the wayside. Although reps are focusing on fewer customers, they still feel stretched thin. Instead of drumming up new business, they are charged with growing the accounts they already have.

"Ninety-eight percent of the time is really account maintenance and growth. There are very few cold calls," says Michael Hillard, national sales manager for the mass bedding division of Fieldcrest Cannon.

Instead, reps are expected to coordinate all facets of the business, from marketing, packaging, dye, and manufacturing cycles to shipping. "The challenge is keeping 1,000 stores in stock on 1,200 items," says Bill Dowling, a Minneapolis-based independent rep for Springs Industries. "Especially with 90-day lead times." Dowling spends most of his time updating sales projections and tweaking computer runs to obtain forecasts for products that have no historical data.

"You get your piece of real estate and you maintain it," says Dowling, summing up the job.

John Ralph, vice president-West Coast for Fieldcrest Cannon and a veteran of home textile sales, misses the excitement of "real" selling. "In the old days, we were opening new accounts, rocking and rolling with selling goods," says Ralph.

For others, the change in the industry is welcome. Jason Aryeh, account manager for the department and specialty store division of WestPoint Stevens, prefers dealing with the same accounts every day and being a resource for his customers. He is relieved to have left behind the aggressive tactics of his first sales job, in real estate.

Home textiles still have the cachet of being part of the fashion industry, and salespeople enjoy keeping up with the trends, anticipating new ones, and trying to persuade their companies to produce what's hot. There's a certain satisfaction in selling a textured, tangible product. "It appeals to the senses, so it generates feedback. You get an emotional response. That's fun," says Mark Bakutis, vice president of sales-department stores for Home Innovations, a mill in Mooresville, N.C.

To some reps, the industry has become just another commodities business; others see it as an opportunity to be creative. Customization, a growing trend in the industry, helps differentiate between products. As Patrick Hayes, national account executive for WestPoint Stevens, points out, the possibilities are endless. Towels can differ by size, weight, color, and by their decorative dobbies (the borders). Packaging can also vary, not only in design but in content. Sheets, comforters, shams, and dust ruffles can be packaged together in any number of combinations.

"I think it's a terrific industry," says Hayes. "It's not just like selling 12-ounce toothpaste for Procter & Gamble: 'This is the price, this is the quantity, these are the ship dates.' You can be much more creative, resourceful."

Creativity does not always come easily, however. To deliver a new fashion or customized product line, salespeople must first sell their own companies—from top executives down through merchandising, service, and mill managers. Pushing a mill that has always been manufacturing-driven to become customer-driven might be the greatest challenge of all. "If I need more colors or faster turn times or certain packaging, manufacturing's attitude is, 'We've been doing it this way for 100 years. We're not going to do it that way,'" says one salesperson from a major mill. "That's a challenge. Turning a big ship is tough."

The pressure to create new custom lines has been steadily mounting in recent years. It began when the mass merchants decided that they wanted to sell some brand names. Then, as the brands that had been in department stores exclusively began to appear on mass merchants' shelves, the department stores sought exclusive lines to maintain their edge. "They all want different products and packaging, and they all want to be first," says Robert Gehm, vice president of mass merchants for WestPoint Stevens.

In home textiles, there are three main customer groups—mass merchants, department and specialty stores, and so-called private ticket customers—and sales forces are divided along the same lines. These channels carry equal status and pay, so preference for one over another is largely a matter of taste. For many, like Gehm of WestPoint, selling to mass merchants is the plum job. Mass merchants have risen in stature as they have upgraded their merchandise. Now, as the channel with the most growth potential, it is the focus of most manufacturers' resources.

"I'd much rather be where the action is," says Gehm. "My division is 40 percent of the company."

Selling to mass merchants often is a team effort, so reps get to work closely with such departments as planning, customer service, logistics, and traffic. They also have fewer details to handle, since mass retailers standardize the operations of their stores.

Sales to specialty and department stores are more individualized and benefit from high product turnover. A rep who misses out on one buy can get back in sooner. While department stores are fold-

ing and merging, specialty outlets and catalogues are proliferating. Selling private ticket or "custom brands," meanwhile, affords the most opportunity to create products, special packaging, styling, and special shipping arrangements.

If home textiles is short on growth, it is long on growth opportunities. Because salespeople engage in a wide range of activities, they have a wide range of career options, both in sales management and in other areas. "Sales is a direct route to anywhere in the company because you're involved in all aspects," says Gary Droeger, Western regional sales manager for WestPoint Stevens.

And while the business has contracted over the years, it's unlikely to disappear altogether. Says Fieldcrest Cannon's Hillard, "I can't imagine there will be something that will replace towels. It's a staying industry."

Reprinted with the permission of SELL!NG magazine.

method allows the data pattern underlying past sales to be systematically evaluated so that the correct pattern can be identified and the best forecasting model selected.

The problems with the Box-Jenkins method center on the availability of information and costs. Often, in a particular forecasting problem, the method cannot be used because too little sales data exist to provide a basis for model selection. In addition, in smaller or start-up companies, computer algorithms often are not available to determine the best parameters for the model.

Implementing Sales Forecasts

In order to ensure that the best sales forecasts will occur and then be used in marketing and management decision making, management should have a positive attitude about forecasting. This attitude is in part dependent on management's familiarity with forecasting techniques and understanding of the usefulness of the resulting forecasts. The implementation of the sales forecasts as well as a general forecasting procedure in a firm can require a behavior change. Sometimes, not only must the behavior of marketing and corporate managers who use the forecast be changed but that of the preparer of the forecast as well.

SALES BUDGETS

One of the major responsibilities of sales managers is to prepare sales budgets and monitor actual versus projected expenditures.[12] A **sales budget** is a financial sales plan indicating the manner in which resources and selling efforts need to be allocated to achieve the forecasted level of sales. The various levels of sales that can be obtained with a given budget are then evaluated in light of the expenditures required to reach the sales level forecasted. The sales budget serves three primary purposes: planning, coordination, and control of selling activities.

Planning

To achieve a particular sales forecast, the selling tasks and support services that are needed must be specified. These tasks and their estimated costs are determined by the sales manager for a particular period of time. Although the time period is usually one year, it can be as short as three to six months.

Coordination

To forecast sales and positively impact the profits of the company, the forecast must be closely integrated with other marketing and financial budgets. All budgets, such as the promotional budget or the amount set aside for bad debts, must reflect the sales budget and the needed selling activities that are forecasted for the period of time.[13]

Control

Sales budgets also establish the financial benchmark for evaluating the actual results. An alert sales manager constantly monitors the budget, looking for any significant variations—the difference between actual results and budgeted (projected) results—that may be occurring.

PREPARING THE SALES BUDGET

The preparation of the sales budget, although considered a onerous task by most sales managers, is an opportunity for careful resource allocation and profit planning. Several steps are typically followed in preparing most sales budgets.

The first step is to review the previous year's outcome, beginning with the previous selling period. The variations that occur most frequently should be noted. These usually center on such line items as salaries, direct selling expenses, commissions and bonuses, in-house support, benefit packages, promotional materials, and achievements. Upon completing the review, the sales manager establishes sales goals and objectives and communicates them to all managers. Every relevant employee should be included in helping to establish the goals and objectives and other items in the budgetary process. This involvement helps to commit individuals to the budget, and this commitment will assist in its successful implementation.

Any problems or specific market opportunities are identified and specific resources set aside in the budget to deal with these unique aspects. Then an initial budget is prepared that allocates specific selling efforts and resources to particular activities, customers, product lines, and sales territories. Although the initial budget should be as accurate as possible, it is usually revised several times before the final budget emerges. Finally, a budget presentation is developed and presented to upper management. This presentation is usually a sales job in itself, particularly if increased funds are being requested. As with any sales presentation, a successful budget presentation requires a succinct summary of the proposed budget along with alternative scenarios.

The last step is implementing the budget and closely monitoring the results. Close monitoring allows resulting variations to be dealt with quickly, enabling budget goals to be met. Although it is the responsibility of each group to stay within its budget, the sales manager is ultimately responsible for ensuring that the overall sales budget is met.

SALES QUOTAS

After the sales force and sales budget have been prepared, the sales manager needs to establish specific goals or quotas for each selling activity and develop plans that will help salespeople meet these quotas. Quotas are usually established in terms of sales volume, but they can also be done for gross margins, selling expenses, profits, or a combination of these. The established quotas are used as standards to indicate the desired level of performance of the individual salesperson, sales territory, district, and/or region. Quotas are very useful in providing goals, controlling the activities of the sales force, controlling the selling expenses, improving the compensation package, and evaluating performance.

Providing Goals

Given the competitive nature of salespeople, it is important that a benchmark figure be established for distinguishing success and failure. The quota provides such a quantitative measure of selling ability and should be the goal of each salesperson. It is, therefore, most important that the quota be realistic and attainable. When attainable quotas are established, they motivate the sales force.

Controlling Activity

Because salespeople are responsible for obtaining the established quotas, these quotas, in effect, enable management to direct and control the selling activities. By establishing a specific number of sales calls per day, a specific amount of a product to be sold, or a specific number of new customer calls, the sales manager can clearly guide the activities of the sales force so that the objectives of the company are achieved within the budget.

Controlling Selling Expenses

Similarly, quotas can be used to control the amount of money spent on meals, lodging, and entertainment. This helps to control the costs of selling and keep them at a minimum. If the quotas are not met or exceeded, the increased expenses can be charged against the salesperson's compensation as well as being noted in the next performance review.

Improving Compensation

Sales quotas can play a role in the salesperson's overall compensation package. In some companies, for example, the quota must be exceeded before a commission is paid. For example, a salesperson can be given a quota of $300,000 in sales for the year and receive a 7 percent commission on every sale above the quota. On a sale of $400,000, the salesperson receives a commission of 7 percent $\times$ ($400,000 – $300,000), or $7000. This type of quota provides a strong incentive for significant sales performance because there is no cap on the amount of commissions that can be earned.

Another company may use a different approach to compensation through quotas. The quota in this case is the basis for calculating the bonus and is usually set quite high and the bonus limited to a maximum amount. If the salesperson does not make the quota, the percentage of the quota is calculated with the bonus set at the percentage of the maximum bonus amount. For example, if a salesperson can earn $4000 for obtaining his or her quota of $300,000 in sales but achieves sales of only $250,000 (83 percent of the quota), the salesperson receives a bonus of 83 percent $\times$ $4000, or $3320.

Quotas can also be used for sales contests, which are excellent short-term incentive tools. The quota for sales contests should be established so that each salesperson has an equal opportunity of winning. A well-designed contest that everyone can win can positively impact sales performance in a particular time period.

Evaluating Performance

Probably the best-known purpose of a sales quota is to measure the performance of the salesperson. However, care must be taken in using a quota as a measure. If a sales quota is exceeded, this either indicates that the salesperson is working extra hard or that the quota is too low. Similarly, a quota that is not met may indicate that the salesperson is not working hard, the territory has problems, or the quota is too high.

TYPES OF QUOTAS

Five basic types of quotas are used by companies: sales volume quotas, financial quotas, expense quotas, sales activity quotas, and combination quotas. The company can use any or all of these quotas, depending on the product, industry, and specific company situation.

Sales Volume Quotas

By far the most commonly used quotas are those based on sales volume; this usually means dollar sales, not unit sales volume. Sales volume quotas are ordinarily based on sales of particular products, sales of new products, or sales to new customers. These quotas are used in performance evaluation by providing the minimum expected performance level during a specific period of time.

Sales volume quotas measured on either a dollar or unit basis are established for a specific period of time, usually for a product or product line, customer or prospect type, or geographic area. The smaller the marketing unit and the shorter the time period, the better the quota is. Using a small marketing unit provides better control and can be combined, when needed, across many units. Unless sales are seasonal, quotas should be established on a monthly or quarterly basis.

Dollar versus Unit Sales Quotas. A question frequently arises about using either a dollar or unit basis for quotas. Both are used by companies and each provides advantages to the sales manager. Sales volume quotas expressed in dollars are the usual measure for product activity and are easily understood by the salesperson and management. They are particularly useful when the salesperson is responsible for selling many different products because a dollar sales volume figure can be established for groups of products. Dollar sales volume figures also make it easier to evaluate and calculate the comparative financial ratios, such as selling costs to quotas and selling expenses to sales, that are used in sales and company evaluation.

When only a few products are sold, unit sales volume quotas are more useful, particularly during rapid price increases or decreases. When there is extreme price volatility, as, for example, during the oil price fluctuations in the late 1980s and early 1990s, dollar sales volume quotas are extremely inappropriate and may lead to frustration on the part of salespeople as well as poor performance appraisal. The unit sales volume basis is more appropriate when products are expensive. A quota of $500,000 may appear more difficult to obtain than a quota of 10 units at $50,000 per unit.

Basis for Sales Volume Quotas. The basis for establishing sales volume quotas is past sales, sales potential, market estimates, or a combination of these. By far the easiest (and most frequently used) method for setting sales volume quotas is to base them on past sales in the territory. The quota is established by increasing last year's quota by the percentage amount the market should increase. If the market is expected to increase 5 percent next year, the quota for each salesperson is last year's quota plus 5 percent, or 105 percent of last year's quota.

A second basis for establishing a sales volume quota is to use the sales manager's estimate of market opportunity and the effort needed by the salesperson. This procedure uses the company's sales forecast, not the sales potential. The salesperson has an input into the quota by providing an estimate of the territory's potential. The sales manager then adjusts this estimate upward or downward, taking into account such factors as the ability and characteristics of the salesperson. This new estimate is adjusted again based on the company's future marketing plans. The sales manager then converts these estimates into sales quotas, which are summed over all salespeople to determine the company's total sales forecast.

Some companies that are very small or very new base their company's sale estimate on market estimates. In these companies, top management establishes the quotas, which are agreed to by the salespeople using one of two different methods. In the first method, the total company sales forecast is divided into territorial estimates and adjusted accordingly. Recognizing that adjustments at the corporate level are different than adjustments at the territorial level, the second method first adjusts the company's forecasted sales based on future company marketing efforts. These adjusted estimates are then broken down into territories and adjusted accordingly.

Financial Quotas

Financial quotas are used when a company is interested in impacting and controlling gross margins or net profit. The quotas indicate to the salesperson that the company prefers to make profits rather than sell larger volumes. Financial quotas help modify the salesperson's natural tendency to sell as much product as possible regardless of the profit. A salesperson may be doing the company a disservice and minimizing the opportunity of the company to earn higher profits from higher margin items if too much time is spent on less profitable, easy-to-sell products. Salespeople also tend to spend more time with customers with whom they feel more comfortable regardless of the profitability of the customer. By placing a quota on net profits, salespeople are encouraged to spend more selling time on more profitable products and with more profitable customers.

In emphasizing profit, financial quotas do have some disadvantages. First, financial quotas are harder for salespeople to understand. Because the net profit goal is composed of a range of products and their respective margins, it is difficult for salespeople, at any given point of time, to determine how well they are doing. This can cause frustration and even a lack of motivation. Second, it takes more time to calculate the net profit, which leads to additional clerical and administrative costs. Finally, because a salesperson's salary, based on the net profit, is much more sensitive to various external and internal factors, financial quotas may be viewed as less fair.

Expense Quotas

Expense quotas are used to highlight the selling costs to salespeople and therefore help control those costs. To try to contain the rapidly escalating costs of travel, food, and lodging, a sales manager can tie reimbursement of these expenses directly to the sales volume or compensation plan. For example, a salesperson may be allowed 4 percent of the sales volume as an expense account. Another way is simply to determine maximum amounts that can be spent per day on food and accommodations. A third method is to use an expense-to-sales ratio in determining the amount of expenses allowed. Because a salesperson's job is to sell, when using expense quotas, care must be taken that the sales performance is not hindered just so costs can be contained. Also, territory differences need to be taken into account as some territories are more expensive to operate than other territories. Each salesperson's expense quota must be based on a realistic assessment of the territory.

Sales Activity Quotas

Because salespeople are given latitude to plan and carry out their daily activities, some companies require each salesperson to follow and meet an established activity quota. Activity quotas may be particularly beneficial for younger, inexperienced salespeople. In setting appropriate activity quotas, managers must first determine the most important activities of the sales force. These activities can include making sales calls, establishing new accounts, obtaining better distribution for products, launching new products, selling a merchandising or advertising program, and demonstrating products. Managers then evaluate each activity to determine an average completion time. Finally, they assign each activity a frequency that will become the target level of performance (see Table 15-7).

TABLE 15-7 Commonly Used Activity Quotas

- Number of calls made
- Number of sales calls on present customers
- Number of sales calls on new customers
- Number of demonstrations
- Number of service calls
- Number of training sessions given
- Number of store advertisements sold
- Number of new accounts established

Establishing activity quotas allows salespeople to better plan their daily activities and routing and make more efficient use of their time. This allows management to control and reward salespeople for performing tasks related to but not involved in a direct sale, such as rearranging a shelf in a supermarket or calling on customers who purchase infrequently. To ensure that appropriate attention and effort are given to achieving sales volume, activity quotas are frequently used in conjunction with sales volume quotas. This eliminates the problem of not focusing on the task of selling while rewarding salespeople for undertaking many nonselling functions.

Combination Quotas

Combination quotas, such as the activity and sales volume quotas, are used when the sales manager wants to control several aspects of the selling task. When a single index of measurement is desired, managers can convert the measurement unit of each quota into points. This can be accomplished most easily by computing the percentage (which now has no unit of measurement) by a weight indicating the importance of the quota to management. An example is given in Table 15-8. In the table the sales manager has assigned weights of 4 to sales volume, 3 to net profit, and 1 to the number of advertisements obtained. Kelly achieved the quota and has the best record in terms of number of advertisements obtained, but Kary outperformed Kelly overall, with a score of 87.75 versus Kelly's score of 75.13. Obviously, Kary was better in both of the more important areas of sales volume and net profits.

Like net profit quotas, combination quotas are somewhat more difficult for salespeople to understand, thereby making it difficult for them to gauge their performance levels. Despite this disadvantage, combination quotas are an excellent way for the sales manager to direct and control the sales force on an activity or individual product basis.

TABLE 15-8 Use of Combination Quotes

Salesperson: Kelly Jones

Area	Quota	Actual Salesperson:	% of Quota	Weight	Quota × Weight
Volume	$200,000	$180,000	75	4	300
Net profit	$75,000	$50,000	67	3	201
Number of advertisements obtained	20	200	100	1	100
					601

Salesperson: Kary Hughes

Area	Quota	Actual Salesperson:	% of Quota	Weight	Quota × Weight
Volume	$300,000	$280,000	93	4	372
Net profit	$150,000	$120,000	80	3	240
Number of advertisements obtained	20	200	90	1	90
		18			702

Score: Kelly—601/8 = 75.13
Kary—702/8 = 87.75

ADMINISTERING QUOTAS

Regardless of the quota system employed, it will be ineffective unless it is properly and carefully administered. In order to ensure that salespeople do not become anxious and nervous, sales managers must establish realistic and understandable quotas.

Establish Realistic Quotas

Since successful sales management involves motivating salespeople, managers should remember that salespeople are only motivated by quotas that are attainable and resulting rewards that are valuable. Quotas are established based on different theories of motivation and attainability. Some companies establish an average quota and reward salespeople based on the percentage of quota achieved, believing that salespeople should be motivated to continue to work hard. Other companies establish high quotas and reward salespeople for performance above these quotas believing that salespeople should be rewarded only for excellent performance. This type of company usually has a higher base salary for the salesperson than the first company to help compensate for the potential difference in earnings. Regardless of the one used, it is important that the sales force view the quota system as fair, realistic, and attainable.

Establish Understandable Quotas

Part of the problem of quotas lies in their perception. Giving a clear explanation of the quotas and the methods by which they were established helps gain the cooperation and acceptance of the sales force. The sales manager can help the sales force understand quotas by including each salesperson in the quota-setting procedure and ensuring that each is informed on a regular basis regarding performance relative to quotas as well as any changes in the procedure. A clear understanding allows the quota system to be an effective method for motivating, evaluating, and controlling the sales force.

CHAPTER SUMMARY

Forecasting sales is an important area of sales planning. Managers must take into account both controllable and uncontrollable factors when making the forecast and the sale plan. Good information can be obtained for estimating consumer or industrial demand from a wide variety of reference material. Specific sales forecasting methods include: jury of executive opinion, sales force composite, buyer expectation method, Delphi technique, scenario technique, regression analysis, time series analysis, and the Box-Jenkins method.

   Sales budgets and quotas are important aspects of strategic planning to assist in the planning, evaluating, and control of selling activities. Preparation of a sales budget involves reviewing the activities and results of the previous years, establishing sales goals and objectives, identifying any problems and market opportunities, preparing an initial budget, making a presentation to upper management, implementing the budget, and monitoring the results. Sales quotas are helpful in establishing objectives and monitoring the results of the established budget. The four basic types of quotas most frequently used are sales volume, financial, sales activity, and combination quotas. Any quota system must be carefully implemented to obtain optimum results.

KEY TERMS

Box-Jenkins method, p. 358
buyers' expectation method, p. 352
buying power index (BPI), p. 348
coincident (simultaneous) indicators,
   p. 348
controllable factors, p. 347
curve fitting, p. 356

Delphi method, p. 353
exponential smoothing, p. 357
jury of executive opinion, p. 350
lagging indicators, p. 348
leading indicators, p. 347
market potential, p. 348
market size, p. 348

CHAPTER QUESTIONS

1. Because budgeting is one of the most important areas of the sales manager's job, discuss the need for flexibility in the budgeting process and the problems involved in budgeting flexibility, including evaluation.

2. A company that wholesales office furniture has the following pay structure for its salespeople: salary plus a fixed percentage of sales revenue for expenses. The sales manager of the company believes that this approach provides good incentive because a salesperson who wants more expense money to attract new accounts and increase old ones must achieve more sales. Comment on the appropriateness of this plan in terms of the budget and salesperson motivation. Devise a better plan if you think an improvement is needed.

3. You are a sales manager for a company in Cleveland, Ohio, who must establish a sales budget. Using the latest edition of the "Sales Manager's Budget Planner" (a special report of *Sales & Marketing Management*) or some other source, determine the costs (including transportation) of a three-day trip for one salesperson in each of the following three cities: Boston, Dallas, and St. Louis.

4. Design a general quota system for a company with well-established products and territories and one for a new company with new products and territories. Both companies are in the same industry. Compare the two quota systems.

5. If a company uses manufacturer's representatives on a commission-only basis, should these reps have quotas established by the company? Discuss the advantages and disadvantages of these quotas.

6. Discuss the length of a good quota period and the advantages and disadvantages of setting monthly quotas, quarterly quotas, and yearly quotas.

7. Discuss the impact of a quota that is set too high on a salesperson's job satisfaction, morale, and performance. Discuss the impact of quotas set too low for the same three variables.

8. For each of the following products, discuss the factors that you would use in estimating market potential (be specific):
   a. Swatch watches
   b. Riding lawn mowers

    c. Large industrial machinery for the plastics industry

    d. Bayer aspirin

    e. Laptop computers

    f. McDonalds hamburgers

    g. Yoplait yogurt

    h. Michael Jordan–autographed basketballs

9. As sales manager, you are given the responsibility of forecasting the sales for next year of a new cake mix that will be introduced next week. Discuss the factors and the process you would use in forecasting the sales for this product.

10. Your company produces a regional beer and has the following five-year sales history: $52,743, $61,920, $67,320, $72,980, and $79,120. What techniques would you use to forecast sales for next year? Justify your choice.

11. Discuss the benefits and problems of having each salesperson estimate the buying potential and next year's sales of each account for each of the firm's 20 product lines.

NOTES

1. Offbeat options for any budget. *Sales & Marketing Management* (April 1992), 88–96.

2. Ibid., p. 89.

3. For a detailed discussion of various types of forecasting techniques, see Spyros Makridakis and Steven C. Wheelwright, *Forecasting: Methods and applications* (New York: Wiley, 1978); Spyros Makridakis, *Handbook of forecasters: A manager's guide*, 2nd ed. (New York: Wiley, 1987); and Frank H. Eby, Jr., and William J. O'Neill, *The management of sales forecasting* (Lexington, MA: Heath, 1977).

4. A discussion of the advantages and disadvantages of this technique as well as the sales force composite and buyers' expectation method can be found in *Forecasting sales* (New York: National Industrial Conference Board, 1964), 13, 21, and 31, respectively.

5. The Delphi technique was devised by the RAND Corporation to forecast the likely state of technology in the future. It has since been adopted for use in sales forecasting and in marketing decisions. See Norman C. Dalkey, *The Delphi method: An experimental study of group opinion* (Santa Monica, CA: RAND Corp., 1969); Marvin Jolson and Gerald Rossow, The Delphi method in marketing decision marketing. *Journal of Marketing Research* 8 (November 1971), 443–448; and C. L. Join, Delphi—Forecast with experts' opinions. *Journal of Business Forecasting* 4 (Winter 1985–1986), 22–23.

6. Charles I. Clarke and Lawrence L. Schkade, *Statistical methods for business decisions* (Cincinnati, OH: South-Western, 1969), 657.

7. The moving average is often centered at the midpoint of the series being averaged. For the case at hand, the 11.8 moving average would be the midpoint of the series being averaged. A discussion of centering can be found in Charles W. Gross and Robin I. Peterson, *Business forecasting* (Boston: Houghton Mifflin, 1976), 125–142.

8. For a thorough discussion of exponential smoothing and its use in business forecasting, see Robert G. Brown, *Smoothing, forecasting and prediction of discrete time series* (Englewood Cliffs, NJ: Prentice Hall, 1963); and Cyril Anson, How to use exponential smoothing techniques in sales forecasting. *Scientific Business* (May 1965), 15–23.

9. The technique used for correlation analysis discussed here is usually Pearson product-moment correlation. Other correlation coefficients include Spearman's rank correlation coefficient and Kendall's coefficient of concordance.

10. For a discussion of regression analysis, see J. R. Draper and H. Smith, *Applied regression analysis* (New York: Wiley, 1966); and Gross and Peterson, *Business forecasting*, 80–117.

11. A discussion of this method can be found in Mokridakis and Wheelwright, *Forecasting*, 131–143.

12. For examples of interesting ways companies establish budgets and quotas, see Creating budgets: Is a shop at Heublein. *Sales and Marketing Management* (January 1987), 76–77; Robert A. Morris, How to manage your sales force. *Inc.* 12 (January 1990), 120–122; and Michael Barrier, The power of a good idea. *Nation's Business* 78 (November 1990), 34–36.

13. For a discussion of one type of expenses—automation expenses—see Donald J. Plumley, All right, how much will it cost. *Sales and Marketing Management* (December 1989), 50–55.

SUGGESTED READINGS

Chase, Charles W., Jr. Forecasting computer products. *Journal of Business Forecasting* (Spring 1991), 2–6.

> There are two categories for forecasting sales—quantitative and qualitative methods. A step-by-step account to forecasting sales is given. The main thrust of the article centers on gathering appropriate independent variables and data to figure and accurately forecast each product or brand.

Davis, Mark M., and Paul D. Berger. Sales forecasting in a retail service environment. *Journal of Business Forecasting* (Winter 1988–1989), 8–11, 17.

> A forecast can be made by assessing the historical information for a day, month, or year. Monthly data are useful for companies that pay their employees on a monthly or bimonthly basis; however, the day of the week is generally seen as the most important forecast information. An hourly sales and item requirement within each day can be examined after forecasting the total dollar sales for each weekday has been completed. This can be computed by taking a weighted average of the fraction of total daily dollar sales for each hour of each day within the previous three-week interval. The three-week sales for the indicated hour are then added and divided by the total sum of the daily sales values.

Easingwood, Christopher J. An analogical approach to the long term forecasting of major new product sales. *International Journal of Forecasting* (1989), 69–82.

> Diffusion modeling is important for making an adoption and forecast analysis. Product diffusion patterns vary among product groups. Therefore, a new product's success or failure may be predicted. If a location of a diffusion map can be pinpointed, it is possible to make accurate projections.

Filip, Christine S. Beyond the crystal ball: Forecasting sales results. *Sales & Marketing Management* (July 1990), 10, 12.

> A sales manager can create a reliable forecast by using appointment calendars of each member of the sales force and a list of possible closes and revenues. The manager can then evaluate the sales personnel's performance to ensure that they have handled each case appropriately. By comparing these two reports and discussing the information with the salespeople, a sales manager can better make an accurate sales forecast.

Gross, Charles W., and Jeffrey E. Sohl. Disaggregation methods to expedite product line forecasting. *Journal of Forecasting* (May–June 1990), 233–254.

> An outline of problems that develop when forecasting sales within a company that has many product lines is developed. Three desegregated models are shown that help locate the necessary desegregated methodologies and compare the accuracy of individual products' forecast to desegregated totals. Twenty-one disaggregation schemes are studied.

Hamlin, Henry A., and Jason O'Neal. Sales forecasting without tears. *CFO: The Magazine for Senior Financial Executives* (June 1991), 56–61.

> A computer spreadsheet is not always a reliable way to forecast a company's budget. The template given can be changed in order to make any alterations that a company finds necessary. This template is simple to use and produces an accurate budget that can be changed according to any alterations made in percentages.

Silham, Peter A. Using quarterly sales and margins to predict corporate earnings: A time series perspective. *Journal of Business and Finance Accounting* (Spring 1989), 131–141.

> The effects of income announcements on stock prices and the net impact of accounting decisions on the time series behavior and predictive ability of quarterly earnings can be studied by quarterly univariate earnings (UE). It is also possible to predict earnings by multiplying predicted sales (PS) by predicted margins (PM).

Triantis, John E., Praces Libsci, and Robert A. Forrest. Forecasting sales of products with asymmetric demands. *Journal of Business Forecasting* (Summer 1989), 20–23.

> An asymmetric product demand occurs when the quantity demand remains the same if a product increases or decreases in price. A traditional demand model estimated with ordinary least squares (OLS) is unable to handle asymmetry in demand responses associated with price fluctuations. OLS models are able to show demand asymmetry with little alterations. This can be done by utilizing the Wolffram technique, the varying parameter regression technique, or two other Laspeyre's price Indices in the demand model.

Wright, David J. Decision support oriented sales forecasting. *Journal of the Academy of Marketing Science* (Fall 1988), 71–78.

> When using alternative forecasting methods, it is essential to look at the factors involved in each individual situation. It is not always a good idea to assess alternative forecasting methods only according to forecast accuracy. An example illustration is presented using two companies in terms of sales forecasts for market share and control.

Chapter 16 _____

Rewarding the Sales Force

_____

OPENING SCENARIO

It was not a good day for Phil Kary, sales manager of Dumas Makt., H.K. One of the company's salespeople had just turned in his two-week notice and was going to work for another company. Also, Kary had heard rumors that his best salesperson, Marcia Dubrowski, was considering another job opportunity. What was causing this exodus? Was it just the usual sales turnovers that occurred in the industry? Were there problems with the company's management? Or was it the company's reward system for its sales force? Kary made a note to review the company's compensation package that afternoon to make sure the combination plan of salary plus commission was on par with those of other companies. He wanted his salespeople to receive good compensation. Perhaps there was a problem in the company's fringe benefit package. Kary knew he might have to make some adjustments given the changes occurring in the tax laws and health-care delivery system. No matter what the problem. Kary knew that he had to identify it and develop a solution. The sales force was one of the company's most important assets.

Chapter Objectives

After reading this chapter, you should be able to

- Understand the three basic compensation plans.
- Select the appropriate compensation method for a particular organizational circumstance.
- Understand methods for controlling expenses.

INTRODUCTION

Motivating the sales force is addressed regularly by most companies. Establishing the correct compensation package is a critical factor in obtaining the sales and profits desired. Most executives feel that money is the most important part of any incentive plan, creating the excitement and desire to obtain the goals established. According to R. J. Cortopassi, sales manager of Carl Eric Johnson in Georgia, "Any program without a direct financial return will not succeed. Fixed cash bonuses may be very time consuming to administer, but they work."[1] Suzette Key, regional sales manager of Action Telcom in Texas, suggests, "If you really want to see people produce, try dropping or freezing base salaries, increasing commission margins, and adding bonuses."

At Business Interiors, the entire sales team is rewarded when it achieves certain profit levels. According to John Sample, "It's like an instant reward. If they hit it today, then tomorrow they'll be rewarded. There are multiple levels to it, and there's an ultimate goal for team performance and profitability. You still have to make sure there are individual rewards for the salespeople who are actually selling, causing the stuff to happen." At Robinson Brick, a part of every employee's performance bonus is based on the bottom line and/or customer survey responses.

Sales incentives take a wide variety of forms, some of which do not cost a great deal of money. According to Larry Cooper, regional sales manager for Tyson Foods, Arizona, "It does not take a lot of money to get salespeople motivated. Many of these guys are not high-income earners, so a chance to win $500 extra means something."

Regardless of the compensation plan, two basic rules apply: Keep it simple, and review it periodically. Complicated compensation plans create more problems than motivation. According to Donald Quinn, area manager of Exide in Kansas, "The least successful program I was ever involved with was a quarterly incentive that was so complicated it was no longer an incentive. The simple monthly cash bonus based on percent of sales target (and profitability) attained for the month is what I've found to be most effective with my salespeople." James Maule, general manager of Penn Advertising, Pennsylvania, concurs, "These things don't have to be elaborate at all. If you want to jazz it up, you can use the idea of a salesperson of the month contest with, say, a $400 award every month leading to salesperson of the year with a $1,000 award."

Compensation needs to be reviewed regularly with the appropriate changes implemented. Delta Dental has modified its compensation yearly since it changed the way it does business. This can create some problems and stress in the sales force, admits the company's CEO, Bob Hunter, who feels that the sales force accepts changes "when they understand and participate in goal setting." Presently Delta Dental has different compensation plans for different salespeople. The company's four salespeople who were responsible for opening doors are paid a small base salary and various commissions tied to regional goals for new accounts, a group goal for adequate rates, and overall corporate goals. The five account executives who take over the account once it is opened from these four salespeople are compensated for maintaining existing business. They receive a higher base salary and are eligible for three possible bonuses: a bonus for retention, a bonus for profitability, and a bonus for corporate goals. Whenever the compensation plan undergoes change, stress and lost sales can occur. When the compensation plan was changed at Business Interiors, the company underwent a three-month phase-in with the salespeople going through training and retraining. According to John Sample, "We took a hit in pay and some sales. Anytime you make a change like that, you've got to be willing to take the hit."

Besides psychological motivations, financial compensation is an important aspect of salesperson motivation. The top salesperson should be one of the highest paid individuals in an organization, earning more than the sales manager and upper-level managers and, in some instances, even more than the president of the company. Given the importance of salespeople, and their potential for high earnings, an organization must design and administer an appropriate financial compensation plan. This chapter looks at basic compensation methods and their advantages and disadvantages, as well as other expenses in selling and their respective compensation and control.

IMPORTANCE OF SALES COMPENSATION

Sales compensation is an issue that no company can ignore. No president, consultant, or academic has been able to come up with a compensation system, because too many variables are involved, such as the corporate culture, the type of salesperson, the industry, the customers, and the need for support services. As incentives for salespeople, compensation plans are used to increase the mix of products sold, increase gross margins of sales, retain customers, increase the number of new accounts, reach team or company goals, or any combination of these.

In establishing an appropriate compensation plan, companies must recognize that salespeople are the critical, and often the only, link with customers. The well-being and happiness of the sales force are important in achieving forecasted sales and company profits. One of the key ingredients to the well-being and effort of the sales force is compensation. Not only does the compensation plan contribute to well-being, it indicates the appropriateness of the performance level and directs the activities of salespeople. Because compensation is by far the largest share of all direct selling costs—about 79 percent—a good compensation plan is needed to maximize the return for the company's investment.

Actual sales compensation plans vary, depending on the industry, company, product, and market situation. Although sales force compensation costs make up about 22 percent of total sales in the direct marketing industry for companies such as Avon and Amway, they are only 4 percent of sales costs in the retail food industry for companies such as Pillsbury and General Mills. Despite this wide variation, three basic methods of sales compensation are used:

Straight-commission plan. The individual receives an amount that varies with results, which are usually measured in terms of sales or sales and profits.

Straight-salary plan. The individual receives a fixed amount of money at fixed intervals (usually weekly or biweekly).

Combination compensation plan. The individual receives a fixed amount of money and an additional amount based on performance in the form of a commission and/or bonus.

Given the hypercompetitive atmosphere of today's markets, and the broader, more international product lines, companies are finding that a single compensation method is difficult to apply universally throughout the company.[2] Multiple methods are used so that products can be sold, customers satisfied, and top salespeople appropriately rewarded.

Customer satisfaction is an important part of implementing a compensation package, because the level of customer satisfaction is negatively affected by high turnover of salespeople. Only with a solid and competitive compensation plan can companies retain and motivate top-performing salespeople. More than any other employees, salespeople respond to monetary compensation. Salaries and compensation packages vary greatly, with some top salespeople earning $1.5 million a year. (The salaries and total compensation packages of salespeople are surveyed yearly by *Sales & Marketing Management*.) Salespeople, like entrepreneurs, view compensation as a way of keeping score among their peers, and are highly motivated by compensation plans. Yet, money is a more effective incentive for some individuals than others. Its usefulness also depends on the earnings level of a particular salesperson.

DESIGNING A SALES COMPENSATION PACKAGE

Although there are several methods for designing a sales compensation program, one useful approach consists of five steps:

1. Prepare job descriptions.
2. Establish sales and other objectives.
3. Determine appropriate general categories of compensation.
4. Develop and pretest the compensation plan.
5. Implement and evaluate the plan.

Preparing Job Descriptions

Before a compensation plan can be established, a company must prepare detailed job descriptions for each category of salesperson and manager. Each job description should specify the responsibilities and performance criteria of the position. Some sales jobs may involve little direct selling, but be heavily involved in "missionary work" or "support services." Other sales jobs involve more direct customer contact and actual selling. The company must carefully analyze the tasks necessary for each job and then write a description for each category. A job description establishes the basis for developing the most appropriate compensation plan as the tasks involved, the level of creativity needed, and the degree of difficulty are delineated. Sales jobs of like value should receive similar levels of compensation.

Establishing Sales and Other Objectives

A principal purpose of a compensation plan is to achieve the organization's established objectives. In addition to total sales volume and profitability, other specific objectives that may be important in developing the compensation plan include

- The number of sales presentations made to customers
- The number of new products sold to established customers
- The sales of specific products
- The use by customers of company promotional material and displays
- The number of times the company's products are advertised by customers
- The level of **conversion ratio**—that is, the number of orders as a percentage of sales presentations
- The number of new customers obtained
- The **operating efficiency,** the level of costs per sale, in a sales territory
- The number of old customers retained

Because sales data for each salesperson are readily available, managers can easily measure the productivity of each member of the sales force against the established objectives.

Although sales objectives reflect the company's point of view, the compensation plan must reflect both the company's and the salespeople's vantage points. For the company, a good compensation plan is simple to administer, offers maximum control over the sales effort, and provides a balance between sales results and sales costs. For salespeople, a good compensation plan reflects their ability and experience, provides a regular income, and provides substantial rewards for good performance. These different objectives make it difficult for a single compensation plan to be implemented in a company.

Determining Categories of Compensation. Because too low a level of compensation tends to create high turnover, the general level of sales compensation must be high enough to attract and retain quality salespeople. Several factors affect the appropriate base level of pay for a sales force: the education, experience, and skills required to sell successfully; the income level for comparable jobs in the company; and the income level for comparable sales jobs in the industry.

An initial approach to establishing general categories of compensation assigns numerical values to each job requirement that reflect the most significant factors of success in the selling task. The maximum value is then calculated, and each sales job compared to this value. Table 16-1 gives an example based on education, experience, and sales skills. The table presents a numerical ranking of the

TABLE 16-1 Establishing General Levels of Sales Compensation

Job Requirement	Education	Experience	Sales Skills	Possible Total Score
Numerical value	5	8	10	23

Minimum Score Required for a Sales Position

Sales Position	Education	Experience	Sales Skills	Position Total	Salary Range
Sales trainee	3	4	2	9	$20,000–$26,000
Junior salesperson	4	6	6	16	$25,000–$42,000
Senior salesperson	4	7	8	19	$32,000–$65,000
Territory sales manager	4	8	10	22	$55,000–$85,000

sales jobs and salary range for a particular company. In this example, the company rates sales skills 10, most important, followed by experience and education. The highest possible total score is 23. Each of the other four positions is assessed according to these factors, with the territory sales manager having the highest position total of 22. The overlapping salary range assigned to a particular sales job allows for growth and increased salary, within each position, depending on the individual's abilities and performance.

The level of compensation must be adjusted for any cost of living differences in the sales territories. A good source of reference on living costs in selected metropolitan areas is published annually in *Sales & Marketing Management* under "Survey of Selling Costs." This source is very useful in making the appropriate salary adjustments that reflect the cost of living in different areas.

Developing the Plan

Most compensation plans are a mixture of regular salary, commissions, and/or bonuses, as mixed compensation has been found to be more effective in accomplishing objectives and achieving good sales and profit results. The main compensation decision centers on determining the appropriate mix of regular and incentive salaries. Because a straight-salary plan is least expensive at higher levels of sales, and a straight-compensation plan least expensive at lower levels of sales, a good compensation plan should reflect different sales volumes.

The salary portion of any plan should enable salespeople to meet daily living expenses, while encouraging and "compensating" them for nonselling tasks that are not directly measured in the sales and profit achieved. These nonselling tasks can include customer service, shelf stocking, and gathering comparative product price information or other needed market information. Although these nonselling tasks are very important to the company, the fixed-salary portion of total compensation should not be so high that a salesperson could become complacent and not strive for increased sales. In many sales compensation plans, about 70 percent of the total income of a salesperson is fixed, while the rest, about 30 percent, comes from commissions and bonuses.

Commissions and Bonuses. The size of the commission and bonus part of the compensation plan is based on the salespeople's ability to meet or surpass an established **sales quota,** the minimum sales requirement. Although the relationship between the amount of the compensation package that is incentive (not fixed) and the turnover rates of the sales force has not been definitely established, turnover rates for salespeople in the retail trade, or those who sell technical products to first customers, tend to increase in proportion to the percentage of the compensation package that is fixed. Conversely, turnover rates in a creative or new business sales force tend to increase as the percentage of the total package that is incentive increases.

Fixed commissions and bonuses are much easier to administer, but they do not offer the incentive needed for top salespeople in most companies. Salespeople must feel challenged and be rewarded for obtaining higher, more difficult levels of sales volume. Progressive commission rates can reward these high achievers. With **progressive commission rates,** the commission percentage increases as the sales volume increases. For example, a company may offer a 5 percent commission for all sales up to 2000 units, a 4 percent commission for all sales from 2000 to 3000 units, and a 3 percent commission for all sales 3000 units and over. Sometimes, particularly when there is a high probability of windfall sales (sales that are not due to the effort of the salesperson), companies use **regressive commission rates,** in which the commission percentage decreases as sales increase. The type of commission plan used—fixed, regressive, or progressive—should reflect the objectives of the company, the capability of the sales force, and the profit potential of the various products being sold.

Even more difficult than establishing the basic commission plan is establishing a system for dividing commissions when two or more sales representatives are involved in the sale. This problem frequently occurs when one sales representative calls on a customer's headquarters, and other sales representatives call on divisions, local branches, or outlets of the same company. In some cases, the commissions should be divided to reward each individual proportionately for the effort involved in the sale while at the same time continuing to provide motivation to all the other salespeople. For example, if the sales representative calling on a branch office persuaded the manager to ask corporate headquarters to order a product, he or she might receive 90 percent of the commission for the products sold to the branch office, and the sales representative calling on the headquarters might receive 10 percent.

Stock Options. The problem of retaining top-quality salespeople can sometimes be solved by offering stock options. With a **stock option,** salespeople have the right to purchase stock in the company, at a future date, at the present price, that should be lower than the market value. If the price of the stock rises (which usually occurs in fast-growing, dynamic companies), salespeople can buy the stock at the lower, established price and then sell the stock, if desired, at the higher market value. When the company is growing, and the stock price is increasing, salespeople are more reluctant to leave the company, because depending on the terms of the plan, there may not be an opportunity to exercise the stock option and realize the profits at a future date.

This incentive is developed further when stock options are awarded based on performance, or when the company allows top-performing salespeople to contribute to a special equity fund that is matched by the company when specified sales objectives are achieved. If a salesperson leaves the company, he or she receives his or her contribution to the equity fund but forfeits the company's matching contribution.

When the stock of the company is not increasing in price, and therefore has no future incentive value, companies can implement alternatives to stock options in order to retain their top people. Alternatives used most frequently include performance unit plans and stock appreciation rights. Under a typical **performance unit plan,** salespeople receive stock or cash when certain long-range goals or objectives are achieved. These goals can take the form of specified levels of sales, distribution, or profits. Under a **stock appreciation plan,** salespeople actually receive cash or stock equal to the gain that would have been possible by exercising a stock option without being required to actually have the money to purchase the stock.

Other Incentives and Fringe Benefits. Other incentives in the form of **fringe benefits**—the noncash portion of the salesperson's salary—are used to provide motivation and rewards.[3] For example, club memberships, the use of a company airplane, special vacations, trips for salespeople and spouses, financial counseling, loans, and leaves of absence are sometimes used by a company as fringe benefits to further motivate and reward salespeople. Most fringe benefits augment the basic compensation package.[4]

Pretesting the Plan

Given the importance of the sales compensation plan, it should be pretested before being implemented. (Pretesting is not possible for start-up companies because it requires sales data for the preceding three years.) By evaluating the impact on sales of a compensation plan in previous years, a company can evaluate the quality of the plan as well as its deficiencies. In larger, multidivision or multiarea companies, the proposed plan can actually be implemented, and the effects evaluated, in a few areas before it is implemented throughout the entire company.

A pretesting method that can be used in every company, including new companies, involves presenting the proposed compensation plan to a committee of key salespeople for comments and reactions before it is implemented. The approval of this group allows a plan to be more easily accepted by the entire sales force.

Implementing and Evaluating the Plan

Companies can ensure that a compensation plan is accepted with minimum difficulty if the plan is written clearly and is easy to understand, and if the compensation is easy to calculate, fair, flexible, and quickly paid. Significant changes in the market, or company conditions, require that the compensation plan be evaluated and altered as needed. Sometimes, particularly when a "hot product" is introduced, or shortages occur for other reasons, the plan must be revised immediately. Changing the compensation plan to reflect shortages and attempting to allocate available products equitably minimize ill will among salespeople and customers alike. Furthermore, any changes in the time involved in nonselling activities also require that the compensation plan be revised.

One concern in administering sales compensation plans is whether to disclose salaries of salespeople and managers. Providing salary information usually causes friction and jealousy among the sales force, in addition to greater demands for pay justifications and more objective performance measures. This can lead to increased dissatisfaction with the sales managers, others in positions of responsibility, and the entire company.

A well-administered plan requires periodic review and evaluation to determine its continued effectiveness in attracting, motivating, and maintaining a quality sales force. This review should be done regularly, on at least an annual basis.

RELATIVE BENEFITS
OF ALTERNATIVE COMPENSATION PLANS

In designing an effective sales compensation plan, companies must consider the advantages and disadvantages of alternative plans in light of various market and company conditions. Managers must consider the basic plans—straight commission, straight salary, or a combination—as well as the issues of expense accounts and fringe benefits.

Straight Commission

The **straight-commission** compensation plan maximizes incentives, minimizes security, and frequently results in very high productivity and earning levels for salespeople. This plan is usually employed in direct marketing, some industrial sales, retail furniture sales, automotive sales, international sales of the company's local salespeople selling in their country's market, real estate transactions, and group sales. Under this plan, unproductive salespeople eventually resign because their salaries are derived from paid commissions based only on performance, as measured in terms of sales and sometimes profits.

When establishing a straight-commission plan, the company first must establish the base or unit. This becomes the basis for paying commissions, and is usually stated in units of sale, dollar sales, gross profits, or some sales/profit combination. Second, the company must determine the rate that will be paid per unit, which is often expressed as a percentage of gross profit or sales. Third, the company must establish the starting point for commissions. This point can be the first unit sold, the first unit sold after obtaining a specific level of sales, or an established sales quota. Finally, the company must decide on the time period for payment of commissions, as well as the method for handling sales returns, canceled orders, and nonpayment.

Commissions are usually paid when the order is received, goods are shipped, or payment is received. Commissions are usually adjusted in the next payment period for nonpayment, canceled orders, or returned merchandise in the previous period. To help ensure prompt delivery and build customer relations, most companies usually pay commissions once the order is shipped. Under this system, salespeople work with production and shipping to ensure that the order is sent on a timely basis, and is not canceled because of delay.

To help offset fluctuations in salary, and to help salespeople on straight commission, some companies establish a draw, in addition to the established commission plan. A **draw** is a sum of money paid to salespeople against future commissions. The money obtained from the draw is deducted by the company from commissions earned in the next payment period. The remaining amount of commissions is then paid to the salesperson. A **guaranteed draw** extends the conditions of the draw, and need not be repaid by the salesperson if earned commissions are not enough to offset the draw. A draw against future commissions provides some security for salespeople while also providing incentive to perform and produce.[5] With an upper limit placed on the size of the draw, a negative draw position, even for several weeks, does not pose a problem.

A draw is particularly effective for new salespeople because it provides necessary income while they establish a customer sales base. An example of cash flow for a salesperson with a $200 weekly guaranteed draw and a 12 percent commission on sales is illustrated in Table 16-2. In week 1, the salesperson made no sales, and took a draw of $200. This left a negative balance of $200. In week 2, sales of $1500, at a 12 percent commission rate, yielded earned commissions of

TABLE 16-2 Salesperson Commission Structure (Based on a $200 Weekly Draw and a 12 Percent Commission on Sales Volume)

Week	Sales Volume	Earned Commissions	Weekly Draw	Balance
1	$ 0	$ 0	$ –200	$ –200
2	1500	180	200	–220
3	2000	240	200	–180
4	2500	300	200	–80
5	3000	360	200	+80
6	5000	600	200	+480
7	7000	840	200	+1120
8	2500	300	200	+1220
9	3500	420	200	+1440
10	1500	180	200	+1420
Totals	$28,500	$3420	$2000	$1420

$180. With a draw of $200, the salesperson had a negative balance of $220. This negative balance continued until week 5, when sales of $3000 earned commissions of $360, and a positive balance of $80 was reached.

With or without a guaranteed or unguaranteed draw, straight-commission plans are used in many industries, particularly when the company wants a strong incentive to sell. Some industries, such as the consumer packaged goods industry, tend not to use a straight-commission plan because of the difficulty in relating sales volume to the efforts of a particular salesperson. For example, the sale of a 96-ounce box of Ultra Tide at a Stop-n-Shop store in Cleveland, Ohio, might have been the result of a manufacturer's coupon from Procter & Gamble, not the work of the salesperson calling on the account. It may also have resulted from a call by the sales manager to Stop-n-Shop's headquarters, a display allowance given by Procter & Gamble to the Stop-n-Shop store for displaying the product, a product advertisement in the Cleveland *Plain Dealer*, or the salesperson's call on the manager of another Stop-n-Shop store in the area. In all likelihood, a combination of several of these affected the sale.

The straight-commission method has several advantages and disadvantages. Advantages include the following:

- The incomes of salespeople are a direct result of their productivity.
- Salespeople can earn significant salaries with no ceiling.
- Salespeople can easily keep track of their performance and earnings.
- No company money is tied up because costs (exceeding a draw) occur only when a sale is made.

- Salespeople have maximum freedom and incentive to perform.
- Poorly performing salespeople usually quit on their own.

The distinct disadvantages to the straight-commission method include the following:

- Salespeople develop little, if any, company loyalty.
- Salespeople must live with a great deal of uncertainty and anxiety about future income.
- Larger than normal turnover occurs when business is low.
- Salespeople have little reason to do anything but sell.
- Salespeople tend to sell more product than the specific customer situation warrants; this can result in customers with too much inventory, causing customer dissatisfaction.
- Salespeople strongly resist any changes in sales territories.

Straight-Salary Plan

Even though individuals with good selling ability are better rewarded (if they can perform) under a straight-commission plan, many people do not like to work under conditions of uncertainty and potential for wide fluctuations in income. These more security-minded salespeople prefer a dependable, regular income rather than making a larger amount of money under the uncertain straight-commission plan. Security with a straight-salary plan is particularly important in widely fluctuating company and market situations and when the company's sales are periodic or seasonal.

A company should definitely consider a **straight-salary plan** under the following circumstances, even though the incentive for higher sales volume may be reduced:

1. *When a long learning period is needed for salespeople to perform effectively.* A straight salary is needed, at least in the beginning, to cover the training period until commissions are large enough to provide an adequate standard of living. Initially, without a straight-salary plan, it would be very difficult to recruit good salespeople.

2. *When a major capital expenditure is involved with an extended negotiation period in the selling process.* A company may take more than a year to make such a big decision. A salesperson might be calling on, and working with, a company during this entire period in order to make the final sale, and yet would not earn any commission during that time.

3. *When sales, usually those more technical in nature, require team selling among a salesperson, a marketing support person, a technical engineer, and an upper-level man-*

ager. Because each individual plays a role in the final sale, it is difficult to assign total credit to the salesperson.

4. *When advertising, sales promotion, and/or a direct-mail piece have a significant effect on the final sale, and when the extent of that effect with respect to the efforts of the salesperson is difficult to evaluate.* A straight-salary plan in this case also rewards nonselling activities, commonly called **missionary selling.** These include providing customer assistance, setting up in-store displays, redesigning an entire area of a store for introducing a new line of products, or calling on potential new customers.

Because a salesperson's compensation in a straight-salary plan is not based on productivity, which is usually measured by sales and/or profits, this compensation plan provides salespeople with the most security and allows the company to direct all the sales activities. This helps to ensure that the company will reach its established objectives. In industries such as heavy machinery, aerospace, chemical, petroleum, and consumer nondurable goods, a straight-salary compensation plan is widely used. Sometimes salespeople are even called consultants or engineers, with sales not even being part of their title.

The straight-salary compensation plan also has several advantages and disadvantages. The advantages include the following:

- It provides security for salespeople.
- It directs all the activities of the sales force.
- It provides flexibility and adaptability in territorial assignments and sales activities.
- It is very easy to administer.

The disadvantages of using the plan sometimes outweigh the advantages, however. Disadvantages include the following:

- It provides no financial incentive to maximize productivity and the selling effort.
- It gives a fixed selling cost regardless of sales.
- It allows income inequities to develop, with the least productive salespeople being overpaid and the most productive salespeople being underpaid.
- It tends to cause turnover among the most productive salespeople.

Combination Compensation Plans

A **combination compensation plan** combines characteristics of both the straight-salary and straight-commission plans. The salary part of the compensation package provides security and a base reward for minimal level of sales performance. The commission and/or bonus part of the compensation package is a reward for achieving or exceeding volume and/or profit goals. The critical factor in developing an effective combination compensation plan is the proportion of salary to

SELL!NG
THE FRONT LINES OF BUSINESS

How They're Making It
Linda Corman

No two salespeople react the same way to a new compensation plan. Bell Atlantic's Linda Zemke swallowed hard and turned to spreadsheet analysis. Reebok's Chris Walsh breathed a sigh of relief and started filling out mortgage applications. Brigitte Sabar of The Knoll Group confronted the realities of a non-team, every-salesperson-for-himself environment.

Staring down the barrel of a new compensation plan for 1995? Confused? If it's any comfort, you have a lot of company. Chances are, even your employer has some questions about the latest pay scheme. Some of the biggest companies in the country are dismantling their old plans, rethinking the value of their salespeople, and imposing tremendous changes in an effort to improve productivity and profitability.

Reebok has laid a foundation of base pay as it looks to its salespeople to provide merchandising and marketing support—tasks that aren't easily commissionable. Baxter Health Care has moved to a salary-plus scheme, and made teamwork a factor in incentive pay. The Knoll Group, meanwhile, backed off the team approach and is paying instead for individual performance and profitability. And

Pitney Bowes created a new yardstick for bonus rewards: year-to-date performance.

What's the best way to pay salespeople? Where better to look for answers to that question than on the front lines of business. We interviewed half a dozen salespeople who have seen their compensation plans change recently, and asked them to weigh in on the pros and cons of the different approaches. Among this vocal group, there is a clear consensus about what works and what doesn't.

The best plans, say many, are simple. The best plans are equitable. The best plans reward extraordinary results extraordinarily—and not always just in cold cash.

The best plans, it seems, take into account what salespeople think about the increasingly various ways they're paid.

Listen in.

EVERY SALESPERSON FOR HIMSELF: THE PROFITABILITY PLAN AT KNOLL

Brigitte Sabar's new compensation scheme has turned her into something of a spy and pitted her against her fellow reps. After 14 years at The Knoll Group, a furniture manufacturer in East Greenville, Pa., she no longer shares information or group commissions with the company's other reps. Instead, Sabar, who is based in Bedminster, N.J., spends time checking up on her colleagues to make sure that none of them is selling to one of her clients behind her back. "You have to spy on other regions to make sure you don't get cheated," says Sabar. "It's a waste of time, and it breeds mistrust."

In the old days, before Westinghouse acquired Knoll in 1990, Sabar was happy to cooperate with other reps. In fact, the company made it worth her while. Reps earned a base salary of $22,000 a year, and a commission on all new business. More important, they each contributed 25 percent of their commissions to a pool that was divided evenly among reps in a given region. Teamwork truly paid off.

Under the new plan, Sabar gets paid a base salary more than triple her previous one. But her commissions are based mainly on individual performance and the profitability of her deals. Despite the increase in salary, the change has been decidedly *unprofitable* for Sabar.

Where once she was rewarded for handling large accounts—including Sony, BASF, and Schering-Plough—Sabar now finds herself being penalized. Big clients expect big price breaks, Sabar explains. "You can't get big projects unless they're 60 percent to 65 percent off," she says. But under the new plan, the higher the discount, the smaller the commission.

Sabar estimates that four years ago, if she had a $6 million year, she would have made $180,000; just $22,000 would have been base pay. With the new plan, in a $6 million year, she would make $110,000, of which $70,000 would be base.

Worse than the pay cut, however, is the erosion in team spirit. Five years ago, Sabar remembers, she would steer new reps through customer projects. Now, she says, she barely knows who the new reps are. "There's no teamwork at all. I have no incentive to take on a new person and show them the ropes. Everything I learned, I learned from other reps," says Sabar, who started with the company as a sales assistant.

If another rep sells to Sabar's clients, Sabar is entitled to a 25 percent cut. But because cooperation is no longer built in to the compensation plan, Sabar says that salespeople find ways to cut each other out, particularly by selling through furniture brokers to the end customer. Sabar says she can understand such temptations. "I've been reluctant to inform the right person whose account it is," she admits.

Sabar does not know for sure that the move away from team selling is directly responsible for her drop in income. But she guesses that Knoll is missing out on some projects because reps are not sharing information with each other.

AHEAD OF THE GAME: BONUS BOOM AT PITNEY BOWES

Dennis Farrell is the first to admit his new compensation plan is complex. But he understands it well enough to know that it keeps him running hard. Farrell, a major account executive for Pitney Bowes based in Baltimore, makes the bulk of his annual income in bonuses.

But that's only because he far exceeds his annual quota.

For years Pitney Bowes paid its sales force a draw against commissions. In the past two years, however, the Stamford, Conn., company, has moved almost 20 percent of its 2,600 salespeople to a plan that offers a combination of base compensation and incentive bonuses. Here's how it works.

Salespeople at Pitney Bowes get annual quotas that are set according to their positions within the company. Their base salary also is determined by position, and is contingent on eight factors, including product knowledge, customer satisfaction, and cooperation with other departments. Reps also get monthly incentive bonuses that hinge upon their year-to-date performance.

If Farrell were running at 100 percent of his quota in a given month, his pay would be 50 percent salary, 50 percent bonus. In other words, his bonus rate would be 100 percent of salary. But if he slipped to 75 percent of quota, his bonus rate, according to the Pitney Bowes formula, would slide to 33 percent. And it would not come up again until he was back on track at 100 percent of quota. Conversely, if he were selling at 120 percent of quota, his bonus rate would jump to 150 percent. And selling key products would add to the bonus.

Under the old system, a bad month would also mean less pay. Draws at Pitney Bowes were relatively conservative, says Farrell, and most of the salespeople made their money on end-of-month commissions. If sales would fall, commissions would fall. But it was easier to dismiss a bad period because it did not have ongoing ramifications. "If you were struggling in a given month, you'd think, 'I'll be okay,' so long as you can live off your draw," says Farrell. Now, he says, you can withstand a bad month due to the base salary. The difference is that now there isn't the proverbial clean slate at the end of every month; every day your performance is measured against your projections for the year.

While the bonus plan might not have much impact on total annual income, Farrell finds the accountability to be a real incentive—so much so, in fact, that he is running at 175 percent of his quota. "Since you're paid on year-to-date performance, you're much more motivated to meet and exceed your quota," he says. And if you push certain products, you can earn another 25 percent in bonus. "This compensation plan drives me harder," he says.

Farrell was far less bullish on the new plan when he first heard about it in 1993. "There was a concern in terms of change: What does it really mean to me?" recalls Farrell, who has been with the company for nine years. But, he stresses, management went to great lengths in openly discussing the plan and trying to allay salespeople's fears.

Pitney Bowes expects to convert the rest of its sales force to the new program within two years. The changes were made to complement a reorganization that split up customers according to size and product usage. Also, the company wanted salespeople to concentrate more on developing relationships with their customers and meeting their needs, and it developed this plan as a way to reward salespeople for these efforts, explains Deborah

Hoffman, the company's manager of sales compensation.

Farrell, who has large national accounts, has always focused on customer service. But, he says, it's nice to get "rubber-stamped approval for something you're already doing."

RISK FACTOR:
THE "BOTTOM'S-UP" PLAN
AT BELL ATLANTIC

At the heart of the profit-driven bonus plan that Bell Atlantic in Philadelphia began rolling out two years ago is a simple premise: It's not what you earn that counts, but how you earn it. The concept may be simple, but the plan has left Linda Zemke, and others in the 170-member sales force, struggling with some very complex emotions. Like confusion. And fear.

"I have really, really mixed feelings about it," says Zemke, a team leader for the large business group.

For starters, she says, "you need to do a spreadsheet analysis" to determine a reasonable quota. Then there's a laundry list of factors, packaged in a 100-page compensation guide, that can greatly affect bonuses. To be sure, the plan is far more unpredictable—and onerous—than the old salary-plus-commission program.

Now compensation revolves around quotas, and there are five different schemes depending on the size of those goals. Salespeople start the year with a quota and a projected income level. Under a typical scenario, they receive 60 percent of their income in the form of salary. The balance, paid out in monthly bonuses, depends on four components: volume and product targets, client retention, individual challenge objectives, and quarterly goals.

Most of the incentive pay, some 60 percent to 70 percent, is based on monthly attainment of the annual quotas. The plan features a sliding bonus rate that greatly rewards people who are running ahead of projections, and penalizes those who are falling behind. The new arrangement puts salespeople on the hook, not only for annual volume estimates, but also for the profitability of products they sell.

In a process known as "bottoms-up," salespeople are asked in the fall to estimate their volume for the coming year. After assessing their customer base and the opportunity in their territory, the company assigns them a quota in January. The quotas are high, admits Sheryl Richeson, director of compensation for Bell Atlantic large business.

"The problem is, people try to get a low quota so they can blow it out," says Richeson. "We're trying to put more risk in the plan without reducing salaries."

Take this hypothetical example. If a salesperson has a quota of $1 million, and a total projected income of $80,000, he can expect to earn $48,000 in salary and $32,000 in bonuses. The majority of that incentive pay, about $22,000, will come from meeting his annual quota. If in any given month, he is running at 61 percent to 100 percent of plan, he will get $175 for every percent of quota he attains. But if he's selling at a rate of less than 60 percent, he only gets $50 for every percent of quota attained. Therein lies the downside.

The upside? If a salesperson sells at more than 100 percent of plan, he gets

$300 for every percent of quota he reaches. He also gets quarterly bonuses of $500 just for keeping up the pace. And if his sales involve certain "strategic" products, he will earn additional bonus dollars.

For salespeople, the profitability quotient translates into paperwork. Zemke says every sale requires 50 percent more time in paperwork, since she has to document the profitability of the products when she claims credit for their sale. Still, Zemke says she enjoys the feeling of managing a business rather than pushing volume. "The job seems more important, more challenging," she says. "Before, the products were not as complex and the accounts were not as complex. This is a service business now. It's not just pushing boxes."

ALL FOR ONE AND ONE FOR ALL: TEAM INCENTIVES AT AT&T GLOBAL INFORMATION SOLUTIONS

The day they changed the way he gets paid, Ken Daniels began changing the way he works. The team leader for AT&T Global Information Solutions (AT&T GIS) has found more time for himself and his customer, the Cincinnati-based Kroger supermarket chain, since his company switched to a team-based plan in December 1993. Before that, when individual performance determined incentive pay, ambitious sellers like Daniels would overload themselves with responsibilities. Now the team won't let them.

"If 21 people are responsible instead of just one, it makes time away a little easier," says Daniels, who oversees a team of 21, including 11 salespeople. "I'm taking [vacation] this year where I never used to take time off."

More important, Daniels says he now devotes 75 percent of his time to clients compared with 25 percent under the former plan. As a sales manager under the old plan, he was far busier reviewing his reps than rallying them. "An inordinate amount of time was spent reviewing the historic performance of individual reps," he says. All that changed last year when AT&T GIS moved to interdisciplinary team selling.

The Dayton, Ohio, company (formerly NCR) used to compensate its 12,000-member sales force with a base salary plus commission determined by individual performance against a revenue quota. Under the new plan, Daniels and his teammates still receive base salaries of 60 percent to 70 percent of their compensation. But now they make up the balance with four types of bonuses—the customer satisfaction bonus, the associate satisfaction bonus, the profit bonus, and the revenue bonus—paid out at different intervals.

The switch prompted the 29-year company vet to rethink his entire approach. Since team members are now more willing to take on problem-solving responsibilities, he finds himself relieved of the authoritarian role he had assumed as sales manager. "I used to be a dictatorial-type manager," says Daniels. "I now delegate the whole thing. I try to let the team go."

Knowing that he is being rated by his team also has made him less self-centered than before. In the past, for example, if he thought he was the best person to give a presentation, he would dictate that he did it. Now the team decides who's best, he says. "I needed to learn to hold back. I saw some reactions. You start analyzing the looks."

Here's the plan. AT&T GIS sets company-wide customer satisfaction goals at the beginning of each year and hires outside firms to conduct customer surveys. In Daniels's case, the customer satisfaction bonus depends on his individual scores. (Now his rating is compared to a composite of similar grades in the retail industry. Eventually, the rating will be just the Kroger evaluation.) Associate satisfaction, meanwhile, is determined by internal surveys—and that bonus is based on the aggregate satisfaction of teams throughout the division, not just Daniels's own team. The profit bonus is based on his team alone, and the revenue bonus reflects both individual and team performance. Daniels wishes that associate satisfaction was based on his team's performance alone. Then, he says, the rating would be in "direct association to what you're doing rather than a national composite. We all believe that we do better than the average composite score."

In the first year of the plan, Daniels reports that his entire team saw an increase in their incomes.

THE BUCK STOPS HERE: STRAIGHT SALARY AT BAXTER HEALTH CARE

For the first time in 21 years, Mike Gorby knows exactly what to expect from his annual income. A year ago his long-time employer, Baxter Health Care of Deerfield, Ill., moved some account managers, including Gorby, from a straight commission structure to a straight salary program, and switched most of its salespeople from commissions to a salary-plus-commissions-plus-bonuses plan. Moreover, it factored customer satisfaction, teamwork, and overall company performance into the new system.

The result for Gorby? More predictability, less potential.

"There is not as much upside for me," he admits. But, Gorby adds, "there is a comfort level to being on salary instead of on commission."

For Gorby, based in Cincinnati, the change in compensation forced major adjustments in how he views both his job and his earning potential. Still, Gorby never feared for his livelihood. "Baxter had always treated me fairly," he says. "To retain the quality of sales force the company had, it would have to pay fairly."

Under the new arrangement, 10 percent of Gorby's salary is held back until the end of the year. He receives the balance only if he gets adequate ratings for customer satisfaction and team selling, and if the company meets its targets. Customer satisfaction ratings are determined by samplings of customer opinion. Team selling ratings are based on surveys of team members, who evaluate each other.

The salespeople, some 2,500 of them, earn 60 percent of their projected annual incomes as salary, and have another 10 percent held back for teamwork and customer satisfaction bonuses at the end of the year. Reps earn the balance of their incomes in monthly commissions, which are based on individual performance and profitability.

Under that scenario, 20 percent of the total incentive compensation is based on teamwork. But individual regions can choose to make that proportion larger, says Tom Hill, vice president of human resources for Baxter Diagnostics. Hill predicts that under the new scheme, most people will earn about the same as they have in the past. In fact, Baxter guaranteed the commissions of its reps during the transition year to allow them to focus more on teamwork and less on personal gain. In the end, the company decided that its first year's worth of customer satisfaction surveys were incomplete. So it left 1994 bonuses up to management.

While the new plan may limit his upside potential, it has made account manager Gorby anything but complacent. "I'm self-motivated," he says. "I want to have the best team."

With the new compensation program has come a new sense of cooperation and a greater appreciation of colleagues and clients. "I've changed my thought processes," explains Gorby. "I look longer range instead of just selling individual product. I think about what products my customers need, regardless of what division [they would come from]."

Under the old plan, Gorby adds, "I'd be in the hospital, working independent of other Baxter resources, not caring about what other Baxter divisions did." At most, he might have worked with 60 percent of the other Baxter sales reps calling on the same client. The others he wouldn't even know.

In an effort to help its sales force adapt to the company's new team approach, Baxter sponsored a three-day adventure called the Pecos Experience. One of the team-building exercises had salespeople scaling 42-foot walls carrying pitchers of water. Says Gorby, "The experience taught me that there are a lot of other resources in the company."

BETTER SAFE THAN SORRY: MORE SALARY THAN INCENTIVES AT REEBOK

There was a time when Reebok's Chris Walsh wouldn't have dreamed of applying for a mortgage. Back when he was an outside representative for the Stoughton, Mass., company, getting paid straight commissions, his income was too unpredictable for such a commitment. Then, five years ago, Reebok brought its sales operation inside, and gradually made base salary a growing component of its compensation plan.

Within the first year, Walsh, who is based in Atlanta, was comfortable enough with his partial salary to buy a house. Less than two years later he was confident enough to trade up for another. Now, after five years on salary with Reebok, he and his wife are building a future with their infant son.

"I have a nest egg to retire on and medical benefits as well," says Walsh, who was promoted last year to region footwear sales manager for Reebok Southeast. "That's a big change in your life. With 100 percent commission, there's a lot of stress. If the economy goes bad," he says, "your income can vary radically."

With a solid base, he says, "you aren't always worrying about where your income is coming from," and he thinks that makes employees more valuable to Reebok. Walsh has not gotten too comfortable, though. He says, in fact, that he's working harder now than when his income hinged on the outcome of every single sales call.

That's exactly what Reebok hoped would happen. In part, the compensation change was designed to encourage the sales force, now 500 strong in the U.S., to do more than sell, according to Tom Carmody, senior vice president/general manager for Reebok North America. "We're asking them to be marketers, merchandisers, and put on events," says Carmody. "You want them at your beck and call."

To determine salespeople's incomes, Reebok averages their earnings for the previous two years. Then, depending on prospects in their territories, it projects their volume for the year. Merit and promotion increases, based on the rep's activities in merchandising, marketing, and administrative responsibilities, are added on top of that. Salary is then set at 70 percent of that total projected income. Beyond that, reps earn monthly commissions; if they sell the projected volume, they will earn their projected income. For managers like Walsh, salary is 80 percent of total income, and the rest is commission on total regional sales.

The commission amount varies, depending on projected sales and projected earnings. But the total is invariably lower than it used to be, according to Walsh. Still, he says, that trade-off is worth it for the security gained from having a base salary and benefits. "If your territory is falling off, the downside risk is also less," stresses Walsh, who says his income has risen steadily, even with the compensation change.

Reebok converted to the new plan gradually because "people are averse to change," says Carmody. In the first half-year the company brought salespeople in-house, reps received their full commission plus a salary. In the second year they received 50 percent base pay and 50 percent commission. In the past two years they have received 70 percent base and 30 percent commission. Walsh said the gradual shift helped provide a "base of stability" amid all the change.

Walsh gives Reebok a lot of credit for having worked out the fairest way to treat its employees in a stagnant market. He notes, "When you've been in the growth part of the business and then seen it flatten out, and then the company says they'll provide a salary, that's heartening and motivating."

Reprinted with the permission of SELL!NG magazine.

---

commission incentive. The ideal combination is a salary large enough to attract talented salespeople coupled with an incentive plan large enough to strongly motivate them. Although the salary-incentive mix varies depending on the industry, the competition, and the nature of the selling task, a compensation package that is 70 to 80 percent salary and 20 to 30 percent incentive is usually considered balanced and attractive.[6]

Because a single compensation plan is usually not flexible enough to use throughout an entire company, various combination plans tend to provide the greatest flexibility. There are four basic types of combination plans:

1. Salary plus commission. This plan is used most frequently. It allows a company to obtain a high sales volume without sacrificing customer service. It provides security for the sales force and yet motivates them for strong sales performance.

2. Salary plus bonus. This plan is usually the best combination for achieving long-run sales objectives. It helps to motivate a salesperson to achieve a particular customer mix or to sell specific large capital expenditure items. A bonus differs from a commission in that it provides a lump sum of money (or stock) for a specified performance, such as making a quota, making a certain profit, obtaining a specified number of new accounts, or selling a new product to a specified number of existing accounts.

Bonuses can be paid for individual or group performance, and can be distributed in the next pay period or over several time periods, or even deferred until retirement. Depending on the tax structure, the latter arrangement is often favored by highly paid salespeople or sales managers because the income may be taxed at a lower rate, as retirement benefits, rather than at the higher rate of regular income. Unless there is an overriding reason, it is better to pay a bonus as soon as possible after it is earned in order to maximize its effect in stimulating performance. Bonus plans provide flexibility in stimulating the sales force on an individual or group basis to achieve whatever objectives have been established.

3. Commission plus bonus. This plan is frequently used for group sales. When a team effort is needed to sell to a buying committee, or different salespeople are calling on different managers in the company, this compensation plan is one of the easiest to administer and provides a fair compensation to everyone involved in the sale.

4. Salary plus commission plus bonus. This plan combines the elements of the previous two plans. It provides the greatest flexibility while stimulating sales and providing security, as it allows management to focus the sales force on achieving certain objectives, such as new product introduction or specified product or customer sales. This compensation plan is particularly useful in eliminating inventory imbalances or minimizing the extreme fluctuations in seasonal sales.

EXPENSE ACCOUNTS

A significant part of sales costs and the sale compensation plan are fringe benefits and expense accounts.[7] The fringe benefit package, in particular, is a way the company can provide job satisfaction and establish company loyalty, thereby minimizing turnover. Companies are also faced with significantly increasing selling expenses in the form of travel, meals, and lodging. These selling expenses have significantly raised the average cost of a typical sales call, and have increased faster than any other sales cost. While every company needs to recognize that selling costs and entertainment expenses are part of the cost of doing business, managers should carefully monitor these costs for compliance to company policy. Companies should also reimburse these costs quickly, particularly when they are personal outlays paid for by salespeople. The policy of most companies is to reimburse for such expenses as travel, automobile, telephone, meals, lodging, drinks, and laundry.

The Expense Plan

Because expense reimbursement is examined very carefully by the sales manager, an expense plan should be carefully designed to make sure it is equitable, flexible, and easy to administer.

Equitable. By far the most important factor in designing an expense reimbursement plan is that it is equitable to the company and to its salespeople as well. The expense plan should reimburse all legitimate selling expenses incurred by salespeople without profit or loss. Legitimate expenses should reflect regional cost differences in lodging, travel, food, and entertainment, as well as the costs of dealing with different types of customers, selling different products, or performing different selling tasks. A company can obtain an initial understanding of the costs of doing business in a major metropolitan market by looking at the yearly selling cost index (SCI) in *Sales & Marketing Management.*

Flexible. As with all aspects of sales compensation, the expense plan needs to be flexible. Constantly changing market conditions require that salespeople have the freedom to respond in order to maintain established customers and product bases as well as obtain new ones. This may mean that a large potential customer may need to be especially catered to at a greater cost than is usually allowed. A sales expense plan needs to be flexible enough to allow and even encourage this type of activity when it is necessary.

Easily Administered. Finally, the expense plan must be easily understood and easy to administer. Some companies have made their expense plans so full of legalese that they are difficult to understand and administer. A company must establish clear guidelines so that salespeople can easily understand which expenses are reimbursable. These expenses should then be reimbursed efficiently and quickly with minimum clerical costs and effort.

Types of Reimbursement Plans

Given the increasing burden of selling expenses, it is important for a company to implement a good reimbursement plan when the expenses are not paid by salespeople. This frequently occurs in a straight-commission reimbursement plan. Three reimbursement plans are widely used: limited, unlimited, and combination.

Limited Reimbursement Plan. In this plan, salespeople are restricted either to a fixed amount of money for a period of time or a specified allowance amount per item. In the former case, a company establishes a fixed amount of money per day, or per week, above which expenses are not reimbursed. Under the specified amount per item method, a company sets a fixed amount for lodging, meals, or per mile traveled. This plan, by establishing very clear guidelines, leaves little chance of misunderstanding and expense account padding, a practice that is, of course, very unethical. It also allows expenses to be predicted and budgeted more accurately.

There are some disadvantages to a limited reimbursement plan. It can make salespeople too expense conscious. When this occurs, they may not incur some expenses that may increase sales or save a customer or product line. Sometimes the benefits of larger expenses outweigh the costs incurred. The plan can also damage the esprit de corps of salespeople by giving them the feeling that management does not have faith or trust in them. Frequent revision of the established expense figures is also needed, particularly in a time of high inflation. When revisions are made, management must also ensure that the changes are clear, and the timing of their implementation is well understood to avoid confusion among the sales force.

Unlimited Reimbursement Plan. An unlimited reimbursement plan is the most widely used method for reimbursing all necessary selling and travel expenses. To be reimbursed, salespeople must submit itemized expense reports with the necessary receipts. This flexibility allows the expense differences in territories, customers, or products to be taken into account. The sales manager must ensure that salespeople do not operate too inefficiently or pad the expense account. However, the plan makes it very difficult to forecast expenses accurately.

Combination Reimbursement Plan. A combination of the reimbursement plans often provides the greatest flexibility and control. One common combination plan sets limits on certain items, such as food and lodging, but has unlimited travel expenses. Another combination plan relates the expenses to sales. For example, a salesperson may be reimbursed for all expenses up to 3 percent of net sales and can also be rewarded with a bonus, depending on the level of expenses below 3 percent of net sales. If net sales are $30,000 and expenses $940, the salesperson would be reimbursed only $900 (3 percent of $30,000), not the $940 actually incurred.

SPECIAL INCENTIVE PROGRAMS

Probably the most mismanaged part of the sales compensation package is the special incentive programs.[8] These programs are most frequently dropped in a flat economy or when a company is in trouble. In spite of this, the amount spent on sales incentive programs has been increasing each year, reaching $7.3 billion in 1994.

The goals of sales managers in implementing incentive programs are listed in Table 16-3. Although sales volume—increasing overall demand—remains the leading goal of incentive programs, other goals, including skill-based objectives, are also important. Selling new accounts (39 percent), introducing new products (37 percent), and building dealer traffic (14 percent) are also goals of incentive programs. Also, incentive programs still are used to accomplish the traditional goal of improving morale and goodwill.

Sales managers often need to justify the additional expense of a proposed incentive program, particularly when management is overly concerned about keeping costs down. These concerns can be addressed in several ways. First, the additional sales from an incentive program almost always make up for the additional costs. Second, an incentive program should be thought of as a method to produce specific results, and not just as an extra perk. If the sales manager talks about an incentive program as a prize, it will be looked at as an additional unwarranted expense by management. Instead, the sales manager should introduce the incentive program as meeting the company's long-term needs, such as increasing market share, reducing turnover, or successfully introducing more new products.

Some resources available to help design and implement a good incentive program are listed in Table 16-4. Associations, trade shows, publications, and resources can be of great assistance in designing and implementing a successful incentive program. They are especially helpful in implementing programs in more difficult times when motivation of the sales force becomes even more important.

TABLE 16-3 Goals of Sales Managers in Implementing a Sales Incentive Program

Objective	Percentage of Respondents Reporting
Increase overall demand	65%
Feature selected items	48
Promoting the full line	42
Sell new accounts	39
Introduce new product	37
Improve morale and goodwill	28
Bolster slow season	22
Move full line of slow items	19
Offset competition	16
Support consumer promotion	16
Prepare for strong season	15
Build dealer traffic	14

Source: Facts Survey. *Incentive* (September 1992). Reproduced with permission.

TABLE 16-4 Resources for Planning an Incentive Program

Associations

- **Association of Incentive Marketers (AIM),** 1600 Route 22, Union, NJ 07083; 908-687-3090, fax: 908-687-0977. This association, with over 400 members representing every segment of the incentive distribution industry including manufacturers, incentive reps, promotion agencies, and fulfillment houses, offers seminars for professionals within the industry and also maintains a speakers' bureau.
- **Association of Retail Marketing Services (ARMS),** 3 Caro Court, Red Bank, NJ 07701; 908-842-5070, fax: 902-219-1938. Focuses on incentive promotion at the retail level, offers legal and legislative services to the industry, conducts research programs, and compiles statistics.
- **Incentive Federation, Inc.,** P.O. Box 774, Madison Square Station, New York, NY 10159; no phone. Acts as the government relations arm of promotion marketing professionals, and is particularly concerned with working against legislation that would, in its view, unfairly restrict incentive marketers and corporations from competition.
- **Incentive Manufacturers Representatives Association (IMRA),** 1555 Napierville/Wheaton Road, Suite 103 B, Napierville, IL 60563; 708-369-3466, fax: 708-369-3773. Comprises over 300 incentive suppliers that are either independent manufacturer's reps or use reps; offers many resources to members and suppliers, including lists of reps in a particular area, video programs, manuals for new suppliers, and educational seminars throughout the year.
- **Society of Incentive Travel Executives (SITE),** 21 West 38 Street, 10th floor, New York, NY 10028; 212-575-0910, fax: 212-575-1838. This international association, with over 2000 members primarily representing hotels and resorts, incentive houses, and tourist organizations, provides educational seminars and information services to anyone involved in organizing incentive programs.

Trade Shows

- **Premium Incentive Show**

Dates: Annually, May

Where: Jacob Javits Convention Center, New York, NY

Contact: Carl Hen (registration) or Liz Shubert (education), Miller Freeman, 1515 Broadway, New York, NY 10036; 212-626-2375/800-950-1314, fax: 212-768-0015

- **California Premium and Incentive Travel Show**

Dates: Annually, June

Where: Anaheim Convention Center, Anaheim, CA

Contact: Sarah Adamson, AMC Trade Shows East, 240 Peachtree Street N.W., Suite 2200, Atlanta, GA 30303; 404-220-2218, fax: 404-220-3030

- **Motivation Show**

Dates: Annually, September

Where: McCormack Place, Chicago, IL

Contact: Hall-Erikson, Inc., 150 Burlington Avenue, Clarendon Hills, IL 60514; 708-950-7779, fax: 708-950-7843

Publications

- *Business and Incentives Strategies,* 1515 Broadway, 32nd floor, New York, NY 10036; 212-869-1300, fax: 212-302-6273
- *Incentive,* 335 Park Avenue South, 5th floor, New York, NY 10010-1789; 212-592-6456, fax: 212-592-6459

Reference Guides

- **The 1993 Premium, Incentive and Travel Buyers Guide,** Reed Reference Publishing, 121 Chanlon Road, New Providence, NJ 07974. Contact Allyn Gilhooly; 908-665-3563/800-321-8110 (ext. 3563), fax: 908-665-3560. Published every February by *The Salesman's Guide,* this book lists nearly 12,000 firms that use premiums and/or incentive travel as part of their overall marketing efforts.
- **AIM—Incentive Showcase Awards.** This celebrates any program designed by a marketing executive who's directly responsible for using, supplying, or implementing a trade, consumer, or employee incentive program using merchandise incentives. The competition culminates each year at the Motivation Show in Chicago, where six Gold Showcase and six Silver Showcase awards are presented at AIM's Incentive Seminar Luncheon. Contact: Andy Bopp: 908-687-3090.
- **IMRA—Gold Key Awards.** These awards, presented each year at the Motivation Show, recognize incentive users for their achievements in conceiving, planning, and executing outstanding incentive programs, including safety or non-sales-oriented programs. Contact: Karen Renk: 708-369-3466.
- **SITE—Crystal Awards.** These awards, presented each fall at SITE's Crystal Awards Banquet (held during the Motivation Show in Chicago), celebrate companies using incentive travel as a motivational tool. Each year, one winner is chosen in each of six different categories, including Creative Use of Incentive Travel to Solve a Marketing Problem, Promotion and Communications, Best Use of Incentive Travel in a Non-Sales Program, and other specific applications. Contact: Lynel Tully: 212-575-0910.
- **SITE—Signet Awards.** These international awards, which are presented at the Signet Awards Presentation, recognize employers who motivate their employees with incentive travel. Two categories are awarded: (1) companies with up to 500 employees and $200 million in sales, and (2) companies that have more than 500 employees and more than $200 million in sales. Whereas SITE's Crystal Awards recognize specific incentive travel programs, the organization's Signet Awards recognize specific companies. Contact: Maureen Mangan: 212-575-0910.

Source: *Sales & Marketing Management* (April 1993), 44–45. Reprinted with permission of Sales & Marketing Management, April 1993.

CHAPTER SUMMARY

Proper compensation of the sales force remains the most effective means of motivation. Regardless of the compensation method used, it is imperative that managers fully understand the importance of sales compensation because it is directly linked to the well-being of the sales force and the entire company. The three basic methods include the straight-salary plan, which provides an individual with a fixed amount of money at fixed intervals; the straight-commission plan, which pays salespeople an amount that varies with results, usually measured in terms of sales or profits; and a combination plan, which pays the individual a fixed amount of money and then an additional amount based on performance in the form of a commission or bonus.

Determining the appropriate plan for a particular company depends on job descriptions, sales objectives, and general categories of compensation. Compensation plans must be developed, pretested, implemented, and regularly evaluated. To provide further incentive, and to motivate performance, companies also add bonuses, stock options, and other fringe benefits, such as club memberships and company cars or airplanes. A tailored, well-structured compensation plan helps to maintain a satisfied sales force, a necessity in maintaining good customer relations.

The straight-commission compensation plan maximizes incentives, minimizes security, and results in very high productivity and earnings for salespeople. Draws paid on future commissions can offset fluctuations in salary for salespeople on straight commission. The straight-salary plan provides for dependable income for salespeople, and is used in industries with periodic or seasonal sales. Combination compensation plans combine characteristics of both the straight-commission and straight-salary plans. Expense plans that reimburse salespeople's expenses for travel, food, and lodging must be equitable, flexible, and easy to administer. They may be limited, unlimited, or combined plans, but they always require monitoring by managers. Special sales incentive programs can achieve specific sales goals.

KEY TERMS

combination compensation plan, p. 387

commission plus bonus, p. 396

conversion ratio, p. 379

draw, p. 384

fringe benefits, p. 382

guaranteed draw, p. 384

missionary selling, p. 387

operating efficiency, p. 379

performance unit plan, p. 382

progressive commission rates, p. 381

regressive commission rates, p. 381

salary plus bonus, p. 396

salary plus commission, p. 396

salary plus commission plus bonus, p. 396

sales quota, p. 381

stock appreciation plan, p. 382

stock option, p. 382

straight-commission plan, p. 384

straight-salary plan, p. 386

CHAPTER QUESTIONS

1. Discuss the advantages and disadvantages of using job evaluations versus the supply and demand conditions in the labor market in determining the appropriate pay levels of a company's sales force.

2. Survey results indicate that companies are not happy with their compensation methods. If this is the case, discuss the reasons why these companies don't change them. Do you believe that the majority of salespeople can be directed by financial compensation? Discuss.

3. Develop the best compensation plan for the following situations:
   a. Creative selling of an intangible good
   b. Ensuring salespeople set up and monitor displays in retail stores

    c. Selling large factory modules

    d. Capturing market share

    e. Emphasizing selling a new product

    f. Clearing out inventory of a product prior to the introduction of its replacement

    g. Selling office equipment

4. As a regional sales manager, you have given one of your salespeople, Pat Grachev, a very small salary adjustment that is below average. Pat has made an appointment with you to discuss this. Prepare a script of the conversation you will have with Pat that will both explain the reasons behind the small salary increase and inspire Pat to work harder in the future.

5. Discuss at least three different ways to design a sales compensation plan that will motivate salespeople to sell the higher-profit items in the product line.

6. Sales incentive contests, although very popular, are sometimes not considered valuable to the firm. Discuss the importance and usefulness of sales incentive contests that will diffuse the usual criticisms.

7. Design an experiment that will determine whether salespeople should be reimbursed for taking customers to sporting events and theaters. Besides the results of the experiment, what other information should you obtain before making this decision?

8. Since compensation is a major factor in attracting and motivating good salespeople, discuss the following issues:

    a. The importance of fringe benefits versus take-home pay

    b. The effect of a bonus as an incentive if it becomes a regular part of the sales compensation plan

    c. The best type of incentive pay for district sales managers

9. Car salespeople are known for switching from one dealership to another, depending in part on what brand is selling the best. Design a compensation plan for a car dealer that will help to decrease the turnover problem and yet still motivate the sales force.

10. Given the importance of successfully launching new products, it is often necessary to change a company's sales incentive compensation plan. In doing this, comment on each of the following questions:

    a. How does the new plan ensure that enough attention will be given to the new products?

    b. How do you establish quotas and goals for each salesperson for the new product when it does not have any sales history?

    c. How does the plan motivate salespeople to maintain and increase the sales of the product after introduction?

    d. How do you determine when the plan will not be effective in a new product introduction?

11. A company recently received a report from a well-recognized consulting firm that its sales compensation plan is more competitive and its mechanics and administration are equitable compared to the plans of similar companies. However, the company is still experiencing a high turnover rate, and those who have left the company indicate that they were not happy with the compensation plan. Discuss this problem, being sure to include the factors contributing to the problem and the appropriate solutions.

NOTES

1. For these and other examples, see: You said it. *Sales & Marketing Management* (April 1993), 10, 11; and Susan Greco, The art of selling. *Inc.* (June 1993), 72–80.
2. These factors are thoroughly discussed in Robert J. Freedman, How to develop a sales compensation plan. *Compensation Benefits Review* (March–April 1986), 41–44.
3. One of the most important benefits, the automobile, is discussed in Richard Szathmary, The company car: Still king of the road. *Sales & Marketing Management* (October 1990), 71.
4. The difference for services are discussed in William Keenon, Sr., The difference in selling services. *Sales & Marketing Management* (October 1990), 71.
5. This is discussed in Joanne Dahm, Using draws wisely in your sales compensation plan. *Sales & Marketing Management* (August 1990), 92–93.
6. For a discussion of the importance of blending sales management and compensation control, see: David W. Cravens, Thomas N. Ingram, Raymond W. LaForge, and Clifford E. Young, Behavior-based and outcome-based salesforce control systems. *Journal of Marketing* 57, no. 4 (October 1993), 47–59.
7. For a survey and studies concerning these and other compensation plans, see Jerry McAdams, Rewarding sales and marketing performance. *Management Review* (April 1987), 33–38; George John and Barton Weitz, Salesforce compensation: An empirical investigation of factors related to use of salary versus incentive compensation. *Journal of Marketing Research* 26 (February 1989), 1–14; and *Current practices in sales incentives* (New York: Alexander Group, 1988).
8. For a discussion of various incentive programs, see Incentives in times like these. *Sales & Marketing Management* (April 1992), 98–99, 104–105, 108; Better than cash. *Sales & Marketing Management* (April 1992), 110–112; and What motivates best. *Sales & Marketing Management* (April 1992), 113–114.

SUGGESTED READINGS

Buhl, William E. Compensation management in practice: Keeping incentives simple for nonexempt employees. *Compensation and Benefits Review* (March–April 1989), 14–19.

> Increasingly, companies are giving nontraditional compensation to their hourly and nonexempt employees. The Fair Labor Standards Act must be followed when designing these alternative compensation plans. Regularly paid bonuses are included when figuring overtime pay rates, but certain bonuses may be excluded.

Gilman, Alan L. Smart compensation and smart selling. *Chain Store Age Executive* (September 1992), 134.

Commissions have been used widely in the past by retailers as a method to motivate salespeople. However, research has discovered that a 2 percent increase in customer retention is the equivalent of a 10 percent cut in costs. Companies have found that commissions that were anticipated to improve productivity, employee satisfaction, and customer retention have actually hurt these areas. This article looks at examples of some retailers' alternative compensation methods.

Hubbartt, William S. Money talks: How to use financial incentives to motivate employees. *Office Systems* (April 1991), 76–80.

Some companies reward their employees for overtime, holidays, or unusual working conditions by giving an extra hourly pay rate. An employee who works to gain more knowledge about his or her job and the company may be rewarded by a pay-for-knowledge plan. This article addresses profit sharing, stock purchases, and other forms of employee incentives.

Keenan, William, Jr. Should sales support employees get incentive pay? *Sales & Marketing Management* (January 1989), 30–33.

Companies are attempting to develop programs for compensation of nonsales employees who help with a sale. All employees benefit from incentive compensation programs to replace or to add to merit rewards. Some companies are reluctant to implement compensation programs for nonsales employees because such programs have the potential to disrupt the goals of the complete employee compensation program. Companies where the salespeople work closely with sales support personnel benefit most from alternative incentive programs.

Matejka, J. Kenneth, Neil O. Ashworth, and Diane Dodd-McCue. Pay for performance vs. performance for pay. *Supervision* (April 1989), 14–16.

A consistent incentive pay system best serves the needs of employees. It makes room not only for past performances but for any future compensation. These plans are also in the company's best interest because they are more cost-effective.

Mika, Peggy. Motivating CSR's. *Rough Notes* (August 1991), 14–16.

Female customer service representatives (CSRs) are attracted to more inventive forms of compensation rather than to the usual monetary awards. Because they make up 95 percent of CSRs in the industry, it is necessary for companies to take their interests into consideration. Some imaginative ways are employee shopping sprees, grab bags, vacations, and bonuses. Money from sales commissions can be used toward bonuses for CSRs.

Nicosia, Robert A. Who says commissions are too high? *Bests Review* (March 1990), 46–48, 88.

Due to consumer demand for lower premiums and increased competition, companies have been forced to lower commissions. Underwriting, claims, indirect expenses, agency profits, processing, and salesperson commissions are dependent on a 15 percent agency commission. An agent's actual commission is in the range of 6 percent, comparable to the 6 to 8 percent commission paid by direct writers to their salespeople. An independent agency does more for its commission than the sales personnel of direct writers. This article lists criteria for comparison of businesses.

Chapter 17

Evaluating the Sales Force

OPENING SCENARIO

Mark Bowers was about to embark on one of those tasks he detested: annual performance evaluations. This was the end of his third year as the district manager (DM) for Martin Papers, a producer of office forms and various other commercial paper products. His district included Arizona, New Mexico, Colorado, and Nevada. He had 12 sales reps who reported to him.

One of the reasons for Mark's dislike of the process was that it seemed to be constantly changing. For example, he had just taken over as the DM when the annual evaluation process was scheduled, and so he sat down with the outgoing DM, Gail Jackson, and went through the process. That was the last year for the "old system," which really amounted only to looking at sales figures and sales costs, and rating performance based on that. Then they established quotas for the next year and were finished. Altogether, the process took about four hours to complete by the time they had done all the paperwork. Jackson told him that the human resource management (HRM) people were making a "few changes" in the evaluation process for the coming year and that he would be adequately briefed on them.

The "few changes" amounted to a complete revamping of the system. The next year, he still had to consider sales volume and sales costs, but he also had to look at sales mix and profitability. Additionally, he had to compute indexes for the various measures and draw up comparisons of them. This year, the HRM department had added a whole series of "qualitative" measures that needed evaluation. For example, he had to rate his people on customer service, professionalism, and time management, as well as various other dimensions. He was frustrated because the qualitative measures were "soft" and difficult to evaluate. He also knew that they were more subjective and therefore subject to bias.

Finally, he was frustrated because what had started out as a four-hour exercise three years ago had turned into an affair that ate up an entire week by the time he sat down with each of his reps to go over the evaluations and to establish goals for the next year.

Chapter Objectives

After reading this chapter, you should be able to

- Understand the importance of performance evaluations in company operations.
- Know the critical elements in a performance evaluation and the best way to measure them.
- Appreciate the difficulty of measuring qualitative aspects of performance.
- Understand the implications of different quantitative measures of performance.
- Recognize the difficulty of providing performance feedback to salespeople.

INTRODUCTION

A major portion of sales managers' time is spent evaluating the efforts of their salespeople. The process is complicated by the many factors, both within and outside the organization, that can affect performance. It is also complicated by the fact that a number of elements must be considered in what we call "performance." Although sales volume is critical, if that were the only criterion to be concerned about, evaluation would be greatly simplified. Sales managers must evaluate not only salespeople's output but also their inputs. Salespeople need to receive feedback not only on relative sales volume but also on how well they are servicing customers.

Sales managers should ensure that they are conducting fair evaluations. They also want to ensure that the appraisal does not undermine performance but leads to improved performance. Additionally, sales managers are plagued by the difficulty of translating that evaluation into some useful feedback for each salesperson.

LEGAL ASPECTS OF EVALUATIONS

Performance evaluations are important for several reasons. They are used as criteria for such purposes as

- Salary adjustments
- Promotions

- Termination decisions
- Motivation
- Training decisions
- Territory/duty assignments
- Feedback
- Strategic planning

Because the performance evaluation serves all these purposes, sales managers need to provide excellent reports. Additionally, performance evaluations must meet legal standards. As in hiring decisions, performance evaluations cannot be discriminatory. Instruments used in performance evaluations must meet tests of validity and reliability, and the way these instruments are applied must not violate the intent of the law.

For example, a sales manager gives a salesperson a low rating on the dimension of "professionalism." She tells him he was given the low rating because his sales volume was down from last year's figures. She explains that truly "professional" salespeople have steadily increasing sales volume. While his sales volume may be down due to some action or inaction on his part (although it may very well be due to some other factor), it is probably not a reflection on his professionalism but on some other dimension. In this case, the evaluation is unfair.

Dena Schneier states that, in general, courts have found appraisals to be discriminatory in the following instances:[1]

1. Appraisals were based on subjective, ill-defined criteria.
2. The items in the appraisal instruments were not based on elements in the job.
3. The appraisal instruments were not properly validated; the instruments did not relate to level of performance.
4. The appraisal instruments were not administered in a standardized manner, which affected their validity.
5. The evaluations seemed to be affected by sexual and/or racial bias.

Furthermore, the 1970 Equal Employment Opportunity Commission (EEOC) guidelines on evaluations state the following:

> The work behaviors or other criteria of employee adequacy which the test is intended to predict or identify must be fully described; and, additionally, in the case of rating techniques, the appraisal form(s) and instructions to the rater(s) must be included as a part of the validation evidence. Such criteria may include measures other than actual work proficiency, such as training time, supervisory ratings, regularity of attendance and tenure. Whatever criteria are used they must represent major or critical work behaviors as revealed by careful job analyses.[2]

In general, the guidelines that apply to hiring practices also apply to conducting evaluations. The instruments employed must not be discriminatory, and, as in hiring, once a discriminatory practice has been uncovered, the burden of proof rests on the company being sued.

ELEMENTS IN THE EVALUATION PROCESS

There are five general dimensions of the salesperson's job that need to be evaluated. Even though they are interrelated, they are best evaluated separately. They include

1. Output
2. Customer relations
3. Job skills
4. Company relations
5. Personal characteristics

These five dimensions can be broken down into two broad categories—outcome-based and behavior-based, representing two schools of thought about performance appraisal.[3] The **outcome-based measures** are concerned principally with the "bottom line." They include such dimensions as sales volume, sales mix, sales costs, and profitability. Generally speaking, with these measures, sales managers take a bit less proactive approach to management, and the salesperson assumes the major responsibility for his or her performance. The outcome-based approach is easier to measure, and in one sense, tends to be more objective. However, even though more objective, they can be affected by factors other than performance.[4]

The **behavior-based measures** are founded on the idea that if salespeople "do the right things," their outcome measures will be in line with expectations. Sales managers get more involved in working with salespeople during the course of the sales cycle and, therefore, evaluations really become an ongoing process. According to Jack Falvey, contributing editor of *Sales & Marketing Management*, this day-to-day approach to managing salespeople is the most effective. He makes a compelling argument:

> If you're doing your job everyday as a field manager, there's no need for an annual or semi-annual performance review procedure. No one working for you should go home on a Friday night without knowing what you think of what they did that week. It's that simple—and that difficult. If your people have to wait for a formal performance review to know how they're doing, you've failed as a manager. After all, how can you expect anyone to grow and improve if he or she is only given feedback once or twice a year?[5]

In other words, managers who are doing their job effectively work with their people on an ongoing basis. Certainly, there is the need for a time once or twice a year where the sales manager and the salesperson go over the year's performance and begin to set the stage for the next year. However, that should be in addition to the ongoing process of providing feedback.

In general, the outcome-based measures and the behavior-based measures are best used in conjunction with each other. Their mix is dependent on a number of factors, such as type of industry, characteristics of the marketplace, and characteristics of the sales force itself. For example, in regard to the type of organization, a study by Donald Jackson, Janet Keith, and John Schlacter found a significant difference between manufacturing firms and service firms on the performance measures considered in the evaluations of their sales forces. Specifically, their findings revealed that sales volume and selling costs were used significantly more by manufacturing firms than by service firms in evaluating performance. Service firms were more likely than manufacturers to consider number of accounts lost and order cancellation rate as measures of performance.

In that same study, there were no significant differences between large and small firms in either their evaluation procedures or their performance bases.[6] However, evidence from another source suggests that, in fact, the size of the organization has an impact not only on what dimensions are evaluated but also on the procedures used in evaluations.[7]

Output measures deal with what we traditionally think of as "productivity measures," such as sales volume, sales mix, sales costs, profitability, number of sales calls, allocation of effort, and so forth. However, output measures historically have been dominant in assessing performance.[8] According to a study of sales managers, **sales volume** (how much is sold) was the most important criterion of evaluation, with sales as a percentage of quota ranking third.[9]

Although sales volume has traditionally been viewed as the major measure of salespeople's productivity, increasingly sales managers are recognizing that simply being concerned with volume can lead to less than optimal profit being generated by the sales unit. **Sales mix,** the combination of products or product lines sold in a given period, has become much more of a focus of attention, because, without a good sales mix salespeople will not generate as much profit as they otherwise could. Commensurate with this move away from simply looking at sales volume, many sales organizations have begun to treat sales territories as "profit centers" rather than as sources of revenue. Although this may sound like semantics, its real impact is to provide a different view of the responsibility of salespeople and the role of the territory in the overall plan of the company.

There are a number of approaches to evaluating the profitability of salespeople. The simplest approach is a sales volume analysis. For example, Allied Electric may evaluate a salesperson using the information listed in Table 17-1. Based on this information, the sales manager can get an idea of how salespeople are performing in sales relative to each other. A sales manager can look at the information in this table and have an idea not only of overall sales but also of the relative success of each salesperson in increasing sales from the previous year relative to the overall increase. The salesperson in Territory 2 had the highest overall sales but had the lowest increase in sales, and was significantly lower than the average increase. At the same time, the person in Territory 3 had the lowest sales volume with the highest increase.

Although we could speculate on what these figures mean, there is no clear-cut message, and the sales manager who relies strictly on them will be operating

TABLE 17-1 Allied Electric Sales Figures

Year	Territory	Sales (000)	Percentage Change	Company	Percentage Change
1993	1	1900	5.0	12,250	4.5
	2	2050	2.9		
	3	1400	6.1		
	4	1750	4.5		
	5	1550	4.5		
	6	1850	5.5		
	7	1750	3.0		

with incomplete information. The person in Territory 2 may well have reached a plateau and may need some additional encouragement, whereas the person in Territory 3 may need some additional resources to develop the territory. But to know any of this for sure, the sales manager needs to do some additional investigating.

A number of factors may have affected the sales results shown in the table. For example, if housing starts were down and the overall growth rate in the electrical supply industry were only 2.5 percent for the past year, Allied would be doing quite well, and what appears to be relatively poor growth in Territory 2 may actually be quite good, given the situation in the industry.

One of the issues in measuring performance output is the problem of regular and irregular fluctuations in sales. For instance, in some industries sales are seasonal, and a firm can do little to overcome this seasonality. This would be considered a "regular" fluctuation in that it is recurring and predictable. An irregular fluctuation is when company employees go on strike or when a raw materials shortage occurs. In either of these cases salespeople can do nothing to affect the situation, and yet their sales need to be evaluated.

Dick Berry has suggested using a combination of a **moving average** and an indexing approach in conducting evaluations as a way to overcome this problem.[10] In such a scheme, the sales manager, instead of simply looking at month-by-month figures, would take a three-month moving average and use that figure for comparison. For example, as shown in Table 17-2, instead of simply comparing Sara Lunsford's May 1994 figure ($109,000) with the May 1993 figure ($122,000), the manager would get a more accurate picture by taking the average for the 1994 quarter ($124,000) and comparing that with the comparable figure for 1993 ($122,000). Sara's performance for May 1994 would not compare favorably to that of May 1993, but her overall performance for the quarter was superior to the previous year's performance for that same time period. There may be a number of reasons for the relatively poor performance in May, but she seems to have made up for it in June.

TABLE 17-2 Sara Lunsford's Three-Month Sales Figures

1993	Sales	1994	Sales
April	125,000	April	137,000
May	122,000	May	109,000
June	119,000	June	126,000
Three-month average	122,000	Three-month average	124,000

Sales managers have always evaluated the activity of the salespeople as a component of productivity. Hence, companies generally have had a system for reporting the number of sales calls, the number of new accounts opened, and the like. However, given the increasing cost per sales call, firms are recognizing that they need to increase their efficiency by a better allocation of effort. Therefore, sales managers need some way of making a relative evaluation of the activities of salespeople as to their efficiency and effectiveness.

One approach that is growing in popularity is using the **return on assets managed (ROAM)** as a measure of output. ROAM is a salesperson performance measure that takes into account not only the volume of sales but also the profitability of a territory relative to the asset turnover. This measure provides sales managers with some additional information.

$$\text{ROAM} = \frac{\text{contribution margin as}}{\text{percentage of sales}} \times \frac{\text{asset}}{\text{turnover}}_{\text{rate}}$$

$$= \text{profit contribution/sales} \times \text{sales/assets managed}$$

For example, in Table 17-3, Territories 4 and 7 show the same overall sales for the period, but are these territories equivalent in their overall output? Using the ROAM formula and the information in Table 17-3, we gain some additional insights into how well these territories are doing relative to each other. Overall, Territory 7 has almost twice the ROAM as does Territory 4, which would indicate not only greater profitability but also greater efficiency in the use of assets.

As we look more closely at the figures, several things become apparent about the nature of this difference in the ROAM of the two territories. First, although the sales are the same and Territory 4 seems to be increasing sales at a faster rate (see Table 17-1), it is doing so at the expense of **profit contribution.** It would appear that the salesperson in Territory 4 is selling a large quantity of lower profit items. Also, although both territories are handling the same amount of inventory, Territory 4 accounts receivables are considerably higher, which may mean that the salesperson is "stretching" the credit limits and terms of his or her customers. Finally, it should be noted, however, that the salesperson in Territory

TABLE 17-3 Territory ROAM Data

	Territory 4	Territory 7
Sales	1,750,000	1,750,000
Cost of goods	1,250,000	1,050,000
Gross margin	500,000	700,000
Selling costs	160,000	150,000
Profit contribution	340,000	550,000
Accounts receivable	750,000	500,000
Inventory	850,000	850,000
Assets managed	1,600,000	1,350,000
Contribution Percentage	19%	31%
Asset turnover	1.09	1.30
ROAM	21%	40%

4 does not have significantly greater selling costs than the person in Territory 7. Using ROAM, the sales manager has the opportunity to gain a greater depth of understanding of where corrective action might be needed.

Aside from sales-oriented and profit-oriented measures, there are several other facets of output that sales managers need to consider. For example, the number of new accounts represents a critical aspect of performance because new accounts reflect the future viability of a territory. Salespeople often hesitate to develop new accounts because they are difficult to develop and because many sales organizations do not reward such development.

Given the increasingly long-term nature of the relationship between suppliers and customers, an important measure of performance is the level of service being provided. Often companies use the "back-door" approach by considering the number of complaints customers make about salespeople. Although this does provide some information, there is a whole segment of the market that will not register a complaint about a salesperson but will simply take its business elsewhere. One approach to measuring this aspect of "output" is by periodically sending out brief questionnaires to a sample of customers in each territory. This not only provides information for the sales manager but also sends a signal to customers that the company is concerned about providing good service.

For each company, there are unique factors of output, some of which are more readily quantifiable than others. Generally, most companies will wish to measure such things as the number of calls per day as part of output. A good evaluation system considers all the important aspects of output. If a company only looks at sales volume, the message is conveyed to salespeople that this is the

SELL!NG
THE FRONT LINES OF BUSINESS

21 Ways to Sharpen Your Selling Edge
Shane Tritsch

Face the ugly truth: The greasy wheel eventually will squeak. To the benefit of moss everywhere, the rolling stone finally will stop rolling. Even a decent steak knife, in time, can't cut butter. Neither, alas, can some salespeople.

While such circumstances may not be the end of the world for the wheel, the stone, or the steak knife, they can be the death of a salesperson. If you've ever lost your selling edge, you know what that means. Salespeople lose their edge for all kinds of reasons and one inescapable truth: They're human, and subject to the forces that get most of us sooner or later. Skills rust. Novelty fades. Passion flickers. Energy wanes.

That big deal you sweated over for years falls apart, and now it's hard to muster the energy or conviction to start over again. Or maybe you've recited the same pitch so many times, it begins to replay in your mind like some stupid song. Perhaps you've endured a year's worth of bad months, and you doubt business will ever improve. Or maybe you've worked with the same customer for so long, you've stopped asking the questions and doing the little things that got you the business in the first place.

"Like anyone, you get lazy, you take shortcuts," says Dick Aderman, director of global hemostasis and former vice president of sales at Baxter Diagnostics in Miami, a division of Baxter Healthcare Corp. "You win for so long that you forget what got you there," he says. "Or you get into a losing streak and start on a downward spiral. You start blaming your luck or your personality, and you stop thinking about the fundamentals of good selling."

For Lyn Eisenhower, a sales representative for CB Commercial Real Estate Group in Los Angeles, losing her edge means "letting any competitor take business I could have gotten. It's taking your eye off the ball, not paying attention to what's going on around you, not listening to the marketplace. It's getting worn out, frustrated, exhausted. It's negativity—being the dark cloud rather than the silver lining."

To Jeff Maher, assistant to the chairman at Miglin-Beitler, a commercial real estate management firm in Chicago, it's just another way of saying you've developed bad habits. "You get stale," he says. "You keep calling on the same customers. Or you stop cold calling to expand your customer base. Or you say, 'I'll make that call tomorrow rather than today.'"

Complacency, frustration, defeat, stagnation, and routine are some of the forces that blunt the selling edge. The best salespeople understand intuitively how to stay sharp. They know more than their rivals about their customers' industries and businesses. They brush up on the latest selling techniques. They read, talk, and listen in an effort to give their clients the most informed service. They aspire to be the best, and know that good selling boils down to fundamentals. They work hard to keep their edge. Here are some ways to sharpen yours.

NO. 2: HAVE A BROAD PURPOSE

Once a year Miglin-Beitler's Maher writes down his goals for the next 12 months on a sheet of paper. And each morning before work he re-reads that sheet of paper. This is his long-range plan, the career road map that keeps him moving in the right direction, not circling on the side streets. "It reminds me that I have a larger purpose," he says. "That puts me in the right frame of mind to go out and accomplish today, not put off till the end of the month."

NO. 3: HAVE A SPECIFIC PURPOSE—LOTS OF THEM

Shrink down the big picture to postcard size but keep the focus. That is, have a clear sense of mission for each day and for each call you make. Understand as much as you can about your customer and plan your call in advance.

"What are you really trying to accomplish?" asks Thomas Smith, director of professional education and corporate communications for CB Commercial Real Estate and the author of *Winning in Commercial Real Estate Sales: An Action Plan for Success*. "Do you really have an unclouded understanding of what you're trying to do every day and on every call, and ultimately, how that activity translates into a strategic approach to your marketplace?"

NO. 4: KEEP EARNING YOUR BUSINESS

If you've had someone's business for a long time, it's easy to start taking it for granted and to stop doing the things that earned you the business.

"You need to realize that just as you have stolen accounts from the competition, so can you lose them," says Lisa Earle McLeod, vice president of national accounts for Vital Learning Corp., a training company based in Omaha. "Don't delude yourself into thinking you have them forever. I have stolen business from competitors because they weren't aware of how the customer's situation had changed, and that made them more receptive to me. I sold to their changed business environment, whereas the competition was still selling to issues of a year ago. If they had been smart, they would have been in there positioning themselves against current issues in business." Which leads to the corollary commandment:

NO. 5: KNOW THY CUSTOMER

"Don't ever consider yourself in an account service role," advises McLeod. "Always be in a selling role. And don't consider the account sold forever. Always ask what is changing with the customer. If you don't, you could be out before it even hits you."

Aderman knows just what McLeod means. When he was vice president of sales at Baxter Diagnostics, the company lost a longtime account, worth $1 million a year, to a competitor. Puzzling over why the customer jumped ship, management concluded that Baxter had let a good relationship go to seed. "We took it for granted," says Aderman. "We lost sight of the fundamentals. Even today we are uncertain who was making the buying decisions there; we no longer understood their buying criteria."

Now Aderman is responsible for keeping in close contact with Baxter's biggest clients. His mission is to make sure his company never again fails to stay abreast of a customer's changing business needs.

"One of the most important ways to gain an edge or sustain a competitive advantage is to learn as much as you can about your customer or client's business," says Smith. "That means not just learning all you can about the customer's company but also about his or her industry and job—things like how he is measured for performance, how they do their job, and how they sell your product or service within their own organization."

NO. 6: TALK TO
THE DECISION-MAKER

Often salespeople are unable to reach the ultimate decision-maker. The question is, how can you get past the pickets and reach that person? One way is simply to ask. But failing that, Bill Foster, president

of The Institute for Innovation, a management consultancy in Greenwich, Conn., suggests asking questions that your contact may not be able to answer, including: "What are your client's five top business goals or needs for the coming year? What are the biggest barriers against achieving those goals or satisfying those needs?" If they can answer, then you get important information that helps you position your product or service. "If they can't answer," says Foster, "they're more sympathetic to your need to talk to their boss. Once you get in, you can learn things that will help you position your line in an additive way that suddenly makes it look different."

NO. 7: TALK TO
THE END USER

One reason salespeople lose touch with their customers is because they don't get beneath the purchasing agent to talk to the people who actually use their product. "Go into the bowels of the organization and find out how many times it's late, how often it breaks, how it could be improved," Foster says. "You need to listen to your customer, and your customer is not just the purchasing agent."

NO. 8: KEEP IT FRESH

Do you ever find yourself repeating the same stock phrases in your sales presentations? Although you may have sold a product a thousand times, your customer may be seeing it for the first. If you're bored with your pitch, your customer will be, too. "One of the oldest adages of selling is that you've got to be sold on your own product," says Foster. "You can be sold on it and still present it in a boring way." His advice: Think of new ways to communicate your message, and vary your pitch according to your audience. "The typical salesperson tends not to segment his audience," Foster says. "They tend to make their sales calls the same way, every day, with the same amount of preparation."

NO. 9: BE NIMBLE, BE QUICK

The clientele at Eisenhower's commercial real estate company has changed in recent years from largely entrepreneurs to institutions. So has the kind of services expected. "Controlling and minimizing risk is important to them," Eisenhower says. How has her company responded? By providing much more service in the form of analyses, reports, and research—all things that prolong the selling cycle and demand greater patience and persistence on the part of the sellers. "You've got to change to meet the needs of your clientele, or you're out of that business," Eisenhower says.

NO. 10: MAKE LEARNING CALLS

One way to rejuvenate yourself is to make a call for the purpose of listening, not selling. Once a year tell your customer that all you want to do is understand where he is going with his business. Ask questions and listen to answers. Or simply say, "I've been calling on you for X years. Today I'd like you to tell me

how my company and I can serve you better." What could you improve about your sales calls, your presentation, confirmation of orders, your company's billing procedures, shipping, and communications when the customer has a problem?

NO. 11: NEVER STOP ACQUIRING SKILLS AND KNOWLEDGE

"Jack Nicklaus still goes out every day and hits practice balls," explains Foster. "Sales training should not be seen as an insult. It's practice.

"Sometimes salespeople object to sales training. They say, 'I've been selling for 20 years. What do I need to learn?' One of the big dangers is that experienced salespeople often are selling 10 years behind the times. They're doing what made them successful back then, and they've lost product knowledge, style, touch. That's why you find that the bottom third of your sales force tends to be the older people. They tend to take things for granted. They're tired. You can't let their years of experience keep them from seeing that they have to keep working to get better."

Related learning helps, too. Monica Finnegan, a broker with CB Commercial Real Estate, has taken continuing education courses on construction, finance, and facility management—"all things that help me understand my customers' world better," she says. Continuing education keeps you fresh because you get involved with other people who have new ideas and different points of view that can shake you free of entrenched ways of thinking and selling.

NO. 12: DON'T OVERLOOK NEW OPPORTUNITIES WITH EXISTING CUSTOMERS

It seems obvious, but salespeople often fail to mine existing customers. "New business comes up with our customers all the time, but my salespeople don't even know about it," says McLeod. "That should be the easiest business to get. Yet they end up missing a lot of good sales opportunities and going out and reinventing business the hard way."

NO. 13: TAKE LITTLE BREAKS

People who push themselves too hard are like sprinters in a marathon. Eventually, the tortoise passes these hares. Take breaks during the day to stay refreshed, and keep a manageable pace.

Similarly, try to carve out a few hours of quiet time on a Monday or Friday to think about business problems. Sometimes setting something aside can yield new solutions to seemingly intractable problems. "There are times when you want to rip your hair out," says Eisenhower. "If you let things alone and divert yourself, you can shed light on the situation. Walk away from it, do something else, then come back to it."

NO. 14: TAKE BIG BREAKS

You know the type—the ones who work all the time, who haven't vacationed in five years and are proud of it. Maybe they shouldn't be. "You need to take a break," says Aderman. "Take a vacation. It gives you distance." It also recharges your cre-

ative batteries, lets you see the forest where once you saw just trees, and enables you to attack old problems from new angles and with renewed vigor.

NO. 15: SEEK MORALE BOOSTERS

If you work on a deal for a long time—say, a period of years—it can be easy to lose sight of your objective. It's okay. Go to a manager or a colleague and admit that you're getting down, that you don't see an end in sight. Say you need someone to get you charged up again. "Many people are reluctant to go to a manager and say they need help," says McLeod. "Because they're saying, 'I know what I have to do, but I'm not motivated.' Any good manager should be receptive to that."

NO. 16: SEE THE WORLD THROUGH YOUR CUSTOMER'S EYES, NOT YOUR OWN

If you are really focusing on the customer, then your sales will happen in time. Priorities get distorted when you begin to zero in on making this month's numbers or to calculate how much money you're going to make on that deal. Thinking about yourself distracts you from thinking about your customer—which is a good way to fall short of this month's numbers.

NO. 17: EXPECT SUCCESS

Great generals often possess a confidence that buoys their troops. Great salespeople often have a winning attitude that contributes to their sales success. Don't just hope for success or want it. Treat it as your birthright. Confidently visualize yourself receiving a commission or shaking hands to cement a deal. But beware the pitfalls of seeing things this way, and heed the following thoughts.

NO. 18: THE GLASS IS HALF FULL

Sure, this is the cornerstone of generations of sales motivation-speak. And for a good reason. Having a positive attitude is crucial to selling. So even if you're sure the glass is half empty, train yourself to think half full.

NO. 19: OKAY, THE GLASS IS HALF EMPTY—BUT NOT FOR LONG

It's easy to be positive when things are going well. But how do you bounce back after adversity strikes? Even the greatest salespeople have their low moments, but they know how to regain altitude in a hurry. How you talk to yourself when you're down can make a big difference in whether you jump up off the canvas. "There are times when I get down on myself," says Eisenhower. "It's natural, and that's okay. But I don't stay there. I talk to myself. I say things like, 'Come on, pull yourself up. Don't panic. You can do it.'"

NO. 20: BE GOOD TO OTHERS

Simple recognition of others takes little effort but can repay you many times over. It could mean saying thanks when someone gives you business, or recognizing a birthday or a graduation. It could mean sending a note to someone's boss to acknowledge a job well done. It could mean sincerely and enthusiastically greeting everyone you come in contact with, from the company president to the receptionist.

"A great salesperson will always reach out, regardless of station," says Smith. "They're consistent in the way they deal with people. Because ultimately, what you have to hang your hat on is the quality of your relationships and service. You've got to be willing to acknowledge others and show respect. It gives you more job satisfaction and meaning, but it's also a way to position yourself apart."

NO. 21: WORK ON THE FUNDAMENTALS

If you asked the 20 best NFL quarterbacks for the five most important things that make a good quarterback, you would have 98 percent duplication of answers after talking to a few of them, says Foster. "And it will all be fundamentals," he says. In the end, keeping your selling edge comes down to basics. "The fact that it isn't new doesn't mean people are doing it," says Foster. "And the fact that it isn't esoteric should not be cause for saying there must be some other secret. You've got to do the fundamentals better. Realizing that is the easy part. Doing it is the hard part."

Reprinted with the permission of SELL!NG magazine.

only thing that is really important. The sales manager may talk at length about the need for salespeople to provide good service to existing accounts and the need for prospecting for new accounts, but salespeople will respond to those things for which they are rewarded.

The other four elements that sales managers need to look at in performing evaluations are behavior-based measures. They include customer relations, job skills, company relations, and personal characteristics. More qualitative than quantitative and thus more difficult to evaluate, nonetheless, these are important parts of the sales job and are typically part of the evaluation in most companies. According to the Patton and King study cited earlier, among the qualitative measures that were found to be important was product knowledge, which was the second most important criterion, along with customer relations, sales presentation skills, and appearance.[11] Additionally, "citizenship" has often been an element in performance evaluations.[12] Table 17-4 shows the results of another study of how firms evaluate their sales forces.

These qualitative elements of the job are more difficult to evaluate because they require that sales managers spend time with individual salespeople to get a firsthand opinion of how well each person is doing. Also, sales managers must

TABLE 17-4 Qualitative Aspects of Sales Force Evaluation

Characteristic Evaluated	Percentage of Sample Considering
Attitude	90
Product knowledge	89
Selling skills	85
Appearance and manner	82
Communication skills	81
Initiative and aggressiveness	80
Planning ability	78
Time management	73
Knowledge of competition	72
Judgment	69
Creativity	61
Knowledge of company policies	59
Report preparation and submission	59
Customer goodwill generated	50
Degree of respect from trade and competition	34
Good citizenship	23

Source: Donald W. Jackson, Jr., Janet E. Keith, and John L. Schlacter, Evaluation of selling performance: A study of current practices. *Journal of Personal Selling & Sales Management* (November 1983), 43–51. Reproduced with permission.

make an evaluation of each salesperson in relation to other salespeople, and in an impartial, legally sound fashion.

Although there are a number of ways sales managers might evaluate these elements, generally they employ some type of scale. One popular form is a **graphic rating scale.** For example, if sales manager wished to evaluate a salesperson on "time management," one of the elements in Table 17-4, he or she might use one of the following three scale forms:

	Poor					Exceptional	
Time Management	0	1	2	3	4	5	6

	Below Average	Average	Above Average	Exceptional
Time Management	1	2	3	4

1. Allocates enough time to the better accounts to provide them with a good level of service.

Almost Never	1	2	3	4	5	6	7	Almost Always

These scales allow the manager to make a value judgment with the aid of a numerical scale that can differentiate levels of performance on a particular dimension. Although these do not eliminate bias, they at least force the manager to give a relative rating to his or her salesperson.

Another approach that seeks to define more specifically the important elements of the sales job is the **behaviorally anchored rating scale (BARS).**[13] This is a multistep process of delineating the behaviors related to a given aspect of sales. The steps are

1. Individuals who are familiar with the job are asked to detail the critical incidents of effective and ineffective behavior. This set of incidents is then reduced into a smaller set.
2. The group developing the BARS reviews the set of critical incidents and groups them into a smaller set of performance dimensions that are stated in general terms.
3. The set of critical incidents is presented to another group of salespeople who are also provided with the performance dimensions outlined in step 2. They are asked to assign the critical incidents to the appropriate dimension of performance. A critical incident statement is retained if 60 percent or more of the group assign it to the same performance dimension.
4. The second group is then asked to rate the behavior described in the critical incident on a 7- to 10-point scale as to how effectively or ineffectively it represents performance on the dimension.
5. A set of six to eight incidents that seem to have the highest rating by the group as being related to the dimension is then selected for the BARS.

The final product is similar to what is shown in Table 17-5, which uses the performance dimension of time management.

TABLE 17-5 A BARS for Time Management

	Time Management	
Performance Categories and Definitions of the Dimension		Behavioral Anchor Statements
Very High This indicates a very good use of time management.	10 9	Allocates time well, gets reports completed when or before they are due, and uses scheduled appointments.
	8 7	Allocates time well, is seldom late with reports, and often uses scheduled appointments.
	7	Does a fair job with time allocation, gets many reports in on time, and occasionally uses scheduled appointments.
Moderate This indicates an average level of time management.	6 5 4	Does a fair job with time allocation, gets many reports in on time, and occasionally uses scheduled appointments.
	5 4	Does not spend enough time with better customers, turns many reports in late, and seldom uses appointments.
	3 2	Spends excessive time on low-yield accounts, turns very few reports in on time, and only rarely schedules appointments.
Very Low This indicates a very poor level of applying time management principles.	2 1 0	Does not prioritize accounts into a hierarchy, consistently turns reports in late, and does not schedule appointments.

The BARS approach to rating offers a number of advantages that the graphic rating scales do not. First, it involves several persons in the process of development, which means that sales managers can take advantage of the expertise of others in the company. Related is the fact that when people become involved in the development of the system in which they work, they will generally be much more accepting of the results of the system. The third major advantage of the BARS is that it provides concrete descriptions of behaviors related to a particular dimension of the sales job. That makes it easier for sales managers to pinpoint how a salesperson should be rated on a given aspect of job performance.

Errors in Performance Evaluations

Just as in so many other areas of business, performance appraisals have many potential pitfalls. There are many more ways to do them poorly than to do them well. Laurence Siegal and Irving Lane outline five major errors that often occur in doing evaluations:[14]

1. **Distributional errors.** Theoretically, there is some "true" distribution of performance among any group of people. Generally, this distribution will approximate a "normal curve." There are three types of distributional errors—central tendency, severity, and leniency. Central tendency is where an average rating is given to all employees. Severity is when most individuals are rated as poor performers, and leniency takes place when most are given high ratings.

2. **Halo effect.** This is the tendency to generalize from an initial set of experiences to subsequent ones. For example, if a salesperson has been a good performer for the past several years but in the past year performed poorly, a supervisor may still see him as a good performer and rate him higher than he should be rated.

3. **Egocentric effects.** The tendency of the evaluator to use his self-perception as the standard against which subordinates are evaluated. Another effect, contrast error, refers to the tendency to feel that subordinates are different from managers; generally, it is the feeling that they are not as good given that they are subordinates. Similarity error is viewing subordinates as similar to one's self.

4. **Sequential effects.** Many rating instruments use a series of scales that deal with different dimensions of the job. Often in their effort to be consistent, raters tend to give similar ratings on all the scales.

5. **Evaluator bias.** Bias takes place when a series of factors that are irrelevant to performance are taken into consideration when raters are doing performance appraisals. For example, the sales manager who believes that individuals who have moved into sales from other occupations are destined to be poor salespeople would be biased in his evaluation. Also, the sales manager who harbors racial prejudices and allows those to effect the way she evaluates salespeople is engaging in evaluator bias.

The first four types of errors can be adequately dealt with through training. However, evaluator bias is more difficult to overcome because any discussion of it may be threatening to trainees; but, in general, training has proven to be useful in sensitizing managers that bias can affect their decisions and evaluations.[15]

All of these approaches to rating performance have both strengths and weaknesses. Sales managers must develop the approach and the tools that best apply in their own companies. The point of rating scales is to force the evaluator to break the job down into its components, to judge each of those components separately, and to eliminate, as much as possible, any personal bias that the rater might bring to the evaluation table. All salespeople will have areas where they do well and areas that present problems for them. However, the evaluation process should result in sales managers' being able to provide adequate feedback to their salespeople and help them make mid-course corrections. The only way to do that is to obtain as specific information about salespeople and their circumstances as is possible.

When evaluating salespeople, sales managers should remember the following considerations:

1. Be aware of the halo effect when making the evaluation.
2. Base ratings on observed performance and not perceived potential.
3. Do not allow personalities to affect your perception of the person and his or her performance.

4. Do not rate the person on a few instances of good or poor work but, rather, on general success or failure in performing duties.

5. Recognize that all people will have some areas where they will excel and other areas in which they will struggle, and remember that they will often differ from your areas of strength and weaknesses.

6. Resist the temptation of making too close a comparison between the person and the top performer in the company.

7. Realize that over time people will change, and sometimes those changes can positively or negatively affect how they perform in certain dimensions of the sales job.

MANAGEMENT BY OBJECTIVES AND PERFORMANCE APPRAISAL

Since **management by objectives (MBO)** was introduced in the 1950s by Peter Drucker, it has played a major part in corporate America.[16] The reason for its success is that it takes a teamwork approach to deciding employees' future, and therefore employees feel that they play some part in making decisions concerning their career. Wendell French defines MBO as

> a system that features a periodic agreement between a superior and a subordinate on the subordinate's objectives for a particular period and a periodic review of how well the subordinate achieved those objectives.[17]

Certainly with a group such as salespeople, who generally enjoy a certain amount of autonomy, such a system fits well. It is also beneficial to sales managers because working with salespeople to set objectives has the benefit of providing them with more information than might be available otherwise. Obviously, also, because salespeople have some say in what those objectives are, they will feel some sense of ownership.

An inherent part of MBO is the performance appraisal. During the appraisal feedback session, the objectives are established for the next period. When the evaluation is discussed, the salesperson is less likely to question the validity of the objectives and the time spent rehashing such things, and more time can be devoted to discussing what the salesperson can do to accomplish those objectives.

MEANINGFUL FEEDBACK

One of the most difficult things for an evaluator to do is to provide **feedback** that is meaningful to the listener. It is difficult because the information must be couched in terms that the listener will understand and relate to. Another difficulty is that often there is a tendency to forget the reason for feedback. Often managers have some things that they "want to get off their chest," which usually translates into blowing off steam. Feedback, however, should be mainly for providing guidance. In other words, the feedback session is the forum for developing future performance, and when used as such can be a key to the long-term success of the sales organization.

Morey Stettner, president of MAS Communications, a consulting firm that advises Fortune 500 companies, suggests that much of the reason for problems arising from evaluations is due to the way managers go about the process.[18] Often the way managers say things and the words they use bring about a defensive reaction, which effectively negates any good the feedback session might accomplish. He cautions that managers should avoid words like "never" or "always" and should refer to observable facts rather than impressions. Additionally, putting things in the form of questions rather than statements will help ease the idea that the person is being condemned without a fair hearing.

Often feedback sessions are ineffective because the sales manager's remarks are contradictory and do not deal with relevant issues. According to Jack Carew, president of Carew Positional Systems, Inc., much of the reason for this lies in the fact that sales managers do not listen to the concerns of their salespeople.[19] Carew, as well as a survey conducted by *Sales & Marketing Management*, suggests that having salespeople evaluate their managers might be a useful exercise for both groups in that it will let each experience what it is like from a different perspective.[20] Salespeople are interested in getting help to diagnose and solve their problems, not in having their problems solved by them. According to Carew, the tendency for many managers is to jump into the situation personally and resolve it without using the problem as a forum for teaching the salesperson how to deal with it. Additionally, salespeople are interested in working with sales managers to set goals and generally want to receive honest feedback and not simply be told that they are doing okay.

The following guidelines will be useful for sales managers to keep in mind during the feedback session:

1. Evaluations should be discussed with each salesperson individually.
2. Any evaluation should contain positive suggestions for improvement in weak areas. These suggestions should be in addition to the ongoing "coaching" process. These suggestions should contain specific information and support for assertions.
3. Evaluation meetings should be the forum for establishing goals for the next period and for developing plans for meeting those goals.
4. Avoid being overly critical of the individual, especially if that criticism begins with "when I was in your shoes."
5. If the evaluation process involves discussing a pay raise, it is better that the salesperson be given an idea of the average raise given so that he or she has an overall idea of how well his or her performance compares with others' in the organization. If you do not provide that information, there is a tendency to underestimate how relatively good a raise the person received if doing well, and he or she has the tendency to underestimate the average if the person is doing poorly and received a poor raise.

Performance evaluations are a major element in the sales manager's job. Like so many other aspects of that job, this evaluation is rapidly changing. For example, the increased emphasis on total quality management (TQM) is having an impact on our approach to evaluating sales force performance.[21] There are more tools available to assist the sales manager in more fairly conducting evaluations.[22] Also, the move toward developing more partnering relationships with customers means that salespeople are changing their approach to the sales job, and, therefore, the way their performance is evaluated needs to be changed.

CHAPTER SUMMARY

In this chapter, we presented issues related to evaluating salespeople. Legal requirements of evaluations include validity, reliability, and job relatedness. These are the same requirements that apply to hiring practices. They were put in place to eliminate discrimination in performance evaluation because evaluations are used to determine pay raises, promotions, duty assignments, and termination decisions.

Elements that should be part of a performance evaluation of salespeople include both behavioral and output components of performance. For example, sales managers need to consider not only sales volume and profitability but also job skills, level of customer service provided, and product knowledge. Although the former are critical, the latter are important because they have a direct impact on sales performance. However, the latter are the more difficult to measure.

Even with the "easier to measure" elements such as sales volume, some complications arise. Just considering sales volume provides an incomplete picture of how well salespeople are doing. If a salesperson does not have the right sales mix and reasonable sales costs, he or she will not yield adequate profitability. Sales managers, then, must look beyond the sales volume and consider other issues. One approach to doing so involves calculating the return on assets managed (ROAM).

Sales managers face a number of complications when evaluating the behavioral aspects of salespeople's performance. Measuring customer service, for instance, is complicated because of the difficulty of defining what is an appropriate level of customer service and what it means to provide such a level. Sales managers can use a variety of techniques to make such evaluations, but perhaps the best approach is to employ a behaviorally anchored rating scale (BARS). This provides some specificity when determining how well a person is performing.

We closed the chapter with a discussion of some guidelines in conducting evaluations. The essence of these is that sales managers must look at several elements when conducting an evaluation, must be evenhanded in administering evaluations, must give an adequate level of feedback, and must monitor the progress of their salespeople.

KEY TERMS

behavior-based
  measures, p. 409
behaviorally anchored rating scale
  (BARS), p. 421
distributional errors, p. 423
egocentric effects, p. 423
evaluator bias, p. 423
feedback, p. 424
graphic rating scale, p. 421
halo effect, p. 423

management by objectives
  (MBO), p. 424
moving average, p. 411
outcome-based measures, p. 409
profit contribution, p. 412
return on assets managed
  (ROAM), p. 412
sales mix, p. 410
sales volume, p. 410
sequential effects, p. 423

CHAPTER QUESTIONS

1. Why are validity and reliability important in performance evaluations?
2. What is the difference between behavior-based and outcome-based performance measures?
3. What are the difficulties related to behavior-based measures of performance?
4. Why is sales volume often an inadequate measure of performance?
5. How does a BARS help sales managers assess outcome-based performance?
6. Describe how an MBO approach works and the part it plays in performance evaluations.
7. Why is providing feedback a critical element in the performance appraisal process?

NOTES

1. Dena B. Schneier, The impact of EEO legislation on performance appraisal. *Personnel* (July–August 1978), 25.
2. Wendell L. French, *The personnel management process* (Boston: Houghton Mifflin, 1987), 321.
3. Erin Anderson and Richard L. Oliver, Perspectives on behavior-based versus outcome-based salesforce control systems. *Journal of Marketing* 51 (October 1987), 76–88.
4. Greg W. Marshall, John C. Mowen, and Keith J. Fabes, The impact of territory difficulty and self versus other ratings on managerial evaluations of sales personnel. *Journal of Personal Selling & Sales Management* 12 (Fall 1992), 35–47; Greg W. Marshall and John C. Marshall, An experimental investigation of the outcome bias in salesperson performance evaluations. *Journal of Personal Selling & Sales Management* 13 (Summer 1993), 31–47.
5. Jack Falvey, Preappraising performance appraisal. *Sales & Marketing Management* (March 1992), 9–10.
6. Donald W. Jackson, Jr., Janet E. Keith, and John L. Schlacter, Evaluation of selling performance: A study of current practices. *Journal of Personal Selling & Sales Management* (November 1983), 43–51.

7. David Jobber, Graham J. Hooley, and David Shipley, Organizational size and salesforce evaluation practices. *Journal of Personal Selling & Sales Management* 13 (Spring 1993), 37–48.

8. Gilbert A. Churchill, Jr., Neil M. Ford, Steven W. Hartley, and Oliver C. Walker, Jr., The determinants of salesperson performance: A meta-analysis. *Journal of Marketing Research* 22 (May 1985), 103–118.

9. W. E. Patton III and Ronald H. King, The use of human judgment models in evaluating sales force performance. *Journal of Personal Selling & Sales Management* (May 1985), 1–14.

10. Dick Berry, Sales performance: Fact or fiction. *Journal of Personal Selling & Sales Management* (August 1986), 71–79.

11. Patton and King, The use of human judgment models.

12. Scott B. MacKenzie, Philip M. Podsakoff, and Richard Fetter, The Impact of organizational citizenship behavior on evaluations of salesperson performance. *Journal of Marketing* 57 (January 1993), 70–80; Philip M. Podsakoff and Scott B. MacKenzie, Organizational citizenship behaviors and sales unit effectiveness. *Journal of Marketing Research* 31 (August 1994), 351–363.

13. A. Benton Cocanougher and John M. Ivancevich, BARS performance rating for sales force personnel. *Journal of Marketing* 42 (July 1978), 87–95.

14. Laurence Siegal and Irving M. Lane, *Personnel and organizational psychological* (Homewood, IL: Irwin, 1982).

15. Ibid. 93; John C. Mowen and Gary J. Gaeth, The evaluation stage in marketing decision making. *Journal of the Academy of Marketing Science* 20 (Spring 1992), 177–187.

16. Peter F. Drucker, *The practice of management* (New York: Harper & Row, 1954).

17. French, *The personnel management process*, 341.

18. Morey Stettner, The delicate art of criticism. *Sales & Marketing Management* (October 1989), 104, 107.

19. Jack Carew, When salespeople evaluate their managers. *Sales & Marketing Management* (March 1989), 24–27.

20. Executive Advisory Panel, Should managers be evaluated by those they manage? *Sales & Marketing Management* (August 1989), 10–11.

21. David W. Cravens, Raymond W. LaForge, Gregory M. Pickett, and Clifford E. Young, Incorporating a quality improvement perspective into measures of salesperson performance. *Journal of Personal Selling & Sales Management* 13 (Winter 1993), 1–14.

22. Gene Brown, Robert E. Widing, II and Ronald L. Coulter, "Customer Evaluation of Retail Salespeople Utilizing the SOCO Scale: A Replication, Extension, and Application," *Journal of the Academy of Marketing Science*, 19, Fall 1991, 347–351.

SUGGESTED READINGS

French, Wendell L. *Human resource management*. Boston: Houghton Mifflin, 1990.

> Organizations today need to strive not only to be effective but also to have a high quality of life within the organization. This means going beyond simply motivating people to achieve the goals of the organization but also enhancing the quality of their own lives. By doing so, organizations will realize tangible benefits.

Hickman, Craig R. *Mind of a manager—soul of a leader*. New York: Wiley, 1990.

> Managers today are faced with a number of conflicting demands, some that require a careful manager, others that demand a dynamic leader. This creates a tension that is often not fully appreciated but, if unresolved, can lead to major difficulties. Bridging the gap requires that the manager come to have a good self-awareness as well as an understanding of those with whom he or she interacts.

Siegel, Laurence, and Irving M. Lane. *Personnel and organizational psychology.* Homewood, IL: Irwin, 1982.

> Performance in organizations is brought about by applying sound principles of human behavior. Performance is not a universally understood and accept concept, and therefore how organizations define good performance varies a good deal and affects such things as facilitating and measuring performance. Bringing about good performance begins at the individual level.

Cases

Case 1

Dell Computer Corporation

Bill J. Middlebrook
Michael J. Keeffe
John K. Ross III
Southwest Texas State University

Customer satisfaction and customer service are two of the most repeated catchphrases in major corporations, especially from the producer rather than the consumer side of the equation. Michael Dell does not want service and satisfaction to simply be repeated by his corporate employees and support staffs; he requires them to practice what he preaches. In fact the corporate culture—as clearly stated by Michael Dell (*Personal Selling Power,* March 1993)—"is very simple. Responsive, customer focus, high intensity level."

Dell's commitment to this concept of customer satisfaction and service—known at Dell as Direct Relationship Marketing—can be shown through the policies of the corporation. First, there is an unconditional, 30-day money-back guarantee for all of Dell's computer systems and a "no questions asked" return policy.

Second, Dell's toll-free technical support organization is available from 7:00 A.M. to 7:00 P.M., coast to coast (including Mexico). These technicians solve 95 percent of customer problems in less than 6 minutes. Additionally, a TechFax system is available 24 hours a day, 7 days a week. Customers can request technical information through a fax catalog, and problem-solving instructions are returned by fax. A third-party network of on-site service representatives can be dispatched when problems are not solved over the phone. If necessary, unresolved problems are expedited to the design engineers to ensure complete customer satisfaction. Dell users can also access an on-line technical support group via CompuServe.

Finally, Michael Dell openly invites customers to write or call him with comments about the quality of Dell's products and the level of support received from service and support personnel.

This emphasis on quality and service has won accolades from customers and industry analysts. Dell has consistently been recognized as the best in customer support and satisfaction, ahead of all other computer manufacturers. J. D. Power and Associates, known for its automobile rankings, again this year rated Dell number one in customer satisfaction in its third annual end-user survey for the computer industry.

The most publicized story of a company start-up in the computer industry is that of Steven Jobs and Stephen Wozniak designing and marketing Apple computers. These young entrepreneurs took a concept from a garage manufacturing arena and evolved Apple into a multi-million-dollar organization. The story of Michael Dell and the development of the Dell Computer Corporation rivals that of Jobs and Wozniak.

In 1983, Dell, then a freshman pre-med student at the University of Texas, decided to earn additional money by selling disk-drive kits and random access memory (RAM) chips at computer user meetings in Austin, Texas. Within a few months he had sufficient funds to acquire excess personal computers (PCs) at reasonable prices from IBM dealers having difficulties meeting their sales quotas. He modified the machines and began selling them through contacts in the local area and was reported to be grossing approximately $80,000 per month by April 1984. In May 1984, Dell formed the Dell Computer Corporation to sell PC's Limited brand computers and conducted operations out of his dormitory room. After dropping out of school (against his parents' wishes) he began attending computer trade fairs where he sold

these IBM PC-compatible computers, one of the first custom "clones" on the market.

The results of Dell's endeavors were immediate. During the first year of business, sales were approximately $6 million and grew to $257 million within the next four years. In 1988 the brand name was changed to Dell and sales continued to grow such that by 1990 the organization had sold $546 million in PC compatibles and peripheral equipment and $2.1 billion in fiscal 1993 (Dell's fiscal year ends February).

In 1987 Dell established its first international subsidiary in the United Kingdom to enter the growing European computer market. European countries had a lower PC saturation rate than the United States, and there were no large PC manufacturers in Europe. From 1988 to 1991 the organization developed wholly owned subsidiaries in Canada, France, Italy, Sweden, Germany, Finland, and the Netherlands and is in the process of launching other subsidiaries in Europe. An Irish manufacturing facility opened in 1991 to provide systems for the European market. In addition, a support center located in Amsterdam provides technical support throughout Europe. Dell reported that fourth-quarter 1991 international sales were up 109 percent over the same quarter in 1990. By February of 1993 European sales totaled $240 million and constituted 30 percent of total sales. Currently, 40 percent of sales are derived from international subsidiaries after only five years of operations.

In January 1993, Dell made a bold move by entering the Japanese market. Dell Computer KK of Japan employs a staff of 40 workers to provide a full range of sales, service, and technical assistance. Telephone sales is supplemented with an outside sales force and through two major retailers in Tokyo. As the first to attempt telemarketing in Japan, Dell was met with skepticism by some industry observers. Initial reports indicate that the Japanese are very enthusiastic about the marketing approach and are responding in greater numbers than originally forecasted. In fact; the 40 people in the Tokyo office are being tested in their ability to handle requests. Although successful, Dell is expected to have less than 1 percent of the Japanese market in 1993.

Dell Computer Corporation is headquartered in Austin, Texas, with approximately 4200 employees worldwide. Dell had the foresight to surround himself with people having expertise in computer engineering and marketing, and he serves as both chief executive officer (CEO) and chairman of the board of directors (see Exhibit C1–1 for corporate officers and members of the board of directors). The company still operates on the principles espoused by Dell during its in-

ception: customer service and a personal relationship with Dell system users.

PERSONAL COMPUTER INDUSTRY OVERVIEW

The short history of the PC industry is one of booms and slumps. The stellar performance of the industry during the early to mid-1980s was followed by a consolidation of existing companies and a slowdown in sales during the 1986–1987 period. Industry sales increased through 1990, and projections show that corporate capital-equipment spending should grow at a 7 to 8 percent annual rate into the early 1990s. Some analysts contend that the growth rate of the PC industry is uncertain as the growth rate of the economy slows. For example, Volpe & Covington, a San Francisco–based PC

EXHIBIT C1–1 Dell Computer Corporation Officers

Dell, Michael S.	28	Chairman of the board, CEO
Kocher, Joel J.	36	President, worldwide marketing, sales, and service
Henry, G. Glenn	50	Senior vice president
Flaig, L. Scott	48	Senior vice president
Meredith, Thomas J.	42	Chief financial officer, treasurer
Thomas, Thomas L.	43	Chief information officer
Ferrales, Savino R.	42	Vice president
Salwen, Richard E.	47	Vice president, legal counsel
Medica, John	34	Vice president, portable products GP

Directors

Dell, Michael S.	28	Chairman of the board, CEO
Hirschbiel, Paul Jr.	40	
Luce, Thomas W. III	52	
Inman, Bobby R.	62	Nominee
Kozmetsky, George	75	Nominee
Jordan, Michael H.	56	Nominee
Malone, Claudine B.	57	

investment consulting firm, believes that a 15 percent long-term growth in revenues for high-end PCs and a 12 percent compound growth rate for the industry is a reasonable assumption. Other analysts contend that PC sales would grow at only 5 to 7 percent in the 1990s, less than half as fast as sales grew in the late 1980s. In 1992 computer and peripheral sales totaled over $142 billion. This amount grew to $155 billion in 1993 and is projected to exceed $167 billion in 1994. (See Exhibits C1–2 and C1–3)

EXHIBIT C1–2 Worldwide Microsystems Shipped (millions)

Company	1989	1993[a]
IBM	2.7	4.4
Apple	1.5	3.2
Compaq	0.7	2.5
Sharp	1.4	1.9
NEC	1.1	1.7
Dell	0.1	1.4
Commodore	1.5	1.3
Packard Bell	0.3	0.9
Toshiba	0.4	0.8
AST	0.2	0.8
All others	13.5	22.2

[a]Projected.
Source: InfoCorp.

EXHIBIT C1–3 United States Microsystems Shipped (millions)

Company	1989	1993[a]
IBM	1.5	1.8
Apple	1.1	1.7
Compaq	0.4	1.1
Dell	0.1	0.9
Packard Bell	0.2	0.8
Gateway 2000	[b]	0.6
Hewlett-Packard	0.1	0.4
AST	0.2	0.4
Tandy	0.6	0.4
Commodore	0.4	0.3
All others	5.0	7.2

[a]Projected.
[b]<100,000.
Source: InfoCorp.

PC Industry Strategies

Two macroindustry strategies for competing in the PC industry can be combined with two macrosegments of the PC market to assess competitors and competitive approaches. First, PC manufacturers can approach the market as either innovators or imitators. IBM is the accepted innovation leader as both computer manufacturers and customers watch IBM's product development and base production and purchase decisions on current IBM products. Other computer manufacturers approach the market as innovators by developing hardware and software to satisfy specific market segments.

Most firms approach the market building clone PCs. These firms (sometimes called value-added remarketers) use the base MS-DOS technology of innovators and attempt to improve on the system configuration and/or differentiate their product on some basis such as marketing channel used, service and support, product reliability, and/or price. Essentially, value-added remarketers buy components and software from various vendors to configure systems sold under their own brand labels. The success of the imitative approaches is evidenced by the performance of companies such as Compaq, Prime Computer, Inc., CompuAdd, and Dell. Many clone firms believe that to be successful in the PC industry they must be concerned with market pressures to reduce price, and thus they constantly monitor costs and search for ways to reduce those costs.

PC Markets

Macrosegments in the PC industry are usually defined as business, home, government, or education users. Business users want high performance, reliability, and value in a system for their computing needs. State-of-the-art technology, the ability to network and communicate with other systems, customer service and support, and cost are primary purchase determinants for the business user. One of the fastest-growing segments in the business market is the portables market, which is expected to grow at an annualized rate of 20 percent for the next few years.

Home market demand was initially created by innovators, early adopters, and the early majority groups of the adoption or diffusion of innovation cycle. Most home users are price conscious, planning to spend less than $1200 for a system, and they value ease of operation and service as well as support from the manufacturer. This market should not be as lucrative as it was in the early to mid-1980s, but replacement sales (sales to previous PC owners) and sales to those still intending to buy a home PC should make this market moderately attractive. (For a list of competitors by market share, see Exhibit C1–4.)

Government and education users make up the remaining macrosegments of the PC market. Both of these segments represent large, important segments, yet typically yield lower margins than either the business or home markets. Typical purchase decisions are based on a bidding system, with the contract going to the lowest qualified bidder. The education market was considered important for its proposed ability to generate long-term brand loyalty among early users (students). Apple was one of the earliest entrants into this market. It is questionable, however, if the long-term benefits of brand loyalty by early users is actually realized.

This segment, like the business segment, is interested in integrated systems designed to perform to buyers' specific needs. Increased competition for this market has led to increased downward pressures on prices.

EXHIBIT C1–4 Market Share, (percentage) 1992–1993[a]

Company	Market Share 1993[a]	Market Share 1992
IBM	13.9	11.7
Apple	13.5	13.0
Compaq	9.5	5.7
AST	6.2	2.7
Dell	5.7	3.8
Top 5	48.8	36.9

[a]Projected
Source: International Data Corp., Wall Street Journal, Oct. 21, 1993, p. B.1

Competitors

Major competitors of Dell include most traditional PC manufacturers such as IBM, Compaq, Zenith, and Tandy. These firms rely on selling through a professional sales force or through retail outlets. Competitors of Dell using a direct marketing and/or retailing approach (primarily value-added remarketers) include CompuAdd, which offers a full line of 386- and 486-based machines; Northgate, which offers machines similar to Dell at savings of up to $2000 over Dell equipment; and Everex, which offers machines similar to Dell but claim that they are faster than Dell PCs. CompuAdd is located in Austin, Texas; Northgate in Plymouth, Minnesota; and Everex in Freemont, California. None of these firms has the service and satisfaction reputation of Dell.

Changes in the industry will be driven by four factors as the market matures. First, the Gartner Group, a market research firm, estimates that the number of customers replacing their outdated systems are expected to outnumber first-time purchasers by 1995.

Second, an investment report on the PC distribution industry shows that PC saturation rates are relatively low. Only about 33 percent of white-collar workers use PCs on the job, and only 17 percent of all domestic households have a PC. This becomes more important when one considers that the largest growth opportunities are in small to medium-sized accounts (businesses with fewer than 500 employees) that employ more than 70 percent of white-collar workers.

Third, the ratio of price to performance for equivalent functions continues to improve approximately 20 to 25 percent per year, which makes the purchase of state-of-the-art machines more attractive to many segments. And fourth, competition should intensify. Value-added remarketers more than doubled during the 1988–1989 period, with the number of firms increasing from 350 to more than 1000. Coupled with increased demand by business users, improved software and networking capabilities, and increased competition through differentiation and focus-oriented marketing strategies, industry analysts forecast additional changes in both market approaches used by major competitors and further segmentation of the market. The 1990s should be a period of change for the industry, rivaling changes that occurred during the 1980s.

DELL COMPUTER OPERATIONS

Dell's success can be attributed to its commitment to customer service and satisfaction and the marketing of state-of-the-art systems to business users through direct marketing strategies.

Product Line

Dell offers an extensive and competitive product line ranging from inexpensive "first-time user" computers to those with the latest technological developments. This strategy has resulted in a continuing evaluation and modification of Dell's product line with new products constantly being offered and other products being discontinued. Currently Dell is working with Microsoft to deliver factory-installed Windows NT in high-end workstations and networks as the software becomes available. Dell also plans to sell IBM's competing OS/2 operating system preinstalled. The ever-changing demands of computer technology and the market have made product forecasting and planning difficult and risky. For example, during the last quarter of fiscal 1989, Dell overestimated demand and had considerable surplus inventories of finished goods. It attacked this problem and reduced inventories by $36 million in fiscal 1990. Inventory levels for the third and fourth quarters of 1991, respectively, were between 8.6 and 10.3 weeks of sales, below industry averages. In 1993, Dell reported a loss of $75.7 on sales of $700.6 million. This action was after taking $71 million in unusual charges which related to the restructuring of European operations. Also included in this action was the value of inventories and the costs related to notebook computer projects. Michael Dell is predicting a revenue growth of about 70 percent in FY 1994, according to the March 10, 1993, *Wall Street Journal.*

Manufacturing

Dell's computers for the domestic market are manufactured in facilities in Austin, Texas. The purchase of a 126,000-square-foot manufacturing facility in 1989 doubled Dell's manufacturing capability. The 135,000-square-foot facility in Limerick, Ireland, is expected to satisfy the growing international demand for Dell Systems.

The manufacturing strategy utilized at Dell is one of building each computer system to the buyer's specifications. Buyers can add options to customize their system for their own needs. The order is then assembled and shipped with peripherals and upgrades requested by the customer. Manufacturing at Dell actually consists of the assembly and testing of vendor-procured parts, assemblies, and subassemblies. The assembly line is not automated at present, and Dell has not indicated plans to automate. In addition, Dell utilizes a total quality approach where enthusiastic workers compete in product-quality competitions for bonuses and recognition.

Marketing

One factor leading to Dell's success is the organization's marketing style. Dell approaches the market from a service and customer satisfaction standpoint combined with lower prices than comparable brands. Sales leads are generated through several sources, the primary source being advertising in PC and business publications. An outside sales force located in major markets addresses the needs of large corporate customers.

Dell's sales force is channelized according to the market it serves: small/medium business and home users, corporate buyers, and government/education/medical. Each of these sales channels is supported by its own marketing, customer service, and technical support organization. This organizational structure ensures high accountability for the satisfaction of each customer, as well as feedback from daily direct contact with the customer. PC makers dealing through the retail channel do not have this advantage and are not able to respond as quickly to market and service demands as the direct channel. Additional face-to-face exposure occurs at industry shows.

Dell's entire product line is sold by telephone sales representatives who answer more than 8000 incoming calls on a busy day. In addition to answering customer-initiated calls, the Austin-based sales force responds to sales leads and supports the efforts of its team members in the field.

Sales orders are downloaded to the manufacturing facility several times each day, and all systems are custom-configured according to the customer's specifications. Trucks load at Dell's manufacturing facility throughout the day, and overnight services are utilized for expedited orders. Lead times on systems vary from three to seven days.

Internationally, Dell is similar in marketing approach and culture to its domestic operation. Dell's wholly owned subsidiaries give it access to over 70 percent of the available worldwide market for PCs.

Dell sells to major buyers through a small (25-person) sales force located in major metropolitan areas throughout the United States and services those accounts with management teams consisting of sales, customer service, and technical support representatives. Dell believes that the small to medium-sized business represents the greatest growth potential for PC-based systems.

Dell has also arranged to sell its systems through integrators like Electronic Data Systems (EDS) and Anderson Consulting, which will increase its sale potential. This move from traditional channels was prompted by the fact that the mail-order market is only 16 percent of a $35 billion to $40 billion market, less than one-fifth the size of sales of computer stores. Dell currently has 25 percent of the mail-order market.

RETAIL

In 1990 Dell contracted with CompUSA, Inc., a Dallas-based chain of 20 superstores, to sell Dell products through 1993. CompUSA is a computer version of Toys-R-Us, with approximately 21,000 square feet of retail space per store, a service center with a fast service pickup for corporate clients, and over 5000 items at discount prices. CEO Nathan Morton, a former senior executive with Home Depot and Target Stores, expected sales to top $1 billion in 1991 after only two years of operations. CompUSA is adding new stores in major metropolitan areas and sells Dell systems for the same prices as Dell's direct sales.

Dell added Staples Office Supply Superstores to its mass merchandising channel in mid-1991 as well. Staples markets to a less sophisticated computer user than does CompUSA. Although Dell systems are sold through this superstore channel, Dell maintains its same level of customer support to these buyers. Users who purchase Dell systems through CompUSA and Staples are entered into Dell's customer database as if they had ordered directly through Dell.

Dell's mass merchandising move may provide a serendipitous opportunity for the company even though computer retailing is seen by some industry analysts as posed for a shakeout. Dataquest, Inc., believes that traditional retailers will see their share of PC sales shrink through 1994. Analysts state that marketers will have to move toward the ends of the retail spectrum by either concentrating on high-volume, low-price selling or specializing in market niches or other customized services that mass marketers neglect in order to be successful. Smaller operations that emphasize service along with price are already showing the greatest gains. Superstores may be one retail format that not only survives the shakeout but prospers. In 1993 Dell began selling its Precision Line of Computers through Sam's Clubs, a division of Wal-Mart Stores Incorporated. This move is in addition to the agreement with Price Club, another mass merchandising chain.

Research and Development

During the last few years, Dell's revenue growth has allowed the organization to devote considerable resources to building a first-class technological capability. Research and development spending in fiscal 1989 increased 29 percent over the previous year, doubled in fiscal 1990, and was estimated to be more than $18 million in 1991. Dell's efforts are enhanced since Intel added Dell to its preferred purchaser list in 1989.

During fiscal 1990, the first products to utilize the Dell proprietary integrated circuit chip were shipped to customers. Dell is no longer restricted to standard vendor technologies when customizing its machines for specific usages. In 1990 Dell filed 45 patent applications to protect Dell-developed technologies and designs. It has currently been awarded six patents.

Finance

Financial summaries of Dell are presented in Exhibits C1–5 and C1–6. The organization does not pay dividends to investors, instead relying on appreciation of stock price. It has experienced good sales and profit growth, especially after instituting tighter inventory controls following the overstock of 1989. The 1989 inventory problem caused the stock price to drop 42 percent, from a high of $12 to $7 per share. Dell is currently searching for ways to reduce costs without sacrificing customer service and technological performance of its systems.

ISSUES AND CONCERNS

The most pressing concern of investors regarding Dell operations is Michael Dell. Dell has been very successful in building his organization with an entrepreneurial style of management; in fact, Dell contends that he is not an analysis person, preferring to be a mover rather than an analyst. On a scale of 1 to 10, Dell rates himself 10 as a competitor, innovator, goal setter, entrepreneur, and exporter. He rates himself lowest in the areas of production and finance. Although Dell was cited as Entrepreneur of the Year by *Inc.* magazine, his critics wonder if he is capable of making the transition of moving the corporation from a stage 1 entrepreneurial mode to a stage 2 professional management company.

Another concern is Dell's current move to include retail sales in addition to its traditional strength of telemarketing. This move is designed to broaden Dell's appeal to small businesses and the home PC user, but retailers historically have not shown loyalty to any particular brand of machine and may stock several different brands in their stores.

EXHIBIT C1–5 Dell Computer Corporation Condensed Consolidated Balance Sheet (in thousands)

	Jan 31 1993	Feb 2 1992	Feb 3 1991	Feb 2 1990
Assets				
Current Assets:				
Cash & Cash Equivalents	$14,948	$55,460	$36,627	NA
Accounts Receivable, Net	$374,013	$164,960	$89,699	$60,042
Inventories	$303,220	$126,554	$88,462	$68,246
Other Current Assets	$80,239	$65,814	$21,480	$14,228
Total Current Assets	$852,787	$512,180	$236,268	$142,516
Property and Equipment, Net	$70,464	$44,661	$26,483	$26,170
Other Assets	$3,756	$2,722	$1,471	$3,088
Total Assets	$927,005	$559,563	$264,222	$171,774
Liabilities and Stockholders' Equity				
Current Liabilities:				
Notes Payable		NA		$6,500
Accounts Payable	$295,133	$97,389	$77,911	$51,475
Other Current Liabilities	$198,706	$132,145	$70,099	NA
Total Current Liabilities	$493,839	$229,534	$148,010	$84,546
Long-Term Debt	$48,373	$41,450		
Other Liabilities	$15,593	$14,399		
Common Stock	$369	$358		
Additional Paid in Capital	$177,978	$165,745		
Retained Earnings	$208,544	$106,902		
Obligations under Capital Leases			$4,207	$6,041
Deferred Income Taxes		NA		NA
Redeemable Convertible Preferred Stock		NA		NA
Stockholders' Equity	$369,200	$274,180	$112,005	$79,761
Cumulative Translation Adjustment	($17,691)	$1,175		
Total Liabilities & Net Worth	$927,005	$559,563	$264,222	$171,774

Additionally, Dell's emphasis on telemarketing is a double-edged sword. Telemarketing does reduce the need for a field sales force and eliminates channel markups, but Dell is considered by some to be little more than a dim, dusty warehouse that sells cheap, undistinguished PCs.

Lastly, the question also arises whether Dell can continue to grow as quickly as it would like and still have the same emphasis on service, performance, and satisfaction. There is also the situation of more intense competition as the industry matures and growth slows. Dell is still one of the infants in an industry populated by giants, and it must be wary of these financial and technological colossuses potentially entering its market niche.

EXHIBIT C1–6 Five Year Summary

Date	Sales (000)	Net Income	EPS
1992	2,013,924	101,642	2.59
1991	889,939	50,911	1.40
1990	546,235	27,232	0.91
1989	388,558	5,114	0.18
1988	257,810	14,428	0.53
Growth Rate	67.1	62.9	48.6

EXTERNAL AUDIT

In the PC industry, the threat of lower-cost products subsuming market share from premium brands has persisted for many years. Only recently has this actually been realized. In the early years of the industry, compatibility and quality problems frustrated similar attempts. Now, third parties are capable of offering essentially the same level of compatibility and reliability as the branded vendors. The industry members involved in this endeavor have devised better ways to provide customer support, such as toll free numbers and third party on-site support contracts. Better pricing, similar perceived quality and reliability, and better support have led to dramatic market share shifts among industry participants.

Opportunities

1. Unit growth prospects for the PC industry remain attractive. A 15 percent growth rate in revenues for high-end PCs and a compound growth rate of 12 percent for the industry is expected for the next few years.
2. One of the fastest growing segments for business use is the laptop system. This segment is expected to grow at 20 percent per year for the next few years.
3. State-of-the-art technology, networking, customer service and support, and cost are primary determinants of business computer system purchases.
4. Customers replacing outdated systems will outnumber first-time purchasers by 1995.
5. The European market is one of the least saturated markets.
6. PC saturation rates are relatively low. Only about 33 percent of white-collar workers use PCs on the job. Only 17 percent of all domestic households have a PC.
7. Largest growth opportunities are in small to medium-size accounts (businesses with fewer than 500 employees).

Threats

1. Competition is intense in the PC industry given traditional manufacturers such as IBM and Compaq along with the increased number of value-added remarketers of clones and custom clones.
2. Reliance on component manufacturers makes resellers vulnerable to price changes and availability of components.
3. Retail computer stores have traditionally not shown loyalty to any particular brand of system sold in their stores.
4. Some industry analysts contend that the growth rate of the PC industry is uncertain as the growth rate of the economy slows.
5. Research and development by larger, resource-rich competitors may render some of proprietary technology developments obsolete.
6. The home market, initially created by innovators and early adopters, is forecasted to be relatively stagnant for the next few years. Over 75 percent of shoppers cannot justify the purchase of a home computer system.
7. The recession slows the market for upgrades.

Strengths

1. More than 70 percent of Dell's customers have already become repeat buyers.

2. Dell's corporate culture is performance oriented and emphasizes customer satisfaction.

3. Dell offers a complete line of high-performance and low-cost desk and laptop systems relative to generic systems offered by major manufacturers.

4. Dell is developing proprietary technologies to enhance the performance of its systems and to improve its image as a developer of custom systems.

5. Dell is recognized as being one of the industry leaders in customer satisfaction and service after the sale. In 1991 Dell was awarded top recognition in several customer satisfaction surveys conducted in the United States, United Kingdom, Germany, and France.

6. International demand for Dell-configured systems has increased over the last two years, and Dell's move into European markets gives it access to over 70 percent of the world PC market. International sales increased to 34 percent of revenues in 1991. Dell has wholly-owned subsidiaries in Sweden and Italy.

7. 1991 earnings per share quadrupled to $1.36, compared with earnings per share of $.27 in 1990.

8. Dell has a contract with Xerox Corporation for on-site service of Dell PCs. Over 97 percent of Dell customers are within Xerox's standard service radius.

9. Net sales for fiscal 1991 increased 40.6 percent, to $546.2 million from $388.6 million in fiscal 1990. International sales more than doubled for the third consecutive year, reflecting gains in all subsidiary operations and the first full year of operations in France and Sweden.

10. The company introduced eight new products in fiscal 1991.

11. In fiscal 1991, Dell entered into an exclusive sales agreement with CompUSA. Under this agreement, a full line of Dell products is offered through CompUSA computer superstores in the United States.

12. Dell reported a 54 percent increase in sales to major corporate, governmental, and educational accounts.

Weaknesses

1. Michael Dell has been criticized for a lack of patience as well as failure to listen to his managerial staff. Some industry observers question whether Michael Dell will be able to professionalize his management approach as the firm grows and matures.

2. The composition of Dell's work force reflects potential weaknesses in the organization because of the lack of staff depth in terms of experience as well as that of tenure with the company. Although the work force is approximately 50 percent male and 50 percent female, only one female manager, manager of customer service, appears in the management ranks.

3. Dell controls only 2 percent of the IBM-compatible personal computer industry in the United States.

4. Dell is lagging behind competitors with fewer product announcements and delayed new product introductions.

5. The company has focused on a telemarketing strategy for sales promotion. Dell has not capitalized on the other channels to promote products.

6. Dell lacks product selection on the lower end of the marketing scale.

7. Dell has obligated itself to substantial lease payments until 1994.

8. Receivables and receivable days continue to increase.

9. Dell has no expertise in retail.

Automation Partners:
Human Resource Management
In a High-Technology Firm

Dale Jasinski (primary author)
Dr. David B. Balkin
(faculty supervisor)
University of Colorado at Boulder

Jim McBee, Automation Partners' West Coast regional technical consulting manager, walked into Kevin Hobbs's office and began screaming at the regional director.

> I've been busting my back for the last three months on the Quarles job, going the extra mile like I have always done. While the overtime isn't a lot of fun, I realize that to satisfy our commitment to the client sometimes takes an extra effort. That's not the issue. What ticks me off is that I'm working with one of the guys from the DC office on this job and he tells me all kinds of things that make me feel like you've been taking advantage of me. For instance, did you know that all of their technical staff receive company credit cards to use for travel expenses instead of personally foot-

> ing the bill and waiting forever like we do to get reimbursed? Also, he informed me that the salesman in their office, some joker who wouldn't know the difference between a fax board and a motherboard, pulls down over $100,000. Give me a break. I'm making $55,000 with all my incentives and my top paid technicians are lucky to see $40,000. On top of that, they are hiring a new technical manager and no one here is even given a chance to post for the job. He also . . .

At that point, Hobbs cut him off. "Jim, I'm really sorry you had to hear these things during the middle of what I know already is a stressful situation. As a regional director, I've played by the rules as they've been laid

down to me since the merger last year (1990). It's about time that some changes occurred here. Look, next week is our quarterly management meeting, I promise I will bring up the whole spectrum of human resource issues and get back to you on Thursday. Can you hang in there until then?"

Jim nodded yes, thanked Kevin for his time, and departed for the client to begin another all-nighter to install some new software on the system. Kevin sighed and began to replay the course of events that led to this situation.

COMPANY HISTORY

Automation Partners was formed from the December 1990 merger of the Stratcon and Portola Systems, two leading regional law office automation companies located on the East and West Coasts, respectively. These separate companies began operations in late 1986, were venture-backed startups, and enjoyed similar success in the years leading up to the merger. A major distinction between the two, however, was that Portola grew its company by merging in 1988 with Hobbs & Jasinski, Ltd., while Stratcon grew through internal growth in sales. Because of this, centralized internal support systems at Stratcon were created and implemented to assist the firm in its rapid growth, while Portola preferred to maintain to a large degree the independent status of Hobbs & Jasinski. This resulted in the creation of independent branches that almost functioned as franchises on the West Coast (San Diego, San Francisco, and Los Angeles), while the eastern offices (Washington, D.C., New York, and Chicago) were tightly controlled through the Washington, D.C., headquarters.

The goal of Automation Partners was to be the dominant provider of automation products and services to the legal market. Even the name, Automation Partners, was chosen as part of a plan to establish strategic relationships with law firms and corporate law departments for the analysis, design, procurement, implementation, consulting, training, and ongoing support of their automation solutions. In law firm vernacular, the goal was to become the firm's "automation partner." To achieve that goal, the company established a four-pronged strategy that entailed establishing a quality national service organization, hiring and retaining the best people in the industry, developing a comprehensive portfolio of products and services, and cultivating a prestigious client base.

The key to the entire strategy, however, was the company's personnel. As stated by company president John Morton in the company's 1991 annual report:

> As a service provider, people are the most important asset we have as a company. Automation Partners has invested in bringing together a group of people who have created an organization that can sustain rapid growth and provide the infrastructure to reach well into the future. Over 120 people work for the company (as of 1/1/91), with over 80 percent of the staff in the six regional offices. Due to the specific industry focus, many of the employees come from legal backgrounds, including attorneys who have practiced law prior to joining AP. We are able to attract and keep recognized industry leaders who regularly publish in leading trade journals and are in demand for speaking engagements and industry symposiums. Without the contributions of every member of this organization, the past and future success of this company would not be possible.

By 1992, the company had accomplished its objective of being a national player by having offices in six of the major legal markets in the United States: San Francisco, Los

Angeles, San Diego, Chicago, Washington, D.C., and New York. These branch offices were grouped administratively into two separate profit and loss centers (Western Region and Eastern Region) managed by a regional director. The Western Region was headquartered in San Diego, and the Eastern Region was run out of the Chicago office. To support each branch office in the region, central support services such as strategic planning, on-line customer support, purchasing, and marketing were developed in the respective regional headquarters (San Diego or Chicago). This organization is depicted in organization charts in Exhibits C2–1 and C2–2. The New York and Los Angeles offices were managed by newly hired branch managers, while the original four offices were run by the founders of the respective companies (San Francisco, Portola; San Diego, Hobbs & Jasinski, Ltd.; Washington and Chicago, Stratcon).

John Morton, the CEO, was brought in by the venture capitalists to consummate the merger and direct the future activities of the nationwide company. They felt the founders of the former companies (Kevin Hobbs, David Timmons, Richard Hitt, and Robert Messman), who had an average age of 27, lacked the experience necessary in running an operation the size of the newly created Automation Partners. Moreover, the VCs were concerned that the founders' egos and expectations regarding this new nationwide entity might not coincide with their own plans for this venture. Morton's directive from the venture capitalists was straightforward: Make their investment liquid within two to three years. Based on his personal background, he saw this best accomplished through increasing sales revenue through geographic growth and a concentration on hardware sales. While the hardware sales produced greater volume, this type of revenue had lesser margins than the consulting activities. The founders' backgrounds were primarily in the consulting arena, however, and they would be reluctant to give up their traditional emphasis on these services. Morton felt it necessary, therefore, to build up a corporate staff to assist him in implementing this strategy

EXHIBIT C2–1 Automation Partners Organization

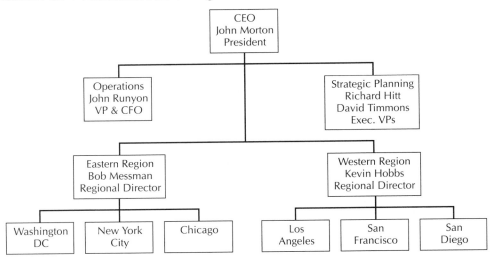

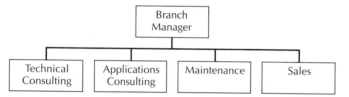

EXHIBIT C2–2 Automation Partners Organization Branch Office

within the branch offices. As a result of this practice and his own personality, which was self-described as "gruff," over time the founders became increasingly distanced from Morton.

A more detailed background of the law office automation industry can be found in the Industry Background section of this case, with résumés of key employees in the Biographies of Key Personnel section. Financial data are included in Exhibit C2–3. Finally, a memo from Morton announcing the merger to the employees is included as Exhibit C2–4.

EXHIBIT C2–3 Comparative Financial Statements (in thousands of dollars)

	1990[a]			1991			1992 (six months)		
	East	West	Total	East	West	Total	East	West	Total
Revenue									
Hardware and software	5,511	4,377	9,888	11,356	4,407	15,763	3,998	1,571	5,569
Services[b]	1,871	1,965	3,836	4,016	2,891	6,907	1,027	886	1,913
Total Revenue	7,382	6,342	13,724	15,372	7,298	22,670	5,025	2,457	7,482
Cost of Sales									
Hardware and software	4,836	3,355	8,191	10,490	3,793	14,283	3,540	1,420	4,960
Gross margin	2,546	2,987	5,533	4,882	3,505	8,387	1,485	1,037	2,522
Operating Expenses									
Salaries and wages	1,346	1,397	2,743	1,934	1,564	3,498	1,047	825	1,872
Commissions	324	102	426	251	45	296	79	19	98
Benefits	339	298	637	163	249	412	83	117	200
Facility costs	259	202	461	277	282	559	157	137	294
All other	436	878	1,314	783	532	1,315	453	291	744
Total expenses	2,704	2,877	5,581	3,408	2,672	6,080	1,819	1,389	3,208
Contribution Margin	−158	110	−48	1,474	833	2,307	−334	−352	−686
Overhead Allocation[c]				2,084	839	2,923	957	279	1,236
Net Profit/Loss	−158	110	−48	−610	−6	−616	−1,291	−631	−1,922

[a]The 1990 divisions reflect performance of the companies prior to the merger with the East Region being Stratcon and the West Region representing Portola.
[b]Services comprised the revenue activities such as consulting, system implementation, training, and system support.
[c]As 1990 represented the separate companies' individual performances, no overhead allocation was necessary. After the merger, centralized services such as strategic management, accounting, purchasing, etc., were allocated based on gross sales.

EXHIBIT C2–4

MEMORANDUM

TO: All Automation Partners

FROM: John Morton

DATE: December 14, 1990

RE: The new Automation Partners

The merger of Portola and Stratcon is complete!!

On November 29, 1990 Dick Hitt and I executed the final documents and completed the merger of our two companies. This is an exciting time for all of us. The enthusiasm throughout the combined companies as well as the reaction to the merger throughout the industry reinforces our belief in the market opportunity, the concept upon which we have built our respective businesses, and the people who have brought us to this point and will carry us to even greater successes.

Congratulations to all of you!

Now we begin the consolidation of the two companies from two, separate and independent regional entities into a unified, national industry leader. While at times the consolidation effort will seem difficult and cumbersome (compared to the past) the benefit to the company and to each of you in your daily activities will be well worth the investment. During this process we will undergo numerous changes that will include changing the company name, changing the administrative procedures for tracking expenses and time, modifications to the services and products we offer and how we offer them, differences in reporting lines and responsibilities and so on. We will even be changing our office location to accommodate the increased staff in the Bay Area. This memo is intended to help provide you with the information you need to better understand some of the changes.

Please find enclosed several documents which reflect our consolidation efforts:

1. *Corporate Capabilities:* This is the text we use to describe the company and the merger to our prospective clients. This document also provides a description of our corporate mission as well as our products and services.
2. *Organization Chart:* The attached chart provides an overview of the new structure we have moved to as Automation Partners. We have invested a great deal of time in designing an organization which best mirrors our

current needs and puts us in the best position to maximize the market opportunity.

3. *Decision Authority Matrix:* In an effort to better define the new organization and the role of the various departments or groups, we have developed a matrix which assigns responsibilities for the tasks which comprise our business. This is a living document which will be updated and modified to reflect the changing environment.

4. *Employee Handbook:* To be provided at a later date. This document will serve to define the procedures and terms of employment.

As we develop additional procedures and policies which reflect the new company, I will make every effort to keep each of you informed either through memos like this or through your respective manager.

Thank you for your cooperation and patience during this critical phase of a new company.

Best wishes for a happy, healthy and prosperous New Year.

Regards,

John

John

Staffing

As a systems integrator, Automation Partners takes responsibility for designing, implementing, training, and supporting computer systems for its clients. This requires both a great deal of technical expertise, and because of the specific market niche, an understanding of the workings of law firms.

Although each branch office independently chose an organizational structure, a basic hierarchy existed in all, as shown in Exhibit C2–2. The duties of the branch manager included responsibility for the revenue and profitability of the region, client relations, personnel, and day-to-day management of their office. There was little doubt, however, as to the most critical function: meeting financial objectives. As Kevin Hobbs, the Western regional director put it:

Our company president, John Morton, instituted a weekly Monday phone call immediately after the merger was complete. The initial purpose of these calls was to be a forum where each of the six branch managers and the two directors could share information about their branch amongst each other and with John. The goal was to assist the new guys in LA and NY in ramping up their operations as well as share experiences with all sorts of matters such as client problems, sales opportunities, employee relations, etc. John quickly made it clear that "problems" were not welcomed and within a few weeks it became nothing more than a sales and revenue report. Any gripes you might have or especially your people had with the way things were going were classified as "whining" and John had no time for whiners!

The New York, Washington, D.C., and Chicago offices each had their own salesperson who was directly responsible for originating business with new clients and the related marketing to accomplish this task. The West Coast offices, as a result of their past emphasis on consulting, had the branch managers assume this responsibility.

The technical consulting manager was responsible for providing the salesperson or director with the basic system design based on the individual client's needs which was relayed to the client in the form of a pricing proposal. Because each system was so extensively tailored to the individual client, this duty required a great deal of knowledge about the ever-changing personal computer technology, especially LANs (local area networks). In addition, this manager was also charged with supervising anywhere from three to ten technicians who actually performed the system installations. These technicians had to possess not only technical knowledge, but because they were dealing in a service business, had to be able to represent themselves in a professional manner and develop client relations skills. Finally, the consulting managers were routinely called in to resolve serious technical or client relations problems. Jim McBee, summarized the role of a technical manager as:

> Basically thankless! I've got pressures from the clients who always assume they are my only responsibility and always want problems fixed yesterday. Lawyers love to threaten and until one of my technicians has been around them for a while, well, he'll melt down almost immediately at the threat of a lawsuit and call me in to resolve the problem. The technical stuff wouldn't be a problem if I could find the time, or the company would cough up the money to send my guys to training once in a

while. What I object to most though is the almost daily reinvention of the wheel around this place. Each of us encounters problems or finds unique ways to tweak the most out of a particular product, yet the information stays with that person. We don't have any ability to share this valuable, and in my opinion, profitable information with our peers. I remember all of the hype about the merger and how wonderful it would be to pool all of this great know-how into one big family. Well, I haven't seen any of it yet, and to make things even worse, now I am losing some of my technicians to help out in the other regions which only makes my clients angry as things aren't getting done like they used to. But from what I hear, I've got it made compared to my counterparts back east. They've got to deal with some prima donna salesman with a commission to collect and doesn't care how he chops up your design to make a sale. He doesn't take the phone call complaining that the system doesn't do what it's supposed to. Out here, we've got directors who know the business and work with us and the clients to make sure things work out the way they should.

The application consulting manager works closely with the technical consulting manager but differs from him in that his responsibility is to design the components that relate specifically to the practice of law, such as litigation support, time and billing, and case management software, and provide the necessary training to the client to ensure proper use of the system. Although understanding the technical implications of the software, this person must be able to fully comprehend the workings of an attorney and a law firm. The typical manager has worked either as a paralegal or attorney and developed an interest in computers that overwhelmed his or her interest in law. Their role is to translate "legalese" into "computerese," and vice versa. Unlike their technical counterparts, application managers' typical engagement is much smaller in duration (weeks rather than months) but greater in exposure in that they work directly with the attorneys, whereas the technical staff typically deal with the support staff of the law firm. A final distinction between the two is that the application consultants are viewed as professional consultants. They bill by the hour rather than in the fixed price arrangement done by their technical counterparts and hence are subject to individual revenue targets rather than the collective goals set for the technical consultant department. Because of the commission's structure emphasis on volume and new sales, the sales function performed by the salespeople usually does not generate any application consulting fees. The responsibility for obtaining these lower volume but higher margin engagements therefore falls on the application consulting manager.

The final department within each region is maintenance. The maintenance staff, or systems engineers as they are called internally, are responsible for responding to customer reports of system problems (either hardware or software) based on their maintenance contracts and performing routine scheduled maintenance on the hardware provided by API. The three eastern branch offices have implemented a common customer support 800 number to centralize this function.

EMPLOYEE BENEFITS

Before the merger, Dick Hitt, Portola's president, had promised the maintenance of what he affectionately referred to as the "Silicon Valley" suite of employee benefits enjoyed by the Portola employees. These included employer-paid premium health insurance with a minimal deductible, tuition reimbursement for attendance at any college or university (no restriction on the type of

courses or degree plan, although work related was encouraged), parking or the mass transit monthly pass equivalent, and membership in a health club. Finally, he hoped to maintain the tradition of an annual company-wide retreat weekend where all employees and their significant others could gather to celebrate the success of the prior year and plan for the next. The last such retreat was held at the beautiful Spanish Bay resort in Monterey, California, and featured a Scottish bagpiper who "piped in the sunset" on the Pacific Ocean as well as golf on the famous Pebble Beach golf course. As Hitt said later when he had to justify this expense to the board:

> Our people work hard in a very demanding environment. The ability to relax during the day through a good workout keeps them at the maximum energy for what typically is a 12 or more hour workday. The health club membership, then, encourages them to do that, and since the clubs are all located downtown, it minimizes the employee's time away from the office. It's the same thing for the annual retreat. Their coworkers should be more than a voice on the other end of the phone. I strongly believe that the personal bonds created at this function contribute greatly to the fantastic productivity and efficiency we get from our people. Moreover, by creating our plan for the next year *together* I get ownership from each and every person, manager to receptionist. The results speak for themselves, Portola has never had an unprofitable month under my stewardship!

The East Coast company, Stratcon, had a different philosophy regarding employee benefits. The health club and tuition policies were not offered, and the health insurance, although with the same carrier (Aetna), had a higher deductible and the company only paid the employee's portion of the premium, whereas Portola paid the entire premium, including spouse and any dependents. Because of the complete centralization of facilities,

Stratcon felt communication and "bonding" was in place among the employees due to their physical proximity. Each manager had a limited "pizza and beer" budget to reward his or her individual department for a job well done. The high amount of travel necessitated by both the centralization and client location did lead the company to provide each employee who traveled with a company American Express card, rather than submit travel reports as Portola required. Moreover, recognizing the personal hardship imposed by frequent, unscheduled travel, Stratcon established a policy whereby employees received bonuses each time they spent more than 10 nights out of town.

Although the merger had been consummated months ago, the reconciliation of these employee benefit policies had not even been started. The new CEO, John Morton, summed it up by stating:

> The least of our worries right now is making a level playing field for the staff regarding these various and sundry benefit plans. We've got more important things to worry about such as establishing good budgeting control systems, more detailed employee time reporting, im-

proved accounts receivable collection. Once I've got the numbers under control, I'll worry about insurance policies and education allowances. As for Spanish Bay, I've always felt that it's the director's job to maintain morale and communicate company policy so I see no need to continue that extravagance. Besides, we had a dinner at my home after the merger announcement where the directors and their spouses were flown in to celebrate.

Compensation Plans

Each regional office was free to determine the compensation levels of their employees, but approval was needed from the CEO on all wage increases, bonuses, and new hires. No attempt was made to alter the compensation programs already in place in the offices established prior to the merger, so there was wide fluctuation in the salaries earned by personnel performing the same basic function, as shown in Exhibit C2–5.

Another result of the independent compensation systems was the variety in incentive plans. For instance, salespeople in the Eastern Region received a commission only on sales to *new* clients. Additional or

EXHIBIT C2–5 Employee Compensation, by Region[a]

Position	Western Region	Eastern Region	Company Average
Technical consultant	$36,000	$50,000	$43,000
Application consultant	42,000	52,000	47,000
Trainer	40,000	55,000	47,500
Maintenance engineers	34,000	38,000	36,000
Sales	N/A	100,000	100,000
Technical manager	55,000	75,000	65,000
Applications manager	60,000	75,000	67,500
Branch manager	75,000	85,000	80,000

[a]Denotes average salary for the three branches in that region.

follow-up sales to existing clients were not included in their commission calculation, which provided for earning 3 percent on hardware and software sales and 5 percent on services sold. A typical engagement was usually composed of 60 percent hardware, 20 percent software, and 20 percent services. The unintended result of this policy was to emphasize hardware sales to new clients at the sake of the higher margin service revenue from existing clients. Moreover, because there was no additional compensation to the salesperson from existing clients, their personal incentive to ensure a smooth implementation consistent with their representation of the system's capabilities was minimal, as was their empathy with their compatriots tasked with this assignment. Bob Messman, Eastern regional director, recognized the problem, but

> What can I do about it? Morton's budgets are a product of his interpretation that both our board and the venture capital market that we need to hit for additional capital want this company to reach $30 million in sales this year. It just can't happen without pushing a lot of hardware, especially personal computer workstations. Besides the shrinking margins we get on this stuff, its creating a real division in my staff. Tim Smith, our salesperson, has a $100,000 target this year, $50,000 in salary and $50,000 in commission potential. There is no way he can achieve it without "moving boxes" to new clients at the expense of cultivating our most important sales asset, our current customers. We are in real danger of losing our image as consultants and becoming just another Wang or NBI who will push whatever product they can on you and leave you high and dry after the check's in the bank. My field guys feel it all the time when customers ask, "Why don't we see Tim anymore?" or even worse, the dreaded, "Tim promised it would work this way and now you're telling me it can't be done." We really need to pull together again as a team like in the old days before it's too late.

The directors and managers also had an incentive system put in place by Morton. He replaced the old plans that existed in each company which called for bonuses paid annually based solely upon departmental or regional achievement of revenue targets. The new plan set up the targets based on net profit after allocation of company-wide overhead and was subject to the company achieving certain profit levels. Thus, even if an individual attained his level of profitability, if the company failed to meet its target, no bonuses were paid.

Training and Development

Prior to the merger, both companies allocated approximately 10 percent of their budgets to employee education, primarily in the form of industry-sponsored training and attendance at key trade shows throughout the year. As a result of the larger than anticipated merger expenses, along with a sharp drop in net profit, these expenses were eliminated entirely from the post-merger budget submitted to the regions by John Morton. Any attendance at trade shows or training had to be approved first by the controller and then by Morton.

To integrate the accumulated knowledge of the two organizations, a technology committee was established. Its mission was to provide a forum to gather and evaluate the various products and services offered by each company and consolidate the best of both into one standard strategy. A key element was the creation of "product specialists" whose responsibilities were to focus on one particular aspect of the technology offered by API (e.g., legal-specific software, general applications, file servers, workstations) and continually work with each of the regional offices to ensure that their staff received the proper training and background in the use of this product or service. After one meeting six weeks after the memo was issued, the first product specialist, Steve Shafford of the former Stratcon Company, made an ill-fated trip to the West Coast as described by Kevin Hobbs, Western regional director:

> You knew from that first meeting of the technology committee that things were not going to go as smooth as John and Dick envisioned when they signed the merger documents. Since neither of them were all that technically proficient, they glossed over some of the major differences in implementation and customer service strategies utilized by the two companies. Just because we both sold WordPerfect, for instance, didn't mean that we set it up the same, exploited the same capabilities of this full-featured software, or even instructed our clients in its use in a similar fashion. These things became obvious at the one and only technology committee meeting. Because of the new budgets, we could only meet for a day (John didn't want the extra night of hotel bills), which wasn't going to be enough time even if things were like they thought. As it was, we spent most of the time arguing about the relative merits of each company's strategy, the quality of their people, and who had the most obnoxious attorney to handle. Steve was especially stubborn, so it came as no surprise that when he came out here, his presentation was met with open resistance by my guys and even by myself. The biggest problem was that the infrastructure wasn't in place to utilize his methodology and, given the budgets, wasn't going to be for quite some time. Accordingly, we basically told him that we would continue to do business as usual. Well, I'm sure when he got home, he was steaming because all of the Stratcon folks just assumed we would buy into their methods 100 percent. After that, the committee tried to set up a teleconference, but one thing or another kept coming up and as I think about it, we never met again.

INDUSTRY BACKGROUND

The law office automation market is a substantial vertical market within the computer industry that is undergoing rapid growth driven by the increasing automation requirements of law firms. These requirements will likely grow at an increasing rate due to geographic dispersion of firms' offices, client-driven pricing pressures, demonstrated successes in the use of automation to win lawsuits, and increased PC acceptance by attorneys. The result is the creation of a substantial market to assist law firms in the migration from their old systems, characterized by closed architecture, proprietary minicomputer solutions to the open architecture, flexible personal computer network solutions.

This has resulted in the law office information systems and services market growing from $1.3 billion in 1989 to over $2 billion in 1991, according to the Impact Research Group study. Significantly, approximately one third (33 percent) of these expenditures, or about $700 million, will be for the integration of application software products and associated services. These purchases represent the high profit margin work for vendors who have seen their margins on other items, especially hardware sales, erode significantly in the past several years. Another major trend documented in this study is the increased emphasis on attorney productivity or "front office" rather than the traditional "back office" applications of timekeeping and billing, accounting, and word processing. As seen in Exhibit C2–6, these back office applications will decrease over the next five years while attorney productivity software such as litigation support, case management, and document assembly will increase.

This reflects the fact that during the initial stages of automation in law firms, the

EXHIBIT C2–6 Changes in Market Share of Legal Software Applications (percent of software revenues)

Application type	Percent of Market (software revenues)	
	1990	1995
Time and billing	18%	13%
Accounting	18	11
Word processing	9	7
Library	8	6
Litigation support	8	10
Case management	8	19
Document assembly	6	14
Other	25	20

Source: Impact Research Group, *Information Systems in the US Legal Market 1990–1995,* Vancouver, 1991.

primary applications were basic word processing along with timekeeping and accounting. The technology was proprietary, that is, it required the purchase of hardware, software, and maintenance through a single vendor such as IBM, Wang, NBI, or Barrister. As firms recognized the inflexibility of these systems, they began to purchase standalone personal computers (PCs), which provided access to a greater number of applications but lacked the ability to provide firmwide access to critical centrally maintained information.

Thus, the current phase of the back office to front office evolution pulls together all of the firms' disparate investments in technology, including their standalone PCs and back office mini-computers. This is being done primarily by the use of LANs or, in the case of multioffice firms, wide area networks (WANs). Again, quoting from the Impact Research group study:

> Larger firms need multi-user systems. These larger firms have or had a minicomputer system and are now looking to replace older systems with networked personal computers which have the power and flexibility to handle the current workload and have an ability to be expanded to handle anticipated future growth. As a result, the use of LANs in law firms is becoming more important and more widespread. These LANs are networked PCs and workstations and connecting personal computers to larger systems which may have already been installed. Networks are becoming more popular because as PCs continue to spread in small, medium-sized and large firms, lawyers and office managers need to control the flow of information in the office. Networks allow lawyers to share information and allows office managers to exercise some control over the flow of data and the use of computer systems in the office.

This trend is reflected in Exhibit C2–7, which shows computer purchases by large law firms (over 20 attorneys in 1991). Thus, there is a substantial market opportunity to assist law firms in the migration that will allow them to take advantage of the new technology being developed in areas such as imaging and multimedia. Automation Partners saw this opportunity and attempted to capitalize on it nationwide.

EXHIBIT C2–7 System Purchases
by Large Law Firms, 1991

Type of System	Percent of Total
PC/LANs	50%
Unix	15
Mini	14
OS/2	8
Other	13

Source: Impact Research Group, *Information Systems in the US Legal Market 1990–1995,* Vancouver, 1991.

Competition

Automation Partners is not alone in recognizing opportunity in its industry. Most firms in this industry attempt to provide their customers with the total solution, that is, hardware, software, training, and support. Very few, however, have attempted to develop their own hardware or software, on the premise that the customer fear of being stuck with proprietary systems is still great. This leaves a niche, according to the Impact Research group study, for a financially sound, nationwide player to take the gamble that the bigger law firms, which stuck with the proprietary systems longer because of their size and large amount of investment in systems, will want to pay a premium for the advantages of an integrated personal computer turnkey system, that is, information sharing among all of the various applications.

Historically, the law office automation market has been served by mini-computer companies that focused on the back office systems, such as Barrister, Syntrex, CCI, NBI, and Wang. All were experiencing severe financial problems and have lost significant market share since 1988. The major competitors were divided into three groups: national, regional, and local companies.

National competitors for multicity, large law firm integration projects include hardware manufacturers (IBM, Apple, Hewlett-Packard), some of the Big Six accounting/consulting firms (primarily Arthur Andersen and Price Waterhouse), and horizontal integrators like Evernet and Network Management, Inc., which specialize not in a particular industry segment but, rather, in the ability to implement large network systems.

There are a limited number of regional competitors. LAN Systems and Lynch Marks & Associates provide stiff competition on the West Coast, as does Micro One in the Midwest and I.C.L. and Kraft & Kennedy in the eastern United States. Each of these firms has annual sales between $7 million and $10 million. A large number of relatively small, local competitors exist in virtually all of the markets served by API. They compete mostly on price and basically sell hardware and software components and will subcontract out the training and support. When the prospective client does not feel the need for a coordinated information systems strategy or believes that it has sufficient industry knowledge and expertise in law office automation, these competitors do well.

Barriers to entry on a local level are minimal, as virtually any systems integrator can buy market share with small law firms via severe pricing discounts. On the regional and national levels, however, barriers include the ability to service a diverse geographic region, financial strength and stability (law firms are very conservative consumers and are slow payers), and the ability to secure aggressive pricing from hardware and software manufacturers based on volume purchases.

Competition in the legal automation market can be segmented by products and services offered, as well as the geographic coverage of the competitor. Viewing this in a matrix with geographic coverage on one axis and products/services on another is helpful, as shown in Exhibit C2–8.

BIOGRAPHIES OF KEY PERSONNEL

John M. Morton, President and Chief Executive Officer. Prior to joining the newly merged Automation Partners, Morton had a distinguished 25-year career in the field of information technology. Morton was most recently a partner with an international management consulting firm, where as one of the worldwide leaders of its information technology practice, he directed studies for Fortune 500 providers and users of information technology. Morton was an executive vice president at Bank of America earlier in his career, with total corporate responsibility for Electronic Banking Services including data processing, systems, and telecommunications. In this capacity, he managed over 7000 employees with an annual operating budget in excess of $750 million. Morton subsequently assumed responsibility for Bank of America's successful Consumer Financial Services area, introducing a wide array of new products, including the bank's first automated teller machines network

EXHIBIT C2–8 Industry Competition by Type and Location

Products and Services: Entry Points	National	Regional	Local
Automation planning and implementation consulting Platform design and implementation	Law office management consulting companies Mini-computer vendors, hardware manufacturers, horizontal integrators	National players have regional strengths Horizontal integrators, Micro One (legal focus in Midwest)	Several in each city Several in each city
Legal-specific application software selection and implementation	None	None	None
Training	None with legal focus	None with legal focus	Several in each city
Network maintenance services (reactive)	Small number of third-party horizontal equipment maintenance providers	Several in each region (none with legal focus)	Several in each city (but none with legal focus)
Network support services (proactive)	None	None	None
Licensed products and materials (legal-specific integration utilities and extensions to third-party software products)	None	None	None

(Versatel) and California's first point of sale interchange network (Interlink).

Morton originally joined Bank of America via the bank's acquisition of Decimus Corporation. He was one of the founders of Decimus, a computer leasing and service bureau company. Serving as chief operating officer, Morton grew Decimus from a start-up to approximately $50 million in assets before it was acquired by BankAmerica Corporation. After the acquisition, he continued to run Decimus as a nonbank subsidiary, growing it to over $900 million in assets. Morton began his career with IBM Corporation in systems engineering and marketing management. He is a graduate of Harvard Business School's Advanced Management Program and has a B.A. in mathematics from Northwestern University.

Richard M. Hitt, Executive Vice President. Hitt has over 15 years' experience in the information systems marketplace working with various organizations throughout the United States, Canada, and Europe. As former president/CEO of Portola Systems, Hitt was responsible for growing the company from a start-up to $9 million in sales. Hitt has participated in growing three other information systems companies into worldwide market leaders. Prior to joining Portola, Hitt served as managing director and vice president of international operations for Page Software, Inc. As executive vice president for Automation Partners, Hitt directs the corporation's product research, development, strategic planning, and support services organizations. He graduated from the University of Kansas with a B.S. in business administration.

John L. Runyon, Chief Financial Officer. Runyon has over ten years' experience in financial management of multi-million-dollar hi-tech corporations, including four years in the legal vertical market. His responsibilities at Automation Partners include all financial and administrative management for the company. He also oversees the Operations group. Prior to joining the company, Runyon was the financial officer for Design and Production, Inc. This $20 million firm designs, fabricates, and supplies ongoing support services for hi-tech marketing exhibits for the Fortune 500. Runyon has a B.B.A. degree in finance from George Washington University. Additional academic accomplishments include successful completion of the CPA exam.

David H. Timmons, Senior Vice President. Prior to founding Stratcon, Timmons was with the law firm of Jones, Low & Samuelson. Timmons has consulted with many of the nation's top law firms in the development of strategic automation plans to serve the needs of attorneys as well as support staff. With primary emphasis on attorney automation, Timmons has assisted many client firms in the development of practice-specific applications addressing such areas as document generation, document management, archiving solutions, litigation management, and file room automation. Timmons recently directed Automation Partners' participation in creating the Advanced Technology Law Office (ALTO) exhibit featured at the 1991 National Association of Legal Administrators symposium in Nashville. He is a frequent speaker at legal association meetings for attorneys and administrators. Timmons directs the company's strategic planning efforts. He is a graduate of George Washington University with a B.B.A. in business economics and has done extensive work toward his Ph.D. in operations research.

Kevin Hobbs, Western Regional Director. Prior to co-founding Hobbs & Jasinski, a law office automation consulting practice that was acquired by Portola Systems in 1989, Hobbs was employed by Arthur Andersen & Company and was extensively involved in law office automation. He was responsible for the installation of large litigation document management systems. Over the last five years Hobbs has designed over 40 major local area network–based solutions for legal clients. He graduated with honors from California State University at Fresno with a B.S. degree in accounting.

Robert Messman, Eastern Regional Director. Messman has over 12 years of industry experience, the first 5 years at IBM. As executive vice president of Informatics, Messman was responsible for development of a nationwide organization, which provided automation products and services to the legal profession. While there, his strategic direction, tactical marketing, and sales campaigns helped establish Informatics as a significant vendor in the industry with over 300 law firm clients nationwide and 30 in the Midwest Region. Most recently, Messman was a principal in an acquisition firm, where he successfully closed two major contracts within an 18-month period. He graduated with honors from the University of Indiana with a B.A. in marketing and finance.

Case 3

ISM Engineering

Lester A. Neidell
University of Tulsa

Paul Olson, director of marketing for ISM Engineering, leaned back in his chair, and looked at the telephone. For the past 10 minutes he had listened to a tirade from Jean Moret, purchasing agent for Snecma (France), one of ISM's largest customers. Snecma maintained all of Air France's jet engines and provided similar services to other European airlines. ISM's first quarter 1993 sales figures, which were displayed prominently on a wall sales chart, did little to alleviate his foul mood. He thought about the situation he faced, and the options open to him. "April 1993—we're 27 percent under the sales forecast for the year, and Pete Adams [acting CEO] has put a hold on $328,000 of completed parts scheduled to be shipped to Snecma. I've got one angry customer on my hands."

Paul pressed his intercom button, "Jessica, better book us on an early flight to Paris tomorrow, and make hotel reservations for 2 nights . . . no, better make it until Saturday, at the Orly Hilton."

THE COMPANY

ISM Engineering is a repair facility for aircraft turbine (engine) parts. Its customers include the United States Armed Forces and major airlines in the United States and around the world. A list of ISM's ten largest customers for each of the preceding four years is contained in Exhibit C3–1. Financial statements for the two previous years are contained in Exhibit C3–2. ISM is a subsidiary of Air Services, Inc., a publicly traded company with 1992 sales of $125 million.

Prior to its purchase by Air Services, the company was called ISM Fabrication, and was operated as a partnership. A net profit of $450,000 was recorded in 1990, but in the

EXHIBIT C3–1 Yearly Sales by Top Ten Customers

	Percent of Annual Sales			
CUSTOMER	1989	1990	1991	1992
U.S. Armed Forces	35.9	44.9	32.6	11.5
KLM (Holland)	12.1	11.7	24.2	32.9
Snecma (France)	9.1	12.8	16.1	16.7
McDonnell Douglas	6.9	5.5	4.1	2.4
Korean Airlines (Korea)	5.4	1.8	—	—
Alitalia (Italy)	2.2	1.8	2.3	3.7
Avianca	2.2	—	—	—
General Electric	1.9	—	—	—
Western Airlines	1.5	4.6	3.4	4.4
Rolls-Royce (England)	1.4	—	—	—
American Airlines	—	1.8	1.9	—
Varig Airlines (Brazil)	—	1.7	1.2	—
Republic Airlines	—	1.7	1.7	2.4
Pacific Southwest	—	—	1.5	1.5
Continental Airlines	—	—	—	6.1
Air Ground	—	—	—	1.3
Total company sales ($ millions)	11.8	11.3	13.6	16.8

previous two years losses had been sustained. Financial statements for the partnership years are not available.

Company History

In 1967, three former college roommates from Georgia Tech founded a specialty steel fabrication business, Automatic Welding, in Atlanta, Georgia. John Isom, vice president of sales, and Elliott Stevens, treasurer, had obtained business degrees, while Lawrence Martin, president, was a mechanical engineer. Shortly after startup, Martin was in the machine shop of Delta Airlines, where Delta machinists were trying to repair a jet engine part. After watching several failures, Martin asked if he could take the part back to his

shop for repair. In about a week's time, a superior repair was developed. News of this spread rapidly by word of mouth through the U.S. commercial aircraft industry, and the small welding business was soon overwhelmed with orders from other airlines. In 1966, Specialty Welding became ISM Fabrication. The informal business objective of this new company was to repair an aircraft engine part so that it met or exceeded all OEM specifications, and to do it for less than half the price of a new part.

In 1975, the largest customer of ISM was the U.S. Army. Business with the army began when the army purchased a "repairable" part from KLM Airlines, but was not able to complete the repair satisfactorily. ISM's expertise provided a solution, with the result that almost all U.S. Army aircraft turbine repair work was routed to ISM. When KLM heard of the repair through its army contacts, ISM received its first international order.

Two years later, John Isom spent 100 consecutive days in Europe marketing ISM's know-how to European airlines. Toward the end of this time period, because of his lack of cultural knowledge and "contacts," Isom decided to hire a manufacturer's representative for Europe. Kirk Dhouw, a Swiss citizen fluent in six languages, was selected.

While the European market was being opened, there were significant sales problems in the United States and in other foreign markets. The sales organization was unable to market repairs as fast as Larry

EXHIBIT C3–2
ISM Engineering Consolidated Statements of Income and Retained Earnings

Years ended December 31, 1991 and 1992

	1992	1991
Net sales	$16,781,317	$13,620,979
Cost of sales	12,246,093	10,136,844
Gross profit	4,535,224	3,484,135
Selling, general and administrative expenses	2,422,979	1,729,426
Operating income	2,112,245	1,754,709
Other income (expense)		1,007,437
(see Note 1)	(544,100)	(435,807)
	(544,100)	571,630
Income before income taxes	1,568,145	2,326,339
Provision for income taxes	557,715	850,247
Net income	1,010,430	1,476,092
Net loss for the period from December 9, 1990 through December 31, 1990 (Note 2)		(25,967)
Retained earnings, beginning of year	3,123,122	1,672,997
Dividends paid	(678,928)	..
Retained earnings, end of year	$3,454,624	$3,123,122

Note 1: *Related Party Transactions:* The Company purchased approximately $300,000 of raw materials from its parent in each of the years 1986 and 1985. The Company paid $478,680 in 1986 and $80,056 in 1985 to an affiliate in sales commissions. In 1985, the Company received $1,007,437 in sales commissions from its parent. A management fee of $81,804 and $72,608 was paid to its parent in 1986 and 1985, respectively.
Note 2: *Accounting Period:* Beginning in 1985, the Company changed its year-end from a 52–53 week fiscal year to a calendar year. The 1984 fiscal year was a 53 week period ending December 8, 1984. This change was made to conform the Company's year-end with that of its parent.

(exhibit continues)

EXHIBIT C3–2 (*continued*)
ISM Engineering Consolidated Balance Sheets

	December 31, 1992 and 1991	
Assets	1992	1991
Current assets		
Cash	$317,033	$362,341
Accounts receivable	3,460,616	2,113,485
Due from parent		1,010,412
Claim for income tax refund	73,559	
Inventories	4,627,351	2,370,824
Other	47,289	42,024
Total current assets	8,525,848	5,899,086
Property and equipment, less accumulated depreciation	4,620,012	2,948,608
Due from parent		415,000
Other assets	340,705	405,081
	$13,486,565	$9,667,775

Liabilities and Stockholders' Equity		
Current liabilities:		
Note payable	$250,000	$250,000
Accounts payable	1,232,929	514,834
Accrued payroll	496,206	398,188
Other accrued liabilities	163,240	273,270
Due to parent	335,304	
Income taxes payable		716,552
Current maturities of long-term debt	3,743,506	680,974
Total current liabilities	6,221,185	2,833,818
Long-term debt	2,556,787	2,609,279
Deferred income taxes	555,732	413,319
Stockholders' equity:		
Common stock, $1 par—shares authorized, 1,000,000; outstanding 688,237	688,237	688,237
Retained earnings	3,454,624	3,123,122
Total stockholders' equity	4,142,861	3,811,359
	$13,486,565	$9,667,775

Martin developed them. Seven manufacturer's representatives were added, three for the U.S. market and four for international sales. The 1977 "rep" organization and the commission structure are shown in Exhibit C3–3.

By 1986, ISM had lost its technical differential advantage. Other repair facilities developed similar repair procedures for older jet engines, while the three Western OEM engine manufacturers (General Electric, Pratt & Whitney, Rolls-Royce) warranted

EXHIBIT C3–3 Reps and Their Commission Structure, 1977

Location of Representative	Territory	Commission (%)
Switzerland	Europe (except Portugal)	5
Rio de Janeiro, Brazil	Brazil	7
Bogota, Colombia	Colombia	7
Miami, Florida	U.S. east of Mississippi, Canada (except house accounts)	5
Bombay, India	India	5
Buenos Aires, Argentina	Argentina	7
St. Louis, Missouri	McDonnell Douglas	5
Lisbon, Portugal	Portugal	7
Los Angeles, California	United Airlines	5

their new products in such a way that many of ISM's repairs would have voided the warranty. Repair volume was maintained due to an increase in air travel, but the company's market share declined. More frequently ISM was winning orders based on price and turnaround time instead of on technology.

The three partners disagreed on how to compete in this new environment. John Isom wanted to expand to take advantage of volume pricing, but Elliott Stevens and Larry Martin were more conservative. Stevens finally decided that he had had enough and offered to sell his share of the partnership. Unable to come up with the money to buy out Stevens, and unable to find a new investor/partner, the three founders agreed to sell ISM.

In July 1989, Air Services, Inc., purchased all outstanding stock of ISM, and established a subsidiary, ISM Engineering. John Isom remained as marketing director of the new subsidiary until March 1990, when he was replaced by Paul Olson. Olson was experienced in international marketing, and had a broad background in the airline and heavy equipment industries. (See Exhibit C3–4 for a summary of his experience.) Shortly before Olson was hired, the other of the two remaining original owners, Larry Martin, resigned from the presidency. Peter Adams, formerly contract administrator and director of purchasing of the parent company, was appointed acting CEO but was not given the title of president. Instead, a new position, assistant to the president, was created for him, and the president's position was left vacant. Adams was a native Atlantan, had no prior line experience, and had not traveled outside the United States. His primary responsibility was to oversee the financial side of the company. Exhibit C3–5 is the organizational chart of the new company.

EXHIBIT C3–4

RÉSUMÉ OF PAUL OLSON

Birth Date: September 12, 1950
Career Objective: Senior Sales Management in Aircraft Industry
Education: University of Georgia, BBA 1971
        Major: Corporate Finance
        Minor: Transportation
        Graduated top 15% of class

        Georgia State University
        10 hours toward MBA

        Florida International University, MBA 1987
        Major: International Business

EXPERIENCE

March 1984– December 1989	Eastern Airlines, Miami, Florida Purchasing Agent, Repair and Overhaul Section
June 1983– January 1984	Great Lakes Dredge & Dock Company Jebal Ali, United Arab Republic On-Site Administrative Manager/Diving Superintendent
January 1982– March 1983	Gulf Standard Dredging Company Manama, Bahrain Operations Manager
December 1981– December 1982	Gulf Standard Dredging Company Basra, Iraq Welder
March 1977– November 1980	Brussels Development Company Limited Atlanta, Georgia President (site developers of real estate)
January 1972– February 1977	U.S. Army Medical Corps Company commander of medical company Honorably discharged with rank of major

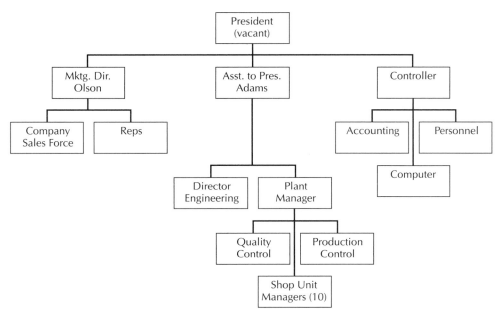

EXHIBIT C3–5 Organizational Chart, March 1991

Paul Olson Talks About His New Job

"When I first came to ISM, it was apparent that I was an unwanted outsider. Larry Martin, the former president, had just left the company, and there was much fear of the unknown. Martin had managed the company very conservatively. Everyone seemed to move in slow motion and no one wanted to make a decision. Group management existed, which is good for the communication factor, but unfortunately even minor issues were hashed to death. It was a very close group, a family; each member covering the other's mistakes when necessary, and each very skeptical of new ideas. For many years these people had worked under no pressure. Sales volume had increased very little, and the emphasis was on efficiency, especially on the Snecma project. The learning curve for Snecma had been long and costly, but this customer was now producing a profit.

"I was enthusiastic and ready to help this company grow. My idea was to involve everyone, to develop a full team effort. I held a meeting to introduce myself and to spread my enthusiasm. Few people laughed at my jokes. I felt like a Democrat in a Republican Congress."

New Strategy

Paul Olson began immediately to revamp the sales force. In his first six months on the job, four new salespeople were hired, and the manufacturer's representative network that Isom had developed was largely disbanded. The world was divided into six territories (see Exhibit C3–6), and the new sales force went on the road. However, the U.S. government, KLM, and Snecma were re-

EXHIBIT C3–6 Sales Territory and Representative Structure, July 1991

Position	Territory	Payment
Director of marketing (Paul Olson)	Far East, Middle East, Africa	Salary
Company salesman	Europe, Canada	Salary
Company salesman	West of Mississippi	Salary
Company salesman	East of Mississippi	Salary
Company salesman	Special large accounts	Salary
Company salesman	U.S. government	Salary
Representative	South America, Mexico	Commission (10 percent)

tained as "house" accounts, to be serviced personally by Olson.

In Olson's view, "Sales growth in this industry requires frequent direct contact with the customer. Reps sell everyone's services, and have little or no loyalty. We have no control of their time or efforts. I use them only in developing markets or when absolutely necessary to penetrate the market, as in South America.

"ISM's reputation in the industry was not good. Previous promises had not been fulfilled. We had to convince lost customers that our organization was under new leadership and things would be different. I begged, borrowed on old friendships and called in markers for a chance to prove this."

Frequent company meetings were held in which Olson explained his operations, marketing, and sales goals. "I was determined that everyone in the organization would be prepared to service the increased volume. Sarcastically, I was told, 'Bring it in; we'll get it out.' Six months after I initiated the new sales program, the backlog had tripled. Production just wasn't prepared for the new surge in orders."

Advertising and Sales Promotion

For the first time in the company's history, ads were placed in trade publications. Promotional activity, which had been largely the domain of the now terminated manufacturer's reps, became a major thrust. Professional consultants were hired to develop trade show booths, and to instruct the new sales force on how to "work" trade shows. Customer give-aways and organized outings (fishing trips in Mexico and Hawaii, hunting trip in Canada) also became part of the communication program.

Key Current Problems

A summary of the company's major problems, as developed during a staff meeting in December 1992, is contained below:

Pricing: There is a trend toward cutthroat competition among U.S. airlines as a result of deregulation. This fare competition is reflected in the airlines' efforts to reduce costs elsewhere. Profits on domestic repairs will become more limited.

Production: Lack of computer capability limits ability to control and track material. Scheduling is manual and ineffective. Poor employee attitude due to inconsistent management policies and turbulent union contract negotiations has hurt job commitment. There have been isolated incidences of slow down and sabotage.

Engineering (R&D): Innovations have been slow, and the area is understaffed.

COMPETITION

Olson discussed the competition. "Only one 'non-captive' competitor exists in the United States—Chromalloy, Inc. Other competition is from airlines' in-house repair facilities, from the OEMs, and from engine overhaul shops. But these companies are also customers. ISM gets overflow from all, and in the case of the airlines and OEMs, gets business for processes that they have not developed internally. Quality is not a major competitive issue, as all work must meet specifications. Inspection is very involved and tedious; all parts not meeting standards are returned for rework. The most important competitive factor, now that technology is about even, seems to be 'turn time,' how quickly the job can be done. Price occasionally becomes a marketing issue, but an acceptable price range is typically dictated by the market. A company must decide if repairs can be profitably done within that price range. Price is more important internally; at different times it's necessary to give extremely low prices in order to obtain volume necessary to cover overhead. We marketing people are often at odds with accounting people, who continually complains about low margin items."

MARKETS

For much of its history, ISM depended on three accounts for half to two thirds of its annual volume. These were the U.S. military,

typically contributing 30 to 40 percent of annual volume, and KLM and Snecma, which combined for 20 to 25 percent each year. Olson was determined to reduce this dependence, and was particularly fearful of losing American military contracts as defense budgets came under pressure. A massive, worldwide marketing campaign was developed and implemented. As a result of the new marketing emphasis, several new accounts were developed, and older, smaller accounts were expanded, lessening dependence on the three major customers. While the largest single air travel market is the United States, several factors favor expanded international marketing efforts.

First, air travel in many third world countries is underdeveloped. As incomes increase so will air travel. Second, as mentioned earlier, there are three jet engine manufacturers in the Western world: General Electric, Pratt & Whitney, and Rolls-Royce.[1] The first two are headquartered in the United States, and it is likely that foreign airlines will look to the United States for repair of their GE and P&W engines.[2] Third, ISM has been successful in obtaining foreign business, as Exhibit C3–7 indicates. In 1992 more than 20 foreign accounts were active.

Olson's assessment of foreign markets follows:

Europe. Europe has the most potential of the international markets. There are some nationalistic tendencies, but most airlines, even though state-owned, will go where they get the best combination of price and turn-around time.

East Asia. This is a tough market. Most routes are long haul; long-haul carriers have less per mile seat cost and require less maintenance. Most engine wear is on takeoff and during low atmospheric travel. Low atmospheric travel produces more sand, dust, and

EXHIBIT C3–7   List of ISM's
                          International Accounts[a]

Alitalia
Canadian Pacific Airlines
Pratt & Whitney of Canada
Cruzeiro do Sul S A—Servicos Aereos (Brazil)
VASP (Brazil)
Ansett Industries, Australia
Air India
Far Eastern Air Transport
Japan Air Lines
Air New Zealand
Pakistan International Airlines
Caledonian Airmotive, Ltd. (England)
Iberia Air Lines (Spain)
KLM (Holland)
Lufthansa German Airlines
South African Airways
Air France
Scandinavian Airlines System
Swissair
Transportes Aereos Portuguese

[a]From company accounts receivables, August 1986.

other atmospheric engine pollution. Engines used for long haul may fly 10,000 hours before repairs are required, and the extent of repairs is less. Short-haul carriers normally overhaul their engines after approximately 4000 hours flight time. Nevertheless, the Far East remains a priority market for ISM because we see a significant increase in air travel. Some of the country markets are more promising than others.

Japan. Japan is extremely nationalistic. The government provides protective trade policies, and the country has overhaul companies that get most of the repair business.

Korea. Korean Airlines is a small, long-time, solid account. There are prospects for additional work when some of the R&D we have currently in process becomes usable.

Singapore. Little business can be obtained here because of internal airline policies. Aircraft are usually replaced in four or five years, when the manufacturer's warranty runs out.

Indonesia and Thailand. There is good potential here, especially when the individual airlines develop in-house overhaul capability. Currently, these airlines send the entire engine to a major overhaul company, where it is broken down, repaired, and parts sent out to a company like ISM for repair. As these airlines begin to disassemble their own engines, they will require more outside repair work than the overhaul companies.

Australia and New Zealand. Currently ISM has a limited amount of work from both countries. Distance is an important factor governing turn time. These airlines freight their own parts, and shipments wait at their docks until there is a cargo vacancy. Australia in particular has a policy of keeping work at home as much as possible, but volume and lack of technology require that some parts repair be sent outside the country.

South and Central America. Unlike other parts of the world, local sales reps are a must. Most deals are "under the table," involving large commissions and kickbacks, and cannot be handled by U.S. personnel. Also, many countries are extremely nationalistic, and governments typically restrict or tax currency transactions. We have paid as much as 25 cents on the dollar surcharge. Even though technology is limited, each airline tries to keep as much work in the country as possible. Aircraft flown in South America are typically flown in worse condition than allowed in the United States. Despite this, ISM has had small but steady business from Brazil and Venezuela. However, collection of receivables has run as long as six months, and we need to consider this when pricing in this market. A list of accounts receivable (see Exhibit C3–8) shows the difference between foreign and domestic payments.

Africa. South Africa is the only country where local overhaul capability exists. Olson has no reservations about South African business. "Business is business and I don't confuse business with politics." In all other African countries, engines are sent to the country of old colonial rule for repair. Corruption and government regulation cause problems.

THE SNECMA DISPUTE

As noted earlier, Snecma had been one of the company mainstays. This was achieved from the R&D efforts the founding CEO, Larry Martin, had expended and from the close personal relationship that had developed between Snecma personnel and another of the company's founders, John Isom. However, the French were also shrewd negotiators, and it wasn't until 1989 that ISM had achieved "satisfactory" profits from the Snecma account. The French were continually trading volume for price.

Through the years, the French had never contracted to the price/volume terms requested by ISM, but had always sent the required number of parts once ISM agreed to the French price. In other words, ISM had always capitulated to a price without receiving volume guarantees. The French always met the desired, but informally agreed upon, volume. It was a risky game, but ISM management accepted this method in order to retain the business.

Pete Adams, as contract administrator of the parent company, had been involved with the Snecma account before Paul Olson was hired. When John Isom was preparing to leave he turned Snecma over to Adams because he was the only one who was at all familiar with the account. Snecma was the last account Paul Olson actually took over. Paul attempted to "ease" his way into the account, continuing to include Adams in the negotiations in order to maintain continuity.

Paul Olson had shrewdly sized up Snecma and its purchasing agent, Jean Moret. Jessica Winters had been in the Accounting Department and had knowledge of the Snecma account. Jessica went with Paul and Pete on their first combined negotiations with Moret. She got along very well with Moret, and in Olson's words, "softened" the atmosphere. When Olson was absent from the office, Jessica often handled Moret's inquiries.

EXHIBIT C3–8 Status of Accounts Receivables (percent)

	Domestic Accounts	Foreign Accounts
Current	48.5%	21.1%
31–60 days	26.5	21.0
61–90 days	9.4	16.3
Over 90 days	15.6	41.6

Jean Moret,
Snecma Purchasing Agent

Jean Moret assumed the position of Snecma purchasing agent in 1985. He was a tough negotiator and very nationalistic. One of his primary goals was to build a comprehensive turbine repair source within his native France. In addition to servicing all of Air France's turbine repair needs, Snecma also performed work for other European airlines. It was an important gesture to have as much French content as possible.[3] But, due to Snecma's volume, it was necessary for them to go outside of France for many different repairs. Also, Snecma's in-house R&D efforts for the type of repair in which ISM specialized had not been very productive. As a result, funds and manpower were routed to more profitable areas within Snecma. Despite this, Moret continued to use the threat of in-house capability in his annual contract negotiations with ISM. Thus, the "game" followed for several years was as follows: Moret was probably bluffing, but the founders of ISM, and last year, Olson, were unwilling to call his bluff.

1993 Contract

Olson and Adams were well aware of this game when they arrived in Paris in November 1991 to negotiate the next year's contract. They were determined to obtain a long-term volume commitment from Snecma, one that extended several years. In this way, ISM could plan better for facilities expansion, for the purchase of new equipment, and for the hiring and training of new personnel.

The proposal they planned to present to Moret was

1. Continue to repair units at the rate of 12 per month at $20,500 per unit until current orders were completed.

2. Reduce price to $18,500 per unit based on receiving a multi-year commitment of a minimum of 16 units per month.

Moret opened the meeting with the following information. He had promised his superiors a $2000 per unit price decrease for 1993. Before Paul Olson could reply, Peter Adams assumed control. Adams responded that he would agree to this price reduction if the annual repair was increased from 144 units to 192 units. As in the past, Moret refused to sign such a contract, but gave broad assurances that the need was there for 192 units. Adams held firm. Snecma would sign a contract guaranteeing the volume increase or the previous price stood.

No contract was signed, and the ISM contingent returned unhappily to Atlanta.

Orders and shipments continued to flow without a signed agreement. ISM billed at the $20,500 price; Snecma paid $18,500. After 90 days of underpayments, the controller brought the situation to Adams's attention. Adams sent a telex to Moret, informing him that all work in-house for Snecma was to be terminated, and no completed product would be shipped until Snecma paid the additional $2000 per unit for all 1993 work, which amounted to 21 units or $42,000.

Moret called Olson on Monday, April 6, 1993. However, Olson was not in the office and Jessica Winters took the call.

Tuesday morning Jessica relayed the conversation with Moret to Paul Olson. "I can't believe how angry Jean was. He said that he had never been so insulted in all his life, and he refuses to negotiate with Pete Adams. However, after talking for a while, Jean did authorize release of payment of $2000 additional for 20 units.

"Paul, in my opinion we're in serious danger of losing the Snecma business."

Paul Olson then called Jean Moret. The conversation was entirely one-sided; Moret shouted in the telephone at Paul for 10 minutes, sometimes in English and sometimes in French.

"I have never been so affronted. First, my contract with you remains unsigned. Then Monsieur Adams sends me a telex telling me that our orders are being stopped. We have been doing business for eight years, and never do I get such an insulting message. Monsieur Isom was a gentleman—a man of honor. I can't do business with someone with no honor."

Then Jean Moret dropped a bombshell, "You know, my friend Paul, that we just lost two large contracts, UTA [Union de Transports Ariens] and LTU [Luftransport-Unternehmen, West Germany]. Many of my employees will be leaving this division to work repairing cases. I know we're not competitive with your work, but *mon dieu*, I can't fire any workers. So I don't know if we'll be needing any more work done by ISM."

It was after this conversation that Paul called Jessica and asked her to book the both of them for Paris.

NOTES

1. A joint venture between GE and Snecma, CFM International, is producing GE-designed engines in France for Airbus Industrie, a European consortium.

2. Transportation of entire engines to and from the United States is usually accomplished by "hanging" a nonoperating engine on the wing of an aircraft that is regularly scheduled to the U.S. That is, regularly scheduled passenger aircraft "ferry" engines back and forth.

3. Snecma was wholly owned by the French government.

Case 4

Calox Machinery Corporation (A)

Lester A. Neidell
University of Tulsa

Mike Brown, international sales manager, tapped his pencil on the notepad and contemplated his upcoming discussion with Calox's executive committee concerning the distributor situation in New Zealand. The Labor Day weekend break had not been especially conducive to his sorting out the conflicting information and varied opinions concerning the New Zealand predicament. After only 3 months on the job Mike had not expected to be involved in a decision that would have such far-reaching consequences.

On paper the decision looked simple: whether or not to adhere to his earlier decision to replace the original New Zealand distributor, Glade Industries, with a newly formed company, Calox New Zealand, Ltd. Despite his newness to the company, Mike was confident that Calox's executive committee would agree with whatever recommendations he made in this situation, since he had been charged with "solidifying" the International Sales Division. If he decided to reverse his decision to terminate Glade Industries, could he "undo" any damage done so far?

Three previous faxes were spread on his desk along with the brief notes that he had jotted down during Thursday's conference call between Calox's executives and the company's legal counsel. Mike swung back to the PC behind his desk and began to draft what he hoped would be the definitive Calox policy for New Zealand.

THE COMPANY

Calox Machinery Company began in 1946 as a partnership between John Caliguri and William Oxley. The two engineers met during World War II and discovered mutual interests in mechanical engineering and construction. Both were natives of Kansas City, and at the end of the war they established a partnership with the expressed purpose of developing high-quality excavation equipment and accessories. Their first product was an innovative hydraulically operated replacement blade for a light-duty scraper.

Calox's principal customers were independent contractors engaged in excavation of building sites, and airport and highway construction and maintenance. Calox's products were primarily replacement items for OEM (original equipment manufacturer) parts and accessories. Some OEM sales were achieved; that is, contractors could order new equipment from OEMs with Calox blades and accessories already installed. Growth over the years was slow, but steady.

The product line expanded to include payloader buckets, a number of dozer and scraper blades, and parts for aerial equipment including construction forklifts and snorkels. A key to the company's success was their specialty status; their products were used to enhance the performance of expensive equipment produced by Caterpillar, Eaton, International Harvester, Case, and other OEMs. Calox's strategy was simply to provide a better part, often at a premium price, and to have it readily available in the field through a network of strong distributors. Direct competitors in the United States included small specialty producers such as Bobcat, Dresser, and Gradall, as well as the parts divisions of the large OEM manufacturers. Primary competitors in international markets included Terex, Deutsch, Takeuchi, and Hitachi. William Oxley compared Calox to the Cummins Engine Company, which had achieved a superior position in the diesel engine market through a similar strategy.

The partnership was replaced by an incorporated structure in 1970, when Bill Oxley, Jr., became CEO. Despite slow growth of the U.S. economy, both 1990 and 1991 were very good years for Calox; annual sales increases of 12 percent were achieved, and the company set profit records each year. Sales for the 1991 fiscal year broke the $70 million barrier for the first time in the company's history. That year, approximately 280 people were employed at the single location in Kansas City, of which three-fourths were hourly workers engaged in fabrication.

INTERNATIONAL SALES

Calox's first international sale occurred in 1971, when the company responded to an unsolicited inquiry and shipped a small order to Canada. International sales languished throughout the 1970s, when a great deal of construction was put on hold due to the "energy crisis." Channels of distribution for international sales were much the same as for domestic sales. Independent distributors were given nonexclusive rights, although in practice most countries had only one distributor. Forty of Calox's 110 distributors were located outside the United States. In 1991 almost 25 percent of Calox's sales were generated internationally. In the 1988 to 1991 period, aided by the relative decline of the U.S. dollar against most other currencies, international sales grew at an annual rate of 16 percent.

Prior to Mike's arrival, there was no uniform procedure by which Calox investigated foreign markets and appointed distributors outside the United States. Bill Lawrence, Mike Brown's predecessor, essentially ran export sales as a one-man operation. Since Calox had very limited international experience, and most international markets were relatively small compared to the United States, primary market research was considered to be an unnecessary expense. In those countries guesstimated to have large enough markets, Bill obtained a list of potential distributors by advertising in that country's construction journal(s) (if available) and principal newspapers. He then made a personal visit to interview and select distributors. In smaller markets, distributors were appointed through one of two methods. Most commonly, Bill appointed a distributor after receiving an unsolicited request. In a very few cases, distributor applications were solicited via advertisements as in "large" markets, which were then reviewed in Kansas City. In all cases in which personal visits were not made, distributor applicants had to submit financial statements. Efforts to interview distributor applicants by telephone were not always successful, due to time constraints and the lack of a suitable translation service.

The New Zealand Distributorship

In 1986 Calox appointed G. W. Diggers, Ltd., as its agent for New Zealand. This arrangement was a novel one, for G. W. Diggers was also a producer of excavating equipment. Because of some earlier poor experiences in certain foreign markets, Calox had instituted a policy of not distributing through any company that also manufactured excavating equipment. This policy was not followed in New Zealand because of the limited distributorship options available. At the time of the appointment, the owner of G. W. Diggers, Geoffrey Wiggins, assured Calox that the two lines were complementary rather than competitive, and that he intended to keep it that way. During 1989, G. W. Diggers purchased $800,000 of equipment and supplies from Calox.

In 1990 an abrupt change occurred in what had been a very successful, if short, relationship. G. W. Diggers was purchased by a large New Zealand conglomerate, Excel Ltd., which gave a new name, Glade Industries, to its excavating facility. The former owner of G. W. Diggers, Geoff Wiggins, was not associated with Glade Industries. Mike Brown's predecessor felt that the acquisition by Glade could only help Calox's position in New Zealand, because the resources available through Excel, Glade's parent company, were so much greater than what had been available to G. W. Diggers.

However, it soon became apparent that working with Glade was going to be very challenging. Glade raised prices on all Calox products in stock. Then they complained that Calox products were not selling well and that a "rebate" was needed to make Calox's products competitive in the New Zealand market. Simultaneously, Glade began production of a line of products competitive with Calox, but of a substantially poorer quality. During 1991 sales to Glade were virtually zero, and market information obtained by Calox indicated that Calox's former position in the New Zealand market was being occupied by Wescot Industries, with products imported from Great Britain. Exhibit C4–1 gives annual sales of Calox products to G. W. Diggers and to its successor, Glade Industries.

EXHIBIT C4–1 Annual Sales to G. W. Diggers and Glade Industries (in thousands of U.S. dollars)

Sales to G.W. Diggers				Sales to Glade		
1986	1987	1988	1989	1990	1991	1992 (6 months)
21	310	535	801	105	70	10

Mike Brown began his new job as international sales manager for Calox in June 1992. A few weeks after arriving at Calox, Mike received a long letter from Geoff Wiggins. Geoff suggested that the situation in New Zealand was critical, and that he would be willing and able to establish a new distributorship, Calox New Zealand, Ltd., to be exclusive distributors of the Calox product line. Mike then invited Geoff to come to Kansas City the last week of July to discuss the proposal. Mike found Geoff to be very affable, technically knowledgeable, and an excellent marketing person. In the time period since selling his business to Excel Ltd. Geoff had been working as a general contractor. The 24-month "no-compete" clause Geoff had signed when he sold G. W. Diggers had expired. Geoff provided figures that indicated New Zealand's 1991 imports of excavating equipment were roughly NZ$2 million, out of a total domestic market of nearly NZ$3 million. (In 1991, US$1 NZ$0.62.) He claimed that G. W. Diggers had achieved, at the height of its success, almost a 50 percent share of the New Zealand market. Geoff argued persuasively that with his personal knowledge of New Zealand's needs, Calox could once again achieve a dominant market position. With the blessing of the vice president of marketing, Mike and Geoff shook hands on a deal, with the exact details to be worked out by mail and faxed over the next few weeks. Geoff urged that time was of the essence if Wescot's market advances were to be slowed, and left a $100,000 order for 75 units to be shipped in 120 days, but not later than November 15, 1992.

Communications with Glade

Mike began to prepare a letter of termination to Glade. However, before this was completed, Calox received three mailed orders from Glade, totaling $81,000. This was the first contact Mike had with Glade and the first order received from Glade in 5 months. Because the standard distributor's agreement required a 60-day termination notice, Mike felt the Glade orders had to be honored.

A short time later Calox received a letter in the mail from Glade stating that they had heard rumors that another company was going to supply Calox products to Glade's customers and that delivery had been promised within 150 days. The letter continued by saying that this information could not possibly be true because Glade had an exclusive distributor agreement. This was news to Mike as well as to others at Calox headquarters because it was against company policy to grant exclusive distributorships. A search of Bill Lawrence's files turned up a copy of the initial correspondence to Geoff Wiggins, in which Geoff was thanked for his hospitality and a sole distributorship arrangement was mentioned. However, the distributorship agreement signed with Wiggins was the standard one, giving either party the ability to cancel the agreement with 60 days' notice.

Mike and the other senior Calox executives assessed the situation at length. The letter mentioning the "sole distributor agreement" was in a file separate from all other New Zealand correspondence. It was nothing more than a statement of intent and probably not legally binding in the United States. However, New Zealand courts might not agree. Further, the distributorship agreement should have been renegotiated when Excel purchased G. W. Diggers, but this had not happened. Glade could make a case that the distributorship had endured for 2 years under the existing agreements, which included the letter in which exclusivity was mentioned.

Mike determined that the "sole distributorship" letter also contained "extenuating circumstances" language which Calox could use to justify supplying the new New Zealand distributorship:

> [T]here may be occasions in the future, when, due to unforeseen circumstances, some entity in your nation refuses to purchase any other way than direct from our factory. We do not want to lose any potential sales, however we pledge our best efforts to cooperate with you for any such possible sales should they present themselves and provided there is a reasonable profit to be made on such sales by us and cooperation can be worked out.

The letter also specifically stated that all agreements between Calox and G. W. Diggers were subject to the laws of Missouri. Furthermore, Mike felt that Glade had not lived up to the actual signed distributorship agreement in that Glade had not promoted Calox products, had not maintained adequate inventory, and had engaged in activities and trade practices that were injurious to Calox's good name.

Armed with this information, Mike sought legal counsel, both in the United States and New Zealand. After a week, Calox's U.S. attorney, based on their own investigations and those of a law firm in Christchurch, New Zealand, offered four "unofficial" observations:

1. New Zealand is a "common law" nation, whose commercial law is similar to that of the United States.
2. It was possible to argue that because G. W. Diggers had changed ownership, previous agreements might not be binding. However, the most likely court finding would be that there was an implied contract between Calox and Glade on the same terms as with G. W. Diggers, because numerous business dealings between Calox and Glade had occurred after the takeover.
3. Calox was required to give Glade 60 days' termination notice.
4. There was a possibility that a New Zealand court would agree to assume jurisdiction of the case.

After reviewing the above issues Mike suggested to Calox senior management that Glade be terminated. Mike reasoned that Glade would react in one of two ways. One possibility was that they would accept termination, perhaps suggesting some minor compensation. A second scenario was that Glade would attempt to renegotiate the distributorship agreement. Mike was instructed to draft and fax a termination letter to Glade. This letter, sent by fax on August 20, is reproduced in Exhibit C4–2. The next day the first order for the new distributorship was shipped; the expected arrival date in New Zealand was October 10, 1992.

Glade's faxed reply, dated August 24, was not encouraging (see Exhibit C4–3). It appeared that Mike and the rest of the Calox

EXHIBIT C4–2 Fax from Calox to Glade, August 20, 1992

Calox Company, Inc.   August 20, 1992
P.O. Box 21110
Kansas City, MO 64002
U.S.A.

Mr. Ian Wells
Group General Manager
Glade Industries
39 Ames Road
Christchurch, New Zealand 2221

Dear Mr. Wells:

This letter is to inform you that Calox Company terminates any International Distributor's Sales Agreement or other Distribution Agreement that you may have or be a party to as Distributor expressly or impliedly with Calox Co. as Manufacturer. Said termination is effective 60 days from the date of this letter.

During the past year the following have gravely concerned us and effectively shut off our sales to the New Zealand market.

Reorganization of G. W. Diggers under Glade leading to continuous loss of personnel knowledgeable of the excavation business and difficulty for Calox's understanding with whom we are doing business. In June 1990, we were advised by telex that we were dealing with Excel Ltd., not G. W. Diggers or Glade.

Only $10,000 purchases for an eight-month long period from us, which we clearly found led to major loss of Calox sales to the marketplace and a complete domination of the excavation business by Wescot Industries, a major competitor.

Lack of effort on the part of Glade in promoting our product and maintaining effective selling facilities.

Numerous complaints to us from Customers in New Zealand about Glade continually changing policies, lack of stock, and wildly increasing prices have clearly pointed out that our reputation, as well as G. W. Diggers, has been badly hurt and will impair sales for some time to come.

No progress has been made in introducing our heavy industrial line to the New Zealand market despite assurances from Glade personnel that progress would be made.

We have thoroughly investigated the New Zealand Market and now have firmly decided that it is time for Calox to make a change in its distribution of products.

For the long term, this will allow us to best carve out a full niche in a market we and you have allowed competitors to dominate for too long. We must guarantee ourselves a consistent, aggressive sales effort in the market, which will not be subject to the effects of major policy changes such as those we have seen from Glade.

While two shipments are already en route to you, order number 52557 has not yet been completed for shipment. Since it will be ready imminently, please let us know immediately whether you wish, under the circumstances, to receive shipment or to cancel this order.

Sincerely,

Michael Brown
International Sales Manager

management team had miscalculated. Despite the tone of the Glade letter, and the expressed request to ship order #52557, Mike suggested to the executive committee that no additional product be shipped to Glade.

While Mike and the rest of Calox management was deciding how to respond to Glade's initial rejection of the termination letter, a longer fax, one with a more conciliatory tone, dated August 31, was received from Glade (see Exhibit C4–4). In this letter Glade argued that Calox's best interests were served by working with Glade and mentioned an order for approximately 10 times the "normal" amount of product. However, the order was not transmitted with the fax letter. Glade offered (for the first time) to come to Kansas City for a visit.

Glade's conciliatory letter created a great deal of consternation at Calox headquarters. Its arrival the week before Labor Day meant that holiday plans would have to be placed on the back burner while a suitable response was formulated. Two distinct camps developed within Calox.

One set of managers, whose position was supported by Mike Brown, felt strongly that despite potential legal risks, retaining Glade as a distributor would be a bad business decision. Although Glade had made promises and was offering to renegotiate, it was still producing a competitive line. Also, Glade's historical performance did not augur well for Calox's long-term competitive situation in New Zealand. The "extraordinary" order was viewed as a ploy to entice Calox into continuing the relationship. It was likely to take upwards of 2 years for all that machinery to clear the New Zealand market. Cognizant of Glade's earlier price manipulations, many of this group felt that Glade might resort to "fire sale" prices when confronted with a large inventory, further damaging Calox's reputation as a premier supplier.

EXHIBIT C4–3 Fax from Glade to Calox, August 24, 1992

Glade Industries   24 August 1992
39 Ames Road
Christchurch, New Zealand 2221

Mr. Michael Brown
International Sales Manager
Calox Company, Inc.
P.O. Box 21110
Kansas City, MO 64002
U.S.A.

Dear Sir:

We acknowledge receipt of your letter dated 20 August 1992.

We are currently discussing its contents with our solicitors. They are also reviewing the distribution agreement.

Please proceed with the shipment of order #52557.

Yours faithfully,

GLADE INDUSTRIES LTD.
Ian Wells
Group General Manager

This camp considered that Calox's long-term interests would best be served by terminating the Glade distributorship and completing a formal agreement with Geoff Wiggins. However, there was concern that outright rejection of the Glade order would add to potential legal problems.

These managers also suggested that any further correspondence with Glade should emphasize that Calox could and would exercise a unique product repurchase option upon termination of the distributorship. This provision in the distributorship contract provided that Calox, upon proper termination of the distributorship by either party, could repurchase all remaining Calox inventory from the distributor at 80 percent of its net sales price to the distributor. Thus, if Calox did produce and ship the large Glade order, Calox would, if the order were shipped normally via sea freight, be able to buy it back for 80 percent of the price paid by Glade before it ever reached New Zealand.

The alternative camp wanted to forestall any legal battles. Headed by the U.S. sales manager and the comptroller, they argued

EXHIBIT C4–4 Fax from Glade to Calox, August 31, 1992

Glade Industries   31 August 1992
39 Ames Road
Christchurch, New Zealand 2221

Mr. Michael Brown
International Sales Manager
Calox Company, Inc.
P. O. Box 21110
Kansas City, MO 64002
U.S.A.

Dear Sir:

I refer to your letter dated 20 August 1992, terminating our agreement which was exe-cuted on 28 February 1986.

In accordance with this agreement and attached to this letter is our order #A1036, for 600 products and parts. We would be pleased if you would confirm this order in due course.

We respectfully ask that you reconsider your termination decision as we believe that it is not in your best interests for the following reasons:

1. G. W. Diggers/Glade were not achieving an adequate return on investment until June 1991. An unprofitable distributor certainly is not in your best interests as princi-pal.

2. The individuals that contributed to that unprofitable performance are no longer working for our company. Incidentally I understand that you have appointed Mr. Geoffrey Wiggins to a position as distributor in New Zealand. How can you justify ap-pointing the person responsible for your market share decline over the past three years?

3. Our purchases certainly have been reduced the last nine months due to our need to get inventory down to lift overall return on investment. That situation has now been corrected with the order attached to this letter.

4. We now have a young aggressive marketing team, all highly experienced in market-ing products of a similar nature to yours. When Bill Lawrence was in New Zealand, I advised him that I was restructuring our marketing group. A resume on our three se-nior marketing men is attached. These men have all commenced in the last four

months. I am confident that this team will achieve market leadership in New Zealand and selected export markets with or without Calox's involvement. We have already commenced targeting Wescot's customers. Our recommendation is that you renegotiate your distribution agreement with us, with the inclusion of mutually agreed performance targets which will satisfy your objectives in terms of profitability and market share from the New Zealand market. I would like you to advise me a time which is convenient to you, for me to meet with you in Kansas City to commence negotiation of this distributor agreement.

Yours faithfully,

GLADE INDUSTRIES LTD
Ian Wells
Group General Manager

————

These are the three new men who have commenced to work for us:

Sean Cox, Sales Manager
35 years old. Formerly CEO of Sean Cox Industries of Christchurch. SCI was the chief contractor for the Auckland airport, but sold its business to Midland Industries. Mr. Cox has fifteen years experience in the construction industry.

Joshua Dunn, Sales Representative, North Island
46 years old. Formerly an independent sales representative for various equipment manufacturers, including Hitachi and Ford New Holland.

Brian Muldoon, Sales Representative, South Island
23 years old. Construction engineering degree from New South Wales Institute of Technology (Sydney, Australia). Formerly a management trainee with our parent company, Excel Ltd.

that Glade had finally "gotten its act together" and that the new Glade team of three sales executives would provide greater market coverage than Geoff Wiggins's "one man show." This group introduced the possibility of reopening negotiations with Glade, supplying Glade by diverting the order already shipped to Geoff Wiggins, and producing the (yet unreceived) large Glade order.

By Wednesday, September 2, the two sides had hardened their positions. Mike was determined to break with Glade and begin anew in New Zealand. However, he was concerned about legal ramifications, and, on Thursday, September 3, Calox's executive committee and Mike conferred with their Kansas City attorneys via a conference call.

The lawyers agreed that any further business conducted with Glade would be detrimental to a termination decision. They warned that despite the termination letter (Exhibit C4–1) any further shipments to Glade would likely yield a court ruling that the distributorship was still in effect and, furthermore, that the buyback provision could not be enacted. They also said that if all business with Glade were terminated, and Glade did come to the United States to file, the most they would be likely to receive if they won the court case were the profits on the new sales to Geoff Wiggins, which amounted to $10,000. This sum was probably not large enough to warrant legal action by Glade, especially considering the apparently poor financial situation at Glade and the expense of initiating legal action in the United States.

At the end of this conference call, which lasted about 30 minutes, Bill Oxley, Jr., turned to Mike and said, "Mike, I'm off to the lake now for the holiday. I'd like your recommendation Tuesday morning on this Glade thing."

Calox Machinery Corporation (B)

Lester A. Neidell
University of Tulsa

Mike Brown decided that, despite the potential legal risks, sound business practice dictated that he follow through with the termination of Glade's distributorship, and his recommendation to that effect was accepted by the Calox executive committee. Mike's letter fax of September 9 (Exhibit C4–5) was very specific. First, he restated that it was in the best interests of both parties to terminate the distributorship. Second, since there was no prospect that the Glade order could be completed and delivered prior to the termination date of October 20, 1992 (60 days from the first letter; see Case A, Exhibit C4–2), he made it known that Calox would exercise its buyback option if Glade did indeed forward the missing order. Following

legal advice, Mike added the caveat, "We are open to your comments, of course." The legal reasoning behind this was that if Calox did begin producing the large Glade order, and then bought it back while it was on the open seas, it could be interpreted by the courts that Calox was deliberately attempting to damage Glade financially.

Glade's "hardball" reply (Exhibit C4–6) was discouraging. In it Glade requested an accounting of sales to other distributors, claiming that they (Glade) were legally entitled to recover all Calox profits from these sales. Several Glade executives began to waffle, and proposed again the solution of diverting the order already shipped to Geoff Wiggins, producing the (still unreceived)

EXHIBIT C4–5 Fax from Calox to Glade, September 9, 1992

Calox Company, Inc.   September 9, 1992
P.O. 21110
Kansas City, MO 64002
U.S.A.

Mr. Ian Wells
Group General Manager
Glade Industries
39 Ames Road
Christchurch, New Zealand 2221

Dear Mr. Wells:

Reference your 31 August letter, we must regretfully advise that we feel it is in our best interest to continue with our termination of sales to Glade Ltd. as we explained. We appreciate the points you made in your letter, but nevertheless remain convinced that working with Glade Industries Ltd. is not the best way for Calox to achieve its goals in New Zealand.

While we have not yet received your order number A1036 for 600 items referenced in your letter, I should point out that first, Calox is not able to complete an order for all 600 items prior to the termination date, and second, we would want to exercise our option to purchase back all good outstanding products at 80% of our net selling price.

In consideration of these factors, we do not believe it advisable to accept your offer. We feel that this would only affect your situation and we do not seek to take advantage of you in this regard. We are open to your comments, of course.

Sincerely,

Michael Brown
International Sales Manager

---

large Glade order, and renegotiating with Glade (see Case A).

Before an acceptable response could be agreed upon, another fax (Exhibit C4–7) was received from Glade. In this conciliatory letter, Glade offered to forgo any claims if their large order was completed and if Calox agreed not to exercise their buyback right.

Calox management breathed a huge sigh of relief and instructed Mike to inquire

EXHIBIT C4–6 Fax from Glade to Calox, September 14, 1992

Glade Industries   14 September 1992
39 Ames Road
Christchurch, New Zealand 2221

Mr. Michael Brown
International Sales Manager
Calox Company, Inc.
P.O. Box 21110
Kansas City, MO 64002
U.S.A.

Dear Sir:

I acknowledge receipt of your letter of 9 September 1992.

I am very concerned at the position in which Calox Co. has been selling direct into New Zealand to Glade's customers. This is in direct contravention of your obligations and undertakings under the Distributor Agreement between us and in particular in breach of the undertaking contained in your letter of 27th January 1986.

We have clearly suffered loss and damage as a result of these actions on your part in breach of the Distributor Agreement which we would be entitled to recover in legal proceedings.

We therefore seek from you a full account of all sales made by you direct into New Zealand in breach of the agreement and payment to us of all profits made by you in respect of those sales.

Yours faithfully

Glade Industries, Ltd.
Ian Wells
Group General Manager

about the specifics of the order, complete it, ship it to Glade, and be done with them! Mike, however, felt it was necessary to obtain additional legal counsel before doing this.

The lawyers were emphatically negative. They felt quite strongly that if Calox shipped the large order, the courts would rule the original agreement binding, despite all the communication about termination.

EXHIBIT C4–7 Fax from Glade to Calox, September 17, 1992

Glade Industries   17 September, 1992
39 Ames Road
Christchurch, New Zealand 2221

Mr. Michael Brown
International Sales Manager
Calox Company, Inc.
P.O. Box 21110
Kansas City, MO 64002
U.S.A.

Dear Sir:

I refer to my open letter of 14 September 1992.

As indicated in that letter we are most concerned at the loss and damage we have suffered by your acting contrary to the terms of the existing Distributor Agreement.

We are, however, prepared to forgo our rights in relation to those breaches in return for your agreeing to supply the 600 items referred to in our order #A1036 and not to seek to exercise any rights of repurchase in relation to those items upon termination of the agreement.

Yours faithfully,

Glade Industries Ltd.
Ian Wells
Group General Manager

The courts would interpret the correspondence as a ploy by Calox designed to coerce Glade into placing a large order. They reiterated their previous advice that at the current time, Glade could only obtain minimal damages in U.S. courts; it would hardly be worth Glade's time and energy.

Mike and the company's legal counsel agreed that a final letter had to be written to Glade that would summarize the communications between Calox and Glade and make perfectly clear Calox's position. This letter had to clearly impart that Calox, with the advice of legal counsel, did not recognize as valid Glade's claim that any agreement had been breached. Glade, in fact, had violated the previous distributorship agreement by failing to market Calox's products. Due to Glade's negligence, Calox had sustained damage to their reputation and good name, so that any legal recompense would be forthcoming to Calox. Calox's intent in the New Zealand market was to repair the damage that Glade had done to Calox' reputation by forging ahead with an aggressive new distributor.

What Happened to the Effective and Productive Managers Who Became Less Effective and Productive Overseas?

Doris Eschbach
and Gerald E. Parker, Ph.D.
Saint Louis University

Six years ago, Smallappliance Corporation selected effective, productive managers for expansion into several foreign locations. Many of these managers were not as effective and productive in their assignments as anticipated. Others returned early and/or went to other companies, including competitors. What can be handled differently in the current expansion to ensure that managers remain effective and productive in their new positions overseas and continue to be an asset to the company at the end of their overseas assignment?

EXPANSION

You are the assistant to the executive vice president of human resources of Small-appliance, a multinational corporation. The president has asked you to select managers for overseas assignments in the current expansion. Because of global competition in the new areas, management would like to gain market share in these new areas more quickly than the company did in the last expansion of international locations six years ago. It is imperative to gain market share relatively quickly this time because several of your competitors, including two from Germany and Korea, have entered or are expected to enter the same new markets. As improvements have been made to several appliances, it is imperative to gain market share before competitors also make improvements to their product line.

CHANCE FOR ADVANCEMENT

The vice president of human resources, your boss, is in ill health, and he is expected to retire soon. You are being considered for his job; however, much depends on whether you can handle the successful placement for these overseas assignments.

POOR PAST PERFORMANCE

Six years ago, when managers were also chosen for expansion into several foreign locations, effective, productive managers were selected. No training was provided by the organization, as these managers were familiar with company operations. No plans were made for repatriation at that time, as the managers were to be on the international assignments for several years. Although effective, productive managers were selected for the previous expansion, many did not perform as well as expected, or worse, returned earlier than planned, and several left the company. Now executives, especially the vice president of marketing, are asking if something can be handled differently by your human resources department in this expansion in order to ensure that the managers who are selected and sent overseas remain effective and productive, and that these managers will remain an asset to the company when they return.

HOW CAN POOR PAST PERFORMANCE BE EXPLAINED?

The executives are asking you why the managers who were sent previously did not perform as anticipated, based on their past effectiveness and productivity in their assignments in the United States. They also want to know why these fast-track managers did not remain with Smallappliance.

As you were not involved in the earlier selection process, you list items to investigate. You are hopeful that the personnel files of the expatriate managers who were not very productive, who returned early, or who left Smallappliance will provide you with some insights, because if the managers selected in the current expansion do not remain productive when sent overseas, someone else will become the new vice president of human resources.

ISSUES

You wonder if other multinationals send their effective managers overseas and whether any other selection criteria are used. You are planning to ask the members of the Human Resource Management Association how their firms handle the selection of expatriates, if any training is provided, what type of training, and how repatriation is handled. Questions need to be answered in three major areas: selection, training, and repatriation.

1. What criteria, if any, besides being an effective and productive manager are necessary? Do expatriates from other multinationals remain effective and productive overseas? Were the wrong managers selected six years ago?
2. Could cross-cultural training for the specific location enable the expatriate managers to remain successful and productive overseas as

they are in the United States? Would poor productivity have been avoided if cross-cultural training and/or language training had been provided? If so, what kind of training would be needed, and how will you convince the executives to make the investment in training? Do other corporations provide training? What kind of training? Is it successful?

3. Why are many of the managers who are returning leaving Smallappliance for other companies? What can be planned now so that the managers in the new locations will remain with the firm.

The answers to these questions will enable you to answer the executives' questions and will give you the information to propose how you will handle the selection of the managers and begin making plans for their return. You begin by reading the personnel files from the earlier international expansion. Then you will talk to the experts from other companies.

EXPATRIATE RECORDS

Jack Wright's file indicates a productive manager who was well liked by his subordinates. He and his wife frequently traveled for pleasure, and both were anxious for the overseas assignment. Jack was sent to Spain and after about six months he was performing adequately in his new position. Upon his return to the States, he reported to the person who had taken over his job at the time of the transfer. Jack left the company shortly afterward.

Michael Kelly was assigned to Mexico. Mike had given no indication of interest in this assignment. His parents, brothers, sisters, and friends lived nearby, and Mike had been happy with his job in the United States. Mike made no effort to learn Spanish or to adapt to Mexican customs. He alienated customers, and did not get along well with his staff, although he did not appear to exert much control. Mike stayed in Mexico for nine months. Then he quit to take a job with another company back in his hometown.

Ron Smith and family were sent to Saudi Arabia where they lived in a compound with other expatriates. However the Saudis required that they send their 13- and 14-year-old sons to school outside the country; the Smiths requested an early return. Ron has indicated that he does not want any foreign assignments in the future.

Steve Hogan's file indicates that his assignment in Kuwait was cut short because his wife did not like the country. Everything was different; she found little of interest to do; she was not allowed to work as she had in the United States. Steve requested to return after only six months.

Henry Schmidt was a successful manager in the United States despite always requiring everything to be done his way and not tolerating any questioning from subordinates. He was sent to Australia, where he had trouble meeting his objectives. He complained that his subordinates were disrespectful and did not follow orders. Henry was not meeting deadlines and had cost overruns.

Robert Wren was noted for getting jobs done on time and on budget in the United States, for following rules, regulations, etc., to the letter. Robert was sent to Panama, where he felt the operation was loosely run with employees expecting time off for Carnival and other events, taking too long for lunch, and not finishing work promptly. New work rules were put into effect and many employees quit, which affected the operation adversely. Robert reported that the employees had bad attitudes toward work and that close supervision was needed to keep them working.

Jennifer Adams was sent to Korea. Her file indicated that she had requested extensive information before the assignment, and that she had studied about the country and had taken language lessons. However, Jennifer seemed to have difficulty in managing overseas and after the first nine months she was not as productive as in the States. Korean customers directed much of their communications to her male subordinates, who then had to come to Jennifer, making tasks take longer than necessary and causing deadlines to be missed.

Tom Hancock felt that an overseas assignment would broaden his knowledge of company operations. He began studying about the country, Brazil, and about the Latin American area, as well as the Portuguese language, as soon as he learned about the assignment. Tom was an effective and productive manager soon after his arrival, and remained effective until he was transferred back to the home office. Tom has been transferred frequently since his return and keeps asking for a position where his skills could be better utilized. You are aware that he has become more and more involved in activities outside the company and seems to seek satisfaction away from his job.

The other files indicate similar situations.

WHAT CAUSED PREVIOUS FAILURES?

What insights can be drawn from the files of managers from the previous international expansion? What do these files indicate that you can do, or should not do, as you learn what was done, or was not done, in selecting, preparing, and retaining managers who are assigned overseas? As you answer the questions listed in the Issues section, in preparation for formulating a plan for selection and preparation of the managers to be assigned to the new overseas posts by Smallappliance, indicate the file(s) to which you are referring.

Case 6

Phoenix Holdings' Troubled Acquisition

Joseph Wolfe
Bradley W. Miller
University of Tulsa

By early 1991 it was obvious to J. "Mike" Miller, president and CEO of Phoenix Holdings, Inc., that something had gone wrong with his company's purchase of the Western Aero Supply Corporation, a San Antonio aircraft parts wholesaler. His banks were wondering about Western Aero's low performance, many of his suppliers had frequently placed it on a COD-only delivery basis, and employee morale had deteriorated. More importantly, the San Antonio operation, which was the foundation for a newly created regional wholesale branch, had been discontinued for over a year, thus destroying one of the acquisition's key assets and much of the synergies Mike wanted for the two additional branches he had created. Although it was known that numerous short-term transition costs would be involved with the March 1988 acquisition, he now wondered into what kind of mess he had gotten Phoenix Holdings.

After collecting various internal reports and his thoughts on the company's situation, Mike wanted to bounce his ideas off some of his top executives. As a result of these discussions, Western Aero's ultimate future was to be decided, as it was now May 1991, and

This case does not indicate either correct or incorrect managerial actions or decisions and is intended to promote a discussion of the issues and alternatives associated with this industry and company. Many of the materials employed in this case were initially gathered as a student case-writing project conducted by Bradley W. Miller.

some type of action had to be taken. Would a little more fine tuning in the company's Dallas branch and with its new catalog sales operation turn this acquisition around, or was the purchase of Western Aero a basically flawed idea? Should Phoenix hang tough a little longer or should basic changes be set into motion?

GENERAL AVIATION INDUSTRY

The aviation industry's customers can be broken down into two major categories: military and civilian sales. Within the civilian category there exists the broad categories of commercial and general aviation. General aviation is composed of all civil flying, excluding certificated route air carriers, supplemental operators, large aircraft commercial operators, and commuter airlines. This aviation group is made up mostly of privately owned aircraft, but a small proportion consists of light demand air taxis, agricultural applications of insecticides and fertilizers, and power-line patrols and observation.

For a number of business cycles the demand for general aviation equipment appeared to be tied to the nation's gross national product (GNP). If GNP increased 1 percent, general aviation shipments increased 4 percent, and this relationship held true until the late 1970s. Thereafter, despite a relatively robust economy from 1983 to 1989, general aviation shipments fell during the same period. For example from 1978 to 1979, real GNP rose about 3.2 percent while general aviation shipments fell 1.1 percent. Exhibit C6–1 demonstrates the previous and current relationships between GNP and general aviation aircraft shipments. The Federal Aviation Administration (FAA) believes the industry's departure from its historic demand relationship can be attributed to a number of price and operating expense factors—higher prices charged for new airplanes, raising fuel and maintenance costs for owners and operators, and increased product liability by the manufacturers.

EXHIBIT C6–1 GNP Levels and General Aviation Aircraft Shipments

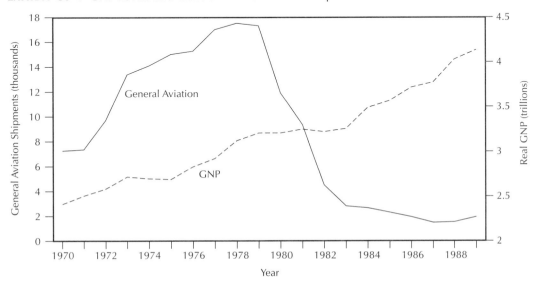

Between 1972 and 1987, the purchase price of a single-engine airplane rose 240 percent, and multiengine and turboprop airplane prices, respectively, rose 300 percent and 220 percent from 1972 to 1989. While these price increases dampen the demand for new aircraft which ultimately have to be serviced, the absolute size and cost of operating and maintaining America's fleet of active general aviation aircraft, as well as the number of pilots available and their number of logged flight hours, have the most direct effect on the aircraft service industry. Exhibit C6–2 provides information on the value of all civil aeronautic shipments made in the United States for selected years from 1972 to 1991. Exhibit C6–3 gives various measures of flying activity, such as the number of airports

EXHIBIT C6–2 Civil and Military Aerospace Industry Sales, 1975–1991
(in billions of current dollars)

Group	1975	1980	1985	1989	1990	1991
Civil	6.5	16.3	13.7	22.1	31.4	38.1
Military	10.0	15.2	36.8	38.9	38.3	32.1
Total	16.4	31.5	50.5	61.0	69.7	70.2

Note: Preliminary data for 1990 and estimated data for 1991.
Source: Statistical Abstract of the United States 1991 (Washington, DC: Bureau of the Census, U.S. Department of Commerce), Table 1086.

EXHIBIT C6–3 Civil Flying, 1983–1989

Item	Unit	1983	1985	1987	1988	1989
Public airports	1000	4.8	5.9	5.0	5.0	5.1
Private airports	1000	11.2	10.5	12.0	12.3	12.4
Total	1000	16.0	16.4	17.0	17.3	17.5
Fixed-wing aircraft	1000	200.8	198.0	204.1	197.0	204.5
Multiengine	1000	34.5	33.6	33.0	32.2	33.2[a]
Single-engine						
4-place and over	1000	107.2	105.6	107.5	105.2	108.5[a]
3-place and less	1000	59.2	58.8	63.5	59.6	62.8[a]
Rotorcraft	1000	6.5	6.4	6.3	6.4	7.5
Pilot licenses						
Commercial	1000	159	152	144	143	145
Private	1000	319	311	301	300	293
Student	1000	147	147	146	137	143
General aviation						
Hours flown	Million	35.2	34.1	33.4	33.6	35.0
Fuel consumed:						
Gasoline	Mil. gal.	428	420	402	398	418[a]
Jet fuel	Mil. gal.	613	691	672	746	741[a]

[a]Estimated by the case writers.
Source: Statistical Abstract of the United States 1991 (Washington, DC: Bureau of the Census, U.S. Department of Commerce), Table 1081; and *FAA Statistical Handbook of Aviation: Calendar Year 1989* (Washington, DC: U.S. Department of Transportation), Tables 8.2 and 8.3.

available, the number and classes of pilot licenses held and general aviation-type airplanes being flown, and the number of flight hours recorded and airplane fuel consumed for the years 1983 to 1989. Exhibit C6–4 displays the FAA's forecasts of flying activity for the years 1993 to 2001.

Regarding the variable costs associated with private flying, Exhibits C6–5 and C6–6 reveal the historical cost trends for general aviation's two largest airplane categories. In constant 1972 dollars the operating costs of flying a single-engine piston airplane peaked in 1983 and then fell about 10 percent to a fairly constant rate from 1987 to 1989. Maintenance costs, however, for this same type of airplane have risen almost constantly since 1971, although the overall increase has been less than the aircraft's operating costs.

EXHIBIT C6–4 Selected FAA General Aviation Forecasts for 1993–2001

Item	Unit	1993	1995	1997	1999	2001
Active aircraft	Thousands	220.0	220.5	223.5	225.0	227.0
Hours flown	Millions	35.0	36.5	38.0	38.5	39.7
Private pilots	Thousands	305.0	306.0	307.0	308.0	310.0
Student pilots	Thousands	145.0	148.0	149.0	149.5	150.0

Source: Interpreted from graphs in *FAA Aviation Forecasts Fiscal Years 1990–2001,* FAA-APO 90-1 (Washington, DC: U.S. Department of Transportation, March 1990), 100, 102, 103.

EXHIBIT C6–5 Single-Engine Operating and Maintenance Costs (*Source:* Adapted from *FAA Statistical Handbook of Aviation: Calendar Year 1989* [Washington, DC: U.S. Department of Transportation, 95].)

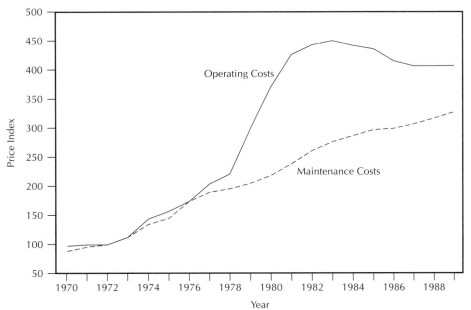

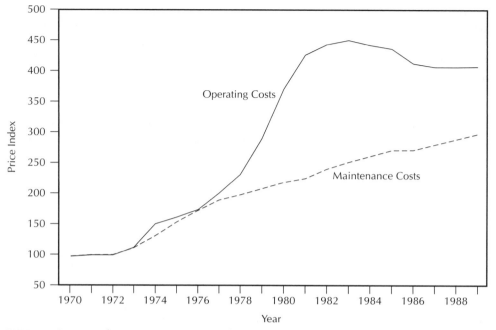

EXHIBIT C6–6 Multi-Engine Operating and Maintenance Costs (*Source:* Adapted from *FAA Statistical Handbook of Aviation: Calendar Year 1989* [Washington, DC: U.S. Department of Transportation, 96].)

Although many relatively low growth indicators exist for this industry, the FAA notes a number of encouraging signs. In recent years, the cost of purchasing turbojet aircraft has actually fallen, and only moderate price increases for multiengine piston and turboprop aircraft have been experienced. This has resulted in an annual growth rate of 3.6 percent for turbine-powered aircraft from 1989 to 2001 and an annual increase of 4.3 percent for turbine rotorcraft. Respective annual flight hour increases of 3.8 percent and 6.5 percent for these aircraft have been forecasted by the FAA for the same time period. Additional encouraging signs for the industry have appeared. Based on marketing research it has been estimated that 3.6 million American households have a family member who wants to learn how to fly and can afford to

do so. Sales of business-type jets should accelerate by 1995 as deliveries of the new Cessna CitationJet and Swearingen SJ-30 begin in 1992 and 1993. Learjet, Inc., expects to deliver thirty new aircraft in 1993 with four Model 60s and twenty-six 30-Series being planned for production. The piston-powered, single-engine aircraft segment, however, is expected to experience little, if any, growth for the rest of the 1990s.

WHOLESALE GENERAL AIRCRAFT PARTS INDUSTRY STRUCTURE

The manufacturers of general aviation aircraft use a large number of American parts suppliers when they make their airplanes. These suppliers, in turn, appoint a number of local distributors/wholesalers to make their parts and supplies available for after-market repairs and maintenance that inevitably follow from the use of the aircraft in which their parts are used. Of the two groups, commercial versus general, the latter market is the largest, broadest, most fragmented, and more easily entered. If the requisite distributorships can be obtained, a local wholesaler can supply the complete overhaul servicing needs of one single-engined airplane with a parts inventory amounting to between $8000 and $10,000; an inventory of about $2000 can overhaul the typical small airplane engine. Given parts manufacturers will directly airship parts to end users under emergency, aircraft-on-the-ground situations (AOG orders), a wholesale distributor does not even need a complete inventory to obtain credit for customer purchases and to service the majority of that customer's needs. Accordingly, a wholesale distributor can enter this industry with a relatively small capital investment in a minimum-sized inventory, depending on the number of customers and competitors in a given market area.

Until 1986 the wholesale airplane parts industry was dominated by two key players—Aviall, Inc., and Van Dusen Air, Inc. Between them they garnered about 40 percent of the industry's $500 million to $600 million in annual sales. In November 1985, Aviall was acquired by Ryder System, Inc., for $149 million, and in 1986 it purchased Van Dusen Air's aircraft parts distribution business. In its newly combined form Aviall operates over 80 stocking locations with 700 employees throughout the world. It has over 65,000 active parts numbers, represents over 200 major product lines and 1000 suppliers, and it possesses a working base of more than 25,000 customers. Despite its size and supposed economies of scale, Ryder System's aviation businesses experienced losses in 1989, while in 1990 they accounted for 23.3 percent of the company's overall sales but only 17.6 percent of its operating profits.

In late 1989, Global Aircraft Parts, Ltd., a new entrant into this industry, estimated the annual domestic sales and the number of locations for this industry's major participants as shown in Exhibit C6–7. Industry experts

EXHIBIT C6–7 Major Domestic Participants, Late 1989

Company	Annual Sales	Locations
Aviall, Inc.	$370,000,000	70
Piedmont Aircraft Supply	35,000,000	18
Cooper Aircraft Supply	35,000,000	7
Atlantic Aviation	15,000,000+	1
Less than $15,000,000 annual sales		
AAR Western Skyways		2
Aircraft Service		1
Cosgrove Aircraft Service		1
Omaha Airline Supply		3
Precision Aeromotive		1
Western Aero Supply		2

Source: Business plan, Global Aircraft Parts, Ltd., March 1990, 22–23.

have noted the constant dilemmas faced by those in the distribution channels for general aviation parts and supplies. The typical wholesaler employs a "hub and spoke" distribution system. In this type of operation a central warehouse or distribution center is created along with a number of "spokes" or local branch offices which take and solicit orders from regional customers. Each local branch also maintains inventories for making immediate deliveries. Should a branch be out of stock on specific items, sometimes amounting to 25 to 30 percent of the customer's original order, those items available are delivered immediately and the branch attempts to provide the remaining items from inventories held at the company's "hub" or other branches. To be financially successful, a parts wholesaler must minimize inventory levels both at each branch and within its overall system to maximize the return on its major asset while providing optimal "fill rates" for its customers. Although a typical branch might obtain five to seven stock turns a year, an overall system with many branches might obtain less than three turns a year. A low fill rate is the result of inadequate inventory levels and results in a higher stock turn and lower inventory investment for the wholesaler. Customers must then pay for additional delivery costs on back-ordered items while having their important revenue-producing airplane on the ground for an unnecessarily long time. In this regard, while customers are generally price sensitive, immediate and complete deliveries are the deciding factor in emergency, nonscheduled repair situations. For scheduled maintenance checks and overhauls, where parts can be ordered many weeks in advance, price is a greater factor than speedy and complete deliveries.

At one time competition in this industry's parts segment was waged at the local level between isolated local participants. With the advent of telemarketing and fast overnight deliveries provided by carriers such as Federal Express, United Parcel Service, and DHL Worldwide Express, national catalog wholesalers have entered the scene. Working from one large and efficient "paper-free" warehouse using highly automated inventory tracking systems and very accurate sales forecasting techniques, they compete by offering very low prices on what are basically commodity-type items while simultaneously providing relatively speedy deliveries. They accomplish this while maintaining minimum inventory levels for both themselves and their customers, although some feel their service is very impersonal and unsupportive.

Service is another key to success in this industry. While service is a function of the distributor's in-stock position, it is also dependent on how well the company relates to its customers. For most transactions this is manifested in the knowledge the company's salespeople possess when taking orders or suggesting parts and supplies that should be purchased. This translates into customer loyalty that can partially offset a competitor's lower prices. A good salesperson knows engines, can help customers with superseded parts numbers, is knowledgeable about FAA regulations regarding parts and component upgrades, and can quickly locate information in the numerous parts reference manuals. Over the years such a person can cultivate a following among purchasing agents, mechanics, and engineers in the local area. This service aspect frequently influences the distributor chosen by the industry's service stations, known as fixed-base operators (FBOs).

Although many wholesalers have attempted to improve their service levels while implementing operating efficiencies so they can be profitable with lower margins, many FBOs are unhappy with the overall distribution system they must use. First, although fill rates have often been low, wholesalers typically provide little information regarding what parts ordered will be shipped immediately and what parts are back-ordered for what time period. The back order itself causes an inordinate amount of "downtime" on an aircraft, while the lack of shipping information wastes mechanics' time and interferes with the rational scheduling of aircraft maintenance and service. Second, because back-ordered items must be shipped separately, the FBO must pay freight charges on each separate shipment. For a typical order this could result in four or five separate shipments. And third, the frequency of back orders and out-of-stock situations frustrates the FBO's desires to implement just-in-time (JIT) inventory systems. Although the use of JIT exacerbates the problem caused by the wholesalers, it is a viable way to lower the service station's inventory investment. Any wholesaler that could help the FBO accomplish a reasonable JIT inventory system would prove to be a strong partner in containing overall airplane service costs.

WESTERN AERO SUPPLY CORPORATION

Western Aero Supply is a 5.5-million-dollar-a-year company engaged in the wholesale distribution of new aircraft parts (SIC 5088, CLs 2612 and 2613). It was incorporated in San Antonio, Texas, in late 1946 by William B. Matthews. For almost 40 years it had been a good performer at its single location. By the early 1980s, however, its profitability began to suffer due to Matthews' declining interest and advancing age and the competitive pressures exerted by Aviall's San

Antonio branch. Aviall, Inc., featured a complete line of parts and supplies, had lower prices, and provided superior service by maintaining a better systemwide in-stock position.

Mike Miller purchased Western Aero for $650,000. At the time of the purchase, Western's year-to-date losses had amounted to about $20,000, with the year's projected losses amounting to over $45,000. He believed the price was justified based on the company's assets, the distribution rights it held, and the goodwill it had created over the years. About two thirds of Western's value consisted of its parts inventories, about $30,000 worth of office equipment, and its receivables less payables. The remainder of the purchase price was based on the value of good will, a noncompetitive covenant on William Matthews, and the exclusive right to distribute various manufacturer's products in the San Antonio area. In negotiating Western Aero's price it was believed about 75 percent of the receivables would be collected, about 20 percent of the inventory was almost worthless, and another 20 percent could only be sold at prices substantially below original cost. As part of the final agreement Matthews was allowed to keep his former office and retain the use of his telephone and secretary. Additionally the company's name could not be changed while he was still alive, and two of his favorite employees received guaranteed employment at Western Aero.

Almost immediately after the deal had been closed, Western Aero's headquarters was moved to Tulsa, Oklahoma, where the wholly owned subsidiary shared office space and expected synergies with Phoenix Holdings' two other operations. As shown in Exhibit C6–8, all subsidiaries serviced the general aviation industry with Mid-States Aircraft repairing and overhauling general

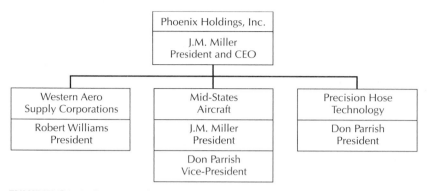

EXHIBIT C6–8 Corporate Structure (*Source:* Created by the case writers.)

aircraft engines and Precision Hose Technology servicing the end user's needs for flexible tubing and hoses. A number of internal benefits were anticipated. Mid-States Aircraft, Phoenix's largest subsidiary with about 60 percent of its total sales, could have about 40 percent of its parts supplied by Western Aero. Although Precision Hose Technology already had a Stratoflex hose distributorship, it could now combine its purchases with those of Western's, thereby obtaining a larger volume discount. In addition to moving Western's headquarters to Tulsa, branch operations were begun in that city, as well as in Dallas, Texas, in September 1988. With these additions, Phoenix Holdings, Inc., became a company with revenues amounting to $15 million to $16 million per year.

At the time of the Dallas branch's creation, numerous attractions appeared to exist. Inexpensive office and warehouse space was available, and the logistics were good. Dallas was a major market. It was only a 50-minute flight from Tulsa, so the inventories from both branches could service each other, and it was a market midway between Tulsa and San Antonio. Additionally Western Aero had the chance to hire two people with business dealings in the Dallas market. John Henderson was hired from

Aviall and John Hassel was engaged after having worked for Omni Air, an insolvent Dallas parts distributor. It was believed that, through their hiring, a number of major accounts would automatically be brought to the new branch. In justifying the Dallas operation, Mike Miller said "I was led to believe by the two Aviall people I had hired that customers were so displeased with Aviall's service we would be successful with any branch we opened against them."

Others in the company were less confident about the operation's chances for success. Daus Decker, Western's San Antonio manager, thought Western Aero's overall priorities were wrong. He argued, "Before going blindly into the wind in Dallas we should rebuild San Antonio. It will take over a year to build up San Antonio with only one manager there all the time. We don't have enough resources to build a branch in Dallas while trying to make San Antonio successful at the same time. What's worse, we'll be fighting Aviall in its own hub city." Exhibit C6–9 presents various market and population statistics associated with cities located in the Southwest.

With branch operations now in San Antonio, Dallas, and Tulsa at the end of 1988, Western Aero had created a regional "hub and spoke" distribution system, and

EXHIBIT C6–9 Statistics for Selected Cities

City	Metropolitan Population (1000)	10-Year Growth (percent)	Local Airports (number)	Local Wholesalers (number)	Aircraft Schools (number)
Austin	782	45.6	4	8	14
Dallas	3885	32.6	11	137	42
Houston	3302	20.7	11	26	25
Kansas City	1566	9.3	12	34	17
Little Rock	513	8.1	2	6	8
Oklahoma City	959	11.4	9	21	18
San Antonio	1302	21.5	4	44	13
Tulsa	709	7.9	6	28	17

Notes: Population reported for 1990; population growth from 1980 to 1990.
Sources: Statistical Abstract of the United States 1991 (Washington, DC: Bureau of the Census, U.S. Department of Commerce), Tables 36 ad 38 for population statistics. 1991 respective city telephone directory *Yellow Pages* for all remaining information.

Phoenix Holdings was expecting a large turnaround in the following year. Management thought that work force reductions, efficiencies brought about through the use of a new automated system, and more branches to cover the company's higher fixed costs would be reflected in profitable returns. Western Aero also invested money in marketing efforts and the hiring of skilled salespeople and managers to handle the new computerized system in the two additional branches. Five new people were hired, with three others moving over from the company's Mid-States Aircraft operation.

As shown in the company's 1988–1990 income statements and balance sheets in Exhibits C6–10 and C6–11, J. M. Miller's expected turnaround did not materialize. To

EXHIBIT C6–10 Western Aero Supply Income Statements Years Ending December 31

	1988[a]	1989	1990
Customer Sales[b]	$ 810,845	$5,056,108	$4,314,106
NAPDA Sales	240,834	1,476,331	1,216,000
Total Sales	1,051,679	6,532,439	5,530,106
Cost of Sales	781,902	5,331,491	4,766,055
Gross Profit on Sales	269,777	1,200,948	764,051
Selling and General Administration Expense	279,084	1,095,819	763,926
Income from Operations	(9,307)	105,129	125
Net Other Expense	(2,973)	(85,700)	(56,641)
Income before taxes	(12,280)	19,429	(56,516)
Taxes/Tax Recovery	(1,200)	3,475	(3,500)
Net Income	(11,080)	15,954	(53,016)

[a]Results for the year's last eight months.
[b]Includes transfer sales to affiliates at 5 percent over cost.
Source: Audited company reports.

EXHIBIT C6–11 Western Aero Supply Balance Sheets Years Ending December 31

	1988[a]	1989	1990
ASSETS			
CURRENT:			
Cash	$ 103,007	$ —	$ —
Trade accounts receivable	197,834	430,402	385,580
Parts inventories	517,621	960,818	1,037,848
Due from parent and affiliates	—	403,523	478,051
Covenant not to compete, current	43,729	43,729	43,729
Prepaid expenses and other	9,355	10,757	12,573
TOTAL CURRENT ASSETS	871,546	1,849,229	1,957,781
NET PROPERTY AND EQUIPMENT	56,958	32,747	16,229
OTHER:			
Unamortized covenant not to compete	145,764	102,035	58,306
Other assets	3,872	7,480	9,513
TOTAL OTHER ASSETS	149,636	109,515	67,819
TOTAL ASSETS	$1,078,140	$1,991,491	$2,041,829
LIABILITIES AND STOCKHOLDERS' EQUITY			
CURRENT LIABILITIES:			
Notes payable	$ —	$ 445,770	$ 645,770
Accrued expenses	3,187	—	—
Due to affiliate	95,634	—	—
Accounts payable and accrued expenses	236,419	881,110	844,194
Current maturities of long-term debt	77,529	60,730	57,888
TOTAL CURRENT LIABILITIES	412,769	1,387,610	1,547,852
LONG-TERM DEBT, less current maturities	236,684	159,240	102,352
TOTAL LIABILITIES	649,453	1,546,850	1,650,204
STOCKHOLDERS' EQUITY:			
Preferred stock, 5.0%, cumulative $5.00 par	15,500	15,500	15,500
Common stock, $.50 par	37,187	37,187	37,187
Additional paid-in capital	30,410	30,410	30,410
Retained earnings	390,721	406,675	353,659
	473,818	489,772	436,756
Less: Treasury stock, at cost	(45,131)	(45,131)	(45,131)
TOTAL STOCKHOLDERS' EQUITY	428,687	444,641	391,625
TOTAL LIABILITIES AND STOCKHOLDERS' EQUITY	$1,078,140	$1,991,491	$2,041,829

[a]Liabilities and equity created and held during the time of possession of Western Aero by Phoenix Holdings, Inc.
Source: Audited company reports.

become more competitive, Western Aero continued its membership in the National Aircraft Parts Distribution Association (NAPDA), spent more on advertising, and began catalog sales in late December 1990 with full-page parts listings in *Trade-A-Plane*, a trimonthly "Yellow Pages" newspaper. NAPDA is a voluntary association that, for a $1000 monthly fee, allows its members to fill each other's stock outs at 5 percent above cost, thereby ensuring the complete shipment of any customer's order. With Western Aero's use of catalog sales, it entered a hotly contested and price-competitive arena while also angering many of its local customers. Its goal was to undersell all competitors on the industry's most visible items. Exhibit C6–12 displays Western Aero's quoted prices in *Trade-A-Plane* on a sample of airplane parts and supplies versus those of its two major full-line catalog

competitors, Chief Aircraft, Inc., in Oregon on California's northern border, and San-Val Discount located in Van Nuys, California. Exhibit C6–13 lists the major product categories carried by Western Aero and the typical markups recently obtained on those goods.

CLOSING THE SAN ANTONIO BRANCH

As branch operations settled down, Mike Miller almost immediately became concerned about the poor monthly sales and gross profits being generated in San Antonio. Given its high wage costs, it was selling too few big-ticket items such as engines and cylinders and too many high-margin but low-ticket items such as masking tape, paint cans, hose fittings, and sectionals. Daus

EXHIBIT C6–12 Sample of Catalog Items and Prices

	Listed Price		
Items	Western Aero	San-Val Discount	Chief Aircraft
Lord Engine Mount—Cessna 180-182	$ 180.00	$ 186.00	$ 204.95
Alcor Single CHT set	175.00	179.95	172.95
Concorde Battery CB25 (12-9)	73.00	75.00	75.00
Cleveland Conversion Kit—Piper J-3	445.00	454.95	499.95
4522 Landing Lights	21.00	22.50	22.25
RN-2100 Scott oil pressure gauge	22.00	24.95	22.95
McCreary Tire—600-6 4 Ply Air-trac	43.00	45.00	45.00
Goodyear Tire—650-8 8 Ply Special II	91.00	95.00	106.00
Slick Magneto—4271	275.00	283.95	279.95
Slick Harness—6 cylinder	190.00	185.00	196.00
Concorde Battery—CB24-11 (G242)	158.00	164.00	157.00
O-Ring sets	50.00	56.95	64.95
Total	$1723.00	$1773.25	$1846.95

Source: Trade-A-Plane 54, no. 18 (May 1991), 11–13, 15, 20–21.

EXHIBIT C6–13 Product Categories and Expected Gross Margin Ranges

Product Category	Gross Margin Percent
Pilot supplies	35–45
Engine parts	10–20
Engines	5–10
Ignition products	15–20
Pumps and filters	15–25
Tires and tubes	25–35
Navigation and communication	25–30
Batteries	20–30
Harnesses and accessories	25–35
Hardware	50–70
Lighting systems	30–40
Lights	35–45
Paint, chemicals, and lubricants	30–40
Wheels and brakes	15–30
Heating and exhaust systems	20–30
Miscellaneous	30–35
Average	15–20

Note: The proportion of engine sales made during a period is the major contributor to the range in obtained margins.
Source: Management's estimates.

Decker, the branch's manager, started off well by selling old inventory purchased at comparatively low costs given their current inventory replacement value. The operation's gross profits started to decline, however, as soon as he had to work with fresh, high-cost inventories. In November 1988, Daus was transferred to Dallas as a salesman and Paul Feltes was sent to San Antonio from Tulsa's branch where he served as branch manager until March 1989.

Paul experienced only limited success at selling the company's bigger ticketed items, although he had been very successful at this in Tulsa. When the operation showed no real profit improvement, Mike Allen was hired to replace Paul Feltes in April 1989. Given monthly losses ranging from $5000 to $10,000, and Mike's cumulative branch tallies on their profits and losses summarized for the year in Exhibit C6–14, it was concluded in September that the San Antonio sales force lacked both the product and customer knowledge, as well as the necessary charisma, to make the branch a success. Additionally the branch had become a joke within the company, and most customers in the San Antonio area itself felt Western Aero was more a hardware vendor than an engine and airframe supplier.

Once Mike had made the shutdown decision, Robert Williams was dispatched to

EXHIBIT C6–14 Branch Income Statements Year Ending December 31, 1989

	Dallas	San Antonio	Tulsa
Sales	$1,054,345.78	$614,625.57	$2,862,947.07
Cost of Sales	892,774.92	498,034.02	2,288,939.92
Gross Profit	161,570.86	116,591.55	574,007.15
Direct Expenses:			
Wages	92,417.06	122,739.34	195,068.82
Automobile	5,959.61	2,833.48	13,084.61
Discounts Taken	7,795.28	4,144.26	16,024.15
Benefits	n.a.	820.48	1,568.82
Telephone	16,517.94	23,529.04	35,821.26
Freight	10,017.02	22,626.26	43,671.26
Office Supplies	579.73	n.a.	8,932.94
Rent	15,600.00	3,273.50	6,000.00
Employee Insurance	4,428.72	20,850.05	15,436.90
Utilities	1,355.00	(3,681.89)	1,897.29
Warehouse	1,944.83	2,759.36	9,055.78
Operating Expenses	156,615.19	199,893.88	346,561.83
Overhead Contribution	$ 4,955.67	$ (83,302.33)	$ 227,445.32

Source: Reconstructed from internal company records.

San Antonio in December to make the pronouncement to its employees. All were given four weeks' severance pay. Although not the reflective type, Mike Miller exclaimed in the aftermath "If I had it to do all over again I would have hired a whole new staff right away in the very beginning." Certainly this move might have minimized the effects of William Matthews' habit of coming to the office everyday where he would reminisce about the "good old days" and act like he still owned the business.

REFERENCES

1987 census of wholesale trade: Commodity line sales, United States. Washington, DC: Bureau of the Census, U.S. Department of Commerce.

A flying start. *Express Magazine* (Winter 1990), 8.

Business plan. Global Aircraft Parts, Ltd., March 1990.

FAA aviation forecasts fiscal years 1990–2001, FAA-APO 90-1. Washington, DC: U.S. Department of Transportation, March 1990.

FAA statistical handbook of aviation: Calendar year 1989. Washington, DC: U.S. Department of Transportation.

Kolcum, Edward H. Ryder managers predict aviation units will show moderate growth in 1990. *Aviation Week & Space Technology,* March 26, 1990, 77.

Newitt, Jane. Gray skies forever? *American Demographics* 11, no. 11 (November 1989), 36–39.

Phillips, Edward H. Business aircraft sales linked to global economic recovery. *Aviation Week & Space Technology,* March 16, 1992, 136–138.

Statistical abstract of the United States 1991. Washington, DC: Bureau of the Census, U.S. Department of Commerce.

Case 7

Trucking Plus Company in France

Hayet Kbaier
Lester A. Neidell
University of Tulsa

"I cannot postpone the final decision on our distribution problem in France any longer," was the spoken reflection of Ronald Baxter, Trucking Plus Company's (TPC) vice president of marketing. The report of Hans Brawns, international sales manager, and Curtis Slater, European area manager, lay on Ron's desk.

The French market had been a particularly difficult one to deal with ever since TPC initiated European export sales. Originally, a two-tiered European distribution plan serviced the European market. TPC sold its products to a "head" distributor or sales agent located in Switzerland, which then resold the products to "subdistributors" in each of the Western European countries. In 1982, a single-tier distribution plan was begun, in which each country's distributor placed orders directly with TPC. Bernard Clotier, who was the original French subdistributor, was elevated to head distributor. But sales in France remained below target. One year later, in 1983, a second head distributor, Jean Claude Palmer, was appointed. Since then, annual sales in France exceeded TPC targets. By the end of 1986, both French distributors were at the same level of sales, and each demanded revision to the customary exclusive distribution system.

HISTORY OF THE COMPANY

Trucking Plus Company began business in 1965. The original owner, Brian Norris, a skilled tool and die maker, recognized the future growth prospect of the trucking industry and initiated manufacture of truck wheels and drive parts. By 1970, the company had grown from a local Connecticut firm to a national sales volume of $2 million. Technological development allowed Trucking Plus Company to enlarge its product line with new products such as hydraulic suspension equipment and electrical life gates. When first introduced, these new products performed extremely well in the U.S. industrial market, with TPC obtaining a 50 percent share of its target markets. However, the 1973 oil crisis halted growth in industrial markets.

After his father's death, in late 1974, Don Norris was appointed president. He immediately hired professional managers to help him run the business. This initiative proved successful. TPC's industrial sales resumed their upward trend, and the company's product line was broadened to include suspension equipment and lift gates of different sizes for the consumer market. In 1976, the company's share was 9 percent of the U.S. consumer market for its products, which grew to a 40 percent share by 1986. Export sales of industrial and consumer products were initiated with various countries in Europe, Latin America, and the Middle East. In 1986, TPC achieved export volume of $2.7 million, almost 30 percent of its total dollar volume of this original product line.

In 1983, Trucking Plus Company acquired a $5.5 million (sales) company specializing in the manufacture of equipment for heavy trucks. As of the end of the 1985 fiscal year, sales of the acquired company reached $10 million, half of TPC total sales.

Don Norris considered TPC's growth and profitability at both the domestic and international levels to be very satisfactory. TPC's marketing organization is shown in Exhibit C7–1.

EXHIBIT C7–1 Trucking Plus Company

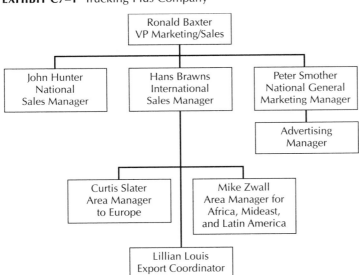

EUROPE'S EXPORT BUSINESS

When hit by the energy crisis of the 1970s, the company decided to investigate the international market. It observed a great potential for its products, especially in the European consumer market, where it was becoming faddish to drive trucks.

The first European export sale was in 1976. The two-tier distribution system described earlier was used. For the next five years, European sales were slow and no significant market share was gained. In 1982, Ronald Baxter was hired as marketing vice-president. One of Ron's assets was that he was fluent in French, German, and Japanese. Ron quickly recognized that the distribution system in Europe was not efficient and needed to be changed. The two-tier process of selling through a master distributor based in Geneva, Switzerland, which then resold to subdistributors in each country was not price competitive. TPC's competitors sold directly to distributors in the individual European countries. Soon after he took over the business, Ron changed entirely the European distribution system. The company's most important subdistributor in each country was appointed as the main distributor in the country in question. The new distribution system proved very successful for much of Europe. European sales doubled in the 1983–1986 time period.

THE FRENCH MARKET

The 1982–1983 performance of the appointed main distributor in France, Bernard Clotier, was substandard. He was selling the TPC products under his own trademark "JECIVMACISA," was taking high profit margin at the expense of greater market share, and was "cheating" on the company by buying parts from other competitors in the United States. In 1984, after detailed consideration of the situation, TPC's international sales manager, Hans Brawns, was given permission to appoint Jean Claude Palmer of Palmer S.A. as the company's second main distributor in France. This initiative was the start of the French distribution dilemma now facing Ron Baxter.

Distribution in France

Unlike in the United States, the distribution network in France is not broad and the demographics are such that customers don't have to drive long distances to find the parts they need. Rarely would there be more than one distributor carrying a particular manufacturer's product line in one city, thus allowing direct product and price competition to be kept at a minimum. All distributors requested exclusive distribution. When denied, they retaliated by not putting the effort, money, and time needed to promote and develop a market for the product.

The French Distribution Dilemma

But, when Jean Claude Palmer joined Bernard Clotier as second distributor of the company products, he defied tradition. On his own, he decided to lower prices and to increase promotion, advertising the company product line under TPC's own trade name. He also started using TPC products in the manufacturing of his own Auto Hauley, opening a greater market potential for the company in France. His aggressive actions were not intended against other competitors alone but also against Bernard Clotier, who soon retaliated by lowering his prices too. A price war was triggered in the French market. At the time TPC welcomed the competition. In just one year its exports to France doubled.

By the middle of 1985, Jean Claude Palmer's monthly import's volume grew to reach the same level as Bernard Clotier's. Realizing his strengthened position, he decided to "strong-arm" TPC's Connecticut headquarters to grant him sole distribution in the French market. Bernard Clotier, after learning about Jean Claude's approach, contacted Connecticut to announce his intention to promote and sell TPC's products under their own trademark and he too requested that exclusive distribution be granted to him.

Ron Baxter decided to buy time with both and to decide within a year or two according to performance. Meanwhile, the situation in France intensified, prices continued to drop, and TPC's sales increased.

In February 1986, Jean Claude Palmer went into joint partnership with Mouroux S.A.R.L., one of Europe's largest auto carrier manufacturers. The new partnership strengthened his financial and bargaining position with TPC. Finally, at the October 1986, Frankfurt Motor Show in Germany, Jean Claude met with Ron and demanded sole distribution be granted to him by Christmas 1986. Until exclusive distribution was granted, no new orders would be forwarded to Connecticut. Caught in the middle, Baxter proposed a visit to Connecticut. Upon his return to Connecticut, the vice president of marketing was unexpectedly visited by Bernard Clotier, who came to present his case for appointment as exclusive French distributor. Clotier made no assurances other than pointing out that business reasons now compelled him to promote TPC's name, and that market conditions in France would force him to keep prices competitive.

Three weeks after Bernard's departure, Jean Claude arrived in Connecticut to strongly emphasize his demand for sole distribution and delivered an ultimatum—if by the end of January 1987 sole distribution was not granted to him, he would cancel all business with TPC.

Upon Jean Claude's departure, Ronald Baxter contacted his international sales manager and his area manager in Europe for a comparative analysis on both distributors, and for recommendations.

They both concluded that Jean Claude be appointed as the exclusive distributor for France on the basis that he offered greater future growth than Bernard Clotier. Exhibit C7–2 reports Brawns' and Slater's assessment and recommendations.

ADDITIONAL INFORMATION

Jean Claude Palmer had become increasingly testy as TPC considered its alternatives. On December 29, 1986, Curtis Slater received a long telex from Jean Claude, which is reproduced in Exhibit C7–3.

EXHIBIT C7–2 Trucking Plus Company

Hans Brawns/Curtis Slater   January 22, 1987

Interoffice Memo

Subject: French market

As discussed during several occasions since end of fiscal year 1985 our two distributors in France ask now for our decision on distribution in this country. Both visited Fairfield in December to present their arguments for becoming the only distributor.

After our visit mid January we have put old and new facts together on attached list to show advantages and disadvantages for both companies and to make our recommendation understood.

After long and thorough discussion we have come to the conclusion to recommend

Jean Claude of Palmer-Mouraux S.A.R.L.

as the leading distributor for France on the facts that he gives Trucking Plus Company the best efforts and success for future business. He is able to open the best of opportunities that exist.

At the same time we would like to recommend to keep Bernard Clotier on a direct sales line, but not as a main distributor. A commission deal with Jean Claude Palmer should be worked out and Jean Claude would agree to that.

Hans Brawns
Curtis Slater

French Market Distributor Comparison

C.A.S., Bernard Clotier	Palmer-Mouraux S.A.R.L.

1. Company News

Enlarged with new large building for more production (platforms) and assembling. Also new shop built on old building for more exhibits of products.

Merger with Mouraux, leading car-carrier manufacturer in Europe (600 people) and worldwide sales. Partnership is 50:50 (Jean Claude) maybe 49:51 (others). Jean Claude has taken over Mouraux's activities in France and will be assembling/mounting at Saint Mihiel. Car carrier platforms and equipment will be manufactured at Hangenbieten-Strassburg with new Palmer workshop (about 80 people). Distribution of Trucking Plus Company's products will remain with Palmer.

2. Market Activities

Sales 1985 vs. 1986 $229–$338,000
Increase of *47.6%*
Sales activities: no change
Hates to follow Jean Claude in prices.
Losing original equipment business. Promotes no manufacturer names on products.

Sales 1985 vs. 1986 = $115–$355 (incl. subdistr)
Increase of *208.7%*
Sales activities: very aggressive sales all over France to all levels of customers' work shops, wholesalers, OE, etc.
Price calculation leaves him with satisfactory margin, works also on commission basis for orders with OE's if necessary. Promotes strongly Trucking Plus Company products to make them as popular as possible in France.

3. Product Mix (wheels, drive parts, and lift gates)

Sells different lines of products with his name, but now mainly Trucking Plus Company products and some other brands.

Promotes and sells total company product line, only in case we do not have application needed, takes RULE (a competitive product) or one or two specialties.

4. Cooperation

Bernard Clotier and his son Philip are fine businessmen, and our advice given last year has led to an increase that we didn't really expect. Attitude is very conservative, and cooperation as far as market information about activities is rather poor. They do not like any kind of interference with their customers and would not like business on commission basis, if it had to be necessary with regard to competition. To cover their businesses they prefer to build consumer image to their own name. Innovations with regard to OE possibilities are not forthcoming.

Jean Claude is very aggressive and he motivates his people in same direction.
His promised increase in business was held and he reached an outstanding performance.
He wants to become the best distributor, and Trucking Plus Company the best known manufacturer in the market to replace WARN.[a] He feels that within the next year he can come close to this target, especially since he found the backup from Mr. Mouroux.
Cooperation in respect of market information and technical support for Trucking Plus Company is excellent. He devotes all his efforts to the goal.

[a]Well known manufacturer of trucking equipment in France.

EXHIBIT C7–3

TRUCKING PLUS COMPANY—FRANCE

JEAN CLAUDE PALMER

TELEX NO 3002

HERE JEAN CLAUDE PALMER/PALMER MOUROUX SARL
LE 29 DECEMBER 1986

TO CURTIS SLATER

DEAR CURTIS.

PLEASE STOP SENDING A TELEX PER DAY ASKING ME MY NEXT ORDER. AS FAR AS YOU DO NOT TAKE ANY DECISION WITH DISTRIBUTION. I CONSIDER THAT I HAVE NO LIABILITY OF ANY SORT WITH YOUR FIRM. IT IS CLEAR THAT I ORDER WHAT I WANT WHEN I WANT. I DECIDED NOT CONTINUING AGGRESSIVE MARKET PENETRATION. WHOLE SALER PERSONNEL VISIT. ADVERTISEMENT AND EXHIBITION BECAUSE IT DOESN'T GIVE ME ANYTHING MORE THAN CLOTIER C.S.A., WHO IS TRANSGRESSING IN THE WHOLESALE AGREEMENT SIGNED WITH YOUR DISTRIBUTORS. YOU HAVE TO TAKE A DECISION. I'LL NOT BE INVESTING IN CSA TRUCKING PLUS COMPANY TRADEMARK PROMOTION WHEN FRENCH TERRITORY IS COVERED BY THE SAME PRODUCT UNDER DISTRIBUTOR TRADEMARK. I INTEND ALSO THEN TO COMMERCIALIZE UNDER MY OWN TRADEMARK "PALMER MOUROUX" THAT WILL AUTHORISE ME TO INCREASE MY RANGE OF PRODUCT LINES AND TO BUY FOLLOWING US DOLLARS RATE AT THE BEST OF MY INTEREST TO BE JUST IN FAIR COMPETITION WITH CSA.
IT IS CLEAR I DO NOT ORDER ANYTHING UNTIL DECISION IS TAKEN. C.S.A. JUST STARTS TO MAKE ADVERTISEMENT UNDER YOUR NAME CLAIMING HE IS YOUR GENERAL DISTRIBUTOR FOR FRANCE FOR 10 YEARS. IT SEEMS HE IS CHANGING HIS MIND AND COMING ON MY TRACK. IT IS QUITE CLEVER BECAUSE IT LEAVES PEOPLE THINK THAT WE ARE NOTHING HERE AND I CAN'T STAND THAT. MISTER MOUROUX, MY PARTNER, SAID ALSO YOU HAD TO BE PRECISE AND LET US KNOW IF WE CAN CONTINUE INVESTING IN YOUR PRODUCT PROMOTION IN FRANCE. WE ARE NOT PHILANTHROPIC AT ALL AND IF WE DO NOT SEE REWARD IN THE FUTURE WE LEAVE.

BEST REGARDS.
JEAN CLAUDE PALMER

Case 8

Southeastern Directory

Ralph W. Jackson
University of Tulsa

Tina Spaulding set down at the desk in her apartment, exhausted from the trying day she had just completed. It was 7:15 P.M., and she had not yet had dinner, and was not even sure that she wanted to. As she sat looking over the results of her day's efforts, she thought back on the previous four months. That was how long it had been since she had completed training with Southeastern Directory, and had been in the field selling yellow page advertising. These had been perhaps the most frustrating four months of her life, and she hoped that somehow things would get better soon.

HER BACKGROUND

Tina had graduated from the University of Kentucky with a major in marketing six years before. Upon graduating, she went to work as an inside salesperson at Allied Industrial Supply, an industrial wholesaler, in Louisville, Kentucky. She hoped to move from that position into outside sales. Two years later, when it did not appear that she would move into outside sales in the near future, she applied for a position as a project buyer at Badger Construction Company in Tampa, Florida. She would be purchasing the same types of items that she had sold at Allied. The buyer position paid 25 percent more than her inside sales job, and she thought she might like living in Florida. After an initial interview in Louisville, Badger flew her to Tampa for another interview, after which they made her an offer, which she accepted. She was with Badger for about three and a half years. She enjoyed her job there and liked Tampa, but had gotten to the point of feeling that she had mastered the job and there were limited opportunities within Badger.

THE SOUTHEASTERN SCREENING PROCESS

While visiting Atlanta, her hometown, a friend told her of the earning opportunities at Southeastern, and informed her that he had heard there were some openings in the Atlanta district. He said that directory reps earned a base salary with a potentially lucrative commission structure. Additionally, they paid a car allowance and had excellent benefits. Fortunately, Southeastern had a branch office in Tampa where she could apply.

Southeastern used a three-stage screening process. Very few applicants made it through two of the three stages, much less through all three. The three stages were (1) application and initial interview; (2) aptitude and personality testing; and (3) role-play interview. Tina easily made it through the first two stages. The third stage involved a series of three role-plays and took almost an entire day to complete.

In the first role-play, she was to play the part of a marketing manager who had to develop a promotional campaign to introduce a new product. She was given an hour and a half to develop the campaign while staying within a budget, and prepare a presentation for the "president" of the company. She had 45 minutes to make the presentation. Although the president asked a number of questions and raised some objections, the presentation went well.

In the second role-play, she played the part of a marketing manager who had to decide on one of three advertising campaigns, and present her choice. She was given an hour to decide on the campaign and to prepare to present her choice to the "president" and "sales manager" and "comptroller" of the company. She had an hour to present and defend her choice. Each of the three raised some objections; however, things seemed to go well.

In the final role-play, Tina was to play the role of a supervisor who had to decide on which of three subordinates to promote. She was to review the three profiles she was given, make her decision, and present the decision to two people playing the roles of her "supervisor" and the "vp of personnel." She was given an hour to make her decision and prepare to present it. When she made the presentation, the vp of personnel seemed to initially agree with her choice, while her supervisor strongly disagreed with her decision. Gradually, as the presentation progressed, the vp of personnel began to side with her supervisor. Finally, at the end of the presentation, her supervisor said, "Well, this concludes the role play, but off the record, Tina you made the wrong decision. If you care to change before we enter it into our log, I will let you." Tina felt like this was a test of her persistence, and replied, "I think I made the right decision. If you think I am wrong, so be it, but I will not change my mind." The other two looked at each other for a moment, then the person playing her supervisor said: "Good, I had hoped you wouldn't back down. This part of the interview is now really over, and you have done well. From what I understand, you did well in your earlier role-plays. We'll be making a decision in the next few days, and will get back to you." The next week, Tina received a phone call followed by a letter offering her a job, and telling her that a training class was scheduled to begin in four weeks in Atlanta, Georgia.

THE SOUTHEASTERN TRAINING PROGRAM

Training for directory representatives lasted four weeks. There were anywhere from four to seven trainees per training group, and these would generally be assigned to the same region after training. There were five in Tina's class, and they were from various backgrounds. Two had been in sales, Cindy Havner had sold securities and Josh McGovern had sold commercial real estate. Bill Briggs had been a high school football coach, and Will Tomkins had been in banking. There were several such training groups going through the program simultaneously in Atlanta. The groups were each assigned a trainer who had been a successful yellow page salesperson at Southeastern.

The four weeks of training program had three phases. Phase I presented basic selling techniques, and lasted for two weeks. During these two weeks, trainees were introduced to the six-step sales approach. The six steps were (1) preparation; (2) the approach; (3) information gathering; (4) the presentation; (5) handling objections; and (6) closing the sale. In teaching these six steps, trainers used tapes and role-plays extensively. During the two weeks, trainees were also taught the Southeastern approach to organizing accounts and time management. Additionally, trainees were given a session on goal setting and one on the Southeastern philosophy.

The philosophy that was presented was that the directory representative was always to put the customer's interest first. Although representatives should strive to sell customers as large an ad as possible, they should never sell customers advertising they did not honestly feel the customer needed. This philosophy was constantly reinforced throughout the training program.

During the phase II of the program, trainees were given a week of training regarding the mechanics of setting up a yellow page ad. They were exposed to the entire process of how a yellow page directory was developed and published. In phase III of the program, trainees had to make an initial presentation to one of their classmates and then two to the trainer. These latter two were taped. After each trainee had been taped, the tapes were critiqued by the entire class. The trainee and the trainer together chose which of the two would become part of the trainee's permanent record and be sent to his or her initial supervisor. On Wednesday of the final week, trainees would be given their account packets for their first canvass, and were told who their supervisors would be. Thursday and Friday were used to prepare 20 to 25 accounts for their first canvass. The trainers helped in the process and signed off on the prepared packets. For the first two months in the field, new reps were required to have their supervisors sign off on their packets.

A yellow page canvass involves calling on each customer who had a business phone that would be listed in a particular directory. These customers had business phones with Southeastern General Telephone Company (SGTC). SGTC operated in Georgia, Alabama, Florida, South Carolina, North Carolina, and Tennessee. Its district offices were located in Atlanta, Tampa, Charlotte, Knoxville, and Montgomery. Southeastern Directory Company was a wholly owned subsidiary of SGTC. Customers who had not purchased ads in three years were contacted via telephone by inside sales reps. Customers who had an advertisement in the yellow pages, as well as new customers, were personally called on by directory reps during the canvass. Directory reps in the Atlanta district worked not only on the Atlanta canvass, which took about eight months to complete, but also on canvasses in Macon, Marietta, Columbus, Athens, and Augusta, which altogether accounted for the other four months of the year. The Macon canvass lasted for three weeks, Marietta for two weeks, Columbus for four weeks, Athens for three weeks, and Augusta for four weeks.

Tina's first canvass would be Macon, Georgia. The Atlanta canvass would not start for another three weeks, and the trainer told the group that beginning in a smaller book would be good practice for the Atlanta canvass, which was certainly the most critical one for them. The account packets each trainee received were roughly equal in the amount of total advertising revenue they contained. Each packet had a mixture of types of businesses.

Interestingly, Tina would be part of one of the few unionized sales forces. About 97 percent of the directory representatives joined the Communication Workers of America (CWA). It was also interesting that the trainers, though part of management and therefore no longer members of the union, encouraged the trainees to join the CWA.

THE SOUTHEASTERN SYSTEM

Directory representatives earned a base salary of $800 per month plus a commission. The commission was based on the monthly price of an ad. The percentage commission varied with each different directory. For example, the percentage of commission for the

Atlanta directory was smaller than for the smaller directories serviced by the Atlanta office. However, the cost of the ads in Atlanta was much higher than the cost in the smaller cities, so directory reps typically made more money in the Atlanta canvass than they would in the other canvasses. For example, in Atlanta, reps received an 81 percent commission, while in Macon, they received a commission of 143 percent. However, with the differences in the cost of ads in Atlanta, reps would make more than in Macon. Exhibit C8–1 gives a comparison of Atlanta and Macon in the ad rates and the commissions earned for the various sizes of ads. The rate structures and commissions for the other smaller cities the Atlanta office serviced are similar to those of Macon. In addition to being paid a commission on ads, reps also received commission on any in-column listings. For example, each commercial phone customer automatically received a regular listing (RL) in the yellow pages at no additional charge. However, if a customer wished his company to be listed in bold print, he would pay $18.50 per month in Atlanta, and $10 per month in Macon. In addition to a bold listing, which resulted in revenue, there were other in-column listings as well as other products,

EXHIBIT C8–1 Comparison of the Monthly Ad Rates and Resulting Commissions in the Atlanta and Macon Directories

	Atlanta		Macon	
Ad Size	Rate/Mo.	Commission	Rate/Mo.	Commission
Quarter column (2″ × 2″ ad)	$147.50	$119.50	$55.00	$78.65
Double quarter column (2″ × 4″)	$295.00	$238.95	$110.00	$157.30
Triple quarter column (2″ × 6″)	$442.50	$358.45	$165.00	$235.95
Double half column (1/4 page)	$590.00	$477.90	$220.00	$314.60
Triple half column (3/8 page)	$885.00	$716.85	$330.00	$471.90
Double column (1/2 page)	$1180.00	$955.80	$440.00	$629.20

such as coupons and restaurant guides, that were revenue producers for reps.

In addition to their salary plus commission, reps were paid 25 cents per mile for car expenses. When they were working a "road book," that is, a directory outside Atlanta, they were reimbursed up to $45 per night for lodging and received a food per diem of $40 per day.

Although directory reps were on their own during the day, they had to turn in an activity report each morning by 8:30 A.M. that showed the previous day's results. This activity report contained information on the five areas in which reps had to meet daily quotas:

1. Number of closes (contracts signed by the customer)
2. Amount of revenue handled (total value of contracts)
3. Amount of new business sold (new advertising)
4. Net sales to existing advertising (advertising sold in addition to ads bought previously by the customer)
5. Amount of old business lost (ads that customers refused to renew)

The specific quotas varied by canvass. The information gleaned from these reports was listed on tote boards. There was a tote board for each unit, one for the region, and one for the entire canvass. These were publicly displayed in prominent places in the office. The unit tote board showed the results for every person in the unit, while the ones for the region and the canvass only showed the top ten people.

THE "REAL WORLD" OF SELLING

On Monday, Tina reported to the Atlanta office of Southeastern Directory. She and her colleagues in the training program had a variety of paperwork to fill out. Additionally, they sat through a morning orientation session. After lunch, Tina, along with the other new reps, departed for Macon. The canvass had begun that day and so they would not be too far behind when they reported to the headquarters hotel in Macon. She arrived in Macon about 2:30 P.M. and checked into the headquarters hotel. Southeastern would establish a "command center" at the headquarters where each salesperson had a desk and a phone, and where each would report to work in the morning and turn in their reports from the previous day's activities. After checking in, she went to the command center to try and meet her new supervisor, and to find her desk so she could get organized to begin making calls. Fortunately, her supervisor, Elizabeth Cartwright was there, and Tina got the chance to introduce herself. Elizabeth informed Tina she would ride with her either later in the week or early next week. Southeastern required that supervisors ride with new reps within a week of their starting work, and after that, they ride with the new reps at least once every two weeks for the first two months. Although Elizabeth seemed very professional to Tina, she also seemed a bit "cold." Upon meeting Tina, Elizabeth commented "Welcome to the 'real world'—I hope you're ready to be the pacesetter for our unit." Tina's friend, Ron Marcus, who was a veteran salesperson with Southeastern and one of the top five Atlanta producers, had told her that Elizabeth Cartwright had the reputation for being one of the most difficult supervisors in the Atlanta office.

After visiting briefly with Elizabeth, Tina, being anxious to get started, left the hotel to try to make at least two calls that afternoon. That evening, she saw Cindy and Josh, with whom she had gone through training, and four other sales reps going to dinner. They invited her along, and she joined them so she could get to meet some of the other directory reps. After some of the veteran salespeople had a few drinks, they began the process of "enlightening" the new reps on how things really worked. One of the veteran salespeople, Todd Johnston, who had been with Southeastern for 12 years, summed up the feelings of the group of veterans by saying: "Forget all that crap you learned in training—all the company really cares about is how much advertising you sell!" Another of the group who had been with the company for seven years, John Williford, added: "This is a numbers game, and those who make their numbers are heroes, and those who don't are gone. The company doesn't care about your personal problems, and the company has never heard of the concept of loyalty, either to the customers or to its salespeople." The rest of the conversation of that evening followed along similar lines. Tina went back to her room about 8:30 P.M. She wasn't too bothered by what she heard because she had been warned to expect to hear some of that kind of talk. Also, she knew that some of the guys had had a bit too much to drink and were probably just talking.

Tina's first week went well. She made a number of good sales, and none of her accounts had cancelled their ads. At the end of the week, she was number two out of the seven reps in her unit in the Macon canvass. She felt good about her results, but as she was preparing to leave for her home in Atlanta at 4:00 P.M. on Friday, Elizabeth told that she expected her to be leading her unit by this time next week. She had said it in such a way that Tina came away feeling like she had been chastised.

On the following Tuesday, Elizabeth rode with Tina. Although she knew that Elizabeth would ride with her that week, she was extremely nervous and made a few minor blunders in a couple of her presentations. However, she survived the day and managed to make quota in all five areas. Elizabeth did not have much to say about her presentations despite the fact that Tina asked her several questions. By the end of the week, she had slipped to third place in her unit. This was partly due to one of the reps having a "windfall" in that one of his customers bought half-page ads under two listings as well as two quarter-page ads under two other listings. The canvass was completed by Thursday of the third week. Tina ended up at number two in her unit, and tenth overall for the canvass. Josh, who had gone through training with her, was the only other one in her training group to make the top ten.

On Friday, they were to report to the Atlanta sales office to draw for the Atlanta canvass which was due to be kicked off the next Monday. The draw consisted literally of each rep drawing a large envelope out of a box. The envelope contained the computerized printout of each account the reps would handle during the canvass. The envelopes were equal in total revenue, and contained a variety of businesses randomly sorted by the computer which meant that reps typically did not have the same customers from year to year. Tina spent the rest of Friday preparing accounts so she could let Elizabeth review and initial them before she began calling on her Atlanta accounts.

In the second week of the Atlanta canvass, Elizabeth rode with Tina. Again, Tina was nervous, but had done a better job of planning than she had the first time

Elizabeth rode with her. She had a number of apparently good prospects lined up, and called and made appointments with six of them. In spite of having the appointments set ahead of time, the first two customers did not have time to see her. Elizabeth was a bit agitated by this, and seemed to blame Tina. The third appointment was with the owner of a tire store. He seemed to be cordial enough initially, but when he found out that Elizabeth was Tina's supervisor and that Tina was a relatively new rep, he seemed to give Tina a more difficult time. He became somewhat obstinate and appeared to delight in raising difficult objections. Tina handled the situation well, although she was a bit unnerved by it. In the end, he bought the ad she proposed.

Since they had a little extra time, Tina decided to call on one of her customers, a furniture store, even though she did not have an appointment. She had planned her route to this customer, however, there was some major construction going on, and when they took the detour, Tina got lost for about twenty minutes. This customer renewed his double quarter column ad, although he complained about the 10 percent increase in ad rates, and would not even consider buying a larger ad. They then broke for lunch. During lunch, Elizabeth let Tina know that they had wasted much of the morning. She then asked Tina what job she had prior to becoming a directory rep. Tina responded that she had been a buyer for an engineering firm in Tampa. Elizabeth inquired as to whether she had ever been in outside sales. Tina explained that she had not, but that she had been in inside sales with the idea of moving into an outside sales job with the company. Elizabeth then stated: "Well, if you haven't been in outside

sales before, you'll never make it selling yellow pages."

The next two months and three weeks in the Atlanta canvass went okay for Tina. She had made quota most days, and was currently third in her unit in sales. She had a number of disappointments with accounts that should have bought advertising but for some reason did not. However, she had made some good sales, and overall her earnings had been good. However, Elizabeth reminded Tina on several occasions that, as a new rep, she should be leading her unit, and that she felt Tina's performance was below par. During one such conversation, Elizabeth told Tina, "Your sales must improve. Do anything you have to do to improve improve sales, just don't tell me what you do. I can't object to what I don't know about." Tina responded that she would improve her sales but that she would not compromise her personal ethics. Despite the criticism, Tina kept plugging away, determined to prove to Elizabeth that she could make it as a directory rep. If she held out for a year, she could transfer to another unit.

In the past two weeks, Elizabeth had made a couple of off-the-cuff comments that Tina's performance had better improve, or she would seek to have her terminated. Two of the people in her training group, Cindy Havner and Will Tomkins, had already left Southeastern. In her entire working career, Elizabeth Cartwright had been the first person that she absolutely despised working for. It seemed to Tina that Elizabeth had a personal vendetta against her. Elizabeth had made a couple of disparaging remarks about the fact that Tina was a college graduate. Only one other person in her unit had a degree. Elizabeth Cartwright had gotten into sales by transferring from the repair division of SGTC, and had been a successful directory rep. After two years as a directory rep, she was offered a supervisor's position. Supervisors are evaluated based on their unit's performance. That was seven years ago, and she had not been in line for any promotions since then, partly due to the fact that she did not have a degree.

Case 9

Texas Timber Products, Inc.

Marlene Kahla
Stephen F. Austin State University

INTRODUCTION

Texas Timber Products, Inc. (TTPI), grew, harvested, processed, and sold timber products, plywood, and particleboard. The company employed about 10,000 people in its operations in the southern Gulf states.

Kenny Smith, export sales manager for TTPI, was faced with several problems. Sale of timber products to overseas customers had been increasing at a fairly rapid rate over the last five years and the company had not altered its operating procedures or organizational structure to accommodate the nondomestic market. Kenny's department essentially operated outside the company's regular sales department. This resulted in tension, misunderstanding, and low morale among the domestic sales staff.

On another level, Kenny faced somewhat of an ethical dilemma—the better grades of lumber were being shipped overseas where prices were substantially higher than here in the States. This meant that domestic customers were being sold an inferior product. While this practice meant higher profit for the company, there was a question as to whether domestic customers, whose patronage had helped build the company to its present position, were being treated fairly.

A procedural problem nagged Kenny. A situation had developed involving nonpayment by a Cuban customer who owed the company $300,000. Since Kenny was relatively new at handling international transactions, he was curious as to how the customer was able to take possession of the shipment (at a foreign port) without presenting proper documentation from the bank. He also had to come up with a way to get the Cuban customer to pay the $300,000 due TTPI.

Kenny was frustrated. He could do only so much. He often wondered what was really expected of him at TTPI. His job description focused on sales and sales force management. He had a sales staff of one order taker who was also his secretary. And international sales, for yet another year, was not mentioned in the most recent company report.

CASE STUDY

It was an unusually brisk day in May. Kenny Smith, export sales manager for Texas Timber Products, Inc. (TTPI), sat at his desk gazing over the rolling hills of a well-manicured golf course. He thought about his current position with the company and how far he had come since his early years of stacking boards in a Houston warehouse. As export sales manager for TTPI he was in a more responsible position than any he had held before. He was aware, however, that his 15 years' experience in the lumber and building supply business had taught him little about how to deal with jealous colleagues, too few qualified people to do the best job, no special recognition within the company, and international contractors, banks, and agencies.

Kenny wished he was on that golf course right now. He had just received word from the Credit Department that a Cuban contractor, Mr. Heredia, had not paid for a sizable shipment of plywood. The shipment, which Kenny had authorized, was picked up by Heredia at a Puerto Rican port over six months ago.

Julia Munez, his secretary and order taker, was on break, and one of the salesmen, Roy, from domestic sales just barged into his office and chewed him out. One of his customers had complained about the quality of lumber in a #1 load of boards delivered to the job site. Roy was anything but happy about the increase in Kenny's sales, "Damn it, Kenny, we here in the homefront

have few quality boards for our customers—lighten up on those foreign sales—they're kill'n us with our customers!"

COMPANY BACKGROUND

Recently the building products group experienced its most profitable year in history and established production records in most product categories. Sales totaled $419.3 million, earnings were up by 151 percent, lumber production was up 67 percent, and plywood and gypsum production were up by 27 percent and 19 percent, respectively.

Specialty lumber and plywood products were developed for export to Mexico. Overall, export sales were expected to increase at an accelerated rate over the next two years.

The company employed about 10,000 people in its operations in the southern Gulf states. The majority of company sales (about 60 percent) were made to lumber and building supply companies (including four company-owned retail outlets) and 15 percent was to large building contractors who bought direct. Export sales accounted for the remaining 25 percent of building products sales.

Andrew Summitt was the company president. The Summitt family founded the firm in 1923 and it was incorporated and went public in 1983. Andrew Summitt was a highly respected leader and was the motivating force behind the company's success. His current focus was on expanding lumber production because he expected demand for pine lumber products to increase and was afraid that additional environmental restrictions might hamper future fiber conversion.

Because of preoccupation with activities at higher levels of the business, Andrew Summit was not fully aware of how fast the company's exporting division was growing. In fact, exports of company products were experiencing exceptional growth and were the primary reason for the company's sales increase the previous year. The Building Products Division would have had a somewhat disappointing year had there not been a sizable increase in export sales. The exceptional performance of the export division was due to a combination of high quality products produced in plants located near Gulf Coast ports. This permitted ready penetration of European lumber markets. In addition, close proximity to Mexico had given the company a competitive edge in this fast growing market.

Unfortunately for Kenny, the significance of the export division was not fully appreciated by upper level management since domestic and foreign sales were not recorded and reported separately in the company's financial reports (see Exhibit C9–1). To Summitt, sales were sales—regardless of whether made to domestic or foreign customers.

Organizationally, the Export Sales Department was under the vice president of marketing, Joe Chumley. Chumley gave Kenny Smith a free rein in operating his department as long as sales were increasing and no major problems developed. While Kenny appreciated the confidence placed in him by Joe and other company officials, he was very much aware of the responsibilities and pressures that accompanied his position.

THE CURRENT DILEMMA

Kenny continued to ponder his delinquent customer. He knew that some delinquent accounts could be expected when orders were shipped without requiring advanced payment. As Kenny confided to a colleague: "In the wholesale business there were always some stable ones that paid their bills. But there were others that never really settled up. We used to keep a list of welshers that circulated among the wholesalers in Houston. But we later found out that Robinson-Patman, or something like it, made the list illegal. I guess we made mental notes instead. Most of the wholesalers knew that not everyone

EXHIBIT C9–1 Building Products Sales

Product	Sales (in millions)			
	1993	1992	1991	1990
Pine lumber	$90.8	$82.1	$78.3	$69.4
Fiberboard	58.2	48.3	46.4	43.7
Particleboard	80.2	67.2	64.7	59.4
Plywood	60.3	49.3	47.5	40.5
Gypsum wallboard	53.1	42.1	40.2	36.6
Foam insulation	9.3	6.2	5.4	4.4
Retail distribution	57.3	43.1	40.3	37.5
Other	10.1	7.2	6.2	5.8
Total	$419.3	$345.5	$329.0	$297.3

was going to pay for all the lumber and supplies. When the bottom fell out of the market in Houston, we were really forced to watch who we made deals with. Now that I've gone international, it looks like I have to do the same thing. Except this time it is with those Cubans. It seems as though they take advantage of every little mistake made in documentation."

Because of the extended channels involved in dealing with overseas accounts, there were many opportunities for mistakes to be made. The international sale of lumber involved: TTPI, the foreign customer, the U.S. Department of Agriculture, the Export-Import Bank in New York, the bank in the country of destination (in this case, Puerto Rico), and marine and surface transportation companies.

Kenny realized that exporting was a growing opportunity for the lumber industry and for his company. What bothered him was that he essentially operated outside of the company's regular sales department. His department consisted only of himself and one secretary/order taker. Although foreign sales depleted the supply of pine available for the domestic market, they were not coordinated with sales and supply reports or with the company's other sales representatives. Kenny commented: "When they discover that they have 25 percent less pine to sell [domestically], they will want some immediate answers. But what am I supposed to do? Exporting is hot! It is in vogue; anybody who's anybody exports—it is the thing to talk about at parties. Until two years ago one telemarketing person handled all of our export sales, which never exceeded $13 million per year. So far this year [July] our export sales are almost $40 million. What really bothers me is that we are still such a small department—just Julie [the secretary/order taker] and me."

Kenny continued to ponder some of the problems of his department: "It's tough trying to keep good relations with everyone in the sales department—and with my boss. When my department is pushing to expand export sales, supply for domestic sales suffers. One problem is the mill itself. It's difficult to explain to the 40-hour-per-week mill supervisors that I need my board feet in millimeters. They look at me like I'm from another planet when I talk metric. I am trying to market to the world when the millers just want to talk about drinking beer and fishing.

"If it's not the millers it's the salespeople. They are mad as hell as it is. Some, like Wally Lumpkin, won't even try to understand that my telemarketers and I are just trying to do our jobs. All they see is less to sell [domestically] and unhappy customers. No attempt at coordination! On top of that, they blame me for the declining quality of their domestic lumber supply. Western Europe, the United Kingdom in particular, will pay $925 per 1000 board feet of Southern Yellow 1 (SY1) pine. The U.S. contractors will pay only $325 per 1000 board feet. Sure, much of the SY1 pine will go to the U.K. while little, if any, gets into the domestic market. Domestic contractors, the ones that keep us in business during the off years, are not getting actual #1 grade lumber. Before, they were getting a much better grade. Joe Chumley, my boss, stresses me out, too. He keeps pushing me for more export sales."

Kenny's thoughts were interrupted by Julie Kemp, the secretary/telemarketer. She handed him a memo from the Puerto Rican Bank which was working with Heredia's account. The memo indicated that Heredia had not responded to any letters or calls concerning his past-due account. Julie asked Kenny: "Why is this so important? All we have done today is work on this, this Cuban Connection!" Frustrated, Kenny replied: "It's just important! That's all! And don't ask anybody but me questions. If you want to know anything about this 'Cuban Connection,' please talk to me—no one else, just me!"

Kenny swung around in his chair, looked at the golf course again and thought: "Don't I know how to fill out papers by now? A consignee* should never go to the dock and pick up the materials without stopping by the bank first. Three hundred thousand dollars won't break the company, but it is a sizable amount. This error is my responsibility. If Chumley finds out about it I will be listening to lectures from here to retirement—if he doesn't fire me first. Damn, what a tough call! If I can fix it, maybe he won't find out."

Kenny decided to contact the Export-Import Bank (Eximbank) and ask for their assistance. He hoped they would help col-

lect from Heredia or at least assist in finding out who failed to get the required documentation before releasing the shipment. Kenny asked Julie to get someone at the bank on the phone for him.

At this point Kenny's door opened and Chumley entered. "Well, 'Mr. Productive,' how is the guy heading the fastest growing department at TTPI? I want you to know that your figures are surprisingly steady compared to domestic. Old man Summit and I are getting ready to make some capital investments and re-tool the mill to accommodate international standards. The revenue from your department is helping everybody."

The phone rang, and Julie notified Kenny that Ms. Smart from Eximbank was on the line. Kenny realized that temperatures would soon be rising. He asked Joe if he would mind waiting in the outer office while he took a personal call.

*Mr. Heredia had the lumber shipped to Puerto Rico because U.S. businesses could not export to Cuba at that time. However, the lumber should not have been released without first being cleared by the bank. A mistake in documentation occurred between Kenny's desk and delivery to Heredia. Someone at some point did not follow standard procedures.

Case 10

Ideal Brands, Inc.

James W. Cagley
Dale A. Lunsford
University of Tulsa

David Johnson, group research manager at Ideal Brands, looked at the envelope and its contents again. The check for $1000 was made out to him and the accompanying note said only "Thank you." It was signed by the owner of Creative Research, Inc., a supplier to which Johnson had just awarded a $220,000 contract. No other explanation was needed. Johnson knew the check was a "gift" in exchange for the contract. But what should he do with the check? This was the first time he had received anything other than a thank you from a supplier

BACKGROUND INFORMATION

David Johnson received his M.S. in marketing from the University of Minnesota in 1990 with minors in statistics and psychology, and joined Ideal Brands, Inc., as a research analyst in the Consumer Research Department. His first assignments related to research on two of the company's smaller entries in the soft-drink market.

In 1992, Johnson was promoted to research manager and in 1993 to group research manager. He supervised all research on three brands that accounted for approximately $525 million in annual sales. Ideal Brands has eight different brands in the soft-drink market. Company sales for fiscal 1993 were $850 million.

Organization of the Consumer Research Department

The Consumer Research Department reported directly to the vice president of marketing. (An abbreviated organization chart for Marketing is presented in Exhibit C10–1

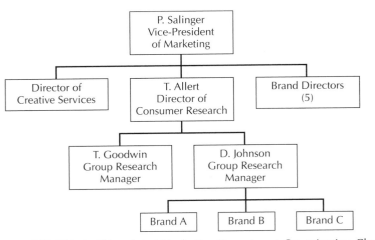

EXHIBIT C10–1 Abbreviated Marketing Department Organization Chart

and shows the reporting relationships within the department.) In addition to Johnson, the principals in the department were the director of consumer research, Ted Allert, and the other group research manager, Tom Goodwin.

Ted Allert had been with Ideal for nine years, having been hired as a group research manager. He had previously been a project manager for a coffee marketer after leaving an academic position for a corporate career in marketing research. Tom Goodwin, after completing college, worked for NASA as a systems engineer. He had been with Ideal for 12 years in various positions in planning, sales, marketing, and research. His expertise was computer systems and forecasting.

Johnson's Responsibilities

As previously mentioned, Johnson was responsible for all research on three of Ideal's brands. He had control of a $2 million research budget that was distributed approximately as follows:

—Advertising creative studies	30%
—Problem market studies	30
—Product concept testing	20
—Test market/market tracking	10
—Miscellaneous	10
Total	100%

Seventy-five percent of Johnson's research budget was used for outside suppliers. The decision to use external firms for research was based on such considerations as expertise, experience, credibility with both advertising agency and Ideal management, expedience, a cost-benefit evaluation, and a general "feel" or "comfort level" between project supervisor and supplier.

Introduction of Peter Sallinger

Some uncertainty had been introduced in the spring of 1994 when Peter Sallinger was appointed as the new vice president of marketing. He was new to the soft-drink industry after having spent 15 years with two cereal marketers in brand management and marketing. His most recent position had been as director of marketing for the third largest cereal marketer. He had been extremely successful in expanding both sales and share of market and was, of course, expected to do similarly well with Ideal Brands.

Johnson, Tom Goodwin, and Ted Allert had spent a great deal of time bringing Sallinger "up to speed" on all research that impacted his decision areas. Johnson was impressed with Sallinger—his grasp of the importance of research and his ability to synthesize findings from disparate studies and methodologies.

THE PROPOSED RESEARCH PROJECT

At Ideal Brands, individual projects were developed by research groups and presented to the marketing group for discussion and "blessing" before research was fielded. In June, Johnson, Allert, and Sallinger were discussing preliminary plans for a large-scale study related to the 1996 advertising pool. The pool represented $40 million that would be expended on advertising Ideal's three leading soft-drink brands. Sallinger asked about recent approaches to evaluating advertising creative. The conversation went like this:

Johnson: In the two years I've been involved, we have used primarily qualitative techniques, specifically focus groups, to evaluate our creative.

Sallinger: Who have you been using for these groups?

Johnson: We have used a firm named Dynamic Research. They have had a lot of experience in the soft-drink industry and

have brought a lot of insight to our brands.

Allert: We also used them before Dave was put in charge of advertising creative research.

Sallinger: It might be time to seek a fresh approach to our research. While at [previous cereal employer], we used a firm named Creative Research, Inc., for most of our qualitative work. I think it would be appropriate if we would talk to them about the 1995 creative study.

The Research Methodology

The proposed methodology for the 1995 creative study involved an initial set of 24 focus groups in 6 cities to be fielded early in 1995. Results would be presented to a combination of ad agency and Ideal management in May, and creative direction for the 1996 pool would be based largely on this study. A follow-up study using rough creatives (animatics or storyboards) would be conducted in August 1995. This follow-up study was slated to include eight to ten focus groups and would serve as a final concept check before production began for the budgeted $40 million advertising campaign.

Vendors

In the process of developing the final research proposal, Johnson sought proposals from three research firms—Dynamic, Creative Research, and Quality First Research. A brief description of each follows:

Dynamic Research had been involved with Ideal Brands' research for five years and the primary qualitative vendor for the past two years. Allert and Johnson had been pleased with their work, although it bothered them that it appeared as though Ideal was becoming too dependent on Dynamic. The owner of Dynamic was withdrawing from active, hands-on management and had recently hired two people from competitive research houses to handle most of the moderation and analysis.

Creative Research, Inc., was a research firm that specialized in qualitative research applied to advertising creative, basic consumer positioning, and concept testing. Its owner and principal had earned a Ph.D. in social psychology from the University of Southern California and had an impressive list of former and ongoing clients, including automobile companies, financial institutions, and consumer goods firms.

Quality First Research was an unknown quantity to Allert and Johnson but had, at one point, been the primary supplier for one of Ideal's largest competitors. They had a solid reputation for quality in fieldwork, moderation, and analysis but were known as a relatively high-cost firm.

The Supplier Decision

The final supplier decision fell to Johnson and Allert. Each of the potential suppliers' proposals followed the two-stage plan. Johnson was relatively comfortable with each firm and their primary people and felt that any of the three would do an adequate job.

Prices for the proposals ranged from $200,000 (Dynamic) to $245,000 (Quality First). Remembering Sallinger's "suggestion," both Johnson and Allert felt that Creative Research warranted a favored position. Their price of $220,000, plus presentation travel expenses, was not out of line with the budget Johnson envisioned. Creative Research was selected, the final proposal was presented to the marketing group, "blessed," and a contract was signed in November 1994.

THE DILEMMA

On December 5, 1994, Johnson received a letter from Creative Research with "PERSONAL" stamped on the envelope. Inside was a check for $1000 made out to Johnson and a note saying "Thank you" signed by the owner of CRI.

Johnson wondered what to do. This was the first time he had received anything more than a thank-you note from a supplier. He consulted Ideal's Policy Manual. In this case, the manual was somewhat ambiguous: "The purpose of both gifts and entertainment in business is to create good will. If they do more than that and unduly influence the recipient or make that person feel obligated to 'pay back' the other company, then they are unacceptable."

Johnson still wondered what to do. Should he talk to Allert? Should he mention the "thank you" to Sallinger?

Company Index

Index